ENDANGERED SPECIES ACT
Law, Policy, and Perspectives

SECOND EDITION

EDITORS
DONALD C. BAUR
WM. ROBERT IRVIN

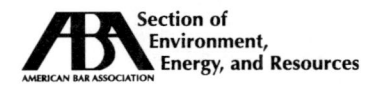

ABA Section of Environment, Energy, and Resources
AMERICAN BAR ASSOCIATION

Cover design by Laurie McDonald.

Cover photograph of polar bears © 2010 Kennan Ward.

The materials contained herein represent the opinions and views of the authors and/or the editors, and should not be construed to be the views or opinions of the law firms or companies with whom such persons are in partnership with, associated with, or employed by, nor of the American Bar Association or the Section of Environment, Energy, and Resources, unless adopted pursuant to the bylaws of the Association.

Nothing contained in this book is to be considered as the rendering of legal advice, either generally or in connection with any specific issue or case; nor do these materials purport to explain or interpret any specific bond or policy, or any provisions thereof, issued by any particular franchise company, or to render franchise or other professional advice. Readers are responsible for obtaining advice from their own lawyers or other professionals. This book and any forms and agreements herein are intended for educational and informational purposes only.

© 2010 American Bar Association. All rights reserved.

No part of this publication may be reproduced, stored in a retrieval system, or transmitted in any form or by any means, electronic, mechanical, photocopying, recording, or otherwise, without the prior written permission of the publisher. For permission, contact the ABA Copyrights and Contracts Department at copyright@abanet.org or via fax at 312-988-6030, or complete the online request form at http://www.abanet.org/policy/reprints.htm.

Printed in the United States of America.

15 5 4 3

Library of Congress Cataloging-in-Publication Data

Endangered Species Act : law, policy, and perspectives / [edited by] Donald C. Baur and Wm. Robert Irvin. — 2nd ed.
   p. cm.
 Includes index.
 ISBN 978-1-60442-580-2
 1. United States. Endangered Species Act of 1973. 2. Endangered species—Law and legislation—United States. I. Baur, Donald C. II. Irvin, William Robert, 1959–

KF5640.A315E53 2009
346.7304'69522—dc22

                                          2009036365

Discounts are available for books ordered in bulk. Special consideration is given to state bars, CLE programs, and other bar-related organizations. Inquire at Book Publishing, ABA Publishing, American Bar Association, 321 North Clark Street, Chicago, Illinois 60654-7598.

www.ShopABA.org

Summary of Contents

Foreword xiii
Preface to the First Edition xv
Acknowledgments. xvii
About the Editors xix
About the Contributors and Peer Reviewer. xxi

Overview. xxxii

   1. Historical Background of the Endangered Species Act 8
   2. Listing Endangered and Threatened Species 16
   3. Critical Habitat 40
   4. Recovery 70
   5. Interagency Consultation Under Section 7 104
   6. Indian Rights and the Endangered Species Act 126
   7. The Take Prohibition 146
   8. Land Use Activities and the Section 9 Take Prohibition 160
   9. Exceptions to the Take Prohibition. 192
  10. Landowner Incentives and the Endangered Species Act 206
  11. Habitat Conservation Plans and the Endangered Species Act 220
  12. Plants. 246
  13. Citizen Suits 260
  14. The Endangered Species Act and the Constitutional
      Takings Issue 292
  15. The Convention on International Trade in Endangered Species
      of Wild Fauna and Flora 316
  16. State Endangered Species Acts 344
  17. Nanotechnology and the Endangered Species Act. 360
  18. Conserving Endangered Species in an Era of Global
      Warming: An Environmental Community Perspective 374
  19. Refocusing the Endangered Species Act: A Regulated
      Community Perspective 394

Table of Cases. 411
Index. 421

Contents

Foreword xiii
Preface to the First Edition xv
Acknowledgments. xvii
About the Editors xix
About the Contributors and Peer Reviewer. xxi

Overview. xxxii
Donald C. Baur and Wm. Robert Irvin
    Introduction 1
    Responsibility for Implementation 1
    The ESA's Goals 2
    Listing, Critical Habitat, Recovery Plans 3
    The Duty to Consult and Avoid Jeopardy. 4
    The Take Prohibition and Its Exemptions. 5
    Conclusion 6

Chapter One
Historical Background of the Endangered Species Act 8
Michael J. Bean

Chapter Two
Listing Endangered and Threatened Species 16
J. B. Ruhl
    Introduction 17
    Current State of the Law 18
        Key Statutory Definitions and Standards 18
        Section 4 Implementing Procedures 19
        Section 4 in the Courts. 22
    Emerging Issues and Future Directions. 31
        Five-Year Status Reviews 31
        Political Interference in Listing Decisions. 32
        Climate Change 33
    Conclusion 35

Chapter Three
Critical Habitat 40
Federico Cheever
    Introduction 41
    Current State of the Law 42
        Definition of Critical Habitat 42
        Designation of Critical Habitat 48
    Emerging Issues and Future Directions 58
        The Regulatory Significance of Critical Habitat Adverse
            Modification on the Ground and in the Water 58
        Critical Habitat Designation and the National Environmental
            Policy Act 60
    Conclusion 62

Chapter Four
Recovery 70
Dale D. Goble
    Introduction 71
    Current State of the Law 71
        The Meaning of Recovery 71
        Recovery Planning 79
    Emerging Issues and Future Directions 85
        Viability Thresholds in Recovery 85
        Recovery Plans as "The Best Scientific . . . Data Available" 87
    Conclusion 90

Chapter Five
Interagency Consultation Under Section 7 104
Patrick W. Ryan and Erika E. Malmen
    Introduction 105
    Current State of the Law 105
        Federal Agency Compliance with Section 7(a)(1) Duty to Conserve 105
        Federal Agency Compliance with Section 7(a)(2) Duty to Consult 105
        Preparing for the Possibility of Formal Consultation 106
        Formal Consultation 111
        Incremental Consultation 116
        Reinitiation of Consultation 116
        Emergency Consultation 117
        The God Squad Exemption 117
        The Role of Indian Tribes 118
    Emerging Issues and Future Directions 118
        Discretionary versus Nondiscretionary Agency Action 118

  Climate Change 119
  Section 7 Consultation Regulations 120
 Conclusion 120

Chapter Six
Indian Rights and the Endangered Species Act 126
Mary Gray Holt

 Introduction 127
 Current State of the Law 127
  Three Pillars of Indian Law 127
  Ambiguity in the Case Law—Did the ESA Abrogate Treaty Rights? 130
  Harmonizing the ESA and Tribal Rights: Secretarial Order No. 3206 . . . 133
 Emerging Issues and Future Directions 136
 Conclusion 139

Chapter Seven
The Take Prohibition 146
Patrick Parenteau

 Introduction 147
 Current State of the Law 147
  Statutory and Regulatory Framework 147
  Constitutional Challenges to the Take Prohibition 148
  Jurisdictional Prerequisites to Bringing Suit Under
   the ESA Citizen Suit Provision 149
 Emerging Issues and Future Directions 150
  Proving Harm from Habitat Modification 150
  Vicarious Liability 152
  Injunctive Relief 153
 Conclusion 154

Chapter Eight
Land Use Activities and the Section 9 Take Prohibition 160
Steven P. Quarles and Thomas R. Lundquist

 Introduction 161
 Current State of the Law 161
  The Basics on Take of Listed Wildlife 161
 The Current Law of ESA Section 9 Take Under FWS's Harm Rule 168
 Emerging Issues and Future Directions 179
  Are Regulators Enjoinable Causes of Take? 179
 Is a Source of Greenhouse Gas Emissions an Enjoinable Cause
  of Take of a Polar Bear? 181
 Conclusion 182

Chapter Nine
Exceptions to the Take Prohibition 192
Sam Kalen and Adam Pan
    Introduction 193
    Current State of the Law 193
        Section 10(a)—Enhancement and Incidental Take Permits 193
        Section 10(j)—Experimental Populations 196
        Other Exceptions to the Take Prohibition 199
    Emerging Issues and Future Directions 201
    Conclusion 202

Chapter Ten
Landowner Incentives and the Endangered Species Act 206
Michael J. Bean
    Introduction 207
    Current State of the Law 208
        Safe Harbor Agreements 208
        Candidate Conservation Agreements with Assurances 211
        Conservation Banking 213
    Emerging and Future Directions 214
    Conclusion 217

Chapter Eleven
Habitat Conservation Plans and the Endangered Species Act 220
Douglas P. Wheeler and Ryan M. Rowberry
    Introduction 221
        Purposes and Perceptions of the Early ESA 221
        1982 ESA Amendment 222
        Babbitt Administrative Reforms 224
    Current State of the Law 225
        The "No Surprises" Rule and the ITP Permit Revocation Rule 225
        Habitat Conservation Plans and Adaptive Management 227
        HCPs/ITPs and NEPA 231
    Future Directions 234
        The Western Riverside County Multiple-Species HCP (MSHCP) 234
        The Role of Mitigation 237
        Lessons Learned 238
    Conclusion 240

Chapter Twelve
Plants 246
Holly Wheeler
    Introduction 247

  Current State of the Law 248
   A Unified Approach to Plant and Wildlife Conservation 248
   The ESA Diverges: Regulatory Differences Between Plants
    and Wildlife. 249
   The Role of CITES in Plant Protection. 251
  Emerging Issues and Future Directions. 252
  Conclusion. 254

Chapter Thirteen
Citizen Suits 260
Eric R. Glitzenstein
  Introduction 261
  Current State of the Law 261
   Standing. 261
   Other Jurisdictional Issues 264
   ESA versus APA Claims Following *Bennett v. Spear*. 265
   Standard of Review 270
   Venue/Transfer Issues. 271
   60-Day Notice Requirement. 273
   Intervention 273
   Relief 274
  Emerging Issues and Future Directions. 275
  Conclusion. 276

Chapter Fourteen
The Endangered Species Act and the Constitutional Takings Issue 292
John D. Echeverria and Glenn P. Sugameli
  Introduction 293
  Overview of Relevant Takings Principles 293
  ESA Provisions Affecting Property Use 295
  Overview of the ESA and Constitutional Takings Claims 297
  Regulatory Restrictions on Natural Resource Use. 298
   Ripeness Issues. 298
   Threshold Property Issue 299
   Takings Analysis. 301
  Restrictions on Defense of Property 306
  Official Access for Survey Purposes 307
  Restrictions on Commercial Dealings. 308
  Conclusion. 309

Chapter Fifteen
The Convention on International Trade in Endangered Species of Wild Fauna and Flora 316
W. Michael Young and Holly Wheeler

    Introduction 317
    Current State of the Law 317
        The Structure of CITES 317
        The Conservation Standards of CITES 319
        The Administrative Procedures of CITES 320
        Specialized CITES Procedures 323
    Emerging Issues and Future Directions 327
        Coordination Between CITES and Other Multilateral Environmental Agreements 327
        The Effects of Conservation Restrictions on People's Livelihoods 332
    Conclusion 335

Chapter Sixteen
State Endangered Species Acts 344
Susan George and William J. Snape III

    Introduction 345
    Current State of the Law 345
        History 346
        Listing 347
        Critical Habitat 348
        Prohibitions 349
        Permits 350
        Conservation Agreements 350
        Penalties and Enforcement 351
        Recovery Plans 352
        Consultation 352
        Plant Protection 353
        Funding 353
        States Without Acts or Provisions 354
    Emerging Issues and Future Directions 355
    Conclusion 355

Chapter Seventeen
Nanotechnology and the Endangered Species Act 360
J. Michael Klise, Steven P. Quarles, and Wm. Robert Irvin

    Introduction 361
        Why Nanotechnology? 361
        Overview of the Endangered Species Act 361

Current State of the Law 362
    The Endangered Species Act and Nanotechnology 362
        Protecting Against Effects of Nanotechnology Using the ESA
            Section 9 Take Prohibition 364
        Protecting Against Effects of Nanotechnology Using Federal Agency
            Consultation with the Services Under ESA Section 7(a)(2) 365
Emerging and Future Directions 367
    Use of the Take Prohibition to Address Nanoscale Materials 367
    Use of ESA Section 7(a)(2) to Address Effects of Nanoscale Materials ... 368
    The ESA's Conservation Goal and Nanotechnology 369
Conclusion 370

Chapter Eighteen
**Conserving Endangered Species in an Era of Global Warming:
An Environmental Community Perspective** 374
John Kostyack and Dan Rohlf
Introduction 375
A Record of Success Despite Significant Obstacles 375
Entering an Era of Rapid Climate Change and Ecosystem Disruptions 378
The Need for Climate Change Safeguards 379
Making the ESA More Effective 380
    Modest Legislative Updates 381
    Using Existing Tools to Enhance the ESA's Effectiveness 382
    New Energy and New Initiatives 385
Integrating the ESA into the Larger Climate Change
    and Conservation Framework 387
Conclusion 389

Chapter Nineteen
Refocusing the Endangered Species Act: A Regulated Community Perspective ... 394
W. H. "Buzz" Fawcett
The Challenge of the Act 395
The Act Is a Reflection of Its Time and Congressional Neglect 395
The Act Is Primarily a Jurisdictional Statute 396
Transparency and the Administration of the Act 398
Critical Habitat: The Agony of Expectations Unfulfilled 399
The Polar Bear Paradox 400
The *Pinchot* Conundrum 402
Toward a Conservation Economy 404

Table of Cases 411
Index 421

Foreword

In 1978, on a windswept wildlife refuge in southwestern Colorado, a young boy peered through the lenses of an old pair of binoculars hoping to see a whooping crane within a cluster of greater sandhill cranes. The boy knew that the whooping crane was an endangered species. He was pleased that the "grown-ups" were trying an experiment of collecting whooping crane eggs and placing them in the nests of greater sandhill cranes where they were to be raised by "foster parents." He hoped the experiment would work because he did not want to see the whooping crane become extinct. Thirty years later, the Fish and Wildlife Service's Web site notes that the experiment the boy was so excited about "has not lived up to expectations" and the whooping crane remains an endangered species.

Like the experiment with the whooping cranes, the execution of the Endangered Species Act (ESA) is viewed by some as not living up to expectations. There is no doubt that purposes of the Act, "to conserve the ecosystems upon which endangered and threatened species depend; provide a program for the conservation of endangered species and threatened species; take the appropriate steps to achieve the purposes of treaties and conventions the United States had chosen to enter into," are sound, if not ambitious.

The enactment of the ESA placed great responsibility and discretion in the hands of the Secretary of the Interior and the Secretary of Commerce. Indeed, much of the controversy regarding the Act has arisen in the manner in which these administrators have attempted to execute congressional will. One surprising reality to an ESA novice is that even with 35 years, and counting, of administrative experience under their belts, and tremendous discretion, these Departments continue to struggle to interpret and implement key terms of this statute.

The contributors to this book are a stellar group of authors who are well prepared to lead a reader through the twists and turns of this statute and its implementation. Starting with a look at the historical background of the ESA, winding through critical sections of the statute, examining cutting-edge issues, and sharing the perspectives of varied interests, this book will be of use to novices and experts alike. Several of the authors have served, or serve, in the federal government, many within the Office of the Solicitor at the Department of the Interior. Over the years, I have learned a great deal from some of these authors, and I believe you will as well.

I believe that future administrators of the Act will continue to refine their understanding and interpretation of a number of key terms, phrases, and sections of the ESA. As they do so, they will recognize new opportunities and confront new challenges regarding the future administration of the ESA. Precisely how the Departments choose to utilize their authority and discretion will be closely and appropriately scrutinized by the public, the courts, and the Congress.

Enjoy the book.

David L. Bernhardt

Preface to the First Edition

Over nearly 30 years of practicing and teaching natural resources law, I've had close encounters with practically all the primary statutes in the area. The most ambitious, complex, and far-reaching of these, I can say without hesitation, is the Endangered Species Act. No other statute has so immodest a goal as preserving life forms on the planet from extinction; no other statute employs such a complex and sweeping array of tools and techniques designed to carry out that goal.

The web of life is unfathomable: "Nature is not only more complex than we think; it's more complex than we *can* think" was an expression often voiced by the participants in the Northwest Forest Plan, which was formulated as a response to spotted owl gridlock in the early 1990s. So it's not surprising that a law designed to preserve viable remnants of the natural world would be complicated too.

The ESA is of interest to lawyers from just about every standpoint: its interface of science and law; its mediation of the tension between executive discretion and judicial review; the interaction between the executive and legislative branches in its administration; the role of citizen suits in its administration; federalism issues; and its overlapping regulatory tools (principally the consultation process of Section 7, the "takings" prohibition of Section 9, and the habitat conservation planning process of Section 10).

The act is having a remarkable effect on land and water management in communities across the country. Its cutting edge is regulatory, and it bristles with opportunities for litigation. There is no gainsaying that the courts have played a large role in its implementation, stepping in at critical moments with decisions such as *Tennessee Valley Authority v. Hill* (snail darter) and *Sweet Home* (take through habitat modification). Yet most of its real gains on the ground have come not from court orders, but from negotiations and settlements that guide undertakings by landowners, water managers, and governmental agencies.

That fact is part of the genesis of this book. Justice Frankfurter once observed that "it would be a narrow conception of jurisprudence to confine the notion of 'laws' to what is found written in statute books, and to disregard the gloss which life has written upon it."[1] The ESA's effects can scarcely be understood by pondering its text or the regulations that implement it, or even the judicial opinions that address it. Life has supplied a gloss that anyone serious about dealing with the ESA must understand.

Over the years, a hardy band of law-trained people have become real experts—indeed, gurus—of the ESA *cum* gloss. Remarkably, nearly all of them have been corralled and persuaded to contribute to this volume. These authors—diverse in their experiences and points of view—eat, drink, and live (okay, they administer, litigate, advocate, and teach) ESA issues, and it shows. They understand the statute's complexity, its subtlety, and (pardon the expression as applied to law that seeks to forestall extinction) where its bodies are buried. A goodly number of these experts, I am proud to report, are currently or were lawyers in the federal government (most in the Interior Department's Solicitor's Office).

In short, the subject is worthy, the authors eminently qualified guides. The result is a superb collection of commentary on a fascinating and challenging law that is remaking land and water use in America.

John Leshy

Note

1. Nashville, C. & St. L. Ry. v. Browning, 310 U.S. 362, 369 (1940).

Acknowledgments

Many individuals have contributed to the development of this book. While it would seem logical that the second edition is easier than the first, that proved not to be the case. The successful completion of this version of *Endangered Species Act: Law, Policy, and Perspectives,* therefore, is due to the assistance of many people. Judy Casey of Perkins Coie was "command central" for most of this effort, until she finally had enough of one of the editors' inability to say no to projects like this and transferred (for good cause) to another practice group. Her hours of hard work are very greatly appreciated. With Judy's change in duty station, we were fortunate to call upon the return services of Rebecca Brezenoff, the veteran coordinator of the first edition, to bring the book across the finish line. Again, we owe thanks to Laurie McDonald for her outstanding cover design and to Kennan Ward for his outstanding photograph of polar bears. Thanks also to Charles Kogod, photo editor at Defenders of Wildlife, who assisted in securing the rights to the photo. Jennifer Carney helped once again, in coordination and production. Adam Pan donated his time for a technical review of the entire book.

As always, the ABA Book Publishing staff provided outstanding support. What the editors failed to do in meeting deadlines, the staff made up for by pushing other aspects of the production. Special thanks to Leslie Keros for guiding the overall effort and to Amelia Stone for her marketing expertise. Thanks also to the members of the section's Book Publishing Board and its two chairs during this project—Sam Kalen and Peter Wright—for support and the occasional kick in the butt. We owe a debt of gratitude as well to our peer reviewer, Murray Feldman, for his thorough review and thoughtful suggestions.

Finally, thanks to our families—Phebe Jensch, Christopher Baur, and Nancy, Tom, and Carrie Irvin—for their love, support, and patience throughout this project.

About the Editors

Donald C. Baur is a partner in the Washington, D.C., office of Perkins Coie LLP. He previously has served as General Counsel of the U.S. Marine Mammal Commission and as an attorney advisor in the Office of the Solicitor for the U.S. Department of the Interior, where he served in the Office's Honors Program. He graduated with highest honors from Trinity College and from the University of Pennsylvania School of Law. Mr. Baur is on the summer faculty of the Vermont Law School, where he teaches ocean and coastal law. He also taught federal wildlife law at the Golden Gate School of Law, and serves as Co-Chair of the ALI-ABA Environmental Institute Conference on Species Protection and the Law and as an instructor in the Environmental Law Institute's Environmental Boot Camp. He is coeditor of and contributor to the ABA's *Ocean and Coastal Law and Policy* (2008, with Tim Eichenberg and Michael Sutton) and coeditor of the first edition of the ABA's *Endangered Species Act: Law, Policy, and Perspectives* (2002, with Wm. Robert Irvin). Mr. Baur serves on the Book Publishing Board of the ABA Section of Environment, Energy, and Resources and has written more than 20 articles published in law reviews and related journals.

Wm. Robert Irvin is Senior Vice President for Conservation Programs at Defenders of Wildlife in Washington, D.C., where he manages conservation policy, litigation, field conservation, and international conservation programs, supervising a staff of policy advocates, scientists, and lawyers in the United States, Mexico, and Canada. Prior to joining Defenders of Wildlife, Mr. Irvin served as Director of U.S. Conservation for World Wildlife Fund; Vice President for Marine Wildlife Conservation and General Counsel for the Center for Marine Conservation; Senior Counsel for Fish and Wildlife on the Majority Staff of the U.S. Senate Committee on Environment and Public Works; Counsel and Director of the Fisheries and Wildlife Division, National Wildlife Federation; Trial Attorney in the Civil Division of the U.S. Department of Justice; and was in private legal practice in Portland, Oregon. Mr. Irvin has written and lectured extensively on biodiversity conservation issues. He is coeditor of the first edition of the ABA's *Endangered Species Act: Law, Policy, and Perspectives* (2002, with Donald C. Baur). He was a member of the IUCN's Red List Criteria Review Working Group, which revised the standards for listing threatened species globally. Mr. Irvin has taught Biodiversity Protection at Vermont Law School and the University of Maryland School of Law. Mr. Irvin graduated magna cum laude with a B.S. degree in Forest Science from Utah State University in 1980. He earned a J.D., Order of the Coif, in 1983 from the University of Oregon School of Law. He has served as co-chair of the Environment, Energy, and Natural Resources Section of the District of Columbia Bar and is on the board of directors of the Environmental Law Institute and the advisory board for the *Environmental Law Reporter*.

About the Contributors and Peer Reviewer

Michael J. Bean headed the Wildlife Program of Environmental Defense from 1977 through 2009. In 2003 he became codirector of its Center for Conservation Incentives. A 1973 graduate of the Yale Law School, he serves on the board of Resources for the Future and is a past member of the Board on Environmental Studies and Toxicology of the National Research Council of the National Academy of Sciences, and the board of directors of the Environmental Law Institute. He was appointed by former Interior Secretary Gale Norton to be one of the 10 members of the National Wildlife Refuge Centennial Commission and until recently served as the director of the Pew Fellows Program in Marine Conservation. His book, *The Evolution of National Wildlife Law*, the third edition of which was written with Melanie J. Rowland in 1997, is generally regarded as the leading text on the subject of wildlife conservation law. Mr. Bean pioneered the use of "safe harbor agreements" as an incentive-based strategy to gain the cooperation of private landowners in conserving endangered species. Mr. Bean's work with safe harbor agreements is part of a larger effort to address the importance of incentives—both financial and regulatory—in accomplishing conservation goals, and was instrumental in Environmental Defense's creation in 2003 of a Center for Conservation Incentives, which is dedicated to exploring, testing, and implementing incentive-based strategies for conserving biodiversity. He now serves as Counselor to the Assistant Secretary for Fish and Wildlife and Parks at the Department of the Interior, having assumed that position in June 2009.

David Bernhardt is a Shareholder at Brownstein Hyatt Farber and Schreck, LLP where he focuses on counseling, litigation, and transactions involving environmental, energy, and natural resource matters. Mr. Bernhardt was unanimously confirmed by the United States Senate to serve as the Solicitor of the Department of the Interior in October 2006, where he served until 2009. In addition, between 2001 and 2006 he served as Deputy Solicitor, Deputy Chief of Staff, Counselor to the Secretary of the Interior, and Director of the Office of Congressional and Legislative Affairs. Prior to serving within the Department of the Interior, Mr. Bernhardt was at Brownstein from 1998 to 2001. Before joining Brownstein in 1998, he served as legislative director and rules committee associate in the U.S. House of Representatives for Congressman Scott McInnis.

Federico Cheever is Professor of Law and Associate Dean of Academic Affairs at the University of Denver Sturm College of Law. He began teaching at the University of Denver College of Law in 1993 specializing in Environmental Law, Wildlife Law, Public Land Law, Land Conservation Transactions, and Property. Professor Cheever writes extensively about the Endangered Species Act, federal public land law, and land conservation transactions. After graduating from Stanford University (B.A./M.A. 1981) and the University of California, Los Angeles (J.D. 1986), and clerking for Judge Harry Pregerson of the United States Court of Appeals for the Ninth Circuit in Los Angeles (1986–1987), he came to Denver as an Associate Attorney for the Sierra Club Legal Defense Fund (1987–1989). Between 1990 and 1993, he was an associate at the law firm Faegre & Benson.

John D. Echeverria is a Professor of Law at Vermont Law School. He was formerly the Executive Director of the Georgetown Environmental Law & Policy Institute at Georgetown University Law Center. Mr. Echeverria also served as the General Counsel of the National Audubon Society and as the General Counsel and Conservation Director of American Rivers, Inc. He is a graduate of the Yale Law School and the Yale School of Forestry and Environmental Studies, and was a law clerk to the Honorable Gerhard Gesell of the U.S. District Court in the District of Columbia. Mr. Echeverria has written extensively on the takings issue and various other aspects of environmental and natural resource law and frequently represents state and local governments, environmental organizations, planning groups, and others in regulatory takings cases at all levels of the federal and state court systems. At the 2007 annual meeting of the American Bar Association, Mr. Echeverria received the Jefferson Fordham Advocacy Award to recognize outstanding excellence within the area of state and local government law over a lifetime of achievement.

W. H. "Buzz" Fawcett is a lawyer in Washington, D.C., representing a wide variety of clients on a wide variety of federal issues. Previously a partner in the Perkins Coie environmental and energy practice group, Mr. Fawcett came to that firm from Capitol Hill where he served as Legislative Director to then Senator Dirk Kempthorne. In that capacity, he led and was responsible for the Senator's efforts to reauthorize the Endangered Species Act and passage of the Safe Drinking Water Act and the landmark Unfunded Mandates Act. Mr. Fawcett began his career as the Boise City Attorney.

Murray Feldman (peer reviewer) is a partner in the Boise, Idaho, office of Holland & Hart LLP. He represents state and local governments, landowners, and others in Endangered Species Act litigation and administrative proceedings on species listing, critical habitat designation, consultation, habitat conservation planning, and related issues. He has worked on ESA matters throughout the Pacific Northwest, and in Alaska, Alabama, Nevada, New Mexico, and Michigan. His practice also includes litigation and regulatory compliance on National Environmental Policy Act, Clean Water Act, public lands, and climate change issues. Mr. Feldman is the author of over 25 published articles and book chapters on environmental law topics. He is a past vice-chair of the ABA Section of Environment, Energy, and Resources' Endangered Species and Public Lands committees and past chair of the Idaho State Bar's Environment and Natural Resources section. He received his J.D. from the University of California, Berkeley (Boalt Hall) School of Law, where he was an associate editor of the *Ecology Law Quarterly*, and his M.S. degree from the University of Idaho College of Natural Resources.

Susan George is a Senior Attorney at the Institute of Public Law, University of New Mexico School of Law, where she practices natural resources and environmental law. She has taught wildlife law and biodiversity and the law as an adjunct professor at the University of New Mexico School of Law, and is the author of numerous publications, including "State-Based Alternatives for Protecting Wildlife," "Conservation in America: State Government Incentives for Habitat Conservation," and "ESA Section 6: The Role of the States." She previously served as State Counsel for Defenders of Wildlife for over 10 years, and has worked at the Western Environmental Law Center and in private practice.

Eric R. Glitzenstein is a founding partner of Meyer Glitzenstein & Crystal, a public-interest law firm in Washington, D.C., that specializes in litigation on issues pertaining to wildlife protection and conservation. He has represented conservation organizations in many significant Endangered Species Act cases, including lawsuits resulting in the protection of the Canada lynx under the ESA, the creation of new sanctuaries and refuges for Florida manatees, the listing of hundreds of animals and plants as endangered or threatened, a strengthened recovery plan for the grizzly bear, and new safeguards for right whales in both the Atlantic and Pacific oceans. He is the Chairman of the Litigation Committee and a member of the Board of Directors of Defenders of Wildlife, Vice Chairman of the American Bar Association's Committee on Animal Law, and a member of the Board of Advisors of the Center for Native Ecosystems. He has testified before congressional committees on ESA and other wildlife issues, and was an Adjunct Professor at Georgetown University Law Center, where he taught courses on public interest advocacy and civil litigation. He is a graduate of the Georgetown University Law Center (J.D. 1981, magna cum laude) and Johns Hopkins University (B.A. 1978), and worked as a law clerk for Judge Thomas Flannery of the United States District Court for the District of Columbia and as a staff attorney with the Public Citizen Litigation Group.

Dale D. Goble is the Margaret Wilson Schimke Distinguished Professor of Law at the University of Idaho. His teaching and research focus on natural resource law and environmental history. In addition to the usual numerous articles, he is the co-author of *Wildlife Law: A Primer* (Island Press 2009), *Wildlife Law: Cases and Materials* (Foundation Press, 2d ed. 2009), *Federal Wildlife Statutes: Texts and Contexts* (Foundation Press 2002), and *Northwest Lands, Northwest Peoples: Readings in Environmental History* (University of Washington Press 1999). He was a co-organizer of the Endangered Species Act at Thirty Projects, a multidisciplinary, multi-interest evaluation of the ESA at its 30th anniversary. In addition to two national conferences, the Project produced nearly a dozen smaller workshops as well as congressional and agency briefings, several journal articles, and two volumes: *The Endangered Species Act at Thirty: Renewing the Conservation Promise* (Island Press 2006) and *The Endangered Species Act at Thirty: Conserving Biodiversity in Human-Dominated Landscapes* (Island Press 2006).

Mary Gray Holt is a senior staff attorney in the Office of General Counsel, National Oceanic Atmospheric Administration. She received her B.A. (Honors) from Brown University in 1978 and her J.D. from the University of Oregon School of Law in 1984. Her areas of practice, since joining NOAA in 1991, include ocean and coastal law, coastal land use and constitutional takings, alternative energy resources, fisheries and protected resources, natural resource damages, and international law related to marine resources. She was a participant in the negotiation of Secretarial Order 3206 American Indian Tribal Rights, Federal-Tribal Trust Responsibilities and the Endangered Species Act in 1997 and continues to enjoy opportunities to work with Indian tribes on coastal issues. The views expressed in this chapter are those of the author and not necessarily those of NOAA or the U.S. Department of Commerce.

Sam Kalen is Of Counsel with Van Ness Feldman, in Washington, D.C., as well as an Assistant Professor of Law at the University of Wyoming School of Law. He also has served as a special assistant to an associate solicitor, in the Office of Solicitor at the Department of the Interior. His areas of practice have been in the environmental, natural resources, and energy areas, focusing on assisting clients on issues involving a host of programs, and in particular he has worked on Endangered Species Act matters for approximately 20 years. His teaching has focused on environmental law and related subjects, and he has published a variety of articles in the field. Mr. Kalen graduated from Clark University (B.A. 1980) and Washington University (J.D. 1984), and after clerking for the Hon. Warren D. Welliver of the Missouri Supreme Court (1984–1986) joined Van Ness Feldman (1986–1994; 1996–present). Mr. Kalen joined the faculty at the University of Wyoming in August 2009, and has taught as a visitor at Florida State University School of Law, Penn State University (Dickinson) School of Law, and as an adjunct at Washington & Lee University School of Law and the University of Baltimore School of Law.

J. Michael Klise is a partner in the Washington, D.C., office of Crowell & Moring LLP. His areas of focus include the Endangered Species Act, National Environmental Policy Act, federal administrative law, and federal appellate litigation. His practice concentrates on the major federal laws regulating land use activities, particularly timber and mining operations. His clients have included individuals, companies, school districts, municipalities, flood control districts, county boards of supervisors, and regional and national trade associations. He has represented them in ESA citizen suits and other litigation at the federal district court and appellate levels, as well as in proceedings before administrative tribunals. In addition, he frequently writes and lectures on the ESA and other topics involving natural resources law. He earned his J.D. at Catholic University Law School in Washington, D.C. He is admitted to practice before the U.S. Supreme Court, most U.S. Courts of Appeals, and in Maryland and the District of Columbia.

John Kostyack is Executive Director of Wildlife Conservation and Global Warming for the National Wildlife Federation, where he leads NWF's effort to safeguard wildlife and ecosystems from the impacts of climate change. Among his responsibilities are the national campaign to incorporate ecosystem safeguards and funding in federal climate change legislation and NWF's advocacy on endangered species, invasive species, and state wildlife action plans. Mr. Kostyack frequently writes and lectures on meeting the challenges of conserving U.S. wildlife and ecosystems. His recent publications include an article on updating the National Flood Insurance Program to address global warming. He is a longtime leader in ESA policy and litigation. He helped to win the endangered species conservation tax incentive for private landowners recently passed by Congress and has won a series of important court rulings through his legal advocacy.

John Leshy is the Harry D. Sunderland Distinguished Professor of Real Property Law at the University of California, Hastings College of the Law in San Francisco, where he teaches property, constitutional law, various natural resources courses, and American Indian law. Previously he was Solicitor (General Counsel) of the Department of the Interior throughout the Clinton administration, special counsel to the Chair of the House Natural Resources Committee, a law professor at Arizona State University, Associate Solicitor of the Department of the Interior for Energy and Resources in the Carter administration, with the Natural Resources Defense Council (NRDC) in California, and a litigator in the Civil Rights Division of the Department of Justice in Washington, D.C. He chaired and co-chaired, respectively, the Interior Department transition team for the Clinton-Gore and Obama-Biden administrations. Mr. Leshy has published widely on public lands, water, and other natural resources issues, and on constitutional and comparative law, including books on the Mining Law of 1872 and the Arizona Constitution. He is coauthor of *Federal Public Land and Resources Law* (2007), currently in its sixth edition, and of *Legal Control of Water Resources* (2006), now in its fourth edition. He has litigated cases in state and federal courts, served on numerous commissions and boards, and since 2002 has been President and then Vice-Chair of the board of the Wyss Foundation, which supports land conservation in the intermountain West. He is currently on the Board of the Grand Canyon Trust and the Natural Heritage Institute, and has thrice been a visiting professor at Harvard Law School, from which he graduated in 1969 after earning an A.B. at Harvard College in 1966.

Thomas R. Lundquist is counsel in the Washington, D.C., office of Crowell & Moring LLP. His areas of focus include the Endangered Species Act, National Environmental Policy Act, public land law, and jurisdiction. He frequently represents land-use and development interests in litigation brought under the Administrative Procedure Act or the ESA. This includes the Supreme Court's ESA section 9 decision in *Sweet Home* and ESA section 7 decision in *National Association of Home Builders v. Defenders of Wildlife*. He received his B.S. in biology/ecology from Union College (magna cum laude, Phi Beta Kappa), and his J.D. from the Harvard Law School.

Erika E. Malmen is a member of the Perkins Coie Environment & Natural Resources group. She practices in the firm's Boise office focusing on environmental, energy, and natural resources law; local, state, and federal government permitting; real estate and land use; and water law. Ms. Malmen has been recognized by Chambers USA as one of "America's Leading Environment & Natural Resource Lawyers," and is listed in the Cambridge Who's Who Registry. She is an active member of the Idaho State Bar Environment and Natural Resources section, serving one year as secretary and treasurer, and currently serving as chairperson. Prior to joining Perkins Coie, Ms. Malmen worked for the U.S. Department of the Interior in Washington,

D.C., where she was first an attorney for the Division of Land and Water and later the Acting Special Assistant to the Solicitor. She also served as legal counsel to the Governor of Idaho's Office of Species Conservation. Ms. Malmen received her law degree from the University of Denver Sturm College of Law and her undergraduate degree in speech communication from the University of Utah.

Patrick Parenteau is Professor of Law and Senior Counsel in the Environmental and Natural Resources Law Clinic at Vermont Law School. He previously served as Director of the Environmental Law Center at VLS from 1993 to 1999. Professor Parenteau also teaches in the Environmental Studies Program at Dartmouth College.

Professor Parenteau has an extensive background in environmental and natural resources law. His previous positions include Vice President for Conservation with the National Wildlife Federation in Washington, D.C. (1976–1984); General Counsel to the New England Regional Office of the Environmental Protection Agency in Boston (1984–1987); Commissioner of the Vermont Department of Environmental Conservation (1987–1989); and Of Counsel with the Perkins Coie law firm in Portland, Oregon (1989–1993).

Professor Parenteau is a nationally recognized expert on the Endangered Species Act and other environmental laws. He has been involved in drafting, litigating, implementing, teaching, and writing about environmental law and policy for over 30 years. He submitted an amicus brief in the U.S. Supreme Court on behalf of Professor E.O. Wilson and other distinguished scientists in *Sweet Home v Babbitt*. He is a recipient of the National Wildlife Federation's Conservation Achievement Award for 2005 in recognition of his contributions to wildlife conservation and environmental education.

Professor Parenteau holds a B.S. from Regis University, a J.D. from Creighton University, and an LL.M. in Environmental Law from the George Washington University.

Steven P. Quarles is a partner in Crowell & Moring LLP, and former chair of that firm's Environment & Natural Resources Group. His broad-ranging practice includes representation of corporate, trade association, state and local governments, and land trust clients before all three branches of government. Before entering private practice, he was a Fulbright Scholar in India, served as counsel to the U.S. Senate Committee on Energy and Natural Resources, and served as Deputy Under Secretary of the U.S. Department of the Interior. Mr. Quarles was an invited participant in the ESA at Thirty project at the University of California at Santa Barbara (2003), the Stanford University Forum on the ESA and Federalism (2005), and the ESA Working Group on Habitat Issues sponsored by The Keystone Center (2006). He is a trustee of the Maryland Environmental Trust and serves on the boards of the American Forest Foundation, the Henry M. Jackson Foundation, and the Resources First Foundation and on the Secretary of the Interior's Wind Power Guidelines Federal Advisory Committee. He is a graduate of Princeton University (and recipient of the Herrick Prize from the Woodrow Wilson School of Public and International Affairs) and Yale Law School.

Dan Rohlf is Professor of Law and Clinical Director of the Pacific Environmental Advocacy Center (PEAC) at Lewis and Clark Law School. His teaching focuses on biodiversity and the intersection of law and science, and includes summer field-based courses co-taught with ecologists. His litigation through PEAC, Lewis and Clark's environmental law clinic, focuses on the Endangered Species Act, and has included high-profile cases such as a series of successful challenges to biological opinions governing operations of the federal dams in the Columbia River Basin. He has authored or co-authored numerous publications on the Endangered Species Act, including the book *The Endangered Species Act: A Guide to Its Protections and Implementation*. He holds a B.A. in geology from Colorado College and a J.D. from Stanford Law School.

Ryan M. Rowberry is an associate in the Environmental Practice Group at Hogan & Hartson, LLP (Washington, D.C.). His practice is primarily focused on land conservation, endangered species, and historic preservation issues. Mr. Rowberry has represented corporate, public interest, and nonprofit organizations in a variety of matters, ranging from compliance with the Convention on International Trade in Endangered Species of Wild Fauna and Flora (CITES) to multistate water litigation. In 2007 he authored "Law School Update: LCCHP Law School Survey Report" in *Yearbook of Cultural Property Law 2007* (Left Coast Press), which documents the results of his nationwide survey of U.S. law school professors regarding cultural property law curricula. Mr. Rowberry holds a B.A. (1999) in English from Brigham Young University and was elected a Rhodes Scholar. He completed an M.Sc. (2001) in Comparative and International Education and an M.St. (2005) in Medieval British Legal History at Oxford University. He received his J.D. (2008) from Harvard Law School.

J. B. Ruhl is the Matthews & Hawkins Professor of Property at Florida State University College of Law, where he teaches courses on environmental law, land use, and property. Previous to joining the FSU in 1999, Professor Ruhl taught at Southern Illinois University in Carbondale (1994–98) and at the George Washington University Law School (1998–99). He served as Visiting Professor of Law at Harvard Law School in spring 2008 and has also visited for summer teaching at Vermont Law School, the University of Texas School of Law, and Lewis & Clark College of Law.

Professor Ruhl is a nationally regarded expert in the fields of endangered species protection, ecosystem services policy, regulation of wetlands, ecosystem management, environmental impact analysis, and related environmental and natural resources fields. His publications in these fields have appeared in the *Stanford Law Review*, *Georgetown Law Review*, *Minnesota Law Review*, *George Washington Law Review*, *Washington University Law Review*, *Boston University Law Review*, *Environmental Law*, and *Ecology Law Quarterly*. He is a co-author of two casebooks, *The Law of Biodiversity and Ecosystem Management* (Foundation Press, 2d ed. 2006), which is the first casebook to organize environmental law under these emerging themes, and the *Practice and Policy of Environmental Law* (Foundation Press 2008), which is the only environmental law casebook incorporating a practice context focus. He also recently published *The Law and Policy of Ecosystem Services* (Island Press 2007).

Prior to entering full-time law teaching, Professor Ruhl was a partner in the law firm of Fulbright & Jaworski, L.L.P., practicing environmental and natural resources law in the firm's Austin, Texas, office. He received his B.A. (1979) and J.D. (1982)

degrees from the University of Virginia, his LL.M. (1986) in Environmental Law from the George Washington University Law School, and a Ph.D. (2006) in Geography from Southern Illinois University.

Patrick W. Ryan is a Seattle-based Partner with Perkins Coie, LLP in its Environment & Natural Resources Group. He is a graduate of Portland State University, B.A., History, with honors (1991), Gonzaga University School of Law, J.D., magna cum laude (1994) and obtained a LL.M., Environmental Law at the George Washington University Law School (1996). He has counseled timber and other clients on numerous state and federal issues regarding forest practices and timber management, habitat conservation plans and section 10 permits, and proposed listings. Mr. Ryan is the past co-author of a chapter on Section 10 planning for the ALI-ABA ESA Law and Policy Treatise (2002) and is a frequent speaker on the ESA and the Migratory Bird Treaty Act at conferences around the country. He has also written numerous articles and client updates on ESA-related topics.

William J. Snape III is Senior Counsel at the Center for Biological Diversity. He is also a Practitioner in Residence at American University Law School and the Head Swim Coach at Gallaudet University. In addition, Mr. Snape is the author of numerous articles on natural resource issues and is the editor of *Biodiversity and the Law*, published by Island Press. For over a decade, Mr. Snape was Vice President and Chief Counsel for Defenders of Wildlife. He received his B.A., magna cum laude, from the University of California, Los Angeles (1986), and his J.D. from the George Washington University Law School, where he was president of the Environmental Law Society.

Glenn P. Sugameli is a staff attorney with Defenders of Wildlife in Washington, D.C., where he heads the Judging the Environment project on judicial nominations, property rights/"takings," and other issues involving environmental protection and the federal courts. He has spoken widely at takings law and other conferences and written extensively on various aspects of takings, including testimony, chapters in books for a lay audience, and the first edition of this book and the ABA books *Taking Sides on Takings Issues: Public and Private Perspectives* (2002) and *Taking Sides on Takings Issues: The Impact of Tahoe-Sierra* (2003). His law review articles have been published in *The Urban Lawyer, Environmental Law, Fordham Environmental Law Journal*, and the *Virginia Environmental Law Journal*. He has been quoted hundreds of times in television and radio interviews, newspaper and magazine articles, Op-Eds, Letters to the Editor, and editorials. His dozens of reported cases include Supreme Court, Federal Circuit, and D.C. Circuit cases and successful appeals from Florida, Michigan, and Wisconsin state court decisions that had found takings. Mr. Sugameli is a 1976 cum laude graduate of Princeton University and received his J.D. in 1979 from the University of Virginia School of Law, where he served on the *Virginia Law Review*.

Douglas P. Wheeler is a partner in Hogan & Hartson, LLP and is a member of the firm's Environmental and Climate Change Practice Groups in its Washington office. Mr. Wheeler provides counsel to corporate, institutional, and individual clients on natural resource and land use issues, including Endangered Species Act and CITES compliance, habitat mitigation and banking, water and wetlands management, sustainable forestry, historic preservation, and markets for ecosystem services. He has worked exclusively with natural resource and environmental issues in the private, public, and nonprofit sectors since joining the U.S. Department of the Interior in 1969, where he served as Assistant Legislative Counsel and Deputy Assistant Secretary for Fish and Wildlife and Parks. He has since served as a senior executive of nonprofit conservation and environmental organizations, including the National Trust for Historic Preservation (Executive Director, 1977–1980), the American Farmland Trust (President, 1980–1985), the Sierra Club (Executive Director, 1985–1987), and the World Wildlife Fund (Vice President, 1987–1991). Before joining Hogan & Hartson in 1999, he served for eight years as California's Secretary for Natural Resources, where he developed nationally recognized strategies, including Natural Communities Conservation Planning, to effectively manage the state's natural resources in an era of rapid growth and development. He serves on the boards of the Lincoln Institute of Land Policy, the American Farmland Trust, and the National Conservation System Foundation, and is an emeritus member of the boards of advisors of the Duke University School of Law and the Bren School of Environmental Science and Management at the University of California, Santa Barbara. He is a graduate of Hamilton College and the Duke University School of Law.

Holly Wheeler is an attorney with the Office of the Solicitor, Branch of Fish and Wildlife, for the U.S. Department of the Interior. Since 2002, Ms. Wheeler has been the primary staff attorney within the Department for issues involving international wildlife law and implementation of the Convention on International Trade in Endangered Species of Wild Fauna and Flora (CITES); marine mammals; and nonnative, invasive species, as well as all matters involving foreign endangered species and specific areas under the Endangered Species Act (ESA) relating to domestic species. She served as chief legal counsel to the U.S. delegation at the 13th (2004) and 14th (2007) Meetings of the Conference of the Parties to CITES and most recently has been the agency's lead staff attorney providing legal counsel and litigation support for the decision to list the polar bear as a threatened species under the ESA. With a Bachelor of Science degree in Fisheries and Wildlife from the University of Missouri, she has worked in the conservation field since 1981. Ms. Wheeler joined the Office of the Solicitor in Washington, D.C., following her graduation from Vermont Law School in 1996 and a judicial clerkship with the Vermont Supreme Court.

W. Michael Young has served as the Assistant Solicitor for Fish and Wildlife at the U.S. Department of the Interior since 2002. During his 27-year tenure as an attorney with the Office of the Solicitor, he has worked on a wide variety of Endangered Species Act (ESA), Marine Mammal Protection Act, and other federal wildlife conservation issues, including the co-authorship of the ESA section 7 consultation regulations in 1986. In recent years, Mr. Young's primary area of practice has involved international wildlife conservation issues under the Convention on International Trade in Endangered Species of Wild Fauna and Flora (CITES), the

Agreement on the Conservation of Polar Bears, and trade and the environment issues under the North American Free Trade Agreement and other multilateral and bilateral international trade agreements. He served as legal counsel to the U.S. Delegation at five meetings of the Conference of the Parties to CITES (Kyoto, Japan, in 1992; Fort Lauderdale, Florida, in 1994; Harare, Zimbabwe, in 1997; Nairobi, Kenya, in 2000; and Santiago, Chile, in 2002). He also served as legal counsel to the U.S. Delegation during negotiations that led to the signing of the U.S.-Russia Agreement on the Conservation and Management of the Alaska-Chukotka Polar Bear Population (signed in Washington, D.C., on October 16, 2000). Prior to joining the Solicitor's Office, Mr. Young was engaged in the private practice of law in Alabama. He also served as the Research Analyst to the Chief Justice of the Supreme Court of Alabama from 1977 to 1978. Mr. Young is a graduate of the University of Montevallo and the Cumberland School of Law of Samford University.

Overview

Donald C. Baur and Wm. Robert Irvin

Introduction

The Endangered Species Act of 1973 (ESA) was born in the heyday of American environmental legislation, a period in the 1960s and 1970s that saw the enactment of numerous environmental statutes, including the Wilderness Act of 1964, the Clean Air Act of 1970, the Federal Water Pollution Control Act of 1972, the Marine Mammal Protection Act of 1972 (MMPA), and the Fishery Conservation and Management Act of 1976. Even among these landmark environmental laws, the ESA stands out, as perhaps the most stringent, most comprehensive, and most controversial. This book, now in its second edition, assembles the thoughts, analyses, and recommendations of a number of experts in the field on the ongoing legal practice that has emerged from this law over more than 35 years.[1]

As Michael Bean explains in his short history of the law (Chapter 1), the ESA provides a comprehensive approach to the complex environmental problem of species extinction. For instance, like the Migratory Bird Treaty Act and the MMPA, the ESA prohibits the take of protected species. Like the Lacey Act, the ESA regulates commerce in wildlife and plants. The ESA also provides for habitat acquisition similar to provisions of the Migratory Bird Conservation Act. Even the ESA's most distinctive provision, the interagency consultation requirements set forth in section 7, finds a progenitor in the Fish and Wildlife Coordination Act. The ESA is unique because it adopts all of these approaches to the battle against extinction and the drive toward species recovery, in recognition of the multiple and diverse causes of species endangerment.

The ESA's comprehensive approach has significant impacts on the management and use of public and private lands and waters. Thus, it is not surprising that the law has engendered much controversy during its first 35 years. At least some of this controversy is due to an inadequate understanding of what the law does and does not require. This misunderstanding is by no means limited to the lay public; even many legal practitioners find themselves at sea when faced with a client's first encounter with the ESA. As with the first edition, this book is intended to serve as a guide for both the novice and the more experienced practitioner to the ins and outs of the ESA.

Responsibility for Implementation

The ESA is administered jointly by the Secretaries of Commerce and the Interior. Within the Department of Commerce, the National Marine Fisheries Service (NMFS) is responsible for carrying out the Act. This agency has jurisdiction over marine species, including anadromous fish. At the Interior Department, lead responsibility for the ESA is vested in the U.S. Fish and Wildlife Service (FWS). FWS applies the ESA to terrestrial species, nonmarine aquatic species, and certain marine species, including sea turtles while on land and sea otters.

Numerous states have their own laws to protect rare and vulnerable species. These laws vary significantly. Some of them closely resemble the federal ESA, while others are much more limited in scope. Still others create even more rigorous standards. As a general rule, however, the requirements of the federal law prevail in situations where there might be a conflict. State laws can control in cases of conflict only where they are more stringent.[2] States can enter into cooperative agreements with FWS and NMFS, and in doing so qualify for federal financial assistance and receive a narrow exception from the take prohibition for certain conservation programs.[3] In Chapter 16, Sue George and William Snape analyze the role and effectiveness of state endangered species laws.

Throughout this book the manner in which FWS and NMFS apply the ESA is discussed in a variety of contexts, such as making listing decisions (Ruhl, Chapter 2), conducting consultations (Ryan and Malmen, Chapter 5), complying with the take prohibition (Quarles and Lundquist, Chapter 8), and applying exemptions to the take prohibition (Kalen and Pan, Chapter 9; Bean, Chapter 10; and Wheeler and Rowberry, Chapter 11). This book also addresses specific issues such as protecting plants (Wheeler, Chapter 12), applying the ESA in international settings (Young and Wheeler, Chapter 15) and to nanotechnology (Klise, Quarles and Irvin, Chapter 17), and reconciling the law with the rights of Native Americans (Holt, Chapter 6).

The ESA's Goals

In 1973, Congress enacted the ESA with a bold declaration of both the reasons it was needed and the goals it was written to achieve. In section 2 of the law, Congress found and declared that "various species of fish, wildlife, and plants in the United States have been rendered extinct as a consequence of economic growth and development untempered by adequate concern and conservation."[4] Furthermore, Congress recognized that other species were in danger of extinction and "these species of fish, wildlife, and plants are of esthetic, ecological, educational, historical, recreational, and scientific value to the Nation and its people."[5] Moreover, Congress recognized that the United States had pledged itself through various international agreements to conserve endangered species.[6]

To address these concerns, Congress clearly established that the purposes of the ESA are "to provide a means whereby the ecosystems upon which endangered species and threatened species depend may be conserved, to provide a program for the conservation of such endangered species and threatened species, and to take such steps as may be appropriate to achieve the purposes of the treaties and conventions" under which the United States pledged to conserve endangered species.[7]

The congressional findings and purposes underlying the ESA are remarkable in two important respects. First, Congress clearly recognized that "economic growth and development, untempered by adequate concern and conservation," was a leading cause of species endangerment. Second, Congress made conservation of ecosystems the first purpose of the ESA, even before conserving endangered species themselves. Thus, Congress demonstrated an important degree of realism about the causes of extinction and foresight about what must be done to stave off extinction.

A central question raised often by the chapter authors is whether Congress provided the tools necessary to achieve these goals. The purposes to which these tools are applied are discussed in several of the chapters in this book including those by Bean (History—Chapter 1), and Goble (Recovery Planning—Chapter 4). The viewpoint of advocates from the environmental community on how well the ESA is accomplishing these goals, as well as the role of the ESA in addressing the causes and impacts of global warming, is provided by John Kostyack and Dan Rohlf in Chapter 18. A different perspective on these issues from the resource development community is set forth in Chapter 19 by Buzz Fawcett.

Listing, Critical Habitat, Recovery Plans

To receive protection under the ESA, a species first must be listed. The listing process involves a detailed technical review that may be initiated by nonfederal parties through a petition, or by FWS or NMFS on their own initiative.[8] Listing decisions must be made on the basis of five criteria set forth in the ESA:

1. The present or threatened destruction, modification, or curtailment of the species' habitat or range;
2. Overutilization of the species for commercial, recreational, scientific, or educational purposes;
3. Disease or predation;
4. The inadequacy of existing regulatory mechanisms; or
5. Other natural or manmade factors affecting the species' continued existence.[9]

Decisions on listing proposals must be made according to specified time frames.[10] Decisions are to be made "solely on the basis of the best scientific and commercial data available,"[11] and economics are not taken into account.[12] As of September 18, 2008, a total of 1,353 species in the United States were listed as endangered or threatened, with 574 foreign species also listed.

Critical habitat is to be designated at the time of listing or within one year. Critical habitat is defined as the specific geographic area that contains the physical and biological features essential to the species' conservation and that may require special management or protection.[13] Critical habitat need not be designated when such identification would increase the risk of harm to the species or when the benefits of exclusion, including economic benefits, outweigh the benefits of designations.[14] Once a critical habitat is designated, federal agencies are prohibited from authorizing (e.g., through permits, licenses, contracts), funding, or carrying out any action that is likely to result in the destruction or adverse modification of the critical habitat.[15] As of September 18, 2008, critical habitat has been designated for 520 of the species listed in the United States.

The important building blocks of listing and critical habitat are dealt with in two chapters in this book. In Chapter 2, J. B. Ruhl discusses the listing process and the manner in which FWS, NMFS, and the courts have interpreted the Act's requirements.

Federico Cheever gives similar treatment to the critical habitat designation process in Chapter 3.

The ultimate goal of the ESA is bringing listed species to a point where they no longer require the Act's protections.[16] The mechanism intended to guide this effort for each listed species is the recovery plan. Section 4(f) of the ESA directs FWS and NMFS to "develop and implement plans for the recovery and survival" of listed species.[17] This duty does not apply if a finding is made that "such a plan will not promote the conservation of the species."[18] These plans generally are quite detailed and identify recovery actions to be taken over an extended period of time. They are non-enforceable and advisory in nature. As of September 18, 2008, recovery plans had been developed for 1,168 of the species listed in the United States. The requirements of section 4(f) and the case law that has grown up around those ESA provisions are discussed in Chapter 4 by Dale Goble.

The Duty to Consult and Avoid Jeopardy

In addition to the prohibitions on take set forth in section 9 of the ESA, the other ban on actions that adversely affect listed species is the jeopardy/critical habitat modification prohibition of section 7(a)(2).[19] This prohibition is carried out through the interagency consultation process, also mandated by section 7(a)(2).

The federal government and each of its agencies have a statutory mandate to use their powers for the conservation of species.[20] Each agency must ensure that any action it authorizes, funds, or carries out is not likely to jeopardize the continued existence of a listed species in the wild, or destroy or adversely modify its critical habitat.[21] If an agency determines that a proposed action may adversely affect a listed species, it must formally consult with FWS or NMFS.[22] If an agency determines that a proposed action may adversely affect a species proposed for listing, it must confer informally with FWS or NMFS, and the results of that conference are nonbinding.[23]

After consultation, FWS or NMFS will issue a biological opinion regarding the effects of the proposed action.[24] If the FWS or NMFS find jeopardy or critical habitat destruction or adverse modification, they must propose reasonable and prudent alternatives to the action, if such alternatives are available.[25] If the action agency rejects these alternatives, it may seek an exemption from the Endangered Species Committee—a Cabinet-level committee, rarely used—or run the legal risk of proceeding in the face of the jeopardy finding. If the action will result in the incidental take of a listed species, the biological opinion will be accompanied by an incidental take statement proposing any measures FWS or NMFS believes necessary to minimize the impact of the taking on the species. Section 7 consultation is discussed by Patrick Ryan and Erika Malmen in Chapter 5.

In addition to the consultation requirements of section 7, federal agencies must also consult with qualifying tribes potentially affected by ESA-related determinations. Under an order issued during the Clinton administration by the Secretaries of

Commerce and the Interior, federal agencies that administer the ESA must also consult with any federally recognized tribe whose lands, trust resources, or treaty rights may be affected by any decision, determination, or activity implementing the ESA. These procedures are described by Mary Gray Holt in Chapter 6.

The Take Prohibition and Its Exemptions

The jeopardy prohibition in section 7 applies only to federal agencies, although it indirectly affects those nonfederal entities that depend upon federal actions for their activities. For nonfederal actions that could independently affect listed species, the section 9 take prohibition applies.[26] Due to its breadth and the consequences that result from violating it, the take prohibition is both the strength of the ESA and the source of much controversy over the law's reach. This section also prohibits the export, import, possession, transportation, or sale of listed species in certain circumstances.[27]

Under section 9, to "take" means "to harass, harm, pursue, hunt, shoot, wound, kill, trap, capture, or collect, or to attempt to engage in any such conduct."[28] Regulations defining "harm" to include habitat modification were upheld by the U.S. Supreme Court.[29] The requirements of section 9 are set forth by Patrick Parenteau in Chapter 7. Steve Quarles and Tom Lundquist describe section 9 compliance issues in Chapter 8. The ESA's special prohibitions regarding threatened and endangered plants are discussed by Holly Wheeler in Chapter 12. International trade restrictions and other international aspects of ESA implementation are described by Michael Young and Holly Wheeler in Chapter 15.

To enforce these prohibitions, the federal government can initiate a civil action to obtain an injunction against activity that may result in a take (e.g., halting an ongoing forest practice), obtain civil penalties for a past take, or initiate a criminal action if the take is "knowing."[30] These prohibitions can also be enforced in a civil action initiated by citizen groups under section 11(g) of the ESA.[31] Citizen suits are discussed by Eric Glitzenstein in Chapter 13.

The section 9 take prohibition is not ironclad; the ESA sets forth important exceptions. As noted above, federal actions that cause incidental take can be excused by an incidental take statement included in a biological opinion issued under section 7(a)(2). This exception is discussed by Patrick Ryan and Erika Malmen in Chapter 5.

Additional exceptions to the take prohibition are set forth in section 10 of the ESA, which is discussed by Sam Kalen and Adam Pan in Chapter 9. These exceptions include those for pre-Act specimens, economic hardship, subsistence, and handicraft use by certain Alaskan residents, and for scientific purposes or propagation.[32] Section 10 also establishes an exemption for so-called "experimental populations."[33] This authority is invoked when necessary to pave the way for the introduction of a population of a listed species in a new area when necessary for conservation purposes. The authority of section 10(j) allows for the application of less restrictive ESA prohibitions, including relaxing the ban on taking. In 1982, Congress amended the

ESA to allow a private applicant to commit a take that would otherwise be prohibited if such taking was "incidental to, and not [for] the purpose of, the carrying out of an otherwise lawful activity."[34] Under section 10 of the ESA, incidental take is currently authorized through a variety of voluntary agreements to conserve or minimize and mitigate impacts to fish and wildlife, including (1) candidate conservation agreements (CCAs), (2) safe harbor agreements, and (3) habitat conservation plans (HCPs).

Using those tools to enlist landowners in ESA conservation measures has increasingly been recognized as important by the environmental and regulated communities alike. Michael Bean discusses these incentives in Chapter 10. At the same time, the implementation and monitoring of HCPs continues to be controversial, as described by Doug Wheeler and Ryan Rowberry in Chapter 11.

A continuing source of controversy under the ESA is the relationship between the enforcement of the law's take prohibition and private property rights. The tension between the ESA and the Constitution's Fifth Amendment takings clause is discussed in Chapter 14 by John Echeverria and Glenn Sugameli.

Conclusion

After more than 35 years, the ESA continues to be one of our most important, yet controversial, conservation laws. Efforts to reauthorize the ESA over the past 20 years have foundered as each side blocks the other's legislative initiatives while failing to reach consensus on what measures are necessary to enhance the ESA's effectiveness and usefulness. Despite the controversies, however, the ESA remains in place, due largely to the overwhelming public support for saving wildlife on the brink of extinction. Accordingly, for conservationists who care about saving endangered wildlife and its habitat, for landowners, businesses, and government agencies whose activities are affected by the ESA's requirements, and for attorneys representing all of these interests, a thorough knowledge of how the law has been interpreted and applied is essential. It is our hope that this new edition of this book will continue to provide that knowledge and that you, as readers, will use that knowledge to further the farsighted and noble purposes for which the ESA was enacted.

Notes

1. Many individuals have contributed to the development of this book. For this second edition, technical assistance has been provided by Rebecca Brezenoff and Judy Casey with Perkins Coie. Adam Pan, an environmental attorney practicing in Washington, D.C., provided editorial assistance.
2. 16 U.S.C. § 1533(f).
3. *Id.* § 1535(d)(2); 50 C.F.R. §§ 17.21(c)(5), 17.31(b).
4. 16 U.S.C. § 1531(a)(1).
5. *Id.* § 1531(a)(3).
6. *Id.* § 1531(a)(4).
7. *Id.* § 1531(b).
8. *Id.* § 1533.
9. *Id.* § 1533(a)(1).

10. *Id.* § 1533(b)(1).
11. *Id.* § 1533(b)(1)(A).
12. *Id.* § 1533(a)(1)(D).
13. *Id.* § 1533(a)(3).
14. 50 C.F.R. § 424.12(a)(1)(i)–(ii).
15. 16 U.S.C. § 1536(a)(2).
16. *Id.* §§ 1531(b), 1532(3).
17. *Id.* § 1533(f).
18. *Id.*
19. *Id.* § 1536(a)(2).
20. *Id.* § 1536(a)(1).
21. *Id.* § 1536(a)(2).
22. 50 C.F.R. § 402.141.
23. 16 U.S.C. § 1536(a)(4); 50 C.F.R. § 402.10.
24. 16 U.S.C. § 1536(a)(3)(A); 50 C.F.R. § 402.14(g)(4).
25. *Id.*; 50 C.F.R. § 402.14(g)(5).
26. *Id.* § 1538(a)(1)(B), (c).
27. *Id.* § 1538(a)(1)(A).
28. *Id.* § 1532(19).
29. Babbitt v. Sweet Home Chapter of Cmtys. for a Great Or., 515 U.S. 687 (1995).
30. 16 U.S.C. § 1540(b).
31. *Id.* § 1540(g).
32. *Id.* § 1539(a)(1), (b), (e), (f), (h).
33. *Id.* § 1539(a)(1).
34. *Id.* § 1539(a)(1)(B).

1

Historical Background of the Endangered Species Act

Michael J. Bean

Herman Melville, it seemed, knew almost everything about whales. His tale of Captain Ahab's obsessive quest for the white Leviathan was woven around chapters that discuss whale anatomy, whales in mythology and the arts, whales in the fossil record, the whaling community of Nantucket, uses of whale oil, and so on. Melville's knowledge of whales was almost encyclopedic.

And yet, on the most important question that Melville asked about whales, he was dead wrong. In Melville's inimitable prose, the question was "whether Leviathan can long endure so wide a chase, and so remorseless a havoc; whether he must not at last be exterminated from the waters, and the last whale, like the last man, smoke his last pipe, and then himself evaporate in the last puff."[1] To this question, Melville emphatically answered in the negative. Whales, he believed, were simply too numerous, their human pursuers too few, and the vast expanses of the ocean too great for extinction to be a possibility.

Melville undoubtedly never heard the modern term "catch per unit effort," but he was aware that whalers in his day had to search longer and farther to bring back the same number of whales as in former days. He dismissed this fact, however, with the argument that whales, "influenced by some views to safety," had simply rearranged their groupings from many small pods to fewer but larger herds and had moved elsewhere: "If one coast is no longer enlivened with their jets, be sure, some other and remoter strand has been very recently startled by the unfamiliar spectacle."

Moreover, Melville argued, even if driven from waters everywhere else, whales could take final refuge in "two firm fortresses, which, in all human probability, will for ever remain impregnable." Like the Swiss retreating from their valleys to the mountains in the face of invaders, whales pursued in the open sea "can at last resort to their Polar citadels, and diving under the ultimate glassy barriers and walls there, come up among icy fields and floes; and in a charmed circle of everlasting December, bid defiance to all pursuit from man." Clearly, Melville never foresaw the melting of the polar ice cap from human-caused climate change that now seems likely.[2]

From the vantage point of a century and a half later, Melville's steadfast refusal to regard the extinction of whales as thinkable seems wholly irrational, a matter of blind faith masquerading behind a facade of learned sophistry. At least Melville was able to acknowledge that some whale fossils were of species no longer in existence. Thomas Jefferson, on the other hand, had argued against the possibility that any fossil creatures were of extinct species. In Jefferson's view, "such is the economy of Nature that no instance can be produced of her having permitted any one race of her animals to become extinct, of her having formed any link in her great work so weak as to be broken."[3]

And yet, even if Melville can be faulted for his steadfast refusal to acknowledge the consequences of the industry he extolled, he should not be judged too harshly. The belief that our means are too limited and the resilience of our fellow creatures too great for our actions ever to drive them to extinction—not just whales, but virtually any other species—is with us still. Indeed, it is the reason that our acknowledgment of a species' endangerment often comes too late. It is, in short, part of the explanation for the fact that meaningful legislation to prevent the extinction of other species was so long in coming.

Melville's *Moby-Dick* was published in 1851. It would be almost another half century before recognition of the true peril that many species faced would be sufficient to prompt action. That recognition stirred the beginning of the American conservation movement. Among its leaders were some of the most distinguished scientists and influential citizens of the day. Theodore Roosevelt, avid outdoorsman and accomplished natural historian, was instrumental in the founding of the New York Zoological Society (now known as the Wildlife Conservation Society) in 1895. Among the first tasks of the society was to rescue the American bison, of which only a handful remained. The National Audubon Society traces its roots to this same era, a response to the decimation of many plumed birds to supply the millinery trade.

The efforts of the early conservationists prompted a legislative response. In 1900, Congress enacted the first significant federal wildlife law, the Lacey Act, named for Iowa Congressman John Lacey, its principal sponsor.[4] The congressional debate that produced the Lacey Act reveals widespread awareness of at least one catastrophic decline in a once-familiar species, the passenger pigeon.

Within the lifetimes of those who debated the Lacey Act, the passenger pigeon had been one of the most abundant birds in the nation. Vast flocks were reported to have literally blackened the skies for extended periods. Yet by the turn of the century, this once-prolific bird had been reduced to a handful of survivors. Congressman Lacey apparently thought the bird had already gone extinct, for he declared that "[t]he wild pigeon, formerly in this country in flocks of millions, has entirely disappeared from the face of the earth."[5]

Lacey wrote the bird's obituary prematurely; the last survivor, a female named Martha by her captors, would die September 1, 1914, in a cage in the Cincinnati Zoo. Martha's death brings to mind the words of one of Roosevelt's compatriots, the scientist William Beebe, in 1906: "The beauty and genius of a work of art may be reconceived, though its first material expression be destroyed; a vanished harmony may yet again inspire the composer; but when the last individual of a race of living things breathes no more, another heaven and another earth must pass before such a one can be again."[6]

The collapse of the passenger pigeon had happened so quickly, and was so evident to so many, that Congress felt compelled to do what it never had done before—enact federal legislation for the conservation of wildlife. Before the Lacey Act, wildlife conservation had been the jealously guarded exclusive prerogative of the states. Indeed, the U.S. Supreme Court had intimated, only four years earlier, that the states were the owners of all wildlife within their borders.[7] Nevertheless, prompted by the slaughter of birds for their meat and feathers, Congress enacted the Lacey Act. The first purpose of the bill, according to Congressman Lacey, was to authorize the Secretary of Agriculture (who oversaw the Bureau of Biological Survey, predecessor to today's U.S. Fish and Wildlife Service) "to utilize his Department for the reintroduction of birds that have become locally extinct or are becoming so."[8] More broadly, the law made it a federal offense to ship unlawfully acquired wildlife—not only birds, but other species as well—in interstate commerce. Federal wildlife conservation law was launched, and it was the endangerment and extinction of species that set it in motion.

The Lacey Act came too late to avert the extinction of the passenger pigeon. Nor did it rescue North America's only native parrot, the Carolina parakeet, the last of which also died in captivity in 1914. The heath hen, a bird that was still somewhat common in Melville's New England, had completely vanished by 1932. By 1941 the extinction of the whooping crane also appeared imminent. The crane had once occupied a breeding range over parts of Iowa, Illinois, Minnesota, North Dakota, and Canada, but by 1941 its entire population had been reduced to only 21 birds.

One year earlier, in 1940, the United States signed a Convention on Nature Protection and Wildlife Preservation in the Western Hemisphere.[9] Among its stated purposes was "to protect and preserve in their natural habitat representatives of all species and genera . . . in sufficient numbers and over areas extensive enough to assure them from becoming extinct through any agency within man's control." World War II soon distracted the nation's attention, and the commitments of the Western Hemisphere Convention were largely unaddressed for another quarter century.

Despite the absence of any statutory authority to seek to conserve endangered species, the Department of the Interior's Bureau of Sport Fisheries and Wildlife, which had been created by executive reorganization in 1939, began modest research and conservation projects directed at a few seriously imperiled species. Preventing the extinction of the whooping crane was one of the first of these projects. Another early object of concern was the nene, or Hawaiian goose. For it, Congress passed a 1958 law authorizing the Secretary of the Interior to carry out a program of research, propagation, and management. Without much notice or fanfare, the Interior Department was steadily building a portfolio of projects aimed at averting the extinction of endangered species.

Eventually, these projects coalesced around a more formal effort to understand the gravity of the extinction threat. In 1964, within the Interior Department's Bureau of Sport Fisheries and Wildlife, the Committee on Rare and Endangered Wildlife Species was established. One of its first products was a preliminary list of rare and endangered vertebrates, informally referred to as "the Redbook." The 63 species it identified represented the first unofficial list of endangered species in the United States.

Contemporaneous with these developments in the United States, a parallel effort was playing out in the international arena. The International Union for the Conservation of Nature, an amalgam of governmental and nongovernmental conservation entities, began to promote the idea of a global treaty to protect endangered species in the early 1960s. The impetus for its efforts was not unlike that which had spurred Congress to action in 1900. The extinction of many of the world's great whales, which Melville had thought inconceivable, was now perceived to be a real possibility.

Similarly vulnerable were many of the world's spotted cats and other familiar species under siege from overexploitation and loss of habitat. (The international effort would eventually bear fruit in 1973 with the negotiation of the Convention on International Trade in Endangered Species of Wild Fauna and Flora.[10])

In the United States, Congress passed its seminal endangered species law in 1966. A catalyst for the law was the fact that Congress had balked at appropriating funds for the nascent endangered species effort initiated by Interior's Committee on Rare and Endangered Wildlife Species. Before it would appropriate significant funds, Congress wanted to make sure that Interior had the necessary authority to initiate such a program. The 1966 Endangered Species Preservation Act was the result.[11]

The 1966 act was a very modest first step into the endangered species arena. It directed the Secretary of the Interior to "carry out a program in the United States of conserving, protecting, restoring and propagating selected species of native fish and wildlife that are threatened with extinction."[12] The contents of that program, however, were largely unspecified. The law authorized the secretary to utilize the then-new Land and Water Conservation Fund to acquire land for the program and directed him to promulgate a list of native endangered species. Significantly, however, it imposed no prohibitions or restrictions with respect to the hunting or selling of such species or the destruction of their habitats. On March 11, 1967, the secretary published the first official list of endangered species. It totaled 78.

The 1966 act focused exclusively on species native to the United States and, implicitly at least, solely on vertebrates. The extinction threat, however, knew no national or taxonomic boundaries; for many of the world's most imperiled species, the American marketplace was the engine driving their overexploitation elsewhere. Recognizing these facts, Congress in 1969 significantly expanded the federal endangered species program by enacting the Endangered Species Conservation Act of 1969.[13] It authorized the Secretary of the Interior to promulgate a list of species—U.S. or foreign—that were "threatened with worldwide extinction." These species could include not only vertebrates but mollusks and crustaceans as well. Importantly, for the first time ever, the 1969 law imposed a clear regulatory prohibition: no endangered species could be imported into the United States except for a limited set of special purposes.[14] Among the first species added to the expanded list were eight of the great whales.

The 1969 law also directed the secretary to "seek the convening of an international ministerial meeting" to conclude "a binding international convention on the conservation of endangered species."[15] That meeting was hosted by the United States in early 1973. From it came a global treaty to regulate international trade in endangered species, including both plants and animals. In the United States, the treaty is known by its formal name, the Convention on International Trade in Endangered Species of Wild Fauna and Flora, or CITES. In much of the rest of the world, it is known simply as "the Washington Convention."

The international meeting that produced CITES gave added impetus to efforts in the United States to revise the endangered species law that had been enacted only four years earlier. To conservationists and to the President's Council on Environmental Quality, which was a very influential voice in the Nixon administration, the 1969 law had a number of serious deficiencies. It encompassed neither plants nor most invertebrates. It did nothing to restrict the "taking" of endangered species. It imposed no real constraints on federal land managers or other federal agencies. It lacked the flexibility to distinguish among populations of a species, some of which might be in serious peril. Finally, beyond land acquisition authority, it had no mechanism to recognize or protect habitats of special significance to endangered species. Congressman John Dingell, a sportsman and wildlife enthusiast, used his subcommittee chairmanship in the House to push a bill remedying these shortcomings.

In hindsight, it is ironic that the provisions of the law enacted late in 1973 that have given rise to so much recent controversy sparked little debate at the time. Instead, one of the most contentious issues was the familiar debate over the relative roles to be given state and federal agencies. Among those who argued most steadfastly for state primacy was the National Wildlife Federation. At hearings it argued that states should "continue to exercise the prime responsibility for managing" endangered species and should "be given an appropriate opportunity to prepare and manage recovery plans, and retain jurisdiction over endangered species."[16] Congress instead chose to give the federal government primary responsibility for endangered species, while encouraging the states to develop parallel conservation programs of their own.

Both the House and Senate gave nearly unanimous approval to the Endangered Species Act of 1973.[17] How much attention the Nixon White House, then engulfed in Watergate and other scandals, gave to the legislation can only be surmised. Just two months before the Act reached the president's desk, Vice President Agnew had resigned, Nixon had prompted an uproar by firing Watergate special prosecutor Archibald Cox, and the House Judiciary Committee had begun impeachment hearings. Despite those serious distractions, President Nixon offered a brief but eloquent statement upon signing the bill into law. "Nothing is more priceless and more worthy of preservation," Nixon noted, "than the rich array of animal life with which our country has been blessed. It is a many-faceted treasure, of value to scholars, scientists, and nature lovers alike, and it forms a vital part of the heritage we all share as Americans."[18] Referring to the "countless future generations" for which that heritage is held in trust, Nixon concluded that "[t]heir lives will be richer, and America will be more beautiful in the years ahead, thanks to the measure that I have the pleasure to sign into law today."[19]

Thirty-five years later, nearly 2,000 species and lesser taxa (more than 1,350 of which occur in the United States) are in peril of extinction. A few have been safely pulled back from the brink, among them the gray whale, wolves in the Great Lakes states, grizzly bears in the Yellowstone ecosystem, and the nation's symbol—the bald eagle. For most, however, their ultimate fate remains unknown and rests on how effectively the Endangered Species Act is implemented and on what future Congresses do with that law. The near unanimity that characterized the political support for the Endangered Species Act in 1973 has given way to sharp partisan and ideological conflict. Congress reauthorized and amended the Endangered Species Act three times in its first decade, but nearly two decades have passed since any significant revisions have been able to muster enough support in a sharply divided Congress to become law.

Notes

1. All quotations from Herman Melville are from chapter 55 of his 1851 classic, *Moby-Dick*. Chapter 55 is entitled "Does the Whale's Magnitude Diminish?—Will He Perish?"
2. For a discussion of the prospects for significant polar ice melting, see the notice listing the polar bear as a threatened species, 73 Fed. Reg. 28,211 (May 15, 2008).
3. THOMAS JEFFERSON, NOTES ON THE STATE OF VIRGINIA 55 (1855).
4. 31 Stat. 187 (1900) (current version at 16 U.S.C. §§ 3371–3378 and 18 U.S.C. § 42).
5. 46 CONG. REC. 4871 (Apr. 30, 1900).
6. C. WILLIAM BEEBE, THE BIRD: ITS FORM AND FUNCTION 18 (1906).
7. Geer v. Connecticut, 161 U.S. 519 (1896).
8. 46 CONG. REC. 4871 (Apr. 30, 1900).
9. 56 Stat. 1534, T.S. No. 981, U.N.T.S. No. 193.
10. 27 U.S.T. 1087, T.I.A.S. No. 8249.
11. Pub. L. No. 89-669, §§ 1–3, 80 Stat. 926.
12. *Id.* § 2(a).
13. Pub. L. No. 91-135, 83 Stat. 275.
14. *Id.* § 2.
15. *Id.* § 5(b).
16. *Hearings on Endangered Species before the Subcommittee on Fisheries and Wildlife Conservation and the Environment*, 93d Cong., 1st Sess. 292–293 (1973) (statement of Louis S. Clapper on behalf of the National Wildlife Federation).
17. 16 U.S.C. §§ 1531 *et seq.*
18. Statement of President Richard M. Nixon, upon signing the Endangered Species Act, San Clemente, CA (Dec. 28, 1973), *reprinted in* S. COMM. ON ENVIRONMENT AND PUBLIC WORKS, A LEGISLATIVE HISTORY OF THE ENDANGERED SPECIES ACT, AS AMENDED IN 1976, 1977, 1978, 1979, AND 1980, at 487 (1982).
19. *Id.*

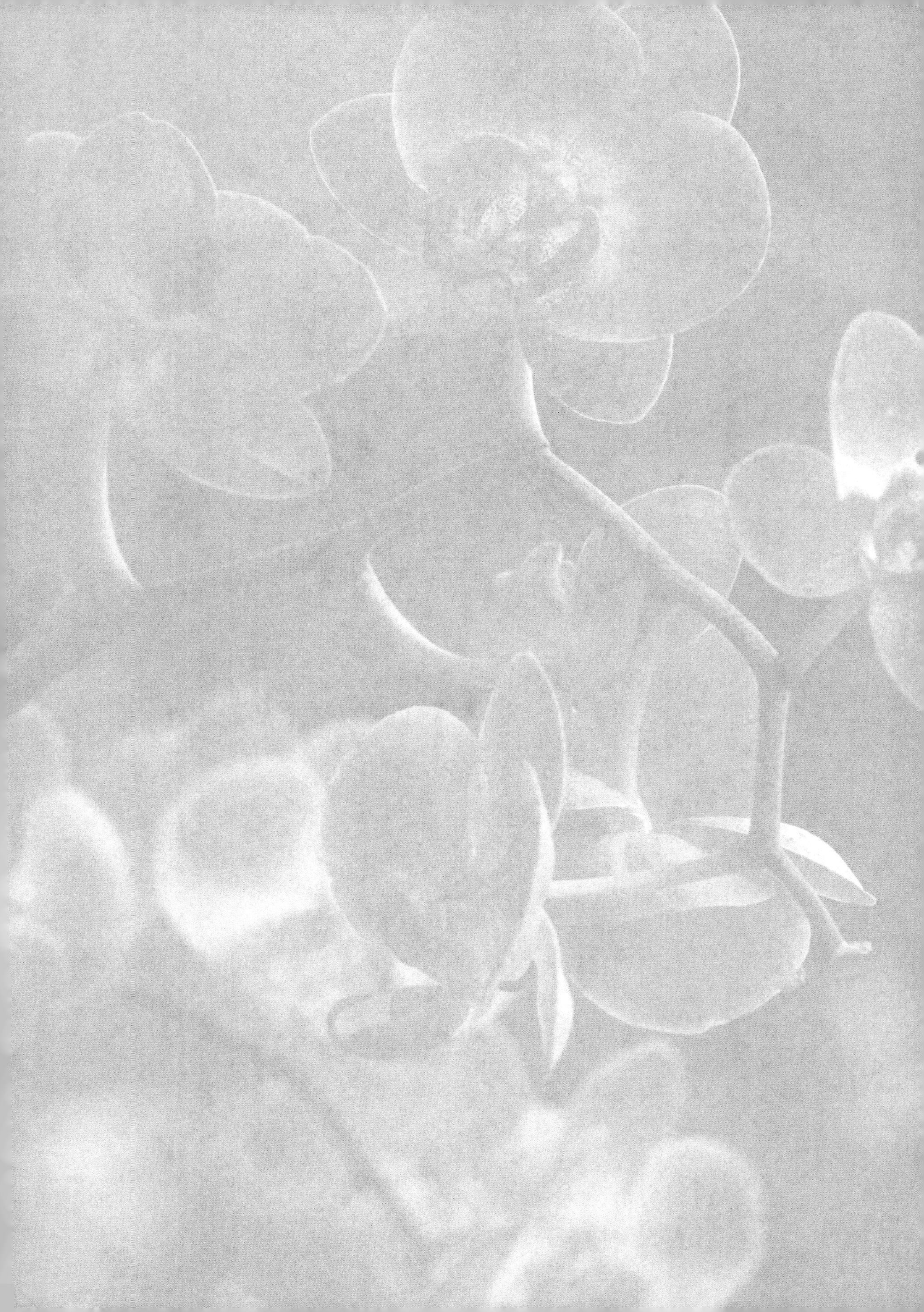

2

Listing Endangered and Threatened Species

J. B. Ruhl

Introduction

The starting point for any comprehensive review of the Endangered Species Act (ESA) should be the procedures for listing endangered and threatened species found in section 4 of the Act.[1] Congress, when reauthorizing the ESA in 1982, confirmed that these procedures are nothing less than the keystone of the nation's first meaningful species protection law.[2] They authorize the Secretary of the Interior, in the case of freshwater and terrestrial species, and the Secretary of Commerce, in the case of marine and anadromous species, to designate species that are endangered or threatened by virtually any natural or human-caused factors affecting their continued existence.

The listing of a species triggers several important duties and prohibitions under the ESA. Under section 7, all federal agencies must ensure that actions that they fund, approve, or carry out do not jeopardize a listed endangered or threatened species or adversely affect designated critical habitat.[3] Federal agencies must also promote conservation of endangered and threatened species through their programs.[4] All persons, public or private, must comply with the prohibitions set forth in section 9, the most familiar of which is the "take" prohibition covering listed endangered fish and wildlife species,[5] which the Secretaries may extend to threatened fish and wildlife species by rulemaking.[6] Finally, the Secretaries in most cases must prepare plans for the recovery of endangered and threatened species.[7] Once a species is listed, the tremendous force of these provisions (particularly the jeopardy prohibition in section 7 and the take prohibition found in section 9) comes to bear—some would say with too great a potency, and some would say without enough. Under either perspective, however, all agree that the species listing process, because it triggers the regulatory and planning provisions of the statute, is "the gateway to the ESA."[8]

Ironically, notwithstanding all the front-page attention the ESA has received since the infamous snail darter case, in which the Supreme Court ruled that the jeopardy prohibition precluded final construction of a federally constructed dam,[9] remarkably little attention was paid to the species listing process during the ESA's first two decades. Most litigation under the Act prior to 1995 involved the effects of a listing, not whether the listing should have occurred. Since then, however, through the surge in the number of species being listed or examined for listing, and through an increasing awareness by environmentalists and industry alike of the broad and deep force of the ESA's prohibitions, the species listing process has become the focus of intensified advocacy and litigation.

With that heightened focus in mind, this chapter provides a blueprint of the listing process as presently structured and an overview of the current issues driving administrative implementation and judicial interpretation. The section on the current state of the law covers key statutory definitions and standards, the statutory procedures for listing decisions, and the key judicial interpretation and agency policy developments. The section on emerging issues briefly covers three topics that are likely to be crucibles of further judicial and administrative attention to the section 4 listing program in the next decade: (1) the upcoming wave of five-year species status reviews; (2) the revelation in 2007 of significant political interference with listing decisions; and (3) unquestionably the most complex of all, climate change.

Current State of the Law

The breadth of the ESA is plainly illustrated by the statutory definitions and criteria relevant to the listing process, which are found in section 3 of the Act. These statutory definitions and criteria are incorporated into the administrative regulations adopted jointly by the U.S. Fish and Wildlife Service (FWS) for the Department of the Interior and the National Marine Fisheries Service (NMFS) for the Department of Commerce.[10] The statute and regulations also specify detailed procedures for carrying out the listing function. For the most part, the administrative regulations for listing definitions and standards do not elaborate substantially on the statutory terms. As with many environmental laws, however, over time court interpretations have added extensively to the content and meaning of the provisions, which in turn has prompted the agencies to promulgate extensive administrative policy guidance and other secondary regulatory materials. The current state of the law for the ESA listing program thus has become an amalgam of statutory provisions, administrative regulations, judicial decisions, and agency policy guidance documents. For a clearer picture of the resulting maze, this section of the chapter unpacks it into its component parts.

Key Statutory Definitions and Standards

The starting point is the statutory definition of species, which includes any "species or any subspecies of fish or wildlife or plants, and any distinct population segment of any species of vertebrate fish or wildlife which interbreeds when mature."[11] A species is endangered if it is "in danger of extinction throughout all or a significant portion of its range,"[12] or a species may be threatened if it is "likely to become an endangered species within the foreseeable future throughout all or a significant portion of its range."[13] Only insects determined to be pests are denied these designations.[14] The agencies' regulations adopt these definitions without material change.[15]

The ESA and its implementing regulations provide several criteria for applying these broad, amorphous statutory definitions. For example, the assessment of the endangered or threatened status of a species is measured under the statute using five factors:

(A) the present or threatened destruction, modification, or curtailment of its habitat or range;
(B) overutilization for commercial, recreational, scientific, or educational purposes;
(C) disease or predation;
(D) the inadequacy of existing regulatory mechanisms;
(E) other natural or manmade factors affecting its continued existence.[16]

The species' status assessment must also take into account the efforts of state and foreign governments to protect the species insofar as they may avoid the need for federal ESA listing.[17] The agency must weigh all of these factors "solely on the basis of the best scientific and commercial data available."[18] This limitation reflects Congress's desire that "economic considerations have no relevance to determinations regarding the status of species."[19]

Although the regulations incorporate the statutory criteria for listing a species as endangered or threatened without material change,[20] only the regulations provide the criteria for delisting (removing a listed species from the list). A species may be delisted if the best scientific and commercial data available substantiate either that it is extinct, that it has recovered, or that the original data used for the listing were in error.[21] A species is extinct if it is extirpated from its previous range.[22] A species is recovered if the best available scientific and commercial evidence shows it is no longer endangered or threatened.[23]

Section 4 Implementing Procedures

Section 4 of the ESA creates four basic programs for implementing the definitions and standards relevant to the species listing process: (1) petition review; (2) listing action rulemaking; (3) emergency rulemaking; and (4) post-listing status review. The Secretary of the Interior has delegated implementation of these functions to the FWS, and the Secretary of Commerce has done so through the NMFS. The agencies have promulgated rules that elaborate upon the statutory programs, and the FWS has also issued the *Endangered Species Listing Handbook*, now in its fourth edition, as internal procedural guidance.[24]

Petition Review

Any person or organization may petition the FWS or NMFS to add a species to the endangered or threatened species list, delist a species, or reclassify a listed species (for example, from threatened to endangered),[25] though no such procedure exists for emergency listings.[26] To the maximum extent practicable, within 90 days of receiving a petition the agency must determine whether the petition presents substantial biological data to indicate that the petitioned action may be warranted.[27] To facilitate that evaluation, the agencies' regulations require that a petition to list, delist, or reclassify a species supply information that:

- Clearly indicates the administrative measure recommended and gives the scientific and any common name of the species involved;
- Contains detailed narrative justification for the recommended measure based on available information, past and present numbers and distribution of the species involved, and any threats faced by the species;
- Provides information regarding the status of the species overall or a significant portion of its range; and

- Is accompanied by appropriate supporting documentation in the form of bibliographic references, reprints of pertinent publications, copies of reports or letters from authorities, and maps.[28]

The data supplied on these subjects satisfies the "substantial information" criterion if it leads a reasonable person to believe that the measure proposed in the petition may be warranted.[29] Although public notice is not required to announce the filing of a petition, the 90-day finding on the petition must be published in the *Federal Register*.[30]

If the petitioned agency finds after its 90-day review that a petition does not satisfy the "substantial information" requirement, the unsuccessful petitioner may appeal that decision directly to federal district court.[31] If the agency determines that a petition presents adequate biological data to suggest the petitioned action may be warranted, the agency must, within 12 months of filing, commence a review of the petitioned action and make a determination as to whether the action is warranted.[32] If the agency decides that the petition may be warranted but that additional data is needed to make a definitive finding, the agency will publish a "notice of review" in the *Federal Register* to solicit additional data.[33]

For listing, delisting, and reclassification petitions, the agency's 12-month finding can determine that the petition is warranted, not warranted, or warranted but precluded.[34] The "warranted but precluded" category is reserved for situations when expeditious progress is being made on other pending listing status decisions that take precedence over the petitioned action.[35] The FWS has established a system for the ranking of species in terms of priority for final action on listing decisions based on taxonomic distinctions and the magnitude and immediacy of threat.[36] The agency also allocates funding for final listing actions based on a ranking system.

The agency's 12-month finding must be published in the *Federal Register*.[37] A petitioner who is unsuccessful in his listing action at this stage also may appeal a "not warranted" or "warranted but precluded" finding directly to federal district court.[38] Warranted but precluded findings on listing action petitions must be reviewed on an annual basis until the petitioned action is found to be warranted or not.[39] If the finding on a listing action petition is that the petitioned action is warranted, the agency must promptly publish in the *Federal Register* a proposed regulation to implement the petitioned action, thus concluding the petition review process.[40]

Listing Action Rulemaking

Species may be listed, delisted, or reclassified either through the petition process or at the initiation of the FWS or NMFS if adequate biological data warrants the action. In either case, the agency must publish a proposed rule in the *Federal Register* to begin the listing status decision process.[41] As a general rule the ESA makes all listing decisions subject to Administrative Procedure Act notice and comment rulemaking procedures.[42] Pursuant to specific ESA mandates, the agency also must supply notice directly to each state and foreign nation in which the species is believed to occur; to federal agencies, local authorities, and private individuals known to be affected by the rule; to such professional scientific organizations deemed appropriate; and to the affected public through newspapers.[43] The agency must accept public comment on the proposed rule for at least 60 days following such publication and must hold at least one public hearing within 45 days of publication if any person so requests.[44]

Within one year after publishing the proposed rule, the agency must adopt one of three positions: (1) promulgate a final rule implementing the listing action or find that the listing action should not be made; (2) withdraw the proposed rule if available evidence does not adequately support either of those two actions; or (3) extend the review period for no more than six months if there is disagreement regarding the sufficiency or accuracy of the available biological data.[45] If the agency decides to list a species as threatened rather than endangered, it must decide which of several protective features will apply to the species. Some of the ESA's prohibitory provisions and other requirements do not apply automatically to threatened species as they do for endangered species,[46] but under section 4(d) the listing agency may apply the section 9(a) endangered species protections to threatened species.[47] The FWS has extended such protections to all threatened species under a general regulation unless rules adopted for a particular species or special permit terms provide otherwise,[48] whereas the NMFS uses a species-by-species rulemaking approach for its section 4(d) authority.[49]

Emergency Rulemaking

Notwithstanding the ESA and Administrative Procedure Act procedures required for petitions and listing actions, the FWS and NMFS may at any time issue a regulation to implement any listing action in response to an emergency that poses a significant risk to the well-being of a species of fish, wildlife, or plant.[50] An emergency rule may take effect immediately upon publication in the *Federal Register*; however, the listing agency must supply notice to each state in which the species is believed to occur and must provide a detailed explanation in the published rule as to why the emergency action is necessary.[51] The emergency rule ceases to have effect if the agency later determines that substantial evidence does not exist to warrant the rule, or in all cases 240 days after publication, within which time the agency must initiate and complete normal rulemaking procedures for the species to remain listed.[52]

Post-Decisional Listing Program Duties

Several ESA programs are designed to continue the pursuit of species study and conservation objectives following a listing action. These include (1) list publication; (2) delisted species monitoring, and (5) listed species five-year status reviews.

List Publication

List publication applies to the Secretary of the Interior, requiring the FWS to publish in the *Federal Register* a list of all species the FWS and NMFS determine are endangered or threatened.[53] The lists must include scientific and common names, the portion of the species' range in which it is endangered or threatened, and any critical habitat. The lists must also be revised periodically to reflect new listing status decisions.[54] The FWS has published these lists at 50 C.F.R. §§ 17.11 (wildlife species) and 17.12 (plant species).[55] For example, as of January 2008, 607 animal species and 744 plant species that live totally or partly in the United States were listed as endangered or threatened.[56] Forty-two percent of listed animal species were mammals, and 43 percent were other vertebrate species.[57] Sixty-three threatened species, all of which were animals, had specialized section 4(d) rules.[58]

Delisted Species Monitoring

A species that is delisted because it has been found to have recovered from its endangered or threatened status must be monitored.[59] Although a delisted species is no longer protected by the regulatory provisions found elsewhere in the ESA, the FWS or NMFS must monitor the species for not less than five years following the delisting decision and, if necessary, make prompt use of the emergency rulemaking authorities to protect the well-being of the species.[60]

Five-Year Status Review

At least once every five years, FWS and NMFS must conduct a review of all listed species under their respective jurisdictions and determine which should be removed from the lists or changed in status in accordance with the listing status rulemaking procedures.[61]

Section 4 in the Courts

Before the 1990s, judicial examination of the ESA section 4 programs was insignificant. One early case addressed standing to challenge listing decisions, ruling that one must show, as a result of the administrative action, a concrete injury that is likely to be redressed by a favorable judicial decision.[62] That decision may have been a harbinger of the Supreme Court's later standing decision under another section of the ESA, which rejected assertions of abstract, tenuous standing theories such as impaired use of the ecosystem.[63] During the 1980s, however, case law on section 4 actions increased, and it worked up to a fast pace by the mid-1990s and into the 2000s on both substantive and procedural fronts.

Substantive Challenges

The first case to tackle the merits of a listing decision on substantive grounds, *Northern Spotted Owl v. Hodel*,[64] followed the FWS's December 1987 "not warranted" verdict on the petition that was filed to list the northern spotted owl, which at the time was a candidate species. The court confirmed that listing decisions are to be reviewed under the "arbitrary and capricious" standard of the Administrative Procedure Act, which is narrow and presumes agency action is valid.[65] In the case of the northern spotted owl, however, none of the consultants involved in the species status review, which the FWS used to support the agency's decision, had concluded that the species was not at risk of extinction.[66] Since no expert testimony in the record supported a "not warranted" finding, the agency's decision could not be accepted as a matter of administrative expertise and, thus, was remanded.[67] *Hodel* opened the floodgates to a wave of substantive litigation under section 4 that has grown progressively wider in scope and deeper in detail. Several of the major battleground issues are summarized below.

Insufficient Biological Support in the Record

Many decisions in the 1990s followed *Hodel*'s lead in finding that FWS or NMFS failed to build an adequate record to support its listing decision. For example, when the FWS decided not to reclassify two subpopulations of grizzly bear from threatened to endangered, the D.C. federal district court concluded that the FWS had not sufficiently addressed the ESA listing criteria for one of the subpopulations.[68] Later, the court ruled that the FWS's decision not to list a population of grizzly bears as endangered was arbitrary and capricious because of a failure to explain adequately the basis for the decision and for lack of sufficient record evidence in support of not listing.[69] In particular, the FWS failed to establish that the population could withstand the current rate of human-caused mortality, that the population was not endangered simply by virtue of its small size, that present regulatory mechanisms were adequate to protect the population, and that Canadian habitat will continue to be available to the population.

Another district court overturned the FWS's decision not to list the contiguous U.S. population of the Canada lynx as arbitrary and capricious because it was not supported in the administrative record and because the FWS had demanded conclusive evidence of endangerment, whereas the ESA requires only a likelihood.[70] Still another court ordered the FWS to reconsider its decision to list only two of five populations of bull trout that had been petitioned for listing.[71] The court ordered the agency to consider listing the species throughout its entire range.

The trend of closer judicial scrutiny of FWS and NMFS listing decisions has continued to build into the 2000s, with many decisions falling in line with *Hodel* but some upholding the agency decision.[72]

The decisions discussed so far all involve courts examining FWS or NMFS decisions *not* to list a species or population. In a first-of-its-kind case, in 2000 a court struck down a decision to list a species on substantive grounds.[73] The court found that FWS's decision to list the Sacramento splittail as threatened was arbitrary and capricious because FWS did not state why the population size was inadequate and did not show the relationship between the data received, particularly from the state wildlife protection agency contrary to listing, and the conclusion to list the species. The case focused on FWS's selective use of population abundance data to support the listing decision, and the agency's failure to explain why it ignored some data evidencing continued high abundance while relying on other low-abundance data. The agency, in the court's view, failed "to acquire a broader range of unbiased data or address critiques of the studies they used, which appear biased."

On only one occasion has a court defined the standard of review applied to emergency listings. The city of Las Vegas and other public and private entities sued to enjoin

Listing Endangered and Threatened Species | 23

implementation of the FWS's emergency listing of the Mojave Desert population of the desert tortoise.[74] The court noted that the emergency listing procedure requires the agency to withdraw the emergency rule if at any time within the 240-day effective period after the emergency listing the agency finds that substantial evidence does not exist to support the rule.[75] The court reasoned, therefore, that substantial evidence cannot be the standard used to validate the initial emergency listing itself, because the statute contemplates that the agency will not have made that determination, if at all, until after the emergency listing. Moreover, because a normal rulemaking must follow the emergency rulemaking for the listing to survive, applying the same standard of evidence would not make sense. Hence, an emergency listing is subject to a "somewhat less rigorous process of investigation and explanation ... than for normal rulemaking."[76] The court suggested that an emergency listing would be deemed invalid only if the agency completely disregarded superior scientific evidence or completely failed to discuss state and local efforts.[77]

Distinct Population Segments

In August 2007, the FWS delisted the Idaho springsnail on the basis that "it is now considered to be part of a more widely distributed taxon, the Jackson Lake springsnail."[78] The Idaho springsnail was not a species and thus not a "listable entity." What makes a "listable entity," in other words, is everything under the ESA and thus often is, not surprisingly, a matter of heated litigation.

Most of the "listable entity" litigation has centered around agency decisions about distinct population segments (DPS) and the agencies' policy of requiring that the DPS be "significant" to the species as a whole in order to deserve listing. A number of decisions uphold agency designations of DPS status and the agencies' "significance" standard,[79] but a few significant decisions have overturned agency DPS findings.

A blockbuster case in this regard involved the Arizona population of the pygmy owl. In a complex analysis of the decision by FWS to assign DPS status to the birds, the Ninth Circuit ruled that FWS had properly found the group was "distinct," but had improperly concluded the group was also "significant."[80] The Arizona population was too small a percentage of the western range of the species to be considered significant. The agency later delisted the Arizona population, a decision upheld in the courts.[81]

Many of the DPS decisions involve decisions about what NMFS calls "evolutionarily significant units" (ESU) of Pacific salmon—i.e., the salmon version of a DPS. These decisions are complicated by the presence of hatchery spawned and naturally spawned salmon of the same species in the same waters, the question being whether the ESU includes both or may include only the natural fish. In *Alsea Valley Alliance v. Evans*,[82] a federal district court from Oregon ruled that because NMFS considered hatchery and natural fish as part of the same ESU, it could not exclude hatchery salmon from its listing status review. This decision called into question numerous ESU listings, but the government did not appeal. Rather, in 2005 NMFS developed a new hatchery listing policy for considering hatchery salmon that was consistent with *Alsea*.[83] In 2007, however, a federal district court in a case from Washington, *Trout*

Unlimited v. Lohn,[84] invalidated the new policy, holding that listing decisions must be based exclusively on the status of naturally spawning fish. The status of hatchery salmon in the listing decision calculus thus remains uncertain. As the *Trout Unlimited* court noted, "to the extent this Court's order can be read to conflict with *Alsea*, perhaps this will have the happy result of instigating needed appellate review." That result seems likely sooner or later, meaning the salmon sagas of the Northwest will experience another wave of listing litigation regardless of how an appellate court rules.

Conservation Efforts

In recent years, the extent to which FWS and NMFS can recognize ongoing and prospective species conservation efforts in its listing decisions has led to some courts invalidating decisions not to list. For example, in a case involving the Barton Springs salamander in Austin, Texas, the district court found that the FWS had improperly relied upon a state-initiated conservation plan as a basis for declining to list the species, primarily because the agreement called for prospective actions by the state and, thus, had no track record of success.[85] Another court held that the NMFS acted improperly when it adopted a two-year horizon as the "foreseeable future" criterion for its decision not to list the Oregon coast coho salmon as threatened. The NMFS reasoned that the species was not threatened with endangerment within the two-year post-decision period in which Oregon would implement protective measures, but the court held that two years "fall[s] far short of any reasonable definition of foreseeable future."[86] In several other cases, courts ruled that the agency improperly decided not to list a species as endangered or threatened because it had improperly considered the potential future beneficial effects of conservation actions planned by other federal agencies rather than focusing on the present status of the species.[87] On the other hand, several district courts held that the agency is permitted to consider the effects of state conservation plans that are already in place when deciding whether to list species under the ESA.[88] As discussed below, this front of litigation led the agencies to develop a more comprehensive policy guidance to govern the consideration of conservation efforts.

Threatened Species

The decision to list a species as threatened instead of endangered occasionally comes under scrutiny. For example, one court rejected FWS's basis for concluding that a distinct population segment of the lynx was threatened, not endangered.[89]

Recent decisions have also considered the agencies' exercise of discretion under section 4 to extend protections to threatened species, particularly decisions whether to allow regulated taking of such species.[90] By statute, threatened species are not automatically protected under the take prohibition of section 9. The FWS's general regulation extending the take prohibition to threatened species in the absence of a specific regulation to the contrary[91] has been upheld.[92] The FWS has departed from that general rule on many occasions without judicial interference.[93] Regardless of the agency's decision under section 9, however, threatened species are entitled to the same level of conservation as endangered species under section 7.[94] The statutory framework for conservation, however, accounts for the possibility of regulated taking "where population pressures within a given ecosystem cannot otherwise be relieved."[95] Accordingly, courts have found that as long as the agency has a rational basis for finding that population pressures exist, the decision to allow regulated takings of a threatened species is permissible.[96]

Best Available Science

Although the ESA leaves the "best scientific data available" standard of evidentiary quality undefined, in *Bennett v. Spear* the Supreme Court explained that its "obvious purpose . . . is to ensure that the ESA not be implemented haphazardly, on the basis of speculation or surmise . . . [and] to avoid needless economic dislocation produced by agency officials zealously but unintelligently pursuing their environmental objectives."[97] It is, in other words, a check on both the hasty application of regulatory power and the uninformed use of science. Accordingly, the courts have interpreted it to impose several practical guidelines on the agencies:[98]

- The agencies may not manipulate their decisions by unreasonably relying on certain sources to the exclusion of others.
- The agencies may not disregard scientifically superior evidence.
- Relatively minor flaws in scientific data do not render that information unreliable.
- The agencies must use the best data available, not the best data possible.
- The agencies may not insist on conclusive data in order to make a decision.
- The agencies are not required to conduct independent research to improve the pool of available data.
- The agencies thus must rely on even inconclusive or uncertain information if that is the best available at the time of the decision.
- The agencies must manage and consider the data in a transparent administrative process.

Consistent with that theme, one court declined to require FWS to conduct population surveys of the goshawk to determine whether listing is appropriate.[99] The "best available" standard imposes no obligation on FWS or NMFS to conduct independent studies; rather, the agency must "find and consider any information that is arguably susceptible to discovery." Some courts—all confined to the Ninth Circuit—have suggested that the "best available evidence" standard embeds a "benefit of the doubt" standard when listing species, but others disagree.[100]

Other Statutory Standards

A few cases have found that the listing agency improperly interpreted other statutory standards for listing. For example, one court held that FWS improperly applied the "in the foreseeable future" and "risk of extinction" standards when it declined to list a species on the basis that there was only a 64 percent chance of extinction within 100 years.[101] And several courts have held that FWS improperly required "conclusive evidence" in support of listing when it denied a listing petition.[102]

Procedural Challenges

Just as substantive challenges to section 4 listing actions have been on the rise, allegations of procedural deficiencies have also given the agencies trouble in court. The challenges involve not only procedures specified in the ESA, but also the National Environmental Policy Act, the Administrative Procedure Act, and other procedural laws.

ESA Procedures

For example, in one case the procedural requirements for listing were used as a basis to vacate a listing in a case that involved a small snail found in Idaho. During the comment period, the FWS had failed to provide the public with essential studies of the species and had also failed to list the species before the conclusion of the six-month extension of the one-year period following the proposed rule. Significantly, however, the district court noted that its decision was not to be construed as a comment on the substantive merit of the listing. The appeals court later concluded that the listing could not be vacated on the grounds used by the district court.[103]

Another listing procedure case addresses the findings needed to justify extension of the one-year period following the proposed rule. The court held that the provision that there be "substantial disagreement regarding the sufficiency or accuracy of the available data" requires FWS to describe in its decision document a rational basis for concluding that disagreement exists *and* why the extension would be helpful in resolving the controversy.[104]

The FWS's track record of compliance with the listing procedure time deadlines has led to controversy and litigation that is unlikely to abate soon. For example, through 1991 the FWS was on time for 90-day petition findings only 26 percent of the time and more than four months late 25 percent of the time.[105] The requirement that final listing rules be promulgated within one year of the proposed rule had been missed by over six months 13 percent of the time through 1991.[106] The backlog shows no sign of letting up—as of January 2008 there were nine species formally proposed for listing and 282 "warranted but precluded" candidates for listing for which final action had yet to take place.[107] Not surprisingly, therefore, the deadlines specified in section 4 also have led to numerous challenges. For example, a district court ruled that the FWS failed to present evidence that during the 23-month period between the filing of a petition to list the Baird's sparrow and the issuance of the 90-day finding, it was working at all times on other species in the priority prescribed by the Listing Priority Guidance. Thus the clock for the 12-month finding was not tolled by the extended 90-day period.[108] The court found particularly relevant an internal FWS e-mail that openly stated that the FWS regional office responsible for the listing decision had not made 90-day findings on several petitions in order to toll the 12-month finding. By contrast, although FWS failed to make a timely 12-month finding on a petition to list the yellow-billed cuckoo, a district court held that it must consider "the equities of the situation" to determine the date by which the agency must complete the finding.[109] FWS had argued for additional time to complete a genetic study of the bird, and the court found the study sufficiently important to deny plaintiffs' request to order the agency to reach its decision immediately.

National Environmental Policy Act

Because section 4 lays out tightly defined substantive standards and assessment procedures, one early decision concluded that listing decisions are exempt from the environmental impact statement requirements of the National Environmental Policy Act (NEPA).[110] The court reasoned that the ESA's strictly confined species listing criteria prevent the FWS/NMFS from taking the NEPA's broader environmental impact criteria into consideration and that, in any event, the ESA listing process includes sufficient procedural safeguards to ensure full evaluation of its environmental objectives.[111] Another court more recently held that the decision to list a species as threatened and develop special rules under section 4(d) also is not subject to NEPA.[112] In other words, the ESA listing process simply does not need the NEPA's help.

Administrative Procedure Act

A strong reminder that listing decisions are subject to the Administrative Procedure Act, except where specifically excluded (as in emergency listings), came in a decision regarding the FWS listing of the gnatcatcher as a threatened species. Members of the public had requested to review the background data of a report on which the FWS based its decision as to where the species' range extended. The FWS, which had never obtained or reviewed the background data before the listing, refused in spite of the fact that the version of the report in question reached conclusions diametrically opposed to an earlier draft. The court held that "there could hardly be any greater abuse of discretion than for an adjudicating official to rely on a report where the underlying data has been denied to that official," and that "where the Secretary relies on one of [a scientist's two] contradictory conclusions, the interested parties should be allowed access to the underlying data."[113] The district court, which in an earlier decision had ordered the species delisted, allowed the FWS to retain the species as listed but ordered the FWS to release the data, allow public comment on it, and decide whether the species should continue to be listed.

Other Procedural Laws

The Federal Advisory Committee Act (FACA) proved to be the downfall of another listing action when a court enjoined the FWS from using an advisory committee's report on the Alabama sturgeon in its listing deliberations. The FWS, according to the court, had not followed the FACA procedures for compiling the report and thus could not use the report in making its decision.[114]

Administrative Reform

Although criticism of the ESA generally and of the FWS's implementation policies specifically has been mounting since 1990 from several fronts, by 1994 Congress had not taken action to reaffirm or reform the law despite many attempts (and still has not as of this writing). In 1994, the FWS launched an effort to address some of the criticism ahead of legislative action, including measures to address the section 4 programs. For example, in July 1994, the FWS and NMFS released a series of policy statements addressing several aspects of ESA administration, including the listing program under section 4. One policy deals with the role of peer review as a complement to the public comment process in listing decisions and related functions under section 4. The agencies announced that it would now be their policy to incorporate independent peer review in those functions during the public comment period. In listings, that peer review would involve soliciting the opinions of "three appropriate and independent specialists regarding pertinent scientific and commercial data and assumptions" and would result in the agency "summariz[ing] in the final decision document ... the opinions of all independent peer reviewers received on the species."[115] The agencies also reserved the right to commission a special peer review, to be conducted in the six-month statutory extension period, to address special questions raised in the initial comment and peer review periods.

Another policy addresses how the agencies will ensure that their section 4 decisions "represent the best scientific and commercial data available."[116] The policy promises impartial review of data, full documentation of all information that supports or does not support the agency's position, and the use of primary and original sources of information as the basis for formulating agency decisions.

To address the concern that listing rules often are uninformative with respect to what actions will or will not cause take of the species, another of the 1994 policies promises "to identify, to the extent known at the time a species is listed, specific activities that will not be considered likely to result in violation of section 9" and to identify a contact in the agency "to assist the public in determining whether a particular activity would constitute a prohibited act under section 9."[117]

Recognizing that it had been criticized often for not including state input in listing decisions, the agencies stated in another July 1994 policy that it would use the expertise of state agencies to compile information relevant to listing actions.

Finally, another of the July 1994 policies states that the agencies will "group listing decisions on a geographic, taxonomic, or ecosystem basis where possible" and will use partnerships with other agencies to enhance "ecosystem management."[118] That policy does not define "ecosystem."

Later in 1994, the FWS and NMFS announced adoption of an internal guidance manual for management of listing petitions, one aspect of which is to more rigorously define what level and type of evidence is needed to advance a petition through the 90-day and 12-month findings process.[119] The agencies revised and reissued the policy in 1996.[120]

Administrative reform efforts experienced another surge forward in March 1995 when the FWS released its comprehensive agenda for administrative reform—basically summarizing what the agency had done in 1994—and its proposals for legislative reform.[121] The agency explained that its administrative reform measures reflect efforts to respond to some of the problems asserted with respect to the listing process, though the added steps do not suggest speedier decisions.

Later, in 1996, the agencies also developed three policies dealing with technical and procedural aspects of the section 4 listing process: (1) a proposed policy statement describing the criteria for determining distinct vertebrate populations;[122] (2) the updated policy for listing petition evaluation and management;[123] and (3) a final revised listing priority guidance statement designed to prioritize the backlog of pending species listing actions.[124]

For many years the FWS and NMFS gathered data on species for listing consideration and divided these species into three categories. Category 1 comprised species for which the agency had substantial information on hand to support the biological appropriateness of proposing to list as endangered or threatened. Development and publication of proposed rules on these species, though anticipated, were precluded by other listing activity. Category 2 comprised species for which information indicated listing was possibly appropriate but conclusive evidence on biological vulnerability and threat were not yet available. No specific plans for proposed listing existed for such species, and it was recognized that further information may ultimately point against listing. Category 3 comprised species that were at one time under consideration for listing but were removed from such consideration because persuasive evidence suggested they were extinct (subcategory 3A); were taxa, which did not satisfy the ESA definition of species (subcategory 3B); or were more abundant than previously thought (subcategory 3C). Although no candidate species received ESA protection, the agencies periodically published the candidate lists and solicited data on the named species and nominations for new candidates.[125] In 1996, the FWS announced it would no longer maintain the Category 2 and Category 3 species on the candidate species list, thus reducing candidate species to only those for which the FWS has determined there is evidence to support a proposal for listing (i.e., the old Category 1).[126] The agency explained that the old system led many people to the mistaken conclusion that the thousands of species in Category 2 would be listed in the near future.

Of significant relevance to the listing process, in 1999 the FWS adopted a rule that would allow it to issue enhancement of survival permits under section 10(a)(1) of the ESA to private persons and public agencies who commit to conserve candidate species' habitat on their property.[127] The FWS will issue such permits based on a finding that the measures, if adopted by similarly situated property owners and agencies, would obviate the need to list the species. The permit would specify the allowable take should the species subsequently be listed and would put a cap on the conservation measures that would be required of the permittee. The agencies also jointly published a revised policy supporting these initiatives, which previously had been embodied only in internal guidance and informal publications.[128] The NMFS may propose its own rule codifying the policy in the future.

Also in 1999, the FWS issued the new Listing Priority Guidance, which removes all critical habitat actions from priority guidance, leaving them to case-by-case funding and processing prioritization, and replacing the tiered priority system with a similar priority list.[129] The new Listing Priority Guidance addressed (1) emergency listings, (2) final decisions on proposed listings, (3) the status of candidate species, and (4) processing listing petitions.[130] FWS provides annual reports summarizing the progress on these listing actions.[131]

In 2000, following defeats in the courts when listing was deferred based on state, local, and private conservation agreements, FWS and NMFS issued a draft policy for evaluation of conservation efforts when making listing decisions.[132] The agency adopted the final policy, known as the Policy for Evaluation of Conservation Efforts When Making Listing Decisions (PECE), in 2003.[133] It focuses on the criteria the agencies will use in determining whether formalized conservation efforts contribute to making listing a species unnecessary. Formalized conservation efforts include conservation agreements, conservation plans, management plans, or similar documents entered into by federal, state, local, and tribal governments, businesses, organizations, and individuals.

Also in 2000, FWS announced that "because all available funding must be allocated to conduct critical habitat designations required by court orders or settlement agreements," the agency "will be unable to consider adding any new species to the Endangered Species List, except on an emergency basis, for the remainder of the 2001 Fiscal Year."[134] The agency said it would process listing actions under court order or settlement agreement, actions already processed into the headquarters, and those sufficiently funded with FY 2000 funds. The agency also said it would not respond to any new petitions. With litigation not letting up and budgets not going up, this kind of listing program "shutdown" or "slowdown" could become a recurring event in listing program implementation.

Emerging Issues and Future Directions

Predicting where the listing program is headed over the next decade is at best a guesstimate. Like other sections of the ESA, citizen petitions and citizen suits drive the directions of litigation over the listing program, which in turn drives agency policy reactions. A number of the issues discussed above, such as the meaning of "significant portion of the range," have been heating up for a while and now are coming to a boil in the courts and the agencies as of this writing. They are likely to play out over the next few years. But another set of issues on the horizon has the potential to impose pressure on the listing program in ways not yet experienced. In the absence of congressional intervention, these are likely to gain momentum over the next few years and, if this estimate is anywhere on point, they will dominate the listing program well into the 2010s. The three issues in this category are the upcoming wave of five-year reviews, the revelation in 2007 of significant political interference with listing decisions, and climate change.

Five-Year Status Reviews

One criticism of the ESA's performance focuses on how many species have been listed relative to the number recovered under the Act's protective measures. Responding to this criticism, in 1998 the FWS declared that it would emphasize delisting and described 29 species potentially eligible for delisting or downlisting for various reasons.[135] As of January 2008, however, only 21 species had actually been recovered to the point of delisting.[136] Frustration with the pace of recovery-based delistings, industry groups have discovered the five-year status review procedure. The post-listing five-year status review requirement of section 4 had been a sleepy corner of the listing program until recently, when industry groups appear to have decided it may work to their advantage to put pressure on FWS and NMFS to conduct timely and comprehensive status reviews, presumably to prompt the agency into delisting decisions or to provide the basis for litigation if the agency retains the species' listing. One of the first cases on the topic, decided in 2000, involved an industry group claim that if the FWS fails to conduct the required post-listing five-year review of a species' status the ESA requires automatic de-listing of the species, a claim the court rejected.[137] However, FWS later settled litigation brought by agricultural and water supply interests after conceding that no status review had been conducted for the delta smelt, a small fish found in the Bay-Delta Estuary of California that was listed in 1993.[138] In 2007, a court agreed with the Florida Home Builders Association that FWS must conduct and complete reviews on 89 listed species by September 30, 2010.[139] It is likely that as the agencies are forced into completing more five-year reviews over the next several years, litigation will follow on the heels of their decisions and stretch well into the 2010s. Indeed, seeing this prospect on their horizon, in 2006 the FWS and NMFS adopted a guidance document outlining the five-year status review standards and procedures.[140]

Political Interference in Listing Decisions

With so much riding on the "gateway" listing decisions, it has not been uncommon to hear claims that "political" influence had tainted a listing action decision, though only in the rare case has hard evidence been produced to back up such allegations. That changed in 2007 with the investigation of allegations that Julie MacDonald, when serving as Deputy Assistant Secretary for Fish, Wildlife, and Parks at the Department of the Interior, "bullied, insulted, and harassed the professional staff of the U.S. Fish and Wildlife Service (FWS) to change documents and alter biological reporting regarding the Endangered Species Program."[141] According to the results of the Interior Department investigation, MacDonald, who at the time had no formal education in natural sciences, had "been heavily involved with editing, commenting on, and reshaping the Endangered Species Program's scientific reports from the field."[142] "MacDonald said she views her involvement in the Endangered Species Program as part of her duties, and she challenges the science produced by FWS field personnel and makes them accountable for the citations and rules they refer to in field reports,"[143] whereas numerous scientists in the agency perceived her behavior—particularly her direct contact with field-level agency scientists—as inappropriate.[144] The investigation found that MacDonald committed no illegal acts in this regard,[145] and it reached no conclusions with regard to whether her behavior was an appropriate exercise of her duties.[146]

Did Julie MacDonald cross the line, or was she just doing her job? On the one hand, science produced within an agency by field personnel cannot be treated as sacrosanct, immune from scrutiny by nonscience personnel responsible for using science (and other factors) in the exercise of professional judgment. Agency decision makers have a responsibility to ensure that the science upon which they base decisions is reliable. On the other hand, if in doing so the decision makers supplant the scientists and take over the job of producing the science, they have become the problem with regard to the reliability of the agency's decision process.

Based strictly on the information contained in the investigation report, MacDonald clearly satisfied her role of holding scientists accountable, albeit in a manner that was by all accounts extremely combative and likely corrosive to the integrity of the agency's decision process. Also according to the report, she appears not to have unilaterally altered scientific findings, although she came as close to doing so as one possibly could without crossing the line. If the investigation report is accurate, however, she appears to have pressured scientists into making the changes. The report recounts numerous instances where MacDonald ordered that reports be altered or insisted on the integration of scientific information that she independently collected.[147] There is no evidence in the report to suggest she commissioned anything remotely like independent, external peer review to resolve differences between her and the field scientists. When brought to light through the investigation, the consequences of her behavior in 2007 were nothing short of an unraveling of agency listing (and other) decisions made under her oversight.[148] It is likely the FWS will be reviewing, revising, and litigating over those decisions for years to come, and it may take longer for the listing process to regain its integrity in the eyes of stakeholders.

Climate Change

Recall that section 4(a)(1) of the ESA requires the FWS and NMFS to determine whether any species is an endangered species or a threatened species because of any of the following factors:

> (A) the present or threatened destruction, modification, or curtailment of its habitat or range;
> (B) overutilization for commercial, recreational, scientific, or educational purposes;
> (C) disease or predation;
> (D) the inadequacy of existing regulatory mechanisms;
> (E) other natural or manmade factors affecting its continued existence.[149]

There could hardly be a more definitive mandate to consider the effects of greenhouse gas emissions and climate change on species. Greenhouse gas emissions are unquestionably a "man-made factor," and if, as abundant evidence suggests, they are contributing to climate change, they are potentially "affecting ... [the] continued existence" of climate-threatened species. Regardless of their causal agents, atmospheric warming, sea level rise, and other primary ecological effects of climate change involve "the destruction, modification, or curtailment of ... [species'] habitat or range." Furthermore, the ecological disruption effects of climate change contribute to secondary ecological effects such as "disease or predation." The effects of climate change, therefore, are unambiguously within the ambit of the listing criteria, leaving no room for argument that it may be left out of the listing calculus. Hence, over the next decade the agencies are likely to confront a growing challenge of identifying which species are endangered or threatened partly or primarily because of climate change. The staghorn corals, which NMFS has listed in part based on climate change effects, and the polar bear, which FWS has listed as threatened, are just at the front of what is likely to be a long queue of listing decisions based on climate change, followed by litigation over the results.

Of course, although section 4 leaves no room for debate over whether the agency must integrate climate change effects in the listing decision, the statute provides considerable flexibility for how the listing agency does so. For example, a species is endangered if it is "in danger of extinction throughout all or a significant portion of its range"[150] and is threatened if it "is likely to become an endangered species within the foreseeable future throughout all or a significant portion of its range."[151] These are not precise concepts. For example, what does "all or a significant portion of its range" mean? As noted above, one court described the passage as "odd phraseology" and an "enigmatic phrase,"[152] and recently it took the lawyers at the Department of the Interior 19 single-spaced pages of dense legal analysis, accompanied by 17 single-spaced pages of probing discussion of the ESA's legislative history, to explain to the FWS what the lawyers believe this phrase means.[153] Between this interpretational difficulty and phrases such as "in danger of," "is likely to," and "foreseeable future," the FWS and NMFS may not be so hemmed in after all. Given the extent of agency expertise that must necessarily go into making such judgments, and given the uncertainty associated with downscaling global climate change effects to local species-specific ecological contexts, the FWS likely has considerable play in terms of matching different climate change threat scenarios with the ESA's endangered/threatened/not threatened matrix. Some species may present such compelling cases of climate change threat that even aggressive use of discretion could not support a decision not to list, but many will present more ambiguous scenarios.

Another source of discretion in the listing function rests in section 4(d). The discretion to tailor special rules for threatened species may prove especially useful for the FWS and NMFS with respect to a climate-threatened species. It may allow the agencies to identify and regulate the specific effects of human adaptation to climate change that pose significant obstacles to the survival and recovery of a species, whereas broad, dispersed actions such as greenhouse gas emissions could be entirely excluded from regulation. Of course, the success of this strategy depends on a scientifically credible basis for designating the species as threatened. Moreover, the condition that protective regulations be "necessary and advisable to provide for the conservation of such species" has not been tested in a context like that suggested—i.e., to exclude one set of causal factors, ostensibly because the cause, effect, and response associated with them is so complex, so as to focus conservation resources on a more manageable set of factors.

Conclusion

Although ESA listings were a relatively sleepy area of law under the Act for its first 20 years of implementation, the 1990s witnessed a surge in judicial and administrative attention to the listing process as the keystone of the ESA program. Courts have become increasingly willing to probe the agencies' decisions on procedural and substantive grounds, and the agencies have become more willing to address criticisms of their performance with tangible administrative reforms. Due to environmentalist and industry stakeholders realizing that virtually all ESA issues start with the listing question, it is likely that these trends will continue. Whether the agencies' reform efforts fully resolve the concerns expressed from both fronts is yet to be seen. In the end, only Congress can decide that, and it has yet to coalesce around any definitive answer.

Notes

1. 16 U.S.C. § 1533.
2. *See* H.R. REP. NO. 97-567, at 8, *reprinted in* 1982 U.S.C.C.A.N. 2807, 2810.
3. 16 U.S.C. § 1536(a)(2)–(3).
4. *Id.* § 1536(a)(1).
5. *Id.* § 1538(a)(1).
6. *Id.* § 1533(d).
7. *Id.* § 1533(f).
8. Cal. Plant Soc'y v. Norton, 2005 WL 768444, at *6 (D.D.C. Mar. 24, 2005)
9. TVA v. Hill, 437 U.S. 153 (1978).
10. 50 C.F.R. § 424.
11. 16 U.S.C. § 1532(16).
12. *Id.* § 1532(6).
13. *Id.* § 1532(20).
14. *Id.*
15. 50 C.F.R. § 424.02(e), (k), (m).
16. 16 U.S.C. § 1533(a)(1)(A)–(E).
17. *Id.* § 1533(b)(1)(A).
18. *Id.*
19. H.R. CONF. REP. NO. 97-835, at 20, *reprinted in* 1982 U.S.C.C.A.N. 2807, 2861.
20. 50 C.F.R. § 424.11(c).
21. *Id.* § 424.11(d).
22. *Id.* § 424.11(d)(1).
23. *Id.* § 424.11(d)(2).
24. U.S. FISH & WILDLIFE SERV., ENDANGERED SPECIES LISTING HANDBOOK: PROCEDURAL GUIDANCE FOR THE PREPARATION AND PROCESSING OF RULES AND NOTICES PURSUANT TO THE ENDANGERED SPECIES ACT (1994).
25. 16 U.S.C. § 1533(b)(3)(A); 50 C.F.R. § 424.14(b)(1).
26. Fund for Animals v. Hogan, 428 F.3d 1059, 1063–64 (D.C. Cir. 2005).

27. 16 U.S.C. § 1533(b)(3)(A); 50 C.F.R. § 424.14(b)(1).
28. Id. § 424.14(b)(2)(i)–(iv).
29. Id. § 424.14(b)(1).
30. 16 U.S.C. § 1533(b)(3)(A) (listing actions), (D)(i) (critical habitat revisions); 50 C.F.R. § 424.14(b)(1) (listing actions), (c)(1) (critical habitat revisions).
31. 16 U.S.C. § 1533(b)(3)(C)(ii).
32. Id. § 1533(b)(3)(B) (listing actions), (D)(ii) (critical habitat revisions); 50 C.F.R. § 424.14(b)(3) (listing actions), 424.14(c)(3) (1997) (critical habitat revisions).
33. 50 C.F.R. § 424.15(a).
34. 16 U.S.C. § 1533(b)(3)(B)(i)–(iii); 50 C.F.R. § 424.14(b)(3)(i)–(iii).
35. 16 U.S.C. § 1533(b)(3)(B)(iii); 50 C.F.R. § 424.14(b)(3)(iii).
36. See 48 Fed. Reg. 43,098 (1983).
37. 16 U.S.C. § 1533(b)(3)(B) (listing actions), (D)(ii) (critical habitat revisions); 50 C.F.R. § 424.14(b)(3)(i)–(iii) (listing actions), 424.14(c)(3) (1997) (critical habitat revisions).
38. 16 U.S.C. § 1533(b)(3)(C)(ii).
39. Id. § 1533(b)(3)(B)(iii); 50 C.F.R. § 424.14(b)(4).
40. 16 U.S.C. § 1533(b)(3)(B)(ii) (1994); 50 C.F.R. § 424.14(b)(3)(ii).
41. 16 U.S.C. § 1533(b)(5)(A)(i); 50 C.F.R. § 424.16(c)(1)(i).
42. See 16 U.S.C. § 1533(b)(4) (incorporating APA provisions at 5 U.S.C. § 553).
43. Id. § 1533(b)(5)(A)(ii), (B)–(D) (1994); 50 C.F.R. § 424.16(c)(1)(ii)–(vi).
44. 16 U.S.C. § 1533(b)(5)(E) (hearing); 50 C.F.R. § 424.16(c)(2)–(3) (comment period and hearing).
45. 16 U.S.C. § 1533(b)(6)(A)–(B); 50 C.F.R. § 424.17(a)(1)(i)–(iv).
46. See generally Enos v. Marsh, 769 F.2d 1363, 1368–70 (9th Cir. 1985).
47. 16 U.S.C. § 1533(d).
48. See 50 C.F.R. § 17.31(a) (1998).
49. See, e.g., 50 C.F.R. § 227.21(a) (extending take prohibition to threatened salmon species).
50. 16 U.S.C. § 1533(b)(7); 50 C.F.R. § 424.20.
51. 16 U.S.C. § 1533(b)(7)(B) (1994); 50 C.F.R. § 424.20(a).
52. 16 U.S.C. § 1533(b)(7) (1994); 50 C.F.R. § 424.20(b).
53. 16 U.S.C. § 1533(c).
54. Id.
55. See also 50 C.F.R. §§ 222.23(a), 227.4 (1997) (designating specific listed species for which NMFS is responsible).
56. For updates, see U.S. Fish & Wildlife Serv., Species Reports, Summary of Listed Species Listed Populations and Recovery Plans, http://ecos.fws.gov/tess_public/Boxscore.do.
57. For updates, see id.
58. For updates, see U.S. Fish & Wildlife Serv., Species Reports, Special Rule Report, http://ecos.fws.gov/tess_public/SpecialRule.do?listings=0&type=4d.
59. 16 U.S.C. § 1533(g).
60. Id.
61. 16 U.S.C. § 1533(c)(2); 50 C.F.R. § 424.21.
62. Glover River Org. v. U.S. Dep't of Interior, 675 F.2d 251 (10th Cir. 1982).
63. Lujan v. Defenders of Wildlife, 112 S. Ct. 2130 (1992).
64. N. Spotted Owl v. Hodel, 716 F. Supp. 479 (W.D. Wash. 1988).
65. Id. at 481.
66. Id. at 482.
67. Id. at 483.
68. See Carlton v. Interior Dep't, 42 Env't Rep. Cas. (BNA) 1082, 1995 U.S. Dist. LEXIS 14738 (D.D.C. Sept. 29, 1995).
69. Carlton v. Babbitt, 1998 WL 761479 (D.D.C. 1998).
70. Defenders of Wildlife v. Babbitt, 958 F. Supp. 670 (D.D.C. 1997).
71. Friends of the Wild Swan v. U.S. Fish & Wildlife Serv., No. 94-1318-JO, 1996 U.S. Dist. LEXIS 17111 (D. Or. Dec. 4, 1997).

72. *See, e.g.*, Am. Wildlands v. Kempthorne, 2007 U.S. Dist. LEXIS 20851 (D.D.C. Mar. 26, 2007) (upholding decision not to list the westslope cutthroat trout).
73. Sw. Ctr. for Biological Diversity v. Babbitt, 215 F.3d 58 (D.C. Cir. 2000).
74. City of Las Vegas v. Lujan, 891 F.2d 927 (D.C. Cir. 1989).
75. *Id*. at 932.
76. *Id*.
77. *Id*. at 933.
78. 72 Fed. Reg. 43,560, 43,560 (Aug. 6, 2007).
79. *See, e.g.*, Nw. Ecosystem Alliance v. U.S. Fish & Wildlife Serv., 475 F.3d 1136 (9th Cir. 2007); W. Watersheds Project v. Hall, 2007 WL 2790404 (D. Idaho Sept. 24, 2007).
80. Nat'l Ass'n of Home Builders v. Norton, 340 F.3d 835 (9th Cir. 2003).
81. Nat'l Ass'n of Home Builders v. Kempthorne, No. 02-903 (D. Ariz. Mar. 12, 2007).
82. 161 F. Supp. 2d 1154 (D. Or. 2001).
83. 70 Fed. Reg. 37,204 (June 28, 2005).
84. 2007 WL 1795036 (W.D. Wash. June 13, 2007).
85. Save Our Springs v. Babbitt, No. MO-96-CA-168 (W.D. Tex. Mar. 25, 1997).
86. Or. Natural Res. Council v. Daley, 6 F. Supp. 2d 1139 (D. Or. 1998).
87. *See* Friends of the Wild Swan v. U.S. Fish & Wildlife Serv., No. 94-1318-JO, 1996 U.S. Dist. LEXIS 17111 (D. Or. Nov. 13, 1996) (bull trout); Biodiversity Legal Found. v. Babbitt, No. 96-00227-SS, 1996 U.S. Dist. LEXIS 15322 (D.D.C. Oct. 10, 1996) (Alexander Archipelago wolf); Sw. Ctr. for Biological Diversity v. Babbitt, 939 F. Supp. 49 (D.D.C. 1996) (Queen Charlotte goshawk).
88. San Luis & Delta-Mendota Water Auth. v. Badgley, No. 99-5658 (E.D. Cal. June 23, 2000), *aff'd*, 2000 U.S. App. LEXIS 23983 (9th Cir. Sept. 11, 2000) (without opinion).
89. Defenders of Wildlife v. Norton, 340 F. Supp. 2d 9 (D.D.C. 2002).
90. *See* 16 U.S.C. § 1533(d).
91. 50 C.F.R. § 17.31(a).
92. Sweet Home Chapter of Cmtys. for a Greater Or. v. Babbitt, 1 F.3d 1 (D.C. Cir. 1993), *modified on other grounds*, 17 F.3d 463 (D.C. Cir.), *rev'd on other grounds*, 515 U.S. 687 (1995).
93. *See, e.g.*, 58 Fed. Reg. 16,758 (1993) (proposed rule to allow incidental take of the threatened coastal California gnatcatcher).
94. *See* 16 U.S.C. §§ 1538(a), 1536(a)(1).
95. *Id*. § 1532(3).
96. *See* Christy v. Hodel, 857 F.2d 1324, 1333 (9th Cir. 1988), *cert. denied*, Christy v. Lujan, 490 U.S. 1114 (1989) (rational basis existed); Sierra Club v. Clark, 755 F.2d 608, 613–19 (8th Cir. 1985) (remanded for findings on basis).
97. 520 U.S. 154, 169 (1997).
98. *See* Sw. Ctr. for Biological Diversity v. Norton, 2002 WL 1733618, at *8 (D.D.C. 2002) (summarizing the existing body of case law).
99. *See* Or. Natural Res. Council v. Brown, 1997 WL 464826 (N.D. Cal. July 29, 1997); Defenders of Wildlife v. Babbitt, 1999 U.S. Dist. LEXIS 10366 (S.D. Cal. June 14, 1999).
100. *Compare* Ctr. for Biological Diversity v. Lohn, 2003 WL 23004985, at *12 (W.D. Wash. Dec. 17, 2003) (benefit of the doubt applies), *with* Envtl. Prot. Info. Ctr. v. NMFS, No. C-02-5401 EDL, 15 (N.D. Cal. Mar. 2, 2004) (no benefit of the doubt standard).
101. W. Watersheds Project v. Foss, 2005 WL 2002473 (D. Idaho Aug. 19, 2005).
102. Ctr. for Biological Diversity v. Morganweck, 351 F. Supp. 2d 1137 (D. Colo. 2004); *see also* Moden v. U.S. Fish & Wildlife Serv., 281 F. Supp. 2d 1193, 1203 (D. Or. 2003).
103. Idaho Farm Bureau Fed'n v. Babbitt, 839 F. Supp. 3d (D. Idaho 1993), *rev'd*, 58 F.3d 1392 (9th Cir. 1995).
104. Marbled Murrelet v. Lujan, No. 91-522, 1992 U.S. Dist. LEXIS 14645 (W.D. Wash. Sept. 16, 1992), *motion for stay denied*, No. 92-36705 (9th Cir. Sept. 24, 1992).
105. *Endangered Species Act—Types and Numbers of Implementing Actions*, GAO/RCED-92-131BR, at 23 (May 1992).

106. *Id.* at 24.
107. For updates, see U.S. Fish & Wildlife Serv., Species Reports, Listing Status: Proposed Endangered, Proposed Threatened, http://ecos.fws.gov/tess_public/SpeciesReport.do?listingType=P, and Listing Status: Candidates for Listing, http://ecos.fws.gov/tess_public/SpeciesReport.do?listingType=C.
108. Ctr. for Biological Diversity v. Badgley, 2000 U.S. Dist. LEXIS 15155 (D. Or. Oct. 11, 2000).
109. Biodiversity Legal Found. v. Babbitt, 63 F. Supp. 2d 31 (D.D.C. 1999). *See also* Biodiversity Legal Found. v. Badgley, 1999 WL 1042567 (D. Or. 1999) (same result, different species).
110. Pac. Legal Found. v. Andrus, 657 F.2d 829 (6th Cir. 1981).
111. *Id.* at 835–37.
112. Ctr. for Biological Diversity v. U.S. Fish & Wildlife Serv., 2005 WL 2000928 (N.D. Cal. Aug. 19, 2005).
113. Endangered Species Comm'n v. Babbitt, 852 F. Supp. 32 (D.D.C. 1994).
114. Alabama-Tombigbee Rivers Coal. v. Dep't of Interior, 26 F.3d 1103 (11th Cir. 1994).
115. 59 Fed. Reg. 34,270 (1994).
116. 59 Fed. Reg. 34,271 (1994).
117. *Id.* at 34,272 (1994).
118. *Id.* at 34,274 (1994). A recent example of this policy being put into practice is the proposal to list 47 species (45 plants, two birds, and one fly) as a group based on their common ecosystem. *See* 73 Fed. Reg. 62,591 (2008).
119. 59 Fed. Reg. 65,781 (1994).
120. 61 Fed. Reg. 36,075 (1996).
121. *See* U.S. Fish & Wildlife Serv., Protecting America's Heritage: A Fair, Cooperative and Scientifically Sound Approach to Improving the Endangered Species Act (1995).
122. 61 Fed. Reg. 4710 (1996).
123. *Id.* at 36,075 (1996).
124. *Id.* at 64,475 (1996).
125. 50 C.F.R. § 424.15(b); *see, e.g.*, 54 Fed. Reg. 554 (Jan. 6, 1989).
126. *See* 61 Fed. Reg. 64,481 (1996).
127. 64 Fed. Reg. 32,706 (June 17, 1999).
128. *Id.* at 32,717 (June 17, 1999).
129. *Id.* at 57,114 (Oct. 22, 1999).
130. *Id.* at 57,114 (Oct. 22, 1999).
131. *See, e.g.*, 72 Fed. Reg. 69,034 (Dec. 6, 2007) (2007 annual report).
132. 65 Fed. Reg. 37,102 (2000).
133. 68 Fed. Reg. 15,100 (Mar. 28, 2003).
134. Memorandum from Jamie Rappaport Clark, Dir., U.S. Fish & Wildlife Serv., to Reg'l Directors, Re: Listing Workload (Nov. 17, 2000); *see also* News Release, U.S. Fish & Wildlife Serv., Flood of Court Orders Precludes New Listings of Threatened and Endangered Species in FY 2001 (Nov. 22, 2000), *available at* http://news.fws.gov/NewsReleases.
135. 63 Fed. Reg. 25,502 (1998).
136. For updates, see U.S. Fish & Wildlife Serv., Species Reports, Delisting Report, http://ecos.fws.gov/tess_public/DelistingReport.do.
137. Bernstein/Glazer, LLC v. Babbitt, 2000 U.S. Dist. LEXIS 3813 (S.D.N.Y. Mar. 28, 2000).
138. News Release, U.S. Fish & Wildlife Serv., Service to Conduct Review of Threatened Delta Smelt (Aug. 1, 2005). The litigation involved two lawsuits. *See* Cal. Farm Bureau Fed'n v. Dep't of Interior, No. 1:02CV02328 (D.D.C.); San Luis & Delta Mendota Water Auth. v. Dep't of Interior, No. CIV-F-02-6461 (E.D. Cal.).
139. Fla. Home Builders Ass'n v. Kempthorne, 496 F. Supp. 2d 1330 (M.D. Fla. 2007).

140. Nat'l Oceanic & Atmospheric Admin. & U.S. Fish & Wildlife Serv., 5-Year Review Guidance: Procedures for Conducting 5-Year Reviews Under the Endangered Species Act (July 2006), *available at* http://www.nmfs.noaa.gov/pr/pdfs/laws/guidance_5_year_review.pdf.
141. Dep't of Interior, Office of Inspector Gen., Report of Investigation of Julie MacDonald 2 (2007) [hereinafter MacDonald Report].
142. *Id.*
143. *Id.* at 17.
144. *See id.* at 4–16.
145. *See id.* at 2.
146. Leaked copies of the investigation report began to circulate in early April 2007. *See* Erik Stokstad, *Appointee "Reshaped" Science, Says Report*, 316 Science 37 (2007). MacDonald resigned from her position on April 30, 2007, and several days later Department of the Interior officials testified in Congress that the Department is committed to "the integrity of science." *See Interior Commits to "Integrity of Science" in Aftermath of Appointee's Resignation*, Daily Env't Rep. (BNA), May 10, 2007, at A-10.
147. *See* MacDonald Report, supra note 141, at 4–5.
148. The immediate fallout was swift and decisive. In July 2007, the Fish and Wildlife Service announced it would review eight species listing and critical habitat designation decisions made under MacDonald's supervision. *See* News Release, U.S. Fish & Wildlife Serv., U.S. Fish and Wildlife Service to Review 8 Endangered Species Decisions (July 20, 2007), http://www.fws.gov/news/NewsReleases/showNews.cfm?newsId=E54AFD13-CC75-4E83-9780C462E13BA6E2 (last visited Sept. 12, 2007). In August 2007, Judge Gladys Kessler of the D.C. federal district court ordered the agency to inform the court "what action, if any, the Department will take regarding the involvement of Julie MacDonald in the designation of critical habitat for the Canada lynx." Defenders of Wildlife v. Norton, Civ. A. No. 04-1230 (D.D.C., Aug. 27, 2007) (order to the Department of the Interior). Shortly thereafter, the Center for Biological Diversity announced plans to sue the agency over 55 decisions it believes were subject to MacDonald's influence. *See* Mike Ferullo, *Environmental Organization Seeks to Reverse 55 Species Decisions Made by Administration*, Daily Env't Rep. (BNA), Aug. 29, 2007, at A-1. In December 2007 FWS announced that at least seven of the decisions required revision.
149. 16 U.S.C. § 1533(a)(1).
150. *Id.* § 1532(6).
151. *Id.* § 1532(20).
152. Defenders of Wildlife v. Norton, 258 F.3d 1136, 1141 (9th Cir. 2001).
153. Memorandum from Solicitor, U.S. Dep't of the Interior, to Director, U.S. Fish and Wildlife Serv., The Meaning of "In Danger of Extinction Throughout All or a Significant Portion of Its Range" (Mar. 16, 2007).

3

Critical Habitat

Federico Cheever

Introduction

As the Supreme Court noted in *Tennessee Valley Authority v. Hill*,[1] in enacting the Endangered Species Act (ESA), Congress explicitly recognized that the greatest threat to endangered and threatened species is the destruction of "natural habitats."[2] Congress made it clear that one of the Act's principal purposes—if not its primary purpose—is to "provide a means whereby the ecosystems upon which endangered species and threatened species depend may be conserved."[3] "Conservation" as defined in the Act includes "the use of all methods and procedures which are necessary to bring any endangered species or threatened species to the point at which the measures provided pursuant to this chapter are no longer necessary."[4] In other words, the Act seeks to provide habitat for "conservation," and "conservation" means recovery of species.

Congress expressed its concern for habitat conservation in a variety of provisions in the Act.[5] Congress expressed this concern most plainly in the Act's provisions for (1) the designation of critical habitat and (2) the prohibition against federal agency actions that destroy or adversely modify designated critical habitat.[6] Although central to the Act's mission, the critical habitat provisions have had few powerful friends. The agencies charged with administration and enforcement of the Endangered Species Act have downplayed the significance and utility of critical habitat protection.

Section 4(a)(3)(A) provides that "[t]he Secretary . . . to the maximum extent prudent and determinable . . . shall, *concurrently* with making a determination . . . that a species is an endangered species or a threatened species, designate any habitat of such species which is then considered to be critical habitat."[7] Of the 1,231 domestic species of plants and animals listed as of April 30, 2000 (when this chapter was first prepared), only 124 had designated critical habitat.[8] By April 2009, 544[9] of 1,317[10] listed domestic species had designated critical habitat. However, this significant proportional increase in the number of species with designated critical habitat was not the function of a shift in internal agency priorities, but rather a shift in priorities imposed by the federal courts. Federal courts applying the language of the Act to the cases before them have consistently required reluctant agencies to designate critical habitat and to do so in compliance with the statutory deadlines mandated by Congress.

In May 2003, the Department of the Interior issued an unprecedented press release declaring: "The Endangered Species Act is broken. The flood of litigation over critical habitat designation is preventing the Fish and Wildlife Service from protecting new species and reducing its ability to recover plants and animals already listed as threatened or endangered."[11]

A U.S. General Accounting Office (GAO) report released in June 2002 presented a different picture. First, the GAO report pointed out that the U.S. Fish and Wildlife Service (FWS) "separately allocates its endangered species program funds by distinct subcategories corresponding to the program areas of recovery, consultation, candidate conservation, listing [including designation of critical habitat] and landowner incentives."[12] It is therefore unlikely that litigation over "critical habitat designation" could prevent the Fish and Wildlife Service from "recover[ing] plants and animals."

Second, "staff reported spending 10 percent of their time on listing activities, including designation of critical habitat."[13]

In 2005, the U.S. House of Representatives passed HR 3824: "To amend and reauthorize the Endangered Species Act of 1973 to provide greater results conserving and recovering listed species, and for other purposes." Section 5 of the bill would have repealed all critical habitat requirements. The U.S. Senate never voted on the legislation.

Despite its lack of friends in the executive and legislative branches of government, critical habitat designation and protection remain part of the Endangered Species Act. The combination of agency reluctance to enforce the law and the continued commitment of many environmental groups to the concept of critical habitat has generated a considerable body of case law.

The significance of the courts in interpreting the meaning of critical habitat has increased. A number of circuit courts have struck down the Reagan-era regulatory definition of "destruction or adverse modification"[14] of critical habitat, which required injury to both survival *and* recovery prospects of a listed species. This definition is an essential component in application of critical habitat designations in the protection of species. As of this publication, FWS and National Marine Fisheries Service or NOAA Fisheries (NMFS) have not promulgated a new definition.[15]

At the same time, new concern about climate change and the consequent projected shift of species habitat over time calls for new thinking about the role of critical habitat designation and protection as a component in the preservation of threatened and endangered species.[16]

Thirty years after the creation of the statutory processes for designating and protecting critical habitat, a significant number of basic legal questions about critical habitat remain unresolved.

Current State of the Law

Definition of Critical Habitat

Origins

As enacted in 1973, section 7 of the ESA mandated that federal agency actions not destroy or adversely modify the habitat of endangered or threatened species determined by the Secretary to be "critical."[17] As enacted, however, the ESA did not provide any mechanism or criteria for determining what constituted a listed species' "critical habitat."

In 1975, FWS and NMFS, in a "Notice on Critical Habitat,"[18] enumerated specific criteria relevant for determining what should be conserved as critical habitat. These included "(1) Space for normal growth, movements, or territorial behavior; (2) Nutritional requirements such as food, water, minerals; (3) Sites for breeding, reproduction or rearing of offspring; (4) Cover or shelter; or (5) Other biological, physical, or behavioral requirements."[19]

In January 1978, FWS and NMFS promulgated regulations that defined "critical habitat" broadly. The regulations defined critical habitat as "any air, land or water area . . . and constituent elements thereof, the loss of which would appreciably decrease the likelihood of the survival and recovery of a listed species or a distinct population segment of its population."[20] Here the agencies specifically noted the significance of critical habitat both for survival and recovery. Under this definition, critical habitat could include both portions of a listed species' present habitat and additional areas needed for reasonable expansion or recovery of the species' population.

In November 1978, Congress amended the ESA to add a definition of critical habitat and a process for its designation. These changes were part of Congress's general reassessment of the ESA after the U.S. Supreme Court's decision in *Tennessee Valley Authority v. Hill*.[21] The House Report on the 1978 ESA Amendments recognized that the new statutory definition of critical habitat "[was] modeled after that found in present Department of [the] Interior regulations." However, the House Report also noted with disapproval that "the existing regulatory definition could conceivably lead to the designation of virtually all of the habitat of a listed species as its critical habitat."[22] The Senate Report echoed this sentiment, stating that FWS and NMFS definition would "substantially increase the amount of area involved in critical habitat designation and therefore increase proportionately the area that is subject to the regulations and prohibitions which apply to critical habitat."[23] These passages suggest that Congress intended to impose a somewhat narrower view of critical habitat.

Statutory Language

In November 1978, Congress added a definition of critical habitat to the ESA very similar to the regulatory definition promulgated by FWS and NMFS in January 1978. The definition, found in section 3(5) of the Act, states that critical habitat for a listed species means:

> (i) the specific areas within the geographical area occupied by the species, at the time it is listed . . . on which are found those physical and biological features (I) essential to the conservation of the species and (II) which may require special management considerations or protection; and
> (ii) specific areas outside the geographical area occupied by the species at the time it is listed . . . upon a determination by the Secretary that such areas are essential for the conservation of the species.[24]

This definition is incomprehensible without reference to the Endangered Species Act's definition of "conservation" discussed above.[25] Congress defined "critical habitat" with the recovery of listed species in mind.

As FWS put it in its original 1994 determination of critical habitat for four species of endangered fish on the Colorado River:

> In the case of critical habitat, conservation represents the areas required to recover a species to the point of delisting (i.e., the species is recovered and is removed from the list of endangered and threatened species). *In this context, critical habitat preserves options for a species' eventual recovery. . . .*[26]

On the other hand, as FWS notes in the more recent boilerplate language from both the Proposed Revised Designation of Critical Habitat for the Northern Spotted Owl[27] and the Revised Critical Habitat for the San Bernardino Kangaroo Rat:[28]

> [C]ritical habitat designations ... will not control the direction and substance of future recovery plans, habitat conservation plans, or other species conservation planning efforts if new information available to these planning efforts calls for a different outcome.

One part of the statutory definition of critical habitat appears to limit the areas that may be designated. Section 3(5)(c) directs that "critical habitat shall not include the entire geographical area which can be occupied by the endangered or threatened species" except "in circumstances to be determined by the Secretary."[29] A House Report accompanying the bill that would become the 1978 ESA Amendments cautioned that "the Secretary should be exceedingly circumspect in the designation of critical habitat outside of the presently occupied area of the species."[30]

It is at least equally important that another part of the definition of critical habitat specifically contemplates identifying and protecting significant *unoccupied* habitat. "[S]pecific areas outside the geographic area occupied by the species at the time it is listed" can be designated as critical habitat if the Secretary finds that such areas are "essential to the conservation of the species."[31] Indeed, the critical habitat designation and protection process provides the ESA's only direct protection of unoccupied habitat.

Examination of the language employed in the statutory definition of critical habitat adopted by Congress suggests that there is no great difference between the test to be applied in identifying critical habitat "within the geographical area occupied by the species" and "outside the geographical area occupied by the species."[32] In practical terms it can be impossible to identify what habitat is "occupied" and what habitat is "unoccupied" at any given time.[33]

Still, the statute does make *some* distinction between occupied and unoccupied habitat. Section 3(5)(A)(i) defines critical habitat as an area, occupied by the species at the time of listing, with features (1) "essential to the conservation of the species" and (2) requiring special management considerations or protection.[34] Section 3(5)(A)(ii) defines critical habitat outside the range occupied at the time of listing as those areas determined to be "essential to the conservation of the species."[35] With occupied areas, some, but not necessarily all, areas with features "essential to the conservation of the species" may be designated. For unoccupied habitat the area *itself* must somehow be "essential."[36] What this distinction means in practice is unclear. In either case, a finding that the habitat is "essential to the conservation of the species" is the touchstone for lands *inside* the occupied range of the species and *outside* the occupied range of the species.

The statutory definition for critical habitat located *inside* the occupied range of a species requires an additional finding of an actual or potential need for "special management considerations or protection." Recently, the U.S. District Court for the District of Columbia in *Cape Hatteras Access Preservation Alliance v. U.S. Department of the Interior*[37] and the U.S. District Court of the Eastern District of California in *Home Builders Association of Northern California v. U.S. Fish and Wildlife Service*[38] have held that this language requires the agency designating critical habitat to make a finding regarding the possible need for "special management considerations or protection."

The U.S. District Court for the District of Arizona in *Center for Biological Diversity v. Norton*[39] rejected a Department of the Interior argument that Forest Service lands in Arizona and New Mexico could not be designated as critical habitat for the Mexican spotted owl. The Department of the Interior argued that "special management considerations or protection" were unnecessary because, under current land and resource management plans, the lands were already being adequately managed and therefore the land could not be designated as "critical habitat." The court observed:

> Whether habitat does or does not require special management by Defendant or FWS is not determinative on whether or not that habitat is "critical" to a threatened or endangered species. What is determinative is whether or not the habitat is "essential to the conservation of the species" and special management of that habitat is possibly necessary. . . . Thus, the fact that a particular habitat does, in fact, require special management is demonstrative evidence that the habitat is "critical." Defendant, on the other hand, takes the position that if a habitat is actually under "adequate" management, then that habitat is per se not "critical." This makes no sense.[40]

On the other hand, the U.S. District Court for the Eastern District of California, in *Home Builders Association of Northern California*,[41] offered a different but not necessarily inconsistent analysis of the significance of the "special management considerations or protection" language in the statutory definition of critical habitat:

> What Defendants argue, in essence, is that the Service considered whether specific activities, carried out by various governmental entities on the land designated as critical habitat, might require special management considerations. What the Service was required to do, however, was different. It was required to make a finding, prior to designating a particular area as critical habitat, that the area in question might require special management considerations and protections at some time in the future.[42]

Under the ESA, the concept of critical habitat assumes significance for the protection of species almost exclusively through the operation of section 7, which requires all federal agencies to ensure that actions they fund, authorize, or carry out are not likely to either "jeopardize the continued existence of" a listed species or destroy or adversely modify critical habitat.[43] To ensure compliance with these prohibitions, section 7 requires federal agencies to consult with FWS or NMFS to ensure that any agency action will not "jeopardize" or "result in the destruction or adverse modification" of critical habitat.[44] No other regulatory constraints flow from an area's designation as critical habitat.[45] Unless there is a federal nexus with the action that has the potential to adversely modify critical habitat (thereby triggering the section 7 obligation to consult), the fact that an area has been designated as critical habitat is inconsequential. However, as discussed elsewhere in this book, the federal nexus can take a variety of forms including federal funding and issuance of a federal permit under, for example, section 404 of the Clean Water Act.[46]

Regulatory Interpretation

In contrast to the statutory definitions, joint Reagan-era FWS/NMFS regulations governing designation of critical habitat make a clear distinction between occupied and unoccupied habitat.[47] The joint regulations specify that habitat outside of the geographic area presently occupied by a listed species can be designated as critical habitat "only when a designation limited to its present range would be inadequate to ensure the conservation of the species."[48] In response to comments accompanying promulgation of this regulation, FWS and NMFS accepted the assertion of Conoco, North American Production, that designating unoccupied areas as critical habitat required a "positive showing of need."[49]

The joint FWS/NMFS regulations elaborate the statutory elements of critical habitat strikingly similar to those regulatory elements first set forth in the 1975 notice. Physical and biological features whose presence may warrant an area's designation as critical habitat include:

1. Space for individual and population growth, and for normal behavior;
2. Food, water, air, light, minerals, or other nutritional or physiological requirements;
3. Cover or shelter;
4. Sites for breeding, reproduction, rearing of offspring, germination, or seed dispersal; and generally;
5. Habitats that are protected from disturbance or are representative of the historic geographical and ecological distributions of a species.[50]

The regulations go on to provide:

> When considering the designation of critical habitat, the Secretary shall focus on the principal biological or physical constituent elements within the defined area that are essential to the conservation of the species. Known *primary constituent elements* shall be listed with the critical habitat description.[51]

FWS and NMFS use the term "primary constituent elements," or PCEs, to identify "those physical and biological features . . . that are essential to the conservation of the [species or] subspecies and that may require special management considerations or protection."[52] "Primary constituent elements" may include, but are not limited to, "roost sites, nesting grounds, spawning sites, feeding sites, seasonal wetland or dryland, water quality or quantity, host species or plant pollinator, geological formation, vegetation type, tide, and specific soil types."[53] Failure to adequately identify primary constituent elements may result in invalidation of critical habitat designation.[54] Absent an adequate record to support their conclusion, agencies cannot include land within a critical habitat designation because it *might* include primary constituent elements sometime in the future.[55] There are, however, limitations to the specificity the regulation requires. In the November 2006 opinion in *Home Builders Association of Northern California v. U.S. Fish and Wildlife Service*, plaintiff Homebuilders argued that the designation of critical habitat for 15 vernal pool species "improperly included structures and other developed areas that do not contain the primary constituent elements (PCEs) essential to conservation of the fifteen species."[56] The court disagreed, finding FWS functional description of PCEs in upland habitat necessary to provide nutrients to vernal pool species "reasonably specific."[57]

Under the joint regulations (and agency practice[58]), absent a determination by the Secretary that a broader geographic area needs to be identified as critical habitat to conserve a species, the critical habitat of a listed species will include only specific areas occupied by the species, at the time of listing, with features "essential to the conservation of the species."[59] Once again, in understanding the meaning of "essential" one must consider the recovery-oriented nature of the definition of conservation. As FWS observed in its influential 1993 critical habitat determination for the Northern Spotted Owl:

> Critical habitat identifies specific areas essential to the conservation of a species. Areas not currently containing all of the essential features, but with the capability to do so in the future, may also be essential for the long-term recovery of the species . . . and may be designated as critical habitat.[60]

Judicial Intervention

As noted above, the section 7 consultation process and the determination whether or not an action authorized, funded, or carried out by the federal government may result in "destruction or adverse modification" of designated critical habitat trigger the protection afforded designated critical habitat. The Reagan-era joint regulations defined "destruction or adverse modification" as "a direct or indirect alteration that appreciably diminishes the value of critical habitat for both the survival and recovery of a listed species. Such alterations include, but are not limited to, alterations adversely modifying any of those physical or biological features that were the basis for determining the habitat to be critical."[61] The regulations emphasize that the action subject to consultation must threaten to "appreciably diminish" the value of critical habitat for *both* the survival and recovery of a listed species.

In March 2001, in *Sierra Club v. U.S. Fish and Wildlife Service*,[62] the Fifth Circuit struck down FWS's regulatory definition of "destruction or adverse modification" as inconsistent with the ESA:

> The ESA defines "critical habitat" as areas which are "essential to the conservation" of listed species. . . . "Conservation" is a much broader concept than mere survival. The ESA's definition of "conservation" speaks to the

recovery of a threatened or endangered species. . . . Requiring consultation only where an action affects the value of critical habitat to both the recovery and survival of a species imposes a higher threshold than the statutory language permits.[63]

The court went on to point out:

> We further note that 50 C.F.R. § 402.02 [including the definition of "destruction or adverse modification"] renders it less likely that critical habitat will be designated. Because of the higher threshold imposed by defining the destruction/adverse modification standard in terms of both survival and recovery, federal agencies would be required to consult with the Department of Interior less frequently than if the standard were defined in terms of recovery alone.[64]

In August 2004, in *Gifford Pinchot Task Force v. U.S. Fish and Wildlife Service*,[65] the Ninth Circuit struck down the same regulatory definition. The court noted:

> This regulatory definition explicitly requires appreciable diminishment of the critical habitat necessary for survival before the "destruction or adverse modification" standard could ever be met. Because it is logical and inevitable that a species requires more critical habitat for recovery than is necessary for the species survival, the regulation's singular focus becomes "survival."[66]

The court went on to find:

> Congress, by its own language, viewed conservation and survival as distinct, though complementary, goals, and the requirement to preserve critical habitat is designed to promote both conservation and survival. Congress said that "destruction or adverse modification" could occur when sufficient critical habitat is lost so as to threaten a species' recovery even if there remains sufficient critical habitat for the species' survival. The regulation, by contrast, finds that adverse modification to critical habitat can only occur when there is so much critical habitat lost that a species' very survival is threatened. The agency's interpretation would drastically narrow the scope of protection commanded by Congress under the ESA.[67]

FWS and NMFS have recognized the need to revise the definition regulation in light of these two cases.[68] However, to date, they have not done so.

Designation of Critical Habitat

The Process

In addition to defining critical habitat, the 1978 ESA Amendments established detailed criteria and a rulemaking process for the designation of critical habitat. As amended, section 4 of the Act requires the Secretary to publish the final rule designating critical habitat for a species at the same time the final rule listing the species as endangered or threatened is published "to the maximum extent prudent and determinable."[69]

No similar mandate for designation of critical habitat exists when FWS or NMFS have already made a determination regarding critical habitat and are merely revising that designation. Any critical habitat revision process is subject to the more flexible requirements of ESA section 4(3)(A)(ii), which indicates that the Secretary "may, from time-to-time thereafter, as appropriate, revise such designation."[70] Failure to revise critical habitat may be challenged under the Administrative Procedure Acts provision allowing actions to "compel agency action unlawfully withheld or unreasonably delayed."[71] However, agency failures to revise critical habitat have been upheld even when an original designation was never completed[72] and when a revised recovery plan called for critical habitat revision.[73]

Despite the mandate for simultaneous listing and designation of critical habitat, critical habitat is rarely designated at the time of listing. As of April 2009, critical habitat had been designated for more than one-third of all listed domestic species. Not surprisingly, much of the case law generated under the critical habitat provisions concerns the scope of the exceptions that FWS and NMFS may assert to justify failure to comply with the general mandate for concurrent listing and designation.

In the past eight years, the focus of litigation has shifted from whether FWS or NMFS must designate critical habitat for specific creatures to whether specific designations of critical habitat are valid under the law and regulations introduced above.

Petitions for Designation of Critical Habitat

Critical habitat may be designated by the Director of the FWS or the Director of NMFS or upon the submission of a petition by "any interested person."[74] Under the joint FWS/NMFS regulations, the agency must promptly review any petition to designate critical habitat and take appropriate action.[75] Under the terms of the Act, "to the maximum extent practicable" within 90 days after receiving a petition to "*revise* a critical habitat designation" FWS or NMFS must "make a finding as to whether the petition presents substantial scientific information indicating that the revision may be warranted."[76] Within 12 months after receiving a petition to revise critical habitat that clears the 90-day substantial information hurdle, FWS or NMFS must "determine how [it] intends to proceed with the requested revision, and shall promptly publish notice of such intention in the Federal Register."[77] While the statutory requirements appear to impose a set of prescriptive deadlines, case law suggests that the agencies may be entitled to some flexibility in their application.[78]

FWS and NMFS must publish the notice of the proposed rule designating critical habitat in the *Federal Register* and give the proposal to affected state, federal, and private entities.[79] In addition to the text of the proposed rule and a summary of the data on which it is based, the proposed rule must contain a map of the habitat area and, to the maximum extent practicable, a description and evaluation of those public and private activities that, if undertaken, may adversely modify such habitat or be affected by the critical habitat designation.[80] After publication of the proposed rule, the agency must accept public comments for 60 days and, upon the request of any person, hold a public hearing.[81]

The final rule designating critical habitat must contain the same sort of information as the proposed rule, with a summary of the comments and recommendations received.[82] The agency must publish the final rule within one year of the proposed rule[83] unless the agency finds that a six-month extension is warranted "because there is a substantial disagreement among scientists" about the data relating to the critical habitat designation.[84]

If the agency decides that designation is not prudent or critical habitat is not determinable, the agency must state its reasons for not designating critical habitat in the publication accompanying the proposed and final rules listing the endangered or threatened species.[85]

When May Critical Habitat *Not* Be Designated?

Congress envisioned that FWS and NMFS would designate critical habitat concurrently with a listing decision in the great majority of cases and that such designation would reflect the impacts, including the economic impacts, that critical habitat designation would have on an area. The agency, however, need not designate critical habitat if designation is not "prudent." If the agency finds that critical habitat is not "determinable," it may extend the period in which to designate critical habitat by not more than one year. After 2003, FWS and NMFS may not designate critical habitat on Department of Defense lands subject to an "integrated natural resource management plan" (INRMP) if the FWS or NMFS determine that the INRMP provides a benefit to the species. Existing critical habitat may be revised as new data become available to the agency.[86] Suits to force agencies to designate critical habitat may be barred by 28 U.S.C. § 2401, which requires that civil actions against the United States be brought within six years of the time the cause of action accrues. Finally, FWS has regularly and energetically asserted that lack of funds may relieve it of its obligation to designate critical habitat.

When Is Designating Critical Habitat "Not Prudent"?

FWS and NMFS need not designate critical habitat if designation is not "prudent." The joint FWS/NMFS regulations indicate that designation of critical habitat would not be "prudent" if:

> (i) The species is threatened by taking or other human activity, and identification of critical habitat can be expected to increase the degree of such threat to the species; or
>
> (ii) Such designation of critical habitat would not be beneficial to the species.[87]

Language accompanying the promulgation of these regulations suggests, for example, that designation might not be prudent if it encouraged illegal collection of the species by publicizing the location of the species.[88]

During the 1980s and 1990s, FWS and NMFS routinely declined to designate critical habitat for newly listing species on the ground that it was not prudent.[89]

However, cases in the late 1990s and the early years of the 21st century rejected these determinations in a variety of context and eventually altered agency practice.

In May 1997, in *Natural Resources Defense Council v. U.S. Department of the Interior*,[90] the Ninth Circuit rejected FWS arguments that the designation of critical habitat for the coastal California gnatcatcher was not prudent. The court rejected FWS argument that designation was not prudent because designation "would increase the degree of threat to the gnatcatcher." The court also rejected FWS's argument that designation "would not appreciably benefit the species" because the majority of gnatcatcher habitat was on private land and not subject to section 7, the only section of the Endangered Species Act that protects critical habitat. The court emphasized the narrowness of the "not prudent" exception to the obligation to protect critical habitat.[91]

In July 1997, in *Building Industry Association of Superior California v. Babbitt*,[92] the U.S. District Court for the District of Columbia rejected another FWS argument that designation of critical habitat was not prudent. The agency had determined not to designate critical habitat for various species of fairy shrimp, tiny crustaceans found in vernal pools in California's central valley. FWS decided that it would not be prudent to designate critical fairy shrimp habitat, citing the fear that "the publication of precise maps and descriptions of critical habitat in the Federal Register would make these species more vulnerable to incidents of vandalism."[93] The court rejected the FWS argument for reasons similar to those employed by the Ninth Circuit in *NRDC*.[94] In *Butte Environmental Coalition v. White*,[95] a California district court issued an order requiring FWS to designate critical habitat for the fairy shrimp with six months.[96]

In March 1998, in *Conservation Council of Hawaii v. Babbitt*,[97] the U.S. District Court for the District of Hawaii applied similar reasoning to reject an FWS decision not to designate critical habitat for 245 species of Hawaiian plants. Again the court rejected the agency argument that designation of critical habitat would lead to destruction of protected species and habitat on the ground that FWS had failed to provide evidence that this was the case.[98] The court also rejected the argument that designation of critical habitat on private land was not prudent because it would afford no protection absent the federal connection necessary to invoke the protections of section 7.

In March 2001, in *Sierra Club v. U.S. Fish and Wildlife Service*,[99] the Fifth Circuit overturned yet another FWS determination not to designate critical habitat. FWS had declined to designate critical habitat for the Gulf sturgeon on the grounds (1) that the designation was "not prudent" because the habitat, although necessary for recovery, was not necessary for survival of the species and (2) that designation of critical habitat afforded no protection not afforded by consultation and the jeopardy prohibition. The Fifth Circuit invalidated FWS's regulatory definition of "destruction or adverse modification," discussed above.[100] The court then rejected FWS's assertion that jeopardy consultation was "functionally equivalent" to consultation under the destruction/adverse modification standard as untenable.[101]

By the middle of 2001, almost every argument FWS could muster to defend a "not prudent" determination had been rejected by one district court or another. FWS had failed to win a single case on this point.

When Is Critical Habitat Not Determinable?

Critical habitat designation is not required at the time of species listing if critical habitat is not "determinable."[102] Under the joint FWS/NMFS regulations, critical habitat is not determinable when:

> (i) Information sufficient to perform required analyses of the impacts of the designation is lacking; or
> (ii) The biological needs of the species are not sufficiently well known to permit identification of an area as critical habitat.[103]

Critical habitat is not determinable, for example, when the agency lacks information on a species' need for space to reproduce.

Unlike a finding that designation of habitat is not "prudent," a finding that critical habitat is not determinable only delays the obligation to designate.[104] The agency may extend the time period for finalizing critical habitat designation by an additional year.[105] However, by the end of the additional year, the agency "must publish a final regulation, based on such data as may be available at that time, designating to the maximum extent prudent, such habitat."[106]

In the 1980s, agencies frequently declined to designate critical habitat for listed species on the basis that critical habitat is not determinable.[107] However, decisions in *Center for Biological Diversity v. Evans*,[108] *Forest Guardians v. Babbitt*,[109] *Colorado Wildlife Federation v. U.S. Fish and Wildlife Service*,[110] and *Northern Spotted Owl v. Lujan*[111] demonstrate a judicial willingness to (1) independently examine FWS's claims that critical habitat is not determinable and (2) require FWS to designate critical habitat within the time periods specified by the Act.

In 2005, in *Center for Biological Diversity v. Evans*,[112] the district court rejected a NMFS determination that Pacific Ocean critical habitat for the right whale was not determinable. Atlantic Ocean habitat had already been designated. Accordingly, the Pacific Ocean habitat designation was a critical habitat *revision* and was not subject to the obligation to designate within one year. NMFS asserted that it lacked sufficient information to designate habitat areas. The court found the agency had enough evidence to designate critical habitat under the Act's standard:

> Here, the best available evidence supports critical habitat designation. Beginning in 1996, small groups of right whales—including calves—were seen congregating, feeding and engaging in courtship behavior in the southeast Bering Sea. [T]he Marine Mammal Commission, (a federal body of marine mammal experts charged with making recommendations to NMFS) concluded that
>
>> the repeated occurrence of right whales in summer and fall months, coupled with the fact that the petitioned area lies within a broader area in which whaling records document that right whales were once abundant, provides a reasonable basis for concluding that the petitioned area contains physical or biological features essential for the species' survival.

Under the best available standard, Congress required the agency to consider the scientific information available at the time of consideration, giving the species the benefit of the doubt.[113]

In 1998, in *Forest Guardians v. Babbitt*,[114] the Tenth Circuit reversed a U.S. District Court for the District of New Mexico decision allowing FWS additional time to complete a critical habitat designation of the Rio Grande silvery minnow. FWS admitted its failure to comply with this statutory duty to designate critical habitat for the silvery minnow, but defended its inaction on the ground that "no resources are available at this time to complete a critical habitat determination for the silvery minnow."[115] The court rejected this excuse, pointing out that "'[s]hall' means shall,"[116] and that FWS was required to comply with the statutory deadlines mandated by the Endangered Species Act.

In 1992, in *Colorado Wildlife Federation v. Turner*, the plaintiff sought to compel FWS to designate critical habitat for the razorback sucker, a Colorado River fish species. FWS had listed the razorback sucker as an endangered species but had failed to designate critical habitat within two years of the proposal to list.[117] FWS argued that it had insufficient information to properly designate the razorback sucker's critical habitat.[118] The court rejected this argument, holding that Congress had addressed this situation and FWS must publish a final rule "using all information presently available."[119] The court concluded that it had no discretion to order otherwise despite FWS's claims that prompt designation might result in designation of an unnecessarily large geographic area as critical habitat.

In 1991, in *Northern Spotted Owl v. Lujan*,[120] another federal court rejected a FWS determination that critical habitat was not "determinable." When FWS listed the northern spotted owl as a threatened species, it had deferred designating critical habitat on the grounds that critical habitat was not "determinable."[121] Plaintiffs, 22 environmental groups, challenged this determination and filed a motion for summary judgment to compel FWS to designate critical habitat for the northern spotted owl. The court granted summary judgment, holding that FWS's determination "not to designate critical habitat concurrently with the listing of the northern spotted owl, or to explain any basis for concluding that the critical habitat was not determinable," was arbitrary and capricious.[122] The court based its decision on what it saw as a clear congressional intent that "the designation of critical habitat is to coincide with the final listing decision absent extraordinary circumstances."[123]

The 1991 decision in *Northern Spotted Owl* provided a wake-up call to the agencies and the public that courts would not necessarily defer to a conclusion that critical habitat was not determinable. The 2005 decision in *Center for Biological Diversity v. Norton* indicates that courts may be willing to second-guess agency determinations that the agency lacks necessary information. The decisions in *Forest Guardians* and *Colorado Wildlife Federation* emphasized further that designation must occur within one year of species listing despite information gaps or budgetary constraints.

Department of Defense Integrated Natural Resource Management Plans

In 2003, as part of the National Defense Authorization Act, Congress amended the critical habitat provisions of ESA to prevent FWS or NMFS from designating critical habitat on Department of Defense lands subject to an "integrated natural resource management plan" if the FWS or NMFS determine "in writing" that the INRMP provides a benefit to the species.[124] INRMPs are required for Department of Defense facilities under the 1997 amendments to the Sikes Act unless the Department of Defense "determines that the absence of significant natural resources on a particular installation makes preparation of such a plan inappropriate."[125]

Statute of Limitations

Title 28 U.S.C. § 2401 provides "every civil action commenced against the United States shall be barred unless the complaint is filed within six years after the right of action first accrues." Section 2401 provides the general federal statute of limitations for actions against the U.S. government. In *Center for Biological Diversity v. Hamilton*,[126] environmental groups brought suit to force FWS to designate habitat for the threatened blue shiner and the goldline garter, Alabama and Georgia river minnows. FWS had issued a final rule to list the two species in April 1992. The final rule indicated that the designation of critical habitat "may be prudent but . . . it is not now determinable."[127] FWS took no further action. In September 2004, the Center for Biological Diversity filed suit to force designation of critical habitat. Plaintiffs asserted that their suit was not barred by the six-year statute of limitations because failure to designate critical habitat was a continuing violation of the agency's obligation. "The continuing violation doctrine permits a plaintiff to sue on an otherwise time-barred claim when additional violations of the law occur within the statutory period."[128] The Eleventh Circuit "in a matter of first impression"[129] rejected plaintiffs' continuing violation argument and affirmed the lower court's dismissal of the complaint.

However, in *Schoeffler v. Kempthorne*,[130] the U.S. District Court for the Western District of Louisiana took a different—if not necessarily contrary—position. In January 1992, FWS listed the Louisiana black bear as a threatened species and declared the bear's critical habitat "not then determinable." In December 1993, FWS proposed to designate some critical habitat. FWS never issued a final rule. In March 1994, FWS again proposed designating critical habitat. In September 2005, after a decade of further discussions, plaintiffs sued to force designation of critical habitat. FWS asserted that their claims were barred by the statute of limitations. The court disagreed:

> Defendant's conduct and representations since its initial determination that a critical habitat was prudent, although not yet determinable, evidenced that defendant was taking the necessary steps to designate critical habitat for the Louisiana Black Bear, seemingly at the earliest point possible. The Secretary's not determinable finding was followed by subsequent action whereby the defendant, at least superficially, attempted to comply with the legal mandate by proposing rules, accepting public comments, holding public hearings, and even

promising that critical habitat designation would be forthcoming. This all confirmed plaintiffs' reasonable, good faith belief that the Secretary would ultimately comply with the law, even if at a time after the statutory deadline.[131]

The court did not rely on the "continuing violation" doctrine and limited its discussion of *Center for Biological Diversity v. Hamilton* to the second paragraph of a lengthy footnote.[132]

Lack of Federal Funds

As Judge Inman of the U.S. District Court for the Eastern District of Tennessee put it (in a case requiring designation of critical habitat for 16 species):

> Stated crassly and starkly, it is money—more accurately, the lack of money—that has precipitated this suit and others like it. Congress has charged the Fish and Wildlife Service with the responsibility of identifying endangered or threatened species and the critical habitat for those species. To state the obvious, it requires money to fulfill this statutory duty. Unfortunately for all concerned, Congress has declined to curtail the scope of the Fish and Wildlife Service's duties under the Endangered Species Act, yet has refused to adequately fund the Service to enable it to carry out those duties.[133]

Sometime in the mid-1990s, in the wake of Congress's April 1995 one-year moratorium on funding for the listing of species and designation of critical habitat,[134] the federal government began asserting lack of funds as a legal defense to its statutory obligation to designate critical habitat.[135] While courts were reluctant to allow the funding moratorium to affect compliance with the explicit statutory deadlines in section 4 of the Act, they occasionally bowed to fiscal reality.[136] The lack-of-funds arguments persisted after the moratorium had ended. In 1999, in *Biodiversity Legal Foundation v. Badgley*,[137] the U.S. District Court for the District of Oregon rejected a FWS argument based on budget constraints. As noted above, in *Forest Guardians v. Babbitt*[138] the Tenth Circuit rejected a similar financial "impossibility" defense. In 2003, in *Center for Biological Diversity v. Norton*,[139] the U.S. District Court for the District of Arizona rejected a similar argument presented creatively as a Federal Rule of Civil Procedure 60(b)(5) motion ("it is no longer equitable that the judgment should have prospective application"). However, in an unreported opinion in a different case with the same name, the U.S. District Court for the Southern District of California found that FWS exhaustion of its annual funding for critical habitat designations constituted "changed conditions" and warranted amendment of an order requiring designation of critical habitat for eight plant species.[140]

Designation of Critical Habitat and Conservation Goals

Most courts and commentators have treated the obligations imposed by ESA to identify recovery goals for species[141] and the obligations imposed by the definition of critical habitat to identify habitat "essential to the conservation of the species" as separate.

However, at least one court has pointed out that it is difficult to identify what habitat is "essential" for the conservation of a species, unless one already knows what will be required to conserve the species. In the 2003 opinion in *Home Builders Association of Northern California v. U.S. Fish and Wildlife Service*,[142] Judge Ishii of the U.S. District Court for the Eastern District of California remanded the FWS designation of critical habitat for the Alameda whipsnake for a variety of reasons. Among these reasons was:

> [B]ecause essential physical or biological features must be essential for "the conservation of the species," they must be necessary to bring the species, "to the point at which the measures provided pursuant to [the ESA] are no longer necessary." The court concludes . . . that if the Service has not determined at what point the protections of the ESA will no longer be necessary for the snake, it cannot possibly identify the physical or biological features that are an indispensable part of bringing the snake to that point.[143]

In 2006, in *Home Builders Association of Northern California v. U.S. Fish and Wildlife Service*,[144] a different case (involving 15 vernal pool species) with the same name, Judge Shubb, also of the Eastern District of California, rejected Judge Ishii's logic, declaring:

> Although PCEs must be described in a critical habitat designation, there is no indication in the ESA that the agency must simultaneously prepare objective, measurable criteria indicating when the ultimate goal of conservation of the species will be achieved.[145]

While this may seem no more than a skirmish in the annals of critical habitat litigation, this exchange raises significant unresolved questions about the relationship between critical habitat designation and the establishment of recovery goals.

May Economic Impacts Be Considered in Designation of Critical Habitat?

Congress required that critical habitat be designated on the basis of the "best scientific data available" after considering the "economic impact and any other relevant impact, of specifying any particular area as critical habitat."[146] The regulations require the Secretary to conduct an "impact analysis" to "consider the reasonably probable economic and other impacts of the designation" on "significant activities that would either affect an area considered for designation as Critical Habitat or be likely to be affected by the designation" after an area is proposed for designation and prior to finalizing the critical habitat designation.[147] The designation of critical habitat is the only place in the ESA where Congress has explicitly authorized the Secretary to consider economic impacts. In October 2008, the Office of the Solicitor of the U.S. Department of the Interior issued an opinion emphasizing the "broad discretion" FWS and NMFS have in excluding areas from critical habitat.[148]

In designating an area as critical habitat, Congress directed the agency to consider the "economic impact, the impact on national security, and any other relevant impact, of specifying any particular area as critical habitat."[149] Any portion of an area can be excluded from critical habitat designation if the benefits of exclusion outweigh the benefits of inclusion unless "failure to designate such area as critical habitat will result in the extinction of the species concerned."[150] The October 2008 Department of the Interior Solicitor's Memorandum interprets this provision as preventing only exclusions that constitute the "but for" cause of extinction. "If, in the absence of designating a particular area, the species would go extinct, but the designation of that area would prevent that extinction, the Secretary must designate the area."[151]

Given the significance of critical habitat designation (triggering the obligation to consult under section 7), the requirement to consider the economic impacts of designation translates into an analysis of the costs of enforcing the adverse modification standard imposed by section 7. Economic impacts of designation do not include the costs of enforcing the jeopardy standard of section 7 or any costs associated with the listing of a species.[152]

The agency must calculate the impacts resulting from designation of critical habitat. In *New Mexico Cattle Growers Ass'n v. U.S. Fish and Wildlife Service*,[153] industry groups challenged designation of critical habitat for the southwestern willow flycatcher. The plaintiffs asserted that the designation of critical habitat was illegal because FWS had failed to properly consider the economic impact of habitat designation. The agency previously determined the designation of critical habitat would have *no* incremental economic impact. Accordingly, the agency argued it was not required to fully analyze the economic impact of protection as part of the critical habitat designation process. In 2001, the Tenth Circuit Court of Appeals specifically rejected this "baseline" approach to compliance with a statutory obligation to consider the economic impact of critical habitat designation. The court stated that "the root of the problem lies in FWS's long held policy position that [critical habitat designations] are unhelpful, duplicative, and unnecessary."[154] The court declared that its decision was "compelled by the canons of statutory interpretation to give some effect to the congressional directive that economic impacts be considered at the time of critical habitat designation."[155] While the opinion rejects one defense against preparing a thorough analysis of the economic impacts of critical habitat designation, it provides little guidance for determining what an adequate analysis might be.

In April 2002, in an unreported opinion in *National Association of Home Builders v. Evans*,[156] the U.S. District Court for the District of Columbia implicitly accepted the Tenth Circuit's approach by accepting a consent decree requiring remand of a designation of critical habitat because that designation was inconsistent with the holding in *New Mexico Cattle Growers Association*. The court stated, "[T]he Tenth Circuit's opinion is well-reasoned and comports with the express statutory language of Congress." The court found that Congress required "an analysis of the economic impact of a critical habitat" and that "[u]nder the current 'incremental baseline approach,' any costs associated with listing the species is kept below the 'baseline.'" The court concluded, "[I]n placing the economic impact of the listing (and other relevant factors) below the baseline, as the Court reads it, costs that should be considered in making the critical habitat designation are left entirely out of the picture."[157]

Later that year, in *Home Builders Association of Northern California v. Norton*,[158] in a published opinion, another District of Columbia district judge accepted a similar consent decree on similar grounds.

Emerging Issues and Future Directions

The Regulatory Significance of Critical Habitat Adverse Modification on the Ground and in the Water

Under the terms of the Endangered Species Act, the duty to consult on potential destruction or "adverse modification" of critical habitat is a distinct duty from the duty to avoid "jeopardy."[159] By identifying two different circumstances that trigger the obligation to consult (the potential for "jeopardy" and the potential for destruction or "adverse modification"), and by establishing a scheme whereby some, but not all, habitat of a listed species may be designated as "critical," Congress made it clear that "adverse modification" consultation should be independent from and, in some cases, more stringent than "jeopardy" consultation. Because Congress specified that critical habitat would be designated with the conservation of the species in mind and specifically authorized the designation of unoccupied habitat, it would seem logical that the issue of destruction or "adverse modification" would be considered in light of the recovery prospects of the species.

This point emerged in the 2006 opinion in *Center for Biological Diversity v. Bureau of Land Management*.[160] Environmental plaintiffs challenged a limited FWS critical habitat designation for the Peirson's milk-vetch in the Algodones Dunes in Imperial County in southeastern California. BLM asserted that because the milk-vetch was present in proposed critical habitat areas excluded from its challenged designation, any federal action that might affect those areas also might affect the species, thus triggering the section 7 "jeopardy" consultation. Therefore, BLM argued, additional critical habitat designation was unnecessary. The court responded:

> Defendants' argument misses the point, however, because although they are correct that the critical habitat designation of the excluded areas would not increase the number of opportunities for section 7 consultations, the scope and nature of these consultations would be affected, as would the extent of the protections afforded the excluded areas. . . .
>
> An example is illustrative. The final rule excluded [two areas] from the designated critical habitat. Because milk-vetch is found in the excluded areas, if a federal action is proposed in those areas that may affect the milk-vetch, the agency contemplating the action would be required to consult with the Service pursuant to section 7 of the ESA. That consultation would require the agencies to insure that the action is not likely to jeopardize the continued existence of the milk-vetch. However, because the excluded areas were not designated as critical habitat, the agencies would not be required to insure that, with respect to these areas, the proposed action will not result in the destruction or adverse modification of the designated critical habitat. . . . [T]he focus of

those consultations will be on the species' survival, not recovery. In contrast, if the areas ... had been designated as critical habitat, any future section 7 consultation would be required to also determine whether the proposed action would destroy or adversely modify the critical habitat, an inquiry that is broader than the jeopardy analysis.[161]

While Congress may have intended that critical habitat receive greater protection than listed species habitat not so designated, the 1986 joint FWS/NMFS regulations blurred that distinction and blended the adverse modification and jeopardy standards of section 7 into something approaching a single "no jeopardy" standard.

Invalidation of the regulatory definition of "destruction or adverse modification" and the reassertion of a recovery-based concept of critical habitat in *Sierra Club v. U.S. Fish and Wildlife Service*[162] and *Gifford Pinchot Task Force v. U.S. Fish and Wildlife Service*[163] establish that the destruction or "adverse modification" standard really are different from the "jeopardy" standard. The absence of a new regulation, however, has left the courts to sort out what the distinct meaning of adverse modification might be.

In *National Wildlife Federation v. National Marine Fisheries Service*,[164] environmental groups challenged the NMFS biological opinion for proposed operations of Federal Columbia River Power System dams and related facilities. Plaintiffs challenged both the determination that the proposed operations would not jeopardize the continued existence of listed fish species and that it would not adversely affect the designated critical habitat of those species. In 2007, the Ninth Circuit affirmed the district court ruling that NMFS had failed to ensure that the operation would not adversely modify designated critical habitat. Specifically, the court found that "NMFS's adverse modification analysis did not adequately consider recovery needs "and that the NMFS critical habitat determination "(1) did not adequately consider the proposed action's short-term negative effects in the context of the affected species' life cycles and migration patterns, (2) relied on uncertain long-term improvements to critical habitat to offset certain short-term degradation, and (3) concluded that the species' critical habitat was sufficient for recovery without adequate information to make that determination."[165]

In 2007, in *Oregon Natural Desert Association v. Lohn*,[166] the district court remanded a "no adverse modification" determination in biological opinions regarding the impact of livestock grazing in protected steelhead trout and bull trout in Oregon's Malheur National Forest. The court showed a similar concern with the effect of grazing on species recovery and the government's willingness to balance documented short-term negative impact with speculative long-term mitigation.[167] In responding to the degraded baseline conditions in the designated critical habitat, the court also emphasized the obligation to consider cumulative impacts in consultation involving either a jeopardy determination or adverse modification determination.[168]

In 2007, in *Natural Resources Defense Council v. Kempthorne*,[169] environmental groups challenged the 2005 biological opinion gauging the effect of operation of the federally managed Central Valley Project and the State of California's State Water

Project on the delta smelt, a small indigenous Sacramento River fish. In finding the "no adverse modification" determination inadequate, the court focused on the importance of recovery prospects in assessing adverse modification.[170]

Critical Habitat Designation and the National Environmental Policy Act

Another long-standing issue concerning critical habitat is under what circumstances, if any, FWS and NMFS must comply with the National Environmental Policy Act (NEPA) and prepare an environmental assessment (EA) or environmental impact statement (EIS) in connection with designation. NEPA requires federal agencies to prepare a statement of the environmental impacts for all "Federal actions significantly affecting the quality of the human environment."[171] If an agency is unsure whether a proposed action requires the preparation of an EIS, regulations of the Council on Environmental Quality (CEQ) implementing NEPA direct the agency to prepare an EA to determine whether an EIS must be prepared.[172]

In 1983, FWS published a notice of its determination that EAs need not be prepared for regulations adopted under section 4 of the ESA.[173] Section 4 authorizes the agency to list endangered or threatened species and to designate critical habitat.[174] Prior to 1983, FWS prepared environmental assessments for all regulations listing species or designating critical habitat. However, in 1983, CEQ recommended that FWS listing decisions be exempt from NEPA as a matter of law or, alternatively, because the critical habitat designations could be categorically excluded from NEPA requirements.[175] CEQ based its recommendation on a decision by the Sixth Circuit Court of Appeals in *Pacific Legal Foundation v. Andrus* holding that FWS did not have to comply with NEPA when deciding whether to list a species because the Secretary had no discretion to withhold the listing of an otherwise eligible species because of environmental considerations.[176]

Since the 1983 policy change, FWS has not regularly prepared EAs or EISs for decisions regarding the listing of species or the designation of critical habitat. However, the current validity of this policy as it relates to the designation of critical habitat is uncertain.

In *Douglas County v. Lujan*,[177] the plaintiffs sought to enjoin FWS from implementing a critical habitat designation for the spotted owl until an EA or EIS was prepared. Citing the holding in *Pacific Legal Foundation*, FWS argued that an EA or EIS did not have to be prepared for the designation of critical habitat. The U.S. District Court for the District of Oregon held that the Endangered Species Act did not relieve FWS of the obligation to comply with NEPA as to the designation of 6.9 million acres of critical habitat for the Northern spotted owl.[178]

In 1995, in *Douglas County v. Babbitt*,[179] the Ninth Circuit reversed the district court holding and determined that the Endangered Species Act implicitly exempted the critical habitat designation process from NEPA. The court of appeals stated:

> The purpose of the ESA is to prevent extinction of species, and Congress has allowed the Secretary to consider economic consequences of actions that fur-

ther that purpose. But *Congress has not given the Secretary the discretion to consider environmental factors, other than those related directly to the preservation of the species.* The Secretary cannot engage in the very broad analysis NEPA requires when designating a critical habitat under the ESA. . . .[180]

In 1996, the Tenth Circuit, in *Catron County Board of Commissioners v. U.S. Fish and Wildlife Service*,[181] articulated a position directly contrary to the Ninth Circuit's, holding "that the legislative history . . . indicates that Congress intended that the Secretary comply with NEPA when designating critical habitat . . . when such designations constitute major federal action significantly affecting the quality of the human environment."[182]

In 2004, in *Cape Hatteras Access Preservation Alliance v. U.S. Department of the Interior*,[183] the U.S. District Court for the District of Columbia accepted the Tenth Circuit's reasoning in *Catron County Board of Commissioners* and rejected the Ninth Circuit's approach in *Douglas County*. The court declared, "To ignore NEPA while designating critical habitat is to argue for NEPA's implicit repeal by the ESA and amendments to the ESA, an argument not supported by the ESA's text or the legislative history."[184]

At another level of NEPA compliance, in 2002, in *Middle Rio Grande Conservancy District v. Norton*,[185] the conservancy district and State of New Mexico challenged FWS's revised designation of critical habitat for the Rio Grande silvery minnow. FWS had prepared an EA and made a finding of no significant impact (FONSI) determining that no further NEPA compliance was necessary.[186] The Tenth Circuit upheld a district court opinion requiring FWS to prepare an EIS. In support of this holding, the Court of Appeals cited *Catron County Board of Commissioners* for the proposition that "circumstances in the Tenth Circuit which would relieve the Secretary of the Interior from the duty to prepare an EIS when designating critical habitat will be unquestionably rare."[187] The court justified its decision to order preparation of an EIS rather than remanding to the agency to reassess its own finding by describing the desperate plight of the species and the role FWS delays had played in making it so.[188] The court opined that "there is overwhelming evidence that the designation will significantly affect the quality of the human environment."[189] The court cited the documented need to maintain water in the designated river sections and the fact that the Middle Rio Grande was a "fully appropriated" river and that "[a]ny reallocation of water will be at the expense of water users."[190] And "[i]n response to a questionnaire from FWS, the United States Bureau of Reclamation . . . indicated it might curtail river management practices in response to the designation."[191] Finally, the court observed:

> This court has recognized that the requirements of NEPA can further the objectives of the Endangered Species Act. *See Catron County.* . . . This case demonstrates that the abdication of an agency's responsibilities under NEPA can frustrate the goals of the Endangered Species Act. FWS' delays and inadequate decisionmaking have resulted in the absence of a critical habitat designation eight years after the Silvery Minnow's listing. The protections of a

designation are particularly needed by the Silvery Minnow, a species placed on the brink of extinction by habitat loss. Adherence to the policy objective of the ESA to halt the extinction of the minnow no matter the cost requires that NEPA compliance be completed as expeditiously, yet comprehensively, as possible.[192]

Conclusion

Three decades after Congress added the first detailed critical habitat designation and protection provisions to the Endangered Species Act, critical habitat is beginning to emerge from the shadows. Dozens of federal court decisions have established that critical habitat must be designated for almost all listed endangered or threatened species and that the protections provided by critical habitat designation are different from those provided by the jeopardy prohibition. Beyond that, much remains to be resolved. Critical habitat may become an essential tool for meeting the Endangered Species Act's recovery goals or it may become a burdensome, expensive, largely meaningless paperwork exercise. Much depends on how federal wildlife agencies respond to the complex direction federal courts have given them.

Notes

1. 437 U.S. 153 (1978).
2. *Id.* at 179 ("In shaping legislation . . . Congress started from the finding that '[the] two major causes of extinction are hunting and destruction of natural habitat.' . . . Of these twin threats, Congress was informed that the greatest was destruction of natural habitats").
3. *Id.*
4. *Id.*
5. *See* Babbitt v. Sweet Home Chapter of Cmtys. for a Greater Or., 515 U.S. 687 (1995).
6. 16 U.S.C. §§ 1533(a)(3), 1536(a).
7. *Id.* § 1533(a)(3)(A) (emphasis added).
8. U.S. Fish & Wildlife Serv., Species Reports, Listed Species with Critical Habitat, http://ecos.fws.gov/tess_public/CriticalHabitat.do?nmfs=1 (last visited Sept. 13, 2007).
9. *Id.*
10. U.S. Fish & Wildlife Serv., *Endangered Species Bulletin*, http://www.fws.gov/endangered/bulletin/2007/ES_Bulletin_03-2007.pdf (Mar. 2007).
11. Press Release, U.S. Dep't of Interior, Endangered Species Act "Broken," http://www.doi.gov/news/03_News_Releases/030528a.htm (May 28, 2003).
12. GAO-02-581, Endangered Species Program: Information on How Funds Are Allocated and What Activities Are Emphasized 3 (June 2002).
13. *Id.* at 4.
14. 50 C.F.R. § 402.02; *see* Gifford Pinchot Task Force v. U.S. Fish & Wildlife Serv., 378 F.3d 1059 (9th Cir. 2004); Sierra Club v. U.S. Fish & Wildlife Serv., 245 F.3d 434 (5th Cir. 2001).
15. 50 C.F.R. § 402.02.
16. *See generally* THOMAS LOVEJOY & LEE HANNAH, CLIMATE CHANGE AND BIODIVERSITY (2006).
17. Pub. L. No. 93-205, 87 Stat. 884, 16 U.S.C. § 1536(a) (1976) (current version at 16 U.S.C. § 1536(a)).

18. The ESA delegates joint administrative authority to the Secretary of the Interior and the Secretary of Commerce, who, in turn, have delegated their authority to the Director of the FWS and the Director of NMFS. Together, the FWS and NMFS have promulgated regulations under the ESA, which are located at 50 C.F.R. pts. 401–403 (referred to as the "joint regulations").
19. 40 Fed. Reg. 17,764 (Apr. 22, 1975).
20. 43 Fed. Reg. 870, 874–75 (Jan. 4, 1978).
21. 437 U.S. 153 (1978).
22. H.R. Rep. No. 95-1625, at 25 (1978), *reprinted in* 1978 U.S.C.C.A.N. 9453, 9475.
23. S. Rep. No. 95-874, at 10.
24. Endangered Species Act Amendments of 1978, Pub. L. No. 95-632, § 2, 92 Stat. 3751 (codified at 16 U.S.C. § 1532(5)(A)).
25. 16 U.S.C. § 1532(3).
26. Determination of Critical Habitat for the Colorado River Endangered Fishes: Razorback Sucker, Colorado Squawfish, Humpback Chub, and Bonytail Chub, 59 Fed. Reg. 13,374, 13,377 (Mar. 21, 1994) (emphasis added).
27. Proposed Revised Designation of Critical Habitat for the Northern Spotted Owl (Strix occidentalis caurina), 72 Fed. Reg. 32,450, 32,456 (June 12, 2007).
28. Revised Critical Habitat for the San Bernardino Kangaroo Rat (Dipodomys merriami parvus), 72 Fed. Reg. 33,808, 33,810 (June 19, 2007).
29. 16 U.S.C. § 1532(5)(c).
30. H.R. Rep. 95-632, at 18 (1978), *reprinted in* 1978 U.S.C.C.A.N. 9453, 9468.
31. 16 U.S.C. § 1532(5)(A)(ii).
32. *Id.*
33. *See* Home Builders Ass'n of N. Cal. v. U.S. Fish & Wildlife Serv. 2006 WL 3190518 (E.D. Cal. Nov. 2, 2006) ("[T]here is theoretically no limit to the degree of precision agencies could be compelled to undergo before designating critical habitat under Home Builders' argument [that FWS failed to distinguished adequately between occupied and unoccupied habitat]. Within a critical habitat unit, it is entirely possible that a single square inch of the land at issue would be wholly unoccupied by the relevant species. Clearly, an agency should not have to make a critical habitat determination on such a fine scale, but the logical extension of Home Builders' argument would seem to impose just such a requirement on the agency. Therefore, the critical habitat designation will pass muster regardless of whether the habitat designated was occupied or unoccupied.").
34. 16 U.S.C. § 1532(5)(A)(i).
35. *Id.* § 1532(5)(A)(ii).
36. Cape Hatteras Access Pres. Alliance v. U.S. Dep't of Interior, 344 F. Supp. 2d 108, 119 (D.D.C. 2004) ("[B]oth occupied and unoccupied areas may become critical habitat, but, with unoccupied areas, it is not enough that the area's features be essential to conservation, the area itself must be essential.").
37. *Id.* at 124 ("The Service must focus on the management requirements of the area's features").
38. Homebuilders Ass'n of N. Cal. v. U.S. Fish & Wildlife Serv., 268 F. Supp. 2d 1197, 1218 (E.D. Cal. 2003) (holding that while a present need for special management considerations or protection was not required, the agency was required to "make a finding, prior to designating a particular area as critical habitat, that the area in question might require special management considerations and protections at some time in the future").
39. Ctr. for Biological Diversity v. Norton, 240 F. Supp. 2d 1090, 1098–99 (D. Ariz. 2003) ("The phrase 'which may require special management' can be rephrased as 'can require' or 'possibly requires' without altering its meaning. Hence, a plain reading of the definition of 'critical habitat' means land essential to the conservation of a species for which special management or protection is *possible*.").
40. *Id.* at 1099.
41. 268 F. Supp. 2d 1197 (E.D. Cal. 2003).

42. *Id.* at 1218.
43. 16 U.S.C. 1536(a)(2).
44. *Id.* § 1536(a)(2). Section 7 also imposes an obligation to confer with the Secretary for Federal Agency on actions that are likely to "result in the destruction or adverse modification of proposed critical habitat." 16 U.S.C. § 1536(a)(4). Unlike section 7 consultation, such conferences do not produce binding or mandatory constraints on the action in question. See Chapter 5.
45. Critical habitat may be implicated under the taking prohibition in section 9. Section 9 makes it illegal for any person to "take" an endangered species. 16 U.S.C. § 1538(a) (1988). "Take" is defined by the Act to include "harm," *id.* § 1532(19), which FWS regulations define to include "significant *habitat* modification or degradation where it actually kills or injures wildlife." 50 C.F.R. § 17.3 (1993). Under these definitions, "taking" is tied to significant habitat modification regardless of whether or not the habitat is critical habitat. Nonetheless, as a practical matter, a court may attach greater import to a "taking" caused by habitat modifications to critical habitat. *See* Palila v. Haw. Dep't of Land & Natural Res., 639 F.2d 495 (9th Cir. 1981); Pamela Baldwin, The Role of Designation of Critical Habitat Under the Endangered Species Act (ESA), CRS Report for Congress, Aug. 27, 2004, *available at* http://digital.library.unt.edu/govdocs/crs/permalink/meta-crs-10046:1 (last visited Feb. 22, 2008); *see also* Babbitt v. Sweet Home Chapter of Cmtys. for a Greater Or., 515 U.S. 687 (1995).
46. *See* Chapters 5 and 11.
47. Listing Endangered and Threatened Species and Designating Critical Habitat; Amended Procedures to Comply with the 1982 Amendments to the Endangered Species Act, 49 Fed. Reg. 38,900 (Oct. 1, 1984).
48. 50 C.F.R. § 424.12(e).
49. CNAP expressed the opinion that "there must be a positive showing of need before a critical habitat larger than that currently occupied by the species to be protected can be designated." The Services agree that any designation of critical habitat must be based on a finding that such designated area contains features that are essential in order to conserve the species concerned. This finding of need will be a part of all designations of critical habitat, whether or not they extend beyond the range a species currently occupies. 49 Fed. Reg. 38,900, 38,903 (Oct. 1, 1984).
50. 50 C.F.R. § 424.12(b).
51. *Id.* (emphasis added).
52. *See, e.g.,* Revised Critical Habitat for the San Bernardino Kangaroo Rat, 72 Fed. Reg. 33,808, 33,810–11 (June 19, 2007); Proposed Endangered Status for the Cook Inlet Beluga Whale, 72 Fed. Reg. 19,854, 19,861(Apr. 20, 2007).
53. *Id.* The identification and delineation of areas containing these features, addressed in the rulemaking process, raises a series of technical and scientific issues that are beyond the scope of this chapter.
54. Home Builders Ass'n of N. Cal. v. U.S. Fish & Wildlife Serv., 268 F. Supp. 2d 1197, 1211 (E.D. Cal. 2003) ("[The Critical Habitat Designation Rule for the Alameda Whipsnake] merely describes where the primary constituent elements may be located, using phrases in three of the four sentences indicating that the primary constituent elements 'are in' or 'may be found in' particular areas, or that particular habitat features 'may also contain' the elements. Relatedly, in the first of the four sentences, the Service merely describes the primary constituent elements as essential for five primary biological needs. None of these sentences tell the reader what the primary constituent elements actually are.").
55. The Cape Hatteras Access Pres. Alliance v. U.S. Dep't of Interior, 344 F. Supp. 2d 108, 122–23 (D.D.C. 2004) ("The Service may not statutorily cast a net over tracts of land with the mere hope that they will develop PCEs and be subject to designation.... It might be different if the Service had discussed observations of specific PCEs at one time and had evidence that the PCEs, though not always present, would return during the plover's wintering season.... The agency does not document its PCE findings and, to the extend it has designated areas lacking PCEs, appears to rely on hope.").

56. 2006 WL 3190518, at *13 (E.D. Cal. Nov. 2, 2006).
57. *Id.* at 17.
58. *See, e.g.,* Endangered and Threatened Wildlife and Plants; Final Designation or Non-designation of Critical Habitat for 95 Plant Species from the Islands of Kauai and Niihau, HI, 68 Fed. Reg. 9116, 9168 (Feb. 27, 2003) ("As part of the Service's designation process, the entire geographic area that could be occupied by the threatened or endangered species is never put forth as proposed or final critical habitat, unless circumstances unique to the species require such a designation and only after approval by the Secretary of the Interior (or the Secretary of Commerce)"). In the case of *Astragalus lentiginosus* var. *piscinensis* (Fish Slough milk-vetch), however, the FWS did designate almost the entire geographic range of the species as critical habitat. Designation of Critical Habitat for Astragalus lentiginosus var. piscinensis (Fish Slough Milk-Vetch), 70 Fed. Reg. 33,774, 33,786 (June 9, 2005) ("With the exception of one small area described below, the entire geographic area that is or was known to be occupied by the *Astragalus lentiginosus* var. *piscinensis* is being designated as critical habitat because the taxon occupies a small geographic area, and that area is occupied by plants that are likely to function as one cohesive population. These areas are all considered essential to the conservation of the species, in accordance with section 3(5)(C) of the Act.").
59. Critical Habitat Designation for Northern Spotted Owl, 57 Fed Reg. 1796 (Jan. 15, 1992).
60. *Id.*
61. 50 C.F.R. § 402.02.
62. 245 F.3d 434 (5th Cir. 2001).
63. *Id.* at 441–42.
64. *Id.* at 443.
65. 378 F.3d 1059 (9th Cir. 2004).
66. *Id.* at 1069.
67. *Id.* at 1070.
68. Unified Agenda, Monday, April 30, 2007, Dep't of Interior (DOI), 72 Fed. Reg. 22,705, 22,717 (Apr. 30, 2007).
69. 16 U.S.C. § 1533(a)(3), (b)(6)(C)(ii). Failure to designate critical habitat does not invalidate a species listing. Alabama-Tombigbee Rivers Coal. v. Kempthorne, 477 F.3d 1250 (11th Cir. 2007) (finding listing of Alabama sturgeon valid despite apparently illegal failure to designate critical habitat).
70. 16 U.S.C. § 1533(a)(3)(A)(ii).
71. 5 U.S.C. §§ 555(b), 706(1); *see* Biodiversity Legal Found. v. Norton, 285 F. Supp. 2d 1, 12 (D.D.C. 2003).
72. Ctr. for Biological Diversity v. U.S. Fish & Wildlife Serv., 450 F.3d 930, 935 (9th Cir. 2006).
73. Biodiversity Legal Found. v. Norton, 285 F. Supp. 2d 1, 14–16 (D.D.C. 2003) (The court, however, retained jurisdiction to ensure that the critical habitat revision did eventually take place.).
74. 50 C.F.R. § 424.14(d).
75. *Id.*
76. 16 U.S.C. § 1533(b)(3)(D)(i) (emphasis added).
77. *Id.* § 1533(b)(3)(D)(ii).
78. *See* Biodiversity Legal Found. v. Babbitt, 146 F.3d 1249 (10th Cir. 1998) (upholding Clinton-era FWS listing priority guidance apparently contravening statutory listing deadlines); *but see* Forest Guardians v. Babbitt, 174 F.3d 1178, 1184 (10th Cir. 1998).
79. 50 C.F.R. § 424.16(c)(1).
80. 16 U.S.C. § 1533(b)(8); 50 C.F.R. § 424.16(b).
81. 16 U.S.C. § 1533(b)(5); 50 C.F.R. § 424.16.
82. 50 C.F.R. § 424.18(a).
83. 16 U.S.C. § 1533(b)(6)(A)(ii).
84. 50 C.F.R. § 424.17(a)(iv).
85. *Id.* § 424.12(a).

86. 16 U.S.C. § 1533(a)(3)(B); 50 C.F.R. § 424.12(g).
87. 50 C.F.R. § 424.12(a)(1).
88. The Federal Register language accompanying the promulgation of the regulations reads thus:

> Legislative history makes clear that Congress intended designation of critical habitat to be beneficial to the conservation of species. Experience has shown, nevertheless, that precise identification of habitat of vulnerable species carries inherent risks of vandalism and taking. In some cases, these risks can be controlled through vigorous enforcement of Section 9 of the Act. In other cases, because of enforcement difficulties, or because no violation of Section 9 may be involved (as in taking of plants on nonfederal land or the destruction of plants even on federal land without their reduction to possession), designation of critical habitat may have a net adverse effect on a species. It is this net effect, taking into account potential risks and benefits of a particular designation, that will guide the Services in decisions regarding the prudence of a particular designation.

U.S. Fish & Wildlife Serv. & Nat'l Marine Fisheries Serv., Listing Endangered and Threatened Species and Designating Critical Habitat; Amended Procedures to Comply with the 1982 Amendments to the Endangered Species Act, 49 Fed Reg. 38,900, 38,902 (Oct. 1, 1984).

89. *See, e.g.*, 64 Fed. Reg. 15,691, 15,702 (Apr. 1, 1999) (designation of critical habitat for flatwoods salamander not prudent); 63 Fed. Reg. 26,517, 26,527–28 (May 13, 1998) (designation of critical habitat for the Preble's meadow jumping mouse not prudent); 63 Fed. Reg. 15,152, 15,156 (Mar. 30, 1998) (designation of critical habitat for Cowhead Lake tui chub not prudent); 63 Fed. Reg. 15,164, 15,171 (Mar. 30, 1998) (designation of critical habitat for four plants from south central coastal California not prudent); 63 Fed. Reg. 9967, 9973 (Feb. 27, 1998) (designation of critical habitat for Gulf sturgeon not prudent); 58 Fed. Reg. 34,926, 34,930 (June 30, 1993) (designation for Carolina heelsplitter not prudent due to threat of collection).
90. 113 F.3d 1121 (9th Cir. 1997).
91. "By expanding the imprudence exception to encompass all cases in which designation would fail to control 'the majority of land-use activities occurring within critical habitat' . . . the Service contravenes the clear congressional intent that the imprudence exception be a rare exception." *Id.* at 1126. The court also considered and rejected the FWS argument that the protection afforded by the California State Natural Communities Conservation Program rendered designation of critical habitat unnecessary. The court noted (1) that the existence of another protection regime does not render designation of critical habitat imprudent, and (2) that the voluntary nature of the NCCP program made it an inadequate substitute for the mandatory protections provided by critical habitat designation. *Id.* at 1127.
92. 979 F. Supp. 893 (D.D.C. 1997), *appeal dismissed,* 161 F.3d 740 (D.C. Cir. 1998).
93. *Id.* at 905.
94. The district court reasoned thus:

> The FWS appears to rely on two assumptions, both without any support in the record: first, that owners of critical habitat who learn of the presence of fairy shrimp on their property would increase their developmental pace in direct violation of the ESA, and, second (the other side of the coin perhaps), that so long as critical habitat is not designated such landowners would remain unaware of their potential liability and therefore not develop their property apace. The Court finds this reasoning, if it can be called that, attenuated and unsupported by the record.

Id. at 906. The FWS position was dealt an additional blow in 2002 in the D.C. circuit court in Nat'l Ass'n of Homebuilders v. Norton, 309 F.3d 26 (D.C. Cir. 2002), which

held that specific information about location of cactus ferruginous pygmy owls must be released under the Freedom of Information Act (FOIA), 5 U.S.C. § 552(b)(6).
95. 145 F. Supp. 2d 1180 (E.D. Cal. 2001).
96. *See also* Jumping Frog Research Inst. v. Babbitt, 1999 WL 1244149 (N.D. Cal.) (rejecting another FWS argument that designation of critical habitat was not prudent because it would increase the risk to species members. The court observed that the increased threat rationale failed to balance the pros and cons of critical habitat designation as expressly required by the Act.).
97. 2 F. Supp. 2d 1280 (D. Haw. 1998).
98. *Id.* at 1284.
99. 245 F.3d 434 (5th Cir. 2001).
100. *Id.* at 442 (invalidating 50 C.F.R. § 402.02); see text accompanying notes 63–68.
101. *Id.* at 444–45.
102. 16 U.S.C. § 1533(b)(6)(C)(ii).
103. 50 C.F.R. § 424.12(a)(2).
104. When critical habitat has been deemed "not determinable" within the one-year (or 18-month) period, the initial review period may be extended by not more than one additional year. At the end of the additional year or sooner, critical habitat *must be determined* to "the maximum extent prudent." 48 Fed. Reg. 36,062, 36,062–63 (Aug. 8, 1983) (emphasis added).
105. 16 U.S.C. § 1533(b)(6)(C).
106. *Id.* at § 1533(b)(6)(C)(ii).
107. *See, e.g.,* 63 Fed. Reg. 31,693, 31,707 (June 10, 1998) (critical habitat for Coastal-Puget Sound, Jarbidge River and St. Mary-Belly River population segments of bull trout not determinable); 58 Fed. Reg. 14,248, 14,270 (1993) (critical habitat for Mexican spotted owl not determinable).
108. 2005 WL 1514102 (N.D. Cal.)
109. 164 F.3d 1261, *amended opinion at* Forest Guardians v. Babbitt, 174 F.3d 1178 (10th Cir. 1998).
110. 36 E.R.C. (BNA) 1409 (D. Colo. 1992).
111. 758 F. Supp. 621 (W.D. Wash. 1991).
112. 2005 WL 1514102 (N.D. Cal.)
113. *Id.* at 6 (citations omitted; emphasis in original).
114. 164 F.3d 1261, *amended opinion at* Forest Guardians v. Babbitt, 174 F.3d 1178 (10th Cir. 1998).
115. *Id.* at 1182–83.
116. *Id.* at 1187.
117. 36 E.R.C. (BNA) at 1409, 1410 (D. Colo. 1992).
118. *Id.* at 1412.
119. *Id.* at 1413.
120. 758 F. Supp. 621 (W.D. Wash. 1991).
121. *Id.* at 623.
122. *Id.* at 629.
123. *Id.* at 626.
124. 16 U.S.C. § 1533(a)(3)(B), Pub. L. No. 108-136, 5318(a), 117 Stat. 1433 (2003).
125. 16 U.S.C. § 670a(a)(1)(B).
126. 453 F.3d 1331 (11th Cir. 2006) (per curiam).
127. *Id.* at 1333.
128. *Id.* at 1334.
129. *Id.* at 1333.
130. 493 F. Supp. 2d 805 (W.D. La. 2007)
131. *Id.* at 815.
132. *See id.* n. 29.
133. S. Appalachian Biodiversity Project v. U.S. Fish & Wildlife Serv., 181 F. Supp. 2d 883, 886 (E.D. Tenn. 2001).

134. Department of the Interior and Related Agencies Appropriations Act of 1995, Pub. L. No. 103-332, 109 Stat. 73, 86 (Apr. 1995).
135. *See* Silver v. Thomas, 924 F. Supp. 972 (D. Ariz 1995); Envtl. Def. Ctr. v. Babbitt, 73 F.3d 867 (9th Cir. 1995).
136. *See* Envtl. Def. Ctr. v. Babbitt, 73 F.3d 867, 871 (9th Cir 1995) ("Although the appropriations rider does not repeal the Secretary's duty to make a final determination whether the California red-legged frog is endangered, the rider (and the budget resolution continuing the rider's moratorium on funding) necessarily restrict the Secretary's ability to comply with this duty by denying him funding . . . we find that lack of available appropriated funds prevents the Secretary from complying with the Act. Accordingly, we must vacate and remand to the district court to modify its order and judgment to provide that compliance with the requirement that the Secretary make a final determination as to the endangered status of the California red-legged frog is delayed until a reasonable time after appropriated funds are made available, the time to be specified by the district court.").
137. 1999 WL 1042567 (D. Or. 1999) ("I am sympathetic with FWS' position of being given mandatory duties by Congress without sufficient funds to get the job done. I am also sympathetic with plaintiffs' frustration at multiple year delays in listing species which require quicker attention. Forcing the agency to respond to multiple court orders does not further the purpose of the ESA and may cause the decline of species that do not have an environmental organization advancing their causes through litigation. As a reviewing court, however, our job is not to assess the wisdom of policy choices."), *rev'd on other grounds*, Biodiversity Legal Found. v. Badgley, 309 F.3d 1166 (9th Cir. 2002); *see also* Conservation Council for Haw. v. Babbitt, 24 F. Supp. 2d 1074, 1078–79 (D. Haw. 1998) (quoting Sw. Ctr. for Biological Diversity v. Babbitt, No. 96-1874, slip op. at 7 (D. Ariz. Mar. 20, 1997)) ("[t]o the extent the [FWS] feels aggrieved by Congress' failure to allocate proper resources in which to comply with [its] statutory duty, Congress, not the courts, is the proper governmental body to provide relief.").
138. 174 F.3d 1178, 1192 (10th Cir. 1999).
139. 304 F. Supp. 2d 1174 (D. Ariz. 2003).
140. Ctr. for Biological Diversity v. Norton, 2003 WL 22225620 (S.D. Cal. 2003).
141. *See* section 4(f)(1), 16 U.S.C. 1533(f)(1), to identify "such site-specific management actions as may be necessary to achieve the plan's goal for the conservation and survival of the species" and "objective, measurable criteria which, when met, would result in a determination, in accordance with the provisions of this section, that the species be removed from the list."
142. 268 F. Supp. 2d 1197 (E.D. Cal. 2003).
143. *Id*. at 1214.
144. 2006 WL 3190518 (E.D. Cal. Nov. 2, 2006).
145. *Id*. at 18.
146. 16 U.S.C. § 1533(b)(2).
147. 50 C.F.R. § 424.19.
148. U.S. Dep't of Interior, Solicitor's Opinion M-37016 (Oct. 3, 2008).
149. 16 U.S.C. § 1533(b)(2).
150. *Id*.
151. U.S. Dep't of Interior, Solicitor's Opinion M-37016 at 25 (Oct. 3, 2008).
152. However, if, for the reasons discussed below, the jeopardy and adverse modification standards are identical, then no costs or regulatory impacts are associated with a critical habitat designation nor do any benefits flow from critical habitat designation. Nonetheless, some critical habitat designations, especially some designations done by NMFS, appear to rely upon this rationale in explaining the impact of designating critical habitat. *See* 58 Fed. Reg. 68,543, 68,545 (1993) (no incremental net costs for designating areas within the species' current distribution as critical habitat); *id*. at 45,269, 45,272 (no adverse environmental impacts from designating critical habitat). If the "no impact" analysis is correct, the further argument could be made that designation of critical habitat is not "prudent" because such designation would not be beneficial to the listed spe-

cies. *See* 50 C.F.R. § 424.12(a)(1) (1993). Indeed, the FWS has come close to relying on this exact rationale in not designating critical habitat. *See, e.g.*, 58 Fed. Reg. 14,248, 14,270 (Mar. 16, 1993) (Mexican spotted owl); 58 Fed. Reg. 34,926, 34,930 (June 30, 1993) (Carolina heelsplitter).
153. 248 F.3d 1277 (10th Cir. 2001).
154. 248 F.3d at 1283.
155. *Id*. at 1285.
156. Civ. No. 00-2799, 2002 WL 1205743 (D.D.C.).
157. *Id*. at 3.
158. 293 F. Supp. 2d 1 (D.D.C. 2002).
159. For a thorough discussion of section 7 and the jeopardy standard, see Chapter 5.
160. 422 F. Supp. 2d 1115 (N.D. Cal. 2006).
161. *Id*. at 1144–45.
162. 245 F.3d 434 (5th Cir. 2001).
163. 378 F.3d 1059 (9th Cir. 2004).
164. 481 F.3d 1224 (9th Cir. 2007).
165. *Id*. at 1240.
166. 485 F. Supp. 2d 1190 (D. Or. 2007).
167. *Id*. at 1197–98.
168. *Id*.; *see* 50 C.F.R. 402.14(g).
169. 2007 WL 1577896 (E.D. Cal. 2007).
170. *Id*. at *47–51.
171. 42 U.S.C. § 4332(c).
172. 40 C.F.R. § 1508.9.
173. Preparation of Environmental Assessments for Listing Actions under the Endangered Species Act, 48 Fed. Reg. 49,244 (Oct. 25, 1983).
174. 16 U.S.C. § 1533(a).
175. 48 Fed. Reg. 49,244 (Oct. 25, 1983).
176. 657 F.2d 829 (6th Cir. 1981).
177. 810 F. Supp. 1470 (D. Or. 1992), *aff'd in part, rev'd in part*, 48 F.3d 1495 (9th Cir. 1995).
178. 48 F.3d at 1480.
179. 48 F.3d at 1495.
180. *Id*. at 1507 (emphasis added).
181. 75 F.3d 1429 (10th Cir. 1996).
182. *Id*. at 1439.
183. 344 F. Supp. 2d 108 (D.D.C. 2004).
184. *Id*. at 135.
185. 294 F.3d 1220 (10th Cir. 2002).
186. *Id*. at 1225.
187. *Id*. (quoting Catron County Bd. of Comm'rs v. U.S. Fish & Wildlife Serv., 75 F.3d 1429 (10th Cir. 1996)).
188. *Id*. at 1226 ("Because FWS' delayed and inadequate compliance with NEPA and the ESA have helped to push the Silvery Minnow perilously close to extinction, and because the record contains overwhelming evidence of the environmental impacts of a critical habitat designation, this case represents one of the rare circumstances when a remand to the agency to conduct yet another EA is not appropriate.")
189. *Id*. at 1227.
190. *Id*. at 1228.
191. *Id*.
192. *Id*. at 1230–31.

4

Recovery

Dale D. Goble

Introduction

The drafters of the Endangered Species Act (ESA) envisioned an orderly progression that begins when a species is determined to be at risk of extinction and ends when that risk has been reduced to an acceptable level. Between these risk assessments, the Act mandates two different types of actions: those designed to prevent extinction[1] and those that promote recovery. Although their focus differs, both contribute to the ESA's overarching goal of "conserving" listed species, the first by stabilizing the species and the second by ameliorating the threats it faces to the point at which it is no longer unacceptably at risk of extinction. This is the fundamental objective of the ESA: recovering species so that they no longer require the Act's protection. As the U.S. Court of Appeals for the Ninth Circuit recently commented, "[T]he ESA was enacted not merely to forestall the extinction of species . . . but to allow a species to recover to the point where it may be delisted. . . . [I]t is clear that Congress intended that conservation and survival be two different (though complementary) goals of the ESA."[2]

This chapter examines two related aspects of recovery. The first is the decision that a species has (or has been) recovered. The second topic is recovery planning, the Act's primary tool for achieving the goal of delisting of species. Recovery planning is not, however, the only tool for achieving the delisting species; the Act's recovery provisions also include:

1. Section 7(a)(1), which imposes an affirmative obligation on all federal agencies to "utilize their authorities in furtherance of the purposes of this Act by carrying out programs for the conservation of [listed] species."[3]
2. Section 10(a), which authorizes the federal agencies charged with implementing the Act to issue recovery permits "to enhance the propagation or survival of the affected species."[4]
3. Section 10(j), which authorizes the wildlife agencies to transplant experimental populations of listed species.[5]

Recovery plans—using these and other statutory tools[6]—"help to guide the recovery effort by describing actions considered necessary for the conservation of the species."[7]

Before examining recovery planning, however, it is helpful to begin with an examination of the goal that recovery planning is to advance, the recovery and delisting of species.

Current State of the Law

The Meaning of Recovery

Statutory and Regulatory Definitions of "Recovery"

The ESA does not explicitly define "recovery." Instead, the Act's objective is to "conserve" at-risk species and the ecosystems upon which they depend.[8] This is a more ambitious objective than the traditional, Gifford Pinchot definition of "conservation,"[9] because Congress defined the term as the affirmative obligation to "use . . . all methods and procedures which are necessary to bring any [listed] species to the point at which the measures provided pursuant to this Act are no longer necessary."[10] The Act thus implicitly defines "recovery" as "no longer sufficiently at risk of extinction to be listed as endangered or threatened."

The agencies responsible for implementing the Act, U.S. Fish and Wildlife Service (FWS) and the National Oceanic and Atmospheric Administration-Fisheries (NOAA-Fisheries), have affirmed this understanding of the term in a series of regulations beginning in 1980.[11] For example, the FWS issued guidelines on recovery planning in 1990 that defined "recovery" as

> the process by which the decline of an endangered or threatened species is arrested or reversed, and threats to its survival are neutralized, so that its long-term survival in nature can be ensured. The goal of this process is the maintenance of secure, self-sustaining wild populations of species.[12]

In short, the ESA and its implementing regulations define "recovered" to mean "no longer in need of the Act's protection." A species no longer requires the Act's protection when it is no longer endangered or threatened. Thus, it is the Act's definitions of "endangered" (i.e., "in danger of extinction throughout all or a significant portion of its range"[13]) and "threatened" (i.e., "*likely* to become an endangered species *within the foreseeable future* throughout all or a significant portion of its range"[14]) that provide the applicable standards for determining whether a species has "recovered."

"Recovery" as Risk Assessment

"Endangered" and "threatened" are risk-based standards. As first-year torts students quickly discover, "risk" is the possibility that something bad may happen.[15] Under the ESA, the "something bad" is the extinction of a species. This bad has two components. The first is *uncertainty*: What is the probability that the species will become extinct? The second issue is *time*, since extinction is a process rather than a tort-like calamitous event: What is the temporal scale over which the risk of extinction is to be assessed? Thus, in assessing the status of species (i.e., deciding to list, reclassify, or delist a species), the FWS and NOAA must determine the probability that the species will become extinct over some period of time.

The Act's definitions of "endangered" and "threatened" provide some limited guidance on these questions. To be "endangered," the Act specifies the required probability of extinction as "in danger"; to be "threatened," the probability is that the species is "likely to become" in danger. These are obviously vague and only marginally helpful statements.[16] How much "in danger" must a species be to be "endangered"? Beyond a vague "more," how does that degree of risk differ from the degree of risk that is "likely to become" in danger? Or is the difference between "endangered" and "threatened" to be determined solely on a temporal scale? That is, is an endangered species "in danger" *now* while a threatened species is "in danger" *within the foreseeable future*? How long is "foreseeable" on a planet that is 4.567 billion years old? And, since species have always gone extinct, are there any species that are truly not "foreseeably" at risk of extinction?

Although the Act requires the risk assessment be made "solely on the basis of the best scientific and commercial data available,"[17] as Holly Doremus has noted, neither "threatened" nor "endangered" can be determined solely on the basis of scientific information.[18] Beyond the question of risk (that is, some probability of extinction over some time horizon), there is the question of whether that risk is acceptable—and a decision that a risk is *acceptable* is an ethical/policy judgment. Science can inform this judgment (by providing information on the risk the species faces), but cannot make it.[19]

As with the uncertainty and temporal components of the risk assessment, the Act's drafters provided some guidance on the acceptability question. The Act requires the nation to conserve species at risk of extinction. As the Supreme Court noted in *Tennessee Valley Authority v. Hill*, "[the] plain intent of Congress in enacting th[e] statute was to halt and reverse the trend toward extinction, *whatever the cost*."[20] To that end, Congress drafted a statute that "admits of no exceptions."[21] But the Act is no longer what it was. A combination of legislative and administrative amendments have transformed it from a no-exceptions law into a flexible, permitting statute.[22] As J. B. Ruhl has written, it is now possible "to kill endangered species, legally."[23] Nonetheless, the Act still has an "overarching purpose[:] to protect a species and its habitat from extinction."[24]

Perhaps the best discussion of the probability and time elements of risk within the context of an actual status determination is the FWS decision not to list the cerulean warbler.[25] In assessing the extinction risk, the agency concluded that the best available science indicated that: (1) the total population of the species was 390,000 individuals in 2006 (plus or minus 50 percent); and (2) the population trend of the species was an annual decline of 3.2 percent (between 4.2 and 2.0 percent with a 90 percent certainty).[26] This suggested that the population would decline to 200,000 in 20 years, 80,000 in 50 years, and 15,000 in 100 years. But, as the agency noted,

> the farther into the future we attempt to predict, the less confident we can be that the historical trend will persist. Future population sizes will vary due to a variety of factors, both random events and progressive changes in causal environmental factors that we cannot foresee at this time.[27]

The FWS therefore concluded that the species was not at risk of extinction in the foreseeable future.[28] Although the agency did not explain its ethical/policy judgment, the foreseeable risk to the species was *implicitly* deemed to be acceptable.

The analysis of the petition to list the cerulean warbler was unusual in its explicit discussion of the probability of extinction over time. The fact that it is unusual reflects, in part at least, the Act's requirement that status determinations be made through an evaluation of the threats facing the species.[29] This requirement has shifted the focus of agency decision-making from an explicit evaluation of the risk facing the species (the definitions of "endangered" or "threatened") to an individualized examination of a list of threats potentially facing a species:

1. The present or threatened destruction, modification, or curtailment of its habitat or range;
2. Overutilization for commercial, recreational, scientific, or educational purposes;

3. Disease or predation;
4. The inadequacy of existing regulatory mechanisms; or
5. Other natural or manmade factors affecting its continued existence.[30]

The FWS and NOAA evaluate these factors not only in determining the status of a species but also in drafting recovery plans[31] and making the ultimate delisting decision.[32]

In sum, the ESA defines "recovery" as no longer in need of the Act's protection—that is, when the species is no longer "endangered" or "threatened." The definitions of these terms require the agency to determine the status of a species by assessing the risk of extinction it faces, which (in turn) requires the agency to determine whether the probability of extinction (likely to become in danger of extinction) over some temporal scale (within the foreseeable future) is acceptable. The acceptability judgment requires the decision maker to set a viability threshold for the species being assessed. That is, the agency must determine whether the goal *should* be to conserve a minimally viable, an evolutionarily viable, an ecologically viable, or some other population threshold.

This risk assessment has been obscured because the statute is focused instead on an evaluation of the five factors that emphasize the threats facing the species. The strength of this approach is that it permits an extended, individualized examination of the threats facing a species given what is known about its specific life history and traits.[33] Its weakness is a blurring of the distinction between the scientific issues (the probability and time elements of risk), on the one hand, and the ethical/policy judgment on the acceptability of that risk, on the other. This blurring reduces the transparency of the decision making and doubtless results in inconsistent decisions on the status of different species.[34]

Defining "Recovery" Operationally

Seventeen domestic species have been delisted as recovered.[35] An examination of the status-determination rulemaking packages of these species provide insight into the operational definition(s) that the agencies have employed in determining that a species has recovered.

Although both listing and delisting determinations require a risk assessment (that is, a determination that some risk over some time is acceptable or not), the two determinations differ significantly.[36] Most importantly, the available information about the species—and thus the risk associated with uncertainty—differ substantially. At the time a species is proposed for listing, relatively little is generally known about it. When a species is approaching recovery, on the other hand, there is a body of data on the management actions that have proved successful in conserving the species. A second difference is also important. The decision to delist a species removes the protection it is afforded under the ESA, which creates an additional problem: will removal of the ESA's "existing regulatory mechanisms"[37] again place the species at risk by removing its legal protection?

The problem is that specific species face specific threats that often require continuous monitoring and risk management—actions that are not available under generally applicable statutes such as the Clean Water Act[38] or the Nonindigenous Aquatic Nuisance Prevention and Control Act.[39] Thus, the very strength of the ESA in preventing extinction becomes a deterrent to delisting a species because to do so will frequently remove the protection needed to conserve it and thus lead to a downward spiral that would necessitate relisting. This is the irony of the ESA: it is a powerful statute that can bring species back from the brink of extinction, but its intensely focused power itself can make the statute all but irreplaceable since few federal or state laws provide similarly focused protection against threats such as habitat degradation and nonnative species.

The risk assessment in a decision to delist a species thus requires two types of decisions. First, has the species recovered biologically? Has the chosen ethical/policy objective (i.e., a viability threshold) been met? That is, has its population size and distribution increased sufficiently to provide reasonable assurances that it is no longer unacceptably at risk from stochastic events?[40] Second, is the species' biological recovery threatened by the lack of sufficient legal protection? That is, are there sufficient risk-management/regulatory mechanisms to manage any unremediable threats? An examination of the rulemaking packages of species that have been delisted fall into two broad categories based primarily on the type of ongoing risk management the species requires.

Risk Management Through Existing Regulatory Mechanisms

Most species that have been delisted were at risk primarily as a result of a single, discrete threat. For example, the Aleutian cackling goose was listed in 1967 as a result of population declines attributable to the introduction of a predator (foxes) onto its nesting grounds;[41] removal of the foxes from these islands and hunting closures on the species' migratory route and wintering grounds in Oregon and California allowed its population to climb from 790 individuals in 1975 to 5,800 in 1989 (when it was reclassified as threatened)[42] to 36,978 in 2000 (just before the species was delisted in 2001)[43]; in addition, the species had been reintroduced and was breeding on 11 additional islands from which it had been extirpated.[44] This increase in both population and dispersal reflected the reduction in the threats that had led to the listing of the species and thus met the biological threshold for delisting the species as recovered. Stated differently, the species' population had crossed the agency's viability threshold because it had achieved numbers that permitted recreational hunting.

The risk-management component of recovery was provided by several existing regulatory structures. Since the species nests on islands that are included within the Alaska Maritime National Wildlife Refuge,[45] the FWS has the authority not only to remove foxes from additional islands in the Aleutian chain but also to take whatever additional management actions might be necessary.[46] On the wintering grounds, feeding and roosting habitat was acquired either as fee interests or through conservation easements.[47] More significantly perhaps, the species is monitored and take is managed by the federal, state, and provincial governments through the Pacific Flyway Council[48] established under the Migratory Bird Treaty Act (MBTA).[49] Finally, the species is listed in Appendix I of the Convention on International Trade in Endangered Species of Wild Fauna and Flora (CITES) and is protected against international commercial exploitation.[50]

The goose thus was delisted because (1) it had recovered biologically—the threats it faced had been ameliorated so that its population rebounded and dispersed into its former breeding range in sufficient numbers to permit hunting; and (2) there were sufficient conservation-management mechanisms in place to provide reasonable assurances that the species biological recovery was not at risk.

The gray whale and the American alligator fit the same pattern: both were listed primarily as a result of overharvesting.[51] Following listing and implementation of take prohibitions, the species' populations increased. The necessary risk management to prevent recurrence of the demographic threat posed by overharvest is, in both cases, provided by a number of existing regulatory mechanisms.[52] Similarly, the American peregrine falcon, the arctic peregrine falcon, and the brown pelican were at risk of extinction primarily from exposure to organochlorine pesticides (e.g., dichloro-diphenyl-trichloroethane [DDT]), which caused eggshell thinning that prevented successful nesting.[53] Banning DDT led to population recovery. While the Federal Insecticide, Fungicide, and Rodenticide Act[54] delegates the Environmental Protection Agency sufficient authority to screen chemicals to prevent the reintroduction of organochlorines, additional risks had emerged since the species listings—and other regulatory mechanisms were available to address these potential limiting factors. In delisting the species, the FWS cited the MBTA[55] and CITES,[56] which provide protection against take and commerce; various federal land management statutes that gave the land-managing agencies sufficient authority to manage the habitat to maintain it for the species;[57] as well as state regulatory mechanisms.[58] The combination of these mechanisms provided sufficient assurance of ongoing risk management to satisfy the agency that the species was no longer threatened.

Unfortunately, for most species existing regulatory mechanisms are unlikely to be sufficient given the type of threats they face. The primary causes of imperilment are habitat loss and predation by or competition from nonnative species.[59] These are threats that generally will require continuing conservation management, and thus highlight the irony of the ESA.

Risk Management Through Species-Specific Regulatory Mechanisms

Four delisted species—the Columbian white-tailed deer, Robbins' cinquefoil, Hoover's woolly-star, and bald eagle—are examples of species that lacked sufficient protection under existing regulatory or other conservation mechanisms. These species—like most species—required protection against habitat degradation and introduced, nonnative species. Such threats generally will require ongoing risk management. Their delisting thus required a different approach to risk management and offers a more broadly applicable understanding of recovery.

The Columbian white-tailed deer was once common in the bottomlands and prairie woodlands of the lower Columbia, Willamette, and Umpqua river basins in western Oregon and southwestern Washington. The species declined rapidly following Euro-American settlement as a result of habitat loss, uncontrolled sport and commercial hunting, and "perhaps other factors."[60] By the early 1900s, it had been reduced to two disjunct populations: one along the lower Columbia River and the other in Douglas County in southern Oregon. Following its listing under a predecessor of the ESA in 1967,[61] the Douglas County population increased from an estimated 400–500 animals in 1970[62] to about 6,070 animals in 2002 as a result of the conservation activities initiated pursuant to the ESA.[63] Since the Columbia River population had not increased significantly, the FWS designated the two populations as separate distinct population segments (DPS) and delisted the Douglas County DPS as recovered.[64] Although there was only a single population in each DPS, the increased number of individuals and the concomitant range expansion in the Douglas County DPS led the FWS to conclude that the DPS faced a substantially reduced risk from a stochastic event such as a forest fire.

The delisting of the Columbian white-tailed deer diverges from the delisting of species such as the Aleutian Canada goose and the peregrine falcon on the second requirement—that there be sufficient regulatory or other conservation mechanisms to prevent the species from slipping back into an at-risk status. Although threat factors such as overutilization from hunting can be addressed through traditional game management tools (as was the case with the goose and would be true of risks facing the deer from hunting or poaching), the threat of habitat loss through land conversion to agriculture and residential homesites (which also threatened the deer) differs in two relevant ways. First, given human demographic trends, the threat is unlikely to abate in the foreseeable future. It is not a question of removing a predator or a poison: even if the land were set aside permanently, addressing habitat loss and fragmentation requires ongoing monitoring and management because nature is not static—particularly in an age of global climate change. Habitat changes ripple across space and time because ecosystems respond slowly and often in nonlinear ways; the effects of a change may not be immediately apparent[65] and make continuing risk management all the more crucial.

Second, and more importantly, there were no existing risk-management mechanisms (such as the MBTA) that could manage the range of risks facing the deer from the modification of its habitat. Something else was required. The FWS addressed this need by setting a recovery goal of at least 5,000 acres of "secure habitat." The agency defined "secure" as "areas that are protected from adverse human activities . . . in the foreseeable future, and that are relatively safe from natural phenomena that would destroy their value to the subspecies."[66] This definition has both legal and biological components: the habitat must be legally protected against adverse human actions and it must be managed to continue to meet the biological requirements of the species.

The legal component could be satisfied, the agency concluded, through "zoning ordinances, land-use planning, parks and greenbelts, agreements, memoranda of understanding, and other mechanisms available to local jurisdictions,"[67] as well as public ownership of the land or acquisition of habitat by private conservation organizations through "easements, leases, acquisitions, donations, or trusts."[68] In response, public entities (primarily the Bureau of Land Management (BLM) and Douglas County) acquired over 7,000 acres of habitat.[69] The county also adopted a Columbian White-tailed Deer Habitat Protection Program that imposed land-use controls, including minimum lot sizes and set-back requirements in deer habitat.[70]

Simply setting aside habitat is insufficient, however, because there must also be legal assurances that that habitat will be managed to continue to meet the biological needs of the species. Risk management, in other words, requires *management*. For the Columbian white-tailed deer, the largest publicly owned parcel of habitat is the BLM-managed North Bank Habitat Management Area, a 7,000-acre former cattle ranch that BLM acquired through a land exchange to provide habitat for the species.[71] The BLM management plan includes controlled burns, grazing modifications, and restoration activities to increase the quality of habitat to the deer.[72] In addition, the Douglas County Parks Department manages a 1,100-acre park as a wildlife refuge and a working ranch to provide habitat for the species, and The Nature Conservancy manages a 35-acre site in part to provide deer habitat.[73]

The FWS thus concluded that the Douglas County population of Columbian white-tailed deer could be delisted because (1) its population and distribution had increased to the point that the risk of a stochastic event was reduced to a reasonable level, thus satisfying the threshold biological requirement; and (2) the threat facing the species that required continuing risk management—maintenance of appropriate habitat—was also reduced to a reasonable level through legal protection of the habitat and agreements with the landowners or managers of that habitat to ensure that it would be managed to maintain its biological value to the species.

Robbins' cinquefoil offers a second example. At the time of listing, the cinquefoil had been reduced to a single site in New Hampshire. This site was bisected by the Appalachian Trail and the species' abundance had been substantially reduced due to trampling and habitat destruction by hikers.[74] The demographic component of recovery was met by the establishment of three additional populations and the concomitant growth in the number of individuals from less than 2,000 to more than 14,000 specimens.[75] The risk-management component was satisfied by a series of steps to secure the species' habitat and to provide for the ongoing management of that habitat. The FWS, the land manager (U.S. Forest Service [USFS]), and a conservation organization (the Appalachian Mountain Club) had taken several steps to reduce the impact of hikers: the trail was rerouted away from the original population, and a wall was constructed around the population's location and posted with "closed entry" signs. Finally, a series of conservation-management agreements provided for ongoing risk-management. The Club agreed to provide a naturalist during the summer at a hut near the population who, along with other staff at the hut, monitors human interaction with the population.[76] In December 1994, the FWS and the USFS entered into a memorandum of understanding (MOU) for the conservation of the species under which the USFS agreed to continue to carry out management measures after delisting.[77]

As noted, most species have not been put at risk by single threats such as overharvest, but rather by habitat degradation and invasive species.[78] The Columbian white-tailed deer and Robbins' cinquefoil thus are far more typical than the Aleutian cackling goose or American peregrine falcon. Habitat degradation and invasive species usually will require ongoing human intervention, either to manage the habitat or periodically to remove the invasive species. As the deer and cinquefoil demonstrate, for most listed species there is no specifically targeted legal protection other than the ESA.[79] As a result, conserving such species requires the creation of species-specific protocols to manage the risks facing the species after the ESA's protection is removed.

In sum, the decision that a species has recovered is a determination that the risk of extinction it faces has been reduced to an acceptable level into the foreseeable future. This determination has two elements. First, the threats facing the species must have been ameliorated and its population must be sufficiently large and sufficiently dispersed so that the risk facing the species from both deterministic and stochastic events is acceptable. That is, the species must have achieved some viability threshold. Second, there must be legal structures in place to manage any continuing, unameliorated threats facing the species. This ongoing conservation management can be provided either by previously existing or specifically tailored regulatory or other conservation mechanisms.

Recovery Planning

In commenting on the recovery planning requirements that were being added to the ESA, the 1978 House Report noted that the plans "shall be as long and detailed as is necessary and consonant with their purpose of providing a framework for actions directed at conserving or, at least, insuring the survival of the subject species."[80] The FWS subsequently described a recovery plan as "the 'umbrella' that eventually guides all these [conservation] activities"—referring to the requirement that federal agencies use their authorities to further the conservation of listed species, to the requirement that federal actions do not jeopardize listed species, to the prohibition on taking listed species, and to the limitations imposed on permits based on habitat conservation plans—"and promotes species' conservation and eventually delisting."[81]

There is an intuitive logic to this vision: when a species is sufficiently at risk of extinction to trigger the application of the ESA, biologists describe the threats to its persistence and propose a strategy for preventing its extinction by addressing the threats it faces so that it no longer requires protection. Other federal agencies rely on the recovery plan to assist them in meeting their obligation to conserve (i.e., recover) listed species.[82] This concerted activity addresses the threats facing the species and, as a result, its population increases and disperses. Finally, federal and state agencies and nongovernmental organizations (NGOs) create a risk management structure that provides assurances that there will be ongoing management when the species is delisted.

Recovery planning has fallen short of this vision.

The Statute and Regulations

The FWS began writing recovery plans before Congress amended the Act in 1978 to require the agencies to "develop and implement" plans "for the conservation and survival of [listed] species."[83] The Act was subsequently amended to require each plan to include—"to the maximum extent practicable"—three types of information:

> (i) A description of such site-specific management actions as may be necessary to achieve the plan's goal for the conservation and survival of the species;
>
> (ii) Objective, measurable criteria that, when met, would result in a determination, in accordance with the provisions of this section, that the species be removed from the list; and
>
> (iii) Estimates of the time required and the cost to carry out those measures needed to achieve the plan's goal and to achieve intermediate steps toward that goal.[84]

Both agencies have amplified the statutory requirements in a guidance document.[85] The guidance requires plans to analyze the threats facing the species and determine the actions necessary to remove or mitigate those threats to the point at which the risk to the species has been reduced to an acceptable level.[86]

Recovery Plans

The agencies were slow to develop recovery plans. By 1994, only 54 percent of the then-listed species had recovery plans.[87] Currently, some 86 percent of the 1,320 resident species on the list of threatened and endangered species have a recovery plan.[88] The FWS has also found that the conservation of 1 percent of the species would not be promoted by development of a recovery plan.[89]

Quantity and quality are, of course, often quite different. In the early 1990s, several scientific reports concluded that recovery planners were not setting biologically realistic goals. One study concluded that under a standard measure of extinction risk, some 60 percent of listed vertebrate species had recovery goals that would leave them significantly at risk.[90] The authors concluded that approximately one-third of listed species are being "managed for extinction," which suggested that "political, social, or economic considerations may have been operating that reduced recovery goals so that they were below what might have been set if they had been developed strictly on biologically based estimates."[91] A report by the National Research Council noted that 28 percent of the plans for which data was available had recovery goals set at or below the population size at the time the plan was written, which suggested that "recovery goals are probably too low."[92]

A subsequent research initiative on recovery plans sponsored by the Society for Conservation Biology, the FWS, and the National Center for Ecological Analysis and Synthesis[93] found some improvement, but concluded that much remained to be done. For example, one report that examined the development of plans over time concluded that although the FWS "has made modest improvement in the use of science in recovery plans, many features of recovery plans did not show signs of improvement."[94] Significantly, one finding was that 37 percent of the major threats identified in recovery plans did not have associated recovery tasks.[95] The same patterns were apparent when multispecies recovery plans,[96] recovery criteria,[97] and the relationship between monitoring and the threats facing a species[98] were evaluated.

In part, these shortcomings reflect the perennial problem of inadequate funding.[99] Most commenters agree that "[r]ecovery teams usually work under the constraints of little money, conflicting interest groups, and little time to produce the plan. . . . These problems are exacerbated by the limited information available for most listed species."[100] Regardless of the cause, there is room for improvement in developing recovery plans.

Case Law

Recovery planning has been the focus of relatively little litigation,[101] though this appears to be changing. To date, the case law has focused on three issues. The first is whether the statutory language that "[t]he Secretary shall develop and implement" recovery plans unless she "finds that such a plan will not promote the conservation of the species"[102] is mandatory; that is, can the FWS and NOAA be forced to develop recovery plans for listed species or is the "shall develop" swallowed by the finding exception? A second group of cases has focused on the sufficiency of recovery plans. The Act states that the agency, "to the maximum extent practicable," shall include descriptions, "site-specific management actions" needed to achieve the conservation purpose, "objective, measurable criteria" for delisting the species, and estimates of the time and cost to recover the species.[103] Again, is the statute's mandatory language obviated by the to-the-maximum-extent-practicable exception? Finally, are recovery plans enforceable? The case law on enforceability can be distinguished by two senses of the term "enforceable." The first is captured by the question of whether the agencies can be enjoined to implement a plan's specific recovery measures. The second sense—and the emerging area of dispute—is focused on the use of recovery plans to cabin other types of agency decisions such as biological opinions (BiOps).[104]

In broad strokes, the case law can be summarized as Ad Law 101: courts will defer to agency expertise as long as the agency offers a reasoned explanation for its decisions.

The Obligation to Develop a Recovery Plan

The Edwards Aquifer drains an area of approximately 3,600 square miles before discharging at Comal and San Marcos Springs near San Antonio, Texas.[105] The springs (and the caves from which they issue) are the habitat of several listed species. Pumping from the aquifer upstream from the springs reduces their outflow and threatens the species. By the early 1990s, the FWS had developed a recovery plan for the San Marcos Springs, but not for the Comal Springs.[106] In *Sierra Club v. Lujan,* the conservation group sued the Secretary of the Interior alleging that his failure to develop recovery plans for the listed species at Comal Springs jeopardized their continued existence and was a take.[107] The court rejected the Secretary's argument that he had discretion not to develop recovery plans, noting that section 4 states that the FWS "'shall' develop and implement" recovery plans.[108] "At least in the circumstances of this case," the court concluded, "the ESA section 4 duty to develop and implement a plan is mandatory, not discretionary" because the agency had not availed itself of the statutory exception by finding that a plan "will not promote the conservation of the species."[109] The court emphasized that the Secretary had failed to act for eight years—a delay that was unreasonable given the risks the listed species faced.

A second decision also supports this reading of the statute. *Oregon Natural Resource Council v. Turner* involved a petition for attorney fees based on the decision in an earlier case where the court had determined that the ESA imposed a nondiscretionary duty on the Secretary to develop recovery plans for listed species. Since the Act did not impose a time within which the Secretary must act, the issue that had been set for briefing was "at what point, if ever" the nonperformance became actionable.[110] When the case was mooted by the development of a recovery plan, plaintiff sought to recover attorney fees. The court concluded that, given that the Secretary "is required to develop and implement [recovery] plans . . . , unless he or she finds that such plan will not promote the conservation of the species,"[111] plaintiff was required to prove, inter alia, that the Secretary had either decided not to prepare a plan or that the time that had lapsed since listing the species was so unreasonable as to be a failure to fulfill this statutory duty.[112] In the attorney fees litigation, the court held that the plaintiff failed to meet its burden: because the statute did not include a time limit on developing recovery plans and because Congress recognized that it would take time and resources to develop plans (and thus authorized the Secretary to establish a priority scheme for developing and implementing the plans), the delay (two-and-one-half years) was not unreasonable.[113] As the court stated, this standard reflects the Secretary's "broad discretion to allocate scarce resources to those species that he or she determines would most likely benefit from development of recovery plans."[114]

Thus, the Secretary has a duty to develop a recovery plan—but that duty is not enforceable unless the Secretary has failed to act for a sufficient length of time that the inaction is so unreasonable as to be a failure to fulfill the duty. Given the lack of statutory deadlines and the explicit authority to prioritize recovery planning, a challenger bears a heavy burden.[115]

Contents of the Recovery Plan

In developing recovery plans, section 4(f) requires the agency, "to the maximum extent practicable," to incorporate three types of data: (1) a description of "site-specific management actions . . . necessary to achieve . . . the conservation and survival of the species"; (2) "objective, measurable criteria" for delisting the species; and (3) estimates of "the time required and the cost" to achieve recovery.[116]

These provisions were construed in *Fund for Animals v. Babbitt*, a challenge to the sufficiency of the grizzly bear recovery plan. The court, noting that the ESA "does not detail specific methods or procedures that are necessary to achieve conservation," concluded that the FWS "has the flexibility . . . to recommend a wide range of 'management actions.'"[117] The flexibility is, however, not unlimited:

> [T]he ESA requires . . . the identification of management actions necessary to achieve the Plan's goals for the conservation and survival of the species. A recovery plan that recognizes specific threats to the conservation and survival of a threatened or endangered species, but fails to recommend corrective action or explain why it is impracticable or unnecessary to recommend such action, would not meet the ESA's standard. Nor would a Plan that completely ignores threats to conservation and survival of a species.[118]

Thus, the degree of specificity is tied to the identified threats the species faces—a point that the court reinforces in its discussion of the "objective, measurable criteria" requirement by noting that "the FWS, in designing objective, measurable criteria, must address each of the five statutory delisting factors and measure whether threats to the [species] have been ameliorated."[119]

The specificity of the information and goals in a recovery plan is also bounded by the available scientific information. The Gila trout was listed as endangered in 1967; a revised recovery plan was finalized in 1993.[120] The plan included criteria for reclassifying the species as threatened but did not include delisting criteria. When this was challenged, the court (relying upon *Fund for Animals v. Babbitt*) noted that the statutory language "demonstrates that Congress unambiguously intended that the Secretary be required to incorporate delisting criteria where possible or feasible."[121] Here, the agency had explained its reasons for concluding that delisting criteria could not be immediately specified: floods and fires in 1988 and 1989 destroyed a number of populations and severely damaged habitat, leading the agency to shift its recovery strategy from headwater streams to the renovation of entire drainages. This shift increased uncertainty and required the agency to initiate a substantial genetic and ecological research program.[122] The agency's decision thus was not arbitrary or capricious.

The court in the subsequent decision in *Defenders of Wildlife v. Babbitt* employed the same analytical approach. Beginning with the proposition that the to-the-maximum-extent-practicable language "does not permit an agency unbridled discretion,"[123] it examined the provisions of the recovery plan against the standards enunciated in *Fund for Animals v. Babbitt*, concluding that the agency had failed to provide a sufficient explanation for its decision not to include delisting criteria or more certain time estimates for recovery.[124]

As is to be expected in questions where scientific expertise is paramount, a court will generally defer to the agency if it explains its reasoning—and the reasons reasonable.[125] The case law's touchstones—the threats facing the species and the state of the scientific information—suggest the types of reasoning that the courts are likely to find persuasive.

Direct Implementation of Recovery Plans

The black-letter law is that a recovery plan is not enforceable. The reach of this statement, however, is more constrained than it might appear. It is accurate when "enforceable" is understood to mean that the agency cannot be required to implement a plan's specific recovery measures: "the Recovery Plan is not a document with the force of law divesting all discretion and judgment from the F.W.S."[126] And even then, the issue is whether the agency has exercised its discretion reasonably.

The unenforceability proposition can be traced to two decisions from the mid-1980s. In 1979, FWS wrote a recovery plan for the California condor in cooperation with a consortium of government agencies and NGOs.[127] The plan emphasized two types of recovery actions: (1) a program of captive propagation of birds that were to be reintroduced into the wild and (2) a research program on the remaining wild birds' habits and habitats. In December 1985, FWS reversed its decision to maintain a wild population and ordered the capture of all remaining wild birds. One of the NGOs involved in drafting the recovery plan challenged this decision; the district court enjoined the agency for failing to explain its reasons for abandoning the approach set out in the recovery plan.[128] In *National Audubon Society v. Hester*, the U.S. Court of Appeals for the D.C. Circuit reversed. After noting several changed circumstances, the court concluded that the agency had indeed provided a reasoned explanation of the evolving policy. "The Wildlife Service simply exercised its discretion to 'adapt [its] rules and policies to the demands of changing circumstances.'"[129]

The second—and far less satisfying—decision, *National Wildlife Federation v. National Park Service*, rejected a challenge to the Park Service's decision to keep a campground in Yellowstone National Park open contrary to at least the plaintiff's reading of the grizzly bear recovery plan.[130] The district court summarily rejected the argument as "completely misconstru[ing] congressional intent" since "the Secretary [is] required to develop a recovery plan only insofar as he reasonably believes it would promote conservation."[131] The court's opinion thus is bottomed on the Act's requirement that the Secretary "shall develop and implement" recovery plans "unless he finds that such a plan will not promote the conservation of the species."[132] The court read the finding-exception broadly, concluding that Congress had delegated the Secretary broad discretion over implementation of recovery plans: "This Court will not attempt to second guess the Secretary's motives for not following the recovery plan."[133]

Judicial deference to agency expertise and broad statutory discretion are a powerful combination. It thus is hardly surprising that other courts have also concluded that the content of recovery plans is not binding on the federal wildlife agencies.[134] Discretion can, of course, be abused. In *Sierra Club v. Lujan*, for example, the court concluded that the agency's failure to implement the San Marcos Springs recovery plan was unlawful. In doing so, the court distinguished *National Wildlife Federation v. National Park Service*. The former case stood for the proposition, the court wrote, that where there was a "sufficiently clear justification arising out of facts developed after completion of a recovery plan, the Secretary can temporarily delay [its] implementation."[135] In *Lujan*, on the other hand, the exigencies cut the other way: the agency's failure to implement the recovery plan for eight years was jeopardizing several listed species and the court ordered the agency to take steps to implement the plan.[136] *Lujan* can also be distinguished from *Hester* and *National Wildlife Federa-*

tion by the specificity of the relief being sought. In both *Hester* and *National Wildlife Federation*, the plaintiffs sought to enjoin specific actions—removal of condors from the wild and closure of a campground; in *Lujan*, on the other hand, the plaintiffs sought more general recovery actions to maintain the flow of the springs. How that flow would be achieved was left to the agency's discretion.

A recent decision, however, raises serious questions about the justiciability of the unreasonable-delay claim. In *Conservation Northwest v. Kempthorne,* plaintiff alleged that the Secretary of the Interior had unreasonably delayed implementation of the North Cascades Grizzly Bear Recovery Plan.[137] The court began its analysis with the proposition that the ESA's citizen suit provisions authorize a suit by "any person" who alleges that the Secretary has failed "to perform any act or duty under section 1533 . . . which is not discretionary."[138] It rejected plaintiffs' argument that the duty to implement recovery plans in a timely manner was nondiscretionary. Relying on a 1987 Clean Air Act decision from the D.C. Circuit,[139] the court concluded that a "nondiscretionary duty" required a "date-certain deadline by which the ESA compels the Secretary to implement all of the terms of the recovery plan."[140] Since the ESA imposes no deadline on the implementation of recovery plans, the court held that it lacked jurisdiction over plaintiff's claim.

In sum, the relatively sparse case law on recovery planning has generally followed the black-letter of administrative law. Although the agencies have a duty to develop a recovery plan, the lack of statutory deadlines means that delay in doing so is remediable only when the delay has stretched on for so long as to be an unreasonable dereliction of its duties. Similarly, courts will generally defer to the agencies on the sufficiency of the information in a recovery plan.

Emerging Issues and Future Directions

Viability Thresholds in Recovery

As noted, recovery has been operationally defined as imposing two distinct requirements. The first is biological: the threats facing the species must have been ameliorated to the point at which the number of individuals and populations is such that the risks the species faces are acceptable; that is, the viability threshold for the species has been met. The second requirement is legal: there must be regulatory mechanisms in place that will provide confidence that any remaining threats will be managed so that the species will not fall back below the viability threshold that led to its delisting; that is, there must be a risk-management structure in place. Both recovery requirements have emerged as central issues in the continuing, emotionally charged dispute over the status of the gray wolf in the Northern Rocky Mountains.

In February 2008, the FWS designated the Northern Rocky Mountain (NRM) populations of wolves as a DPS and delisted the DPS as recovered.[141] The agency's decision was vacated by the federal district for Montana in July 2008; the court concluded that the agency had failed to satisfy either prong of the recovery standard.[142] The issue underlying the adequacy of both the biological and legal components of recovery ultimately was the same: what is the appropriate viability threshold? That is, what the Act is designed to conserve?

Previously, no species had been delisted under a post-delisting risk-management program predicated on reducing the number of individuals in the delisted population. Nonetheless, the FWS decided to delist the NRM DPS despite the fact that both Idaho and Wyoming proposed to reduce the wolf populations in their states by killing a substantial number of wolves. At delisting there were nearly 1,000 wolves in Idaho;[143] following delisting, the state authorized the killing of 428 of those wolves.[144] Wyoming's plan was even more extreme: it declared the wolf a predator that could be killed by anyone by any method other than poisoning. As a result, between the publication of the *Federal Register* notice delisting the DPS on February 27 and the district court's issuance of an injunction on July 18, at least 130 wolves—nearly 10 percent of the DPS population—were killed.[145] The agency's decision to authorize the state plans thus was determined to be unreasonable—particularly since the agency had previously concluded that the "goal was, at best, a minimal recovery goal."[146]

Following the district court's decision holding the delisting of the NRM DPS to be illegal, the USFWS reopened the comment period on the remanded rule.[147] On January 14, the agency for the third time announced that it was delisting the NRM DPS; the Obama administration concurred, publishing a final rule delisting the DPS in the *Federal Register* on April 2.[148] The decision to delist differed from its predecessor in delisting the DPS only in Idaho and Montana; the USFWS reevaluated the Wyoming wolf management plan and concluded that it was inadequate because it allowed unregulated take of wolves in 88 percent of the state and regulated take in all of the remaining 12 percent not located in Yellowstone National Park.[149] Both Wyoming and conservationists challenged the decision in June; conservationists are seeking to enjoin a proposed wolf hunt in Idaho that permits killing 220 animals.

The checkered history of wolf recovery in the Northern Rocky Mountains raises fundamental questions of the purpose of the ESA: what *is* recovery? What is it that the ESA is intended to conserve? Is it intended only to prevent extinction?[150] Is a captive population (i.e., zoo specimens) sufficient? Does recovery require only a minimally viable wild population? Does the Act's focus on the future[151] support the conservation of a species' evolutionary potential? Does the ESA's purpose of protecting ecosystems[152] mean that the species role in that ecosystem should be conserved? The Act does not provide a definitive answer—and there are a wide range of conservation viability thresholds. One review, for example, examined 18 alternatives.[153] The list included not only minimally viable populations, but also populations sufficient to maintain evolutionary potential (i.e., sufficient numbers of individuals and populations to adapt to perturbations and trends such as global climate change),[154] ecological function, social dynamics (e.g., sufficient numbers to maintain breeding, migration, and other social life cycles),[155] historical baseline,[156] maximum population, and the status quo.[157]

It is useful to flesh out one of these alternatives—ecological viability, which is conservation of a species' functional role in the ecosystems it occupies—because it is a biologically based standard that is warranted by the statute's language and legislative history.[158] This viability threshold focuses on species as parts of ecosystems; it reflects the fact that species interact with the biotic and abiotic elements of the system and play a dynamic role in shaping the system. Maintaining only a minimally viable number of individuals is likely to change the competitive pressures within the ecosystem and thus to alter the ecosystem—particularly if the species is highly interactive.[159] The ecological effects of reintroducing wolves into Yellowstone National Park offer an instructive example of the impact of a species' ecological function in an ecosystem.

Wolves were reintroduced into Yellowstone National Park in 1995 and 1996.[160] After an absence of nearly 70 years, the species' return was an opportunity to catalog the ecological changes resulting from the reintroduction of a top predator and to shed light on fundamental questions about the structure of ecosystems.[161] Elk are the primary prey for wolves.[162] The reintroduced wolves initially encountered naïve prey since the elk had no familiarity with wolves;[163] the elk (and other prey species such as moose) responded by altering their behavior to avoid areas such as aspen stands that provided wolves cover and the element of surprise.[164] As a result, aspen, cottonwood, and willows, which had declined markedly, began to regenerate.[165] This in turn led to an increase in neotropical bird species (which depend upon such ecosystems for nesting and feeding habitat) and beaver.[166] The return of riparian vegetation appears to also be modifying stream morphology, water temperature (and thus the presence of cold-water fish such as trout), and other key hydrological attributes.[167]

Wolves also reduced the coyote population by half; as a result, rodent populations have increased, providing a larger prey base for midsized carnivores such as foxes, hawks, owls, badgers, and pine martens.[168] The reduction in the numbers of coyotes has also increased pronghorn fawn survival.[169] The carcasses of elk and moose killed by the wolves provide a bonanza for scavengers such as grizzly and black bears, ravens, magpies, and bald and golden eagles.[170] Finally, preliminary data indicates that wolves also buffer the impact of climate change, illustrating "the importance of restoring and maintaining intact food chains in the face of large-scale environmental perturbations such as climate change."[171]

This overview of the impacts of wolf reintroduction on the Yellowstone ecosystem broaches the question of whether recovery of the wolf—and a number of other highly interactive species[172]—should be defined to include their role in the ecosystems they inhabit. Although the science raises the issue, it cannot, of course, resolve it. The question of the acceptability of some level of risk requires an ethical/policy rather than a scientific answer. For example, Idaho has sought to justify its decision to kill nearly half of the wolves in the state as necessary to "protect our hunters and our elk herds."[173] A preference for deer and elk over wolves is not resolvable by appeals to evidence.[174]

Recovery Plans as "The Best Scientific . . . Data Available"

The second emerging issue involves the use of recovery plans to cabin agency discretion when the decision is arguably inconsistent with a plan's provisions. Although it is easy to treat this situation as though it falls within the black-letter-recovery-plans-are-not-enforceable rule, to do so is to blur two meanings of "enforceable." The first, discussed above, involves litigation that seeks to require an agency to do (or to avoid doing) something that a plan states will improve (or harm) a species' status. A recovery plan, however, is a statement of the best available science on the conservation management actions needed to protect and recover a listed species. This information is relevant to a wide range of decisions under the Act. Consultations, for example, must evaluate the effects of the proposed action on both the survival and recovery of the listed species.[175] Similarly, before issuing an incidental take permit for a habitat conservation plan, the wildlife agency must find that the permitted actions "will not appreciably reduce the likelihood of the survival and *recovery* of the species in the wild."[176] More generally, the definition of "conservation," the Act's fundamental evaluative standard, imports recovery into all decisions. Using recovery plans as evidence is a significantly different way of "enforcing" the plans. The courts, however, have been slow to recognize this difference.

Courts have employed the science in recovery plans in a variety of contexts. For example, they have relied upon recovery plans to establish basic facts about the biology of species and their status. In some situations, the use is rather trivial—for example, that entanglement with commercial fishing gear and collisions with ships were significant causes of death for the northern right whale,[177] that the population of the Delhi Sands flower-loving fly was in the "low hundreds,"[178] and that the numbers of grizzly bears had fallen from 50,000 individuals to less than 1,000.[179]

In other cases, however, the courts turned to the recovery plans to provide an independent source of scientific information—for example, how sea turtle hatchlings orient themselves to the sea and thus why beach lights are problematic[180] and the importance of an area used by off-highway vehicles to desert tortoises.[181] Perhaps the best early example of the use of science in a recovery plan as evidence relevant to an issue is *Palila v. Hawaii Department of Land & Natural Resources*.[182] Plaintiff argued that the state agency was taking palilas by maintaining feral sheep and goats in the species' critical habitat since the introduced species were destroying the mamane-naio forest. The agency responded that it had not been established that the species was unable to live without mamane "because no attempts have ever been made to raise Palila in captivity without mamane."[183] The court summarily rejected this argument, relying in part upon the species' recovery plan for the species' habitat requirements.[184]

The fact that many agency decisions are to be based on "the best scientific . . . data available" and that recovery plans are evidence of that science does not mean, of course, that an agency decision that seems to contradict a recovery plan is for that reason alone illegal. But it does suggest that the agency ought to be required to explain why it acted or authorized others to act inconsistently with the plan. For example, shortly after the recovery plan for the Florida panther was completed in 1987, Sarasota County applied to the Army Corps of Engineers for a Clean Water Act section 404 permit to construct a landfill.[185] Following consultation, FWS issued a BiOp concluding that the landfill would not jeopardize the continued existence of the panther. Fund for Animals challenged that decision, arguing that the proposed landfill was in an area that the recovery plan "proposed for habitat preservation" and that "should be monitored to the maximum extent possible to obviate adverse habitat modifications."[186] The U.S. Court of Appeals for the Eleventh Circuit rejected these arguments, concluding that they would "elevate" the recovery plan "into a document with the force of law."[187] Thus the agency had discretion on implementing the plan and it had not abused that discretion since it had provided a reasoned justification in the BiOp.[188]

Agencies do, of course, make decisions that are arbitrary and capricious. For example, in *Southwest Center for Biological Diversity v. Bartel*[189] the FWS proposed to issue an incidental take permit (ITP) to San Diego based on its habitat conservation plan (HCP) for vernal pool species. The court held, inter alia, that the agency was required to reinitiate consultation on the ITP because it had completed a recovery plan after the permit was issued. The court appears to have believed that the ITP was inconsistent with "the strategies and objectives in the recovery plan." Thus, on remand, if the agency determined that the two documents were inconsistent, it "would need to explain why it reached inconsistent conclusions from the same evidence."[190] As the court commented,

> The *Vernal Pool Recovery Plan* is pertinent evidence of the measures necessary to prevent the extinction of the vernal pool species. The language and structure of the ESA's provisions for recovery plans shows that FWS must make a conscientious and educated effort to implement the plans for the recovery of species.[191]

Similarly, in *Carlton v. Babbitt* the plaintiff filed a petition to reclassify the grizzly bear in the Selkirk Mountains from threatened to endangered. The FWS argued that the reclassification was not warranted because the population was stable and capable of sustaining the current level of human-caused mortality.[192] Relying upon a scientific article on the ability of grizzly populations to withstand human-caused mortality, the agency concluded that the Selkirk population could withstand an annual mortality of four percent. The species' recovery plan, however, noted that the article "does not account for demographic, genetic, or other problems that can be dramatically amplified in such small populations."[193] The court concluded that the recovery plan demonstrated that the agency "was fully aware of the limitations on the use of the Harris figure with a population of 26 to 36 bears, making its use arbitrary and capricious."[194]

More recently, the recovery plan for the NRM gray wolves played a crucial role in the court's decision in *Defenders of Wildlife v. Hall*.[195] The recovery plan and the agency's subsequent discussion of the recovery goals emphasized the need for genetic interchange among the three subpopulations to achieve a "high probability of long-term persistence."[196] When the FWS attempted to delist the DPS despite the lack of evidence that there had been any genetic interchange among the populations, the court held that its decision was arbitrary and capricious because it had failed to provide "reasoned analysis" for its decision to change recovery criteria.[197]

The *Defenders* court's decision is eminently appropriate. There are sound reasons not to accord recovery plans automatically binding force; knowledge about a species and what is required to recover it should increase and evolve over time, thus rendering plans potentially outdated. But that fact should not lead courts to the opposite extreme and give them no weight. The plans are, after all, evidence of "the best scientific ... data available" and the agencies' decisions are to be predicated upon precisely such data. Requiring the federal wildlife agency to explain why it acted or authorized others to act inconsistently with the plan is consistent with the broad objectives not only of the ESA, conserving listed species and their habitats, but also of administrative law, requiring agencies to provide reasons for their actions that are rational and reasonable.

Conclusion

The ESA's fundamental purpose is to bring species that are at risk of extinction to the point at which their numbers have grown and dispersed so that the Act's protections are no longer necessary. Though the Act is now more than 30 years old, the questions surrounding recovery are only beginning to be examined and litigated.

To guide the recovery decision as well as the potentially complex mix of management actions necessary to nurture at-risk species to the point of recovery, the Act mandates that the federal wildlife agencies prepare recovery plans. Given the uncertainties and the necessarily iterative learning process inherent in conservation biology, recovery plans are also necessarily tentative. As a result, the courts have been hesitant to require the wildlife agencies to comply with plans. At the same time, however, the plans will generally be evidence of the best available science since they are developed outside the context of any individual dispute; deviations from the plan thus should require justification. These competing interests are reflected in the case law, which exhibits a desire to balance deference to the agency's scientific expertise with a need to ensure transparent decision-making.

Notes

1. The Act's primary extinction-prevention provisions include:
    a. The consultation mandate of § 7(a)(2), 16 U.S.C. § 1536(a)(2).
    b. The prohibitions of section 9, 16 U.S.C. § 1539(a)(1), and the civil and criminal sanctions imposed by section 11, 16 U.S.C. § 1540. *See also id.* §§ 1539(a)(1)(G), 1533(d).
    c. The habitat conservation planning requirements for obtaining an incidental take permit. The § 10(a)(1)(B) incidental take permits operate as a limit on the take and commerce prohibitions by permitting take that is "incidental to, and not the purpose of, the carrying out of an otherwise lawful activity." 16 U.S.C. § 1539(a)(1)(B). Before issuing a permit, the wildlife agency must find that the permitted actions "will not appreciably reduce the likelihood of the survival and *recovery* of the species in the wild." *Id.* § (2)(B)(iv) (emphasis added).

    These extinction-prevention provisions are intended to prevent the continued decline of the species—they are akin to the Hippocratic oath, "First, do no harm."
2. Gifford Pinchot Task Force v. U.S. Fish & Wildlife Serv., 378 F.3d 1059, 1070 (9th Cir. 2004).
3. 16 U.S.C. § 1536(a)(1). *See generally* Pyramid Lake Paiute Tribe of Indians v. U.S. Dep't of Navy, 898 F.2d 1210 (9th Cir. 1990); House v. U.S. Forest Serv., 974 F. Supp. 1022

(E.D. Ky. 1997); J. B. Ruhl, *Section 7(a)(1) of the "New" Endangered Species Act: Rediscovering and Redefining the Untapped Power of Federal Agencies Duty to Conserve*, 25 ENVTL. L. 1107 (1995).
4. 16 U.S.C. § 1539(a)(1)(A).
5. *Id.* § 1539(j). *See generally* Wyo. Farm Bureau Fed'n v. Babbitt, 199 F.3d 1224 (10th Cir. 2000); Dale D. Goble, *Experimental Populations: Reintroducing the Missing Parts, in* THE ENDANGERED SPECIES ACT 379 (Donald C. Baur & Wm. Robert Irvin eds., 2002).
6. The Act's definition of "conserve" includes a nonexclusive list of conservation tools, including "all activities associated with scientific resources management such as research, census, law enforcement, habitat acquisition and maintenance, propagation, live trapping, and transplantation." 16 U.S.C. § 1532(3).
7. Draft Recovery Plan for the Northern Spotted Owl, 72 Fed. Reg. 32,857 (2007).
8. "The purposes of this Act are to provide a means whereby the ecosystems upon which endangered species and threatened species depend may be conserved, [and] to provide a program for the conservation of such endangered species and threatened species." 16 U.S.C. § 1531(b); *see also id.* § 1536(a)(1) ("All federal agencies shall ... utilize their authorities in furtherance of the purposes of this Act by carrying our programs for the conservation of [listed] species.").
9. Pinchot, who created the term to fill a descriptive void, defined it as use for the greatest good for the greatest number for the longest time. GIFFORD PINCHOT, BREAKING NEW GROUND 326 (1947).
10. 16 U.S.C. § 1532(3). In 1988, Congress linked recovery to conservation in requiring the Secretary to "implement a system ... to monitor ... the status of all species which have recovered to the point at which the measures provided pursuant to this Act are no longer necessary" and which been delisted. Endangered Species Amendments of 1988, Pub. L. No. 100-478, § 1004, 102 Stat. 2306, 2307 (1988) (currently codified at 16 U.S.C. § 1533(g)).
11. Rules for Listing Endangered and Threatened Species, Designating Critical Habitat, and Maintaining the Lists, 45 Fed. Reg. 13,010, 13,023 (1980) (a species could be removed from the list as recovered when "the evidence shows that it is no longer Endangered or Threatened"). When the rules were amended in 1984, the definition of "recovery" remained unchanged. Listing Endangered and Threatened Species and Designating Critical Habitat; Amended Procedures to Comply with the 1982 Amendments to the Endangered Species Act, 49 Fed. Reg. 38,900, 38,909 (1984) (codified at 50 C.F.R. § 424.11(d)(2)). The term was formally defined by the agencies in 1986 as part of the consultation regulations to mean the "improvement in the status of listed species to the point at which the listing is no longer appropriate under the criteria set out in section 4(a)(1) of the Act." Interagency Cooperation—Endangered Species Act of 1973, as Amended; Final Rule, 51 Fed. Reg. 19,926, 19,958 (1986) (codified at 50 C.F.R. § 402.02).
12. Fish & Wildlife Serv., Policy and Guidelines for Planning and Coordinating Recovery of Endangered and Threatened Species 1 (May 25, 1990). NOAA's new, interim guidance on recovery planning offers a similar statement: "Recovery is the process by which listed species and their ecosystems are restored and their future is safeguarded to the point that protections under the ESA are no longer necessary." Nat'l Marine Fisheries Serv., Interim Endangered and Threatened Species Recovery Planning Guidance 1.1-1 (July 2006). It is important to note the implicit point: recovery is about ameliorating the threats the species faces. Increased numbers of individuals and populations, while likely evidence of the amelioration of the threats, are in themselves insufficient. *See* Fish and Wildlife Serv. & Nat'l Oceanic & Atmospheric Admin., Interagency Cooperation—Endangered Species Act of 1973, as Amended; Final Rule, 51 Fed. Reg. 19,926, 19,935 (1986) ("recovery is not attained until the threats to the species as analyzed under section 4(a)(1) of the Act have been removed").
13. 16 U.S.C. § 1532(6). The definition might be literally more accurate if it read "in danger of extinction or of extirpation throughout a significant portion of its range."

14. *Id.* § 1532(20). For recovery, the crucial definition is "threatened" since a species that is threatened is less at-risk than a species that is endangered—and thus a step closer to recovered.
15. *See* United States v. Carroll Towing Co., 159 F.2d 169, 173 (2d Cir. 1947) (Hand, J.).
16. As Oliver Wendell Holmes put it, "the question of where to draw the line . . . is the question in pretty much everything worth arguing about in the law. Day and night, youth and age are only types." *Irwin v. Gavit*, 268 U.S. 161, 168 (1925).
17. 16 U.S.C. § 1533(b)(1)(A).
18. Holly Doremus, *Listing Decisions Under the Endangered Species Act: Why Better Science Isn't Always Better Policy*, 75 WASH. U.L.Q. 1029, 1088 (1997). *See also* D. DeMaster et al., Recommendations to NOAA Fisheries: ESA Listing Criteria 2–3 (June 10, 2004).
19. It should be noted that the relevant science is also subject to substantial epistemic uncertainties. *See* Helen M. Regan et al., *A Taxonomy and Treatment of Uncertainty for Ecology and Conservation Biology*, 12 ECOLOGICAL APPLICATIONS 618, 618 (2002). Conservation biologists generally speak of "viable populations." But there is no greater chance of defining a "viable" population solely on the basis of science than there is a "threatened" species. Mark Shaffer, for example, "arbitrarily propose[d]" a definition of minimum viable population as "the smallest isolated population having a 99% chance of remaining extant for 1000 years despite the *foreseeable* effects of demographic, environmental, and genetic stochasticity, and natural catastrophes." Mark L. Shaffer, *Minimum Population Sizes for Species Conservation*, 31 BIOSCIENCE 131, 132 (1981) (emphasis added). In addition to raising (again) the question of acceptable risk—rather than Shaffer's 99 percent chance of surviving for 1,000 years, a policymaker might (equally arbitrarily) choose a 85 percent chance of surviving 100 years—Shaffer's definition also involves uncertainty. First, the models that are employed to assess viability and risks are informed guesses based on (unavoidable) simplifying assumptions about something (extinction) that is itself only poorly understood. *E.g.*, Barry W. Brook et al., *Predictive Accuracy of Population Viability Analysis in Conservation Biology*, 404 NATURE 385 (2000); Tim Coulson et al., *The Use and Abuse of Population Viability Analysis*, 16 TRENDS IN ECOLOGY & EVOLUTION 219 (2001); Brian Dennis et al., *Estimation of Growth and Extinction Parameters for Endangered Species*, 61 ECOLOGICAL MONOGRAPHS 115 (1991). This problem is compounded by the fact that basic data (such as life history traits or current population) are often unknown—a problem that is likely to be particularly acute with at-risk species, which are generally uncommon and thus relatively unstudied. Third, and most importantly, there is question of the uncertainty associated with the risks themselves: these are "stochastic processes," that is, processes "in which the state of the system cannot be precisely predicted given its current state and even with a full knowledge of all the factors affecting the process." Hugh P. Possingham et al., *Population Viability Analysis*, in ENCYCLOPEDIA OF BIODIVERSITY 831, 831 (Simon A. Levin ed., 2001). The ultimately stochastic nature of nature means that biology is a probabilistic science—and the uncertainty of probability is the core of risk. As one review concluded, given the scientific uncertainty "our ability to accurately assess the extinction probability of a species is questionable." *Id.* at 832. *See also* Steven R. Beissinger & M. Ian Westphal, *On the Use of Demographic Models of Population Viability in Endangered Species Management*, 62 J. WILDLIFE MGMT. 821, 831–32 (1998).
20. 437 U.S. 153, 184 (1978) (emphasis added).
21. *Id.* at 173.
22. *See* Dale D. Goble, *The Evolution of At-Risk Species Protection, in* THE ENDANGERED SPECIES ACT AT THIRTY: CONSERVING BIODIVERSITY IN HUMAN-DOMINATED LANDSCAPES 6, 17–23 (J. Michael Scott et al. eds. 2006); Oliver A. Houck, *The Endangered Species Act and Its Implementation by the U.S. Departments of the Interior and Commerce*, 64 U. COLO. L. REV. 277 (1993).
23. J. B. Ruhl, *How to Kill Endangered Species, Legally: The Nuts and Bolts of Endangered Species Act "HCP" Permits for Real Estate Development*, 5 ENVTL. LAW. 345 (1998).
24. Nat'l Wildlife Fed'n v. Norton, 386 F. Supp. 2d 553, 565 (D. Vt. 2005).

25. 12-Month Finding on a Petition to List the Cerulean Warbler as Threatened with Critical Habitat, 71 Fed. Reg. 70,717, 70,718 (2006).). Recently, both FWS and NOAA have become more explicit in their risk assessments. In addition to the cerulean warbler decision, *see, e.g.,* Final Listing Determinations for Elkhorn Coral and Staghorn Coral, 71 Fed. Reg. 26,852, 26,856–57 (2006).
26. 71 Fed. Reg. at 70,731, 70,723.
27. *Id.* at 70,731.
28. *Id.* at 70,731–32.
29. 16 U.S.C. § 1533(a)(1). This list of threats reflects the historical understanding of extinction at the time the ESA was enacted: nature was conceived as a mechanical equilibrium system, a conception that is inherently deterministic. Our understanding of nature has undergone a fundamental transformation: it is now conceived as an historical, probabilistic system. The tension between these two conceptions is reflected in the tension between the traditional threats analysis and an explicit risk analysis in the status determination decision.
30. 16 U.S.C. § 1533(a)(1).
31. Fund for Animals v. Babbitt, 903 F. Supp. 96, 111, 113 (D.D.C. 1995).
32. As several courts have noted, "Since the same five statutory factors must be considered in delisting as in listing, the Court necessarily concludes that FWS ... must address each of the five statutory delisting factors and measure whether the threats to the [species] have been ameliorated." Defenders of Wildlife v. Babbitt, 130 F. Supp. 2d 121, 133 (D.D.C. 2001) (quoting *Fund for Animals v. Babbitt,* 903 F. Supp. 96, 111 (D.D.C. 1995)). *See also* Nat'l Wildlife Fed'n v. Norton, 386 F. Supp. 2d 553, 558 (D. Vt. 2005).
33. *E.g.,* Katherine Ralls et al., *Developing Criteria for Delisting the Southern Sea Otter Under the U.S. Endangered Species Act,* 10 CONSERVATION BIOLOGY 1528 (1996).
34. *See, e.g.,* COMM. ON SCIENTIFIC ISSUES IN THE ENDANGERED SPECIES ACT, NAT'L RESEARCH COUNCIL, SCIENCE AND THE ENDANGERED SPECIES ACT 149–50 (1995) [hereinafter COMM. ON SCIENTIFIC ISSUES]; Daniel J. Rohlf, *Six Biological Reasons Why the Endangered Species Act Doesn't Work—And What to Do About It,* 5 CONSERVATION BIOLOGY 273, 275–76 (1991); Timothy H. Tear et al., *Status and Prospects for Success of the Endangered Species Act: A Look at Recovery Plans,* 262 SCIENCE 976 (1993); David S. Wilcove et al., *What Exactly Is an Endangered Species? An Analysis of the U.S. Endangered Species List: 1985–1991,* 7 CONSERVATION BIOLOGY 87 (1993).
35. The species that have been delisted as recovered are American alligator (delisted between 1975 and 1987), brown pelican [U.S. Atlantic Coast population] (delisted 1985), Palau fantail flycatcher (delisted 1985), Palau ground dove (delisted 1985), Palau owl (delisted 1985), gray whale [eastern Pacific Ocean population] (delisted 1994), Arctic peregrine falcon (delisted 1994), American peregrine falcon (delisted 1999), Aleutian cackling goose (delisted 2001), Robbins' cinquefoil (delisted 2002), Columbia white-tailed deer [Douglas County DPS] (delisted 2003), Hoover's woolly-star (delisted 2003), Eggert's sunflower (delisted 2005), grizzly bear [Yellowstone Ecosystem DPS] (delisted 2007), bald eagle (delisted 2007), Virginia northern flying squirrel (delisted 2008), and gray wolf [Northern Rocky Mountain DPS] (delisted 2009).
36. The FWS and NOAA-Fisheries have acknowledged this difference in adopting the Policy for Evaluation of Conservation Efforts When Making Listing Decisions (PECE), 68 Fed. Reg. 15,100 (2003). In response to the suggestion of several commenters on the draft Policy that it be applied to all decisions, the agencies stated that "a recovery plan is the appropriate vehicle to provide guidance on actions necessary to delist a species." *Id.* at 15,101. Similarly, the Quantitative Working Group also reported that it was divided over whether the standards for listing should also be applied to delisting and reclassification decisions and therefore recommended considering this question separately. D. DeMaster et al., *supra* note 18, at 5.
37. "Existing regulatory mechanisms" is the fourth factor in the required five-factor analysis. *See* 16 U.S.C. § 1533(a)(1)(D).
38. 33 U.S.C. §§ 1251–1387.

39. 16 U.S.C. §§ 4701–4741.
40. The stochastic processes believed significantly to impact extinction are: demographic stochasticity ("chance events in the survival and reproductive success of a finite number of individuals"), environmental stochasticity ("temporal variation of habitat parameters and the population of competitors, parasites, and diseases"), genetic stochasticity ("changes in gene frequencies due to founder effect, random fixation, or inbreeding"), and natural catastrophes ("floods, fires, droughts, etc., which may occur at random intervals through time"). Shaffer, *supra* note 19, at 131. These four type of risks are examined in more detail in Mark S. Boyce, *Population Viability Analysis*, 23 Ann. Rev. Ecology & Systematics 481, 483–95 (1992); Comm. on Scientific Issues, supra note 34, at 124–43.
41. The species was originally listed as endangered in 1967 under a predecessor of the ESA, the Endangered Species Preservation Act (ESPA) of 1966, Pub. L. No. 89-669, 80 Stat. 926, *repealed by* Endangered Species Act, 16 U.S.C. § 1543. *See* Native Fish and Wildlife: Endangered Species, 32 Fed. Reg. 4001 (1967). Under the ESPA, the Secretary was not required to discuss the risk factors affecting the species; that discussion can be found in the proposal to reclassify the species from endangered to threatened in 1989. *See* Proposed Reclassification of the Aleutian Canada Goose from Endangered to Threatened, 54 Fed. Reg. 40,142 (1989).
42. 54 Fed. Reg. at 40,142.
43. Final Rule to Remove the Aleutian Canada Goose from the Federal List of Endangered and Threatened Wildlife, 66 Fed. Reg. 15,643, 15,645 (2001).
44. *Id.* at 15,645.
45. *See* U.S. Fish & Wildlife Serv.—Alaska, Alaska Maritime National Wildlife Refuge, http://alaska.fws.gov/nwr/akmar/index.htm (last visited Jan. 24, 2006).
46. *See* 16 U.S.C. §§ 668dd–668ee.
47. 66 Fed. Reg. at 15,651–52.
48. The Council is a body that represents the state fish and game commissions of the western states and provinces. *See* Pac. Flyway Council, Coordinated Management, http://pacificflyway.gov/Index.asp (last visited Sept. 9, 2005). The Council has prepared a management plan for the Aleutian cackling goose. *See* Pac. Flyway Council, Pacific Flyway Management Plan for the Aleutian cackling Goose http://pacificflyway.gov/Abstracts.asp#acg (July 30, 1999) (last visited Sept. 9, 2005).
49. 16 U.S.C. §§ 703–711. The MBTA federalized the conservation of migratory birds: it begins, for example, with a broad declaration that "it shall be unlawful to . . . take, . . . kill, . . . possess, . . . sell, . . . ship, [or] export . . . any migratory bird." *Id.* § 703. Federal protection extends to "any product . . . which . . . is composed in whole or part, of any such bird or any part, nest or egg thereof." *Id.*
50. Convention on International Trade in Endangered Species of Wild Fauna and Flora, Mar. 3, 1973, 27 U.S.T. 1087, 993 U.N.T.S. 243.
51. The gray whale was listed because of severe depletion as a result of harvest, particularly shore-based whaling operations. Gray Whale, 58 Fed. Reg. 3121, 3125 (1993). The alligator was listed "due to concern over poorly regulated or unregulated harvests." Reclassification of American Alligator as Threatened Due to Similarity of Appearance Throughout the Remainder of its Range, 52 Fed. Reg. 21,059, 21,059 (1987).
52. The gray whale remains subject to an extensive array of regulatory mechanisms. Internationally, the species is regulated by the International Whaling Commission under the International Convention for the Regulation of Whaling, Dec. 2, 1946, 10 U.S.T. 952, 161 U.N.T.S. 72, and CITES. It also protected under federal law when it is within U.S. territorial waters, most significantly the take prohibitions of the Marine Mammal Protection Act (MMPA). 16 U.S.C. §§ 1361–1407. Additional federal laws that are also applicable and offer additional protection include the National Environmental Policy Act, 42 U.S.C. §§ 4321, 4331–4335; the Clean Water Act, 33 U.S.C. §§ 1251–1387; the Act to Prevent Pollution from Ships, 33 U.S.C. §§ 1901–1909; the Marine Protection, Research, and Sanctuaries Act, 33 U.S.C. §§ 1401–1447f, 2801–2805; the Oil Pollution Act of 1990,

33 U.S.C. §§ 2701–2719, 2731–2738, 2751–2761; and the Outer Continental Shelf Lands Act Amendments, 43 U.S.C. §§ 1344–1355, 1801–1802, 1841–1845, 1862–1866.

The alligator continues to be managed pursuant to three federal regulatory mechanisms: the Lacey Act, which prohibits interstate shipment of wildlife taken contrary to state or federal law, 16 U.S.C. §§ 701, 3371–3378; a special rule promulgated under the ESA's similarity of appearance provisions (since the alligator is similar to other crocodilians that are still listed), 50 C.F.R. § 17.42 (2004); and listing under Appendix I of CITES, which prohibits international commerce in the species. 52 Fed. Reg. at 21,062.

53. Final Rule to Remove the American Peregrine Falcon from the Federal List of Endangered and Threatened Wildlife, and to Remove the Similarity of Appearance Provision for Free-flying Peregrines in the Conterminous United States, 64 Fed. Reg. 46,542, 46,452 (1999); Removal of Arctic Peregrine Falcon from the List of Endangered and Threatened Wildlife, 59 Fed. Reg. 50,796 (1994); Removal of the Brown Pelican in the Southeastern United States from the List of Endangered and Threatened Wildlife, 50 Fed. Reg. 4938, 4938 (1985) (organochlorine pesticides were also directly toxic to pelicans).
54. 7 U.S.C. §§ 136–136y.
55. 64 Fed. Reg. at 46,554–55; 59 Fed. Reg. at 50,800; 50 Fed. Reg. at 4941–42.
56. 64 Fed. Reg. at 46,554–55; 59 Fed. Reg. at 50,801.
57. For the peregrine falcon subspecies, the agency cited the National Forest Management Act, 16 U.S.C. §§ 1600–1616; Federal Land Policy and Management Act, 43 U.S.C. §§ 1701–1784; and the various management requirements applicable to the National Wildlife Refuge System, *see* Dale D. Goble & Eric T. Freyfogle, Wildlife Law 219–37 (2002). For the brown pelican, the similar statute is the Estuary Protection Act, 16 U.S.C. §§ 1221–1226, and the refuge system statutes.
58. 64 Fed. Reg. at 46,555; 50 Fed. Reg. at 4941–42.
59. *See, e.g.,* David S. Wilcove et al., *Leading Threats to Biodiversity: What's Imperiling U.S. Species, in* Precious Heritage 239 (Bruce A. Stein et al. eds., 2000) [hereinafter Wilcove et al., *Leading Threats*]; David S. Wilcove et al., *Quantifying Threats to Imperiled Species in the United States: Assessing the Relative Importance of Habitat Destruction, Alien Species, Pollution, Overexploitation, and Disease,* 48 BioScience 607 (1998) [hereinafter Wilcove et al., *Quantifying Threats*].
60. Final Rule to Remove the Douglas County Distinct Population Segment of Columbian White-Tailed Deer from the Federal List of Endangered and Threatened Wildlife, 68 Fed. Reg. 43,647, 43,647 (2003).
61. The species was listed as endangered in 1967, Native Fish and Wildlife; Endangered Species, 32 Fed. Reg. 4001 (1967), under the Endangered Species Preservation Act, Pub. L. No. 89-669, 80 Stat. 926 (*repealed by* Endangered Species Act of 1973, Pub. L. No. 93-205, § 14, 87 Stat. 884, 903 (1973)).
62. Proposed Rule to Delist the Douglas County Population of Columbian White-Tailed Deer, 64 Fed. Reg. 25,263, 25,624 (1999).
63. 68 Fed. Reg. at 43,648.
64. 64 Fed. Reg. at 25,625; *see also* Notice of Public Hearing, 67 Fed. Reg. 42,217, 42,220 (2002). On DPS, *see generally* Policy Regarding the Recognition of Distinct Vertebrate Population Segments Under the Endangered Species Act, 61 Fed. Reg. 4722, 4725 (1996).
65. *See generally* Dale D. Goble, *What Are Slugs Good For? Ecosystem Services and the Conservation of Biodiversity,* 22 J. Land Use & Envtl. L. 411 (2007).
66. 68 Fed. Reg. at 43,651.
67. *Id.*
68. *Id.*
69. *Id.* at 43,653–54.
70. *Id.* at 43,654–55.
71. *Id.* at 43,653.
72. *Id.* at 43,653–54.
73. *Id.* at 43,654.

74. Determination of Pontententilla [sic] robbinsiana to Be an Endangered Species, with Critical Habitat, 45 Fed. Reg. 61,944, 61,945 (1980).
75. Removal of Potentilla robbinsiana (Robbins' cinquefoil) from the Federal List of Endangered and Threatened Plants, 67 Fed. Reg. 54,968, 54,973 (2002).
76. *Id.* at 54,970, 54,972–73.
77. The USFS agreed to provide "long-term protection on the Forest irrespective of the species standing under the Endangered Species Act." U.S. Forest Serv. and U.S. Fish & Wildlife Serv., Memorandum of Understanding for the Conservation of Robbins' Cinquefoil (*Potentilla robbinsiana*) 1 (Dec. 2, 1994). The FWS agreed to maintain the Monroe Flats habitat, to "vigorously protect[]" the species from take through human disturbance, to train personnel, and to provide educational and interpretational information to visitors to the forest. *Id.* at 3.
78. Wilcove et al., *Leading Threats*, *supra* note 59; Wilcove et al., *Quantifying Threats*, *supra* note 59.
79. Holly Doremus, *Delisting Endangered Species: An Aspirational Goal, Not a Realistic Expectation*, 30 ENVTL. L. REP. (Envtl. L. Inst.) 10,434 (2000); Jack E. Williams et al., *Prospects for Recovering Endemic Fishes Pursuant to the U.S. Endangered Species Act*, 30:6 FISHERIES 24, 24 (2005). This is particularly true for plants and invertebrates, which are often entirely without legal protection.
80. H.R. REP. NO. 95-1625, at 19 (1978), *reprinted in* 1978 U.S.C.C.A.N. 9453, 9469.
81. Proposed Designation of Critical Habitat for the Pacific Coast Population of Western Snowy Plover, 60 Fed. Reg. 11,768, 11,770 (1995).
82. 16 U.S.C. § 1536(a)(1). *See generally* Federico Cheever, *The Road to Recovery: A New Way of Thinking About the Endangered Species Act*, 23 ECOLOGY L.Q. 1 (1996); Robert L. Fischman, *Endangered Species Conservation: What Should We Expect from Federal Agencies?*, 13 PUB. LAND L. REV. 1 (1992); DANIEL J. ROHLF, THE ENDANGERED SPECIES ACT (1989).
83. Endangered Species Act Amendments of 1978, Pub. L. No. 95-632, § 11(5), 92 Stat. 3751, 3766 (codified as amended at 16 U.S.C. § 1533(f)). The amendment included an exception to the requirement if the agency finds that "such a plan will not promote the conservation of the species." *Id.* The amendment also ratified the existing agency practice of establishing recovery teams composed of agency and nonagency experts to draft the plans. *Id.*
84. *Id.* § 1533(f)(1)(B).
85. U.S. Fish & Wildlife Serv., Policy and Guidelines for Planning and Coordinating Recovery of Threatened and Endangered Species (May 1990) [hereinafter 1990 Recovery Guidelines], *available at* http://www.fws.gov/endangered/pdfs/recovery/90guide.pdf; Nat'l Marine Fisheries Serv., Interim Endangered and Threatened Species Recovery Planning Guidance (July 2006).
86. The 1990 Recovery Guidelines outline the process: the agency is to appoint a team of biologists familiar with the species to draft a recovery plan. The plan itself must contain three types of information. The first is a summary of what is known about the species, including its distribution, habitat, and life history, and the threat factors that prompted its listing. The second section contains the criteria for determining when the species is recovered. The criteria will often be a specified population size, but may include additional requirements, such as a minimum number of populations or specified habitat requirements. Finally, the plan details the actions required to address the threats to the species and an implementation schedule for the actions needed to meet the plan's objectives. *Id.* at App. I, 9–20. Timothy H. Tear et al., *Recovery Plans and the Endangered Species Act: Are Criticisms Supported by Data?*, 9 CONSERVATION BIOLOGY 182, 184–87, 190 (1995). *See, e.g.,* Fund for Animals v. Babbitt, 903 F. Supp. 96, 108–10 (D.D.C. 1995).
87. U.S. FISH & WILDLIFE SERV., REPORT TO CONGRESS ON THE RECOVERY OF THREATENED AND ENDANGERED SPECIES: FISCAL YEARS 2003–2004, at 18 (2006) [hereinafter 2004 RECOVERY REPORT].

88. There were 592 active recovery plans covering 1135 species. U.S. Fish & Wildlife Serv., Boxscore, http://ecos.fws.gov/tess_public/Boxscore.do (through Aug. 28, 2009). Recovery plans are developed only for U.S. species since the FWS has no authority to engage in recovery actions for non-U.S. species.
89. 2004 RECOVERY REPORT, *supra* note 87, at 18. Examples of times in which the conservation of a species would not be promoted by development of a recovery plan are situations in which the species does not exist in the wild or is thought to be extinct, or a state management plan is an effective substitute. *See* TONY A. SULLINS, ESA 34 n.22 (2001) (citing an FWS "frequently asked questions" page that has been removed).
90. The species would face a 20 percent chance of extinction within 20 years or 10 generations, whichever is longer. Tear et al., *supra* note 34, at 76.
91. *Id.* at 976–77.
92. COMM. ON SCIENTIFIC ISSUES, supra note 34, at 150.
93. The study and its methods are described in Jonathan M. Hoekstra et al., *A Comprehensive Review of Endangered Species Act Recovery Plans*, 12 ECOLOGICAL APPLICATIONS 630 (2002); J. Alan Clark et al., *Improving U.S. Endangered Species Act Recovery Plans: Key Findings and Recommendations of the SCB Recovery Plan Project*, 16 CONSERVATION BIOLOGY 1510 (2002).
94. Cheryl Schultz & Leah R. Gerber, *Are Recovery Plans Improving with Practice?* 12 ECOLOGICAL APPLICATIONS 541, 646 (2002).
95. Joshua J. Lawler et al., *The Scope and Treatment of Threats in Endangered Species Recovery Plans*, 12 ECOLOGICAL APPLICATIONS 663, 665 (2002).
96. J. Alan Clark & Erick Harvey, *Assessing Multi-Species Recovery Plans Under the Endangered Species Act*, 12 ECOLOGICAL APPLICATIONS 655 (2002).
97. Leah R. Gerber & Leila T. Hatch, *Are We Recovering? An Evaluation of Recovery Criteria Under the U.S. Endangered Species Act*, 12 ECOLOGICAL APPLICATIONS 668 (2002).
98. Steven P. Campbell et al., *An Assessment of Monitoring Efforts in Endangered Species Recovery Plans*, 12 ECOLOGICAL APPLICATIONS 674 (2002).
99. *See, e.g.*, Julie K. Miller et al., *The Endangered Species Act: Dollars and Sense?*, 52 BIOSCIENCE 163 (2002).
100 Theodore C. Foin et al., *Improving Recovery Planning for Threatened and Endangered Species: Comparative Analysis of Recovery Plans Can Contribute to More Effective Recovery Planning*, 48 BIOSCIENCE 177, 178 (1998).
101. And relatively little scholarly comment. By far the best is Fred Cheever's piece, to I am indebted. *See* Cheever, *supra* note 82.
102. Endangered Species Act Amendments of 1978, Pub. L. No. 95-632, § 11(5), 92 Stat. 3751, 3766 (codified as amended at 16 U.S.C. § 1533(f)).
103 16 U.S.C. § 1533(f)(1)(B).
104. A BiOp is issued at the end of a formal consultation between the federal wildlife agency and the federal action agency. *See generally* 16 U.S.C. § 1536(b)(3).
105 Sierra Club v. Lujan, 36 Envt. Rep. Cas. (BNA) 1533, 1535–39 (W.D. Tex. 1993), *appeal dismissed sub nom.* Sierra Club v. Babbitt, 995 F.2d 571 (5th Cir. 1993).
106. *Id.* at 1541–42, 1546.
107 *Id.* at 1541–47.
108. *Id.* at 1541.
109. *Id.*
110. Or. Natural Res. Council v. Turner, 863 F. Supp. 1277, 1279–80 (D. Or. 1994).
111. *Id.* at 1283.
112. *Id.* at 1282–83.
113. *Id.* at 1283.
114. *Id.*
115. Strahan v. Linnon, 967 F. Supp. 581, 597 (D. Mass. 1997) (since the agency had developed a priority system for developing plans, the fact that plans had not been issued for several whale species was not a violation of § 4(f)). *Cf.* Fund for Animals v. Babbitt,

903 F. Supp. 96, 104 (D.D.C. 1995) (agency is "required in most cases" to develop a recovery plan).
116. 16 U.S.C. § 1533(f)(1)(B).
117. 903 F. Supp. 96, 106 (D.D.C. 1995).
118. *Id.* at 108. *Cf. id* at 107 ("the phrase 'to the maximum extent practicable' does not permit an agency unbridled discretion"). Recall that 37 percent of the major threats identified in recovery plans did not have associated recovery tasks. Lawler et al., *supra* note 95, at 665.
119. 903 F. Supp. at 111.
120. Sw. Ctr. for Biological Diversity v. Babbitt, 1999 WL 33438081, at *1 (D. Ariz. Sept. 3, 1999).
121. *Id.* at *5.
122. *Id.* at *6–7.
123. 130 F. Supp. 2d 121, 131 (D.D.C. 2001).
124. *Id.* at 133–35.
125. *E.g.,* Sw. Ctr. for Biological Diversity v. Bartel, 470 F. Supp. 2d at 1137 n.16 (S.D. Cal. 2006); Grand Canyon Trust v. Norton, 2006 WL 167560, at *2 (D. Ariz. Jan. 18, 2006); Strahan v. Linnon, 967 F. Supp. 581, 597–98 (D. Mass. 1997); Morrill v. Lujan, 802 F. Supp. 424, 433 (S.D. Ala. 1992).
126. Fund for Animals v. Rice, 85 F.3d 535, 548 (11th Cir. 1996).
127. Nat'l Audubon Soc'y v. Hester, 801 F.2d 405, 406 (D.C. Cir. 1986) (*per curiam*).
128. Nat'l Audubon Soc'y v. Hester, 627 F. Supp. 1419, 1422–23 (D.D.C. 1986), *rev'd*, 801 F.2d 405 (D.C. Cir. 1986).
129. 801 F.2d at 408 (quoting Permian Base Area Rate Cases, 390 U.S. 747, 784 (1968)). Furthermore, the court noted, even if there were no changed circumstances, "agencies are entitled to alter their policies 'with or *without* a change in circumstances,' so long as they satisfactorily explain why they have done so." *Id.* (quoting Motor Vehicles Mfrs. Ass'n v. State Farm Mut. Ins. Co., 463 U.S. 29, 57 (1983)).
130. Nat'l Wildlife Fed'n v. Nat'l Park Serv., 669 F. Supp. 384 (D. Wyo. 1987). The decision is not entirely clear on whether the recovery plan spoke directly to the campground question or only recommended minimizing human-bear contact. The decision also blurs the distinction between the FWS (which drafted the recovery plan) and the NPS (which was being sued for failing to follow the plan) by referring simply to "the Secretary"—which is both agencies. Finally, the court failed to explain why discretion to develop a plan was also discretion not to implement it.
131. *Id.* at 388–89.
132. 16 U.S.C. § 1533(f)(1).
133. 669 F. Supp. at 389.
134. *See, e.g.,* Defenders of Wildlife v. Lujan, 792 F. Supp. 834, 835 (D.D.C. 1992) (plaintiff sought to require agency to introduce wolves into Yellowstone as provided in the species recovery plan; court held, inter alia, that "[t]he Recovery Plan itself has never been an action document" and refused to issue injunction).
135. Sierra Club v. Lujan, 36 Envt. Rep. Cas. (BNA) at 1541.
136. *Id.* at 1541–42, 1543–45.
137. 2007 WL 1847143, at *1–2 (W.D. Wash. June 25, 2007).
138. *Id.* at *3 (quoting 16 U.S.C. § 1549(g)(1)).
139. *Id.* (citing Sierra Club v. Thomas, 828 F.2d 783 (D.C. Cir. 1987)).
140. *Id.*
141. Final Rule Designating the Northern Rocky Mountain Population of Gray Wolf as a Distinct Population Segment and Removing This Distinct Population Segment from the Federal List of Endangered and Threatened Wildlife, 73 Fed. Reg. 10,514 (2008). This was the agency's second attempt to delist the wolf in the Northern Rockies. On April 1, 2003, the agency had delisted and reclassified the species (with the exception of the Mexican wolf) across the conterminous United States. Final Rule to Reclassify and

Remove the Gray Wolf from the List of Endangered and Threatened Wildlife in Portions of the Conterminous United States; Establishment of Two Special Regulations for Threatened Gray Wolves, 68 Fed. Reg. 15,804 (2003). These decisions were held to be violations of the ESA by federal district courts in Oregon and Vermont. Nat'l Wildlife Fed'n v. Norton, 386 F. Supp. 2d 553 (D. Vt. 2005); Defenders of Wildlife v. Norton, 354 F. Supp. 2d 1156 (D. Or. 2005). In addition to delisting the NRM wolf population in 2008, the agency also sought to delist the species in the western Great Lakes region. *See* Final Rule Designating the Western Great Lakes Population of Gray Wolves as a Distinct Population Segment; Removing the Western Great Lakes Distinct Population Segment of the Gray Wolf from Federal List of Endangered and Threatened Wildlife, 72 Fed. Reg. 6052 (2007). *See also* Humane Soc'y v. Kempthorne, 2008 WL 4378080 (D.D.C. Sept. 29, 2008) (vacating delisting of the wolf populations in the Great Lakes region).

142. The district court held that the agency had failed to satisfy either element of recovery. *See* Defenders of Wildlife v. Hall, 565 F. Supp. 2d 1160, 1163–64 (D. Mont. 2008). First, the court concluded that the FWS had failed to establish that the DPS had recovered biologically since there was no "evidence of genetic exchange between subpopulations." *Id.* at 1163. The agency had itself previously concluded that "without ongoing genetic exchange, isolated subpopulations of merely 100 individuals and 10 breeding pairs [the numerical recovery goal] will not exhibit genetic diversity sufficient to withstand environmental variability and stochastic events." *Id.* at 1168. Since the agency simply asserted that genetic exchange is unnecessary, it failed to provide a reasoned explanation for its decision to change course. *Id.* at 1170–71. Second, the court held that the agency had not met the requirement for post-delisting risk management because it failed to offer a reasonable explanation of why the Wyoming wolf management plan was sufficient when there were no significant differences between the state's 2003 wolf management plan that FWS had determined to be insufficient and the 2007 plan that it approved. *Id.* at 1172–75.

143 73 Fed. Reg. at 10,525.

144. Roger Phillips, *F&G Rules Could Slash Idaho Wolf Numbers in Half*, IDAHO DAILY STATESMAN, May 23, 2008. This would have reduced the number of individuals to nearly the minimal recovery goal for the species. Since Idaho established a hunting season and required licenses, no wolves were killed under Idaho's management plan.

145. *See* Julie Cart, *Delisting Endangers Wolves*, L.A. TIMES, Sept. 28, 2008, *available at* http://articles.latimes.com/2008/sep/28/nation/na-wolf28 (last visited Sept. 28, 2008). Since Wyoming did not require licenses, "[h]unters from around the state flocked to rural Sublette County to bag a wolf." *Id.*

146. 71 Fed. Reg. at 6635. The EIS had "reviewed ... the adequacy of the recovery goals because we [FWS] were concerned that the 1987 goals might be insufficient." 73 Fed. Reg. 10,521.

147. Endangered and Threatened Wildlife and Plants; Designating the Northern Rocky Mountain Population of Gray Wolf as a Distinct Population Segment and Removing This Distinct Population Segment From the Federal List of Endangered and Threatened Wildlife, 73 Fed. Reg. 63,926 (2008). *See also* Rocky Barker, *Feds Push to End Wolf Protections*, SEATTLE TIMES, Nov. 28, 2008, *available at* http://seattletimes.nwsource.com/html/nationworld/2008446620_wolves29.html.

148. Endangered and Threatened Wildlife and Plants; Final Rule to Identify the Northern Rocky Mountain Population of Gray Wolf as a Distinct Population Segment and to Revise the List of Endangered and Threatened Wildlife, 74 Fed. Reg. 15,123 (2009). Simultaneously, the agency also delisted the WGL DPS: Endangered and Threatened Wildlife and Plants; Final Rule to Identify the Western Great Lakes Populations of Gray Wolf as a Distinct Population Segment and to Revise the List of Endangered and Threatened Wildlife, 74 Fed. Reg. 15,070 (2009). FWS subsequently agreed to reinstate protections for the WGL DPS pending reproposal of the delisting.

149. 74 Fed. Reg. at 15,170-72.

150. "[T]he ESA was enacted not merely to forestall the extinction of species . . . but to allow a species to recover to the point where it may be delisted. . . . [I]t is clear that Congress intended that conservation and survival be two different (though complementary) goals of the ESA." Gifford Pinchot Task Force v. U.S. Fish & Wildlife Serv., 378 F.3d 1059, 1070 (9th Cir. 2004).
151. The Act's risk assessment is based on the "foreseeable future." 16 U.S.C. § 1532(20).
152. *See* 16 U.S.C. § 1531(b).
153. Eric W. Sanderson, *How Many Animals Do We Want to Save? The Many Ways of Setting Population Target Levels for Conservation*, 56 BioScience 911, 912 (2006).
154. Adaptation to forces such as climate change requires sufficient genetic diversity in the population so that enough individuals survive the change to avoid genetic problems such as inbreeding depression. Estimates of the number of individuals necessary to achieve this level of viability has varied. *See, e.g., id.* at 914 (an effective population of 50 individuals); L. Scott Mills & Fred W. Allendorf, *The One-Migrant-per-Generation Rule in Conservation and Management*, 10 Conservation Biology 1509 (1996) (one migrant per generation); *cf.* Final Rule Designating the Greater Yellowstone Area Population of Grizzly Bears as a Distinct Population Segment; Removing the Yellowstone Distinct Population Segment from the Federal List of Endangered and Threatened Wildlife, 72 Fed. Reg. 14,866, 14,926–27 (2007) (one to two migrants per generation); Daniel Simberloff, *The Contribution of Population and Community Biology to Conservation*, 19 Ann. Rev. Ecology & Systematics 473, 480–85 (1988) (500 individuals); Brian Czech, *The Capacity of the National Wildlife Refuge System to Conserve Threatened and Endangered Animal Species in the United States*, 19 Conservation Biology 1246, 1247 (2005) (species with tens of individuals "are unlikely to encounter inbreeding depression"; species with hundreds of individuals "are unlikely to experience decimating genetic drift or demographic stochasticity"; and species with thousands of individuals "are unlikely to succumb to environmental catastrophe"). *See generally* J. Michael Scott et al., *Representation of Natural Vegetation in Protected Areas: Capturing the Geographic Range*, 10 Biodiversity & Conservation 1297 (2001).
155. Laura L. Anthony & Daniel T. Blumstein, *Integrating Behaviour into Wildlife Conservation: The Multiple Ways that Behaviour Can Reduce Ne*, 95 Biological Conservation 303 (2000); Timothy H. Tear & Ernest D. Ables, *Social System Development and Variability in a Reintroduced Arabian Oryx Population*, 89 Biological Conservation 199 (2000) (social structure dependent at least in part on population density).
156. Historical baselines can provide valuable information both on numbers of individuals and on processes. Peter B. Landres et al., *Overview of the Use of Natural Variability Concepts in Managing Ecological Systems*, 9 Ecological Applications 1179 (1999); Mark V. Lomolino, *Space, Time, and Conservation Biogeography*, in The Endangered Species Act at Thirty: Conserving Biodiversity in Human-Dominated Landscapes 61 (J. Michael Scott et al. eds. 2006). The information can be particularly important given the dramatic collapse of many populations. *See, e.g.,* Jeremy B. C. Jackson, *What Was Natural in the Coastal Oceans?*, 98 Proc. Nat'l Acad. Scis. 5411 (2001).
157. One review of the goals established by recovery plans for species listed under the ESA determined that 28 percent of the plans had goals set below the existing population at the time the plan was written. Tear et al., *supra* note 34, at 376.
158. "The purposes of this Act are to provide a means whereby the ecosystems upon which endangered species and threatened species depend may be conserved [and] to provide a program for the conservation of such endangered species and threatened species." 16 U.S.C. § 1531(b). *Cf.* S. Rep. No. 97-14, at 14 (1982) ("Biologically, it makes sense to treat all taxonomic groups equally or even to place some special emphasis on protecting plants and invertebrates since they form the bases of ecosystems and food chains upon which all other life depends. The Act's stated purpose is to conserve ecosystems.").
159. Michael E. Soule et al., *Ecological Effectiveness: Conservation Goals for Interactive Species*, 17 Conservation Biology 1238 (2003).

160. Establishment of a Nonessential Experimental Population of Gray Wolves in Yellowstone National Park in Wyoming, Idaho, and Montana, 59 Fed. Reg. 60,252 (1994); Establishment of a Nonessential Experimental Population of Gray Wolves in Central Idaho and Southwestern Montana, 59 Fed. Reg. 60,266 (1994). *See generally* Goble, *supra* note 5.
161. For ecologists the reintroduction was an experiment that could provide evidence on the basic nature of terrestrial ecosystems: Are they structured from the top-down or the bottom-up? Is the primary driver of the ecosystem its predators (i.e., top down) or resources (i.e., bottom up)? That is, do predators (the secondary consumers, which are the top trophic level of food webs) influence not only populations of prey species but also lower trophic levels such as primary producers (i.e., would the reintroduction of wolves affect aspen, cottonwoods, and willows)? The bottom-up thesis, on the other hand, focuses on how resources (most notably energy) influence organisms in higher trophic levels. A "trophic cascade"—changes in the ecosystem a level below the trophic level directly affected by the predator—is evidence for the top-down thesis. *See generally* James A. Estes, *Predators and Ecosystem Management*, 24 WILDLIFE SOC'Y BULL. 390 (1996); Mark D. Hunter & Peter W. Price, *Playing Chutes and Ladders: Heterogeneity and the Relative Roles of Bottom-Up and Top-Down Forces in Natural Communities*, 73 ECOLOGY 724 (1992); Mary E. Power, *Top-Down and Bottom-Up Forces in Food Webs: Do Plants Have Primacy?*, 73 ECOLOGY 733 (1992); Robert T. Paine, *Food Web Complexity and Species Diversity*, 100 AM. NATURALIST 65 (1966). The opportunity to investigate such a fundamental question produced intense interest and extensive investigation of variables such as the numbers of aspen and coyotes.
162. Douglas W. Smith et al., *Yellowstone After Wolves*, 53 BIOSCIENCE 330, 335 (2003) (92 percent of all wolf kills).
163. Joel Berger et al., *Recolonizing Carnivores and Naive Prey: Conservation Lessons from Pleistocene Extinctions*, 291 SCIENCE 1036 (2001).
164. *See, e.g.,* Daniel Fortin et al., *Wolves Influence Elk Movements: Behavior Shapes a Trophic Cascade in Yellowstone National Park*, 86 ECOLOGY 1320–30 (2005); John W. Laundre et al., *Wolves, Elk, and Bison: Reestablishing the "Landscape of Fear" in Yellowstone National Park, U.S.A.*, 79 CANADIAN J. ZOOLOGY 1401 (2001); William J. Ripple & Robert L. Beschta, *Wolves and the Ecology of Fear: Can Predation Risk Structure Ecosystems?*, 54 BIOSCIENCE 755 (2004); Clifford A. White et al., *Predation Risk and the Functional Response of Elk-Aspen Herbivory*, 181 FOREST ECOLOGY & MGMT. 77–97 (2003).
165. *See, e.g.,* Robert L. Beschta, *Cottonwoods, Elk, and Wolves in the Lamar Valley of Yellowstone National Park*, 13 ECOLOGICAL APPLICATIONS 1295 (2003); William J. Ripple et al., *Trophic Cascades among Wolves, Elk, and Aspen on Yellowstone National Park's Northern Range*, 102 BIOLOGICAL CONSERVATION 227 (2001); William J. Ripple & Robert L. Beschta, *Wolf Reintroduction, Predation Risk, and Cottonwood Recovery in Yellowstone National Park*, 184 FOREST ECOLOGY & MGMT. 299 (2003); William J. Ripple & Robert L. Beschta, *Restoring Yellowstone's Aspen with Wolves*, 138 BIOLOGICAL CONSERVATION 514 (2007).
166. Joel Berger et al., *A Mammalian Predator-Prey Imbalance: Grizzly Bear and Wolf Extinction Affect Avian Neotropical Migrants*, 11 ECOLOGICAL APPLICATIONS 947 (2001); Smith et al., *supra* note 162, at 33–38; Christopher C. Wilmers et al., *Trophic Facilitation by Introduced Top Predators: Grey Wolf Subsidies to Scavengers in Yellowstone National Park*, 72 J. ANIMAL ECOLOGY 909 (2003).
167. Robert L. Beschta & W. J. Ripple, *River Channel Dynamics Following Extirpation of Wolves in Northwestern Yellowstone National Park, USA*, 31 EARTH SURFACE PROCESSES & LANDFORMS 1525–39 (2006).
168. Robert L. Crabtree & Jennifer W. Sheldon, *The Ecological Role of Coyotes on Yellowstone's Northern Range*, 7(2) YELLOWSTONE SCI. 15, 22–23 (1999); Smith et al., *supra* note 162, at 335–36.
169. Smith et al., *supra* note 162, at 335.

179. *Id.* at 336; Daniel Stahler et al., *Common Ravens*, Corvus corax, *Preferentially Associate with Grey Wolves*, Canis lupus, *as a Foraging Strategy in Winter*, 64 ANIMAL BEHAVIOR 283–90 (2002); Wilmers et al., *supra* note 166.
171. Christopher C. Wilmers & Wayne M. Getz, *Gray Wolves as Climate Change Buffers in Yellowstone*, 3(4) PLoS BIOLOGY e92 at 0571, *available at* http://plosbiology.org. *Cf.* Eric Post & Christian Pederson, *Opposing Plant Community Responses to Warming with and without Herbivores*, 105 PROC. NATL. ACAD. SCIS. 12,353 (2008) (herbivores mitigated the impact of warming on plant species).
172. Examples can be readily multiplied. The anadromous salmonids of the Pacific Northwest, for example, were ecologically crucial in ways that are only becoming apparent. For example, salmon carcasses were a major source of primary nutrients such as nitrogen and carbon in spawning streams. *See, e.g.*, Robert E. Bilby et al., *Incorporation of Nitrogen and Carbon from Spawning Coho Salmon into the Trophic System of Small Streams: Evidence from Isotopes*, 53 CANADIAN J. FISHERIES & AQUATIC SCIS. 164 (1996); C. Jeff Cederholm et al., *Pacific Salmon Carcasses: Essential Contributions of Nutrients and Energy for Aquatic and Terrestrial Ecosystems*, 24 FISHERIES 6 (Oct. 1999); Scott M. Gende et al., *Pacific Salmon in Aquatic and Terrestrial Ecosystems*, 52 BIOSCIENCE 917 (2002); Thomas C. Kline, Jr., et al., *Recycling of Elements Transported Upstream by Runs of Pacific Salmon: N. and C. Evidence in Sashin Creek, Southeastern Alaska*, 47 CANADIAN J. FISHERIES & AQUATIC SCIS. 136 (1990); Mary F. Willson & Karl C. Halupka, *Anadromous Fish as Keystone Species in Vertebrate Communities*, 9 CONSERVATION BIOLOGY 489 (1995). Salmon were also important prey species. Even in the upper watersheds of the Columbia basin, up to 90 percent of a grizzly bear's diet was salmon, and the salmon-eating bears, doing what bears do in the woods, fertilized the forest with some 400 pounds of nitrogen and phosphorus each year. As a result, salmon accounted for approximately 20 percent of the metabolism of an average tree. Dale D. Goble, *Salmon in the Columbia: From Abundance to Extinction, in* NORTHWEST LANDS AND PEOPLES: READINGS IN ENVIRONMENTAL HISTORY 229, 234 (Dale D. Goble & Paul W. Hirt eds., 1999) (reporting preliminary results of a study by Charlie Robbins, a Washington State University biologist). The ecological impacts of recovering salmon only to minimally viable populations are likely to become increasingly apparent over time. A review of the recovery objectives for the species suggest that ecologically viable recovery targets would be at an order of magnitude greater than the current recovery objectives. Christopher A. Peery et al., *Pacific Salmon: Setting Ecologically Defensible Recovery Goals*, 53 BIOSCIENCE 622 (2003). Similarly, recent genetic studies of gray whales in the eastern Pacific concluded that pre-whaling, long-term average populations were between 78,500 and 117,700 individuals, a number three to five times the current population estimate of the now delisted-as-recovered species. S. Elizabeth Alter et al., *DNA Evidence for Historic Population Size and Past Ecosystem Impacts of Gray Whales*, 104 PROC. NAT'L ACAD. SCIS. 15,162, 15,165 (2007). Given the species' ecological role as a bottom feeder, the report's authors suggest that the reduced number of whales had altered nutrient recycling and benthic community structures, reduced the numbers of seabird species that feed on benthic crustaceans brought to the surface by feeding whales, and negatively affected populations of predators (such as orcas) and scavengers (such as California condors). *Id.* at 15,166. *See generally* A. M. Springer et al., *Sequential Megafaunal Collapse in the North Pacific Ocean: An Ongoing Legacy of Industrial Whaling?*, 100 PROC. NAT'L ACAD. SCIS. 12,223 (2003).
173. Phillips, *supra* note 144.
174. Although the available data indicates that elk harvests within the state have remained stable for the past five years, the overall data on the impact of wolves in elk herds is unclear. *See, e.g.*, Robert A. Garrott et al., *Generalizing Wolf Effects Across the Greater Yellowstone Area: A Cautionary Note*, 33 WILDLIFE SOC'Y BULL. 1245 (2005).
175. Nat'l Wildlife Fed'n v. Nat'l Marine Fisheries Serv., 524 F.3d 917, 931–33 (9th Cir. 2008); Gifford Pinchot Task Force v. U.S. Fish & Wildlife Serv., 378 F.3d 1059, 1069–70 (9th Cir. 2004).

176. 16 U.S.C. § 1539(2)(B)(iv).
177. Strahan v. Coxe, 127 F.3d 155, 158–59 (1st Cir. 1997).
178. Nat'l Ass'n of Homebuilders v. Babbitt, 130 F.3d 1041, 1044 (D.C. Cir. 1997).
179. Carlton v. Babbitt, 26 F. Supp. 2d 102, 105 (D.D.C. 1998).
180. Loggerhead Turtle v. County Council of Volusia County, Fla., 92 F. Supp. 2d 1296, 1304 (M.D. Fla. 2000).
181. Ctr. for Biological Diversity v. Bureau of Land Mgmt., 422 F. Supp. 2d 1115, 1125 (N.D. Cal. 2006).
182. 471 F. Supp. 985 (D. Haw. 1979), *aff'd*, 639 F.2d 495 (9th Cir. 1981).
183. 471 F. Supp. at 989 n.7.
184. *Id.*
185. Fund for Animals v. Rice, 85 F.3d 535, 538, 547 (11th Cir. 1996).
186. *Id.* at 547.
187. *Id.*
188. *Id.* at 547–48. A similar result was reached in Cabinet Res. Group v. U.S. Forest Serv. involving a BiOp issued on a road through grizzly bear habitat. 2004 WL 966086 (D. Mont. Mar. 30, 2004). The court rejected plaintiff's argument that "the project impermissibly conflicts with the grizzly bear recovery plan," concluding that it had failed to establish "that the agencies . . . are obligated to do anything more than take into consideration the grizzly bear recovery plan" in issuing the BiOp. *Id.* at *8. *See also* Ctr. for Biological Diversity v. U.S. Fish & Wildlife Serv., 202 F. Supp. 2d 594, 632 (W.D. Tex. 2002) (rejecting claim that incidental take permit issued pursuant to habitat conservation plan that did not meet the standards of a recovery plan was invalid because the FWS HCP Handbook had concluded that the Act "does not explicitly *require* an HCP to recover listed species, or contribute to their recovery objectives").
189. 470 F. Supp. 2d 1118 (S.D. Cal. 2006).
190. *Id.* at 1136.
191. *Id.* at 1136–37. In a footnote to this statement, the court amplified its decision: "FWS has discretion, using its expertise, to decide the content of the recovery plan; however, the ESA clearly requires FWS to follow through with the measures identified in recovery plans." *Id.* at 1137 n.16. Other courts have relied upon recovery plans in challenges to a decision not to prepare an environmental impact statement, Middle Rio Grande Conservancy Dist. v. Norton, 294 F.3d 1220 (10th Cir. 2002), the need to initiate consultation, Bensman v. U.S. Forest Serv., 984 F. Supp. 1242 (W.D. Mo. 1997), and the conclusion of a BiOp, Rio Grande Silvery Minnow v. Keys, 469 F. Supp. 2d 973 (D.N.M. 2002), Heartwood v. U.S. Forest Serv., 380 F.3d 428 (8th Cir. 2004), and Ctr. for Biological Diversity v. Bureau of Land Mgmt., 422 F. Supp. 2d 1115, 1125 (N.D. Cal. 2006).
192. 26 F. Supp. 2d 102, 105–06 (D.D.C. 1998). This was the second appeal. The court had previously remanded the decision to the agency to explain several decisions. The FWS issued supplemental findings and plaintiff again appealed the agency's decision not to reclassify the species.
193. *Id.* at 110.
194. *Id. See also* Biodiversity Legal Found. v. Norton, 285 F. Supp. 2d 1, 14 (D.D.C. 2003) (FWS's assessment of the species' "dire" status and the specificity of its discussion of the problems with (and solutions to) the species' critical habitat in a multi-species recovery plan led the court to conclude that the document was "a manifestation of FWS's intention finally to revise the critical habitat designation" so that its subsequent failure to act was unreasonable).
195. Defenders of Wildlife v. Hall, 565 F. Supp. 2d 1160 (D. Mont. 2008).
196. *See* 71 Fed. Reg. at 6635; 565 F. Supp. 2d at 1168–72.
197. 565 F. Supp. 2d at 1170.

5

Interagency Consultation Under Section 7

Patrick W. Ryan and Erika E. Malmen

Introduction

The Endangered Species Act of 1973 (ESA) section 7[1] and its implementing regulations[2] impose requirements on federal agencies for the protection of listed species[3] as well as species proposed for listing.[4] The requirements of section 7 are both substantive and procedural with inherent potential to affect a wide range of public and private activities. Section 7 is frequently litigated—attributable in part to section 7's status as a powerful land management regulatory tool in a climate of competing land-use interests, confusion surrounding section 7's implementing regulations, and seemingly inconsistent judicial interpretations of federal agency action subject to section 7 compliance.

The majority of compliance litigation revolves around the section 7(a)(2) duty to avoid jeopardy and adverse habitat modification, and thus section 7(a)(2) is the primary focus of this chapter.

Current State of the Law

Federal Agency Compliance with Section 7(a)(1) Duty to Conserve

Section 7(a)(1)[5] should not be overlooked. Courts have held that *all* federal agencies must carry out programs for the conservation of threatened and endangered species,[6] not just the Service.[7] "Conservation" has been defined to mean "to use and the use of all methods and procedures which are necessary to bring any endangered species or threatened species to the point at which the measures provided pursuant to [the Act] are no longer necessary."[8]

However, section 7(a)(1) does not confer any additional statutory authority upon an agency beyond those authorities articulated in any enabling legislation.[9] The methods and procedures used by the agency to comply with section 7(a)(1) must be within the bounds of an agency's statutory authority. Further, courts have afforded federal agencies wide latitude in determining how to best fulfill their duties under section 7(a)(1).[10] Section 7(a)(1) programs may come up in a variety of contexts, including hydropower licensing, ESA conservation agreements between the government and private actors, and in the National Environmental Policy Act (NEPA) process.

Case law involving section 7(a)(1) is not well developed. There appears, for example, to be disagreement among the courts over the issue of whether conservation programs must be carried out for each and every listed species.[11] Agency compliance with section 7(a)(1) is reviewed under the "arbitrary and capricious" standard of the Administrative Procedure Act.[12] A cause of action against the government for failure to comply with section 7(a)(1) may be brought pursuant to the citizen suit provision[13] of the ESA as well.[14]

Federal Agency Compliance with Section 7(a)(2) Duty to Consult

Federal agencies are required under section 7(a)(2) to "insure that any action authorized, funded, or carried out by such agency . . . is not likely to jeopardize the continued existence of any endangered species or threatened species or result in the destruction or adverse modification of habitat of such species which is determined by the Secretary . . . to be critical."[15]

The first inquiry in any section 7(a)(2) analysis concerns whether section 7(a)(2) applies at all.[16] In order for section 7(a)(2) to apply, there must be *discretionary federal agency action*.[17] Federal agency "action" is defined by regulation[18] and broadly construed by the courts to include any action in which there is some federal discretionary involvement or control.[19] Often, discretionary federal agency action is found in the context of reviewing an application for a federal license or permit.

For section 7 to apply, an agency's action must be "affirmative"; an agency that is merely providing advice[20] or declining to act in a certain way[21] is generally not engaging in agency action subject to section 7. Additionally, agency action must also be within the decision-making authority of an agency and unconstrained by any earlier agency commitments for the consultation requirements of section 7 to apply.[22]

Whenever a nonfederal entity seeks a license or permit to proceed with a project or activity, compliance with section 7(a)(2) is almost always implicated. For example, when an applicant applies for a dredge and fill permit under Clean Water Act section 404,[23] the U.S. Army Corps of Engineers must notify the Service of such application if there are listed or proposed listed species in the "action area."[24] Another example would be when a utility seeks Federal Energy Regulatory Commission licensing for a hydroelectric facility. Consultation can also be required for mining activity on national forests subject to the Federal Land Policy and Management Act[25] and for federally financed state highway projects authorized by the Federal-Aid Highway Act.[26]

Determining where there is "action" subject to section 7(a)(2) is not as easy as it may seem. One particular area of difficulty arises when a species is listed in the middle of an ongoing, long-term project. The Ninth Circuit, for example, has held that the continued operation of a hydroelectric project during the last few years of a 30-year license was not "final agency action," subject to the consultation requirement of section 7(a)(2),[27] yet a land resource management plan administered by the U.S. Forest Service (USFS) was held to be "ongoing agency action" subject to section 7.[28]

Consultation may be formal and/or informal as will be discussed later in this chapter. At the end of the formal[29] consultation process, the Service must provide the agency with a written Biological Opinion (BiOp) explaining how the proposed action will affect the species and/or its critical habitat.

Preparing for the Possibility of Formal Consultation

Biological Assessments

A federal action agency[30] may begin its process of complying with its duties under section 7(a)(2) by developing a biological assessment (BA) for its proposed action.[31] The federal action agency commences the BA process by requesting information from the Service regarding any proposed or listed species or proposed or designated critical habitat that may be in or near the action area. The consulting Service has 30 days to provide this information to the action agency.[32] If no proposed or listed species and no proposed or designated critical habitat are within the action area, the section 7 consultation process is generally concluded.

Under ESA section 7(d),[33] once consultation is initiated, neither federal agencies nor permit applicants may make any "irreversible or irretrievable commitment of resources with respect to the agency action which has the effect of foreclosing the formulation or implementation of any reasonable and prudent alternative measures which would not violate subsection (a)(2) of this section." The intent of section 7(d) is essentially to "prevent incidents such as the more than $50 million loss at Tellico Dam as a result of *TVA v. Hill*."[34] The limitations imposed by section 7(d) remain in force during the consultation process and continue until the requirements of section 7(a)(2) are satisfied. If reinitiation of consultation occurs, the prohibition on further commitment of irreversible or irretrievable resources resumes and may block any further agency action until consultation is complete.[35]

If the Service determines that listed species or designated critical habitat may be present, the federal action agency generally must complete a BA within 180 calendar days of receipt of a species list from the Service. The BA is often prepared by a private consultant with input from the action agency and the consulting Service.[36] The accuracy of the species list will require verification if it is more than 90 days old and preparation of the BA has yet to begin.[37] The purpose of the BA is to evaluate the potential effects of the action on the species and critical habitat and determine whether those effects are likely to be adverse.[38] The regulations do not provide for specific contents of a BA but provide that BAs may include the results of on-site inspections, the views of relevant experts, a literature review, and an analysis of the potential effects of the action on listed species or critical habitat.[39]

If the BA finds that the proposed federal action will "not affect," or "is not likely to adversely affect" (NLAA) any listed species or designated critical habitat and the consulting Service concurs in writing with the NLAA finding, the section 7 consultation process is concluded. The consulting Service has 30 days from receipt of a completed BA to issue its concurrence with the NLAA finding. The Service may, however, include modifications to the proposed action that must be implemented by the federal action agency to attain the Service's written concurrence.

There are three possible outcomes of a BA for any proposed agency action:

1. *No effect.* The action agency informs the consulting Service that its proposed action will not affect a listed (or proposed) species or its designated (or proposed) critical habitat.
2. *Is not likely to adversely affect.* Any effects on the listed (or proposed) species or critical habitat will be "discountable, insignificant, or completely beneficial."[40]
3. *Is likely to adversely affect.* The proposed action, or actions interrelated or interdependent with the proposed action, may directly or indirectly result in an adverse effect to a listed species, and the effect is not discountable, insignificant, or beneficial.[41]

If listed species or critical habitat is not present and the activity is not a "major construction activity,"[42] the federal action agency is not required to prepare a BA before deciding whether the proposed action is likely to adversely affect a listed species or its critical habitat. A letter of concurrence from the consulting Service to the federal action agency ends the consultation process. The action agency has the option, however, to informally discuss the project with the consulting Service to assure the accuracy of its determination. During the course of these discussions, the consulting Service may recommend measures that, if implemented, would diminish or avoid adverse impacts to listed species or their critical habitats. If the action agency finds that its proposed action will "not affect" or "is not likely to adversely affect" any listed species or designated critical habitat, and the consulting Service concurs, the section 7 consultation process is concluded.

If the consulting Service does not concur with the BA's findings, the action agency and consulting Service may also informally discuss the project and BA to resolve any conflict. The Service and action agency may agree on additional information or modifications to the proposed action that will result in the Service's concurrence that the action "is not likely to adversely affect" any listed species or designated critical habitat. The BA may also conclude that the proposed action, even with any suggested modifications, "is likely to adversely affect" a listed species or designated critical habitat. If the BA reaches this finding and the underlying issues are not resolved, formal consultation is required.

Informal Consultation

Most consultations are conducted informally between the consulting Service and the federal agency or a "designated nonfederal representative" (such as a private or state applicant, or their consultant).[43] Unlike formal consultation, the informal consultation is an *optional process* created entirely by regulation.[44] Further, this process does not have a clear timetable for conducting the informal consultation and rests solely on the Service's discretion to determine under what circumstances formal consultation is required. The informal consultation process is described by regulation as "an optional process that includes all discussions, correspondence, etc. between the Service and the Federal agency or designated nonfederal representative, designed to assist the Federal agency in determining whether formal consultation or a conference is required."[45] Informal consultations therefore include phone contacts, meetings, discussions, project modifications, and any concurrence that occur prior to the initiation of formal consultation or the Service's concurrence, if any, that formal consultation (or conferencing) is not required. Participants in this process may include the federal action agency or a designated nonfederal representative, the applicants or permittee, and consultants working for any of the first three.

The informal consultation process is generally initiated by a telephone call or letter from the federal action agency to the applicable Service inquiring whether any proposed or listed species or critical habitat may occur within an action area. If it is determined through the initial inquiry that proposed or listed species or critical habitat does not occur within the action area, the section 7 consultation process is concluded. If only proposed species or proposed critical habitat is present, then only a conference is required. If any listed species or designated critical habitat is present, then the federal action agency or designated nonfederal representative generally has the option of evaluating the effects informally with the consulting Service or preparing a BA. As noted above, however, a BA is required if listed species or designated critical habitat occur within an action area and the project is a "major construction activity."

Proper documentation of the informal consultation process is essential to applicants and agencies. The administrative files should contain records of phone contacts, the purpose of the call as it relates to the proposed action or area, and any biological or technical advice or recommendations given by the Service. Meetings should be well documented and can be summarized to help facilitate the completion of the process.

If potential adverse effects are discovered during the informal consultation, however, the consulting Service may recommend modifications to the proposed action to diminish or avoid those effects. If agreed to by the federal action agency, the modifications will be incorporated as a condition in the consulting Service's letter of concurrence, if any, that the proposed action is not likely to adversely affect a listed species or its designated critical habitat. If the underlying issues are not informally resolved, a determination of "is likely to adversely affect" will require formal consultation.

Section 7(a)(4) Conferencing as Informal Consultation

Section 7(a)(4)[46] of the ESA requires federal agencies to "confer" with the Service on any proposed federal action that is likely to jeopardize a species *proposed for listing* or adversely modify any *proposed critical habitat*. Although similar to section 7(a)(2) consultations, there are significant substantive and procedural differences for "conferences." Most notably, the conference results in *nonbinding* recommendations for federal agencies to avoid jeopardy or adverse impacts to proposed species and their habitats.

Under the conference process, an action agency may initiate informal discussions with the Service concerning a proposed action that may affect a proposed species or its habitat.[47] The purpose of the informal discussion is to ascertain whether the proposed action is likely to result in jeopardy of a proposed species or adversely modify proposed critical habitat. If the Service finds that the proposed action is not likely to result in jeopardy or adverse modification, the Service will issue a "conference report" (similar to a letter of concurrence in consultations) completing the conferencing process. During informal discussions, the Service may make advisory recommendations to the federal agency on ways to minimize or avoid adverse effects.[48] If the species is subsequently listed, the federal agency will review the action to determine if formal consultation is required.

If the proposed action would likely result in jeopardy of a proposed species or adverse modification of proposed critical habitat, or if otherwise requested by the federal agency and deemed appropriate by the Service, the federal agency may enter into a formal conference.[49] If a formal conference is commenced, the Service will develop and issue a written conference opinion according to the same procedures as those required for the BiOps prepared during formal consultation. The conference opinion may subsequently be adopted as a final BiOp after the species is listed or the critical habitat is designated if no significant new information has developed concerning the species or habit and the federal action has not significantly changed. Further, any incidental take statement (ITS) contained within the opinion becomes effective once the species is listed and the conference opinion is adopted as a final BiOp.[50]

Early Consultation

When an applicant for a federal permit or license believes that the underlying activity may affect a listed species or its designated habitat, section 7(a)(3)[51] and its implementing regulations[52] provide a means for an applicant-driven approach to section 7 consultations. Early consultation is an *optional process* for applicants for a federal permit or license who believe that the underlying actions may affect a listed species or designated critical habitat. Early consultation occurs before the prospective applicant files the application for the federal permit or license.

The prospective applicant begins the process by requesting the permitting federal agency to initiate early consultation with the applicable Service. The applicant must also certify in writing to the agency that (1) it has a definite proposal outlining the action and its effects; and (2) it intends, if authorized, to implement the proposal. If the underlying action is a "major construction activity," the action agency will also require a BA before starting early consultation.[53] Once this information is received by the federal action agency, the section 7 regulations[54] require the action agency to initiate early consultation with the applicable Service. This request contains the same information required for formal consultation.

Federal action agencies conducting an early consultation are obligated to follow the same procedures and time frames as are required for formal consultations.[55] As a result, the consulting Service issues a preliminary BiOp within 135 days (unless extended) after initiation of early consultation.[56] A preliminary BiOp prepared for early consultation has the same format and contents as a final BiOp prepared for formal consultation. The significant difference between a preliminary BiOp and a final BiOp is that the ITS in a preliminary BiOp will not be effective until the BiOp is adopted by the consulting Service as final.

Once the prospective applicant formally applies for the permit or license from the federal action agency, but prior to the issuance of the permit or license, the action agency can request confirmation of a preliminary BiOp as a final BiOp.[57] If there are no significant changes in the proposed action or information used in the early consultation, the consulting Service will within 45 days confirm or deny in writing the action agency's request to adopt the preliminary opinion as final.[58] If the Service confirms the preliminary opinion as final, the action agency's section 7 obligations are satisfied. Further, the ITS contained in the adopted opinion will be effective for the listed species and activities covered by the statement. If the consulting Service denies the action agency's request, formal consultation is required. In practice, however, the consulting Service, action agency, and applicant will attempt to avoid this result by identifying and resolving any underlying adverse issues during the early consultation period.

Formal Consultation

Once the BA has been completed and submitted, a federal action agency may initiate formal consultation by submitting a written request, called an "initiation package," to the Service.[59] There is no specific timetable for when an action agency must initiate consultation. However, an agency must review its actions "at the earliest possible time" to determine any effect upon listed species or designated habitat.[60] Once initiated, formal consultation must be concluded within 90 calendar days unless an alternative agreement is reached by the action agency and the Secretary of the Interior.[61] After formal consultation is completed, the Service has 45 days in which to issue a BiOp, including any ITS.[62]

The clock does not begin to run on the formal consultation process until the Service receives a complete consultation package. Pursuant to regulation[63] a written request must contain:

1. A description of the action to be considered;
2. A description of the specific area that may be affected by the action;
3. A description of any listed species or critical habitat that may be affected by the action;
4. A description of the manner in which the action may affect any listed species or critical habitat and an analysis of any cumulative effects;
5. Relevant reports, including any environmental impact statement, environmental assessment, or biological assessment prepared; and
6. Any other relevant available information on the action or on the affected listed species or critical habitat.

Within 30 days, the Service will notify the action agency to acknowledge the receipt of the consultation package, and to specify whether there were any deficiencies or gaps in the required data.[64] In the latter case, the action agency must either supply the missing data or inform the service of its nonexistence before formal consultation can officially commence.[65]

Biological Opinion

The BiOp is the documented summary of formal consultation and contains the Service's conclusions as to the effects of the federal agency action at issue. If requested, the Service and/or cooperating agencies in the consultation will issue a draft BiOp in order for the applicant and other interested parties to comment on information and conclusions contained therein. It is not uncommon to note differences between a draft and a final BiOp. Comments received by the Service often enable the Service to fill in information gaps or otherwise improve the draft BiOp. Formal consultation is complete once a final BiOp is rendered. A BiOp determines whether agency action may violate section 7 by jeopardizing the continued existence of a listed species or result in the destruction or adverse modification of designated critical habitat.[66] If the BiOp concludes that a proposed agency action will result in "jeopardy" and/or "adverse modification" then the Service may recommend reasonable and prudent alternatives that an action agency may take to ensure compliance with section 7. In addition to considering the direct effects of a proposed agency action, the Service must also consider the species' "environmental baseline," the "effect of actions," and the "cumulative effects upon a species."[67]

Environmental Baseline

The environmental baseline is the description in the BiOp of the current "state of the environment" within the action area and is the starting point or basis for any effects analysis. The environmental baseline is essentially a composite sketch of the human and natural factors that presently impact a species within an action area. An environmental baseline must include (1) the past and present impact on the species of all federal, state, or private actions; (2) the anticipated impacts of all federal projects in the action area that have already undergone section 7 consultation; and (3) the impact of state or private actions that are contemporaneous with the consultation in process.[68]

Agency actions that have been proposed, but not implemented, are not added to the environmental baseline.[69] Additionally, federal actions where section 7 consultation has been reinitiated or where all of the adverse effects of the project have been removed through the implementation of alternatives do not need to be added to the baseline.[70] In some instances it is not clear exactly what should be included in the environmental baseline and what should not. Recently, the Ninth Circuit upheld a challenge to a BiOp issued by the National Marine Fisheries Service (NMFS)[71] regarding hydroelectric dams in Washington, Oregon, and Idaho. The court found that the NMFS had committed a "substantial procedural violation" by including 14 existing dams and a hypothetical procedure for operating them (intended to mitigate the impact of the dams upon the fish) to the environmental baseline. The court held that by placing the existence of the dams in the "baseline" instead of assessing them as part of the "proposed action," the agencies had consulted on only part of their "action" in violation of the ESA's consultation requirement.[72]

Effects of Actions

The "effects of actions," which are added to the environmental baseline, "refers to the direct and indirect effects of an action on the species or critical habitat, together with the effects of other activities that are interrelated or interdependent with that action."[73] Direct effects, as the phrase implies, are those effects that immediately result from an agency action. Indirect effects are those which emerge "later in time" but are "reasonably certain to occur."[74]

An example of a direct effect would be a species' loss of physical space resulting from a road being constructed through its habitat. An example of an indirect effect would be the future impact upon wetland birds of increased consumption of water made possible by building a dam.[75]

Interrelated actions are "those that are part of a larger action and depend on the larger action for their justification."[76] Interdependent actions "are those that have no independent utility apart from the action under consideration."[77] The Joint U.S. Fish and Wildlife Service (FWS)/NMFS *Endangered Species Consultation Handbook* suggests using a "but for" test to determine whether an action is interdependent or interrelated.[78] For example, the construction of a spill basin to control runoff from a mine would be an interrelated action, because "but for" the larger mine operation, the spill basin would have little justification. Likewise, the construction of a temporary road to remove timber from a forest may be an interdependent action, because "but for" the timber extraction the road may not have utility.

Cumulative Effects

In its initiation package, an action agency must submit an analysis of any "cumulative effects" that may result from the proposed action.[79] The Service is then required to take cumulative effects into account when formulating the BiOp.[80] Cumulative effects are defined as "those effects of future State or private activities not involving federal activities that are reasonably certain to occur within the action area of the Federal action subject to consultation."[81] Thus, cumulative effects describe only *nonfederal* and *future* activities. Past and present impacts of nonfederal activity should be a part of the environmental baseline. Courts may invalidate a BiOp if the "cumulative effects" on a species are not adequately addressed.[82]

What Is Jeopardy?

After considering the environmental baseline, the effects of the proposed action, and any cumulative effects of the proposed action, the Service issues a written BiOp. There are three potential conclusions of a BiOp: (1) a jeopardy determination; (2) a no-jeopardy determination; or (3) a determination that, with "reasonable and prudent alternatives," the action will result in no jeopardy.[83]

The standard for establishing jeopardy is whether an action can reasonably be expected to appreciably reduce "the likelihood of both the survival and recovery of a listed species in the wild."[84] Thus, in determining jeopardy, a service must assess whether, given the many factors affecting the species, the proposed federal action is likely to inhibit the species ability to survive and recover. The Ninth Circuit has recently explained that pursuant to federal regulation,[85] the agencies must consider the impacts of the proposed action on both the survival *and* recovery of the listed species.[86] Thus, even if an agency's action will not result in extinction, that action may still be forbidden by the ESA if it diminishes a species's ability to recover.

If the BiOp concludes in a "no jeopardy" determination, the consultation process is at an end; the project may go forward under the terms of the BiOp, including any ITS.[87] The ITS specifies the impact the agency's action will have on the species, as well as outlining the reasonable and prudent alternatives and the conditions for complying with those alternatives.[88] If the BiOp results in a jeopardy finding, the consulting Service recommends "reasonable and prudent alternatives" to the proposed action that the Service believes will prevent a potential section 7(a)(2) violation.[89]

Even if a proposed action is not likely to jeopardize a listed species, the Service may conclude that the proposed action will nonetheless result in the adverse modification or destruction of critical habitat. Adverse modification or destruction of critical habitat is defined as "a direct or indirect alteration that appreciably diminishes the value of the critical habitat for both the survival and recovery of a listed species."[90] The critical habitat for listed species consists of those areas occupied by the species, at the time of listing, that contain physical or biological features essential to the conservation of the species or unoccupied areas so designated.[91] These "constituent elements" include:

1. Space for individual and population growth, and for normal behavior;
2. Food, water, air, light, and minerals or other nutritional or physiological requirements;
3. Cover or shelter;
4. Sites for breeding, reproduction, rearing of offspring, germination, or seed dispersal; and generally,
5. Habitats that are protected from disturbance or are representative of the historic geographical and ecological distributions of a species.[92]

If an action has some effect on critical habitat but does not decrease the value of the constituent elements for the survival or recovery of a listed species, a finding of adverse modification is unlikely.

Reasonable and Prudent Alternatives

As explained above, the consulting Service may determine that the federal action will jeopardize a listed species or adversely modify its designated critical habitat. In that event, the Service is required to provide the action agency with "reasonable and prudent alternatives" (RPAs) to the proposed action that if undertaken will avoid the likelihood of jeopardy or adverse habitat modification.[93] The action agency and applicant usually participate in the development of RPAs to ensure that alternatives are within their legal authority and jurisdiction, as well as economically and technologically feasible.[94] Under section 7, RPAs are defined as alternatives (1) that the Service believes will avoid the likelihood of jeopardy or adverse modification; (2) that can be implemented in a manner consistent with the intended purpose of the action; (3) that can be implemented in a manner consistent with the scope of the action agency's legal authority and jurisdiction; and (4) that are economically and technologically feasible.[95]

Although limited by the four factors enumerated above, RPAs can be a strong regulatory tool for limiting projects or actions that may otherwise adversely impact fish and wildlife. Moreover, the Service will often look to recovery plans[96] as the best available science in developing RPAs. Furthermore, the Service will often include "conservation recommendations" in the BiOp. Conservation recommendations are discretionary measures suggested to minimize or avoid adverse effects of a proposed action on listed species and their critical habitats, or to develop additional information. Even though the regulations clarify that conservation recommendations "are advisory and not intended to carry any binding legal force,"[97] the action agencies often adopt the recommendations in conjunction with the agency's conservation obligations under section 7(a)(1), as discussed earlier.

In some cases, no RPAs may be available to avoid jeopardy or adverse modification. Examples of circumstances in which RPAs might not be available include actions beyond the scope of consideration (such as locating a project uplands instead of in wetlands requiring a Corps permit); actions of a third party not involved in the proposed action; actions on lands or matters outside the jurisdiction or authority of the action agency; or actions where there is a lack of data on which to base an alternative. In the event the action agency cannot implement the RPA, the agency may (1) decide not to undertake the project; (2) request an exemption from the Endangered Species Committee,[98] or "God Squad" (discussed later in chapter); or (3) modify the action and reinitiate consultation.

In many cases, the Service may defer to the action agency and applicant in determining the feasibility of an RPA. However, the Service retains the final authority over which RPAs are included in the BiOp. Although courts have held that the failure of an action agency to follow the RPAs is not a per se violation of the ESA,[99] the action agency may be at risk of violating its duties under section 7(a)(1). In practice, therefore, federal action agencies will likely ensure implementation of the RPAs as part of the proposed action.

The Incidental Take Statement (ITS)

Federal actions with efforts on listed species or critical habitat that do not rise to the "jeopardy" standard may still result in, or cause, the incidental take of a listed species in violation of section 9. Congress resolved this dilemma by amending section 7 in 1982 to allow a consulting Service to issue BiOps with an ITS. To be covered by an ITS, any taking associated with an agency's proposed action must not be likely to result in jeopardy to a listed species or adverse modification of its designated critical habitat, must result from otherwise lawful activity, and must be incidental to the purpose of the action.[100] An ITS must specify the amount and extent of any incidental taking, provide "reasonable and prudent measures" (RPMs) to minimize the impacts of the taking, and set out "terms and conditions" that the action agency must follow in order to implement the RPMs.[101] The ITS operates to exempt the action agency and permittee from the ESA "take" prohibitions as long as the agency complies with the RPMs and the implementing terms and conditions.[102]

In preparing an ITS, the Service is responsible for documenting the amount or extent of take anticipated; writing RPMs and implementing terms and conditions that are clear, precise, and enforceable; and including reporting requirements that assure timely compliance with the terms and conditions contained in the ITS.[103] RPMs and the implementing terms and conditions should be developed in coordination with the action agency and applicant to ensure that the measures are reasonable, that they cause only minor changes to the proposed project, and that they are within the authority and jurisdiction of the agency or applicant to carry out.[104]

RPMs are those actions "necessary or appropriate to minimize the impacts, i.e., amount or extent, of incidental take."[105] As construed by the Service, RPMs can include only actions within the action area, involve only minor changes to the project, and minimize the level of take associated with the project to the extent reasonable and prudent.[106] RPMs may include training and education for reduction of predation, removal or avoidance of species or habitats, and monitoring. Measures are considered by the Service as reasonable and prudent when they are consistent with the proposed action's basic design, location, scope, duration, and timing.[107]

The "terms and conditions" set forth the specific methods by which the RPMs are implemented, such as who is to be educated, how, and when; how predation will be reduced; who may remove a species or how to avoid the species; or the protocols for monitoring.[108] Terms and conditions of an ITS typically include reporting and monitoring requirements that ensure action agency oversight of any incidental take.[109] Further, the monitoring must be sufficient to determine if the amount or extent[110] of take is approached or exceeded, and the reporting must ensure that the applicable Service will be notified in a timely manner if it does.

Incremental Consultation

Where authorized by statute, an agency may request incremental consultation for each step of a multiphase project. Under incremental consultation the Service will issue a BiOp on each phase or step of a project, as well as provide the agency with the Service's view of the project as a whole. Incremental consultation requires that an action agency satisfy five criteria before going forward with a project: (1) the incremental step must not violate the requirements of section 7(a)(2); (2) the action agency must consult with the Service regarding the entire project and obtain a BiOp for each of the project's stages; (3) the action agency may make no irreversible or irretrievable commitments of resources, pursuant to section 7(d) of the ESA; (4) the action agency must continue to obtain sufficient data upon which a final BiOp can be based; and (5) there must be a reasonable likelihood that the action as a whole will not violate section 7(a)(2).[111]

Some courts have been reluctant to allow action agencies to engage in incremental consultation. In the Ninth Circuit, the Service follows the more restrictive rule laid out in *Conner v. Burford*,[112] which holds that an action agency may not engage in incremental consultation unless a project itself is segmented via statute.[113] Apparently, incremental consultation may still be undertaken outside of the Ninth Circuit.[114]

Reinitiation of Consultation

As long as an agency retains discretionary involvement or control over an action, the possibility exists that consultation may be reinitiated. As a general rule, reinitiation is not appropriate where the project has been completed and the federal role in the project is no longer present. With regard to a permit or license, reinitiation is not available unless the permitting or licensing authority retained a sufficient level of discretionary jurisdiction over the action or unless otherwise authorized by law. Although determining what type of retained authority is necessary for reinitiating consultation is not always easy, some courts have held that consultation is not required unless the scope of agency's discretionary authority over an ongoing federal action may "inure to the benefit" of a listed species.[115] Further, reinitiation of consultation is generally predicated on an affirmative exercise of the federal agency's discretionary authority; the mere retention of a permitting enforcement authority over a project, for example, is generally insufficient to trigger reinitiation.[116]

Assuming there is a sufficient level of discretionary authority over a federal project, and the agency exercises that authority, section 7 regulations require that consultation be reinitiated in at least four scenarios: (1) if the actual take exceeds that which was authorized in the ITS; (2) if new information reveals that the effects on listed species or critical habitat is greater or of a different manner than previously considered; (3) if the action is modified such that it affects listed species or critical habitat in a way not considered in the BiOp; and (4) if a new species is listed or critical habitat designated and is affected by the action.[117] If a court finds reinitiation necessary, the action generally must cease and may not go forward until a new BiOp is issued.[118]

Emergency Consultation

An agency may engage in an emergency informal consultation when listed species or critical habitat are affected by acts of God, disasters, casualties, or national defense or security emergencies.[119] Federal agencies are required to provide the Service with information regarding the emergency and some justification for the expedited consultation. The agency must also disclose the potential impact an emergency may have on any listed species or critical habitat.[120]

As soon as the emergency situation is under control, the action agency must initiate formal consultation.[121] Courts have scrutinized agencies that invoke emergency consultations when addressing emergencies that are predictable or frequently occurring. For example, one district court held that, with regard to the use of fire retardant to fight forest fires, the reliance upon the emergency consultation process by the U.S. Forest Service (USFS) was misplaced. The court held that "the emergency exception is meant for unexpected exigencies" and the USFS's use of retardant during a fire season was "not unexpected but guaranteed; the only question is when and where it will be used."[122] The court ruled that the USFS must undertake formal consultation as to the impact of fire retardant spills on listed species and critical habitat.

The God Squad Exemption

The Endangered Species Committee, or the "God Squad," is empowered to exempt parties from the no-jeopardy requirement of section 7(a)(2). Composed of the Secretaries of Agriculture, the Army, and the Interior, the Chairman of the Council of Economic Advisers, the Administrators of EPA and the National Oceanic and Atmospheric Administration, and a presidential appointee from the affected state, the God Squad was added to the ESA following the famous snail-darter case of *Tennessee Valley Authority v. Hill*.[123] While "God squad exemptions" are a potential means of avoiding ESA regulations, they are rarely sought and even more infrequently granted.[124]

After consultation under section 7(a)(2) is completed, the federal action agency, the governor of a state in which an agency action will occur, or the permit or license applicant may apply for a God Squad Exemption.[125] The Secretary of Interior may initially reject an application if the Secretary determines that the applicant has not fulfilled its consultation responsibilities, has not considered RPAs, or has made an irreversible or irretrievable commitment of resources.[126] If the Secretary does not deny the application, an exemption may be granted if no fewer than five members of the committee determine that (1) there are no reasonable and prudent alternatives to the agency action; (2) the benefits of the action "clearly outweigh" those of alternatives; (3) the action is of regional or national significance; (4) no irreversible or irretrievable commitment of resources has taken place; and (5) appropriate mitigation efforts have been undertaken.[127] The God Squad's decisions are subject to review in the court of appeals in the circuit in which the action takes place.[128]

The Role of Indian Tribes

In addition to the consultation requirements of section 7, the Service must consult with qualifying tribes potentially impacted by ESA-related determinations. Under a joint order[129] issued by the Secretaries of Commerce and the Interior, the Service must consult with any federally recognized tribe whose lands, trust resources, or treaty rights may be impacted by any decision, determination, or activity implementing the ESA. In recent years, tribes have become increasingly protective of their trust resources and treaty rights (such as reserved water rights and hunting and fishing rights). As previously noted, resources not incorporated into the environmental baseline are potentially available for use or consumption by the proposed project to the extent allowable under the ESA and other applicable law. Therefore, tribes are particularly interested in the section 7 consultation process if environmental baselines are composed without incorporating tribal resources protected in trust or by treaty.

Emerging Issues and Future Directions

Discretionary versus Nondiscretionary Agency Action

The Supreme Court decision in *National Association of Home Builders v. Defenders of Wildlife*[130] has confirmed the notion that only discretionary federal agency action is the proper trigger for section 7(a)(2) consultation. However, we anticipate ongoing debate about the discretionary/nondiscretionary distinction. For example, would the result in *National Wildlife Federation v. National Marine Fisheries Service*[131] have been different if the *Defenders* decision had preceded the holding in that case? In

National Marine Fisheries Service, the Ninth Circuit was swift to point out that the action agencies in that case (the U.S. Army Corps of Engineers and the U.S. Bureau of Reclamation) had not clarified with sufficient precision (at least up to Ninth Circuit standards) which of their actions were discretionary and which were not.[132] But what if they had?

Section 8 of the Reclamation Act of 1902 is an example of how the discretionary action principle applies.[133] It states, in part, "nothing in this Act shall be construed as affecting or intended to affect or to any way interfere with the laws of any State or Territory relating to the control, appropriation, use, or distribution of water used in irrigation, or any vested right acquired thereunder, and the Secretary of the Interior, in carrying out the provisions of this Act, shall proceed in conformity with such laws, and nothing herein shall in any way affect any right of any State or of the Federal Government or of any landowner, appropriator, or user of water in, to, or from any interstate stream or the waters thereof."

The plain language of section 8 affords the Bureau of Reclamation no discretion in the context of water allocation in an apparent attempt to respect the concepts of federalism and the sovereign interests of the state. Yet, the 2004 Biological Opinion for the Federal Columbia River Power System (FCRPS) at issue in the *National Marine Fisheries Service* case is premised on discretionary action in the context of water allocation. The Ninth Circuit stated that "*[a]ll aspects* of FCRPS operations, and any dam maintenance or structural modifications, are within the agencies' discretion, and accordingly are subject to section 7."[134]

Admittedly the facts in the *Defenders* case are not quite as complex as the facts in the *National Marine Fisheries Service* case, where there are two action agencies and a consultation on the operations of an entire river system. However, one fundamental issue is the same: agency discretion. One can't help but wonder what the result would have been in *National Marine Fisheries Service* if the Ninth Circuit had not been so quick to dismiss agency assertions of nondiscretion.

Climate Change

The issue of climate change has taken center stage in the debate over the proper breadth of the ESA and application of section 7 consultations to proposed activities that would emit greenhouse gases (GHG). Since 2006, the Elkhorn coral,[135] Staghorn coral,[136] and the polar bear[137] have been listed as threatened pursuant to section 4 of the ESA, at least partially based upon habitat degradation attributable to global warming. Although the polar bear was listed during the tenure of Secretary of the Interior Dirk Kempthorne, Secretaries Kempthorne and Salazar have both taken the position that the ESA is not the proper tool to set U.S. climate policy. On October 3, 2008, Department of the Interior Solicitor David Bernhardt issued a Memorandum providing guidance on the application of the ESA's section 7 consultation requirements to proposed actions involving the emission of GHG. This Memorandum concluded that "where the effect at issue is climate change in the form of increased temperatures, a proposed action that will involve the emission of GHG cannot pass the 'may affect' test and is not subject to consultation under the ESA and its implementing regulations."[138] On May 8, 2009, Secretary Salazar announced that Interior will retain the 4(d) rule pertaining to the protection of the polar bear amidst significant pressure from environmental groups to overturn the rule.[139] The Center for Biological Diversity's pending legal complaint regarding the 4(d) rule is among a half-dozen lawsuits Interior faces on the polar bear listing.

Section 7 Consultation Regulations

In part to address the issue of climate change in the section 7 consultation process, the Services jointly proposed several modifications to the ESA section 7 implementing regulations found at 50 C.F.R. part 402.[140] The Services proposed draft rules to "clarify several definitions, to clarify when the section 7 regulations are applicable and the correct standards for effects analysis, and to establish time frames for the consultation process."[141] In doing so, the Services noted that the current regulations have not been substantially revised since their original adoption in 1986.

On December 16, 2008, the final rules revising the section 7 regulations were published in the *Federal Register*.[142] The final rules largely retained the most controversial provisions of the draft rules, such as generally excluding greenhouse gas emissions from section 7 analyses[143] and exempting federal actions from section 7 review if the *action agency* (not a consulting Service) determines the proposed federal action is (1) not anticipated to result in "take" and (2) falls within a category of effects predetermined "not likely to adversely affect" a listed species or critical habitat.[144]

The rules generated tremendous controversy within the federal, state, and private sectors. FWS Director Dale Hall refused to sign off on the rules before they were published. On December 11, 2008, the Center for Biological Diversity, Greenpeace, and Defenders of Wildlife jointly filed a lawsuit challenging the final rules.[145] On January 16, 2009, several states, including California, New York, Massachusetts, Connecticut, and Oregon, also filed suit seeking to overturn the rules.[146] On March 3, 2009, President Obama issued a memorandum to the Secretaries of Interior and Commerce, requesting that the Services review the rules, and further asking all federal agencies to not implement the rules.[147] Congress also took action, authorizing the Secretaries to immediately revoke the rules without any provision for public notice and comment.[148] Pursuant to this authority, Secretaries Locke (Commerce) and Salazar (Interior) announced on April 28, 2009, that they were revoking the rules. The Secretaries also said the Services will conduct a joint review of the 1986 consultation regulations to determine if any improvements should be proposed.

Conclusion

Like other areas of the ESA, section 7 is heavily litigated, often producing conflicting results. One thing we can divine from the case law is that while ESA section 7(a)(2) consultations may prove difficult and time consuming, steps can be taken to address such issues. The informal and early consultation options provide some measure of flexibility in the consultation process. Applicants and federal action agencies are well advised to engage the Service at the earliest appropriate time in the project planning process and keep thorough records. Applicants for federal permits may also want to consider strategically proactive measures to address potential ESA issues on the horizon through the conferencing process. Whether or not the Services amend the section 7 regulations again, the Supreme Court decision in *National Association of Home Builders v. Defenders of Wildlife*[149] may also provide guidance to agencies in regard to what actions section 7 applies to and when consultation is required. In any event, the trend of extensive litigation concerning ESA section 7(a)(2) compliance is likely to continue.

Notes

1. 16 U.S.C. § 1536.
2. 50 C.F.R. pt. 402.
3. 16 U.S.C. § 1536(a)(2).
4. *Id.* § 1536(a)(4).
5. *Id.* § 1536(a)(1) provides: "The Secretary shall review other programs administered by him and utilize such programs in furtherance of the purposes of this chapter. All other Federal agencies shall, in consultation with and with the assistance of the Secretary, utilize their authorities in furtherance of the purposes of this chapter by carrying out programs for the conservation of endangered species and threatened species listed pursuant to section 1533 of this title."
6. Pyramid Lake Paiute Tribe of Indians v. U.S. Dep't. of the Navy, 898 F.2d 1410, 1416 (9th Cir. 1990).
7. The term "Service" as used in this chapter refers to either the U.S. Fish and Wildlife Service or the National Oceanic and Atmospheric Administration, depending on the particular species at issue.
8. 16 U.S.C. § 1532(3).
9. Sierra Club v. Babbitt, 65 F.3d 1502, 1510, 1513 (9th Cir. 1995).
10. Pyramid Lake Paiute Tribe of Indians v. U.S. Dep't. of the Navy, 898 F.2d 1410, 1418 (9th Cir. 1990).
11. *Compare* Sierra Club v. Glickman, 156 F.3d 606, 616 (5th Cir. 1998) ("[W]e conclude that Congress intended to impose an affirmative duty on each federal agency to conserve each of the species listed pursuant to § 1533") *with* Nw. Envtl. Advocates v. U.S. E.P.A., 258 F. Supp. 2d 1255, 2003 WL 21487274, at *16 (D. Or. 2003) ("The statute does not mention species-specific programs. Rather, the agency may reasonably interpret its § 7(a)(1) obligations to extend no further than engaging in conservation programs that benefit threatened species.").
12. Defenders of Wildlife v. Martin, 2007 WL 641439 (E.D. Wash. Feb. 26, 2007).
13. 16 U.S.C. § 1540(g)(1)(A).
14. *See, e.g.,* Sierra Club v. Glickman, 156 F.3d 606, 617 (5th Cir. 1998).
15. 16 U.S.C. § 1536(a)(2).
16. Nat'l Ass'n of Home Builders v. Defenders of Wildlife, 127 S. Ct. 2518, 2530 n.5 (2007).
17. *Id.* at 2534–35.
18. 50 C.F.R. § 402.02 (1998).
19. Pac. Rivers Council v. Thomas, 30 F.3d 1050 (9th Cir. 1994).
20. Marbled Murrelet v. Babbitt, 83 F.3d 1068 (9th Cir. 1996).
21. Int'l Ctr. for Tech. Assessment v. Thompson, 421 F. Supp. 2d 1 (D.D.C. 2006).
22. W. Watersheds Project v. Matejko, 468 F.3d 1099, 1108 (9th Cir. 2006).
23. 33 U.S.C. § 1344.

24. "Action area" is defined by regulation to mean "all areas to be affected directly or indirectly by the Federal action and not merely the immediate area involved in the action." 50 C.F.R. § 402.02.
25. 43 U.S.C. §§ 1701 *et seq.*
26. 23 U.S.C. ch. 1.
27. Cal. Sportfishing Prot. Alliance v. Fed. Energy Regulatory Comm'n, 472 F.3d 593, 598 (9th Cir. 2006).
28. Pac. Rivers Council v. Thomas, 30 F.3d 1050 (9th Cir. 1994).
29. Informal consultations do not result in the issuance of biological opinion because informal consultation generally occurs when the proposed federal action is not anticipated to result in jeopardy, adverse modification of critical habitat, or incidental take of a listed species.
30. The term "action agency" refers to the federal agency charged with Section 7 compliance, typically the permitting agency. Sometimes the term "consulting agency" is used to refer to the Service.
31. 16 U.S.C. § 1536(c).
32. 50 C.F.R. § 402.12(d).
33. 16 U.S.C. § 1536(d).
34. Nat'l Wildlife Fed'n v. Nat'l Park Serv., 669 F. Supp. 384, 390 (D. Wyo. 1987).
35. Sierra Club v. Marsh, 816 F.2d 1376, 1389 (9th Cir. 1987).
36. 16 U.S.C. § 1536(c).
37. 50 C.F.R. § 402.12(e).
38. *Id.* § 402.03.
39. *Id.* § 402.12(f).
40. "Discountable effects" are those effects "extremely unlikely to occur." "Insignificant effects" are those that cannot be "meaningfully measured, detected and evaluated" and must not rise to a level of "take." FISH & WILDLIFE SERV. & NAT'L MARINE FISHERIES SERV., ENDANGERED SPECIES CONSULTATION HANDBOOK: PROCEDURES FOR CONDUCTING CONSULTATION AND CONFERENCE ACTIVITIES UNDER SECTION 7 OF THE ENDANGERED SPECIES ACT 3-12 (Mar. 1998) [hereinafter SECTION 7 CONSULTATION HANDBOOK].
41. *Id.* at 3-13.
42. A BA is required and must be prepared for "major construction activities" considered to be federal actions significantly affecting the quality of the human environment as referred to in the NEPA. 50 C.F.R. § 402.12(b); *see also* 16 U.S.C. § 1536(c). A major construction activity is a construction project or other undertaking having similar physical impacts that qualifies under NEPA as a major federal action. Major construction activities include dams, buildings, pipelines, roads, water resource developments, channel improvements, and other projects that modify the physical environment and constitute major federal actions. As a rule of thumb, if an Environmental Impact Statement is required for the proposed action and construction-type impacts are involved, it is considered a major construction activity.
43. *See* 50 C.F.R. § 402.08 (nonfederal representative designated by action agency by providing written notice to the consulting Service).
44. *Id.* § 402.13.
45. *Id.* § 402.13(a).
46. 16 U.S.C. § 1536(a)(4).
47. 50 C.F.R. § 402.10(b).
48. *Id.* § 402.10(c).
49. *Id.* § 402.10(d).
50. *Id.* As explained in the section The Incidental Take Statement later in this chapter, an incidental take statement authorizes a federal action to proceed even though it may cause the take of a listed species. Given the insulation from the ESA's take prohibition with an ITS when a proposed species is listed, a private permit applicant and action agency may seek to initiate formal conferencing if the proposed action is likely to cause the take of such species.

51. 16 U.S.C. § 1536(a)(3).
52. 50 C.F.R. § 402.11.
53. *Id.* § 402.11(c).
54. *Id.*
55. *Id.* § 402.11(e).
56. *Id.* § 402.14(e).
57. *Id.* § 402.11(f).
58. *Id.*
59. 50 C.F.R. § 402.14(c); Section 7 Consultation Handbook, *supra* note 40, at 4-6. Alternatively, the Services may request a federal agency to initiate formal consultation. 50 C.F.R. § 402.14(a).
60. 50 C.F.R. § 402.14(a).
61. *Id.* § 402.14(e).
62. *Id.*
63. *Id.* § 402.14(c).
64. Section 7 Consultation Handbook, *supra* note 40, at 4-6.
65. 50 C.F.R. § 402.14(f).
66. The BiOp also examines the likelihood of take from the proposed federal action, and will include an ITS if take is expected to occur. 16 U.S.C. § 1536(b)(4); *see also* Ariz. Cattle Growers Ass'n v. FWS, 273 F.3d 1229, 1232 (9th Cir. 2001) (FWS must demonstrate that take is "reasonably likely" to occur in order to impose an ITS in a Bi-Op).
67. 50 C.F.R. § 402.14(g).
68. *Id.* § 402.02.
69. Section 7 Consultation Handbook, *supra* note 40, at 4-23.
70. *Id.*
71. The National Oceanic and Atmospheric Administration (NOAA) was formerly called the NMFS.
72. Nat'l Wildlife Fed'n v. NMFS, 481 F.3d 1224 (9th Cir. 2007).
73. 50 C.F.R. § 402.02.
74. *Id.*
75. Riverside Irrigation Dist. v. Andrews, 758 F.2d 508 (10th Cir. 1985).
76. 50 C.F.R. § 402.02.
77. *Id*
78. Section 7 Consultation Handbook, *supra* note 40, at 4-26.
79. 50 C.F.R. § 402.14(c)(4).
80. *Id.* § 402.14(g)(4).
81. *Id.* § 402.02.
82. *See, e.g.,* Nat'l Wildlife Fed'n v. Norton, 332 F. Supp 2d 179 (D.D.C. 2004).
83. 16 U.S.C. § 1536(3)(A). As explained later in this chapter, the BiOp will address the potential for the proposed federal action to cause the take of a listed species and will typically include an ITS.
84. 50 C.F.R. § 402.02.
85. *Id.*
86. Nat'l Wildlife Fed'n v. Nat'l Marine Fisheries Serv., 481 F.3d 1224, 1238–39 (9th Cir. 2007).
87. 50 C.F.R. § 402.14(i).
88. 16 U.S.C. § 1536(b)(4); see also section titled The Incidental Take Statement, *infra*.
89. *Id.* § 1536(b)(3)(A); see also section titled Reasonable and Prudent Alternatives, *infra*.
90. 50 C.F.R. § 402.02; *but see* Gifford Pinchot Task Force v. FWS, 378 F.3d 1059 (9th Cir. 2004) (holding the regulatory definition of "destruction or adverse modification" impermissible under the ESA because section 7 requires analysis of impacts that would appreciably diminish the value of critical habitat for the survival *or* recovery of a listed species). *See also* Nat'l Wildlife Fed'n v. NMFS, 481 F.3d 1224, 1237 (9th Cir. 2007) (extending *Gifford Pinchot* to jeopardy analysis).
91. 16 U.S.C. § 1532(5)(A).

92. 50 C.F.R. § 424.12(b).
93. *Id.* § 402.02.
94. *Id.*
95. *Id.*
96. 16 U.S.C. § 1533(f).
97. 50 C.F.R. § 402.02.
98. 16 U.S.C. § 1536(e)–(h).
99. Tribal Vill. of Akutan v. Hodel, 859 F.2d 651 (9th Cir. 1988).
100. *See also* Ariz. Cattle Growers Ass'n v. Fish & Wildlife Serv., 273 F.3d 1229, 1232 (9th Cir. 2001) (FWS must demonstrate that take is "reasonably likely" to occur in order to impose ITS in a Bi-Op).
101. 16 U.S.C. § 1536(b); 50 C.F.R. § 402.14(i).
102. 16 U.S.C. § 1536(o)(2).
103. Section 7 Consultation Handbook, *supra* note 40, at 4-46.
104. 50 C.F.R. § 402.14(i)(2).
105. *Id.* § 402.02.
106. Section 7 Consultation Handbook, *supra* note 40, at 4-50.
107. *Id.*
108. 50 C.F.R. § 402.14(i)(iv).
109. *Id.* § 402.14(c)(3).
110. *Id.*
111. 50 C.F.R. § 402.14(k).
112. 848 F.2d 1441 (9th Cir. 1988).
113. Section 7 Consultation Handbook, *supra* note 40, at 5-7 to 5-8.
114. *Id.*
115. *See* Envtl. Prot. Info. Ctr. v. Simpson Timber Co., 255 F.3d 1073, 1080 (9th Cir. 2001); Sierra Club v. Babbitt, 65 F.3d 1502, 1509 (9th Cir. 1995).
116. W. Watersheds Project v. Matejko, 468 F.3d 1099, 1108 (9th Cir. 2006); Salmon Spawning & Recovery Alliance v. Basham, 477 F. Supp. 2d 1301, 1308 (Ct. Int'l Trade 2007); *see also* Nat'l Assoc. of Home Builders v. Defenders of Wildlife, 127 S. Ct. 2518 n. 11 (2007).
117. 50 C.F.R. § 402.16.
118. Envtl. Prot. Info. Ctr. v. Simpson Timber Co., 255 F.3d 1073, 1076 (9th Cir. 2001).
119. 50 C.F.R. § 402.05.
120. *Id.*
121. *Id.*
122. Forest Serv. Employees for Envtl. Ethics v. U.S. Forest Serv., 397 F. Supp. 2d 1241, 1257 (D. Mont. 2005).
123. 437 U.S. 153 (1978).
124. In over 20 years, a "God Squad" exemption has been applied for only six times and has been granted only twice, in the case of the whooping crane in 1978 and the spotted owl in 1991.
125. 16 U.S.C. § 1536(g)(1).
126. *Id.* § 1536(g)(3)(A)(i), (ii) & (iii).
127. *Id.* § 1536(h)(1).
128. *Id.* § 1536(n).
129. Secretarial Order No. 3206, American Indian Tribal Rights, Federal-Tribal Trust Responsibilities, and the Endangered Species Act (June 5, 1997) (cited in Miccosukee v. United States, 528 F. Supp. 2d 1317 (S.D. Fla. 2007)).
130. 127 S. Ct. 2518 (2007).
131. 481 F.3d 1224 (9th Cir. 2007).
132. The Ninth Circuit stated that "[t]he very fact that the agencies are unable to define the limits of their discretion here reveals that all FCRPS operations are intertwined and subject to discretionary control." 481 F.3d at 1235.

133. 43 U.S.C. § 383.
134. 481 F.3d at 1234 (emphasis added).
135. 71 Fed. Reg. 26,852–901 (May 9, 2006).
136. *Id.*
137. 73 Fed. Reg. 28,212 (May 15, 2008).
138. Memorandum from David Bernhardt, Solicitor, U.S. Dep't of the Interior, to Dirk Kempthorne, Secretary of the Interior (Oct. 3, 2008) (on file with author).
139. News Release, U.S. Dep't of the Interior, Sec'y Retains Conservation Rule for Polar Bears (May 8, 2009) (on file with author).
140. 73 Fed. Reg. 47,868 (Aug. 15, 2008).
141. *Id.*
142. 73 Fed. Reg. 76,272.
143. 50 C.F.R. §§ 402.02, 402.03.
144. *Id.* § 402.03.
145. Ctr. for Biological Diversity v. Kempthorne, No. CV-08-5546 (N.D. Cal.).
146. California v. Kempthorne, No. C-08-5775 MHP (N.D. Cal.).
147. 74 Fed. Reg. 9753 (Mar. 6, 2009).
148. *See* Section 429 of the 2009 Omnibus Appropriations Act (H.R. 1105).
149. 127 S. Ct. 2518 (2007).

6

Indian Rights and the Endangered Species Act

Mary Gray Holt

Introduction

The Endangered Species Act (ESA)[1] has become the focus of many resource management disputes, including the management of resources owned or controlled by Indian tribes or to which tribes have a right of use. Increased population and the intensive development of public and private lands have fragmented the American landscape. The increase of urban and industrial land uses in the West has often made Indian lands the last, or nearly last, functioning habitat for listed species. Because so much development has already occurred on non-Indian lands, and so many ecosystems are already on the brink of collapse, tribes now find themselves subject to severe conservation restrictions to protect species and habitat affected by non-Indian economic development.

The United States has important treaty and trust obligations to Indian tribes whose rights, jurisdiction, and land bases vary dramatically. Likewise, the ESA imposes important responsibilities on the federal government for actions it may take affecting listed species or their critical habitat. In 1997, the federal agencies responsible for implementation of the ESA, the Departments of Commerce and the Interior, adopted a policy of working with Indian tribes to achieve species conservation within a framework honoring Indian tribal sovereignty and treaty rights. That policy continues to be implemented as Secretarial Order No. 3206,[2] and its success can largely be measured by the litigation that has not occurred. Secretarial Order No. 3206 has allowed the federal government to avoid answering the ultimate question whether Indian treaty rights were abrogated by Congress's enactment of the ESA. With this 12-year hiatus in litigation, the federal government has been able to explore new ways to ensure access to treaty resources while improving habitat and ecosystem function for listed species.

This chapter provides a basic outline of Indian law as it relates to ESA implementation, the reasons for and development of Secretarial Order No. 3206, and the implications of Indian treaty rights for species conservation.

Current State of the Law

Three Pillars of Indian Law

Indian Tribes as Sovereign Governments

Professor Charles Wilkinson describes Indian tribes as a "third source of sovereignty in the United States."[3] Tribal sovereignty is the primary principle of Indian law and must be kept in mind when considering any legal issue involving tribal rights. Indeed, according to Justice John Marshall, Indian tribes possess a sovereignty that predates the U.S. Constitution.[4] Recognition of tribal sovereignty remains well documented in the current case law.[5] While Congress may exercise plenary authority over Indian tribes,[6] they remain political entities "possessing attributes of sovereignty over both their members and territory."[7] The boundaries of tribal sovereignty can be discerned through the case law and the language of the treaties, statutes, and executive orders.[8]

Justice John Marshall laid the foundation of sovereignty and the federal trust relationship in three cases often referred to as the "Marshall trilogy": *Johnson v. McIntosh*,[9] concluding that the United States had the exclusive right to divest tribes of original possession of their land and that this right was derived from international law concepts of discovery and conquest; *Cherokee Nation v. Georgia*, characterizing the tribes as "domestic dependent nations" and their relation to the United States as that of "ward and guardian," thus articulating the trust relationship between the United States and Indian tribes;[10] and *Worcester v. Georgia*,[11] further articulating the sovereign status of Indian tribes as "distinct political communities" where state law does not apply.[12]

Today, there are more than 500 federally recognized Indian tribes in the United States.[13] Tribes determine qualifications for membership, establish their own form of government,[14] and possess police jurisdiction over tribal members in Indian Country.[15] Tribal jurisdiction over non-Indian lands within Indian Country is constrained and subject to an interest-based test to determine whether the conduct at issue "threatens or has some direct effect on the political integrity, the economic security or health or welfare of the tribe."[16] Tribal sovereignty and jurisdiction over tribal lands and members extends to the regulation of hunting, fishing, and gathering of plant materials on the reservation and, in some circumstances, off of the reservation.[17]

The Federal Trust Responsibility

The second essential principle of Indian law is the trust responsibility of the United States to Indian tribes. The federal trust obligation of the United States for Indian tribes was first articulated by Justice Marshall as he struggled to explain the legal status of Indian tribes within the new nation's boundaries.[18]

In *Cherokee Nation*, Justice Marshall considered the virtual void in the U.S. Constitution regarding the relationship between the new federal government and Indians. Rejecting the notion that Indian tribes are conquered peoples without government, Justice Marshall turned to principles of international law to characterize America's indigenous people as "domestic dependent nations." Then, borrowing from laws of trust and estates, he found that "[the Indian tribes'] relation to the United States resembles that of a ward to his guardian."[19]

In recent times, the Supreme Court has stated that the federal trust responsibility to Indian tribes stems from the treaty obligations of the United States, the "many acts of Congress and numerous decisions of this Court."[20] The Court has determined that the federal government "has charged itself with moral obligations of the highest responsibility and trust" toward the tribes and their members. This obligation continues and extends to all federal executive branch agencies.[21]

When making decisions affecting treaty or trust resources, the executive branch has a substantive duty to protect "to the fullest extent possible" the tribe's treaty rights and the resources on which those rights depend.[22] The trust analogue is that of a trustee's obligation to conserve the "corpus," the body of assets held in trust for the benefit of the beneficiary. The United States has a duty of loyalty to the beneficiary's interests, just like any other trustee.[23] The trust responsibility has a procedural component of requiring the trustee to consult with its tribal beneficiaries to obtain their views of their own interests.[24] While the Supreme Court has been reluctant to develop a detailed articulation of the trust relationship between the U.S. government and Indian tribes, there is no doubt the trust obligation extends to the affirmative protection of treaty rights as well as Indian lands and resources.[25] For a federal agency, however, this can present a conflict with the many statutory obligations imposed upon it by Congress.[26]

The trust relationship has also served as the basis for the judicial construction of treaty rights. The courts have employed the trust responsibility to require Congress to express its intent in "clear and plain" terms in statutory language or legislative history when compromising or abrogating treaty rights.[27] In addition, various statutes obligate the United States to represent the rights and interests of tribes, including tribal land claims and rights to the use of natural resources.[28]

Reserved Rights

The third principle of Indian law relevant to ESA implementation is the concept of Indian reserved rights—those rights not clearly transferred by the tribe to the federal sovereign are impliedly reserved by the tribe. In *United States v. Winans*,[29] the Supreme Court stated that the United States' treaties with the Indian tribes are not "grants of rights to the Indians, but a grant of rights from them—a reservation of those not granted."[30] As the 11th Amendment of the U.S. Constitution reserves those rights to the States that were not granted to the federal government, so Indian treaty rights include the reservation by the tribes of all rights not specifically transferred to the federal government by treaty. When the United States ceased making treaties in 1871, it began legislating tribal reservations through executive orders and statutes. Executive orders ratified by Congress have also been found to possess a reservation of rights previously held by the sovereign tribe.[31] Tribal reserved rights may include water rights as established by the Supreme Court's decision in *United States v. Winters*,[32] as well as the hunting, fishing, and gathering rights articulated in *Winans*.

Reserved rights to hunt, fish, and gather may be either explicitly reserved or inferred from the language, intent, and surrounding circumstances of a treaty, executive order, or statute.[33] Treaties are interpreted as the tribe would have understood them at the time the treaty was executed.[34] Reserved rights to fish and hunt fall into two categories: on-reservation and off-reservation rights. On-reservation rights to hunt and fish are enjoyed only by tribal members and are subject exclusively to tribal jurisdiction,[35] while off-reservation rights may be shared with non-Indians and subject to regulation for conservation purposes by the relevant state.[36] The courts recognize a right of access over private lands to exercise off-reservation fishing rights.[37]

The nature and scope of a tribal reserved right are dependent upon the facts and practices employed by the tribe at the time the treaties were signed. In early judicial discussions of reserved rights, the tribes' reservation of rights was inferred as a practical matter—the treaty was intended to take land from the Indian tribe as well as to allow Indians to sustain themselves on the reservation so that they would not bother settlers or become a burden on the federal treasury.[38] Thus courts have found that

Indian treaties reserved rights necessary to fulfill the purposes of the reservation to which the tribe was confined. In general, the right to fish includes the harvest of those species that historical and anthropological evidence indicates were taken at treaty time and in many instances, when evidence supports it, the use of modern technology is adapted to fulfill the treaty.[39]

The tribal right to hunt and fish can be abrogated at any time by Congress and an abrogation will usually give rise to a claim for compensation under the Fifth Amendment.[40] Abrogation of hunting and fishing rights is subject to the same stringent test as treaty abrogation generally—the intent of Congress to abrogate the specific right must be explicit.[41] The tribal right to off-reservation hunting and fishing has been held to survive even the termination of the tribes' reservation land base by Congress.[42]

Three years after the Supreme Court found a reserved right to fish off-reservation in *Winans*, it found a similar reservation of water rights in *Winters*.[43] The Supreme Court affirmed the *Winters* doctrine in *Arizona v. California*, and as a result, tribes throughout the West possess significant unquantified water rights.[44] Under the *Winters* doctrine, tribal water rights are subject to federal, not state, water law, although tribes and the United States as their trustee can be joined in a general stream adjudication in state court.[45] The Supreme Court's quantification of *Winters* rights, to date, has been limited to the concept of "practicably irrigable acreage" on the reservation.[46] However, some tribes have begun to assert reserved in-stream flows to support on-reservation fishing rights, and courts have agreed.[47]

The body of law governing relations with Indian tribes is constantly evolving, yet still deeply tied to its origins in Justice Marshall's early-19th-century opinions. The seemingly contradictory concepts of sovereignty and the federal trust obligation meet as extensions of each other in the phrase "domestic dependent nations." Tribes are nations whose existence and continued sovereignty is dependent on the protection of the United States. The rights of tribes and the obligations of the United States to both tribes and species listed under the ESA have elevated the potential for conflict in the context of increasingly fragmented ecosystems, competition for financial gain in development of land uses, and the effects of global climate change. As a matter of policy, it is imperative that the obligations to both Indian tribes and listed species be met; as a legal matter, it has been unclear who the winners will be or whether there will be any at all.

Ambiguity in the Case Law—Did the ESA Abrogate Treaty Rights?

There is no clear answer to whether the ESA can be applied to Indian tribes to restrict uses of Indian treaty resources. In dictum, the Supreme Court has inferred that there is no treaty right to hunt or fish to extinction, stating that "the Treaty does not give the Indians a federal right to pursue the last living steelhead until it enters their nets."[48] When given the opportunity in *United States v. Dion*,[49] the Supreme Court refrained from deciding whether the ESA abrogated treaty rights.[50] Yet in *United States v. Billie*, a Florida federal district court, faced squarely with the question, found that the ESA did abrogate a treaty right to kill a species declared endangered under the Act, and that a tribal member may be prosecuted under the ESA for taking a listed species on reservation lands.[51]

To get a sense of the legal debate, it is useful to examine the Supreme Court's analysis in *Dion*. Dwight Dion, a member of the Yankton Sioux tribe, was convicted of violating both the ESA and the Bald and Golden Eagle Protection Act[52] for shooting four bald eagles on the Yankton Sioux reservation.[53] There was no dispute that the treaty rights reserved to Dion as a Yankton Sioux included the exclusive right to hunt and fish on reservation lands.[54] In his examination of the conviction, Justice Thurgood Marshall, writing for a unanimous Supreme Court, restated well-established principles that Congress has the power to abrogate treaty provisions but that such abrogation is not to be lightly imputed. Absent a "clear and plain" or "explicit statement,"[55] no abrogation of a treaty should be found. The Court unanimously restated traditional principles of treaty interpretation, holding that "[w]hat is essential is clear evidence that Congress actually considered the conflict between its intended action on the one hand and Indian treaty rights on the other, and chose to resolve that conflict by abrogating the treaty."[56] The Court did confirm that where Congress did not make "a clear and plain statement," a court may look to the "legislative history" or the "surrounding circumstances" of the legislation to determine congressional intent toward Indian tribes and treaty rights.[57] Perhaps in an effort to apprise Congress of the importance of treaties with Indian tribes, the Court stated that "Indian treaty rights are too fundamental to be easily cast aside" and therefore an "[e]xplicit statement from Congress is preferable for the purpose of ensuring legislative accountability for the abrogation of treaty rights."[58]

Ultimately, however, the Court concluded that the Eagle Protection Act did abrogate the Yankton Sioux's treaty rights to hunt and take eagles. The Court pointed to the Act's "sweepingly framed" list of prohibitions and Congress's explicit choice to control Indian hunting through a permit regime as evidence that Congress had balanced the treaty, religious, and cultural interests of Indians against the need to conserve eagle species.[59]

The Court undertook a thorough examination of the legislative history of the Eagle Protection Act and made specific note of a U.S. House of Representatives report examining the impact of the proposed bill on Indian tribes. An exception for religious uses by Indian tribes was drafted by the Solicitor of the Interior, and the Senate bill had been amended to include it before being reported to the Senate Commerce Committee. Testimony by the Department of the Interior at the Senate hearings stated the importance of golden eagles in Indian religious ceremonies and the need for an exception to the prohibition for Indian religious uses. Finding that at the end of the legislative process:

> Congress expressly chose to set in place a regime in which the Secretary of the Interior had control over Indian hunting [of eagles], rather than one in which Indian on-reservation hunting was unrestricted . . . Congress' 1962 action . . . reflected an unmistakable and explicit legislative policy choice that Indian hunting of the bald or golden eagle . . . is inconsistent with the

need to preserve those species. We [the Court] therefore read the statute as having abrogated that treaty right.[60]

Further, the Court held that that the Eagle Protection Act divested the defendant of any treaty-based defenses to his conviction under the ESA. The Court reasoned that the prior enacted Eagle Protection Act abrogated the right to hunt and kill eagles and therefore, to the extent the ESA prohibited the same conduct and exercise of treaty right, it was also abrogated. Therefore, no defense to the ESA could exist.[61]

The *Dion* Court hinted that Congress may have failed to address Indian treaty rights in the ESA to an extent sufficient to "effect a valid abrogation" but did not directly address the question.[62] Although it outlined the standard analysis for determining whether treaty rights were abrogated by the ESA, the Court did not engage in any analysis and made no finding on whether the ESA itself abrogated treaty rights.

In 1987, one year later, a Florida federal district court held that the ESA abrogated the treaty rights of a Seminole tribal member to hunt and kill the endangered Florida panther on reservation lands.[63] In *United States v. Billie*, rather than follow the Supreme Court's analysis in *Dion* decided just the year before, the district court looked to *Tennessee Valley Authority v. Hill*, a case famous for its statement that the ESA is "the most comprehensive legislation for the preservation of endangered species ever enacted by any nation," [64] for guidance on Congress's policy choices.[65] The district court examined the legislative history of the ESA, noting, as the *Dion* court did with the Eagle Protection Act, that the Department of the Interior had urged Congress to include provisions in the ESA to allow Indian religious and subsistence uses.[66] However, Congress provided an exception from ESA prohibitions only for Alaska natives. Congress's evident rejection of Interior's recommendation encouraged the district court to ignore the fact that Alaska natives do not have treaties with the United States and therefore must have an exception to continue subsistence hunting and fishing, there being no treaty-guaranteed right.

After emphasizing the significance of the ESA's breadth and legislative history, the district court developed its own view of treaty abrogation. The court in *Billie* held that the United States' treaty with the Seminole tribe did not anticipate the circumstances in which there might be a scarcity of wildlife and therefore did not reserve rights to the tribe to hunt and kill such fragile populations. Echoing Justice Douglas's famous cautionary approbation that a treaty does not entitle a tribe to pursue the last fish,[67] the district court concluded that the tribal right to hunt on the reservation could not be absolute when a species "nears extinction."[68] From this point, the court concluded, the ESA abrogated Indian treaty rights to take any species listed as endangered or threatened under the ESA.

The rationale of *Billie* can be criticized as a poor application of the established principles for interpreting Indian treaties and for treaty abrogation. It can also be said that the court demonstrated a poor understanding of both the Supreme Court's decision in *Dion* and the legislative history of the ESA.[69] Nevertheless, the Supreme Court, and others, have acknowledged the existence of a conservation parameter in the implementation of treaty hunting and fishing rights. Unquestionably, neither the federal government nor the Seminole tribe could have anticipated the near extinction of the Florida panther, which has occurred in conjunction with late-20th-century land uses. However, rather than seeing the loss of species and habitat as a loss of the rights guaranteed to the Seminoles by the United States, the district court viewed the ESA's purposes alone, as if in a vacuum. The district court would have acted more in keeping with the general principles of Indian law to have first considered the United States' duties under the treaty to conserve the species for which tribes bargained at treaty time and then looked to the subsequently enacted statute.[70] The court could have identified the conservation of species as a duty owed by the United States under both the treaty and the ESA, but instead, it found that Billie's treaty right to hunt and kill an endangered species was abrogated by the ESA.

These two cases, *Dion* and *Billie*, created a near necessity for Indian tribes to determine whether their members would be subject to criminal prosecution under the ESA for the exercise of their treaty rights, on or off the reservation. In addition to the threat of criminal prosecution, the ambiguity created by the two cases seemed to jeopardize the concept of the trust responsibility as an obligation of the United States to protect treaty-guaranteed rights to hunt and fish. In essence, *Billie*, and to a lesser extent *Dion*, examined statutes intended to address the loss of species and interpreted them in a manner that diminished the tribal rights guaranteed by their treaty.

Harmonizing the ESA and Tribal Rights: Secretarial Order No. 3206

It was in this context, nearly 10 years later, that Secretary of the Interior Bruce Babbitt accepted a request from tribal leaders to convene a meeting of the Interior and Commerce departments to discuss development of a Secretarial Order[71] on the ESA and tribal rights. Tribal leaders presented Secretary Babbitt with a "white paper" outlining their position on application of the ESA in Indian Country, reciting the burdens imposed on the tribes by the implementation of the ESA's regulations and policies. However, the document also recognized that both the federal agencies and Indian tribes must direct their energies toward their mutual goals of conservation of species and ecosystems.[72]

The Joint Secretarial Order on American Indian Tribal Rights, Federal-Tribal Trust Responsibilities, and the Endangered Species Act (Secretarial Order No. 3206) was developed through an extended series of negotiations[73] by a team of federal and tribal representatives. The document is a landmark in many regards. It represents the outcome of true government-to-government consultative negotiations. It is a commitment by the Departments of Commerce and the Interior to "carry out their responsibilities under the [ESA] in a manner that harmonizes the Federal trust responsibility to tribes, tribal sovereignty and the statutory missions of the Departments and that strives to ensure that Indian tribes do not bear a disproportionate burden for the conservation of listed species so as to avoid or minimize the potential for conflict and confrontation."[74]

The Secretarial Order provides policy instruction to the agencies delegated with implementing the ESA, the U.S. Fish and Wildlife Service and the National Marine Fisheries Service ("the Services"). The Secretarial Order does not interpret the ESA, makes no statement concerning the application of the ESA in Indian Country, and makes no change in existing regulations.[75] It does, however, commit the federal government to implement the ESA in a manner cognizant of its trust obligation to Indian tribes.

The Secretarial Order is composed of two parts. The body of the document sets out the principles underlying the integration of statutory ESA obligations with the federal trust responsibility to Indian tribes.[76] These principles recognize that the objectives of the tribes and the ESA are compatible if not the same, but as separate sovereigns the United States and Indian tribal governments must respect each other's need to achieve those goals differently. In many ways the Secretarial Order sets out several elements of tribal sovereignty for consideration in the implementation of the ESA. For instance, the Order states, "The Departments shall recognize that Indian tribes are appropriate governments to manage their lands and tribal trust resources."[77] The Order requires the Departments "to give deference to tribal conservation and management plans for tribal trust resources."[78] The trust responsibility is also well represented throughout the principles stated in the Order. The Order requires the Departments to "assist Indian Tribes in developing and expanding tribal programs so that healthy ecosystems are promoted and conservation restrictions are unnecessary."[79] This includes providing "scientific and technical assistance and information ... for the development of tribal conservation and management plans," implementing the aspect of the trust that supports development of self-determination and self-governance.[80] In addition, Principle 4 requires the Departments to "take into consideration the impact of their actions on Indian use of listed species for cultural and religious purposes."[81] All of these "Principles" call on the Departments to implement species conservation in a manner to meet statutory objectives while considering and giving respect to the rights, governments, cultures, and treaties of Indian tribes.

The second part of the Secretarial Order, entitled Appendix, constitutes direct instruction from the Secretaries to the Services. The Appendix requires the Services to take specific steps to harmonize implementation of the ESA with the trust responsibility and treaty rights. The Appendix instructs the services to consult with, exchange information with, and utilize the expertise of affected tribes during the ESA section 4 listing process and designation of critical habitat. The services are instructed to conduct analyses of the economic impact of critical habitat designation on tribal communities. The Services are to "avoid or minimize effects on tribal management or economic development."[82]

During the ESA section 7 consultation process, the Services are instructed to solicit information and traditional knowledge and to use the expertise of affected tribes.[83] Four important steps for involving tribes in the section 7 process are clearly set out in the Appendix. The Services are instructed to treat affected tribes "as license or permit applicants entitled to full participation" in any formal consultation process undertaken on an activity proposed by the Bureau of Indian Affairs (BIA).[84] This step makes the tribe an active participant in the consultation process for most activities affecting listed species on reservation lands.

When the Services consult on an action proposed by an agency not within the Departments of Commerce or the Interior, the Services are instructed to encourage the action agency to provide for the BIA's participation on behalf of affected tribes and to "strive to ensure" that any reasonable and prudent alternatives do not discriminate against an affected tribe.[85] Toward that end, the Services are required to document (1) that the selection of reasonable and prudent alternatives is consistent with the federal trust responsibility and (2) the extent to which tribal conservation and management plans can be incorporated into any alternative.[86] The integration of tribal interests into the section 7 process is as close to joint implementation of the ESA as can be directed without statutory changes in the ESA itself. It is a tacit acknowledgement of the mutual interest in conservation of species shared by tribes and the federal government.

In the 12 years since the Secretarial Order was signed, there has been no litigation directly confronting the question of whether the ESA abrogates treaty or tribal rights. It may be an open question as to whether Secretarial Order No. 3206 is a success,[87] but certainly avoiding a clash of two such distinct legal frameworks was an important objective for the federal government in signing and implementing the Order. There can be no doubt that the implementation of the Order has included a relinquishment of federal control over tribal resources and a recognition of tribal sovereignty beyond any remedies that tribes were likely to achieve through litigation.

The Secretarial Order is an explicit acknowledgement that both the federal and Indian tribal governments have strong interests in the conservation of species and the habitat upon which they depend. In many regards, the Secretarial Order is a success. In a monograph assessing the effects of Secretarial Order No. 3206 on ESA implementation, Marren Sanders reports that after the Order was issued (June 1997 to January 2006), 27 of the 100 proposed rules to designate critical habitat considered including tribal lands within designation but later excluded them, having determined that tribal lands were not essential to the conservation of the listed species.[88] Sanders concluded that the best predictor of whether tribal lands would be included within a federal critical habitat designation was the existence of a tribal habitat management plan that was viable and being implemented by the tribe.[89] In several instances, tribes had partnered with the U.S. Fish and Wildlife Service in the development or monitoring of their management plans.[90] In many cases Secretarial Order No. 3206 seems to have led to improved relationships, capacity building, and mutual understanding and respect between tribal and federal land managers.

The likelihood that improved relationships between federal agencies and tribal resource managers have contributed to avoiding ESA litigation is high. Secretarial Order No. 3206 undoubtedly provided a framework and an impetus for improving those relationships on the ground and created the necessary bureaucratic justification for the time, effort, and budget spent on building those relationships. The Order's command that the Services provide technical support and assistance to the tribes and for deference to tribal conservation and management plans has contributed to avoiding some critical habitat restrictions on tribal lands. The principles articulated in

Secretarial Order No. 3206 reinforced the mutual federal and tribal interests in habitat restoration. Also, the absence of litigation reflects a mutual understanding that ESA litigation over exercise of treaty rights would be unlikely to improve the status of species, increase the tools available to land managers for ecosystem conservation, or increase access to treaty resources.

Emerging Issues and Future Directions

After 30 years of dormancy, the notion of tribal treaty rights imposing an affirmative obligation on the State to refrain from engaging in actions to diminish the treaty resource has been awakened. During the 1970s, when the Supreme Court and the federal courts of the Pacific Northwest were considering the meaning and implementation of the 19th-century Stevens treaties for the salmon fishery in the rivers and the coasts of Washington and Oregon, many issues were raised and some were left by the wayside to be resolved at a later time, if necessary.[91] With the listing of most Pacific Northwest salmonid species for protection under the ESA in the last decade, necessity may have arrived.

The rights of the Stevens treaty tribes[92] to fish at their usual and accustomed fishing grounds were litigated in two phases. The first phase, *United States v. Washington (Phase I)*, established the tribes' rights to 50 percent of the harvestable surplus of fish passing through their usual and accustomed fishing grounds in the State of Washington, or a sufficient quantity of fish to provide a moderate standard of living.[93] Achieving this determination was sufficiently controversial and its implementation so tenuous that two additional claims were separated and reserved for later determination.[94] Among the issues held for another day was the tribes' claim that the State of Washington impaired their treaty right to fish by authorizing logging practices, industrial pollution, and obstruction of streams. The tribes' theory asserted that treaties impose an affirmative duty on the federal and state governments to refrain from actions that diminish the opportunity to access the treaty resources or diminish the treaty resource itself—an affirmative trust obligation to conserve the basis of the treaty. From the tribes' perspective, however, the second phase was an obvious and logical step toward making the treaty right meaningful—to the extent the fishery is diminished by the actions of the State and the United States, the treaty right is likewise diminished and some form of relief should be available.

In 1980, six years after the first decision in *United States v. Washington*, the federal courts addressed the tribes' environmental degradation claim in *United States v. Washington (Phase II)*.[95] In deciding this case, the district court relied on the *Winters* doctrine to find that the Stevens treaties reserved to the tribes a sufficient quantity of fish to satisfy their moderate living needs. This reservation, the court held, gave rise to a correlative duty "upon the State (as well as the United States and third parties) to refrain from degrading fish habitat to an extent that it would deprive the tribes of their moderate living needs."[96] Like a reserved water right where a quantity of water must be conserved and made available to support the purposes of a treaty and reservation, the court found that a treaty reserving the right to sustenance by fishing required conservation of the fish.

The State did not find immediate relief at the Ninth Circuit,[97] but en banc review brought an end to the "environmental aspect of the case"[98] when a nine-judge panel vacated the district court's decision. The Ninth Circuit did not, however, reject the substance of the tribes' legal theory. Instead, the panel based its rejection of the "environmental issue" on jurisprudential concerns raised by a declaratory relief action. The Ninth Circuit panel expressed concern about the case seeking "legal rules imprecise in definition and uncertain in dimension."[99] The en banc panel did not close the door on the concept that treaty rights may incorporate some level of environmental protection or sustainability, but cautioned that such an obligation "will depend for its precise legal formulation on all of the facts presented by a particular dispute."[100]

Within a decade of the Ninth Circuit's vacation of the *Phase II* decision, most species of salmon and steelhead passing through the usual and accustomed fishing grounds of the Stevens treaty tribes were declared "threatened" under the ESA and habitat degradation was identified as the primary reason for the decline of their populations.[101] In 2001, the tribes resurrected the "environmental aspect" of the *Phase II* decision by bringing "a particular dispute" with "specific facts" to the federal courts. The treaty tribes sought a determination that culverts owned and maintained by the State of Washington impede salmon migration to spawning areas. The tribes argued that by preventing salmon access to habitat necessary for the propagation of the species, the State violated its duty to refrain from impairing the ability of the tribes to their harvest of treaty-reserved fish and to achieve a moderate living.[102] The tribes presented uncontested evidence that State-owned or -maintained culverts block at least 249 linear miles of streams, preventing salmon from reaching 400,000 square meters of spawning habitat and 1.5 million square miles of productive rearing habitat.[103]

On cross-motions for summary judgment, Judge Ramirez of the Western District of Washington concluded that "by the State's own estimates, removal of the obstacles would result in an annual increase in production of 200,000 fish, many of which would be available for Tribal harvest."[104] The court held that the Stevens treaties and law of the case in *United States v. Washington* carry an implied promise that neither the United States nor its successors would take action to significantly degrade the treaty resource and that the treaties do "impose a duty upon the State to refrain from building or maintaining culverts in such a manner as to block the passage of fish upstream or down, to or from the Tribes' usual and accustomed fishing places."[105] In an effort to reduce the State's concerns and perhaps precedential impact of its order, the court assured defendants that the duty upon the State "is not a broad 'environmental servitude' or imposition of affirmative duty to take all possible steps to protect fish runs . . . but rather a narrow directive to refrain from impeding fish runs in one specific manner."[106] The court focused on the evidence of blocked fish runs as a clear violation of a duty that "arises directly from the right of taking fish that was assured to the Tribes in the Treaties, and is necessary to fulfill the promises made to the Tribes regarding the extent of that right."[107]

After the court's summary judgment order in August 2007, the State of Washington and tribes began negotiations on the appropriate scope and schedule of a remedy. Those discussions have failed to produce an agreement, and trial is scheduled for October 2009.

Through the culverts litigation, the Stevens treaty tribes have sought direct improvement in the habitat of listed salmon species—not because they are listed under the ESA, but because their treaty right to harvest demands there be fish to sustainably harvest. With this case the law may well have arrived at the juncture where the interests of Indian treaty harvest and listed species are aligned. In the State of Washington, it appears, Indian treaty rights may offer a form of ecosystem protection not available under federal or state statute. These treaties are the supreme law of the land. The duty of the United States, assumed by its successor in interest the State of Washington, is one of contract and trust to prevent their activities from jeopardizing the sustainability of the treaty-guaranteed resource. In some ways it is only happenstance that the treaty resources at issue are also sufficiently imperiled to be listed species under the ESA. Perhaps in this instance, what has not been achievable through the ESA, improvement of habitat, can be achieved by the affirmative use of the treaty obligations of the United States to Indian tribes.[108]

Needless to say, the financial cost to the State of Washington of improving its culvert system may be significant. However, the State is likely to find that the opportunity to gain access to important salmon habitat is beneficial to non-Indian fishers as well as Indian fishers. It will be interesting to see whether the treaty right to harvest a listed species ultimately improves its habitat, or whether the appellate courts will be asked to take a different view. The importance of this first ruling in *Phase II* cannot be underestimated. The comments of Billy Frank, Nisqually elder and chairman of the Northwest Indian Fish Commission, capture both the emotion associated with the treaties and a profound understanding of the work required to improve habitat in today's urbanized environment:

> If the fish aren't here, what is the treaty all about? What is the thing we signed in good faith, the peace treaty in 1854? What is the meaning of all that? In our time, and for our children and grandchildren and for their children yet unborn, this is what it means: that we have to have our fish here.
>
> I don't think anyone is saying they are going to close down I-5. In order for us all to live together, we are not turning the lights off. But we have to do a better job at what we are doing. We have to have the leadership and the guts to make it happen, and we haven't had the political will for salmon in this state. We need the political will to bring the salmon back and have a home when they get here.[109]

Chairman Frank's reaction to the summary judgment ruling in the culverts litigation reflects the spirit in the Indian Treaty Room on June 5, 1997, when Secretarial Order No. 3206 was signed by Secretaries Babbitt and Daley. That spirit is one of hope. Chairman Frank describes the difficult but necessary partnerships between Indian tribes and citizens of Washington if ESA listed salmon are to recover and their habitat is to be restored. The culverts case may provide the legal basis for working harder toward these goals. Certainly it represents a new use of treaty rights to achieve conservation objectives.

Conclusion

Compromise, mediation, and open processes are among the many tools necessary for resolving conflict outside the courtroom. Avoiding litigation, however, requires acceptance of the fact that one cannot and will not get everything to which one may think one is entitled. When Secretary Babbitt agreed to a "bilateral" negotiation of ESA procedures to avoid conflicts with treaty rights, it was not just from magnanimity. Nor was it from fear of losing in the courts. It was the same hope that Chairman Frank expressed, founded on the understanding that working partnerships can be stronger and more sustainable than the enforcement arm of a federal conservation statute. It was a hope based on the knowledge that maintaining species and their habitat depends on land managers working together, as well as imposing legal obligations. Support for and implementation of Secretarial Order No. 3206 continues because federal agencies and tribal resource managers understand that species and ecosystems are more likely to flourish when all parties have a stake in their success.

Twelve years later, the legal conflict between the traditional canons of Indian law and the Endangered Species Act remains unresolved. It seems quite likely that Secretarial Order No. 3206 successfully holds that conflict in an angle of repose.[110]

Notes

1. 16 U.S.C. §§ 1531 *et seq.*
2. Secretarial Order No. 3206, American Indian Tribal Rights, Federal-Tribal Trust Responsibilities, and the Endangered Species Act (June 5, 1997).
3. CHARLES WILKINSON, AMERICAN INDIANS, TIME AND THE LAW (1987). The states as sovereigns are largely ignored for the purposes of this chapter and its necessary brevity. However, the interaction of state and tribal jurisdiction is a critical area for examination. An explication of the fundamentals and subtleties of state-tribal relationships can be found in F. COHEN, HANDBOOK OF FEDERAL INDIAN LAW § 6 (2005). This text is the standard reference in Indian law; relevant sections will be noted throughout this chapter, and its review by the interested practitioner is encouraged. Another useful reference is THE AMERICAN INDIAN LAW DESKBOOK, CONFERENCE OF WESTERN ATTORNEYS GENERAL (2004, Supplement 2007), and for the general practitioner WILLIAM J. CANBY JR., AMERICAN INDIAN LAW IN A NUTSHELL (2d ed. 2004).
4. Johnson v. McIntosh, 21 U.S. (Wheat.) 543 (1823); Worcester v. Georgia, 31 U.S. (6 Pet.) 515 (1832); Cherokee Nation v. Georgia, 30 U.S. (Pet.) 1 (1831). *See generally* COHEN, *supra* note 2, at 204–10. *See also* WILKINSON, *supra* note 2, at 54–59.
5. *See, e.g.,* McLanahan v. Ariz. State Tax Comm'n, 411 U.S. 164 (1973) ("To state that Indian sovereignty is different than that of Federal, State or local governments does not justify ignoring the principles announced by this Court for determining whether a sovereign has waived its taxing authority. . . . Each of these governments has different attributes of sovereignty, which also may derive from different sources. . . . we perceive no principled reason for holding that the different attributes of Indian sovereignty require different treatment in this regard."). *See also* Merrion v. Jicarilla Apache Tribe, 455 U.S. 130, 148 (1982).
6. Lone Wolf v. Hitchcock, 187 U.S. 543 (1903). *See also* New Mexico v. Mescalero Apache Tribe, 462 U.S. 324 (1983).

7. United States v. Wheeler, 435 U.S. 313, 322 (1978). For a view of *Wheeler* as a seminal case in the modern view of sovereignty, see WILKINSON, *supra* note 2, at 61–63.
8. COHEN, *supra* note 2, at 212–20.
9. 21 U.S. 543 (1823).
10. 30 U.S. 1 (1831).
11. 31 U.S. 515 (1832).
12. COHEN, *supra* note 2, at 207–08.
13. *See* Indian Reorganization Act of 1934, 25 U.S.C. §§ 476 *et seq.*, and regulations at 25 C.F.R. § 83.
14. Santa Clara Pueblo v. Martinez, 436 U.S. 49, 62–63 (1978); Washington v. Confederated Tribes of the Colville Reservation, 447 U.S. 134, 152–54 (1980). *See also* COHEN, *supra* note 2, at 134–43 and 173–82.
15. "Indian Country" is defined at 18 U.S.C. § 1151 for the purposes of determining tribal criminal jurisdiction. *See generally* COHEN, *supra* note 2, at 182–99.
16. Montana v. United States, 450 U.S. 544, 566 (1981) ("[E]xercise of tribal power beyond what is necessary to protect tribal self-government or to control internal relations is inconsistent with the dependent status of the tribes, and so cannot survive without express congressional delegation." (citations omitted)). *Accord* Brendale v. Confederated Tribes and Bands of the Yakima Indian Nation, 492 U.S. 408, 424–30 (1989) (holding that tribal zoning authority did not extend to fee lands within the reservation unless there is a "protectable interest" in the activities taking place on such lands).
17. United States v. Washington, 502 F.2d 676 (9th Cir. 1975); COHEN, *supra* note 2, at 1142 n.167.
18. Cherokee Nation v. Georgia, 30 U.S. 1, 17 (1831); COHEN, *supra* note 2, at 418–23.
19. *Id.* In a subsequent review of the same matter, Justice Marshall found that "[t]he Indian nations had always been considered as distinct, independent political communities retaining their original natural rights, as undisputed possessors of the soil, from time immemorial . . . and the settled doctrine of the law of nations is that a weaker power does not surrender its independence, its right of self-government, by associating with a stronger, taking its protection." Worcester v. Georgia, 31 U.S. (Pet.) 515, 558 (1832).
20. Seminole Nation v. United States, 316 U.S. 286, 297 (1942) ("[T]he acts of those who represent it in dealings with the Indians should therefore be judged by the most exacting fiduciary standards.").
21. *See, e.g.*, Cobell v. Norton, 240 F.3d 1081 (D.C. Cir. 2001); Pyramid Lake Paiute Tribe v. Morton, 354 F. Supp. 252 (D.D.C. 1972–73); Nance v. EPA, 645 F.2d 701, 711 (9th Cir. 1981), *cert. denied*, 454 U.S. 1081 (1981); Covelo Indian Cmty. v. FERC, 895 F.2d 581 (9th Cir. 1990).
22. Pyramid Lake Paiute Tribe v. Morton, 354 F. Supp. 252 (D.D.C. 1972–73). *See also* United States v. Washington, 506 F. Supp. 187 (W.D. Wash. 1980); Confederated Tribes of the Umatilla Reservation v. Alexander, 440 F. Supp. 553 (D. Or. 1977). In addition, a district court has upheld the exercise of those rights to enjoin the U.S. Forest Service from holding timber sales "without . . . ensuring that the resources upon which the Tribes' treaty rights depend are protected." Klamath Tribes v. United States, No. 96-381 (D. Or. Oct. 2, 1996).

    The extent to which the trust relationship/responsibility of the federal government can be extended to protect treaty resources is unclear. A thorough development of this theory can be found in Mary Christina Wood's "Trust Trilogy," a series of law review articles: *Indian Land and the Promise of Native Sovereignty: The Trust Doctrine Revisited*, 1994 UTAH L. REV. 1471; *Protecting the Attributes of Native Sovereignty: A New Trust Paradigm for Federal Actions Affecting Tribal Lands and Resources*, 1995 UTAH L. REV. 109; and *Fulfilling the Executive's Trust Responsibility Toward the Native Nations on Environmental Issues: A Partial Critique of the Clinton Administration's Promises and Performance*, 25 ENVTL. L. 733 (1995).
23. Cobell v. Norton, 240 F.3d 1081, 1099 (D.C. Cir. 2001); United States v. Mitchell, 463 U.S. 206, 224–25 (1983); White Mountain Apache Tribe v. United States, 11 Cl. Ct. 614 (1987); COHEN, *supra* note 2, at 423–32.

24. Pyramid Lake Paiute Tribe v. Morton, 354 F. Supp. 252 (D.D.C. 1972–73).
25. Parravano v. Babbitt, 70 F.3d 539 (9th Cir. 1995), *cert. denied*, 518 U.S. 1016 (1996). *See, e.g.,* Nw. Sea Farms v. Army Corps of Eng'rs, 931 F. Supp. 1515 (W.D. Wash. 1996); Klamath Tribes v. U.S. Forest Serv., No. 96-381 (D. Or. Oct. 2, 1996); Lac Courte Oreilles Band of Indians v. Wisconsin, 668 F. Supp. 1233, 1240 (W.D. Wis. 1987). The principle is also articulated in the Presidential Memorandum on Government-to-Government Relationship with Tribal Governments (Sept. 23, 2004) and Exec. Order No. 13,175, 65 Fed. Reg. 67,249 (Nov. 6, 2000). *See also* Mary Christina Wood, *The Indian Trust Responsibility: Protecting Tribal Lands and Resources Through Claims of Injunctive Relief*, 39 Tulsa L. Rev. 355 (2003).
26. Menominee Tribe v. United States, 391 U.S. 404, 405–06 (1968). Unless Congress has clearly authorized the compromise of Indian interests to other public interests, the interests of the tribe cannot be subverted. *See, e.g.,* Nevada v. United States, 463 U.S. 110, 127–28 (1983) ("The Government's brief is replete with references to its fiduciary obligation to the Pyramid Lake Paiute Tribe of Indians, as it properly should be. But the Government seems wholly to ignore in the same brief the obligations that necessarily devolve upon it from having mere title to water rights . . . when the beneficial ownership of these water rights resides elsewhere. . . . The government does not 'compromise' its obligation to one interest that Congress obliges it to represent by the mere fact that it simultaneously performs another task for another interest that Congress has obligated it by statute to do."); Cohen, *supra* note 2, at 438–42.
27. United States v. Dion, 476 U.S. 734, 738–39 (1986). In Menominee Tribe v. United States, 391 U.S. 404 (1968), the Court held that the termination of the reservation by statute did not abrogate the treaty rights of members to hunt and fish on reservation lands without state regulation. The Court found that absent an "explicit statement" abrogating the treaty hunting and fishing rights, an intent by Congress to abrogate those rights "would not be lightly imputed." In addition, the hunting and fishing rights in dispute were not expressly reserved by treaty; rather, the Court inferred such a right from a clause stating that the reservation lands were to be held "as Indian lands are held," thus liberally construing the treaty language in favor of the Indians and as they would have understood the language at treaty time. 391 U.S. 405–06. Cf. S. Dakota v. Yankton Sioux Tribe, 522 U.S. 329, 118 S. Ct. 789, 794 (1998).
28. Nevada v. United States, 463 U.S. 110 (1983); Cohen, *supra* note 2, at 438–42.
29. 193 U.S. 371 (1905).
30. United States v. Winans, 198 U.S. 371 (1981).
31. Arizona v. California, 373 U.S. 546, 598 (1963); Parravano v. Babbitt, 70 F.3d 539 (9th Cir. 1995), *cert. denied*, 518 U.S. 1016 (1996).
32. 207 U.S. 564 (1908).
33. Most recently these principles were applied in resolving off-reservation hunting and fishing rights in Minnesota v. Mille Lacs Band of Chippewa, 526 U.S. 172, 199 (1999). See discussions in United States v. Washington, 384 F. Supp. 312, 354–56 (W.D. Wash. 1974), *aff'd*, 520 F.2d 676 (9th Cir. 1975), *cert. denied*, 423 U.S. 1086 (1976), and, recently interpreting the same treaty clauses again, United States v. Washington, 135 F.3d 618 (9th Cir. 1998). These cases are important rulings in the area of reserved fishing rights, as are the following: Puyallup Tribe v. Dep't of Game, 391 U.S. 392 (1968) (*Puyallup I*), Dep't of Game v. Puyallup Tribe, 414 U.S. 44 (1973) (*Puyallup II*), and Puyallup Tribe v. Dep't of Game, 443 U.S. 165 (1977) (*Puyallup III*). If nothing else, these cases demonstrate the seriousness of the public controversy surrounding the exercise of Indian fishing rights in the Northwest. Cases from the Midwest include Minnesota v. Mille Lacs Band of Chippewa, 526 U.S. 172 (1999); United States v. Bouchard, 464 F. Supp. 1316 (W.D. Wis. 1978); Lac Courte Oreilles Band of Lake Superior Chippewa Indians v. Voigt, 700 F.2d 341 (7th Cir. 1983); Lac Courte Oreilles Band of Lake Superior Chippewa v. Wisconsin, 653 F. Supp. 1420 (W.D. Wis. 1987), 663 F. Supp. 682 (W.D. Wis. 1987), 829 F.2d 601 (7th Cir. 1987), 686 F. Supp. 226 (W.D. Wis. 1988), and 707 F. Supp. 1034 (W.D. Wis. 1989).
34. For example, in *Menominee* the Supreme Court interpreted a treaty to encompass fishing rights in addition to hunting rights because it found that the tribal language did not

have different verbs for hunting and fishing. When written in English, the treaty used only the single verb referring to hunting rights. However, at the time of treaty negotiation the tribes had understood the agreement to include the full scope of its needs to find food through hunting and fishing. Today the treaty is interpreted as it would have been understood by the tribe at the time of signing—to encompass both hunting and fishing rights. *Menominee*, 391 U.S. 404, 406 (1968). *See also* Washington v. Passenger Fishing Vessel Ass'n, 443 U.S. 658, 667 (1979).

35. United States v. Montana, 101 S. Ct. 1245, 1258 (1981) (nontribal members are not subject to tribal regulation on reservation lands owned by non-Indians unless their "conduct threatens or has some direct effect on the political integrity, the economic security or health or welfare of the tribe."); Kake v. Egan, 369 U.S. 60 (1962) (if a reservation has been terminated, the right of exclusivity no longer applies); Sohappy v. Smith, 302 F. Supp. 899 (D. Or. 1969) (state cannot diminish treaty rights by implementation of some other state objective or policy.)

36. COHEN, *supra* note 2, at 1143–45. *See* Puyallup v. Washington Dep't of Game, 391 U.S. 392 (1968); Menominee v. United States, 391 U.S. 404 (1968); *See generally* Nye, Comment, *Where Do the Buffalo Roam? Determining the Scope of American Indian Off-Reservation Hunting Rights in the Pacific Northwest*, 67 WASH. L. REV. 175 (1992); Comment, *Reaffirming the Guarantee: Indian Treaty Rights to Hunt and Fish Off-Reservation in Minnesota*, 20 WM. MITCHELL L. REV. 1177 (1994).

37. United States v. Winans, 198 U.S. 371, 380–81 (1905); United States v. Washington, 135 F.3d 618 (9th Cir. 1998); COHEN, *supra* note 2, at 1139–41.

38. State v. Tinno, 497 P.2d 1386 (1974); Kimball v. Callahan, 493 F.2d 564, 566 (9th Cir. 1974), *cert. denied*, 419 U.S. 1019 (1974); United States v. Washington, 384 F. Supp. 402 (W.D. Wash. 1974). *See also* Minnesota v. Mille Lacs Band of Chippewa, 526 U.S. 172 (1999).

39. United States v. Washington, 135 F.3d 618 (9th Cir. 1998) (*Shellfish I*).

40. Menominee Tribe v. United States, 391 U.S. 404 (1968); COHEN, *supra* note 2, at 1163–64.

41. *Menominee*, 391 U.S. at 410–12; *see also* United States v. Washington, 626 F. Supp. 1405 (W.D. Wash. 1985).

42. *Menominee*, 391 U.S. at 411–13; Kimball v. Callahan, 493 F.2d 564 (9th Cir.), *cert. denied*, 419 U.S. 1019 (1974) (holding that although the Klamath reservation had been terminated, the right to hunt, fish, and gather on former reservation lands, now National Forest lands, could continue free of state regulation). *See also* Whitefoot v. United States, 293 F.2d 658 (Cl. Ct. 1961), *cert. denied*, 369 U.S. 818 (1962) (holding that Indian rights to fish were not terminated by tribes' agreement to compensation for loss of the Celilo Falls salmon fishery).

43. Winters v. United States, 207 U.S. 564 (1908). The Court found lands ceded by the tribes could not be used in agriculture or for ranching purposes without water. Thus, the Court reasoned, the absence of an express reservation of water could be interpreted two ways: (1) the tribes gave the water to the United States when they executed the agreement, or (2) the tribes knew they would require the use of water for their new life on the reservation and reserved it to themselves. The Court held that the purposes for which the federal government confined the tribes to a reservation was to become an agrarian people attached to a single piece of land and therefore must have reserved sufficient water to accomplish this purpose.

44. Arizona v. California, 373 U.S. 546 (1963). *See also* United States v. New Mexico, 438 U.S. 696 (1968); COHEN, *supra* note 2, at 1174–76. *See, e.g.*, Judith V. Royster, *A Primer on Indian Water Rights: More Questions Than Answers*, 30 TULSA L.J. 61 (1994).

45. Arizona v. California, 373 U.S. 546, 598–601 (1963); Arizona v. San Carlos Apache Tribe, 463 U.S. 545, 571 (1983); Colo. River Water Conservation Dist. v. United States, 424 U.S. 800 (1976).

46. Arizona v. California, 373 U.S. 546 (1963); *cf.* United States v. New Mexico, 438 U.S. 696 (1978) (refusing to increase tribal reserved rights to support increased acreage). *See* Winters v. United States, 207 U.S. 564, 576–77 (1908).
47. Confederated Salish & Kottenai Tribes v. Namen, 665 F.2d 951 (9th Cir. 1982); United States v. Adair, 723 F.2d 1394 (9th Cir. 1983); Kittitas Reclamation Dist. v. Sunnyside Irrigation Dist., 763 F.2d 1032 (9th Cir. 1985); Colville Confederated Tribes v. Walton, 647 F.2d 42 (9th Cir. 1985); Washington Dep't of Fish & Game v. Puyallup Tribe, 414 U.S. 44, 49 (1973) (*Puyallup II*). *See* Michael C. Blumm, *Unconventional Waters: The Quiet Revolution in Federal and Tribal Minimum Streamflows*, 19 Ecol. L.Q. 445 (1992).
48. *Puyallup II*, 414 U.S. at 49.
49. United States v. Dion, 476 U.S. 734 (1986).
50. *Id.*; Cohen, *supra* note 2, at 1158–61.
51. United States v. Billie, 667 F. Supp. 1485 (S.D. Fla. 1985).
52. 16 U.S.C. §§ 668 *et seq.*
53. The American bald eagle was listed as endangered in the contiguous lower 48 states and threatened in Oregon, Washington, Wisconsin, Michigan, and Minnesota in 1978. 43 Fed. Reg. 6230 (Feb. 14, 1978). The bald eagle was delisted throughout the United States and a recovery monitoring effort begun in 2007. 72 Fed. Reg. 37,345 (July 9, 2007). At the time *United States v. Billie* was tried and decided, the eagle was listed as "threatened" under the provisions of the ESA.
54. *Dion*, 476 U.S. at 737.
55. *Id.* at 738–39.
56. *Id.*
57. *Id.* at 739. As stated in *Dion*, this test for determining treaty abrogation has become known as the "consideration and choice test" encapsulating Congress's consideration of treaty rights and choosing to abrogate them. *Cf.* Anderson v. Evans, 371 F.3d 475, 499–501 (9th Cir. 2004) (finding a treaty right may be subjected to the procedural components of a conservation statute without abrogating the treaty).
58. *Dion*, 476 U.S. at 739–40.
59. *Id.* at 740.
60. *Id.* at 745.
61. *Id.* at 746.
62. *Id.* at 744–45.
63. United States v. Billie, 667 F. Supp. 1485 (S.D. Fla. 1985).
64. 437 U.S. 153, 176 (1978) (quoting *Hearings on Endangered Species before the Subcomm. of the H. Comm. on Merchant Marine and Fisheries*, 93d Cong., 1st Sess. 202 (1973) (statement of Assistant Secretary of the Interior)).
65. *Billie*, 667 F. Supp. at 1488.
66. *Id.* at 1492.
67. *Puyallup II*, 414 U.S. at 49.
68. *Billie*, 667 F. Supp. at 1489–90.
69. The court in United States v. Bresette, 761 F. Supp. 658 (D. Minn. 1991), applied the analysis of *Dion* to the Migratory Bird Treaty Act and found no abrogation of the right to hunt on or off the reservation; however, the holding was based in part on the fact that the species at issue were not threatened with endangerment.
70. A district court in Oregon stated, "Moreover, the federal government has a substantive duty to protect to the 'fullest extent possible' the tribes' treaty rights and the resources on which those rights depend . . . including consideration of habitat needs for any species hunted or trapped by tribal members. . . ." Klamath Tribes v. U.S. Forest Serv., No. 96-381 (D. Or. Oct. 2, 1996). *See also* Confederated Tribes of the Umatilla Reservation v. Alexander, 440 F. Supp. 553 (D. Or. 1977) (enjoining a dam that would destroy fish habitat and thus tribal fishing rights); Muckelshoot v. Hall, 698 F. Supp. 1504 (W.D. Wash. 1988) (enjoining a marina that would destroy fishing areas); Kittitas Reclamation Dist. v. Sunnyside Valley Irrigation Dist., 763 F.2d 1032 (9th Cir.), *cert. denied*, 474 U.S. 1032 (1985).

71. A Secretarial Order is an internal guidance mechanism used by the Department of the Interior. Its function is to give policy direction within the department.
72. Tribal Position Paper 2–3, Aug. 28, 1996 (on file with the author.)
73. *See* Charles Wilkinson, *The Role of Bilateralism in Fulfilling the Federal-Tribal Relationship: The Tribal Rights-Endangered Species Secretarial Order*, 72 WASH. L. REV. 1063, 1075–81 (1997).
74. Secretarial Order No. 3206, Sec. 1. It is worth noting that the Secretarial Order was among several initiatives of the Clinton administration to ensure that rights and interests of Native Americans are given appropriate recognition as sovereigns when federal law is executed. For instance, several years before the Secretarial Order was contemplated, a Presidential Memorandum was issued instructing the federal agencies to operate in a government-to-government relationship with federally recognized Indian tribes. Presidential Memorandum, Apr. 29, 1994, 59 Fed. Reg. 22,951 (1994). Later the president issued a more detailed Executive Order on "Consultation and Coordination with Indian Tribal Governments" to enhance the participation and consideration of Indian tribal governments in the regulatory process. Exec. Order No. 13,175, 65 Fed. Reg. 67,249 (2000).
75. At least one court has examined Secretarial Order No. 3206 and found it to be "guidance" for the Department of the Interior and not creating any substantive trust obligation. Miccosukee Tribe of Indians of Fla. v. United States, 430 F. Supp. 2d 1328, 1336 (S.D. Fla. May 12, 2006).
76. Principle 1 provides that "[t]he Departments shall work directly with Indian tribes on a government-to-government basis to promote healthy ecosystems." Principle 2 states, "the Departments shall recognize that Indian lands are not subject to the same controls as federal public lands." Principle 3 is probably the most critical to the success of the Secretarial Order: "[t]he Departments shall assist Indian tribes in developing and expanding tribal programs so that healthy ecosystems are promoted and conservation restrictions are unnecessary." If the services and tribes achieve even a portion of the goals articulated in Principle 3, the Secretarial Order will be considered a breakthrough in developing intergovernmental partnerships managing natural resources.
77. Secretarial Order No. 3206, Principle 2(B).
78. *Id.*
79. *Id.* Principle 3.
80. *Id.* Principle 3(A).
81. *Id.* Principle 4.
82. *Id.* app. § 3(B).
83. *Id.* app. § 3(C).
84. *Id.* app. § 3(C)(3)(a).
85. *Id.* app. § 3(C)(3)(b).
86. *Id.*
87. Marren Sanders, *Implementing the Federal Endangered Species Act in Indian Country: The Promise and Reality of Secretarial Order 3206*, JOINT OCCASIONAL PAPERS ON NATIVE AFFAIRS no. 2007-1, available at http://www.jopna.net.
88. *Id.* at 24.
89. *Id.*
90. *Id.* at 38–39.
91. *See generally* Vincent Mulier, *Recognizing the Full Scope of the Right to Take Fish Under the Stevens Treaties: The History of Fishing Rights Litigation in the Pacific Northwest*, 31 AM. INDIAN L. REV. 41 (2006).
92. The "Stevens Treaties," negotiated in the mid-1850s by Isaac I. Stevens, Superintendent of Indian Affairs of the Washington Territory, involved a number of Indian tribes located in the Pacific Northwest, specifically the Treaty of Medicine Creek, 10 Stat. 1132 (Dec. 26, 1854); Treaty of Point Elliot, 12 Stat. 927 (Jan. 22, 1855); Treaty of Point No Point, 12 Stat. 933 (Jan. 26, 1855); Treaty of Neah Bay, 12 Stat. 939 (Jan. 31, 1855); Treaty with the Yakamas, 12 Stat. 951 (June 9, 1855); Treaty of Olympia, 12 Stat. 971 (July 1, 1855). *See generally* Washington v. Wash. State Commercial Passenger Fishing Vessel

Ass'n, 443 U.S. 658, 661–69, 99 S. Ct. 3055, 61 L. Ed. 2d 823 (1979). Affected Indian tribes include Hoh, Lower Elwha Band of Clallam Indians, Lummi, Makah, Muckleshoot, Nisqually, Nooksack, Port Gamble Band of Clallam Indians, Puyallup, Quileute, Quinault, Sauk Suiattle, Skokomish, Squaxin Island, Stillaguamish, Suquamish, Swinomish, Tulalip, Upper Skagit, and Yakama. The treaties reserved to the signing Tribes certain fishing rights in common with non-Indians. The typical expression of this concept can be found in the Treaty of Point No Point, which provides: "The right of taking fish at usual and accustomed grounds and stations is further secured to said Indians, in common with all citizens of the United States; and of erecting temporary houses for the purpose of curing; together with the privilege of hunting and gathering roots and berries on open and unclaimed lands. *Provided*, however, that they shall not take shell-fish from any beds staked or cultivated by citizens." Treaty of Point No Point 12 Stat. 933, art. 4 (1855). Because this language reserving the rights to fish in all usual and accustomed places was repeated in virtually the same form in all of the treaties negotiated by Stevens, legal decisions affecting one tribe tend to affect all Stevens Treaty Tribes. In addition, there is a tendency for a subset of tribes to become the lead plaintiffs in litigation and the others to intervene to represent their interests in the interpretation of treaty language. *See, e.g.*, Washington v. Wash. State Commercial Passenger Fishing Vessel Ass'n, 443 U.S. 658, 661–69 (1979).

93. 384 F. Supp. 312 (W.D. Wash. Feb. 12, 1974), *aff'd and remanded* 520 F.2d 676 (9th Cir. 1975), *cert. denied*, 423 U.S. 1086 (1976) (*Phase I*).
94. 384 F. Supp at 328.
95. 506 F. Supp. 187, 202 (W.D. Wash. Sept. 26, 1980) *aff'd in part, rev'd in part*, 694 F.2d 1374 (9th Cir. 1982), *vacated* 759 F.2d 1353 (9th Cir. 1985) (en banc).
96. 506 F. Supp. at 208.
97. 694 F.2d 1374 (9th Cir. 1982).
98. 759 F.2d 1353, 1257 (9th Cir. 1985) (en banc), *cert. denied*, 474 U.S. 994 (1985).
99. *Id.*
100. *Id.*
101. 57 Fed. Reg. 14,653 (Apr. 22, 1992); 60 Fed. Reg. 38,011 (July 25, 1995); 61 Fed. Reg. 41,541 (Aug. 9, 1996); 63 Fed. Reg. 11,482 (Mar. 9, 1998).
102. United States v. Washington, No. CV 9213RSM, Aug. 22, 2007, 2007 WL 2437166 (W.D. Wash.).
103. *Id.*, slip op. at 4.
104. *Id.*
105. *Id.*, slip op. at 10. In the course of the litigation, the State of Washington's counterclaims against the United States for placing a disproportionate burden of meeting the treaty-based duties on the State and for managing the federal lands in such a way as to create an unfair burden on the State were dismissed based on the United States' failure to waive sovereign immunity.
106. *Id.* slip op. at 12.
107. *Id.*
108. Lynda Mapes, *Culvert Ruling Backs Tribes*, Seattle Post-Intelligencer, Aug. 23, 2007 ("'This could be very big,' said Mason Morisset, an attorney representing tribes in the case. 'If it stands, you will see tribes assert themselves on a broad range of activities to protect the habitat. Whether it's clearing wetlands or building roads and developments . . . if we can show you are going to have a net loss of habitat, that is a treaty rights violation.'"). See also O. Yale Lewis III, *Treaty Fishing Rights: A Habitat Right as Part of the Trinity of Rights Implied by the Fishing Clause of the Stevens Treaties*, 27 Am. Indian L. Rev. 281 (2003); Ruth Langridge, *The Right to Habitat Protection*, 29 Pub. Land L. Rev. 41 (2008), Wm. Fisher, *The Culverts Opinion and the Need for a Broader Property Based Construct*, J. Envtl. L. & Litig. 491 n.23 (2008).
109. Mapes, *supra* note 107.
110. A turn of phrase borrowed from Wallace Stegner, *Angle of Repose*, meaning the maximum angle of a stable slope determined by friction, cohesion, and the shapes of the particles.

7

The Take Prohibition

Patrick Parenteau

Introduction

On its face, the take prohibition in section 9 of the Endangered Species Act appears to provide stricter and more comprehensive protection than the section 7 jeopardy prohibition. Unlike section 7, which applies only to actions "funded, approved or carried out" by federal agencies, section 9 applies to everyone, individuals and corporations, as well as governmental entities at all levels. While section 7 is mainly concerned with the survival and recovery of entire species, section 9 is concerned about protecting individual animals.[1] Habitat protection is also potentially broader under section 9, because it does not require any formal designation of "critical habitat" as does section 7. And while violations of both section 7 and section 9 are enforceable by civil actions including citizen suits, there are criminal sanctions for section 9 violations.[2] Section 9 is also the principal means of enforcing restrictions on international trade in wildlife under the CITES convention.[3]

Yet over the 35-year history of the ESA, section 9 has not played a prominent role in litigation to enforce the Act. Numerous cases have been brought to enforce the consultation requirements of section 7 and the listing requirements of section 4, but relatively few section 9 cases have been brought.[4] One reason is that section 9 cases are much harder to win because they are fact-intensive and causation can be very difficult to prove, whereas the bulk of section 7 and section 4 cases are procedural in nature and reviewed "on the record." Still, as the following discussion illustrates, section 9 liability should not be taken lightly by anyone engaged in development activities that may have adverse, albeit indirect and hard to foresee, effects on protected species.

Current State of the Law

Statutory and Regulatory Framework

Section 9 makes it unlawful for "any person"[5] to "take" any "endangered species of fish or wildlife."[6] The Act defines "take" to mean "to harass, harm, pursue, hunt, shoot, wound, kill, trap, capture, or collect, or to attempt to engage in any such conduct."[7] By rule, the Secretary of the Interior has defined the term "harm" to include "significant habitat modification or degradation where it actually kills or injures wildlife by significantly impairing essential behavioral patterns, including breeding, feeding or sheltering."[8] The first case to interpret and apply the harm rule was *Palila v. Hawaii Department of Land & Natural Resources*.[9] There the district court held, and the Ninth Circuit affirmed, that habitat destruction caused by feral sheep and goats to the habitat of the endangered palila bird was a take, based on expert testimony that continued habitat loss threatened the bird's survival and recovery.[10] Following this decision, the U.S. Fish and Wildlife Service (FWS) sought to narrow the harm rule, but in *Palila II*, the Ninth Circuit held that the revised regulatory definition did not change the basic thrust of the rule, and once again ordered removal of the offending sheep.[11] However, the court expressly refrained from deciding "whether harm includes habitat degradation that merely retards recovery."[12]

The U.S. Supreme Court upheld (6–3) the Secretary's broad regulatory interpretation of harm in *Babbitt v. Sweet Home Chapter of Communities for a Great Oregon*.[13] *Sweet Home* involved a difficult facial challenge to the rule, and a majority of the Court ruled that the Secretary's interpretation of an ambiguous term was reasonable and entitled to *Chevron* deference.[14] The Court acknowledged that causation could present difficult issues but expressly declined to opine on the outer limits of what the Secretary's authority might be to enforce the take prohibition.[15] In his majority opinion, Justice Stevens noted that the "harm" regulation could be read to "incorporate ordinary requirements of proximate causation and foreseeability."[16] In her concurring opinion, Justice O'Connor disagreed with the rationale adopted by the Ninth Circuit in the *Palila* cases.[17] However, Justice O'Connor also parted company with Justice Scalia's dissenting view that "take" can only mean "affirmative conduct intentionally directed against a particular animal or animals."[18] Justice O'Connor noted that activity making it "impossible" for animals to breed would, in her view, constitute "actual injury."[19] Suffice to say, the *Sweet Home* case has generated considerable commentary and little consensus on how it should be applied.[20]

Constitutional Challenges to the Take Prohibition

Numerous constitutional challenges have been mounted against the take prohibition, but none have succeeded. One set of cases has been based on the commerce clause. Five different circuits have rejected arguments that the application of the take prohibition to a variety of species, mostly of the noncharismatic variety, exceeded Congress's commerce clause authority.[21] In light of the fact that the Supreme Court denied certiorari in all five cases, it appears that the constitutionality of the take prohibition has been largely settled.

Similarly, claims that application of the ESA's take prohibition caused a "taking" under the Fifth Amendment have not fared well. In *Christy v. Hodel*,[22] the Ninth Circuit held that a rancher was not entitled to compensation for sheep eaten by a grizzly bear. In *Boise Cascade Corp. v. United States*,[23] the Federal Circuit ruled that logging restrictions to protect northern spotted owl did not constitute a "physical taking" of the timber. In another case involving logging restrictions in spotted owl habitat, the Federal Circuit applied the "parcel as a whole"[24] rule to deny compensation.[25]

Irrigators in California's Tulare Lake Basin did manage to score a rare victory when the George W. Bush administration decided to settle a takings claim based on flow restrictions to protect endangered salmon following an adverse ruling from the Federal Claims Court in *Tulare Lake Basin v. United States*.[26] However, the reasoning of this decision was sharply rejected in *Klamath Irrigation District v. United States*,[27] where Judge Allegra, in denying a similar takings claim, said: "[W]ith all due respect, *Tulare* appears to be wrong on some counts, incomplete in others and distinguishable at all events."

More recently, however, a panel of the Federal Circuit ruled (2–1) that a biological opinion requiring a municipality to provide water to a fish ladder at a Bureau of

Reclamation facility constituted a "physical appropriation" of the water by the federal government.[28] Judge Mayer filed a vigorous dissent arguing that, under the controlling law of California, the municipality had no property interest in the water.[29] Recently, the Solicitor decided not to file a petition for certiorari. The case is currently on remand to the Federal Claims Court for a trial on the merits, at which the government is free to challenge whether California law in fact recognizes a property right in the water in question.

Finally, the courts have also held that Fifth Amendment takings claims are not ripe until the property owner has applied for an incidental take permit under section 10 of the Act and has attempted to work out an acceptable habitat conservation plan that would allow some economic use of the property.[30] In *Morris v. United States*, for example, the court rejected the landowners' claim that the cost of the permit process would exceed the value of the timber they wanted to cut.[31]

Jurisdictional Prerequisites to Bringing Suit Under the ESA Citizen Suit Provision

Standing

Section 11(g)(1)(A) of the ESA authorizes "any person" to bring suit against "any person" to enforce the take prohibitions of the Act.[32] As mentioned, the statute defines the term "person" very broadly. In *Bennett v. Spear*,[33] the Supreme Court ruled that the all-encompassing nature of this term included ranchers seeking to invalidate a biological opinion in order to protect their economic interests in water deliveries from a federal irrigation project in the Klamath Basin in Oregon. By the same token, this broad definition makes a number of parties potentially liable for violations of the statutory and regulatory restrictions on take. Defendants in these cases have included corporations,[34] federal agencies,[35] state agencies,[36] towns,[37] school districts,[38] irrigation districts,[39] county governments,[40] and even members of Indian tribes.[41]

Notwithstanding the broad scope of the citizen suit provision, plaintiffs must still satisfy Article III standing requirements to provide a jurisdictional basis for federal courts to hear these cases.[42] In accord with the by now familiar three-part test set out in *Lujan*, a plaintiff "must show that: (1) it has suffered an 'injury in fact' that is (a) concrete and particularized and (b) actual or imminent, not conjectural or hypothetical; (2) the injury is fairly traceable to the challenged action of the defendant; and (3) it is likely, as opposed to merely speculative, that the injury will be redressed by a favorable decision."[43] Standing is a jurisdictional issue that can be raised at any stage of the litigation by the parties or by the court *sua sponte*; further, plaintiffs have the affirmative burden to not only allege but prove standing. It is therefore critical to identify the individuals who can provide standing declarations as early as possible. In the D.C. Circuit, a plaintiff whose standing is not "self-evident" is required to file declarations and other proof of standing "at the first appropriate point in the review proceeding," regardless of whether standing has been challenged.[44]

Injury to aesthetic and recreational interests is sufficient to support individual and organizational standing provided the declarations establish the requisite link between the challenged action and the asserted injury.[45] And even though the species of concern is often named as the lead plaintiff, such as in the *Palila* cases, it is their human benefactors who must establish standing.[46]

60-Day Notice

Plaintiffs must also satisfy the 60-day-notice requirement of the ESA citizen suit prior to filing suit.[47] In *Save the Yaak Committee v. Block*,[48] the Ninth Circuit construed the notice requirement as "jurisdictional" and dismissed an ESA claim for failure to provide a timely notice ("Because of the failure to give written notice timely, we lack jurisdiction to reach the ESA claim."). Other courts have ruled that the notice requirement, while not jurisdictional in a strict sense, is nevertheless a mandatory prerequisite and failure to comply results in dismissal of the ESA claim.[49] The notice must be sent to the correct parties,[50] and must contain enough information to put the recipient on notice of the specific violation(s).[51] Some courts have held that plaintiffs who are not named in the notice letter are subject to dismissal.[52]

Standard of Review

The courts apply different standards of review depending on whether the defendant is a federal agency or a nonfederal entity. Where the defendant is a nonfederal party and the activity being challenged has not been authorized under an incidental take statement[53] courts have applied the de novo standard.[54] But where the defendant is a federal agency and the activity being challenged arises out of a section 7 consultation, the courts tend to apply the "arbitrary and capricious" standard of the Administrative Procedure Act.[55] Under the arbitrary and capricious standard, courts typically limit review to the administrative record.[56] However, where injunctive relief is sought courts have allowed "extra-record" evidence or in some cases a modified de novo proceeding.[57]

Emerging Issues and Future Directions

Three aspects of the take prohibition have been the subject of evolving administrative and judicial interpretations. The first is how to establish that take by habitat modification is occurring. The second is the so-called "vicarious liability" issue, in particular to what extent agencies that authorize activities that result in take are liable under section 9. The final issue of ongoing consideration is when an activity can be enjoined in anticipation that it will result in take. Each issue is discussed in this section.

Proving Harm from Habitat Modification

Habitat loss is the greatest threat to species viability.[58] Yet habitat degradation alone is probably not sufficient to prove a take under section 9.[59] The harm rule, as interpreted in *Sweet Home*, requires a causal connection between habitat modification and "actual injury" to an identifiable member of the listed species. The critical question, however, is what constitutes "injury." Is it injury to a population, or injury to a specific individual? Is the loss of breeding habitat enough? Or must there also be proof that a specific animal was unable to breed? The law is still unsettled on this point.

Notwithstanding Justice O'Connor's disparaging remarks in *Sweet Home*, the Ninth Circuit continues to follow the *Palila* rule that habitat loss impairing breeding success is sufficient to constitute harm and therefore violate the take prohibition. In *Marbled Murrelet v. Babbitt*,[60] the court rejected the argument that *Sweet Home* requires evidence of harm to a specific individual as opposed to harm to the population. After reviewing the various opinions in *Sweet Home*, the Ninth Circuit concluded: "Thus, under *Sweet Home*, a habitat modification which significantly impairs the breeding and sheltering of a protected species amounts to 'harm' under the ESA."[61] Outcomes depend heavily on the facts of particular cases. For example, in *American Bald Eagle v. Bhatti*, plaintiffs alleged that state regulations allowing the use of lead shot in deer hunting on state lands threatened bald eagles that might feed on the remains. The First Circuit found that plaintiffs, who acknowledged the risk of harm was "one in a million," failed to meet their burden of proving an imminent threat of actual injury to an identifiable eagle.[62] In *San Carlos Apache Tribe v. United States*,[63] the court ruled that plaintiffs failed to overcome the government's evidence that reservoir drawdown did not pose a serious threat to the bald eagle nesting around it. In *Morril v. Lujan*,[64] the court dismissed an ESA claim that construction of a housing project threatened the Perdido Key beach mouse because plaintiffs failed to prove that the mouse was even present on the site. In *United States v. West Coast Forest Resources*,[65] the court ruled that the United States had failed to prove that logging in spotted owl habitat would injure a specific pair of owls. This decision followed an earlier ruling requiring that the government track the movements of the owls with radio telemetry to determine their exact movements through the forest.[66]

In *Alabama v. Corps of Engineers*,[67] the court denied a motion for a temporary restraining order against the Corps' operation of a dam and lock because the state had not demonstrated a "but for" causation between the Corps' actions and the take of several species of protected mussels. The court also found that an ongoing drought was an intervening cause that insulated the Corps from liability in any event.

On the other hand, a number of courts have given broad scope to the concept of harm from habitat degradation. In *Bensman v. U.S. Forest Service*,[68] the court found that the Forest Service's salvage logging operations on the Mark Twain National Forest posed an imminent threat of harm to the Indiana bat from "(1) the removal of dead or dying trees which could be roost trees used by male bats in the summer; (2) activity in the vicinity of the hibernaculum during the fall swarming season; and (3) disturbance to the roosting male and female bats in the hibernaculum, resulting in the depletion of fat stores." The court forcefully rejected the argument that actual death or physical injury to a specific animal was required:

> A finding of "harm" does not require death to individual members of the species; nor does it require a finding that habitat degradation is presently driving the species further toward extinction. Habitat destruction that prevents the

recovery of the species by affecting essential behavioral patterns causes actual injury to the species and effects a taking under section 9 of the Act.[69]

Similarly, in *House v. U.S. Forest Service* the court found that a proposed timber sale threatened to harm the Indiana bat by eliminating forage habitat.[70] In *Greenpeace v. NMFS*,[71] the court held that fishing quotas were depleting the prey base for the Steller sea lion to such an extent as to cause harm to the population. In *CBD v. Point Marina Development*,[72] the district court ruled that construction of a 200-unit condominium on a lakefront constituted "harassment" of bald eagles by cutting down perches and driving away prey. However, on appeal the Ninth Circuit ruled that the delisting of the bald eagle rendered the case moot and vacated the lower court's judgment.[73]

Vicarious Liability

Governmental agencies and other entities that authorize third-party activities resulting in take may also be liable under the ESA. The first case to establish this principle was *Defenders of Wildlife v. EPA*,[74] where the Eighth Circuit ruled that the Environmental Protection Agency's registration of strychnine under the Federal Insecticide, Fungicide, and Rodenticide Act constituted an illegal take. The court noted that "the record shows endangered species have eaten the strychnine bait, either directly or indirectly, and as a result, they have died."[75] Based on the "clear relationship" between the registration decision and the deaths of endangered species, the court concluded that "EPA's registrations constituted takings of endangered species."[76]

Another seminal decision extending the vicarious liability rule to cover state agencies was *Strahan v. Coxe*,[77] where the First Circuit ruled that the Commonwealth of Massachusetts was liable for injury to the critically endangered Northern right whales resulting from the licensing of gillnets and lobster pots for commercial fishing. The court rejected the Commonwealth's argument that the licensing was not the "proximate cause" of the whales becoming entangled in the nets, stating, "[A] governmental third party pursuant to whose authority an actor directly exacts a taking of an endangered species may be deemed to have violated the provisions of the ESA."[78] The court further ruled that it was not necessary to prove that whales had in fact been killed by fishing gear. Rather, plaintiffs met their burden by introducing uncontroverted expert affidavits showing that whales had become entangled in fishing gear in the waters off Massachusetts.[79] Likewise, the court gave little weight to evidence that Massachusetts had tried to minimize entanglement: "Given that there was evidence that any entanglement with fishing gear injures a Northern Right whale and given that a single injury to one whale is a taking under the ESA, efforts to minimize such entanglements are irrelevant."[80]

The *Strahan* court also rejected the Commonwealth's argument that the 10th Amendment barred the injunctive relief sought. The Commonwealth cited a line of cases holding that the 10th Amendment prevents Congress from enacting laws that have the effect of "coercing" states to enforce federal regulations.[81] The First Circuit disagreed with that characterization of the effect of the lower court's injunction: "Rather, the court directed the defendants to find a means of bringing the Commonwealth's scheme into compliance with federal law."[82] The court further noted that "the Commonwealth has the choice of either regulating in this area according to federal ESA standards or having its regulations preempted by the federal ESA provisions and regulations."[83]

Since the *Strahan* decision, there have been a number of cases finding state and local governments liable for authorizing third parties to undertake activities that take listed species. In *United States v. Town of Plymouth*,[84] the court granted a preliminary injunction against a local ordinance allowing vehicles to drive on beaches where piping plovers were nesting. The court ruled that: "The Service has proved a likelihood of success on its claim that current management practices with respect to ORV [off-road vehicle] access to Plymouth Long Beach have actually harmed piping plovers and will continue to cause harm to the species if they remain unchecked."[85] In *Loggerhead Turtle v. County Council of Volusia*,[86] the county was held liable for adopting an *inadequate* ordinance regulating beach lighting to minimize take of sea turtles through the "disorienting" effect of lights on turtle nestlings seeking to make their way to the sea. This case is notable because the county had received an incidental take permit covering the countywide ordinance but because not all of the communities adopted the beach lighting regulations, the court found that there was ongoing "take" of turtles by the nonparticipating communities: "We agree with the Turtles that they have shown a sufficient causal connection to seek to hold Volusia County liable for 'harmfully' inadequate regulation of artificial beachfront lighting in the nonparty municipalities of Daytona Beach, Daytona Beach Shores, Ormond Beach and New Smyrna Beach."[87]

State hunting and trapping laws have also come under fire. In *Animal Protection Institute v. Holsten*,[88] the court enjoined a state trapping permit program that had been shown to take the threatened Canada lynx. The court rejected the state's argument that the conduct of the trappers is an independent, intervening cause that relieved the state Department of Natural Resources (DNR) of liability.[89] Citing the Restatement (Second) of Torts, the court stated:

> [F]or purposes of determining proximate cause the DNR's licensure and regulation of trapping is the "stimulus" for the trapper's conduct that results in incidental takings. Accordingly, the trapper's conduct is not an independent intervening cause that breaks the chain of causation between the DNR and the incidental takings of lynx.[90]

This case continues the trend of decisions that extend section 9 liability to agencies that authorize the activity that results in the unlawful take.

Injunctive Relief

In *Tennessee Valley Authority v. Hill*,[91] the Supreme Court ruled that Congress explicitly removed the federal judiciary's traditional equitable authority to balance competing interests in deciding whether to issue injunctions under the ESA. The

Court said that the "language, history, and structure of the legislation under review here indicates beyond doubt that Congress intended endangered species to be afforded the highest of priorities."[92] Further, the Court noted that Congress considered and rejected language that would have permitted an agency to weigh the preservation of species against the agency's primary mission: "The pointed omission of the type of qualifying language previously included in endangered species legislation reveals a conscious decision by Congress to give endangered species priority over the 'primary missions' of federal agencies."[93]

Though *TVA v. Hill* dealt with a substantive violation of section 7, the lower courts have also applied it to procedural violations of section 9.[94] Nevertheless, plaintiffs must prove "a reasonably certain threat of future harm" to enjoin a prospective take.[95] Evidence of past take is relevant but not sufficient for this purpose. One of the leading cases is *National Wildlife Federation v. Burlington Northern Railroad, Inc.*[96] There a train derailed near Glacier National Park, spilling grain along the tracks that attracted a number of grizzly bears, at least five of whom were killed when struck by trains.[97] The National Wildlife Federation (NWF) moved for a preliminary injunction to require Burlington Northern (BN) to reduce speed through the area of the spill and to assess other protective measures such as installing air bags on the locomotives. The district court denied the injunction on the ground that NWF failed to prove that more bears would be killed, particularly in light of the preventive actions taken by BN.[98] The Ninth Circuit upheld that decision, reasoning: "While we do not require that future harm be shown with certainty before an injunction may issue, we do require that a future injury be sufficiently *likely*."[99] The court elaborated:

> We are not saying that a threat of extinction to the species is required before an injunction may issue under the ESA. This would be contrary to the spirit of the statute, whose goal of preserving threatened and endangered species can also be achieved through incremental steps. However, what we require is a definitive threat of future harm to protected species, not mere speculation.[100]

As these cases demonstrate, plaintiffs attempting to establish an section 9 violation are advised to have sufficient evidence in hand to show the likelihood of take before filing suit.

Conclusion

Section 9 has not lived up to the expectations that some had for it. It has not become the premier enforcement tool under the ESA, and the law of take is still evolving. Conventional notions of proximate cause do not mesh well with the way that the science of conservation biology evaluates the risk of extinction from multiple factors including habitat loss and fragmentation. Some courts have recognized the ecosystem context in which harm to a species must be considered and have given section 9 a broad reading. Others have taken a narrower view and demanded greater proof of proximate injury to identifiable animals.

Still, section 9 remains a potent weapon in the arsenal of species protection. Perhaps its greatest contribution to species preservation is the incentive it creates for habitat conservation through the incidental take permit and habitat conservation plans.[101] Without the threat of section 9 liability, fewer landowners would be motivated to undertake the substantial conservation efforts these programs require.[102]

Notes

1. The Act also provides protection for plants. Section 9 makes it unlawful "to remove and reduce to possession any such species from areas under federal jurisdiction; maliciously damage or destroy any such species on any such area; or remove, cut, dig up, or damage or destroy any such species on any other area in knowing violation of any law or regulation of any state or in the violation of any state criminal trespass law." 16 U.S.C. § 1538(a)(2)(B). However, there have been no reported decisions enforcing this provision.
2. A person who "knowingly" violates the take prohibition faces a civil penalty of up to $25,000 and a criminal fine of up to $50,000 and imprisonment for up to one year. *See* 16 U.S.C. § 1540(a) (2000) In *United States v. McKittrick*, 142 F.3d 1170, 1176 (9th Cir. 1998), *cert. denied*, 525 U.S. 1072 (1999), defendant was convicted of killing an endangered gray wolf notwithstanding his claim that he did not know he was shooting a wolf. In the 1978 amendments, Congress replaced "willfully" with "knowingly" to make "criminal violations of the act a general rather than a specific intent crime." H.R. CONF. REP. NO. 95-1804, at 26 (1978).
3. CITES (Convention on International Trade in Endangered Species of Wild Fauna and Flora) is an international agreement between governments. Its aim is to ensure that international trade in specimens of wild animals and plants does not threaten their survival. Information available at http://www.cites.org/.
4. *See, e.g.*, Federico Cheever, *An Introduction to the Prohibition Against Takings in Section 9 of the Endangered Species Act of 1973: Learning to Live With a Powerful Species Preservation Law*, 62 U. COLO. L. REV. 109, 192–93 (1991); Steven G. Davison, *Alteration of Wildlife Habitat as a Prohibited Taking Under the Endangered Species Act*, 10 J. LAND USE & ENVTL. L. 155 (1995).
5. The Act defines "person" to mean "an individual, corporation, partnership, trust, association, or any other private entity; or any officer, employee, agent, department, or instrumentality of the Federal Government, of any State, municipality, or political subdivision of a State, or of any foreign government; any State, municipality, or political subdivision of a State; or any other entity subject to the jurisdiction of the United States." 16 U.S.C. § 1532(13).
6. 16 U.S.C. § 1538(a). Though the statute refers only to "endangered species," the Secretary of Interior has expanded the statutory prohibition on take to threatened species except where the Secretary adopts a "special rule" for threatened species pursuant to § 1533(d). 50 C.F.R. § 17.31(a). By contrast, the Secretary of Commerce, who administers the marine species on the list, regulates take of threatened species exclusively through section 4(d) rules.
7. 15 U.S.C. § 1532(19).
8. 50 C.F.R. § 17.3. The term "harass is defined as "an intentional or negligent act or omission which creates the likelihood of injury to wildlife by annoying it to such an extent as to significantly disrupt normal behavioral patterns which include, but are not limited to, breeding, feeding, or sheltering." 50 C.F.R. § 17.3 (2006).
9. 471 F. Supp. 985 (D. Haw. 1979), *aff'd*, 639 F.2d 495 (9th Cir. 1981) (*Palila I*).
10. *Id.*, 639 F.2d at 498.
11. Palila v. Haw. Dep't of Natural Res., 852 F.2d 1106, 1109 (9th Cir. 1988) (*Palila II*).

12. *Id.* at 1110.
13. 115 S. Ct. 2407 (1995) (*Sweet Home*).
14. "We need not decide whether the statutory definition of "take" compels the Secretary's interpretation of "harm," because our conclusions that Congress did not unambiguously manifest its intent to adopt respondents' view and that the Secretary's interpretation is reasonable suffice to decide this case." 115 S. Ct. at 2416.
15. As Justice Stevens observed in his majority opinion: "In the elaboration and enforcement of the ESA, the Secretary and all persons who must comply with the law will confront difficult questions of proximity and degree; for, as all recognize, the Act encompasses a vast range of economic and social enterprises and endeavors. These questions must be addressed in the usual course of the law, through case-by-case resolution and adjudication." 115 S. Ct. at 2418.
16. *Id.* at 2412 n.9.
17. Justice O'Connor stated: "In my view, then, the 'harm' regulation applies where significant habitat modification, by impairing essential behaviors, proximately (foreseeably) causes actual death or injury to identifiable animals that are protected under the Endangered Species Act. Pursuant to my interpretation, *Palila II*—under which the Court of Appeals held that a state agency committed a 'taking' by permitting mouflon sheep to eat mamane-naio seedlings that, when full grown, might have fed and sheltered endangered palila—was wrongly decided according to the regulation's own terms." *Id.* at 2720–21.
18. *Id.* at 2424.
19. Justice O'Connor commented: "One need not subscribe to theories of 'psychic harm,' to recognize that to make it impossible for an animal to reproduce is to impair its most essential physical functions and to render that animal, and its genetic material, biologically obsolete. This, in my view, is actual injury." *Id.* at 2719.
20. *See generally* chapter 8 of this book; James T. Rasband, *Priority, Probability and Proximate Cause, Lessons from Tort Law Imposing ESA Responsibility on Water Users and Other Joint Habitat Modifiers*, 33 ENVTL. LAW 595 (2003); Alan M. Glen & Craig M. Douglas, *Taking Species: Difficult Questions of Proximity and Degree*, 16 NAT. RES. & ENV'T 65, 68 (Fall 2001).
21. Nat'l Ass'n of Homebuilders v. Babbitt, 130 F.3d 1041 (D.C. Cir. 1997), *cert. denied*, 524 U.S. 937 (1998) (Delhi sands flower-loving fly); Gibbs v. Babbitt, 214 F.3d 483 (4th Cir. 2000), *cert. denied*, 531 U.S. 1135 (2001) (red wolf); GDF Realty Ltd. *v.* Norton, 326 F.3d 622 (5th Cir. 2003), *reh'g en banc denied*, 362 F.3d 286 (5th Cir. 2004), *cert. denied*, 125 S. Ct 2898 (2005) (six species of subterranean invertebrates); Rancho Viejo LLC v. Norton, 323 F.3d 1062 (D.C. Cir. 2003), *reh'g en banc denied*, 334 F.3d 1158 (D.C. Cir. 2003), *cert. denied*, 540 U.S. 1218 (2004) (arroyo toad); Alabama-Tombigbee Rivers Coal. v. Kempthorne, 477 F.3d 1250 (11th Cir. 2007), *cert. denied*, 128 S. Ct. 877 (2008) (Alabama sturgeon).
22. 857 F.2d 1324 (9th Cir. 1988).
23. 296 F.3d 1339 (Fed. Cir. 2002).
24. Tahoe-Sierra Pres. Council, Inc. v. Tahoe Reg'l Planning Council, 122 S. Ct. 1465, 1471 (2002).
25. Seiber v. United States, 364 F.3d 1356 (Fed. Cir. 2004). The Oregon Supreme Court reached a similar conclusion in Boise Cascade v. Dep't of Forestry, 63 P.3d 598, 2003 WL 292305 (Or. 2003).
26. 59 Fed. Cl. 246 (Fed. Cl. 2003).
27. 67 Fed. Cl. 504, 537–39 (Fed. Cl. 2005).
28. Casitas Mun. Water Dist. v. United States, 2008 WL 4349234 (Fed. Cir. 2008). The majority noted: "Moreover, in the instant case, the government admissions make clear that the United States did not just require that water be left in the river, but instead physically caused Casitas to divert water away from the Robles-Casitas Canal and toward the fish ladder. Where the government plays an active role and physically appropriates property, the per se taking analysis applies." *Id.* at *13.

29. Judge Mayer noted:

    > Casitas does not own the water in question because all water sources within California belong to the public. [Citation omitted]. Whether Casitas even has a vested property interest in the use of the water is a threshold issue to be determined under California law. California subjects appropriative water rights licenses to the public trust and reasonable use doctrines, so Casitas likely has no property interest in the water, and therefore no takings claim.

    Id. at *14.
30. *Cf.* Morris v. United States, 392 F.3d 1372 (Fed Cir. 2004).
31. The court stated: "The cost of an ITP application is unknowable until the agency has had some meaningful opportunity to exercise its discretion to assist in the process. Because the cost to the Morrises of the ITP application following the exercise of NMFS's discretion may be less than the alleged economic value of their property, deciding whether a taking would occur if the cost is greater is a hypothetical exercise." 392 F.3d at 1377.
32. 16 U.S.C. § 1540(g)(1)(A).
33. 520 S. Ct. 154, 165–66 (1997).
34. Forest Conservation Council v. Roseboro Lumber Co., 50 F.3d 781 (9th Cir. 1995).
35. Sierra Club v. Yeutter, 926 F.2d 429, 438 (5th Cir. 1991).
36. Strahan v. Coxe, 127 F.3d 155 (1st Cir. 1997).
37. United States v. Town of Plymouth, 6 F. Supp. 2d 81 (D. Mass. 1998).
38. Dow v. Bernal, 204 F.3d 920 (9th Cir. 2000).
39. U.S v. Glenn-Colusa Irrigation Dist., 788 F. Supp. 1126 (E.D. Cal. 1992).
40. Loggerhead Turtle v. County of Volusia, 148 F.3d 1231 (11th Cir. 1998).
41. United States v. Billie, 667 F. Supp. 1485 (S.D. Fla. 1987).
42. Lujan v. Defenders of Wildlife, 504 U.S. 555 (1992) (*Lujan*).
43. Friends of the Earth, Inc. v. Laidlaw Envtl. Sys. (TOC), Inc., 528 U.S. 167, 180–81 (1992).
44. Sierra Club v. EPA, 292 F.3d 895, 900 (D.C. Cir. 2002).
45. *See* Lujan v. NWF, 479 U.S. 871 (1990) (injury in fact "is assuredly not satisfied by averments which state only that one of respondent's members uses unspecified portions of an immense tract of territory, on some portions of which mining activity has occurred or probably will occur by virtue of the governmental action.").
46. Cetacean Cmty. v. Bush, 386 F.3d 1169, (9th Cir. 2004) ("There is no hint in the definition of 'person' in § 1532(13) that the 'person' authorized to bring suit to protect an endangered or threatened species can be an animal that is itself endangered or threatened.").
47. Section 11(g)(2)(A) provides: "No action shall be commenced under subparagraph (1)(A) of this section . . . prior to sixty days after written notice has been given to the Secretary and to any alleged violator of any such provision. . . ." 16 U.S.C. § 1540(g)(2)(A).
48. 840 F.2d 714, 721 (9th Cir. 1988).
49. *See* Sierra Club v. Yeutter, 926 F.2d 429, 437 (5th Cir. 1991) (stating that the notice requirement, "though clearly mandatory, is not jurisdictional 'in the strict sense of the term,' and hence may not be availed of for the first time on appeal by an appellant seeking reversal of an adverse trial court judgment on that basis"); *see also* Hallstrom v. Tillamook, 493 U.S. 20, 31 (1989) ("[W]e hold that the notice and 60-day delay requirements are mandatory conditions precedent to commencing suit under the RCRA citizen suit provision.").
50. In Hawksbill Sea Turtle v. FEMA, 126 F.3d 461 (3d Cir. 1997) the court dismissed a section 9 claim for failure to serve *both* the Secretary of Interior and the Secretary of Commerce, who shared management responsibility for the species of sea turtle at issue.
51. *Compare* Marbled Murrelet v. Babbitt, 83 F.3d 1060, 1073 (9th Cir. 1996) (notice was sufficient) *with* Sw. Ctr. for Biological Diversity v. U.S. Bureau of Reclamation, 143 F.3d 515, 517–19 (9th Cir. 1998) (notice was insufficient).
52. Wash. Trout v. McCain Foods, Inc., 45 F.3d 1351, 1354–55 (9th Cir. 1995); N.M. Citizens for Clean Air & Water v. Espanola Mercantile Co., 72 F.3d 830, 833 (10th Cir. 1996).

53. 16 U.S.C. § 1536(3)(B)(4).
54. *Cf.* Dow v. Bernal, 204 F.3d 920 (9th Cir. 2000); Forest Conservation Council v. Roseboro Lumber Co., 50 F.3d 781 (9th Cir. 1995) (*Roseboro*); Am. Bald Eagle v. Bhatti, 9 F.3d 163, 166 (1st Cir. 1993) (*Bhatti*); Loggerhead Turtle v. County of Volusia, 148 F.3d 1231 (11th Cir. 1998).
55. Sierra Club v. Glicksman, 69 F.3d 90, 95 (5th Cir. 1995) ("[T]he appropriate standard of review of federal administrative agency action under both section 7 and section 9 of the ESA is the arbitrary and capricious standard prescribed by the Administrative Procedure Act.").
56. Citizens to Pres. Overton Park v. Volpe, 401 U.S. 400 (1971).
57. *Cf.* Sierra Club v. Peterson, 185 F.2d 349, 369 (5th Cir. 1999).
58. Stuart L. Pimm & Peter Raven, *Biodiversity: Extinction by Numbers*, 403 NATURE 843–45 (2000).
59. In the preamble to the take regulations (50 C.F.R. § 17.3), FWS states that "habitat modification or degradation, standing alone, is not a taking pursuant to section 9." 46 Fed. Reg. 54,748 (1981).
60. 83 F.3d 1060, 1067 (9th Cir. 1996).
61. 255 F.3d 1073 (9th Cir. 2001) ("Eliminating a threatened species' habitat thus can constitute "taking" that species for purposes of section 9."); *but see* DOW v. Bernal (destruction of "unoccupied" habitat is not enough to prove take of pygmy owl). *See also* Envtl. Prot. Info. Ctr. v. Simpson Timber Co.
62. 9 F.3d at 165.
63. 272 F. Supp. 2d 860, 874 (D. Ariz. 2003).
64. 802 F. Supp. 424, 431 (S.D. Ala. 1992).
65. 2000 WL 298707 (D. Or. 2000).
66. United States v. W. Coast Forest Res., 1997 WL 33100698 (D. Or. 1997).
67. 441 F. Supp. 2d 1123, 1132–34 (N.D. Ala. 2006).
68. 984 F. Supp. 1242 (W.D. Mo. 1997).
69. *Id.* at 1248.
70. 974 F. Supp. 1022, 1031–32 (E.D. Ky. 1997) ("[T]he Court concludes that the Indiana bat's foraging habitat may be adversely affected by the Leatherwood Fork timber sale and thus may constitute a "taking" of the Indiana bat, as the timber sale may harass and/or harm the Indiana bat in violation of the ESA."); *see also* Swan View Coal. v. Turner, 824 F. Supp. 923, 939 (D. Mont. 1992) (evidence that road densities were "substantially affecting essential behavioral patterns" and could be a factor in declining population of grizzly bears in the Flathead National Forest was sufficient to survive a motion for summary judgment).
71. 106 F. Supp. 2d 1066, 1073 (W.D. Wash. 2000).
72. 434 F. Supp. 2d 789 (C.D. Cal. 2006).
73. 535 F.3d 1026, 1034 (9th Cir. 2008).
74. 882 F.2d 1294 (8th Cir. 1989).
75. *Id.* at 1301.
76. *Id.* On a related issue, the Ninth Circuit ruled that EPA violated the requirements of section 7 by failing to consult with FWS and NMFS on pesticide registrations affecting listed Pacific salmon. Wash. Toxics Coal. v. EPA, 413 F.3d 1024 (9th Cir. 2005) *cert. denied sub nom.* CropLife Am. v. Wash. Toxics Coal., 546 U.S. 1090. EPA, FWS, and NMFS have adopted Joint Counterpart Endangered Species Act Section 7 Consultation Regulations, 69 Fed. Reg. 4469 (Jan. 30, 2004).
77. 127 F.3d 155 (1st Cir. 1997), *cert. denied*, 525 U.S. 830 (1988) (*Strahan*).
78. *Id.* at 164.
79. *Id.* at 165.
80. *Id.* at 167.
81. *Id.* at 169.
82. *Id.* at 170.

83. *Id.*; *see also* Seattle Audubon v. Sutherland, 2007 WL 1300964 (W.D. Wash. 2007) (holding that neither the 10th nor 11th Amendments barred an ESA action challenging forest practice rules administered by the Washington Department of Forestry that allowed logging in habitat of the northern spotted owl).
84. 6 F. Supp. 2d 81 (D. Mass. 1998).
85. *Id.* at 91.
86. 148 F.3d 1231(11th Cir. 1998).
87. *Id.* at 1250.
88. 2008 WL 839739 (D. Minn. 2007).
89. *Id.* at *3.
90. *Id.* at *5.
91. 437 U.S. 153, 193–95 (1978).
92. *Id.* at 174.
93. *Id.* at 185.
94. *Strahan*, 127 F.3d at 158; *Marbled Murrelet*, 83 F.3d at 1067–68; *Loggerhead Turtle*, 148 F.3d at 1254–55.
95. *Rosboro*, 50 F.3d at 783.
96. 23 F.3d 1508 (9th Cir. 1994).
97. *Id.* at 1509.
98. *Id.* at 1510.
99. *Id.* at 1512.
100. *Id.* at 1512 n.8.
101. More than 430 habitat conservation plans (HCPs) have been approved, covering millions of acres. HCPs are evolving from a process adopted primarily to address single projects to broad-based, landscape-level planning, utilized to achieve long-term biological and regulatory goals. Information available at U.S. Fish & Wildlife Serv., Habitat Conservation Plans, http://www.fws.gov/Endangered/pdfs/HCP/HCP_Incidental_Take.pdf.
102. *See* Karin P. Sheldon, *Habitat Conservation Planning: Addressing the Achilles Heel of the Endangered Species Act*, 6 NYU ENVTL. L.J. 279–340 (1998).

8

Land Use Activities and the Section 9 Take Prohibition

Steven P. Quarles and Thomas R. Lundquist

Introduction

This chapter addresses commonly encountered legal issues in determining whether a land use or habitat modification activity causes take of an endangered species or threatened species of fish or wildlife within the meaning of Endangered Species Act (ESA) section 9 and the regulatory definition of "harm."[1] It provides background information on the "take" and "harm" definitions, and then discusses current issues on the reach of the take prohibition.

Current State of the Law

The Basics on Take of Listed Wildlife

Definitions

The "Secretary" may determine a species to be an "endangered species" or "threatened species" and place it on a list of such species (listed species) in the Code of Federal Regulations through the rulemaking process described in ESA section 4.[2] ESA section 9(a) establishes a series of "prohibited acts" with respect to "endangered species,"[3] but not less-imperiled "threatened species." Most important, ESA section 9(a)(1)(B) declares that "it is unlawful for any person" to "take" any "endangered species of fish or wildlife" anywhere "within the United States."[4] As "person" is defined to include both private individuals and government agencies and officials,[5] the same take prohibition applies to all human actors on all lands (private and public) within the United States.

A different set of ESA and regulatory provisions makes it unlawful to take most *threatened* species of fish or wildlife.[6] ESA section 4(d) grants the Services the discretionary authority to extend or not extend any of the "prohibited acts" in ESA section 9 to a threatened wildlife species.[7] The U.S. Fish and Wildlife Service (FWS) and the National Marine Fisheries Service (NMFS) have adopted different approaches toward take of threatened wildlife species subject to their jurisdiction.

The FWS presumptively extended the take prohibition (and all other ESA section 9(a) prohibitions) to all threatened wildlife species through the general rule codified at 50 C.F.R. § 17.31(a). That regulation was challenged and upheld in the *Sweet Home* litigation on the ground that ESA section 4(d) was ambiguous enough to allow FWS to apply the take prohibition to all threatened species by a "blanket rule."[8] That is, section 4(d) does not require individualized determinations at the time of listing of which prohibitions should apply to each threatened species. However, FWS has addressed the application of the take prohibition to a few individual threatened wildlife species by adopting, at 50 C.F.R. §§ 17.40–17.46, special ESA section 4(d) rules excepting particular species from the blanket rule.

By contrast, the NMFS takes a threatened species-by-species approach. When a threatened wildlife species subject to NMFS's jurisdiction is listed, NMFS typically states which ESA section 9 prohibitions apply to that species and often applies the full set of ESA section 9 prohibitions.[9] NMFS also has issued ESA section 4(d) rules that exceed the mere prohibition of take of a threatened wildlife species. As an example,

NMFS requires the adoption of certain protective measures for such species (e.g., mandating approved turtle excluder devices on certain fishing vessels to reduce the risk of take of listed turtle species). Those regulations have been affirmed in court.[10]

Because section 9(a)(1)(G) makes it unlawful to violate an ESA regulation, it is unlawful to take a threatened wildlife species in violation of an ESA section 4(d) regulation.[11] The bottom line: the same take prohibition applies to all endangered wildlife species and to most threatened wildlife species.

The ESA itself creates no take prohibition for listed plant species. Nonetheless, ESA section 9(a)(2) and Service rules protect listed plants against certain forms of destruction.[12]

ESA section 3(19) defines "take" of wildlife to mean "to harass, harm, pursue, hunt, shoot, wound, kill, trap, capture, or collect" listed wildlife, "or to attempt to engage in any such conduct."[13] While most of those words are well understood, the intended legislative meanings of "harm" and "harass" are unclear. Accordingly, FWS adopted regulations defining both terms in 50 C.F.R. § 17.3. The "harm" definition includes the concept of significant habitat modification that actually kills or injures wildlife. NMFS adopted in 50 C.F.R. § 222.102 a "harm" definition that, on its face, parallels FWS's rule.[14]

ESA section 11[15] describes the enforcement actions available to enjoin or punish the acts, such as take of listed wildlife, prohibited by ESA section 9 and ESA rules. The federal government may bring civil penalty actions under ESA section 11(a), or criminal penalty actions under section 11(b). Suits to enjoin take or other ESA violations may be brought by the government under ESA section 11(e)(6) or by private citizens under ESA section 11(g). ESA citizen suits to enjoin proposed land uses under the significant habitat modification portion of the "harm" definition have been the most common form of enforcement of the "harm" constraint.

Final elements in this statutory overview are the ESA provisions for allowing incidental take. Until 1982, the ESA and regulatory bans against taking listed wildlife were virtually absolute. In the 1982 ESA Amendments, Congress softened the sting of the ESA somewhat. As is explained in other chapters of this book, ESA sections 7(b)(4) and 10(a)(2) provide mechanisms to render lawful the "incidental take" of wildlife associated with some beneficial land use activities.[16]

The History of FWS's Definition of "Harm" Prior to the 1995 *Sweet Home* Decision

One key to discerning the current meanings of the "harm" and "harass" forms of take is an understanding of their historical evolution. This subsection describes, in chronological order, the history of FWS's harm rule prior to the Supreme Court's decision in *Sweet Home*.[17]

FWS issued its first regulatory definitions of "harm" and "harass" in 1975, and revised the harm rule in 1981. The 1975 harm rule included "significant environmental modification" that has the "effects" of "actually injur[ing] or kill[ing] wildlife, including acts which annoy it to such an extent as to significantly disrupt essential behavioral patterns, which include, but are not limited to, breeding, feeding or sheltering."[18] This rule asserted that land use activities that adversely modify habitat used by listed wildlife could be found to be the culpable source of a take of wildlife. The original harm rule, like the 1981-amended rule, requires an "actual injury" to wildlife. However, the 1975 rule was more ambiguous on whether a tangible "injury" (e.g., a wound or disease) to an individual was required, or whether a disruption of a species' historical behavioral patterns was sufficient to establish "injury." For example, if land clearing is predicted to result in a member of listed wildlife species abandoning use of certain lands—but that individual is expected to relocate to, and continue to exist in, suitable habitat elsewhere—is there enjoinable harm?

This ambiguity plagued the early harm cases—and still echoes today. Most notably, the first set of *Palila* decisions concluded that the State of Hawaii, by not removing feral sheep and goats from state lands, was causing harm to the palila bird.[19] The sheep and goats ate mamane tree seedlings, thereby reducing the number of mature mamane trees available to future generations of the palila for food and shelter. The district court and Ninth Circuit found enjoinable harm even though the bird's population seemed stable and the opinions did not describe any actual death or injury to a particular bird.

This prompted a legal opinion from the Interior Department's Office of the Solicitor. The opinion concluded the *Palila* courts had construed FWS's "overly broad definition of 'harm'" in a way that "exceeds the statutory authority conferred by Section 9," by "erroneously support[ing] the view that habitat modifications alone may constitute 'harm.'"[20] FWS's lawyers "recommend[ed] that the Service clarify its definition to prevent the result reached in *Palila*." The preamble to the 1981 proposed rule included a copy of the legal opinion.[21]

In November 1981, FWS adopted its current regulatory definition of "harm." It states:

> *Harm* in the definition of "take" in the Act means an act which actually kills or injures wildlife. Such act may include significant habitat modification or degradation where it actually kills or injures wildlife by significantly impairing essential behavioral patterns, including breeding, feeding or sheltering.[22]

The preamble to the harm rule provides FWS's contemporaneous regulatory intent that (1) a land use activity's adverse modification of habitat of a listed wildlife species alone is not sufficient to prove an ESA section 9 take of wildlife; and (2) at least three elements must be demonstrated to prove "harm." On the former point, FWS's statements include the following:

> Congress ... did not, however, express any intention to protect habitat under section 9 where there was no appurtenant showing of death or injury to a protected species. ... Congress intended to create a definition of take which included all of the various ways of killing or injuring wildlife. ... [FWS] cannot ... convert section 9 into a habitat protection provision; as other comments pointed out, that is the purpose of sections 5 and 7 of the Act. ... To the extent the comment contends that habitat modification alone is a taking, it is without support in the Act or legislative history.[23]

On the latter point, FWS stated that it added a second sentence to clarify that land use activities that adversely modify habitat are potential sources of harm. However, to "be subject to section 9" under the harm rule, the habitat "modification or degradation [1] must be *significant*, [2] must *significantly impair essential* behavioral patterns, and [3] must result in *actual* injury to a protected wildlife species."[24]

Despite FWS's 1981 intent to narrow the regulatory meaning of "harm," this contraction often was not reflected in judicial decisions in the 1980s and early 1990s. For example, in a subsequent *Palila* case concerning the habitat damage to mamane seedlings done by grazing mouflon sheep, the district court concluded that harm "does not necessitate a finding of death to individual species members" or of a "decline in population numbers"—"If the habitat modification prevents the species from recovering, then this causes injury to the species and should be actionable under section 9."[25] On appeal, the United States filed an amicus brief that made a distinction between the long-term impacts of habitat destruction on survival versus recovery of a listed species. The federal amicus brief argued that habitat modification that prevents the recovery of a listed species should not be "harm," and urged reversal of that portion of the district court's logic. But the federal amicus brief supported affirmance on the ground that there was sufficient evidence that the current destruction of future habitat for palila birds (by sheep eating the mamane tree seedlings) would lead to the extinction of the listed species, and that adverse habitat modification that eventually leads to extinction should be within the harm rule. This amicus brief arguably goes beyond take limits expressed in the 1981 Solicitor's opinion and 1981 harm rule.

In an opaque opinion, the Ninth Circuit basically agreed with the federal brief. The district court was affirmed on the basis that "habitat destruction that could result in extinction" is "harm," and "we do not reach whether harm includes habitat degradation that merely retards recovery."[26] Still, because the *Palila* opinions did not recite any evidence that presently living birds were dying early, the *Palila* opinions interpreted "harm" in a broad manner that sounded alarm bells in the regulated community.

The regulated community's concern over the harm regulation intensified after ESA listing of the northern spotted owl. In 1990, an FWS office issued a set of Owl Guidelines. Those Guidelines were originally designed to be a "safe harbor" from prosecution for potential take if a landowner agreed to maintain prescribed acreage of timberlands in conditions that were generally thought to provide for sufficient suitable owl habitat. But FWS field personnel began to equate noncompliance with the recommendations in the Owl Guidelines with a take violation. This seemed to assert that adverse habitat modification alone was a take of wildlife, contrary to FWS's representations in the preamble to the 1981 harm rule.[27]

The *Sweet Home* Suits

The dubious interpretations of "harm" by FWS and some courts led to two related *Sweet Home* suits. They were brought by a group of small landowners and others whose planned timber harvesting had been restricted by a broad view of "harm" that equated habitat loss with "take" and that often prohibited timber harvesting in large areas used by the threatened northern spotted owl in the Pacific Northwest and the endangered red-cockaded woodpecker in the Southeast.

The lesser-known *Sweet Home* case challenged the Owl Guidelines on substantive grounds (e.g., that adverse modification of habitat without a proven injury to wildlife cannot lawfully be take of wildlife within the meaning of ESA section 9) and procedural grounds (e.g., FWS could not establish new standard for harm unless the standard was adopted through notice-and-comment rulemaking). In response, FWS formally rescinded the Owl Guidelines. The suit was dismissed because FWS had agreed it could not enforce the Owl Guidelines.[28]

The other *Sweet Home* case was eventually resolved by the Supreme Court in 1995.[29] *Sweet Home* initiates the modern era in take cases. It remains the leading case construing the limits of FWS's harm rule.

The *Sweet Home* plaintiffs maintained that the harm regulation was ultra vires of the ESA in including "habitat modification" or land use activities as potential sources of take. Plaintiffs contended that wildlife take under the common law and under the ESA is limited to actions directed at wildlife (e.g., hunting, capturing) that have the physical effect of killing, injuring, or collecting listed wildlife. Plaintiffs also argued that the harm regulation is inconsistent with the structure of the ESA. For example, ESA section 7(a)(2) demonstrates a concern over "habitat" only with respect to federally assisted actions, and ESA section 5 suggests that federal land acquisition with compensation was the legislative solution to the problem of habitat degradation on nonfederal lands.[30]

Though the D.C. Circuit set aside the harm rule, the Supreme Court sustained the facial legality of the rule by a 6–3 vote. Justice Stevens authored the majority opinion. Justice O'Connor filed a concurring opinion that emphasized limitations on harm that were briefly mentioned in the majority opinion.

Throughout the briefing in *Sweet Home*, the government's attorneys interpreted the harm regulation narrowly (e.g., as barring only habitat modification activities that definitely would kill or injure a member of a listed wildlife species, and as including a proximate causation limitation). This presumably was done to improve the prospects the rule would be upheld. The majority opinion in *Sweet Home* accepts the government's representations and adopts these narrowing interpretations. The majority opinion finds that, so limited, the harm regulation is facially consistent with the legislative intent of the ESA.[31] In dissent, Justice Scalia colorfully accuses the majority of "incorrectly" construing the harm regulation strictly and the ESA broadly so as to result in a "regulation that the Court has created and held consistent with the statute that it has also created."[32]

The majority opinion essentially finds that it was legally permissible for FWS to define "harm" as the *effect* of a death or actual injury to a member of a listed species proximately caused by *any* activity—even wildlife deaths caused unintentionally by land use activities. Justice Stevens cites at least seven reasons for sustaining that harm regulation.[33]

After *Sweet Home*, it is clear the ESA allows some land use activities to be enjoinable sources of harm to listed wildlife. While that aspect of the harm rule was upheld, in other important ways the Supreme Court's decision cabined the then-common understanding of "harm."

One notable aspect of the Court's decision is the distinction it drew between section 9 and section 7. In particular, the Court noted that ESA section 7, which applies only to federally assisted or permitted actions, "imposes a broad, affirmative duty to avoid adverse habitat modifications that section 9 does not replicate, and section 7 does not limit its admonition to habitat modification that 'actually kills or injures wildlife.' "[34] Thus, after *Sweet Home*, a biologist's prediction that a land use activity will adversely modify habitat occupied or preferred by a listed wildlife species is not enjoinable harm absent proof of some consequent death of or injury to a member of that species.

Also noteworthy is that *Sweet Home* requires proof that death or actual injury to a member of a listed wildlife species is reasonably certain to occur. The harm rule "emphasize[s] that actual death or injury of a protected animal is necessary for a violation"—"every term in the regulation's definition is subservient to the phrase 'an act which actually kills or injures wildlife.' "[35] This seems to mean that (1) "harm" applies to a living individual (a "protected animal"), not at the population level; (2) an "actual injury" (e.g., a wound) is a prerequisite separate from showing impairment of a behavioral pattern; and (3) "actual injury" must be shown or predicted to a reasonable certainty, and claims of potential or speculative harm are not sufficient.[36] Justice O'Connor's concurrence was expressly predicated on the "understanding[ ]" that, under the majority opinion, "the challenged regulation is limited to significant habitat modification that causes actual, as opposed to hypothetical or speculative, death or injury to identifiable protected animals."[37]

A third notable aspect of the decision is that *Sweet Home* narrowed the range of liability for take by interpreting the ESA and implementing rules to limit liability by "ordinary requirements of proximate causation and foreseeability."[38] Justice O'Connor concurred on the understanding that the "regulation's application is limited by ordinary principles of proximate causation."[39]

Sweet Home identifies the standards for, and limitations on, harm that lower courts must apply in assessing whether the facts and scientific opinions regarding a proposed land use activity establish a case for ESA section 9 take of wildlife. In many ways, the Supreme Court's decision in *Sweet Home* limited harm by returning to the original 1981 intent of FWS and the 1981 Interior Solicitor's opinion on harm. As we will discuss in the section on the current state of the law, this has led more lower courts to narrowly interpret "harm" and to increase the burdens on plaintiffs, including the Services, who seek to enjoin land use activities.

FWS's Definition of "Harass"

In 1975, FWS adopted its current definition of "harass" for purposes of ESA section 9 take.

> *Harass* in the definition of "take" in the Act means an intentional or negligent act or omission that creates the likelihood of injury to wildlife by annoying it to such an extent as to significantly disrupt formal behavioral patterns, which include, but are not limited to, breeding, feeding, or sheltering.[40]

Because "harm" demands proof of "actual injury" while "harass" requires only a "likelihood of injury," some plaintiffs are tempted to bring suits alleging that proposed land use activities would "harass" a listed wildlife species to take advantage of a lower burden of proof. Yet such claims usually will be unsuccessful.

In promulgating its definition of "harass," FWS made clear its intent to address any alleged wildlife take that occurs through physical changes to habitat solely by the harm rule (which mentions "habitat modification or degradation"), not the harass rule (which does not purport to cover habitat-disturbing activities). FWS specifically moved the concept of habitat modification causing take from the "harass" definition in the proposed rule to the "harm" definition in the final rule so that land use activities could be enjoined only on a showing of "actual death or injury to a protected species":

> The concept of environmental damage being considered a "taking" has been retained but is now found in a new definition, of the word "harm." . . . By moving the concept of environmental degradation [from the proposed definition of "harass"] to the definition of "harm," potential restrictions on environmental modifications are expressly limited to those actions causing actual death or injury to a protected species of fish or wildlife.[41]

FWS's contemporaneous interpretation of its own rule should be controlling in court.[42]

Instead of covering physical modifications of habitat, the harass rule addresses the annoying effects of persistent noise, light, or motion. Activities that have only transitory, short-term effects on listed wildlife usually do not meet the legal definition of "harass."[43] Still, "harass" is not completely irrelevant to habitat modification activities, as it could cover the noise from bulldozers, chainsaws, and the like under some circumstances.[44] But FWS's own interpretation of "harass" explains why "harass" has a relatively minor role in the modern law of ESA take.

NMFS's Harm Rule

In 1999, NMFS also adopted a harm rule. On its face, NMFS's definition parallels FWS's definition of "harm," with only a few minor word changes concerning anadromous fish (e.g., inclusion of "spawning"):

> *Harm* in the definition of "take" in the Act means an act which actually kills or injures fish or wildlife. Such an act may include significant habitat modification or degradation which actually kills or injures fish or wildlife by significantly impairing essential behavioral patterns, including, breeding, spawning, rearing, migrating, feeding, or sheltering.[45]

For several reasons, it is uncertain whether NMFS's harm rule will be given the same interpretation as the prevailing judicial view of FWS's harm rule discussed in the next section. NMFS's harm rule has not yet been the subject of any notable judicial interpretations.

On the one hand, the preamble to NMFS's final rule is more aggressive in describing the activities that could constitute harm. If that preamble is deemed to be legally controlling, NMFS's harm rule may prove to be more stringent than FWS's.[46] On the other hand, courts may not view NMFS's preamble to be controlling. Courts may be inclined to interpret the two harm rules similarly and to follow the more-established judicial precedents construing FWS's harm rule. Furthermore, if NMFS's harm rule is construed to not require the death or actual injury of a protected animal, that rule could be challenged as being ultra vires of the ESA section 9 concept of take of wildlife.

The Current Law of ESA Section 9 Take Under FWS's Harm Rule

This section describes the prevailing law on several recurring issues regarding harm under FWS's definition. In particular, it considers when proposed land use activities do and do not become unlawful harm under FWS's harm rule. As a general matter, the "post-*Sweet Home* case law appears to be taking a more-restricted view of when habitat modification will be considered the proximate cause of harm to a protected species."[47]

However, the current law is not uniform. This is due to factors such as an imprecise regulatory definition of "harm," differing judicial perceptions on the comparative importance of preserving listed species and of allowing productive land use activities, and what the *Sweet Home* Court called "difficult questions of proximity and degree" as the ESA "encompasses a vast range of economic and social enterprises and endeavors."

Actual Injury to Wildlife Must Be Proven at Least to a Reasonable Certainty to Demonstrate a Harm Violation and to Obtain a Permanent Injunction

ESA section 11(g) provides a private right of action to bring a citizen suit against any "person," and allows courts to enjoin that person from committing any "violation" of the ESA or an ESA rule.[48] In *Sweet Home*, the Supreme Court "emphasize[d] that actual death or injury of a protected animal is necessary for a [harm] violation."[49] The text of the harm regulation states twice that one prerequisite to harm is an "act which actually kills or injures wildlife."[50] The preamble to the final amended regulation confirms that the *potential* for, or risk of, injury to listed wildlife is not harm:

> [T]he word "actually" [has been] reinserted in the definition to bulwark the need for a proven injury to a species due to a party's actions.... "Harm" covers actions... which actually (as opposed to potentially) cause injury....
> [T]he final redefinition... [is] precluding a taking where no actual injury is shown.... The purpose of the rulemaking was to make it clear that an *actual* injury to a listed species must be found for there to be a taking under section 9.... The final definition adds the word "actually" before "kills or

injures" to clarify that a standard of actual, adverse effects applies to section 9 takings.[51]

As a result, most modern harm cases hinge on whether the plaintiffs have proven the "actual injury" (however defined) or death of listed wildlife that is the essence of a take of wildlife. For example, an early First Circuit decision dismissed a harm claim (that deer hunting using lead shot should be enjoined because bald eagles might die due to lead ingested from feeding on deer carcasses), stating:

> [The] proper standard for establishing a taking under the ESA, far from being a numerical probability of harm, has been unequivocally defined as a showing of "actual harm." . . . Accordingly, courts have granted injunctive relief only where petitioners have shown that the alleged activity has actually harmed the species or if continued will actually, as opposed to potentially, cause harm to the species. . . . Our review of the record indicates that bald eagles can be harmed by the ingestion of lead. There is, however, no evidence in the record of any harm to bald eagles at Quabbin as a result of the 1991 deer hunt. . . . By requiring the plaintiffs to show only "a significant risk of harm" instead of "actual harm," the district court required a lower degree of certainty of harm than we interpret the ESA to require. The appellants certainly cannot meet this court's standard of "actual harm" if the district court found that they failed to prove that even a "significant risk of harm" existed.[52]

The Solicitor General, in his brief in *Sweet Home*, informed the Supreme Court that "courts have correctly interpreted the 'harm' prohibition not to extend to activity that only potentially, as opposed to actually, causes (or will cause) harm," citing *Bald Eagle*.[53]

In the Ninth Circuit, it took some time for the limitations in *Sweet Home* to be accepted.[54] The tipping point came in a 2000 decision finding no harm in a suit to enjoin school construction. In *Defenders of Wildlife v. Bernal*, the Ninth Circuit recognized "habitat modification does not constitute harm unless it 'actually kills or injures wildlife'" and stated that plaintiffs must prove a land use activity is "reasonably certain to injure" a member of a listed species.[55] The appellate panel affirmed the district court's conclusion that there was insufficient site-specific evidence that a pygmy-owl used the area in which construction would occur, and affirmed the exclusion of evidence on the general behavior of pygmy-owls.[56]

Bernal concludes that where the risk of take does not rise to the level of reasonable certainty, the proposed use of nonfederal lands cannot be enjoined. Because obtaining an ESA section 10 incidental take permit "is not mandatory,"[57] the landowner cannot be enjoined to bear the costs of preparing and implementing a habitat conservation plan and of obtaining an incidental take permit. Instead, the landowner can proceed with the proposed activity "without a permit, but it risks civil and criminal penalty if a 'take' occurs."[58] In a risk-of-take situation, *Bernal* effectively means the landowner may choose one of three courses of action: (1) not conducting the proposed land use activity, and bearing the economic consequences; (2) attempting to obtain an incidental take permit under ESA section 10 to eliminate potential take liability, with attendant expenditure of time and funds; and (3) conducting the activity, and bearing the risk that take may occur and may be prosecuted. While none of these options may be particularly appealing, this is the dilemma faced by many landowners with listed wildlife on their property. It may be some solace to landowners that the choice among those options should be theirs under the ESA, and not a choice dictated by the Services, plaintiffs, or courts.

After the *Bernal* ruling, the Ninth Circuit again construed "harm" narrowly, this time in an incidental take setting under ESA section 7(b)(4) in *Arizona Cattle v. FWS*, a case concerning grazing leases on federal lands.[59] Under ESA section 7(b)(4), the Service may provide an incidental take statement for a federally assisted action that would not jeopardize the continued existence of a listed species, if the actor agrees to follow the "reasonable and prudent measures" (RPMs) that FWS identifies to minimize the impacts of take.[60] The RPMs (which, as in *Arizona Cattle*, are often imposed by federal land managers on their permittees) often increase the costs of the action and may require some minor modification of the proposed action. As an initial matter, the Ninth Circuit rejected the government's argument that "incidental take" under ESA section 7(b)(4) could be broader than "take" under ESA section 9. The court then stated that FWS and the action agency cannot impose RPMs on permittees and thereby "engage in widespread land regulation even where no Section 9 [take] liability could be imposed."[61]

The court quoted and applied the *Bernal* test that actual injury to wildlife must be "reasonably certain to occur." For particular grazing leases, the panel often found that FWS had not sustained its burden of showing that listed species were present on the leased lands.[62] The *Arizona Cattle* opinion features *Sweet Home* and *Bernal*, reduces the 1996 opinion in *Marbled Murrelet* to one "*see also*" citation, and does not mention the old *Palila* decisions.[63] *Arizona Cattle* also announced the important principles that (1) the Service (and presumably courts) cannot "impose conditions on otherwise lawful land use if a take were not reasonably certain to occur as a result of that activity"; and (2) the burden of proving harm to a reasonable certainty is on plaintiffs, and defendants do not have to "prove a negative" (e.g., that harm could not possibly occur).[64]

Thus, *Arizona Cattle* and *Bernal* suggest that where allegations of ESA take of wildlife bump up against economic land uses, courts will require a relatively high degree of proof of harm to listed wildlife before a land use activity can be enjoined. Many district court opinions also reflect this dominant trend toward requiring detailed proof that actual injury to wildlife is (reasonably) certain to occur at a site-specific location.[65] For example, "courts have granted injunctive relief only where petitioners have shown that the alleged activity has actually harmed the species or if continued will actually, as opposed to potentially, cause harm to the species."[66]

In one noteworthy case, a district court found that general opinions on the behavior of northern spotted owls could not prove harm to a specific owl pair to a reasonable certainty, and imposed a temporary injunction while the FWS plaintiff paid for radio telemetry studies on forest habitat uses by the pair of owls.[67] After those studies showed owl use of a broad range of habitats, including the area scheduled for timber harvesting, the district court ultimately found that federal plaintiffs had not sustained their burden of proving harm. "[I]nterference" with historic "foraging" patterns "is not sufficient"—the take suit failed because plaintiffs could not show "that this interference will 'actually [kill] or [injure]' the owls."[68]

Where plaintiffs seek to enjoin a proposed land use activity that has no history of having demonstrable take of listed wildlife, they typically will find the requirement for a certain "actual injury" difficult to satisfy. Biologists normally cannot predict with certainty that a proposed land use activity will or will not cause the death of or injury to a protected animal. Often, removing the cover of protective habitat just increases certain risk factors for a member of a listed species (e.g., heightening the chances that a predator may discover the individual or diminishing the chances that the member may find sufficient food). In other situations, habitat modification might not injure a particular animal because the animal can move to nearby suitable habitat or because individuals vary in their responses to environmental stresses.

Where the injury or death of a protected animal is not certain, but there is "a significant risk of harm," in most jurisdictions the stringent standard for proving harm has not been met before the land use activity occurs.[69] In this situation, it appears that the landowner may conduct the activity without being enjoined. But, as *Bernal* confirms, if the landowner does pursue the land use activity in a "risk of take" situation, if harm to listed wildlife actually occurs, the landowner remains subject to civil or criminal penalty actions brought by the United States.[70]

To Obtain a Preliminary Injunction, a Plaintiff Must Show That Actual Injury to Listed Wildlife Is at Least Likely to Occur; Other Factors Vary by Jurisdiction

"Under the traditional test for [preliminary] injunctive relief" that is employed by some courts in ESA cases, "a movant must show: (1) a substantial likelihood of success on the merits; (2) that irreparable injury will be suffered if the relief is not granted; (3) that the threatened injury outweighs the harm the relief would inflict on the nonmovant; and (4) that entry of the relief would serve the public interest."[71] In contrast, the Ninth Circuit has found that the "ESA demonstrates that the balance of hardships and the public interest tips heavily in favor of protected species."[72] This eliminates what is described above as showings (3) and (4).

As we have seen, on the merits, proof of harm after a trial or at summary judgment entails proof of "actual injury." A different standard prevails at the preliminary injunction stage. Ordinarily a preliminary injunction can issue if plaintiffs have a "likelihood of success on the merits."[73] This means that one prerequisite to a preliminary injunction is proof that actual injury to wildlife "is at least likely in the future."[74] In practice, preliminary injunctions have been denied more than they are granted in ESA section 9 take cases.[75]

Most courts still require a showing of irreparable injury to obtain a preliminary injunction, in addition to a showing of likelihood of success on the merits. The "basis for injunctive relief in the federal courts has always been irreparable injury."[76] Even in the Ninth Circuit, plaintiffs must "establish the likelihood of irreparable harm in the future."[77]

Several "courts have held that more than the take of a single animal is required to demonstrate irreparable harm."[78] Arguably, the risk of loss of a few members of a viable, stable species while the case is being heard on the merits is not an irreparable injury. Since other members of the species remain to reproduce, the species persists through time—thereby avoiding the irreparable injury of the loss of a species. For example, the First Circuit suggested that where it was unknown how asserted wildlife "deaths may impact the species," irreparable injury had not been shown.[79] As irreparable environmental injury cannot be presumed,[80] this may limit a court's ability to presume that the likely take of one or a few members of a wide-ranging species is an irreparable injury.

If harm is proven at the end of a case, ESA section 11(g) authorizes a court to do what is necessary to enjoin a future violation of the ESA or an ESA rule. But in some courts, a different equitable balance may prevail when a plaintiff seeks an extraordinary preliminary injunction against a private land use activity without substantial proof of an ESA violation.

What Is Meant by "Actual Injury" to Listed Wildlife?

One recurring question in harm cases is: What is meant by an action that "actually kills or injures wildlife" (the "actual injury" requirement)? The meaning of "actually kills" is clear. It requires proof that a protected animal has been killed or actually would be killed by challenged action.

But does "actual injury" similarly require proof of a wound or similar serious injury to a living individual, or does "significantly impairing essential behavioral patterns" constitute "actual injury"?[81] The former answer is more strongly supported by the regulatory text, by FWS's contemporaneous regulatory interpretation, by the *Sweet Home* opinions and the United States' explanation of the harm rule to the Supreme Court, and by the subsequent lower court case law and law review commentary.

The first sentence of the harm regulation shows that "harm" is defined as a specific effect: "an act which actually kills or injures wildlife."[82] This is consistent with the historic concept that taking wildlife means reducing wild "animals, by killing or capturing, to human control."[83] The second sentence clarifies that the actual injury to wildlife could occur through an indirect mechanism: the habitat modification could "significantly impair[] essential behavioral patterns" to the point that this causes actual injury or death to a member of a listed wildlife species (e.g., death from starvation or exposure to the elements or predators from removing some needed habitat).[84]

As previously noted, FWS's contemporaneous regulatory interpretation when it adopted the revised definition of "harm" was that the rule

> makes it clear that habitat modification or degradation, standing alone, is not a taking pursuant to section 9. To be subject to section 9, the modification or degradation [1] must be *significant*, [2] must *significantly impair*

essential behavioral patterns, and [3] must result in *actual* injury to a protected wildlife species.[85]

Thus, FWS described impairing behavioral patterns and actual injury as separate elements that must be proven to demonstrate harm. Under the preamble, "'harm' requires *both* significant impairment of essential behavioral patterns *and* actual injury to a protected animal."[86] "FWS's commentary accompanying its promulgation of its regulation defining 'harm' indicates that significant impairment of an essential behavioral pattern by itself should not be considered an 'injury.'"[87]

Additionally, the regulatory history reveals that FWS proposed to amend the harm regulation in 1981 precisely to clarify that "injury" or "effects" were separate from impairing essential behavioral patterns:

> This [pre-1981] definition contains a significant ambiguity. If the words "such effects" are read to refer to the phrase "significantly disrupt essential behavioral patterns," then any significant environmental modification or degradation that disrupts essential behavioral patterns will fall under the definition of harm, regardless of whether an actual killing or injuring of a listed species of wildlife is demonstrated. . . . In an opinion dated April 17, 1981, the Solicitor's Office concluded that such a result is inconsistent with the intent of Congress.[88]

Prof. Davison explains why impairment of (historic) behavioral patterns often does not tangibly injure individuals, and should not be considered to be the "actual injury" required for a take of wildlife.

> FWS's commentary accompanying its . . . regulation defining "harm" indicates that significant impairment of an essential behavioral pattern by itself should not be considered an "injury." . . . [E]ven a temporary physical wound, injury or disease should be considered to be an "injury" under the regulation, because in unfortunate circumstances . . . [it] may lead to the premature death of the harmed animal. . . . On the other hand, a protected animal should not be considered to be "injured" simply because its breeding, feeding or sheltering is significantly impaired. In such a situation, the animal may be able to adapt to the impairment. . . . For example, when a protected animal's food supply within a habitat is destroyed or reduced, the animal may be able to find sufficient food [elsewhere]. . . . Yet another example of significant impairment of an essential behavioral pattern that does not "injure" a protected animal would be a situation where a protected animal's shelter (nest) is destroyed by habitat modification but the animal is able to establish a new adequate shelter without suffering any adverse effects (even if the new shelter is located outside the animal's present habitat and range).[89]

Similarly, as described in another example in the legal literature, if timber harvesting just makes it "more risky [for a northern spotted owl] to fly through the clear cut, but if it does not get eaten [by a predator], the bird has not suffered any real injury," and therefore the activity "should not satisfy [the harm standard of] either the *Sweet Home* majority or Justice O'Connor."[90]

In *Sweet Home*, the Solicitor General informed the Supreme Court that significantly impairing essential behavioral patterns could be the "means" or mechanism by which a more tangible injury could occur, but that "harm" required a death or a physical injury in the nature of "wounding":

> The second sentence [of the "harm" definition] specifies that an act constituting "harm" may include the actual killing or injuring of wildlife by means of "significant habitat modification or degradation" that "significantly impair[s]" essential behavioral patterns of the wildlife. There is no reason why Congress would have intended to allow the killing or injuring of protected wildlife where that consequence is brought about by the destruction of habitat essential for the wildlife's breeding, feeding, or shelter, rather than by other means, such as the discharge of a firearm.... In this case, the general word "harm" can be understood to apply the statutory term "take" to all conduct of the sort that the other words ("kill," "wound," etc.) merely exemplify, *Brown v. Gardner*, 115 S. Ct. 552, 555 (1994), including conduct that causes such consequences as killing or wounding by means of significant habitat modification."[91]

This concession helps explain why the majority opinion in *Sweet Home* insists that "actual injury" is a separate, unequivocal prerequisite for harm. The majority opinion found inapposite Justice Scalia's criticism that the "impairing essential behavioral patterns" language made the harm regulation impermissibly broad.[92] The phrase "impairing essential behavioral patterns" and every other "term in the regulation's definition of 'harm' is subservient to the phrase 'an act which actually kills or injures wildlife.'"[93] The Supreme Court stated there are "strong arguments that activities that cause minimal ... harm will not violate the Act as construed in the 'harm' regulation,"[94] and that issue is avoided if imperceptible injuries to behavioral patterns alone do not constitute a wildlife take under ESA section 9.

Based on such considerations, most courts since *Sweet Home* have found that actual injury to a protected animal is an element of harm that plaintiffs must prove. That is distinct from significantly impairing that animal's historic use of certain habitats (its "behavioral patterns"). One example is the *West Coast* case.[95] There, radio telemetry showed some usage by an owl pair of the forested lands to be harvested, as well as owl usage of a number of other forested habitats that would not be altered. District Judge Hogan held that "interference" with historic "foraging" patterns "is not sufficient"—the harm suit failed because plaintiffs could not show "that this interference will 'actually kill[ ] or injure[ ]' the owls."[96] "As long as the owl would still have other areas to forage," there is no actual injury to an actual owl and " there was no take" within the meaning of *Sweet Home*.[97]

Similarly, another court found plaintiffs must prove, in addition to impairment of a listed species' behavioral pattern, that the "impairment actually kills or injures wildlife."[98] Another court stated that "impairing essential behavioral patterns is

[not] a sufficient basis on which to infer that death or injury is necessarily occurring. Whether the degree of impairment is so significant that it is actually killing or injuring grizzly bears is" a separate issue for trial.[99]

In *Sweet Home*, there was a notable side debate between Justice Scalia (for the three dissenters) and Justice O'Connor (concurring) on whether interference with breeding is "harm." That issue is, in substantial part, an application of the larger issue of whether significantly impairing essential behavioral patterns (such as breeding or sheltering) is itself "actual injury" or simply the indirect mechanism by which a tangible physical injury could occur.[100]

The three dissenters in *Sweet Home* concluded that since lack of reproductive success really does not injure particular animals at all (it "takes" no lives in being), it is outside the legitimate scope of "harm."[101] Justice O'Connor opined that an action that makes it "impossible for an animal to reproduce" is "harm."[102] However, in Justice O'Connor's view, speculation that an action might reduce the reproductive success rate is not "harm" (that a "protected animal could have eaten the leaves of a fallen tree or could, perhaps, have fruitfully multiplied in its branches is not sufficient under the regulation").[103]

Actual Death or Injury Must Be Proven with Respect to a Living Individual

Another recurring issue in take cases is whether the harm rule applies only to individuals, or whether harm can be demonstrated at the population level (e.g., if the habitat modification would reduce the likelihood of recovery of the wildlife species' population). The former interpretation is better supported by the regulatory text, by *Sweet Home*, and by subsequent lower court case law and legal commentary.

Since only a currently living individual can be "kill[ed]" or "injure[d]," the text of 50 C.F.R. § 17.3 strongly suggests that harm must be proven with respect to a particular protected animal.[104] As the Supreme Court summarized, the harm rule was amended to "emphasize that actual death or injury of a protected animal is necessary for a violation."[105] The majority opinion in *Sweet Home*, by stating that the "dissent incorrectly asserts that the Secretary's regulation . . . fail[s] to require injury to particular animals," has effectively stated that "harm" does "require injury to particular animals."[106]

Justice O'Connor concurred in *Sweet Home* because, under the majority opinion, the "challenged regulation is limited to significant habitat modification that causes actual, as opposed to hypothetical or speculative, death or injury to identifiable protected animals."[107] Justice O'Connor reasoned that the Ninth Circuit's decision in *Palila* "was wrongly decided" because destruction of tree "seedlings did not proximately cause actual death or injury to identifiable birds; it merely prevented the regeneration of forest land not currently sustaining actual birds" but that could sustain birds in the future.[108] Hence, at least in Justice O'Connor's view, the assertion of long-term or speculative injuries to populations and to the recovery potential do not constitute harm in violation of ESA section 9.

Thus, the harm "test applies to individual living animals, not to the species as a whole. All members of the Court [in *Sweet Home*] seem to embrace this view."[109] Some early Ninth Circuit decisions suggesting that harm could be proven by reference to asserted long-term injuries at the population level "are hard to reconcile with *Sweet Home*," which requires proof that the challenged action would "actually kill or injure a particular animal."[110]

Another element that tends to constrain "harm" to the provable imminent death or injury of a currently living animal is the case law construing the citizen suit provision in ESA section 11(g). Section 11(g)'s use of the present tense "alleged to be in violation" of the ESA or ESA rule arguably requires a good-faith allegation of a current ESA violation.[111] Since, under *Sweet Home*, "harm" emphasizes "that actual death or injury of a protected animal is necessary for a violation" and since "the Government cannot enforce the § 9 prohibition until an animal has actually been killed or injured,"[112] there is a credible argument that ESA citizen suits cannot be maintained where there are only allegations of future harm and no allegation of continuing harm. Although the Ninth Circuit rejected that position, it still found that ESA section 11(g) requires a "showing of an imminent threat of injury to wildlife."[113]

Collectively, the ESA section 11(g) limitation to "imminent" harm and the harm requirement of actual injury to a protected animal seem to require a fairly immediate injury to a currently living individual, and to preclude the types of long-term injuries at the population level found to be "harm" in *Palila*.[114] Indicating this trend in the case law, one court stated the "harm that is imminent must be the death or *actual injury* of an identifiable animal."[115] The line for harm "is drawn with existing animals, as opposed to unborn animals," so that one cannot harm "potential additions to the population."[116] Thus, in *Bernal*, there is no "'harm' if the only purpose for protecting the site would be speculative and intended for the future benefit of the pygmy-owl rather than the present needs of the owl. In other words, there is no requirement in the Endangered Species Act that all suitable habitat for the pygmy-owl—regardless of its irreplaceable nature—be held in trust for that animal."[117] Instead, plaintiffs "had the burden of proving . . . that the proposed construction would harm a pygmy-owl by killing or injuring it."[118] As the Solicitor General's brief in *Sweet Home* states, the "harvesting of trees" in an area "not currently inhabited by the species" would "not, however, be prevented by the Section 9 'take' prohibition."[119]

Additionally, several decisions dismiss take allegations where plaintiffs cannot show that a member of a listed species currently occupies the lands to be developed.[120] Those decisions at least implicitly support the conclusion that "harm" applies only to imminent injuries to currently living individuals.

The Harm Rule Does Not Require a Landowner to Fund Creation of Habitat Conditions Favored by Listed Wildlife; Except in Narrow Circumstances, Harm Applies to Human Actions That Modify Habitats, Not Inaction

Some early take cases gave rise to the specter that a landowner had an affirmative take-avoidance duty to expend funds to create the habitat conditions favored by a listed species. *Sweet Home* seems to undercut that rationale.

In *Sierra Club v. Yeutter*, the Fifth Circuit stated the Forest Service was harming the endangered red-cockaded woodpecker (RCW), in part, because "it did not remove midstory hardwood . . . thus leading to RCW abandonment of cavity trees."[121] Read literally, *Yeutter* suggests that in order to avoid a violation of the harm regulation, landowners must do more than simply avoid adverse habitat modifications that injure members of listed wildlife species—landowners must also invest in managing their lands for the express purpose of improving the species' habitat conditions.[122] Since the *Palila* decisions required Hawaii to remove feral, now native, goats and sheep from state lands, they also could be read as requiring affirmative manipulations of habitat to remedy harm.[123]

Yet nothing in the harm rule or its preamble purports to state that the failure to manipulate habitats to favor listed wildlife constitutes harm. The harm regulation suggests there must be an affirmative "act" by a human being that modifies habitat, as contrasted to the companion harass regulation, which refers to either an "act or omission."[124]

In *Sweet Home*, the Solicitor General's opening brief stated that "harm" usually excludes inaction except where law other than ESA section 9 creates a duty to act, such as a Federal Power Act "duty to maintain a licensed dam structure."[125] Outside such narrow circumstances, "harm" does "not encompass passive acts of nonfeasance or create a duty (where none otherwise would exist) to maintain a listed species' habitat."[126] Thus, the litigation position of the United States is that the harm rule itself creates no duty to act to improve a species' habitat.

The Actual Injury Must Be Proximately Caused by the Challenged Land Use Activity

Sweet Home limits the liability for harm by "ordinary requirements of proximate causation and foreseeability."[127] The opinions of Justices O'Connor and Scalia attempt to affix flesh to the majority's skeletal references to "proximate causation and foreseeability." Their positions suggest that "proximate causation" refers to a cause that is both a fairly direct cause of injury and foreseeable.[128]

The Supreme Court has frequently returned to the "familiar doctrine of proximate cause from tort law" to "draw a manageable line between the causal changes that may make an actor responsible for an effect and those that do not."[129] As this suggests, proximate cause involves considerations of public policy and is a malleable concept. Still, one standard definition is that "proximate cause" means the "direct cause . . . ; producing cause; [or] primary cause" and refers to the "cause that directly produces an event."[130]

Several ESA cases touch on issues of proximate causation. One recurring area for litigation is whether states and local regulators are proximate causes of harm, discussed *infra*. Other, more traditional ESA take cases have involved what could be called proximate causation issues. A take claim against the Department of Navy failed where it appeared that the plaintiff did not distinguish between the Navy and others who made water withdrawals that were adverse to a listed fish species.[131] In another water usage case, a preliminary injunction was denied where the evidence suggested that adverse effects to listed wildlife was caused by a natural drought or by actors other than the federal agency defendant.[132] Where an irrigation district's pumping of water was the active cause for the salmon deaths that occurred when they were impinged on a state-required fish screen, the court found that the irrigation district and not the state was the culpable cause of harm.[133] In a final case, though "future development" of nearby properties may cause take, this "cannot be used to stop DeWeese's project which, by itself, does not pose a threat to the beach mouse."[134] These consistent rulings suggest that it is very difficult for plaintiffs to prove causation and to obtain injunctions where multiple parties are modifying the same habitats.[135]

Other Practical Pointers

As described above, landowners in areas inhabited by listed wildlife species face uncertainty as to whether their land use actions will be viewed as take. This springs both from factual uncertainty about whether the land use activity will actually injure a member of a listed wildlife species, and legal uncertainty over the applicable tests for "harm" and "harass."

Landowners do not relish such uncertainty over take liability. There are answers, albeit only partially satisfactory answers, for a landowner who wishes to gain insulation from take liability. The most obvious is that a landowner could decline to undertake any activity that has any possibility of causing a take. This answer will be unwelcome since it denies productive economic uses of land.

Alternatively, landowners can secure immunity from potential take liability in three ways. First, they can prepare conservation plans (often called habitat conservation plans or HCPs) for listed wildlife species on their lands and seek the Service's issuance of incidental take permits under ESA section 10(a)(2). The incidental take permit allows land use activities to proceed under the plan's terms. Second, where the activities involve a federal agency action (such as permitting), landowners can be beneficiaries of incidental take statements issued under ESA section 7(b)(4) following ESA consultations between the federal agency and the Service.[136] Third, FWS has adopted a general "safe harbor" policy under ESA section 10(a)(1)(A) that would encourage landowners to grow habitats preferred by listed wildlife species and, in return, allow incidental takings so long as the current or baseline population of the listed species is maintained on those lands.[137]

There are two other rarely employed alternatives to provide landowners with greater certainty on allowed and prohibited activities. The first alternative is a special ESA section 4(d) rule on lawful and unlawful land use activities that might affect a particular threatened species. This alternative is available only with respect to threatened species, not endangered species.

In the second alternative, the FWS could informally announce that it will not prosecute some types of land use activities that constitute potential takes of listed wildlife. For example, a landowner can encourage the FWS to review a land management plan and issue a so-called "no take" letter—a letter acknowledging that if the landowner follows his or her submitted management plan, no take is likely to occur and no government prosecution will be undertaken.

Though such Service review is not explicitly authorized by the ESA, neither is it prohibited. It is simply the FWS's exercise of prosecutorial discretion based on its good-faith judgment that no ESA take is likely. As long as the guidance is limited to asserting that "if the landowner adopts specified measures, the FWS will not prosecute the following types of land use actions," and does not stray into insisting that "this particular land use action is a 'take,'" the guidance might not create the type of legal norm that requires a rulemaking under the Administrative Procedure Act or run the risk of violating *Sweet Home*'s limitations on take.

Of the two alternatives (and others not mentioned), proceeding by a rulemaking provides greater security for landowners. FWS's informal view might not prevent an ESA citizen suit by an environmental group alleging a violation of the harm regulation, or even a change of mind by FWS itself.[138] However, if FWS does state in a final rule that certain types of activities are exempt from ESA section 9 take, this should bind FWS and all other litigants.

Emerging Issues and Future Directions

Are Regulators Enjoinable Causes of Take?

After *Sweet Home*, it becomes more difficult for plaintiffs to prove that a site-specific land use activity would cause or has caused harm to listed wildlife. Courts have generally become more demanding on the level of proof required on issues such as actual injury to a protected animal, imminent injury, and an injury proximately caused by the challenged land use activity. The increased rigor required of plaintiffs, and their lower success rate, seem to have contributed to a decrease in site-specific take suits since the 1990s.

One emerging area for ESA take suits concerns claims against state and local regulatory agencies. The theory is: when a state or local agency operates in a regulatory arena to the extent that it grants a permit or otherwise "approves" a private land use activity, if take can occur as a result of that privately proposed activity, the agency is an enjoinable "cause" of take unless it utilizes its regulatory program to police against take.[139] This concept is often referred to as "vicarious liability" of state or local governments for takes committed by permittees.

A vicarious liability lawsuit has several advantages for plaintiffs. First, they hope to eliminate the problems posed by small risks of take at individual sites by aggregating those risks and alleging that take is inevitable somewhere in the regulatory program.[140] Second, if the suit is successful, the plaintiff gets more bang for the buck. That is, more people are regulated to reduce the risk of take and the regulatory agency becomes responsible for policing against take.

This theory gains some support in a few cases. In approving a (nonintrusive) preliminary injunction, the First Circuit arguably held that the Commonwealth of Massachusetts was violating the ESA by licensing commercial fishing that carried some risk of entangling and harming listed whales.[141] The 11th Circuit, in an opinion finding that the vicarious liability theory satisfies the more liberal causation or traceability element of standing, suggested that a county could be liable for takes of turtles caused by inadequate regulation of private persons and municipalities with respect to beach lighting that harmed listed turtles.[142] Two district courts have initially been of the view that, where state law required an "authorization " or "written approval" before commencing timber harvesting on private lands, this might provide a viable basis for a take suit against state regulators on a theory that the State was unlawfully authorizing take or unlawfully allowing take to occur.[143]

Such decisions provoked considerable adverse legal commentary. At least five law review articles critically examine the vicarious ESA liability theory and find the theory is not legally supportable. Three articles explain why jurisdictional limitations, the language of ESA sections 6 and 9, the structure of the ESA and the harm rule, and federalism and other constitutional principles (e.g., the Tenth and Eleventh Amendments) prevent holding state regulators liable for private take of listed species.[144] Two articles by law professors conclude that state regulators are not a proximate cause of take and have no duty to enforce the ESA.[145]

The theory of vicarious liability has not succeeded in several recent cases. The district court that initiated the theory in *Strahan v. Coxe* recently stated: "The Court is not persuaded that the [State] defendants are liable for entanglements of endangered whales . . . in fishing gear licensed by the" State.[146] Shortly after deciding *Strahan v. Coxe*, the district court and the First Circuit seemed to pull back from the theory of vicarious ESA take liability by holding that the U.S. Coast Guard bears no ESA take liability when it licenses ships, even though there is an inherent risk that ships operating in certain waters will strike listed whales.[147] The logic was that the "vessel owner or operator is an independent actor who is, himself, responsible for complying with environmental and other laws."[148] And in 2007, the Court of International Trade held that even a federal regulatory agency has no duty to regulate to prevent ESA section 9 violations.[149] Another court dismissed a facial challenge against California's forest practice rules on the ripeness ground that the take claim should not be heard at the programmatic level—rather, plaintiffs should challenge an individual timber harvesting project and then a court can assess the take allegations on a site-specific and fact-specific basis.[150]

Three other suits essentially ended in draws. After the 11th Circuit's remand in *Loggerhead Turtle*, the district court found that the county was not liable on the merits on two bases. One basis was that the county was not the proximate cause of any take (beachfront property owners were) and the county has no duty to regulate under the ESA. The second basis was that the county had enacted a turtle-friendly ordinance and any takes were now caused by private persons disobeying the ordinance.[151] The former ground supports ESA defendants in vicarious liability cases, while the latter ground provides some support for plaintiffs.

After the district court in *Pacific Rivers Council v. Brown* suggested that Oregon regulators might be enjoinable causes of take when they affirmatively authorize private timber harvesting that could harm listed wildlife, the Oregon legislature changed the law to eliminate any concept of state "authorization." Plaintiffs then moved to dismiss their suit, which the district granted in an opinion that mentioned the nonprecedential nature of the earlier preliminary rulings.[152]

In a similar suit brought against state officials who regulated private timber harvesting for some purposes under the Washington Forest Practices Act, District Judge Pechman issued one interlocutory opinion suggesting that state regulators could be enjoinable causes of take under the logic of *Strahan v. Coxe*.[153] But a subsequent opinion denied a preliminary injunction against the state officials on the ground that take was not sufficiently likely throughout the program.[154] After these mixed signals, the parties reached a settlement and *Seattle Audubon Society v. Sutherland* was dismissed by a stipulation in July 2008.

In our subjective view, the *Pacific Rivers* and *Seattle Audubon* litigation illustrate several shortcomings of the theory of vicarious ESA liability of state regulators. The notion that a state regulator is "authorizing" take is mistaken, as (1) States normally do not purport to authorize ESA take and usually lack the authority to do so; (2) a state permit is not a legal cause of take because landowners have the Fifth Amendment right to conduct private land uses and the State's exercise of the police power constrains, but does not authorize, those private rights; and (3) the State is not a proximate cause as the same risk of take would exist if there were no state regulatory program.[155]

Moreover, as the Oregon experience illustrates, if courts stretch ESA concepts to create a state duty to regulate to prevent take in some circumstances, states may react to do what is necessary to avoid placing that unfunded mandate on state taxpayers. The end result is that states will exit regulatory fields in which they are securing environmental benefits. Hence, the vicarious ESA liability theory seems to fail on both legal and policy grounds.

Is a Source of Greenhouse Gas Emissions an Enjoinable Cause of Take of a Polar Bear?

In May 2008, FWS listed the polar bear as a threatened species. This is the first, perhaps of many, species to be listed primarily due to concerns that the species is threatened by current or projected global climate change.[156] The implications for the ESA of global climate change, and vice versa, will no doubt be significant issues in the future.[157]

One emerging issue under ESA section 9 is whether a proposed power plant or other project that emits greenhouse gases (GHG) can be enjoined because it allegedly takes or harms a polar bear.[158] The answer appears to be "no," both under a special 4(d) rule and under normal take principles.

Contemporaneous with the ESA listing of the polar bear as a threatened species, FWS exercised its discretionary ESA section 4(d) authority to not fully extend the take prohibition to a *threatened* species.[159] The special rule provides that any arguable incidental take associated with an "otherwise lawful activity within any area subject to the jurisdiction of the United States except Alaska" is not a violation of the ESA.[160] Under this rule, any suit should be dismissed that alleges that the GHG emissions associated with, for example, an oil refinery or highway in Texas would take a polar bear.

This rule was adopted as part of Interior Secretary Kempthorne's policy that the ESA not be misused as a back-door mechanism to regulate GHG emissions.[161] The legality of the 4(d) rule and of other aspects of the polar bear listing are being challenged in lawsuits brought by environmental groups, the State of Alaska, and regulated groups.

Even in this absence of the 4(d) rule, the theory that a proposed project in the lower 48 states is the proximate cause of the death or injury of a particular member of a listed species seems to be impossible to prove. As the Director of the Center for Biological Diversity is reported to have stated, "any bid to fight the construction of a power plant by arguing that emissions might harm a species would probably be thrown out of court, because such climate-change effects remain speculative."[162] We would add that because there are billions of sources of GHG emissions (past, present, and future) worldwide, a plaintiff seemingly cannot sustain its burdens of (1) proving that the death or injury to a particular member of a listed species will occur to a reasonable certainty; and (2) attributing that harm to a defendant's proposed project, as opposed to other sources of GHGs.

Conclusion

Under the harm regulation and as construed in *Sweet Home*, a land use activity seemingly does not become a prohibited ESA section 9 take of listed wildlife unless (1) there is a significant habitat modification that (2) perhaps directly or perhaps indirectly through the mechanism of significantly impairing an essential behavioral pattern (3) causes the death of or a tangible actual injury to a member of a listed wildlife species. While the Supreme Court's decision in *Sweet Home* and subsequent lower court decisions have generally narrowed the meaning of "harm," legal uncertainty certainly remains.

Notes

1. The authors represented the landowner interests in several of the cases discussed in the text (e.g., *Sweet Home*).
2. 16 U.S.C. § 1533; *see* definitions of endangered species, threatened species, and Secretary in 16 U.S.C. § 1532. "Secretary" refers to the Secretary of Commerce for some listed marine and anadromous fish species, and to the Secretary of the Interior for all other (most) species. The respective Secretaries have delegated their ESA responsibilities to the National Marine Fisheries Service (NMFS, sometimes also known as NOAA-Fisheries) and the U.S. Fish and Wildlife Service (FWS), respectively. *See* 16 U.S.C. § 1532(15); 50 C.F.R. §§ 17.2, 17.11, 17.12; 223.102, 224.101. FWS and NMFS will be referred to collectively as the Services.
3. 16 U.S.C. § 1538(a).
4. 16 U.S.C. § 1538(a)(1)(B).

5. 16 U.S.C. § 1532(13).
6. We will refer to "fish and wildlife" as "wildlife."
7. In pertinent part, ESA § 4(d) provides:

   Whenever any species is listed as a threatened species . . . , the Secretary shall issue such regulations as he deems necessary and advisable to provide for the conservation of such species. The Secretary may by regulation prohibit with respect to any threatened species any act prohibited under section 9(a)(1) . . . with respect to endangered species. . . .

   16 U.S.C. § 1533(d).
8. Sweet Home Chapter of Cmtys. for a Great Or. v. Babbitt, 1 F.3d 1, 5–8 (D.C. Cir. 1993). The D.C. Circuit's opinion suggests that the Services have a broad range of discretion to allow some forms of take of a threatened species. The Services could exempt from take certain land uses that have relatively benign impacts on a threatened species. One recent example is FWS's § 4(d) rule excluding routine ranching activities from being causes of unlawful take of the California tiger salamander—the stock ponds on ranches provide breeding habitats, even though livestock might occasionally trample a salamander. See 50 C.F.R. § 17.43.
9. See 50 C.F.R. §§ 223.203, 223.205.
10. See Louisiana ex rel. Guste v. Verity, 853 F.2d 322 (5th Cir. 1988); Ctr. for Marine Conservation v. Brown, 917 F. Supp. 1128 (S.D. Tex. 1996); 50 C.F.R. §§ 223.206, 223.207.
11. 16 U.S.C. § 1538(a)(1)(G).
12. ESA § 9(a)(2) makes it unlawful to "remove and reduce to possession" an endangered plant from land "areas under Federal jurisdiction." 16 U.S.C. § 1538(a)(2)(B). On non-federal lands, the same provision makes it unlawful to "remove, cut, dig up, or damage or destroy any such [endangered plant] species on any other area in knowing violation of any law or regulation of any State or in the course of any violation of a State criminal trespass law." In most states, the ESA's incorporation of state law allows a landowner to damage or destroy a listed plant species on his or her own land, and merely protects against removal of listed plants by third-party trespassers. However, plants can obtain take protection if a state law makes take of an ESA-listed plant species a violation of law. There, the "violation of any law . . . of any State" language of § 9(a)(2)(B) would federalize the landowner's violation of state law.
13. 16 U.S.C. § 1532(19).
14. See text accompanying notes 40–44 *infra*.
15. 16 U.S.C. § 1540.
16. 16 U.S.C. §§ 1536(b)(4), 1539(a)(2).
17. Babbitt v. Sweet Home Chapter of Cmtys. for a Great Or., 515 U.S. 687 (1995).
18. 50 C.F.R. § 17.3 (1976); 40 Fed. Reg. 44,116 (Sept. 26, 1975).
19. Palila v. Haw. Dep't of Land & Natural Res., 471 F. Supp. 985 (D. Haw. 1979), *aff'd*, 639 F.2d 495 (9th Cir. 1981).
20. 46 Fed. Reg. 29,492 (June 2, 1981) (providing the Interior legal opinion as part of the preamble to a proposed redefinition of "harm").
21. 46 Fed. Reg. 29,490, 29,492 (June 2, 1981).
22. 50 C.F.R. § 17.3.
23. 46 Fed. Reg. 54,748–50 (Nov. 4, 1981).
24. 46 Fed. Reg. 54,750 (italics in original).
25. Palila v. Haw. Dep't of Land & Natural Res., 649 F. Supp. 1070, 1077 (D. Haw. 1986).
26. Palila v. Haw. Dep't of Land & Natural Res., 852 F.2d 1106, 1108, 1110 (9th Cir. 1983).
27. See Albert Gidari, *The Economy of Nature, Private Property, and the Endangered Species Act*, 6 FORDHAM ENVTL. L.J. 661, 675–76 (1995); Robert A. Anthony, *Interpretative Rules, Policy Statements, Guidances, Manuals, and the Like—Should Federal Agencies Use Them to Bind the Public?*, 41 DUKE L.J. 1311, 1366–71 (1992).

28. *See* Sweet Home Chapter of Cmtys. for a Great Or. v. Turner, No. 91-2218 (D.D.C.). That case is discussed in the Gidari and Anthony articles at the pages cited *supra* note 27.
29. Sweet Home Chapter of Cmtys. for a Great Or. v. Lujan, 806 F. Supp. 279 (D.D.C. 1992), *aff'd per curiam sub nom.* Sweet Home Chapter of Cmtys. for a Great Or. v. Babbitt, 1 F.3d 1, 3 (D.C. Cir. 1993), *rev'd as to "harm" on reh'g*, 17 F.3d 1463, 1472 ("we hold invalid the Fish & Wildlife Service regulation defining 'harm' to embrace habitat modifications"), *reh'g en banc denied with accompanying opinions*, 30 F.3d 190 (D.C. Cir. 1994), *rev'd sub nom.* Babbitt v. Sweet Home Chapter of Cmtys. for a Great Or., 515 U.S. 687 (1995).
30. 16 U.S.C. §§ 1534, 1536(a)(2).
31. *See Sweet Home*, 515 U.S. at 691 n.2, 696–703.
    As Prof. Ruhl has summarized:

    > The *Sweet Home* opinion took with one hand while it gave with the other, limiting the breadth of the harm definition as much as it upheld the idea that take extends to habitat losses.... The stiff evidentiary and proof burdens *Sweet Home* imposed largely explain why the government and citizen groups (through citizen suits) so infrequently attempt to prosecute take violation claims.

    J. B. Ruhl, *Climate Change and the Endangered Species Act: Building Bridges to the No-Analog Future*, 88 B.U. L. Rev. 1, 39–40 (2008).
32. 515 U.S. at 735.
33. First, "harm" has a broad common meaning of "injure" through any means that "naturally encompasses habitat modification that results in actual injury or death to members of" a listed wildlife species. 515 U.S. at 697. Second, reading "harm" to include wildlife injuries caused by habitat modifications is consistent with one of the ESA's stated purposes: conserving "the ecosystems upon which endangered species and threatened species depend." 515 U.S. at 698 (quoting 16 U.S.C. § 1531(b)). Third, construing "harm" to protect against habitat modification causing extinction better comports with the Supreme Court's prior jurisprudence in *TVA v. Hill*, 437 U.S. 153, 184 (1978), that the ESA was intended to "reverse the trend toward species extinction, whatever the cost." 515 U.S. at 698–99.

    The fourth reason is that the *Sweet Home* plaintiffs did not satisfy the difficult burden of proof in a facial challenge to a regulation. *Sweet Home* was one of the first decisions to clearly articulate that, in a facial challenge contending that a regulation is ultra vires of its enabling statute (as opposed to a constitutional challenge), the plaintiff must show that the regulation is invalid "in every circumstance." 515 U.S. at 699. The *Sweet Home* majority identified a bleak hypothetical in which a habitat modification activity would cause a take within the meaning allowed by Congress: "when an actor knows that an activity, such as draining a pond, would actually result in the extinction of a listed species by destroying its habitat." 515 U.S. at 699. However, the majority also stated that the plaintiffs in *Sweet Home* "advance strong arguments that activities that cause minimal or unforeseeable harm will not violate the Act." This leaves the door open for later challenges to the legality of the harm regulation "as applied" in particular circumstances (e.g., where there is no proven death or injury to a protected animal).

    Fifth, the *Sweet Home* majority found support for the harm regulation in the text and legislative history of the "incidental take" provisions added by the 1982 ESA amendments. 515 U.S. at 700–01, 707–08. Sixth, the majority found that the legislative history associated with the enactment of the ESA in 1973 does not "undermine[] the reasonableness" of the harm regulation. 515 U.S. at 704–07. Justice Stevens concluded that the statements in Senate and House committee reports that "'take' is defined ... in the broadest possible manner to include every conceivable way in which a person can 'take' or attempt to 'take' any fish or wildlife" authorize an effects test for take (death or injury to listed wildlife) that reaches "far more than the deliberate actions of hunters and trappers." 515 U.S. at 704–05. The majority thought this outweighed the indicia of legislative intent that the Senate committee had deleted "habitat modification" as a form of take and that the Senate and House leaders had distinguished between habitat destruction and take. 515 U.S. at 705–07 & n.19. *Compare* Justice Scalia's recitation of the ESA legislative intent in 515 U.S. at 726–29.

    Seventh and finally, because "Congress did not unambiguously manifest its intent to adopt respondents' view" of the ESA, the Court concluded it must defer to the implementing agency's "reasonable" interpretation of the ambiguous ESA term "harm" under *Chevron*. 515 U.S. at 703, 708 (citing Chevron U.S.A. Inc. v. Natural Res. Def. Council, 467 U.S. 837 (1984)). This suggests the Services have the discretion to define "harm" to include or exclude injuries to listed species that result from land use activities.

34. 515 U.S. at 703.
35. 515 U.S. at 691 n.2, 700 n.13.
36. These themes are developed at text accompanying notes 44–135 *infra*.
37. 515 U.S. at 708–09. Since Justice O'Connor's concurrence came in a 6–3 opinion, it was not necessary for a majority. Hence, the concurrence is not clearly the law of the land. But that concurrence does identify and develop some themes and rulings that are located in footnotes in the majority opinion in *Sweet Home*.

    One interesting aspect of that concurrence is Justice O'Connor's statement that the leading Ninth Circuit decision on "harm" "was wrongly decided" under the "regulation's own limitations." 515 U.S. at 714 (discussing *Palila*, 852 F.2d 1106 (9th Cir. 1988)). In Justice O'Connor's view, destroying tree seedlings that "merely prevented the regeneration of forest land not currently sustaining actual birds" is not harm, even though it has adverse effects on future generations of a listed wildlife species. 515 U.S. at 714.
38. 515 U.S. at 697 n.9; *see* 515 U.S. at n.13.
39. 515 U.S. at 709.
40. 50 C.F.R. § 17.3.
41. 40 Fed. Reg. 44,413 (Sept. 26, 1975).
42. *E.g., Ohio Mfrs. Ass'n v. City of Akron*, 801 F.2d 824, 832–33 (6th Cir. 1986); *Hart v. Lucas*, 535 F.2d 516, 519–20 (9th Cir. 1976). FWS's original regulatory interpretation can be changed only in another notice-and-comment rulemaking. *E.g., Envtl. Integrity Proj. v. EPA*, 425 F.3d 992, 997–98 (D.C. Cir. 2005).
43. *Cold Mountain v. Garber*, 375 F.3d 884, 889–90 (9th Cir. 2004) (no proof that helicopter noise within nest vicinity caused nest failures for bald eagle); *Fund for Animals v. Fla. Game and Fresh Water Fish Comm'n*, 550 F. Supp. 1206 (S.D. Fla. 1982) (finding that temporary boat noise did not harass a listed wildlife species).

    The legislative history on "harass" is consistent. It states: "a 'harassment' form of taking would allow, for example, the Secretary to regulate or prohibit the activities of bird watchers where the effect of those activities might disturb the birds and make it difficult for them to hatch or raise their young." H.R. REP. NO. 93-412, at 11 (1973). The activities of the birdwatchers do not alter the character of the forest itself except when their presence generates noise and activity levels that annoy the protected birds.
44. A district court's finding that construction was harassing bald eagles was vacated and reversed in *Ctr. for Biological Diversity v. Marina Point Dev. Co.*, 535 F.3d 1026, 1036–37 (9th Cir. 2008).
45. 50 C.F.R. § 222.102.
46. *See* 64 Fed. Reg. 60,727–30 (Nov. 8, 1999).
47. James Rasband, *Priority, Probability, and Proximate Cause: Lessons from Tort Law About Imposing ESA Responsibility for Wildlife Harm on Water Users and Other Joint Habitat Modifiers*, 33 ENVTL. L. 595, 618 (2003).
48. 16 U.S.C. § 1540(g).
49. 515 U.S. at 691 n.2; *see id.* at 700 n.13, 703.
50. 50 C.F.R. § 17.3.
51. 46 Fed. Reg. 54,748–50 (Nov. 4, 1981) (emphasis in original).
52. *Am. Bald Eagle v. Bhatti*, 9 F.3d 163, 165–67 (1st Cir. 1993).

53. Brief for Petitioners at 46, *Sweet Home* (U.S.) (No. 94-859), 1995 WL 89293.
54. Some Ninth Circuit opinions decided shortly after *Sweet Home* seemed to prefer to follow the Ninth Circuit's prior case law on "harm," rather than the tenor of the Supreme Court's guidance. *See* Steven P. Quarles & Thomas R. Lundquist, *When Do Land Use Activities "Take" Listed Wildlife Under ESA Section 9 and the "Harm" Regulation? in* ENDANGERED SPECIES ACT: LAW, POLICY, AND PERSPECTIVES 234–35 (Baur & Irvin eds., ABA 2002). For example, portions of Marbled Murrelet v. Babbitt, 83 F.3d 1060, 1067 (9th Cir. 1996), suggest that impaired breeding success is harm, and an injunction was affirmed in a situation where the opinions did not demonstrate that timber harvesting would cause the death of or actual injury to mobile marbled murrelets.
55. Defenders of Wildlife v. Bernal, 204 F.3d 920, 925 (9th Cir. 2005).
56. 204 F.3d at 926–28.
57. 204 F.3d at 927.
58. 204 F.3d at 927.
59. Ariz. Cattle Growers' Ass'n v. U.S. Fish & Wildlife Serv., 273 F.3d 1229 (9th Cir. 2001).
60. 16 U.S.C. § 1536(b)(4).
61. 273 F.3d at 1239–40.
62. 273 F.3d at 1238, 1243–51.
63. 273 F.3d at 1242.
64. 273 F.3d at 1243–44.
65. *E.g.*, Alabama v. U.S. Army Corps of Eng'rs, 441 F. Supp. 2d 1123, 1132–34 (N.D. Ala. 2006) (preliminary injunction denied); Protect Our Water v. Flowers, 377 F. Supp. 2d 844, 879–81 (E.D. Cal. 2004) (inadequate evidence that members of the species are onsite); San Carlos Apache Tribe v. United States, 272 F. Supp. 2d 860, 873–81 (D. Ariz. 2003) (small risk of harm not sufficient); Swan View Coal., Inc. v. Turner, 824 F. Supp. 923, 939–40 (D. Mont. 1992); Morrill v. Lujan, 802 F. Supp. 424, 431–32 (S.D. Ala. 1992); California v. Watt, 520 F. Supp. 1359, 1387–88 (C.D. Cal. 1981) (the possibility or "threat [of future injury] would still not constitute a 'taking' under the statutes"), *aff'd in part*, 683 F.2d 1253 (9th Cir. 1982), *rev'd on other grounds*, 464 U.S. 312 (1984).
66. Hawksbill Sea Turtle v. FEMA, 11 F. Supp. 2d 529, 552 (D.V.I. 1998).
67. United States v. W. Coast Forest Res. Ltd. Partnership, 1997 WL 33100698 (D. Or. 1997). If the preliminary injunction in *West Coast* "was a victory for the government, then it surely was a pyrrhic one. The requirement to radio-tag individual animals in order to prove their taking imposes an enormous practical burden" and the *West Coast* court "held that the government could not prove harm by relying on statistics showing an average home range for owls, but must produce . . . actual habitat use data for the specific owls in question." Michael Bean, *The Endangered Species Act and Private Land: Four Lessons Learned from the Past Quarter Century*, 28 ENVTL. L. REP. 10,701, 10,703 (Dec. 1998).
68. United States v. W. Coast Forest Res. Ltd. Partnership, 2000 WL 298707, at *5 (D. Or. 2000).
69. *Bald Eagle*, 9 F.3d at 165–66 & n.5.
70. *Bernal*, 204 F.3d at 927.
71. Alabama v. U.S. Army Corps of Eng'rs, 441 F. Supp. 2d 1123, 1130 (N.D. Ala. 2006) (denying a preliminary injunction in an ESA take case and disagreeing with the truncated preliminary injunction test used in the Ninth Circuit). These prerequisites to a preliminary injunction may apply to ESA cases in light of Winter v. Natural Resources Defense Council, 129 S. Ct. 365, 374–75 (2009).
72. Nat'l Wildlife Fed'n v. Burlington N. R.R., 23 F.3d 1508, 1511 (9th Cir. 1994).
73. Amoco Prod. Co. v. Vill. of Gambell, 480 U.S. 531, 546 n.12 (1986).
74. *NWF v. BN*, 23 F.3d at 1511. The *NWF v. BN* court denied an injunction where the source of prior harm (a grain spill from one train that lured grizzly bears, who were killed by later trains) had been cleaned up and where harm was unlikely to recur in the future.
75. See the preliminary injunction denials reported in *Bernal*, 204 F.3d 920 (9th Cir. 2000); *NWF v. BN*, 23 F.3d 1508 (9th Cir. 1994); *Bald Eagle*, 9 F.3d 163 (1st Cir. 1993); Stra-

han v. Pritchard, 2007 WL 478237 (D. Mass. 2007); *Protect Our Water*, 377 F. Supp. 2d 844 (E.D. Cal. 2004).
76. Weinberger v. Romero-Barcelo, 456 U.S. 305, 312 (1982).
77. *NWF v. BN*, 23 F.3d at 1511, 1513. "[I]njunctive relief under the ESA is generally mandated where the moving party 1) has had or can likely show success on the merits, and 2) makes the requisite showing of irreparable injury." Pac. Rivers Council v. Brown, 2003 WL 21087974, at *2 (D. Or. 2003).
78. *Alabama v. Army Corps*, 441 F. Supp. 2d at 1135–36 (collecting decisions).
79. Water Keeper Alliance v. U.S. Dep't of Def., 271 F.3d 21, 33–34 (1st Cir. 2001). Another court found no irreparable injury where the proposed action might "stress" some individuals, but would not "eradicate their population." Hamilton v. City of Austin, 8 F. Supp. 2d 886, 896 (N.D. Tex. 1998).
80. *Amoco Prod.*, 480 U.S. at 544–45.
81. 50 C.F.R. § 17.3.
82. 50 C.F.R. § 17.3.
83. *Sweet Home*, 515 U.S. at 717 (Justice Scalia, dissenting on an issue not contested by the majority). The ESA regulatory concept of "harm" expands the historic meaning of taking wildlife in the sense that it makes it unlawful to kill or injure listed wildlife by any act (such as land uses not directed at harming wildlife), instead of being limited to the class of activities directed against wildlife (e.g., hunting and trapping). As FWS stated in the preamble to the final harm rule, "Congress intended to create a definition of take which included all the various ways of killing or injuring protected wildlife." 46 Fed. Reg. 54,749 (Nov. 4, 1981).
84. 50 C.F.R. § 17.3.
85. 46 Fed. Reg. 54,750 (Nov. 4, 1981) (emphasis in original). "Harm" is not limited "to direct[ly caused] physical injury to an individual member of the wildlife species," such as the felling of a tree killing a nesting bird, as FWS "did not intend to imply that significant habitat destruction which could be shown to injure protected wildlife through [the indirect mechanism of] the impairment of its essential behavioral patterns was not subject to the Act." 46 Fed. Reg. 54,748. While it is possible to indirectly cause harm through impairing essential behavioral patterns, the most fundamental element of harm is proof of a resulting actual injury or death of listed wildlife: "The final definition adds the word 'actually' before the words 'kills or injures' in response to comments requesting this addition to clarify that a standard of actual, adverse effects applies to section 9 takings." 46 Fed. Reg. 54,749.
86. BEAN & ROWLAND, THE EVOLUTION OF NATIONAL WILDLIFE LAW 217 n.120 (Praeger 3d ed. 1997).
87. Steven Davison, *The Aftermath of* Sweet Home *Chapter: Modification of Wildlife Habitat as a Prohibited Taking in Violation of the Endangered Species Act*, 27 WM. & MARY ENVTL. L. & POL'Y REV. 541, 577 (2003).
88. 46 Fed. Reg. 29,490 (June 2, 1981). FWS proposed to redefine "harm" to prevent the result reached in *Palila*. That result was: "because the state had allowed the destruction of forest vegetation which provides the Palila's food, shelter and nest sites, a taking had occurred even though no killing or injuring of individual Palilas was demonstrated" and even though the "Palila population . . . actually increased since the onset of the state's grazing program." 46 Fed. Reg. 29,492 (June 2, 1981) (Solicitor's Opinion included with the proposed rulemaking). Thus, even though the long-term essential behavioral patterns of feeding, sheltering, and rearing young had been impaired by sheep devouring mamane tree seedlings, the Solicitor's Office concluded that no harm within the meaning of ESA § 9 had occurred because "no killing or injuring of individual Palilas was demonstrated."
89. Davison, *supra* note 87, at 577–79. *But see* Marbled Murrelet v. Babbitt, 83 F.3d 1060, 1067 (9th Cir. 1996) ("habitat modification which significantly impairs the breeding and sheltering of a protected species amounts to 'harm' under the ESA").
90. Rasband, *supra* note 47, 33 ENVTL. L. at 615.

91. Brief for Petitioners at 21, 23, *Sweet Home* (U.S.) (No. 94-859), 1995 WL 89293.
92. *See* 515 U.S. at 715–19, 731.
93. *Sweet Home*, 515 U.S. at 700 n.13.
94. 515 U.S. at 699.
95. United States v. W. Coast Forest Res. Ltd. Partnership, 2000 WL 298707 (D. Or. 2000).
96. *Id.* at *5.
97. Rasband, *supra* note 47, 33 ENVTL. L. at 615.
98. Hawksbill Sea Turtle v. FEMA, 11 F. Supp. 2d 529, 553–54 (D.V.I. 1998) (denying injunctive relief against building housing after a hurricane).
99. Swan View Coal., Inc. v. Turner, 824 F. Supp. 923, 939 (D. Mont. 1992).
100. BEAN & ROWLAND, THE EVOLUTION OF NATIONAL WILDLIFE LAW 217–18 (Praeger 3d ed. 1997).
101. 515 U.S. at 734–35.
102. 515 U.S. at 710.
103. 515 U.S. at 711. Further, Justice O'Connor's statement that activities that "completely prevent[ ] breeding" are the equivalent of "sterilizing the creature" and, therefore, "harm" (515 U.S. at 710) implies that actions that only temporarily impair breeding (e.g., for one breeding season) may not be "harm." In the final harm rule, "'impair' was substituted for 'disrupt' to limit harm to situations where a behavioral pattern was adversely affected and not simply disturbed on a temporary basis with no consequent injury to the protected species." 46 Fed. Reg. 54,750 (Nov. 4, 1981).
104. The focus on individuals is implicit in FWS's use of the term "wildlife" in 50 C.F.R. § 17.3. Section 17.3 makes the "definitions contained in part 10 applicable." Part 10 defines "wildlife" to mean the same as "fish and wildlife," which is defined as "any wild animal, whether alive or dead." 50 C.F.R. § 10.12. Thus, it appears that "wildlife" refers to an individual "wild animal."
105. *Sweet Home*, 515 U.S. at 691 n.2.
106. 515 U.S. at 700 n.13. *See also* 515 U.S. at 734 (the majority opinion "apparently *concedes* that the statute requires injury *to particular animals*, rather than merely to populations of animals").
107. 515 U.S. at 708–09.
108. 515 U.S. at 714.
109. BEAN & ROWLAND, THE EVOLUTION OF NATIONAL WILDLIFE LAW 218 (Praeger 3d ed. 1997). *Accord* Tony Sullins, ESA: ENDANGERED SPECIES ACT 53 (ABA Basic Practice Series 2001) ("The *Sweet Home* majority apparently would have limited the application of the 'harm' prohibition to injury to 'particular animals.'"). Conceptually, if "harm" did refer to concepts of injury at the population level (e.g., reducing the habitat available for recovery of an expanding population), this would seem to fall down the slippery slope to the result that any human use of habitat that is adverse to the long-term interests of listed wildlife is "harm." Yet it is ESA § 7 that "imposes a broad, affirmative duty to avoid adverse habitat modifications that § 9 [take] does not replicate, and § 7 does not limit its admonition to habitat modification that 'actually kills or injures wildlife.'" *Sweet Home*, 515 U.S. at 703.
110. Rasband, *supra* note 47, 33 ENVTL. L. at 616 & n.80. More particularly, prior to *Sweet Home*, the *Palila* district court concluded that harm "does not necessitate a finding of death to individual species members" or of a "decline in population numbers"—"If the habitat modification prevents the species from recovering, then this causes injury to the species and should be actionable under section 9." Palila v. Haw. Dep't of Land & Natural Res., 649 F. Supp. 1070, 1077 (D. Haw. 1986). The United States took the unusual step of filing an amicus brief in an ESA § 11(g) citizen suit to inform the Ninth Circuit that FWS's harm regulation did not reach "habitat modification that would prevent or delay the recovery of the" listed species. Palila v. Haw. Dep't of Land and Natural Res., 852 F.2d 1106, 1108 n.4 (9th Cir. 1988). The Ninth Circuit affirmed on the basis that "habitat destruction that could result in extinction" of the species is harm, and "we do

not reach whether harm includes habitat degradation that merely retards recovery." 852 F.2d at 1108, 1110. Thus, *Palila* provides some support for the proposition that long-term injuries to the survival of a population (sheep eating mamane tree seedlings, so that there may not be enough mature mamane trees for future generations of palila birds) can be harm, as does FWS's position pre-*Sweet Home*.

As Prof. Rasband describes, this portion of *Palila* likely did not survive *Sweet Home*. Justice O'Connor expressly found that *Palila* "was wrongly decided according to the regulation's own terms." 515 U.S. at 714. There was no proven "actual death or injury to identifiable birds" or "actual birds"—just speculation that sheep grazing on tree seedlings could cause the extinction of future generations of palila birds. 515 U.S. at 713–14. Further, Justice O'Connor "disagree[d]" with Justice Scalia's thesis that the harm regulation (in violation of the ESA) applied to a "*population* of animals." 515 U.S. at 709–10 (emphasis in original). The *Sweet Home* majority opinion seems to capture the same view that "harm" is limited to the "injury of a protected animal" or "injury to particular animals." 515 U.S. at 691 n.2, 700 n.13.

111. 16 U.S.C. § 1540(g)(1)(A); *see also* Gwaltney of Smithfield, Ltd. v. Chesapeake Bay Found., 484 U.S. 49 (1987).
112. *Sweet Home*, 515 U.S. at 691 n.2, 703.
113. Forest Conservation Council v. Rosboro Lumber Co., 50 F.3d 781, 784 (9th Cir. 1995).
114. *Sweet Home* supports *Palila* in the sense that it affirms the Ninth Circuit's *dicta* that the harm regulation is lawful. See 515 U.S. at 695; *Palila*, 852 F.2d at 1108. Yet *Palila* did not involve a claim by the defendant that the harm regulation was ultra vires of the ESA. *See* BEAN & ROWLAND, THE EVOLUTION OF NATIONAL WILDLIFE LAW 214 ("Neither the *Palila* case nor others that followed it seriously questioned whether the Secretary's regulatory definition of 'harm' was in fact authorized by the Endangered Species Act.").
115. United States v. W. Coast Forest Res. Ltd. Partnership, 1997 WL 33100698, at *6 (D. Or. 1997).
116. Defenders of Wildlife v. Bernal, No. CIV-98-120-TUC-FRZ, slip op. at 3 (D. Ariz. Sept. 23, 1998), *aff'd*, 204 F.3d 920 (9th Cir. 2005).
117. Defenders of Wildlife v. Bernal, No. CV-98-120-TUC-FRZ, slip op. at 6 (D. Ariz. June 9, 1998).
118. *Bernal*, 204 F.3d at 925.
119. Brief for Petitioners at 41–42, *Sweet Home* (U.S.) (No. 94-859), 1995 WL 89293.
120. *E.g.*, *Ariz. Cattle*, 273 F.3d at 1246–48; *Bernal*, 204 F.3d at 925–26; Protect Our Water v. Flowers, 377 F. Supp. 2d 844, 880–81 (E.D. Cal. 2004); Coastside Habitat Coal. v. Prime Props., Inc., 1998 WL 231024, at *3 (N.D. Cal. 1998).
121. Sierra Club v. Yeutter, 926 F.2d 429, 438 (5th Cir. 1991).
122. The *Yeutter* decision appears to confuse a federal agency's responsibilities under ESA § 9 with its separate duties under ESA § 7. There, the Fifth Circuit found that the Forest Service's failure to implement certain measures for protection of red-cockaded woodpeckers (including midstory removal standards) that had been approved by the FWS in consultation under ESA § 7(a)(2) violated that section's duty to avoid jeopardy to the species. 926 F.2d at 439. The court inappropriately transferred the federal agency obligation to follow those ESA § 7 measures to the ESA § 9 prohibition on take.
123. The district court approved a state program requiring that the feral goats and sheep be shot through a broader hunting program. *See Palila*, 639 F.2d at 497.
124. 50 C.F.R. § 17.3.
125. Brief for Petitioners at 47, *Sweet Home* (U.S.) (No. 94-859), 1995 WL 89293.
126. *Id. See also Sweet Home*, 515 U.S. at 716 (where Justice Scalia quotes from the federal brief).
127. 515 U.S. at 696–97 n.9, 700 n.13.
128. *See* 515 U.S. at 709–14, 732–33.
129. Dep't of Transp. v. Pub. Citizen, 541 U.S. 752, 767 (2004). In that National Environmental Policy Act (NEPA) case, the Court found that the President's action in opening

U.S. borders to Mexican trucks was the proximate cause of increased air pollution. Since the air pollution impacts were not caused by the federal agency's action, they did not need to be extensively addressed in the agency's NEPA document. 541 U.S. at 769–70.
130. BLACK'S LAW DICTIONARY 234 ("Cause") (8th ed. 2004).
131. Pyramid Lake Paiute Tribe v. U.S. Dep't of Navy, 898 F.2d 1410, 1420 (9th Cir. 1990).
132. Alabama v. Army Corps, 441 F. Supp. 2d at 1132–35.
133. United States v. Glenn-Colusa Irrigation Dist., 788 F. Supp. 1126, 1133 (E.D. Cal. 1992).
134. Morrill v. Lujan, 802 F. Supp. 424, 431–32 (S.D. Ala. 1992).
135. *See* Rasband, *supra* note 47, 33 ENVTL. L. at 610–30.
136. *See* 16 U.S.C. §§ 1536(b)(4), 1539(a)(2).
137. *See* 16 U.S.C. § 1539(a)(1); 50 C.F.R. §§ 17.22(c), 17.32(c). In application of that policy, FWS described land use practices designed to assist the red-cockaded woodpecker in a six-county region in North Carolina and issued an incidental take permit to itself. 60 Fed. Reg. 10,400 (Feb. 24, 1995). This spared landowners the time and expense associated with applying for their own permit. Landowners who desire to take advantage of that incidental take permit must agree to abide by the land use practices described in a side contract or cooperative agreement with the FWS. In other variations, a state or other government entity can apply for a safe harbor agreement or incidental take permit, and private landowners can have the option of enrolling their lands in that program and obtaining the specified ESA benefits.
138. And an FWS employee's informal view (in nonrulemaking situations) that a particular action would not cause a take might not preclude a later prosecution, because estoppel ordinarily does not apply against the government. Office of Pers. Mgmt. v. Richmond, 496 U.S. 414 (1990).
139. As ESA § 9(g) makes it unlawful to "cause to be committed" a violation of the ESA, ESA liability may sometimes extend beyond the person who actually "takes" listed wildlife within the meaning of ESA § 9(a)(1). 16 U.S.C. § 1538(a)(1) and (g).
140. *See* Rasband, *supra* note 47, 33 ENVTL. L. at 623–30.
141. Strahan v. Coxe, 127 F.3d 155 (1st Cir. 1997).
142. Loggerhead Turtle v. County Council of Volusia County, Fla., 148 F.3d 1231, 1251–53 (11th Cir. 1998).
143. Seattle Audubon Soc'y v. Sutherland, 2007 WL 1577756 and 2007 WL 1300964, at *8–15 (W.D. Wash. 2007); Pac. Rivers Council v. Brown, 2002 WL 32356431, at *11–12 (D. Or. 2002), and 2003 WL 21087974, at *3 (D. Or. 2003).
144. Valerie Brader, *Shell Games: Vicarious Liability of State and Local Governments for Insufficiently Protective Regulations Under the ESA*, 45 NAT. RES. J. 103 (2005); J. B. Ruhl, *State and Local Government Vicarious Liability Under the ESA*, 16 NAT. RES. & ENV'T 70 (ABA Fall 2001); Shannon Petersen, *Endangered Species in the Urban Jungle: How the ESA Will Reshape American Cities*, 19 STAN. ENVTL. L.J. 423, 438–54 (2000).
145. Jonathan Adler, *Judicial Federalism and the Future of Federal Environmental Regulation*, 90 IOWA L. REV. 377, 429–30 (2005); James Rasband, *Priority, Probability, and Proximate Cause: Lessons from Tort Law About Imposing ESA Responsibility for Wildlife Harm on Water Users and Other Joint Habitat Modifiers*, 33 ENVTL. L. 595, 623–28 (2003). Those critiques gain further credibility from the Supreme Court's recent ruling that it is reasonable to construe the ESA as not imposing duties and liability for impacts an agency lacks authority to control under its statutory mandate. Nat'l Ass'n of Home Builders v. Defenders of Wildlife, 127 S. Ct. 2518, 2534–35 (2007). Many state agencies lack statutory authority to deny permits and other forms of authorization when the requirements of the specific state law and regulations have been satisfied, but the privately sponsored activity may entail some risk of take under the federal ESA.
146. Strahan v. Pritchard, 2007 WL 478237, at *9 (D. Mass. 2007).
147. Strahan v. Linnon, 967 F. Supp. 581, 599–602 (D. Mass. 1997), *aff'd*, 187 F.3d 623 (table), 1998 WL 1085817 (1st Cir. 1998).

148. 1998 WL 1085817, at *4.
149. Salmon Spawning & Recovery Alliance v. Basham, 2007 WL 666464, at *3–5 (CIT 2007).
150. Envtl. Prot. Info. Ctr. v. Tuttle, 2001 WL 114422 (N.D. Cal. 2001).
151. Loggerhead Turtle v. County Council of Volusia County, Fla., 92 F. Supp. 2d 1296, 1306–08 (M.D. Fla. 2000).
152. Pac. Rivers Council v. Brown, 2004 WL 2091471 (D. Or. 2004).
153. Seattle Audubon Soc'y v. Sutherland, 2007 WL 1300964 (W.D. Wash. 2007).
154. Seattle Audubon Soc'y v. Sutherland, 2007 WL 1577756 (W.D. Wash. 2007).
155. *See* Rasband, *supra* note 47, 33 ENVTL. L. at 625–26.
156. *See* 73 Fed. Reg. 28,212 (May 15, 2008).
157. For one view of the challenges global climate change presents for the ESA, see J. B. Ruhl, *Climate Change and the Endangered Species Act: Building Bridges to the No-Analog Future*, 88 B.U. L. REV. 1 (2008).
158. Another emerging issue is whether ESA § 7 consultation is required if a proposed project would emit GHG and the project needs a federal permit. The Bush and Obama administrations have provided a "no" answer. *See* Steven P. Quarles & Thomas R. Lundquist, *The Endangered Species Act and Greenhouse Gas Emissions—Species, Projects, and Statute at Risk*, 55 ROCKY MT. MIN. L. INST. 10-1 *et seq.* (2009).
159. As one district court stated:

> The language of 4(d) makes it clear that NMFS "may" impose a take prohibition. The unavoidable implication is that NMFS may, in its discretion, choose not to impose a take prohibition. NMFS's decision to craft a limited take prohibition under 4(d) must be, a fortiori under this analysis, within its discretion.

Wash. Envtl. Council v. Nat'l Marine Fisheries Serv., 2002 WL 511479, at *8 (W.D. Wash. 2002). ESA § 4(d)'s second sentence allows the Service to decline to extend the endangered species take prohibition to a particular threatened species, and this is not limited to situations where the absence of a take prohibition would advance "conservation" (language employed in ESA § 4(d)'s separate first sentence). *See* Sweet Home Chapter of Cmtys. for a Great Or. v. Babbitt, 1 F.3d 1, 7–8 (D.C. Cir. 1994).
160. 73 Fed. Reg. 28,306, 28,318 (May 15, 2008) (to be codified as 50 C.F.R. § 17.11(h)(4)).
161. Remarks by Sec'y Kempthorne, Press Conference on Polar Bear Listing, May 14, 2008, *available at* http://www.doi.gov/secretary/speeches/081405_speech.html. Thus far the Obama administration has continued the 4(d) rule for the polar bear and the general policy against construing the ESA to allow regulation of an individual source of GHGs. *See* Quarles & Lundquist, *supra* note 158.
162. Quoted in Ruhl, *supra* note 157, at 41 n.163. Prof. Ruhl agrees that GHG take theories are not tenable. *See* 88 B.U. L. REV. at 40–42.

9

Exceptions to the Take Prohibition

Sam Kalen and Adam Pan

Introduction

Section 10 of the Endangered Species Act (ESA) provides eight categories of activities that either are or can be excluded from the section 9 prohibitions. This is particularly significant in light of the wide variety of activities that are subject to the section 9 prohibition against take. A "taking" is defined broadly to mean "harass, harm, pursue, hunt, shoot, wound, kill, trap, capture or collect, or to attempt to engage in any such conduct," and it includes acts of "significant habitat modification or degradation where it actually kills or injures wildlife by significantly impairing essential behavior patterns, including breeding, feeding or sheltering."[1] With such a vast array of activities subject to the section 9 prohibition, the provisions of section 10 become extremely important. Any person claiming the benefit of a section 10 exclusion, however, must prove that the exemption or permit under section 10 is applicable.[2] The two most highly visible aspects of section 10 are the incidental take permit provisions and the provision governing the release of experimental populations. This chapter briefly reviews these provisions as well as other types of activities that fall within the umbrella of section 10.

Current State of the Law

Section 10(a)—Enhancement and Incidental Take Permits

Originally, section 10(a) authorized only the granting of an exemption for "scientific purposes or to enhance the propagation or survival of the affected species."[3] Activities within this category generally are designed to "conserve" a listed species, a defined term that includes, inter alia, "scientific resources management, such as propagation, live trapping, transplantation," and, in the extraordinary case where population pressures within a given ecosystem cannot be otherwise relieved, may include regulated taking."[4] In *Sierra Club v. Clark*,[5] for instance, the court observed, in dicta, that "[w]hile this exception does not authorize establishment of a public sport season, it does give the Secretary discretion to permit, for example, the removal of depredating animals or the culling of diseased animals." More recently, however, the district court in *Humane Society of the United States v. Kempthorne*,[6] in an opinion subsequently vacated on mootness grounds,[7] held that a permit could not lawfully be issued to shield a lethal depredation control program, allowing the killing of up to 43 endangered gray wolves. Congress contemplated that the Secretary could exempt activities that promoted the propagation or survival of species, whether those activities occurred in captivity, a controlled environment, or an uncontrolled environment.[8] The U.S. Fish and Wildlife Service (FWS), for instance, defines "enhance the propagation or survival" to include activities such as:

> (a) Provision of health care, management of populations by culling, contraception, euthanasia, grouping or handling of wildlife to control survivorship and reproduction, and similar normal practices of animal husbandry

needed to maintain captive populations that are self-sustaining and that possess as much genetic vitality as possible;

(b) Accumulation and holding of living wildlife that is not immediately needed or suitable for propagative or scientific purposes, and the transfer of such wildlife between persons in order to relieve crowding or other problems hindering the propagation or survival of the captive population at the location from which the wildlife would be removed; and

(c) Exhibition of living wildlife in a manner designed to educate the public about the ecological role and conservation needs of the affected species.[9]

Zoos, for example, typically obtain a permit for the importation and captive breeding of species. Later, when Congress included the provision on experimental populations, it also added a clause in section 10(a) confirming that such a permit could encompass "acts necessary for the establishment and maintenance of experimental populations."[10] Sections 13, 17.22, 17.32 and 222.301–308 (50 C.F.R.) of the regulations establish the procedural and substantive requirements for the issuance of these types of permits.[11]

Enhancement (or Recovery) permits have become increasingly popular in recent years as a tool for creative arrangements designed to conserve and enhance the survival of listed and other species. The "safe harbor" agreement is one such arrangement, whereby private landowners can undertake voluntary conservation actions on their lands and receive assurances that certain future land use activities will not be restricted further if those proactive conservation actions are successful. These types of arrangement reduce the disincentive for landowners to undertake land use activities that benefit species for fear of the accompanying regulatory consequences. The East Bay Municipal Utility District, for instance, recently signed an historic safe harbor agreement, covering habitat in the Mokelumne River watershed for three federally protected species.[12] Other similar types of enhancement permits include candidate conservation agreements.[13]

In 1982, Congress expanded section 10(a) to include an incidental take permit provision, now regarded as one of the principal mechanisms for facilitating conservation of listed species consistent with the needs of local communities and development.[14] Pursuant to section 10(a)(1)(B) of the Act, the Secretary "may permit, under such terms and conditions as he shall prescribe . . . any taking otherwise prohibited by section 9(a)(1)(B) if such taking is incidental to, and not the purpose of, the carrying out of an otherwise lawful activity."[15] The regulations repeat this language.[16]

This amendment responded to and became modeled after resolution of a dispute over development at San Bruno Mountain in northern California, an area the FWS intended to designate as critical habitat for the listed mission blue butterfly and another proposed species.[17] The result was a multiparty negotiated habitat conservation plan, through which private funding would be available for habitat acquisition and management. The 1982 amendments sanctioned this approach. The conference committee explained that this provision created a procedure "whereby those persons whose actions may affect endangered or threatened species may receive permits for the incidental taking of such species, provided the action will not jeopardize the continued existence of the species. This provision addresses the concerns of private landowners who are faced with having otherwise lawful actions not taking."[18] The conference committee also anticipated that conservation plans could address both listed as well as unlisted species. This provision, however, remained relatively unused during its first decade. From 1982 until 1991, only 20 incidental take permit applications were filed.[19] Yet by May 2007, the FWS had issued 376 permits and were working on many others.[20] The FWS maintains a database of approved plans at http://ecos.fws.gov/conserv_plans/public.jsp.

Federal regulations contained in 50 C.F.R. §§ 13, 17, and 222 prescribe the procedures for submitting an application for an incidental take permit. In addition to these regulations, the Services have developed a handbook containing guidance on the habitat conservation planning and incidental take permitting process.[21] The applicant may seek authorization for a single transaction, a series of transactions, or a number of activities over a specific time period. For example, an applicant seeking an incidental take permit from the FWS must submit with the application a complete description of the activity sought to be authorized, the species sought to be covered by the permit, and a habitat conservation plan (HCP). The HCP must describe the likely impact of the taking, those measures the applicant will employ to minimize or mitigate any such impacts, and any procedures for resolving problems posed by unforeseen circumstances. The HCP also must identify and analyze alternatives to the incidental taking and state why they are not being utilized, as well as include any such other measures that the Service may require as necessary or appropriate for purposes of the plan. Before formally seeking the permit, applicants are advised that they may discuss with the Service any possible measures and conservation plans. Also, section 10(c) of the Act requires that notice and opportunity for public comment be afforded to all interested parties before the issuance of any permit—an action that is subject to the procedures of the National Environmental Policy Act (NEPA), as well as to an intra-Service ESA section 7 consultation.

Before issuing any permit, the Service must make certain findings. It must initially determine that any authorized activity is not likely to jeopardize the continued existence of any listed species or result in the destruction or adverse modification of any critical habitat, and that the taking will be incidental to, and not the purpose of, the carrying out of an otherwise lawful activity. The Service must also conclude that

- The applicant will, to the maximum extent practicable, minimize and mitigate the impacts of such taking;
- The applicant will ensure that adequate funding for the plan will be provided;
- The taking will not appreciably reduce the likelihood of the survival and recovery of the species in the wild;

- The measures, if any, required by the Service as being necessary or appropriate for purposes of the plan will be met; and
- The Service has received such other assurances as it may require in order to implement the plan.[22]

Furthermore, any permits must contain terms and conditions necessary or appropriate to effectuate the purposes of the HCP, including monitoring and reporting requirements. A permit will be revoked if its terms and conditions are violated.

Section 10(j)—Experimental Populations

Also in 1982, Congress amended section 10 to authorize the release of "experimental populations." Congress intended that these populations could be managed with more flexibility than other listed species.[23] Prior to this amendment, the FWS had the ability to release populations of listed species outside their current ranges.[24] Yet, hoping to avoid vocal opposition from landowners and industry who feared releases could restrict their activities, the agency showed reluctance to exercise this authority.[25]

With the creation of section 10(j), Congress hoped to "[relax] certain restrictions otherwise applicable to listed species and [to authorize] the Secretary to relax others."[26] As noted above, section 10(a) permits the taking of listed species for "acts necessary for the establishment and maintenance of experimental populations."[27] This language shows recognition that relocating a population necessarily involves takings of individuals within that population. Section 10(j) also gives the FWS the ability to "allow for the directed taking of experimental populations" through regulation and lessens the level of protection provided to experimental populations.[28]

Pursuant to section 10(j), the Secretary is authorized to transport and release an experimental population if he or she determines that the release will further the conservation of the endangered or threatened species.[29] In making this determination, the Secretary must use the "best scientific and commercial data available" and must consider:

1. Any possible adverse effects on extant populations of a species as a result of removal of individuals, eggs, or propagules for introduction elsewhere;
2. The likelihood that any such experimental population will become established and survive in the foreseeable future;
3. The relative effects that establishment of an experimental population will have on the recovery of the species; and
4. The extent to which the introduced population may be affected by existing or anticipated Federal or State actions or private activities within or adjacent to the experimental population area.[30]

Before authorizing a release, the Secretary must, by rule, identify the population and "determine, on the basis of the best available information, whether or not such population is essential to the continued existence of an endangered or threatened species."[31] Congress expected that having the requirement proceed by rule would allow the Secretary to develop regulations specifically tailored to the needs and circumstances of a particular experimental population. The Secretary should make the essential or nonessential finding "based solely on the best scientific and commercial data available, and the supporting factual basis."[32]

The essential or nonessential designation determines the extent to which the ESA protects a particular experimental population. Essential populations are those "whose loss would be likely to appreciably reduce the likelihood of the survival of the species in the wild."[33] Solely for the purposes of section 7 of the ESA, essential experimental populations are treated as threatened species and, where appropriate, require the designation of critical habitat; nonessential experimental populations are treated as species proposed for listing under section 4 of the Act.[34] Proposed species trigger less-stringent section 7(a)(4) conferencing requirements. When experimental populations are not essential to the species' continued existence, section 7 consultation does not apply unless the population is in a park or refuge. Congress further requires that the Secretary determine whether experimental populations released prior to the amendment are essential or nonessential.[35]

According to the FWS regulations, the rule identifying an experimental population must also contain "management restrictions, protective measures, or other special management concerns of the population" and "a process for periodic review and evaluation" of the release project.[36] Section 17.82 of the regulations states that such experimental population rules "will contain applicable prohibitions and ... exceptions for that population."[37] This section makes it clear that FWS has discretion to set conditions for permissible taking and must describe them within the regulation identifying the experimental population. The FWS can set conditions for permissive takings to address affected parties' concerns about an experimental release. For example, the gray wolf experimental population rule allowed individuals to kill individual wolves if they attacked livestock on the individual's private land.[38]

The experimental population regulations also state that the Secretary can release experimental populations outside their current range.[39] The Secretary may not, however, release a population outside its historic range "absent a finding by the Director in the extreme case that the primary habitat of the species has been unsuitably and irreversibly altered or destroyed."[40] Additionally, the regulations emphasize collaboration in the experimental population designation process. Section 17.81(d) requires that the FWS "consult with appropriate State fish and wildlife agencies, local governmental entities, affected Federal agencies, and affected private landowners in developing and implementing experimental population rules."[41] It also requires that the regulation "to the maximum extent practicable, represent an agreement" between the FWS and the affected parties.[42]

Populations designated as experimental under the ESA remain experimental only as long as they are "wholly separate geographically from nonexperimental populations of the same species."[43] In *United States v. McKittrick*, the Tenth Circuit indicated that "if [an experimental population] lost its experimental status because of overlap with natural populations," ESA would afford it the same level of protection as the nonexperimental population.[44] The court deferred to the FWS's regulation "[interpreting] the 'wholly separate geographically' requirement to only apply to populations," not individuals.[45] In *Wyoming Farm Bureau Federation v. Babbitt*, the Tenth Circuit reached the same conclusion when deferring to the FWS interpretation.[46] The FWS had defined "'population' as any self-sustaining group 'in common spatial arrangement.'"[47] And the Service determined that a "'geographic separation' is any area outside the area in which a particular population sustains itself."[48] The court agreed that "these definitions preclude the possibility of population overlap as a result of the presence of individual dispersing wolves" from the natural population mixing with the experimental population.[49]

At present, the FWS has designated experimental populations for over 20 vertebrate species. Experimental population programs nevertheless have had a mixed record of success. Though the Secretary must determine that the release "will further the conservation," Congress recognized that such a release is "experimental," recognizing that such releases will not always achieve their intended results.

Between 1987 and 1990, the FWS released an experimental population of 140 southern sea otters on San Nicolas Island off the coast of southern California.[50] Due to high otter mortalities and emigration from San Nicolas Island, FWS scientists monitoring the program observed significantly fewer otters than they had released and were unable to account for half of the released otters.[51] In 2005, in a draft evaluation of this program, experts concluded that the "program [had] failed to fulfill its purpose and that [the] recovery and management goals for the species [could not] be met by continuing the program."[52]

In contrast to the admitted failure of the San Nicholas Island otter program, the reintroduction of nonessential experimental populations of gray wolves in central Idaho and around Yellowstone National Park has exceeded expectations. In 1995 and 1996, FWS released experimental populations into these areas hoping to produce 10 breeding pairs in Central Idaho and Yellowstone.[53] As of 2006, these regions supported 46 breeding pairs and 31 breeding pairs, respectively.[54]

Decisions to release an experimental population are often controversial. Though section 10(j) relaxes ESA protection for experimental populations, decisions to release populations under 10(j) have still attracted criticism from landowners and environmentalists alike. The decision to release gray wolves throughout their historic range, for example, has fueled criticism from farmers and ranchers in the release area. Environmental groups have opposed the designation of experimental populations on the ground that these populations should enjoy the full protection the ESA affords to other members of the listed species. At present, controversy surrounds the FWS's consideration of a proposal to release an experimental population of wood bison in the interior of Alaska. Interests within the state have expressed concerns that introducing the bison would interfere with or impede their ability to engage in certain activities within the intended release area.[55] Consequently, although section

10(j) provides flexibility for the FWS and an opportunity for dialogue between the FWS, environmental groups, and private parties, it has not dispelled the controversy surrounding the ESA.

Other Exceptions to the Take Prohibition

Section 10 contains five additional exceptions to the take prohibition. First, subsection (b) authorizes the Secretary to grant a limited hardship exemption.[56] Upon notice that a species is being considered for listing, a person may apply for an exemption where he or she has previously entered into a contract and the subsequent listing of the species will cause undue economic hardship.[57] The Secretary may grant an exemption from the take prohibition in section 9 of the Act to the extent he or she deems appropriate and to minimize hardship. The exemption may be granted for up to one year from the date of *Federal Register* notice of the proposed listing; it cannot apply to a taking of species in excess of that specified by the Secretary; and it cannot be granted for the importation or exportation of a specimen listed in Appendix I of the Convention on International Trade in Endangered Species of Wild Fauna and Flora (CITES) when such species is to be used in commercial activity.[58] Congress defined "undue economic hardship" as including but not limited to:

> (A) Substantial economic loss resulting from inability caused by this chapter to perform contracts with respect to species of fish and wildlife entered into prior to the date of publication in the Federal Register of a notice of consideration of such species as an endangered species;
> (B) Substantial economic loss to persons who, for the year prior to the notice of consideration of such species as an endangered species, derived a substantial portion of their income from the lawful taking of any listed species, which taking would be made unlawful under this chapter; or
> (C) Curtailment of subsistence taking made unlawful under this chapter by persons (i) not reasonably able to secure other sources of subsistence; and (ii) dependent to a substantial extent upon hunting and fishing for subsistence; and (iii) who must engage in such curtailed taking for subsistence purposes.[59]

The last provision appears to have evolved out of a proposed amendment to this subsection, when Senator Stevens from Alaska sought to further "protect those people who live in a subsistence economy and depend on the animals for food and for their livelihood."[60] In order to obtain a hardship exemption, an applicant must comply with the FWS regulations that specify the information required for a permit and the criteria for issuance of a permit.[61]

Exemptions under this provision, as well as permits sought to enhance the propagation or survival of a species, must further comply with subsections (c) and (d) of section 10. These subsections require *Federal Register* notice of, and an opportunity to comment on, an application for a permit or exemption, except in an emergency situation where the health or life of an endangered animal is threatened and no reasonable alternative is available to the applicant. The Secretary may grant an exception when a finding is made and published in the *Federal Register* that the exception was applied for in good faith, will not operate to disadvantage endangered species, and will be consistent with the congressionally established purposes and policy set forth in section 2 of the Act.

Second, section 10(e) and the corresponding FWS regulation, 50 C.F.R. § 17.5, provide an exemption for Alaskan Native subsistence hunters. During consideration of the proposed ESA, "[i]t became apparent to the Committee in hearings that the case of the Alaskan native Indians, Aleuts, and Eskimos required special attention"; Alaskan Native subsistence practices were not perceived as posing a principal threat to those species, "provided that the action is for the purpose of consumption or use in a native community or for creation and sale of native articles of handicrafts and clothing, and is not accomplished in a wasteful manner."[62] These conclusions prompted Congress to confirm its approach in the Marine Mammal Protection Act of 1972 and include a special exemption for Alaskan Native subsistence practices.[63] In *United States v. Nuesca*,[64] this exemption was held not to apply to native Hawaiians.

The Alaskan Native subsistence exemption allows an Indian, Aleut, or Eskimo who is an Alaskan Native residing in Alaska, or a nonnative permanent resident of an Alaskan native village,[65] to take an endangered or threatened species if primarily for subsistence purposes[66] and if not accomplished in a wasteful manner.[67] The exemption includes the sale of nonedible byproducts from subsistence practices when "made into authentic native articles of handicrafts and clothing," as defined in the statute and regulations.[68] The exemption, however, is not available to a nonnative resident of an Alaskan native village, if the Secretary finds that such person is not primarily dependent upon such activities. Additionally, the Secretary may prescribe specific regulations governing the taking of listed species whether with reference to species, geographic description, season, or any other factor consistent with the Act and related to the reason for the regulation. Yet before the Secretary can issue such regulations, a determination must be made, after notice and opportunity for hearing in the affected judicial district in Alaska and in compliance with section 103 of the Marine Mammal Protection Act, and such regulations must be removed "as soon as the secretary determines that the need for their imposition has disappeared."[69]

Third, section 10(f) provides a limited exemption for certain pre-Act endangered species parts, which are defined as "any sperm whale oil" and "any finished scrimshaw product" lawfully held in the United States prior to December 28, 1973, and in the course of commercial activity. A "scrimshaw product" is further defined as:

> Any art form which involves the substantial etching or engraving of designs upon, or the substantial carving of figures, patterns, or designs from, any

bone or tooth of any marine mammal of the order Cetacea. For the purpose of this subsection, polishing or the adding of minor superficial markings does not constitute substantial etching, engraving, or carving.[70]

As originally enacted, the ESA prohibited the interstate sale of parts and products of endangered marine mammals legally held under the Marine Mammal Protection Act. This created an economic hardship for individuals who, upon enactment, were legally engaged in the commercial trade of whale oil and scrimshaw.[71] In 1976, therefore, Congress added subsections (f) and (g) and authorized a three-year exemption, which was extended for three years in 1979.[72] Although subsequent amendments authorized a continued exemption period, that period now appears to have expired.[73]

Fourth, subsection (h) exempts certain antique articles from the take prohibition and CITES compliance requirement in section 9, as well as from any rule promulgated under section 4(d).[74] This subsection exempts articles that are 100 or more years old, "composed in whole or in part" of any listed species, which have "not been repaired or modified with any part of any such species on or after December 28, 1973," and which are "entered" at a designated port. Ports are designated by the Secretary of the Treasury after consultation with the Interior Secretary. Anyone interested in importing qualifying articles must submit the necessary documentation required by the Treasury Secretary. Congress included a one-year grandfather provision for those who imported such articles after the Act was passed but before Congress added this subsection (November 10, 1978).[75]

Fifth, section 10 allows noncommercial transshipment of listed fish and wildlife while any such species remain in the control of the U.S. Customs Service—if the shipment is lawfully destined to another country and the exporter or owner did everything reasonably possible to avoid U.S. jurisdiction. The applicable requirements of CITES nevertheless must be satisfied.[76]

Emerging Issues and Future Directions

The future of section 10 permits to avoid take liability is likely to continue to expand and evolve as parties present new circumstances that may stretch the original justification for allowing enhancement permits. For instance, the Service has allowed enhancement permits to support the importation of sport-hunted trophies. The justification for such permits is to increase public awareness by having such trophies on display.[77]

While Congress created the experimental population exception in 1982, few cases further clarify the 10(j)'s scope or the requirements set forth in the FWS regulations. Because the process requires substantial research, consideration, and negotiation, the decision to create an experimental population is time-consuming and often controversial. And, while not always successful, the FWS has found 10(j) to be a useful tool to further conservation in some instances and is likely to continue to release experimental populations. Yet parties affected by the experimental releases are likely to challenge decisions to release experimental populations in the future.

The other take exceptions have much more limited scopes, and are not likely to witness any significant developments. And with the exception of 10(a), few cases have dealt with issues related to section 10 exceptions. The law might continue to develop as parties could attempt to invoke these exceptions and courts might then have more opportunities to consider the applicability of the take exceptions.

Conclusion

This overview of section 10 illustrates the need to examine proposed activities carefully for their potential to comply with one of the types of categories that either are or can be excluded from the prohibitions in section 9 of the Act.

Notes

1. 50 C.F.R. § 17.3 (2007).
2. 16 U.S.C. § 1539(g).
3. Pub. L. No. 93-205, 87 Stat. 896 (1973).
4. 16 U.S.C. § 1532(3).
5. 755 F.2d 608, 614 n.8 (8th Cir. 1985).
6. 481 F. Supp. 2d 53 (D.D.C. 2006).
7. 527 F.3d 181 (D.C. Cir. 2008).
8. H.R. REP. NO. 93-412, *reprinted in* CONG. RESEARCH SERV., A LEGISLATIVE HISTORY OF THE ENDANGERED SPECIES ACT OF 1973, AS AMENDED IN 1976, 1977, 1978, 1979 AND 1980, at 396 (1982) [hereinafter CRS LEGISLATIVE HISTORY].
9. 50 C.F.R. § 17.3. *Cf.* 50 C.F.R. § 216.41 (National Marine Fisheries Service definition under the Marine Mammal Protection Act). *See also* CONG. RESEARCH SERV., ENHANCEMENT-OF-SURVIVAL PERMITS: BACKGROUND AND STATUS OF PROPOSED POLICY (April 2006) (for foreign species).
10. Pub. L. No. 97-304, 96 Stat. 1422 (1982).
11. *See* Hamilton v. Babbitt, 8 F. Supp. 2d 886 (W.D. Tex. 1998) (declining to issue an injunction against the issuance of a scientific permit). Although the "taking" of listed plant species is not prohibited in section 9, the Act does prohibit their importation and exportation, interstate shipment during the course of commercial activity, interstate or foreign sales, removal from areas under federal jurisdiction or malicious destruction or damage of species in any such area, or knowing violation of state law, including trespass. *E.g.*, 16 U.S.C. § 1538(a)(2), (d)–(f). Consequently, the FWS has adopted regulations implementing section 10 exemptions for plant species. 50 C.F.R. §§ 17.62 (permits for scientific purposes or for the enhancement of propagation or survival of endangered plants); 17.63 (economic hardship permits for endangered plants); 17.72 (permits for threatened plant species). For the FWS permit application form, expiring Nov. 2010, see http://www.fws.gov/forms/3-200-54.pdf.
12. *See* News Release, U.S. Fish & Wildlife Serv., Landmark Safe Harbor Agreement Signed Today by USFWS/EBMUD (June 2, 2009), *available at* http://www.fws.gov/sacramento/ea/news_releases/2009_News_Releases/EBMUD_final_Safe_Harbor_Agreement.htm (accessed June 15, 2009).
13. *See* Additional Comments Sought on Permit Regulation Relating to Habitat Conservation Plan, Safe Harbor Agreements, and Candidate Conservation Agreements with Assurance, 6 Fed. Reg. 6916 (Feb. 11, 2000); Safe Harbor Agreements and Candidate Conservation Agreements with Assurance, 64 Fed. Reg. 32,706 (June 17, 1999); Devel-

opment of Policy for the Use of Permits as Conservation Tools; Request for Public Comment, 63 Fed. Reg. 42,639 (Aug. 10, 1998); 62 Fed. Reg. 32,177 (June 12, 1997); 62 Fed. Reg. 32,183 (June 12, 1997); 62 Fed. Reg. 32, 189 (June 12, 1997).
14. Pub. L. No. 97-304, 96 Stat. 1411 (Oct. 13, 1982).
15. 16 U.S.C. § 1539(a)(1).
16. 50 C.F.R. § 17.3.
17. H.R. REP. NO. 97-835, at 30–31 (1982).
18. *Id.* at 29.
19. GOV'T ACCOUNTABILITY OFF., ENDANGERED SPECIES ACT: TYPES AND NUMBERS OF IMPLEMENTING ACTIONS 19, 36 (May, 1992).
20. *See* J. B. RUHL, JOHN COPELAND NAGLE & JAMES SALZMAN, THE PRACTICE AND POLICY OF ENVIRONMENTAL LAW 124 (2008).
21. U.S. FISH & WILDLIFE SERV. & NAT'L MARINE FISHERIES SERV., HABITAT CONSERVATION PLANNING HANDBOOK (Nov. 1996), 61 Fed. Reg. 63,854 (1996); 64 Fed. Reg. 11,485 (Mar. 9, 1999) (Notice of Availability of a Draft Addendum to the Final Handbook for Habitat Conservation Planning and Incidental Take Permitting Process).
22. 16 U.S.C. § 1539(a)(2)(B); 50 C.F.R. §§ 17.22(b)(2), 222.307, 64 Fed. Reg. 14,053 (Mar. 23, 1999).
23. *See generally* H.R. REP. NO. 97-835, at 33–34; S. REP. NO. 97-418, at 31–32 (Department of Interior comments); H.R. REP. NO. 97-517, at 33 (Report of the Committee on Merchant Marine and Fisheries), 45–46 (comments of Assistant Secretary for Fish and Wildlife and Parks). *See also* Wyo. Farm Bureau Fed'n v. Babbitt, 199 F.3d 1224 (10th Cir. 2000); United States v. McKittrick, 142 F.3d 1170, 1174 (9th Cir. 1998), *cert. denied*, 119 S. Ct. 806 (1999).
24. Wyo. Farm Bureau Fed'n, 199 F.3d at 1232; *see* 16 U.S.C. § 1539(j)(3).
25. *Id.*
26. H.R. REP. NO. 97-567, at 33 (1982).
27. 16 U.S.C. § 1539(a)(1)(A).
28. *Id.* at 34.
29. 16 U.S.C. § 1539j(2)(A).
30. 50 C.F.R. § 17.81(b)(1)–(4).
31. 16 U.S.C. § 1539(j)(2)(B).
32. 50 C.F.R. § 17.81(c)(2).
33. *Id.* § 17.80.
34. Experimental populations are treated as threatened species for purposes of establishing protective regulations under section 4(d) of the ESA. *See* 50 C.F.R. § 17.82.
35. 16 U.S.C. § 1539(j)(3).
36. 50 C.F.R. § 17.81(c)(3).
37. 50 C.F.R. § 17.82.
38. 50 C.F.R. § 17.84(i)(3)(i) (2005).
39. 50 C.F.R § 17.81(a).
40. *Id.*
41. 50 C.F.R. § 17.81(d).
42. *Id.*
43. 16 U.S.C. § 1539(j)(1).
44. 142 F.3d at 1175.
45. *Id.*
46. *Id.*
47. *Id.*
48. *Id.*
49. *Id.*
50. Appendix C: Draft Evaluation of the Southern Sea Otter Translocation Program 1987–2004, *available at* http://www.fws.gov/ventura/speciesinfo/so_sea_otter/seis/2005sso draftseis-appendixC.pdf.

51. *Id.* at 8.
52. *Id.* at 26.
53. U.S. Fish & Wildlife Serv., Wolf Tracks: A Summary of Gray Wolf Activities and Issues (Feb. 1999), http://www.fws.gov/midwest/wolf/wolftracks/TRACKS1.PDF.
54. U.S. Fish & Wildlife Serv., Gray Wolf Populations in the United States, 2006, http://www.fws.gov/home/feature/2007/gray_wolf_factsheet_populations.pdf.
55. Rena Delbridge, *Bison, Gas Development Plans Clash*, ANCHORAGE DAILY NEWS, Jan. 30, 2009, *available at* http://www.adn.com/oil/story/672792.html.
56. *See* 50 C.F.R. §§ 17.23, 17.63. Courts occasionally reference the limited scope of the hardship exception to illustrate Congress's intent that species protection take precedence over economic considerations. *See* Tenn. Valley Auth. v. Hill, 437 U.S. 153, 188 (1978); Louisiana *ex rel.* Guste v. Verity, 853 F.2d 322, 331 (5th Cir. 1988).
57. *Cf.* Delbay Pharms. v. Dep't of Commerce, 409 F. Supp. 637 (D.D.C. 1976) (court rejected argument that person holding hardship exemption under the 1969 act could continue to sell specimens after 1973); United States v. Species of Wildlife, 404 F. Supp. 1298, 1299 (E.D.N.Y. 1975) (contract must be entered into before species listed for consideration).
58. 16 U.S.C. § 1539(b)(1). Additionally, the Secretary is authorized to require additional information and may, in his or her discretion, limit the exception to "time, area, or other factor or applicability." 16 U.S.C. § 1539(b)(3).
59. 16 U.S.C. § 1539(b)(2).
60. CRS LEGISLATIVE HISTORY, *supra* note 8, at 380. Senator Stevens's original proposal would have required the granting of an exception, where applicable. *Id.* at 378.
61. 50 C.F.R. §§ 17.23, 17.32, 17.63.
62. S. REP. NO. 93-307, at 5 (1973), *reprinted in* CRS LEGISLATIVE HISTORY, *supra* note 8, at 304.
63. As a consequence, the corresponding NMFS regulatory definitions are contained in 50 C.F.R. pt. 216.
64. 945 F.2d 254 (9th Cir. 1991).
65. *See* 50 C.F.R. § 17.3 (definitions of "Alaskan Native" and "Native village or town").
66. 16 U.S.C. § 1539(e)(1). "Subsistence" is defined in the Act to include "selling any edible portion of fish or wildlife in native villages or towns," 16 U.S.C. § 1539(e)(3)(i). FWS regulations, however, define subsistence as: the use of endangered or threatened wildlife for food, clothing, shelter, heating, transportation, and other uses necessary to maintain the life of the taker of the wildlife or those who depend upon the taker to provide them with such subsistence, and includes selling any edible portions of such wildlife in native villages and towns in Alaska for native consumption within native villages and towns. 50 C.F.R. § 17.3.
67. 16 U.S.C. § 1539(e)(2); 50 C.F.R. § 17.5. For the definition of "wasteful manner," see 50 C.F.R. § 17.3.
68. *Id.* § 1539(e)(3)(ii); 50 C.F.R. § 17.3.
69. *Id.* § 1539(e)(4). *E.g.*, 56 Fed. Reg. 42,541 (1991) (correcting rule issued without following procedures for applying take prohibition to Alaskan Natives engaged in subsistence practices).
70. 16 U.S.C. § 1539(f)(1)(B); *see also* 50 C.F.R. § 17.4. For the NMFS pre-Act endangered species parts regulations, see 50 C.F.R. § 222.201–.205, 64 Fed. Reg. 14,053 (Mar. 23, 1999).
71. CRS LEGISLATIVE HISTORY, *supra* note 8, at 539. Congress was equally concerned with the cultural aspect of scrimshaw in our nation's past with the General Services Administration's large stockpile of whale oil that it was otherwise prohibited from selling. *Id.* *See also id.* at 582–97.
72. Pub. L. No. 94-359, 90 Stat. 911 (1976); Pub. L. No. 96-159, 93 Stat. 1230 (1979).
73. Pub. L. No. 97-304, 96 Stat. 1423 (1982). *See also* H.R. REP. NO. 97-567, at 32 (1982); Pub. L. No. 103-238, § 18, 108 Stat. 559 (1994) (authorizing five-year extension for valid certificates of exemption for pre-Act-finished scrimshaw products or raw materials).

74. Originally, the Act required that the articles be made before 1830. Pub. L. No. 95-632, 92 Stat. 3760 (1978). Congress apparently selected the original 1830 date believing that one could readily distinguish pre- and post-1830 products. CRS LEGISLATIVE HISTORY, *supra* note 8, at 1215. *See* Pub. L. No. 97-304, 96 Stat. 1424 (1982).
75. 16 U.S.C. § 1539(h). *See* 19 C.F.R. §§ 10.53(e), 12.26(g). *See also* 50 C.F.R. § 14.22 (FWS).
76. *Id.* § 1539(i). *See generally* H.R. REP. NO. 97-835, at 32–33 (Conference Report).
77. *See, e.g.*, 73 Fed. Reg. 61,161 (Oct. 15, 2008).

10

Landowner Incentives and the Endangered Species Act

Michael J. Bean

Introduction

The fundamental goal of the Endangered Species Act is to achieve the recovery of endangered and threatened species. Once recovered to the point that the various protections afforded by the Act are no longer needed, a species can be "de-listed," or taken off the list of endangered and threatened species maintained by the Secretary of the Interior.[1] In theory, at least, the administrators of the Endangered Species Act are charged with putting themselves out of business by presiding over an ever-diminishing list of imperiled species. In practice, however, it has not worked out that way. The list of imperiled species has steadily grown over time, with the number of new additions to the list regularly outpacing the number of species that have recovered and been delisted.

The reasons for this track record are several. The administrators of the Endangered Species Act have little or no control over the land use and other activities that cause the imperilment of plants and animals in the first place. If the list of protected species is steadily augmented by a stream of newly endangered species, the Act can hardly be faulted for that. As for the relative infrequency of species being recovered and taken off the list, the usual list of suspects include inadequate funding, political interference, overly timid implementation, waiting too long to initiate conservation efforts, and the fact that many of the causes of species endangerment lie largely beyond the reach of the Act's various tools.

To that list of usual suspects, another, less obvious cause should be added: the Act's principal tools are ill suited to achieving its goals. The Act's various tools are predominantly of a prohibitive nature. As other chapters in this volume describe, the Act prohibits the "taking" of endangered wildlife; the importing, exporting, and selling in interstate commerce of endangered plants or wildlife; the removal or destruction of any endangered plant in violation of the laws of a state; and a variety of other harmful activities.[2] To these, the Act adds an additional layer of prohibitions applicable solely to federal agencies. Those agencies are prohibited from authorizing, funding, or carrying out any action that is likely to jeopardize the continued existence of any listed species.[3] They are likewise prohibited from authorizing, funding, or carrying out any action that is likely to destroy or adversely modify the critical habitat of any listed species.[4]

If the primary goal of the Endangered Species Act were to prevent imperiled species from slipping closer to the brink of extinction, its array of prohibitions might be capable of achieving that goal, provided they were vigilantly enforced, adequately funded, and in fact capable of effectively addressing the factors that threaten to push species closer to the abyss. In fact, however, as already noted, the Act has a more ambitious goal, that of bringing imperiled species back from the brink of extinction to a point where their future is reasonably secure. In short, the Act's goal is not simply to keep things from getting worse but to make things better. For that more ambitious goal, prohibitions alone will seldom suffice. The Act's prohibitions are, after all, aimed at deterring harmful actions, rather than stimulating helpful ones. They may prevent a developer from destroying a patch of suitable habitat for a listed species, but they will not compel anyone to restore the habitats whose loss led to the listing, nor will they compel anyone to control the invasive species that threaten to take over the "saved" patch, or to manage that patch with prescribed fire or prescribed grazing so as to mimic natural disturbance regimes.

How then, are the helpful and necessary actions like these that move a species away from the brink of extinction and toward the goal of recovery to be accomplished? The federal government could, of course, acquire the land where such beneficial management is needed and itself provide that management. Section 5 of the Act authorizes the acquisition of land and water for such purposes,[5] but the amount of land (and water) that would need to be acquired in order to accomplish the recovery of currently imperiled species dwarfs what has historically been purchased or what is likely to be purchased in the foreseeable future. A second possibility is to enlist the cooperation of the states through the cooperative agreement mechanism of Section 6, which offers federal financial assistance to states that develop acceptable conservation programs for listed species.[6] Although most states have entered into cooperative agreements under Section 6, most state programs, like their federal counterpart, are built around a set of core prohibitions, aimed at keeping imperiled species from being made worse off, but doing little to make such species better off.

When Congress enacted the Endangered Species Act in 1973, its brief list of formal "findings" concluded with a finding that "a system of incentives" was a key component of any program likely to safeguard the nation's natural heritage.[7] And yet nowhere else in the Act does the word "incentives" even appear, much less a description of anything remotely resembling a "system of incentives." In practice, the job has fallen to the administrators of the Act to fashion incentive mechanisms from broadly worded authorities originally designed for other purposes. The discussion that follows looks at several of the most important of these administratively created incentive mechanisms.

Current State of the Law

Safe Harbor Agreements

In the early 1990s, a North Carolina landowner named Ben Cone generated a great deal of publicity by threatening to clear-cut most of his forested property so as to keep endangered red-cockaded woodpeckers—which occupied a small portion of his property—from "infesting" the remainder of it.[8] Though Cone garnered the spotlight for himself, his apprehensions about the potential costs of hosting endangered species on his property were shared by many others. Moreover, Cone's threatened action was almost certainly legal. For the red-cockaded woodpecker, the U.S. Fish and Wildlife Service had construed the taking prohibition to bar forestry activities that reduced the number of 30-year-old and older pine trees within a specified distance of an active "cluster" (an aggregation of nesting and roosting cavities maintained by a red-cockaded woodpecker family group) below a specified density.[9] As a result, trees not near an active cluster could be cut—all of them. Pine stands less than 30 years old could also be cut and kept from ever reaching the age at which woodpeckers were likely to forage upon them. In short, forest landowners desirous of avoiding the imposition of new regulatory restrictions could do so quite legally—and there is reason to believe that many did.[10] Moreover, forest landowners already subject to regulation because of the presence of red-cockaded woodpeckers on their land could often reduce or eliminate their regulatory exposure through a form of benign neglect. By refraining from prescribed burning or other measures to control hardwood understory, landowners could allow the transformation of relatively open pine savannah habitat—favored by red-cockaded woodpeckers—into dense, mixed pine and hardwood forest habitat generally inhospitable to this species.

In short, as is often the case with regulatory requirements, people had figured out how to frustrate the intent of the law without violating the letter of the law. From a conservation point of view, however, this meant that the Endangered Species Act was sometimes causing landowners to do the opposite of what was needed to improve the security of imperiled species. Rather than creating, restoring, or improving habitat conditions, some landowners were preemptively removing habitat before it could be occupied by listed species. Rather than actively managing their land to promote the recovery of rare species, they were managing it defensively to keep such species away. Sometimes, such aversion to fostering the presence of endangered species even became official policy. Take, for example, California's Reclamation Board, which issues "encroachment permits" for a variety of activities within floodways, including riparian habitat restoration activities.[11] When issuing such permits, the Reclamation Board routinely prohibits the planting of elderberry bushes, because the presence of such bushes—host plants for the endangered Valley elderberry longhorn beetle—potentially complicates floodway maintenance activities.

Problems such as these once seemed insoluble—an unfortunate but unavoidable consequence of the Endangered Species Act's strict regulatory requirements. However, in 1995 the Fish and Wildlife Service found within the Act the flexibility to fashion an effective solution. That solution took the form of a "safe harbor agreement." In a safe harbor agreement, a nonfederal property owner agrees to carry out voluntarily certain management practices expected to benefit a particular listed species and to maintain those practices for a specified period of time.[12] Those beneficial management practices can take a variety of forms, including habitat restoration or enhancement, reintroduction of listed species, or simply an agreement to continue current management for a specified period of time. The agreement further specifies the regulatory restrictions, if any, that are applicable to the property at the time the agreement is signed, the so-called "baseline" conditions. The aim of safe harbor agreements is to improve upon baseline conditions through the implementation of the agreed-upon management activities. In exchange for the property owner's agreement, the government issues a permit that confers upon the property owner a limited right to take the species covered by the agreement. That may include the right to take the species incidental to implementing the specified management practices, and generally includes the right to take the species incidental to any other lawful activity, provided that such taking is consistent with maintaining the property at or above its baseline conditions. In other words, the "baseline" represents a sort of floor, above which the condition of the property will be raised by the management activities, and to which it can be returned if the property owner desires after fully discharging his responsibilities.

The first several safe harbor agreements were done under the authority of Section 10(a)(1)(B) of the Endangered Species Act,[13] essentially treating them as habitat conservation plans. However, under the Safe Harbor Policy[14] jointly promulgated by the Fish and Wildlife Service and National Marine Fisheries Service in 1999, future safe harbor agreements were to be done under the authority of Section 10(a)(1)(A), which authorizes permits to "enhance the . . . survival" of listed species. The standard for approval of a safe harbor agreement is that it must be expected to produce a "net conservation benefit" for the covered species. In practice, this is a relatively low threshold, particularly since the time-limited duration of conservation commitments required in safe harbor agreements necessarily means that the benefits associated with those agreements will likely be only temporary in nature. In short, safe harbor agreements may only buy a little extra time, but for many endangered species time is in desperately short supply, and securing additional time in which to pursue longer-term conservation strategies may be quite important.

Although safe harbor agreements do not create a positive incentive for voluntary conservation actions by private landowners, they do remove a significant disincentive against such actions. For at least some landowners, that alone is sufficient to elicit conservation efforts. For others, however, some additional financial incentive, if only to reduce the cost of management efforts, is needed. Nothing in the Endangered Species Act specifically authorizes such financial incentives to help landowners shoulder the costs of voluntary conservation efforts, although several initiatives outside the Act have recently been undertaken. The second Bush administration, for example, launched two related initiatives to help pay for voluntary conservation efforts by landowners. The Private Stewardship Grants Program (PSGP) and the Landowner Incentive Program (LIP) were both intended to make financial assistance available to landowners carrying out conservation measures for listed and other "at-risk" species.[15] PSGP funds were directly administered by the Fish and Wildlife Service, while LIP funds were administered by the states. Although both programs were announced with considerable fanfare as part of the administration's "cooperative conservation" initiative, funding levels started out modest and declined. By the final year of the administration, no funds for either program were requested as part of the President's budget.

The Fish and Wildlife Service's Partners for Fish and Wildlife Program has been a more enduring source of financial incentives for private efforts benefiting listed species. The Partners Program was launched in 1987 without specific statutory authorization as a cost-sharing program aimed at assisting habitat restoration efforts on behalf of "federal trust species," that is, migratory birds and endangered species.

Typically, the Service provides 90 percent of the cost of implementing a restoration project; the landowner agrees to provide the balance and to maintain the restored habitat for a period of at least 10 years. The major focus of the Partners Program has been on things other than endangered species, in particular on wetland restoration for migratory waterfowl. However, habitat restoration projects benefiting endangered species are an increasingly common component of the Partners Program portfolio. In 2006, Congress enacted the Partner for Fish and Wildlife Act, which provided specific statutory authority to continue the program.[16]

The first federal conservation cost-sharing program to make specific reference to safe harbor agreements was the Healthy Forest Reserve Program, which is administered by the U.S. Department of Agriculture.[17] The goal of that program is to encourage forest landowners to enter into long-term agreements to manage their forest properties so as to improve conditions for endangered species. Because these agreements were of less than permanent duration, however, Congress recognized that participating landowners would likely want an assurance that their voluntarily undertaken management measures did not leave them with continuing regulatory obligations toward endangered species after the terms of their agreements had ended. As a result, Congress provided that in implementing the program, the Secretaries of Agriculture and Interior would cooperate to make available to participating landowners either safe harbor agreements through the Section 10 permitting process or similar assurances through the Section 7 interagency consultation process.

Candidate Conservation Agreements with Assurances

As noted above, the list of endangered and threatened species has steadily grown longer since the Act's enactment. Because the provisions of the Act do not apply to a species until it is formally listed as threatened or endangered, there would seem to be little that could be done under the Endangered Species Act to affect the flow of species heading toward the point of endangerment. In fact, however, once a species is formally identified as a potential candidate for possible future federal listing, one would hope that landowners and agencies would both be motivated to take actions that might reverse the species' decline and avert its endangerment. At the same time, one must acknowledge that the incentives, particularly for landowners, may be to do the opposite. That is because the landowner who actively tries to protect a declining species on his land may discover, once the species is federally listed, that his efforts resulted in more, not fewer, regulatory encumbrances. To create modest incentives to spur conservation efforts for species before they are endangered, two types of agreements have been developed.

Candidate Conservation Agreements (CCAs) are efforts to put in place conservation commitments from federal or state agencies that are sufficient to avert the need to list a species as threatened or endangered. The reliance upon such agreements by the Fish and Wildlife Service as a justification for not listing a species has frequently been challenged successfully by litigants who contended that the agreements lacked specificity.[18] In response to these challenges, in 2003 the Fish and

Wildlife Service and the National Marine Fisheries Service jointly promulgated a "Policy for Evaluation of Conservation Efforts When Making Listing Decisions," the so-called "PECE Policy."[19]

The PECE Policy provides that CCAs and other similar conservation agreements may be taken into account when making listing decisions if two conditions are met. First, at least for those measures not already implemented, the PECE Policy requires that there be reasonable certainty that they will in fact be implemented. Second, the PECE Policy requires a similar reasonable certainty that, once implemented, the promised measures will be effective. For both of these criteria, the PECE Policy spells out in some detail the considerations that will be taken into account in making these determinations. It should be noted that simply because any particular CCA meets these two criteria, it does not necessarily follow that the species covered by the agreement will not in fact be listed. Rather, the more limited purpose of the PECE Policy is simply to delimit those agreements that may be taken into account in making a listing decision. That is, even a CCA that is reasonably certain to be implemented and reasonably certain to be effective will not necessarily preclude the need to list the species, particularly if the agreement does not address all the significant threats to the species. Nevertheless, the typical motivation for entering into a CCA is to avert the need to list a species, since the agency that enters into the agreement gains nothing else by entering into the agreement.

A different conclusion applies to a related type of agreement known as a Candidate Conservation Agreement with Assurances (CCAA). CCAAs are typically not primarily motivated by a desire to avoid the need to list a species. Further, whereas CCAs are typically entered into by state or federal agencies, CCAAs are typically entered into by nonfederal landowners (which may include a state land managing agency). The landowner who enters into a CCAA agrees to make certain conservation commitments toward a candidate species,[20] in return for which the landowner receives an assurance that in the event that the species is subsequently listed, the landowner's obligations toward that species will be defined by the agreement for as long as it remains in force. That is, the landowner who enters into a CCAA receives a permit authorizing the taking of the species incidental to any activity consistent with the CCAA, with the permit becoming legally effective upon the listing of the species.

It should be readily apparent that in all but the most unusual circumstances, no single landowner will have it in his or her power to take action that precludes the need to list a species. The CCAA Policy jointly promulgated by the Fish and Wildlife Service and National Marine Fisheries Service recognizes this fact by setting forth an approval standard that essentially requires that any given landowner simply perform his or her proportionate share of the task. The rather clumsily worded standard for approval of CCAAs is that "the benefits of the conservation measures implemented by a property owner under a Candidate Conservation Agreement with assurances, when combined with those benefits that would be achieved if it is assumed that conservation measures were also to be implemented on other necessary properties, would preclude or remove any need to list the covered species."[21]

The reference in this standard to "other necessary properties" is explained elsewhere in a somewhat circular fashion as referring to "other properties on which conservation measures would have to be implemented in order to preclude or remove any need to list the covered species."[22] What the CCAA Policy fails to clarify is what level of conservation commitment on these other "necessary properties" is to be assumed in determining whether a given landowner's proposed CCAA meets the test. If one is willing to assume heroic efforts on other necessary properties, then what would be needed on the CCAA property could be very modest. Conversely, if one assumes only modest effort on other necessary properties, then it would be extremely hard for a CCAA property ever to meet the test. For that reason, the most logical understanding of the standard for approval is that the CCAA landowner's commitment must be commensurate with the assumed commitments of other landowners, given the inherent differences in property sizes, characteristics, and so on. Nonetheless, the standard for approval remains somewhat ambiguous and difficult, perhaps contributing to the relatively infrequent use of CCAAs as compared to safe harbor agreements.

Conservation Banking

Both safe harbor agreements and CCAAs are examples of administratively created ideas to avoid some of the conservation disincentives that were unintentionally created by the regulatory requirements of the Endangered Species Act. For at least some landowners, conservation banking offers the potential of a positive financial incentive to invest in conservation efforts for listed species.

Typically, when the Fish and Wildlife Service grants an incidental take permit pursuant to Section 10(a)(1)(B) of the Endangered Species Act, it conditions that permit upon implementation of various mitigation actions. Similarly, when approving federal actions under Section 7 of the Act, the Service often accepts measures proposed by the action agency to offset some of the impacts of the proposed agency action (though the Service is generally unwilling to characterize these measures as mitigation requirements). Conservation banking is a means of anticipating future mitigation needs in connection with federal or nonfederal projects and of supplying those needs with already-accomplished conservation efforts. For private landowners, conservation banking is potentially a way to turn the presence of endangered species or endangered species habitat into an asset rather than a liability.

Endangered species conservation banking has much in common with wetlands mitigation banking under the Clean Water Act, although it has a more recent provenance and has yet to become as commonplace as wetlands mitigation banking.[23] The first endangered species conservation banking effort was launched in 1995 in California, which remains the only state where there has been significant utilization of the concept. In 2003, the Fish and Wildlife Service issued its first national guidance on the use of conservation banks in the federal endangered species program. In general, the guidance requires that land included in a conservation bank be permanently protected through a conservation easement or similar deed restriction. In return for permanently protecting a bank property and for agreeing to manage it so as to maintain its ecological value, the bank operator receives "credits" that it can use to meet either its own or another's future mitigation obligations pertaining to the same species.

Essential to the effective working of any conservation banking system is a standardized "currency" by which both the beneficial and the detrimental impacts of actions on a particular species can be measured. The guidance contains only a cursory discussion of this vitally important topic, suggesting a variety of approaches that could be taken. In practice, however, the customary default has been to utilize the number of acres affected as the measure of impact of both beneficial and detrimental impacts.

Less than five years after promulgating its guidance on conservation banking, the Fish and Wildlife Service signaled a willingness to reconsider some of the core principles embodied in that guidance. Specifically, the Service invited comment on an idea it called "recovery crediting," which was essentially a form of conservation banking in which credits could be earned by federal agencies for less-than-permanent conservation efforts that they underwrote on nonfederal land.[24] Credits earned from these less-than-permanent conservation efforts could only be used to offset less-than-permanent impacts of federal agency actions elsewhere. The impetus for the Service's consideration of this idea was a pilot initiative involving Fort Hood Army Base in Texas and nearby private landowners. That initiative entails the Army paying local landowners to enter into term agreements to manage habitat for the endangered golden-cheeked warbler, in return for which the Army earns credits that can be used to offset the impacts of certain temporary disturbances to warbler habitat on Fort Hood. As of this writing, both the recovery crediting concept and the Fort Hood pilot project that gave rise to it are being evaluated by the Service.

Emerging and Future Directions

On the one hand, the need for incentives to encourage conservation efforts by private landowners is abundantly clear. On the other hand, the experience gained during the past decade's efforts to accomplish conservation through incentive mechanisms underscores some major challenges. These include the need to simplify associated administrative processes, provide predictable levels of funding, harmonize state and federal requirements, and clarify the application of existing incentive tools to particular land ownership situations.

For incentive tools such as safe harbor agreements and CCAAs, landowners make voluntary conservation commitments that they have no other legal obligation to undertake. Facilitating such commitments by easing the administrative process for securing such agreements ought to be an obvious objective for the administrators of the Endangered Species Act. In practice, however, the process of securing such agreements is often slow, difficult, and frustrating. An example of that frustration is the following recent e-mail sent by a consultant (who must remain anonymous) working on a proposed safe harbor agreement to the Service biologist with whom he had been negotiating the agreement:

> I think we've been at this for about three years now, with a number of drafts and a fair amount of work by all of us. Bill and I talked yesterday and agreed that the latest version to incorporate the comments from the solicitor seemed to go beyond a review of what we had previously agreed upon through a legal lens and, in fact, seemed to move the goalposts a few yards back. Moreover, the solicitor is faceless, nameless and we don't get to talk to them, except through you. That's pretty hard. If we have to negotiate further, then we want to at least face the folks on the other side of the table and have the opportunity to build the same level of trust and mutual understanding that we have with you. I appreciate your need for a legal review, but don't see why that is an opportunity for the lawyers to demand more than the biologists have already agreed to with the landowner. I've had this "drive by shooting" kind of approach by the solicitor folks at least twice now on various Sec. 10 projects. I would suggest they be brought in early or their review be limited to purely legal issues, not biological or agreement substance if they must be the last stop.

The merits of that particular complaint are not of paramount importance. What is important is that few landowners will have the patience to endure a process that takes three years and multiple drafts, that appears to move the goalposts after the landowner thought the basic elements of the agreement had been settled, and that is aimed at producing a voluntary agreement that the landowner has no legal duty to enter into in the first place.

A related issue pertains to the harmonization of federal and state requirements. As noted previously, both safe harbor agreements and CCAAs were administratively created innovations that mined existing provisions of the Endangered Species Act for previously untapped flexibility. The general rule under the Act is that the states can be more restrictive with respect to the taking of listed species than the federal requirements.[25] As a result, for species that are subject to both the Act and parallel state legislation, agreements of this sort will require separate authorization under state law. Until presented with a proposed federal agreement, most states seem never to have considered whether they have the authority to approve such agreements. At the very least, this situation creates uncertainty and delay in securing needed approvals and may in fact cause more serious roadblocks. In California, for example, several species are considered "fully protected" under legislation that predates the California Endangered Species Act.[26] That legislation disallows virtually any form of taking, even taking in connection with an agreement that produces a net conservation benefit for the species.

Another more recent example of the complexity of harmonizing state and federal requirements can be found in Hawaii. There the Fish and Wildlife Service approved a programmatic safe harbor agreement for several endangered waterbirds. The State of

Hawaii, notwithstanding that it had in fact already approved at least one programmatic safe harbor agreement, began to question whether it had the legal authority to do so. To clarify its authority, it asked the legislature to amend the state's Endangered Species Act. Far from clarifying the state's authority, however, the legislature approved amendments that, as a practical matter, will make programmatic safe harbor agreements difficult and impractical.[27] Thus, a conservation tool that has generally worked well elsewhere, and that is particularly needed in Hawaii, will be largely unavailable there.

Compounding the above challenges is the further challenge of inadequate resources for incentive efforts. The habitat management and other voluntary commitments of landowners always entail costs, and sometimes entail considerable costs. While some landowners are willing to bear those costs themselves, others are likely to require at least some level of assistance. The experience of the Private Stewardship Grants Program and the Landowner Incentive Program over the past half dozen years has underscored the hazards of uncertain funding levels. The Landowner Incentive Program in particular illustrates the perils, since it relied upon the states to deliver incentives to landowners. Those states who stepped up to that challenge by adding staff were left without resources to support those staff when federal funding for the Program evaporated. The ultimate losers, of course, are not the states, but rather the at-risk species that were to have been the beneficiaries of this incentive program.

The problem of unreliable funding for voluntary conservation efforts could be addressed through tax incentives that encourage such efforts. In the Food, Conservation, and Energy Act of 2008 (the Farm Bill), Congress took a limited step in that direction.[28] Section 15303 of that law amends Section 175 of the Internal Revenue Code[29] to allow taxpayers who are engaged in the business of farming to deduct from their income the cost of implementing "site-specific management actions recommended in recovery plans" approved under the Endangered Species Act. While this measure effectively shifts some of the cost of voluntarily implementing recovery measures to the general Treasury, its significance is limited by the fact that it applies only to taxpayers engaged in the business of farming, matters only to the extent that such expenses would not otherwise be deductible under preexisting law, and offsets only a minority of the costs of such measures. More far-reaching tax credits for certain voluntary conservation actions had been included in the Senate-passed version of the bill, but were ultimately dropped from the law.

Assuming that these challenges can be overcome, another emerging issue concerns the application of certain incentive programs, in particular land ownership situations. As noted previously, both safe harbor agreements and CCAAs are limited to nonfederal landowners. The rationale for so limiting them was that federal land managing agencies have affirmative obligations to use their authorities to further the conservation of listed species. As a practical matter, however, in the West, where many ranches are composed of both private and leased federal land, the degree of certainty that can be conveyed by, for example, a CCAA that literally applies only on nonfederal land may be inadequate to stimulate the sort of voluntary conservation effort that would effectively address the threats to a candidate species. Fashioning a workable approach that takes into account the need for conservation efforts across property boundaries while recognizing the legal distinctions that apply to different land ownerships is a major challenge for the future.

Conclusion

Incentives to encourage voluntary conservation commitments by landowners were largely an afterthought when the Endangered Species Act was enacted. The experience of the past three decades, however, has made plain that the Act's goal of recovering species requires not only the prohibition of harmful activities but the implementation of beneficial ones as well. Both regulatory and financial incentives to encourage those beneficial activities are needed. To date, most incentive mechanisms have relied upon administrative ingenuity to fashion new approaches out of existing provisions of the Act. That effort has produced some noteworthy achievements, but much more is needed if the Act's recovery goals are to be met.

Notes

1. The stated purposes of the Act include "provid[ing] a program for the conservation of . . . endangered species and threatened species." 16 U.S.C. § 1531(b). In turn, "conservation" is defined in the Act to mean the use of all means necessary to bring a listed species "to the point at which the measures provided pursuant to this Act are no longer necessary." *Id.* § 1532(3).
2. *Id.* § 1538(a).
3. *Id.* § 1536(a)(2).
4. *Id.*
5. *Id.* § 1534.
6. *Id.* § 1535.
7. *Id.* § 1531(a)(5).
8. Cone's story is told in Robert Bonnie, *From Cone's Folly to Brosnan Forest and Beyond: Protecting Red-cockaded Woodpeckers on Private Land, in* RED-COCKADED WOODPECKER: ROAD TO RECOVERY (R. Costa and S. Daniels eds., 2003).
9. *See* U.S. Fish and Wildlife Serv., *Private Lands Guidelines, in* RECOVERY PLAN FOR THE RED-COCKADED WOODPECKER app. 5 (2003).
10. *See* Daowei Zhang, *Endangered Species and Timber Harvesting: The Case of the Red-Cockaded Woodpecker*, 42(1) ECON. INQUIRY 150–65 (2004).
11. Title 23, section 4 of the California Water Code defines an "encroachment" to include "any obstruction or physical intrusion by construction of works or devices, planting or removal of vegetation, or by whatever means for any purpose, into" any area covered by a flood control plan.
12. Safe harbor agreements are not applicable on federal lands. The rationale for limiting safe harbor agreements to nonfederal property owners was that federal agencies have affirmative duties to utilize their authorities to conserve listed species under Section 7(a)(1) of the Endangered Species Act, 16 U.S.C. § 1536(a)(1), whereas nonfederal landowners have no comparable affirmative obligations.
13. 16 U.S.C. § 1539(a)1)(B).
14. Announcement of Final Safe Harbor Policy, 64 Fed. Reg. 32,717 (June 17, 1999). Regulations implementing the Policy can be found at 50 C.F.R. §§ 17.22(c) and 17.32(c) for endangered and threatened species, respectively.

15. The Private Stewardship Grants Program was initially described in a notice that appeared at 67 Fed. Reg. 39,419 (June 7, 2002). The Landowner Incentive Program was initially described in a notice on the same date at 67 Fed. Reg. 39,414.
16. Pub. L. No. 109-294 (codified at 16 U.S.C. §§ 3771–3774).
17. The Healthy Forest Reserve Program was authorized by Title V of the Healthy Forests Restoration Act of 2003, Pub. L. No. 108-148 (codified at 16 U.S.C. §§ 6571–6578). Regulations to implement the program appear at 7 C.F.R. pt. 625.
18. *See, e.g.*, Friends of the Wild Swan, Inc. v. U.S. Fish and Wildlife Serv., 945 F. Supp. 1388 (D. Or. 1996); Save Our Springs v. Babbitt, 27 F. Supp. 2d 739 (W.D. Tex. 1997); Nat'l Wildlife Fed'n v. Nat'l Marine Fisheries Serv., 254 F. Supp. 1196 (D. Or. 2003); Fed'n of Fly Fishers v. Daley, 131 F. Supp. 2d 1158 (N.D. Cal. 2000).
19. 68 Fed. Reg. 15,100 (Mar. 28, 2003).
20. Species eligible to be covered by a CCAA include not only formal "candidate species" that have been identified as such by the Fish and Wildlife Service or the National Marine Fisheries Service, but also "species likely to become candidates." The latter category is an undefined group that potentially includes almost anything that the Services wish.
21. Announcement of Final Policy for Candidate Conservation Agreements with Assurances, 64 Fed. Reg. 32,726 (June 17, 1999). Regulations pertaining to CCAAs are promulgated at 50 C.F.R. §§ 17.22(d) and 17.32(d).
22. 64 Fed. Reg. 32,727.
23. Both wetland mitigation banks and endangered species conservation banks are discussed at length in MICHAEL BEAN, REBECCA KIHSLINGER & JESSICA WILKINSON, DESIGN OF U.S. HABITAT BANKING SYSTEMS TO SUPPORT THE CONSERVATION OF WILDLIFE HABITAT AND AT-RISK SPECIES (Envtl. Law Inst. 2008).
24. *See* Notice of Availability for Draft Recovery Crediting Guidance, 72 Fed. Reg. 62,258 (Nov. 2, 2007).
25. *See* 16 U.S.C. § 1535(f) ("Any State law or regulation respecting the taking of an endangered species or threatened species may be more restrictive than the exemptions or permits provided for in this Act or in any regulation which implements this Act but not less restrictive than the prohibitions so defined.").
26. *See* CAL. FISH & GAME CODE §§ 4700 (fully protected mammals) and 5050 (fully protected amphibians and reptiles).
27. Hawaii's Endangered Species Act is one of the few state endangered species laws that specifically authorizes safe harbor agreements. See HAW. REV. STAT. § 195D-22. For the text of the 2008 amendments that require separate approval of every landowner agreement included in a programmatic safe harbor agreement, see http://www.capitol.hawaii.gov/session2008/Bills/SB3103_HD2_.htm. The effect of that requirement is to undo the very purpose and value of a programmatic agreement.
28. Pub. L. No. 110-234, 122 Stat. 923.
29. 26 U.S.C. § 175.

11

Habitat Conservation Plans and the Endangered Species Act

Douglas P. Wheeler and Ryan M. Rowberry

Introduction

Today, landowners and cooperating governments—federal, state, and local—increasingly rely on a unique conservation planning tool, habitat conservation plans (HCPs), to accommodate land development and the strict species and habitat protection requirements of the Endangered Species Act (ESA).[1] This, however, is a relatively recent phenomenon. To understand the expanding utility of HCPs, it is necessary to grasp the tensions that prompted their development.

Purposes and Perceptions of the Early ESA

Struggles to precisely comprehend the scope of the ESA dominated its first decade. Although the Act's stated purposes were to "provide a means whereby the ecosystems upon which endangered species and threatened species depend may be conserved, [and] to provide a program for the conservation of such endangered and threatened species," the Act did not define the term "ecosystems."[2] Nor are there any specific prescriptions for conservation of such "ecosystems."[3] ESA sections 4 and 7 contain the term "critical habitat," but this term is tied to specific statutory requirements (listing and agency consultation) that pertain to the conservation of individual species.[4] Thus, while the original purposes of the ESA are said to have included ecosystem conservation, with its attendant broad implications, the bulk of the Act authorizes regulatory programs to conserve, protect, and recover individual species that are deemed to be endangered or threatened.

A broad reading of ESA's section 9 take prohibitions along with a significant court ruling requiring strict enforcement of the ESA bolstered the perception that the ESA was chiefly concerned with the protection of individual species. Section 9 of the ESA prohibits "any person" (private or public) from taking an endangered species listed by the Secretaries of the Interior or Commerce.[5] A "take," as defined in the ESA, is "to harass, harm, pursue, hunt, shoot, kill, wound, kill, trap, capture, or collect, or to attempt to engage in any such conduct."[6] In 1975, the Secretary of the Interior defined "harm" to include "significant environmental modification or degradation" that "actually injures or kills wildlife," thus widening the scope of the ESA's take prohibitions.[7] And by enjoining the completion of a nearly finished, multimillion-dollar federal dam to shield a listed population of snail darters (three-inch, tan-colored fish) from eradication in 1978, the U.S. Supreme Court in *Tennessee Valley Authority v. Hill* sent an early, powerful message that ESA protections pertaining to even the most obscure endangered species were to be strictly enforced.[8] The Ninth Circuit then enlarged take prohibitions even further in a 1981 case involving the palila, a Hawaiian bird, by holding that mere habitat modification may constitute a take.[9]

The inclusion of habitat modification as a take, coupled with the likelihood of rigorous enforcement, understandably disturbed the private sector and local governments. Developers and landowners feared investing large amounts of time, money, and other resources on a project that might be frustrated at any point by the discovery of a listed species at the project site. And local governments faced heightened scrutiny for regulatory decisions surrounding land development. For nearly a decade after its enactment, it appeared that the ESA would meet national biodiversity preservation goals, if at all, through prohibitions that protect individual species.[10]

The risks of liability and probable enforcement acted as a catalyst for the development of an alternative approach. Following a 1980 settlement agreement between developers and local government regarding the proposed development of the San Bruno Mountain in northern California, the FWS discovered that that the Mission Blue butterfly, a listed endangered species, lived on San Bruno Mountain. Developers, citizen groups, and representatives of various governments formed a steering committee to "formulate a plan that would both protect the endangered species and allow some development of the Mountain."[11] The steering committee commissioned a two-year biological study of the Mission Blue butterfly and other species on San Bruno, which concluded that even if the mountain were to remain completely undeveloped, naturally encroaching brush would destroy the butterflies' grassland habitat.

Given this conclusion, the steering committee developed an innovative conservation plan "by which habitat protection and real estate development on the Mountain" would occur simultaneously.[12] The final San Bruno Mountain Area Habitat Conservation Plan recognized that 14 percent of the Mission Blue's habitat would be affected by development, resulting in an otherwise actionable take of some of the butterflies. But other provisions in the San Bruno HCP (e.g., annual financial contributions by future lot owners to a "permanent habitat conservation program" and preservation of 86 percent of the Mission Blue's present habitat) mitigated this take, with the net effect that the San Bruno HCP actually served to enhance the survival of multiple species on the mountain, including the Mission Blue butterfly.[13] However, no provision of the ESA allowed for an exception to the take prohibitions of section 9. This prompted parties associated with the San Bruno HCP to petition Congress for an exemption.

1982 ESA Amendment

Congress responded to the San Bruno petitions by amending the ESA in 1982 to include section 10(a), authorizing the Secretaries of the Interior and Commerce to issue an Incidental Take Permit (ITP) in association with an approved HCP. An ITP exempts the holder from the penalties of ESA section 9 in situations where a take is "incidental to, and not the purpose of, the carrying out of an otherwise lawful activity."[14] By creating this exemption to section 9 of the ESA, Congress intended to achieve two primary purposes: (1) modification of the broad reach of section 9's stringent take prohibitions to encourage long-term "creative partnerships between the public and private sectors and among governmental agencies" in the interest of multiple species and habitat conservation;[15] and (2) a clear commitment to the concept of ecosystem conservation.

Obtaining an ITP, and thus immunity from section 9 take prohibitions, however, requires much more than just asking for one. Depending upon the species involved, an ITP applicant must submit a properly prepared HCP to either the FWS or the

National Marine Fisheries Service (NMFS) for review, both agencies having been delegated joint authority to administer the ITP program. To ensure that applicants thoroughly prepare their HCPs, Congress adopted the San Bruno HCP as its "model plan," incorporating several elements of its outline into the amendment of the ESA.[16] Section 10(a)(2)(A) requires applicants to specify in their HCPs:

> (i) the impact which will likely result from such taking; (ii) what steps the applicant will take to minimize and mitigate such impacts, and the funding that will be available to implement such steps; (iii) what alternative actions to such taking the applicant considered and the reasons why such alternatives are not being utilized; and (iv) such other measures that the Secretary may require as being necessary or appropriate for purposes of the plan.[17]

In addition to an HCP, there are other prerequisites to the issuance of an ITP. An analysis pursuant to the National Environmental Policy Act (NEPA) is mandatory, and a contractual Implementing Agreement that specifies the legal obligations of the applicant is usually required. Federal agencies, including FWS and NMFS, must comply with ESA section 7(a)(2), which requires each federal agency to "insure that any action authorized, funded, or carried out by an agency . . . is not likely to jeopardize the continued existence of any endangered or threatened species."[18] FWS or NMFS must (1) consult with the action agency (or perform an internal self-consultation if it is the action agency); (2) use "the best scientific and commercial data available" to determine whether issuance of the ITP or its agency counterpart, the Incidental Take Statement, meets the "no jeopardy" standard of section 7; and (3) issue a Biological Opinion with their decision.[19]

If the Biological Opinion finds that the ITP will have "no jeopardy" to the covered species or no destruction/adverse modification to designated critical habitat, these documents—HCP, NEPA analysis, Implementing Agreement, Biological Opinion—are submitted for public comment. And an ITP will ensue only if the Services find that:

> (i) the taking will be incidental; (ii) the applicant will, to the maximum extent practicable, minimize and mitigate the impacts of such taking; (iii) the applicant will ensure that adequate funding for the plan will be provided; (iv) the taking will not appreciably reduce the likelihood of the survival and recovery of the species in the wild; and (v) the measures, if any, required [as necessary and appropriate] will be met.[20]

In sum, by amending the ESA to authorize the ITP in 1982, and the parallel provisions of section 7 that provide for issuance of an incidental take statement (ITS) to federal agencies, Congress intended to simultaneously accommodate land development and the conservation of ecosystems inhabited by endangered species.

Although Congress had high hopes for the ITP program, HCP use remained relatively dormant for over a decade. Unfamiliarity with the process of applying for an ITP, along with the time and cost associated with the completion of the requisite biological surveys undoubtedly contributed to this sluggish start. But the overwhelming deterrent to greater use of HCPs remained the looming specter of continuing liability for species not covered by the Plan, and for unanticipated injury to habitat. Such reticence to embrace HCPs can be explained by ongoing disagreement in the 1980s between the FWS and the courts concerning the legal implications of section 9's take provision.[21] By 1992, a decade after the introduction of the ITP program, only 14 ITPs (including that for San Bruno) had been issued.[22] Statistics for the HCPs tied to these 14 permits reveal that HCPs averaged 30 years in duration, covered an average of two listed species (no nonlisted species were covered), and affected nearly 584,000 acres.[23]

Babbitt Administrative Reforms

Despite a decade of lackluster performance, interest in HCPs was revived by the Clinton administration. In 1993, newly confirmed Secretary Bruce Babbitt began pledging and planning regulatory reforms that would modify the ESA's perceived inflexibility and stimulate private sector involvement in conservation. Fostering a cooperative partnership with private landowners and developers was critical to preserving endangered species, given that more than half of endangered or threatened species occupied habitats that over 80 percent of the time were found on private or state lands.[24] The centerpiece in Babbitt's suite of HCP reforms was the "No Surprises" rule, aimed at creating a further incentive for the private sector to participate in sponsorship of HCPs.[25]

In August 1994, the FWS and NFMS announced the "No Surprises" policy. "No Surprises" provided that "no additional land use restrictions or financial compensation" would be required of a nonfederal ITP permit holder over the course of the permit with respect to the covered species, "even if unforeseen circumstances arise after the permit is issued indicating that additional mitigation [for the covered species] is needed."[26] In other words, ITP holders who adhere to the terms of their HCPs could not be required to expend additional resources conserving the endangered species covered by the HCP, even if unforeseen developments warranted the adoption of additional protective measures. Should such circumstances require intervention and/or modification of the HCP, the additional expense is to be borne by the federal government or cooperating public entity, not the landowner. The No Surprises rule diminished the risk of potential take liability by providing additional economic and regulatory certainty regarding the costs for species conservation and mitigation. To streamline and guide applicants through the HCP/ITP application, the Services also introduced the *Habitat Conservation Planning and Incidental Take Permit Processing Handbook* (*HCP Handbook*) in 1996, offering much needed step-by-step instruction.[27] An addendum was added to the *HCP Handbook* in 2000, introducing an adaptive management focus for HCPs.[28]

The effects of these additional assurances and guidance were profound. According to an FWS database, 177 HCPs were approved during Babbitt's eight years as Secretary (1993–2000). These HCPs covered more than 26,575,000 acres in 22 states and the territory of Puerto Rico.[29] This represents an almost 13-fold increase in the number of approved HCPs compared to the previous decade, and the cumulative acreage conserved between 1993 and 2000 increased over 4,400 percent compared to that for 1982–1992.[30] The duration of ITPs was generally tied to the size of the HCP; small-acreage HCPs tended to receive ITPs for fewer years, while larger HCPs generated ITPs ranging from 30 years to 50 years, with a few ITPs issued for 100 years.[31] In addition, 25 percent (45 of 177) of the HCPs from 1993 to 2000 covered both listed and nonlisted species and their supporting habitats, reflecting that HCPs began to fulfill the broad, ecosystem-minded conservation vision that Congress intended for HCPs when amending the ESA in 1982.[32]

Even after Secretary Babbitt's tenure, the foundation of economic and regulatory assurances he laid has continued to provide substantial conservation dividends. From 2001 to 2009, the Services approved 424 HCPs from 23 states and Puerto Rico.[33] These 424 HCPs cumulatively cover over 22,133,000 acres of land, and the duration of the ITPs granted by the Services range from a couple of years up to several decades depending on the size and scope of the attendant HCP. The 424 HCPs approved between 2001 and 2009 represent more than a doubling of the 177 approved from 1993 to 2000, but the average acreage conserved per HCP diminished as did the percentage of HCPs covering both listed and unlisted species.[34] This trend reflects the fact that small land developers and private landowners became increasingly supportive of HCPs during this period.[35] Nonetheless, since Babbitt's HCP reforms in the early 1990s, over 48 million acres of land have become subject to HCP Implementation Agreements, suggesting that in just 15 years HCPs have become a widely accepted means of accommodating development while preserving endangered species and their habitats.[36]

Current State of the Law

The "No Surprises" Rule and the ITP Permit Revocation Rule

Publication of the No Surprises rule in February 1998 sparked contentious litigation that has only recently been resolved.[37] The purpose of the No Surprises rule, first proposed four years earlier, was to "provid[e] regulatory certainty in exchange for conservation commitments."[38] Consequently, the No Surprises rule required the Services approving HCPs to provide private landowners with "assurances" that "no additional land use restrictions or financial compensation" beyond that specified in the HCP would be imposed, even if circumstances changed in such a way as to render the HCP inadequate to conserve the covered species.[39] The No Surprises rule essentially provides a cost ceiling for nonfederal ITP holders with respect to covered species conservation and mitigation; if the need for additional mitigation beyond that specified in the HCP arises due to unforeseen circumstances, the federal government, using its various ESA authorities (e.g., land acquisition, land exchange, translocation of species), must bear the cost. Upon an applicant's request, these No Surprises "assurances" were incorporated into the HCP. As noted, these assurances proved to be a very effective incentive for landowner participation in HCPs, causing them to be much more widely accepted than before the adoption of the rule.

In July 1998, a coalition of six environmental and tribal groups, spearheaded by the Spirit of the Sage Council, challenged the validity of the No Surprises rule in the federal District Court for the District of Columbia. The Council claimed that the No Surprises rule violated the ESA by barring the Services from "making changes to ITPs which may be necessary to ensure the survival or recovery of endangered and threatened species."[40] However, before the court could settle the controversy surrounding the No Surprises rule, the Services anticipated and addressed one of the plaintiffs' strongest arguments.

On June 17, 1999, one month before oral arguments on the No Surprises rule, the Services promulgated another regulation, the ITP Permit Revocation Rule. Addressing the allegation that agency approval of HCPs with No Surprises assurances deprived the Secretaries of authority to intervene where necessary to protect covered species, the revocation rule offered two responses. First, it confirmed that the Services possessed the authority to revoke ITPs in cases where a permittee did not comply with the terms of the ITP and in cases in which "unforeseen circumstances results in likely jeopardy" to a species covered by a properly implemented HCP where "the Service has not been successful in remedying the situation through other means."[41] The Services were also quick to assure nonfederal landowners, however, that they would revoke ITPs in the latter case only "as a last resort."[42] Second, the revocation rule clarified the standard to be used in revoking an ITP. Prior to the promulgation of the revocation rule, the Services could revoke an ITP when permitted activities were "detrimental to the maintenance *or* recovery of the population."[43] Under the revocation rule, however, the ITP permit revocation standard mirrored the language for ITP permit issuance (i.e., an ITP "may not be revoked for any reason . . . unless continuation of the permitted activity would . . . appreciably reduce the likelihood of the survival *and* recovery of the species in the wild").[44] In other words, to revoke an ITP under the old standard, the Services had to find that an ITP holder's activity triggered only one of the tests, while revocation of an ITP under the revocation rule required that both tests be met. Thus, if an ITP holder's permitted activity "reduce[d] the likelihood of survival" of a species covered by the permit but not its ability to "recover" in the wild, the Services could not revoke the ITP under the revocation rule. The revocation rule's new standard signaled to nonfederal landowners that, although the Services retained the authority to revoke an ITP, they would exercise this authority only in extreme circumstances.

Unsurprisingly, the Services' promulgation of the revocation rule did not satisfy the Council. Claiming that the Services drafted the revocation rule to obviate their initial challenge to the validity of the No Surprises rule, the Council amended its original complaint to include a challenge to the revocation rule. The Services' rapid promulgation of the revocation rule, they argued, had violated the public notice and comment requirements of the Administrative Procedure Act (APA).[45] More than three years later, in December 2003, the district court agreed with the Council and held that the Services had promulgated the revocation rule "in violation of the APA's notice and comment requirements." The district court subsequently vacated and remanded the revocation rule to the Services to "begin anew the APA mandated notice and comment procedures."[46] In addition, without reaching the Council's substantive challenge to the No Surprises rule, the district court held that No Surprises was "sufficiently intertwined" with the revocation rule that it too was subject to remand for reconsideration.[47] Thus, the district court required the Services to consider the No Surprises rule in tandem with the revocation rule during their new rulemaking proceedings. To ensure swift agency action, the court ordered that the Services complete all rulemaking proceedings by December 2004 and enjoined the Services from issuing ITPs with "No Surprises" assurances in the interim.[48]

Following a denial by the D.C. Circuit of their motion to stay the district court's 2003 decision pending appeal, the Services complied with the ruling of the district court. On May 25, 2004, the FWS published a Final Rule withdrawing the revocation rule that had been vacated by the district court. On the same day, the FWS also solicited public comments on its proposal to reestablish the revocation rule and on whether the revocation rule contained the appropriate regulatory standard for revoking ITPs with "No Surprises" assurances.[49] After public comment on the proposed rule, the Services repromulgated the revocation rule on December 10, 2004, without substantial changes.[50]

With the requisite APA rulemaking procedures completed, on August 30, 2007, the district court finally addressed the substantive merits of the No Surprises rule and the revocation rule. The Council had argued that the rules violated the ESA because they did not adhere to the general conservation and recovery-based purposes of the ESA as a whole and section 10 in particular.[51] That is, the rules did not promote or maintain the recovery of species because they contemplated and sanctioned some species loss. The district court disagreed with the Council's argument, noting that "the statutory text of ESA section 10 demonstrates Congressional intent to allow the Services to grant ITPs even if they do not protect the recovery of listed species."[52] ITP applicants had only to ensure that they did not reduce the "likelihood of the survival and recovery of the species."[53] Thus, the district court held that since ITPs were not governed by a recovery-based standard, the No Surprises rule, designed to assure the long-term efficacy of an ITP, and the revocation rule, based on the same overarching premise, are both sanctioned by the ESA.[54] As the court explained, "the ESA does not require ITPs to promote or maintain the recovery of species," so regulatory rules attached to ITPs need not do otherwise.[55] This case has been the only substantial challenge to Secretary Babbitt's administrative reforms affecting HCPs.

Habitat Conservation Plans and Adaptive Management

Following adoption of the Babbitt reforms, and to further encourage use of the HCP option, the Services published a comprehensive guidance document, *Handbook for Habitat Conservation Planning and Incidental Take Permitting Process* (*HCP Handbook*), in December 1996.[56] Recognizing the need to improve HCP flexibility in the face of scientific uncertainty, the Services included a section in the *HCP Handbook* on "adaptive management." As defined by the Services, "adaptive management" is a methodological tool that allows for modifications in HCP mitigation strategies to respond to changes in the relevant ecosystem.[57] Adaptive management provisions are particularly "important to the planning process and the long-term interest of the affected species" when data gaps exist about long-term effects of implementing HCPs.[58] Such provisions integrate species and habitat monitoring, means for collecting and analyzing data, and measurable criteria for making HCP adjustments.[59] This new requirement provides a strengthened "feedback loop" for resource managers, but does so at the expense of certainty for landowners, one of the principal benefits of the No Surprises rule.

In further response to increased demand for HCPs and criticism from some skeptics that existing HCPs relied on unproven or uncertain biological models, assumptions, or data regarding the protection of endangered and threatened species, the Services developed a "five-point policy" in 1999. This policy responded to the charge that HCPs were being developed without sufficient scientific grounding by creating a standardized framework for HCP development and implementation based on focused, credible scientific foundations. Following a period of public comment, the five-point policy was formally adopted as an Addendum to the *HCP Handbook* in June 2000.[60] This guidance (1) requires that HCP applicants clearly state biological goals and objectives; (2) emphasizes the importance of including provision for adaptive management whenever there is uncertainty about the scientific evidence and experimental design motivating the HCP's approach to species conservation;[61] (3) clarifies the purpose and means by which to undertake species and habitat monitoring in implementation of HCPs; (4) explains the factors used to establish the term of an ITP; and (5) extends the minimum public comment period from 30 to 60 days for most HCPs.[62] The adaptive management prong of the five-point policy further explains the theory of adaptive management, lists examples of the types of data gaps necessitating an adaptive management strategy, and specifies the recommended elements of an adaptive management strategy.[63] And as adaptive management provisions of HCPs are collaboratively crafted and agreed upon by both the permit applicant and the Services before the issuance of an ITP, all stakeholders are placed on notice of the range of potential HCP mitigation strategy adjustments, making "adaptive management" compatible with "No Surprises" assurances in HCPs.[64]

Since the addition of the Addendum to the *HCP Handbook* in 2000, most HCPs now include adaptive management provisions that are similar in form. J. B. Ruhl cites the example of an adaptive management strategy in an HCP designed to protect the Santa Cruz long-toed salamander.[65] This HCP contains "an overall monitoring and assessment structure, an itemization of foreseeable changed circumstances such as fire, invasive species, and catastrophic resource stress, and a separate detailed monitoring plan."[66] In general, adaptive management provisions are included in HCPs when data or information gaps are substantial enough to pose a significant risk to the species following issuance of the ITP.[67] Long-term HCPs also tend to include adaptive management provisions to provide flexible mitigation strategies for possible future conditions.[68]

Changes to HCP procedure, however, did not come without challenge. While the *HCP Handbook* Addendum (five-point policy) itself has never been directly challenged, several recent cases address the meaning and legal implications of adaptive management. The first major case concerning adaptive management following issuance of the Addendum was *National Wildlife Federation v. Babbitt*.[69] The FWS had worked with landowners and conservationists in the Sacramento Valley to develop an HCP for the Natomas Basin, home to the threatened giant garter snake and Swainson's hawk.[70] After several rounds of revisions and opportunity for public comment, FWS issued a comprehensive 50-year ITP to the City of Sacramento.[71] The final HCP explicitly recognized that "its assumptions as to the amount, location, and pace of development in the Basin" were incomplete, and that its awareness of the needs of the giant garter snake and Swainson's hawk was imperfect.[72] Thus, utilizing adaptive management, the HCP could be modified when research provided new information on the species, when recovery or mitigation strategies in the HCP necessitated adjustments, or when the extent of reserved lands was to be adjusted.[73] The HCP also provided for ongoing monitoring, including multispecies inventories and continuous assessment of specific management programs.

As the U.S. District Court for the Eastern District of California noted, the "nub" of the National Wildlife Federation's challenge to the HCP was its adaptive management strategies.[74] The Federation argued that the adaptive management approach created a process for making future plan adjustments based on new information, but was not intended to accommodate incomplete or inadequate data. Reliance on adaptive management could not be used to justify "uncertainty inherent in the HCP's deferred decision-making scheme."[75] Although the court ultimately overturned Sacramento's ITP as overly broad, it explicitly approved of the HCP's adaptive management strategy, noting that "inconclusive data alone does not render the Service's findings arbitrary" and that adaptive management would likely mitigate any short-term impact to covered species.[76]

Two cases interpreting the *National Wildlife* decision suggest that adaptive management strategies can indeed be written so as to withstand challenges.[77] In *Center for Biological Diversity v. U.S. Fish and Wildlife Service*, the U.S. District Court for the Western District of Texas upheld an HCP that included extensive and detailed adaptive management strategies for protecting the endangered cave-dwelling beetle and spider species at issue. Some of the adaptive management strategies included replacement of fencing and installation of gates in the caves; fire ant control measures; measures to hunt or trap deer and other mammals causing disturbances; and humidity, drainage, and vegetation control.[78] The HCP also included a schedule for surveys and other monitoring that could correctly trigger adaptive management measures.[79] In contrast, the U.S. District Court for the Southern District of California in *Southwestern Center for Biological Diversity v. Bartel* held the adaptive management strategies in an HCP designed to protect vernal pool species (two types of fairy shrimp and five plant species) to be insufficient because they did not "compel those changes needed to save the species from extinction."[80] Contrasting the adaptive management provision in the *Bartel* HCP with that in the *National Wildlife* HCP, the court observed that the *Bartel* HCP did not have specific and constant monitoring on a set time schedule and did not authorize firm adaptive management measures to be utilized in specified situations.[81] The court concluded that the adaptive management provisions in the *Bartel* HCP "violate the ESA because they lock-in ineffective, unstudied, and inadequate mitigation for the vernal pool species for fifty years. The ESA requires useful mitigation."[82]

In *Natural Resources Defense Council v. Kempthorne*, the U.S. District Court for the Eastern District of California expanded on these precedents in 2007 by emphasizing the importance of reasonable certainty of future mitigation strategies and the enforceability of those strategies.[83] The HCP in *Kempthorne* contained an adaptive management risk assessment matrix for the endangered delta smelt—a small, semi-translucent fish—that included regularly scheduled monitoring and threshold criteria that would trigger a working group meeting.[84] After the working group convened, it could recommend several possible adjustments for purposes of mitigating impact on the delta smelt.[85] Noting that adaptive management case law "sheds little light on how to harmonize [the] competing objectives" of flexibility in adaptive management and certainty of enforcement actions when necessary, the court held that the adaptive management provisions in this HCP were insufficiently certain or enforceable.[86] Because the working group had complete discretion over whether to recommend a mitigation action following a triggering criterion, it was held that the adaptive management provision could not guarantee that an enforcement action would be taken to protect the species.[87] The court found that the ESA requires "reasonable certainty, timetables, and enforceability standards" for adaptive management mitigation strategies, and that the adaptive management process embodied in this particular HCP did not contain appropriate quantifiable objectives or required mitigation strategies.[88]

In 2008, the same court found that an HCP with adaptive management strategies designed to protect the Chinook salmon was appropriately sufficient, certain, and enforceable. In *Pacific Coast Federation of Fisherman's Associations v. Gutierrez*, the court upheld an HCP that contained specific temperature controls, river carryover storage provisions, and mandatory remedial action.[89] Because the adaptive management measures were "non-discretionary," the court determined that they were "definite and sufficiently certain to be enforceable."[90] And as the agency was owed some discretion concerning the form of the implementation of the mitigation strategies, the adaptive management provision struck "the appropriate balancing between the needs of certainty and flexibility prescribed by the law."[91]

In sum, adaptive management is now a common feature of HCPs, particularly in the case of long-term HCPs or HCPs that cover large land areas. While the Services encouraged adaptive management strategies for HCPs during the 1990s, the 2000 Addendum to the *HCP Handbook* refined and elevated the importance of adaptive management as a component of HCPs and a means for ensuring long-term species and ecosystem preservation. Today, courts evaluating the legal sufficiency of adaptive management provisions have insisted that these provisions in HCPs contain enforceable, quantifiable, and specific objectives that are sufficient to protect the covered species and its habitat. Such judicial results highlight the inherent tension in crafting adaptive management provisions that are malleable enough to respond to future changes, yet specific enough to allow for legal enforcement and reasonable certainty to the landowner.

HCPs/ITPs and NEPA

The U.S. Fish and Wildlife Service has determined that every HCP must satisfy the procedural requirements of the National Environmental Policy Act (NEPA).[92] NEPA requires federal agencies to evaluate the environmental impacts of their proposed actions with potential for adverse effect, including the issuance of an ITP. More specifically, if issuance of an ITP is deemed to be a "major federal action" that "significantly affects the quality of the human environment," the issuing agency must prepare a detailed environmental impact statement (EIS) or otherwise comply with NEPA, describing the anticipated effects and actions that may be recommended in mitigation of adverse impacts.[93] NEPA analysis does not compel a particular outcome, but must assure that the acting agency has taken a "hard look" at whether to proceed, as when approving an HCP and issuing an ITP. Although the Services are responsible for ensuring NEPA compliance during the development of the HCP, lack of funding and resources often shift that burden to the applicant (which can pay for NEPA compliance work that remains the duty of the agency to oversee). An applicant may also combine HCP and NEPA analyses into one document for later review and approval by the Services.[94] Such integration of the HCP and NEPA analysis may ultimately benefit both the government and the ITP applicant by "expediting the application process and issuance of the permit."[95]

Although significant overlap exists between the conservation/mitigation requirements of ESA section 10 and those of NEPA, "the scope of NEPA goes beyond that of the ESA by considering the impacts of a federal action on nonwildlife resources such as water quality, air quality, and cultural resources."[96] Therefore, a combined HCP/NEPA analysis should cover "direct, indirect, and cumulative effects" of the proposed incidental take along with the corresponding "mitigation and minimization measures proposed from the implementation of the HCP."[97] Given the wide range and complexity of HCPs, the Services evaluate each HCP on a case-by-case basis to decide which of three levels of NEPA analysis is applicable to the HCP and ITP: (1) categorical exclusion; (2) environmental assessment; or (3) environmental impact statement. The level of NEPA analysis required ultimately determines its compatibility with a draft HCP and the time it takes the Services to review the entire ITP application.

"Low-effect HCPs" are categorically excluded from NEPA.[98] Low-effect HCPs are conservation plans that, viewed individually and cumulatively with other permitted projects, involve "(1) minor or negligible effects on federally listed and candidate species and their habitats; and (2) minor or negligible effects on other environmental values or resources."[99] To determine whether a HCP is low-effect, the applicant and Services consider "the effect of the activity on the distribution or the numbers of the species" among other factors.[100] The size and scope of a particular HCP are not necessarily determinative of whether it will be classified as a low-effect HCP (e.g., large-acreage HCPs may have negligible impacts while small-acreage HCPs may generate significant impacts). More often than not, however, low-effect HCPs involve "a single small land or other natural resource owner and relatively few acres of habitat."[101] If an applicant and the Services determine that a HCP qualifies as a low-effect HCP, the Services will prepare an Environmental Action Memorandum. This brief document "explain[s] the reasons the Services concluded that there will be no individual or cumulative significant effects on the environment" and "serves as the Service's record of NEPA compliance for categorically excluded actions."[102] An ITP for a low-effect HCP is usually issued in less than three months from the time the completed application is submitted.[103]

If an HCP is not eligible for a categorical exclusion from NEPA, then an environmental assessment (EA) is prepared. An EA analyzes the impacts of the HCP to determine whether the HCP will have a "significant environmental impact."[104] Council on Environmental Quality regulations identify 10 factors relating to the context and intensity of the proposed action that may be used to determine whether the threatened impact of an action is "significant."[105] The evidence and analysis in the EA leads the Services to issue either (1) a Finding of No Significant Impact (FONSI) for the HCP; or (2) a decision that the HCP will have a significant environmental impact, thus requiring a more thorough examination of its impacts through the preparation of an EIS.[106] In general, the Services presume that an EA-level analysis is sufficient for almost all HCPs because the ESA section 10 already requires ITP applicants to analyze the impacts of their plans and provide mitigation and minimization strategies.[107] The target ITP processing time for an HCP with a completed EA ranges from three to five months, while that for the HCP with a completed EIS is approximately 10 months.[108]

NEPA challenges to HCPs typically assert that the agency improperly arrived at a FONSI for a particular HCP when it should have required that an EIS be conducted—that is, that the Services, given the information in an EA, made an "arbitrary and capricious" decision in determining that the HCP would not have a significant impact.[109] For instance, in *Gerber v. Babbitt*, area homeowners and a wildlife organization in Maryland alleged, among other things, that FWS had violated NEPA by issuing an ITP for the Delmarva fox squirrel to a development company without conducting an EIS.[110] After reviewing the administrative record (the EA), the U.S. District Court for the District of Columbia disagreed with the plaintiffs. Finding that "the Service considered all relevant factors" and "concluded that the mitigation measures proposed in the [HCP] would be more than adequate," the court dismissed the suit.[111] Similarly, the U.S. District Court for the Western District of Texas in *Center for Biological Diversity v. U.S. Fish and Wildlife Service* held that the FWS had performed "a thorough environmental analysis" before concluding that the development of approximately 750 acres of land in northern Bexar County, Texas, would have no significant impact on two endangered beetle species, one endangered spider species, or their cave habitats.[112]

However, if the record describing the rationale for the Services' decision to issue a FONSI for a particular HCP contains uncertainty or substantial internal agency disagreement, courts will require the agency to conduct an EIS. In 2000, the U.S.

District Court for the Eastern District of California held that the FWS "arbitrarily" issued a FONSI (and subsequently an ITP) for a 50-year, 53,000-acre regional HCP in the Natomas Basin, a critical habitat area for the threatened giant garter snake and Swainson's hawk.[113] The court found that the FWS had not adequately considered all of the necessary factors in its EA, especially for a regional HCP that extended "beyond the jurisdiction of any one local government unit" and had close "proximity to the City of Sacramento, prime farmlands, wetlands, and the confluence of the Sacramento and American rivers."[114] And the "substantial controversy as to the efficacy of the mitigation measures contemplated by the HCP" and the "degree of uncertainty conceded by the Service's own experts during the planning process" bolstered the court's decision to require preparation of an EIS.[115] The U.S. District Court for the Southern District of Alabama in *Sierra Club v. Norton* similarly found that the FWS had "arbitrarily" issued a FONSI for an HCP that sanctioned substantial loss of habitat for the Alabama beach mouse. The court noted that the EA contained no reliable data concerning the minimum habitat requirements for survival and recovery of the mouse and had not considered the cumulative effects of issuing the ITP.[116] The court enjoined construction of a condominium development until an EIS for the HCP was prepared, a process that lasted another five years.[117]

Plaintiffs have also recently challenged ITP renewals, amendments, and adaptive management provisions on NEPA grounds—so far with little success. In *Atlantic Green Sea Turtle v. County Council of Volusia County*, the plaintiffs challenged a county's ITP renewal for four listed species of sea turtles and the piping plover on grounds that the FWS had failed to prepare an EA addressing certain permit amendments. The U.S. District Court for the Middle District of Florida dismissed this challenge as premature, however, as the Service had not yet rendered its final determination whether the ITP should be granted.[118] The U.S. District Court for the Northern District of California also dismissed environmentalists' NEPA challenge to Pacific Lumber Company's HCP for forest land in Mendocino County by holding that (1) its ongoing monitoring requirements do not constitute a "major federal action" triggering a supplemental EIS; and that (2) the FWS "may reinitiate section 7 consultation and not necessarily trigger a requirement for a supplemental EIS."[119] And just last year, the U.S. District Court for the Western District of Washington in *Glasser v. National Marine Fisheries Service* dismissed on standing grounds a suit in which plaintiffs alleged that the NMFS had failed to prepare an EA to accompany an ITP amendment.[120]

In sum, NEPA challenges to HCPs/ITPs usually impugn the adequacy of an EA, and sometimes EISs. If an EA results in a FONSI for a HCP, and is carefully prepared, thorough, clear, and reasonable, courts will typically defer to the Services' judgment. On the other hand, if the EA, or an EIS, reflects substantial uncertainty and disagreement concerning the efficacy of its mitigation strategies, courts will require further, in-depth study of environmental impacts in the form of an EIS. Thus, applicants who follow the Services' advice to combine HCP and NEPA analyses are encouraged to conduct a methodical, meticulous examination of environmental impacts if they are to withstand a NEPA challenge.

Future Directions

The Western Riverside County Multiple-Species HCP (MSHCP)

The Board of Supervisors in Riverside County, California, voted in 1999 to embark upon the most comprehensive application yet of habitat conservation planning. The Supervisors were unlikely advocates for an ambitious, costly, multiple-species program. In their 12-year-old attempt to meet state and federal mitigation requirements for a single species, the Supervisors had expended $42 million to acquire 41,000 acres of Stephens' kangaroo rat habitat. The politically conservative Board became objects of public derision for their efforts to comply with the ESA. How did the Supervisors come, then, to "double down" on their investment in wildlife habitat, embracing multiple-species ecosystem planning as a preferred alternative to relentless confrontation with the state and federal resource agencies over protection of 146 threatened and endangered species of plants and animals?

Riverside County, stretching 200 miles from its western boundary with Orange County to the border with Arizona on the Colorado River, is home to more than two million inhabitants, which number may reach three million by 2020. Until the economic downturn of 2008, construction activity accounted for as many new homes annually, some 15,000, as were being built elsewhere throughout the state. Both in economic activity (39th) and the size of its population (35th), Riverside County ranks ahead of many states. The appeal of this "Inland Empire" is attributable to its affordable housing; open, arid landscape with striking desert and mountain topography; and—in the western sector—reasonable proximity to the job-rich Los Angeles basin. Supervisors reasoned in 1999 that this continuing rapid pace of development, including the requisite transportation and utility infrastructure, would lead inevitably to loss of habitat and conflict with species protection requirements.

In this sense, the Riverside Supervisors addressed a dilemma that confounds planners across the south and southwest: species endemism occurs in precisely those Sunbelt states where population pressures are growing most rapidly. By one account, species abundance is greatest in those states (California, Florida, Arizona, and Texas) that have recently sustained the greatest rate of population growth.[121] Many jurisdictions in those states along the sprawling Interstate 10 corridor have adopted expansive HCPs to reconcile development impact with species and habitat protection. In FWS Regions 2, 4 and 8, corresponding roughly to the species-rich Sunbelt zone, more than 25 million acres are now subject to 544 HCPs.[122] Indeed, although the ESA was not conceived in 1973 as a tool for regional land use planning, it is now by default in many instances the legal framework that best meets that need. The FWS acknowledges that "HCPs are evolving from a process primarily to address single projects to broad-based landscape-level planning to achieve long-term biological and regulatory goals."[123]

Thus, despite dissatisfaction with the outcome of its single-species kangaroo rat experience, the Riverside Board adopted a multiple-species strategy, moving to develop and implement an HCP that would ultimately provide coverage for 146 species of plants and animals on 500,000 acres of protected habitat in the western sector of the county. But the Supervisors made a further commitment to comprehensive planning in the form of the Riverside County Integrated Project (RCIP), which combines the Conservation Plan (HCP) with General Plan and Transportation Plan components. Together, they are intended to provide a "Blueprint for Tomorrow" that integrates housing, transportation, and conservation planning on the 1.26 million acre expanse of western Riverside County.

The land acquisition element is especially ambitious. To mitigate for take of multiple species and their habitat, and thus to qualify for an ITP under section 10 of the Endangered Species Act, the County and 14 participating municipalities are committed to perpetual protection of 500,000 acres, or nearly 40 percent of the MSHCP planning area. Having met these habitat acquisition goals, the county and municipal governments could proceed with other elements of their integrated plan, including housing and infrastructure, without concern that these otherwise lawful development activities would result in civil or criminal liability for violations of the Endangered Species Act. Of the total to be protected, 347,000 acres were already in public ownership at the time of plan adoption, leaving 153,000 to be acquired for plan purposes. It was agreed that the cost of this remaining acreage—to be selected from "cells" identified as high-quality habitat by resource agencies—would be shared equally by developers, local government, and state and federal governments. Anticipated sources of revenue included contributions from developers within the reserve, which is mandatory, development fees or exactions, and appropriated funds from state and federal programs for the conservation of natural resources. Land acquisition was to proceed at a pace roughly equivalent to the rate of development, so that adverse impacts of development would be ameliorated as they occur.

Have these ambitious goals been met? Three years after plan adoption, in 2007, the Western Riverside County Regional Conservation Authority (WRCRCA) took stock of progress toward achievement of its land acquisition objectives under the MSHCP. The results offer a glimpse of the challenges ahead: of the 153,000 acres to be acquired, 35,526 acres had been permanently protected, at a total cost (in 2007 dollars) of $282.4 million, or $8,200 an acre. Examining this data closely, however, it becomes apparent that local government has borne most of the land acquisition burden (20,192 acres), and that private developers had made a relatively small contribution of only 657 acres. In reviewing these statistics, it became a matter of considerable concern to WRCRCA and Riverside County that land acquisition costs over the life of the plan would greatly exceed the original estimate. If additional county funds would be needed to complete the plan, they assumed, its benefits would have also to be reassessed and justified, including an analysis of whether infrastructure elements of the integrated project were more readily accomplished when buffered by a habitat conservation plan. To answer these questions of projected costs and anticipated benefits, the WRCRCA commissioned a study by the Rand Corporation.

The Rand study, "Balancing Environment and Development: Costs, Revenues and Benefits of the Western Riverside County Multiple Species Habitat Conservation Plan," was published in late 2008.[124] It is the most exhaustive cost-benefit assessment of an HCP since the adoption of section 10 in 1982, and underscores the difficulty of sustaining a 75-year commitment to habitat and species conservation in the face of ever-changing ecological, economic, and political circumstances. Foremost, the Rand study estimates the cost of completing land acquisition for the MSHCP to be $4.2 billion, a staggering sum by any measure and roughly twice the 2003 estimates. Though only 117,474 acres remain to be acquired, the cost of each acre will be $36,000, or more than four times the average price per acre of habitat acquired prior to 2007. Clearly, early purchases have occurred in remote, less accessible (and therefore less costly) areas within the reserve. Developers who could do so chose not to build within the reserve, thus avoiding the costs of mitigation. Even though housing prices have fallen precipitously in Riverside County since Rand data was compiled, the price of undeveloped land has remained relatively stable. Rand concludes that the least expensive habitat has been acquired first and that future land acquisition costs will rise inexorably.[125]

Rand also addressed the other question of great concern to WRCRCA and Riverside County: can the increased cost of the MSHCP be justified in terms of its contribution to improved infrastructure and mobility within the county? Although planners acknowledge the benefits of habitat protection, they also chose to adopt the MSHCP and its California state-level counterpart, Natural Communities Conservation Planning, in order to facilitate development. "Overall," Rand reported, "the findings on the MSHCP's impact on the permitting process for road transportation projects are encouraging."[126] In other words, reliance on this HCP to meet obligations of federal and state endangered species laws, in lieu of species- and project-specific compliance, had resulted in less cumbersome (and time consuming) permitting processes for highway construction. Costly, protracted lawsuits were avoided as well. In rapidly growing Riverside County, these are important benefits. But they may not extend to other forms of infrastructure development, according to Rand. Stakeholders who responded to a Rand questionnaire reported that, as often as not, permitting for commercial, industrial, and residential development was complicated by the necessity to comply with requirements of the MSHCP. Rand cautions that these reports may be skewed by respondents' unfamiliarity with the relatively new MSHCP. In addition, the procedural benefits are expected to become more pronounced over time, as new development occurs in a more congested environment.[127]

Nonetheless, the projected expense of MSHCP completion has cast doubt on its continued viability. Given the depressed state of government finances at all levels, the prospects for large land acquisition expenditures are uncertain, at best. MSHCP proponents argue that its value to the county in terms of enhanced mobility must be demonstrated anew. If this can be done, and new sources of funding identified, completion of the MSHCP is a reasonable prospect. Remarkably, the strong coalition of environmentalists, planners, government officials, and development interests that opted initially for the MSHCP remain committed to the concept. They argue that the plan must be revised, however, if it is to survive changes in the planning and economic environment that have occurred since MSHCP and RCIP were first proposed in 1999.

In addition to tackling the projected shortfall in revenue for land acquisition, plan proponents have argued for revisions of the plan itself, in order to reflect the realities of a new geopolitical landscape. While they remain committed to large-scale habitat protection, as originally contemplated, proponents question whether Riverside citizens will tax themselves to complete the plan unless there is acknowledgement that other elements of the RCIP—including transportation infrastructure—have failed to keep pace. Unforeseen population growth spilling over from the Los Angeles basin has stressed the existing transportation infrastructure, and additional corridors planned as early as 1999 will not suffice to relieve congestion. Population and traffic densities have grown so abruptly, in fact, that mass transit may now be a viable option in some areas of the county.

And the MSHCP, limited by statute in its consideration of impacts to species and habitat, has failed to engender truly comprehensive environmental planning and permitting.[128] This deficiency is notable with regard to permits for impacts to wetlands and jurisdictional waters of the United States, which, under section 404 of the Clean Water Act, are issued by the U.S. Army Corps of Engineers. Not only must the Corps consult with the FWS pursuant to section 7 of the Endangered Species Act concerning endangered species impacts, even when permittees have already secured an Incidental Take Permit, but the Corp itself has yet to complete a corresponding Special Area Management Plan to expedite the issuance of section 404 permits in western Riverside County. As noted in the Rand study, "When the MSHCP was adopted, it was hoped that a special area management plan (SAMP) would be developed that resulted in an areawide dredge-and-fill permit under CWA, much like the MSHCP does for the incidental take permit required under ESA."[129] Nor was provision made in the MSHCP for the causes and effects of climate change, which are now expected to significantly alter assumptions about the performance of native ecosystems. California has recently enacted SB 375, which seeks to limit emissions of greenhouse gases through development of "sustainable" regional growth plans.[130] Under SB 375, metropolitan regions like Riverside County will be required to demonstrate that transportation and housing plans curtail sprawl while contributing to improved air quality. Little wonder that RCIP proponents are seeking "adaptive management" of a sort, to better integrate multimedia permitting requirements with those of the MSHCP and to bring the plan into closer conformity with the rapidly changing social, environmental, and economic matrix of western Riverside county.

The Role of Mitigation

An important consequence of increased reliance on habitat conservation plans has been the growth in number and sophistication of mitigation strategies. Even prior to the Babbitt-era adoption of the No Surprises policy and the wider acceptance of HCPs, it had become commonplace under section 404 of the Clean Water Act to compensate for impacts to wetlands through on- or off-site replacement of wetlands on a ratio acceptable to the Corps, or to require the restoration or creation of wetlands in cases where comparable biological values could not be attained through replacement.[131] Although environmentalists initially opposed wetlands mitigation because it was thought to facilitate development that might otherwise be thwarted completely, there is general recognition that, when properly applied, off-site mitigation can result in a net gain of wetlands values, both in quantity and quality, over conventional site-specific requirements. Mitigation "banks" were established by environmental entrepreneurs under supervision of resource agencies to protect large areas from which "credits" could later be sold to developers, as needed to mitigate for impacts of a particular project.

In conjunction with its Natural Communities Conservation Planning program (NCCP), which required mitigation of impacts to terrestrial habitat, California sought to encourage the establishment of multiple-species "conservation banks" through promulgation of guidelines in 1995.[132] The FWS issued similar guidance in 2003.[133] California will likely enact explicit authority for use of "advance mitigation" by its infrastructure agencies, in order to secure large areas of qualified habitat that could be "banked" against future needs.

The generally successful experience with mitigation and conservation banks in facilitating implementation of HCPs has given rise to interest in the wide array of "ecosystem services," in addition to wetlands and terrestrial habitat, that might be bought and sold to meet regulatory requirements. The first federal recognition of the market for ecosystem services occurred with enactment of the Food, Conservation, and Energy Act of 2008 (2008 U.S. Farm Bill), which authorized the establishment of an Office of Ecosystem Services and Markets at the U.S. Department of Agriculture.[134]

Although California has sanctioned the establishment of more mitigation and conservation banks than any other state, largely in support of the NCCP program, its experience has not been trouble-free. One large nonprofit conservation bank in San Diego County had accumulated substantial acreage and endowment funds through contributions from developers in discharge of their NCCP mitigation requirements. Owing to a combination of unforeseen circumstances, including inattentive management and a slowdown in the housing market that affected developers' financial contributions, the bank has filed for bankruptcy.[135] Its land and endowment assets will be distributed to cooperating agencies, but, in some instances, without adequate endowments or clear title. There is even the possibility that some mitigation habitat will be "orphaned," possibly thwarting implementation of the mitigation plan, and leaving open to legal challenge the 75-year Incidental Take Permits that were conditioned on satisfactory completion of mitigation requirements. Owing to the perpetual term of conservation easements and the long-term obligations of bank "sponsors," it is obviously essential to assure that adequate resources, including human capital, are committed to the banking enterprise.

Lessons Learned

A legislative stalemate since 1982 has precluded any substantive amendment of the Endangered Species Act, even after its most important provisions have expired and must be reauthorized in appropriations acts from year to year. In periods of conservative influence, environmentalists have balked at the prospect of needed amendments for fear that, once open, the floodgates could not stem a tide of anti-ESA sentiment. When liberals hold sway, conservatives oppose a legislative dialogue that might lead to even more intrusive regulatory provisions.

Thus, the 36-year-old law reflects an outdated understanding of conservation biology that has since been eclipsed by a better understanding of species survival and their interactive relationship with host habitats. Scientists have almost unanimously rejected the reactionary, single-media, single-species approach embodied in the ESA in favor of preventive measures to protect entire ecosystems. Many of the administrative and policy reforms that reflect this understanding, including the Babbitt initiatives, have been force-fitted into a legal framework that was not intended to bear their weight.

Even as some features of the ESA, such as lists of threatened and endangered species, designations of critical habitat, and ever-wider interpretations of the take prohibitions, continue to draw fire, there is a strong consensus in favor of habitat conservation planning.[136] Its emphasis on ecosystem management is preferred by ESA advocates who understand the limitations of the single-species approach, while landowners and their allies are drawn to the certainty of a 50- or 75-year Incidental Take Permit, accompanied by assurances of "no surprises." It would appear, therefore, that modifications of section 10(a) to reflect the lessons of experience since 1982 would attract support from both camps. A bill that is focused on improvements to the HCP process, rather than a comprehensive rewrite of the Endangered Species Act, might elude the stalemate generated by partisan consideration of its more controversial provisions.

The experience in Riverside County with implementation of its MSHCP suggests the need to augment statutory authority in at least five important particulars:

- Development of a reliable federal financing mechanism that would enable sponsors of "mature" plans, like WRCRCA, to complete land acquisition while prices are relatively low. Proponents of the Riverside plan suggest that a federal revolving fund could provide loans for HCP land acquisition, to be repaid over time by proceeds from local sources, including taxes and exactions. Local governments would be willing to commit prospective revenue, they suggest, if the benefits of long-range comprehensive planning—including transportation infrastructure—are evident to taxpayers.
- A related improvement, also related to efficient completion of "expanded" HCPs, would authorize integration of ESA permitting requirements with other federal and state environmental mandates. These include section 404 permits issued by the Corps of Engineers for dredge-and-fill activity in waters of the United States, and permits related to air quality that might arise from planning for land uses, including transportation infrastructure.
- State requirements could also be integrated and addressed at the same time, as in the case of California's newly enacted control of land use-related greenhouse gas emissions (SB 375) and its own Endangered Species Act.[137] Consideration

should also be given to consolidation of overlapping state and federal requirements, and to delegation of authority for implementation of HCPs where states can demonstrate the requisite capacity.
- While protecting the longevity and procedural certainty of HCPs and ITPs, provision must be made for "adaptive management" in the broadest sense, to provide allowance for the unforeseen consequences of global phenomena like climate change.
- Finally, the Congress should lend its imprimatur to the Babbitt reforms, to make them irrevocable. As noted, they are essential to the success of HCPs as a tool for ecosystem management, but remain subject to challenge so long as they are not codified. Although assurances of "no surprises," safe harbors for cooperating landowners, and the inclusion of candidate species have thus far withstood the legal challenges of detractors, their continued use as potent landowner incentives should not be left to chance.

Conclusion

Practitioners and policy makers alike have reason to respect the habitat conservation plan and its sibling, the incidental take permit. For practitioners, the HCP is a device by which landowners can proceed with reasonable certainty to make uses of their domain that might otherwise be proscribed by the strictures of section 9. For policy makers, the habitat planning process represents—quite simply—a mechanism to balance conservation against the demands of development. It may not be an overstatement to suggest that without this mechanism, the notion of federally protected species survival might not have endured beyond its first decade.

Remarkably, the evolution of habitat conservation planning under section 10 has ameliorated a fundamental deficiency of the Endangered Species Act, to wit, its narrow focus on single species in peril. Through administrative action and judicial intervention, but without further legislative refinement, section 10 has been shaped to keep pace with the edict of conservation biology that we proactively protect and manage wildlife habitat, rather than—after the fact—to recover/conserve threatened species. As the understanding of ecosystem function has grown, so too has the use of habitat conservation planning expanded to embrace multiple species and large landscapes. Though more by default than design, the HCP and, more recently, the MSHCP, have become the most widely used incentives for stewardship of biodiversity on private land. No other provision of environmental law has so markedly influenced land use in the United States.

Habitat conservation planning is not a complete success, as we learn from the experience of western Riverside County. Just as it has evolved in practice since 1982, there remains the need for continuing flexibility in the face of evolving local and regional demands. The Western Riverside MSHCP, though only 10 years old, failed to anticipate many of the issues that today bedevil planners and administrators in rapidly growing communities: even this most ambitious of HCPs has failed to account for climate change, escalating land acquisition costs, redundant permitting requirements, and demands for 21st-century infrastructure, including mass transit. Continued political support for implementation of a 75-year plan may well be dependent on taxpayers' appreciation of its long-term benefits, and a means by which to perform "adaptive management" in the broadest sense. Some may disagree with the assumption that HCPs can be made to serve an even broader planning purpose as communities search for tools that might facilitate growth management. In Riverside County, at least, there is a strong continuing commitment to the principles of its far-sighted MSHCP, even as political leadership seeks additional funding and opportunity for adjustment to much-changed circumstances.

Given the very small likelihood that the Congress will soon adopt a more comprehensive update of the Endangered Species Act, proposals for reform of the HCP/ITP provisions might well engender broad support. Practitioners and landowners can be expected to share and to recommend refinement of an experience that has been largely successful in protecting habitat on private land while accommodating development; policy makers and scientists will likely welcome an opportunity to affirm the emergence of ecosystem management as the guiding principle of HCPs, if not for the ESA itself.

Notes

1. 16 U.S.C. §§ 1531 *et seq.*
2. Pub. L. No. 93-205 § 2(b), 87 Stat. 884 (1973) (codified at 16 U.S.C. § 1531(b) (1994)).
3. In the ESA, "the terms 'conserve,' 'conserving,' and 'conservation' mean to use and the use of all methods and procedures which are necessary to bring any endangered species or threatened species to the point at which the measures provided pursuant to this act are no longer necessary." *Id*. § 3(2) (codified at 16 U.S.C. § 1532(2) (1994)).
4. 16 U.S.C. § 1533(a)(1), (a)(3); 16 U.S.C. § 1536(a)(2).
5. 16 U.S.C. § 1536(a)(1)(B).
6. *Id*. § 1532(19).
7. 40 Fed. Reg. 44,412, 44,416 (Sept. 26, 1975).
8. 437 U.S. 153 (1978).
9. Palila v. Haw. Dep't of Land & Natural Res., 471 F. Supp. 985 (D. Haw. 1979), *aff'd*, 639 F.2d 495 (9th Cir. 1981).
10. Civil and criminal penalties for ESA violations are found in 16 U.S.C. § 1540.
11. Friends of Endangered Species v. Jantzen, 760 F.2d 976, 979–80 (9th Cir. 1985).
12. *Id*. at 980.
13. *Id*.
14. 16 U.S.C. § 1539(a)(1)(B).
15. H.R. CONF. REP. NO. 97-835, *reprinted in* 1982 U.S.C.C.A.N. (Sept. 17, 1982); *see also* H.R. REP. NO. 97-567, *reprinted in* 1982 U.S.C.C.A.N. 2807 (May 17, 1982).
16. H.R. CONF. REP. NO. 97-835, *reprinted in* 1982 U.S.C.C.A.N. (Sept. 17, 1982).
17. 16 U.S.C. § 1539(a)(2)(A).
18. *Id*. § 1536(a)(2).
19. *Id*.
20. *Id*. § 1539 (a)(2)(B).
21. In 1981 the FWS promulgated a rule limiting the definition of a "take" to "actual" harm caused to a species. Thus, not all habitat modifications qualify as "takes," but only those that disrupt essential behavioral patterns or cause a significant decline in species

population. Despite agreeing with the FWS that a "take" has limits, the U.S. District Court for Hawaii in what is known as the *Palila II* litigation held more expansively that a habitat modification that prevents the recovery of a species may also constitute a "take." *See* 46 Fed. Reg. 54,748 (1981) (codified at 50 C.F.R. 17.3); Palila v. Haw. Dep't of Land and Natural Res., 649 F. Supp. 1070 (D. Haw. 1986), *aff'd*, 852 F.2d 1106 (9th Cir. 1988).

22. U.S. DEP'T OF INTERIOR, FISH & WILDLIFE SERV., & U.S. DEP'T OF COMMERCE, NAT'L OCEANIC & ATMOSPHERIC ADMIN., NAT'L MARINE FISHERIES SERV., HABITAT CONSERVATION PLANNING AND INCIDENTAL TAKE PERMIT PROCESSING HANDBOOK, at i, (Nov. 4, 1996), *available at* http://www.fws.gov/endangered/hcp/hcpbook.html (last visited June 10, 2009) [hereinafter HCP HANDBOOK].
23. These figures were calculated using data from U.S. Fish & Wildlife Serv., Conservation Plans and Agreements Database, http://ecos.fws.gov/conserv_plans/public.jsp (last visited June 10, 2009).
24. D. S. WILCOVE ET AL., REBUILDING THE ARK: TOWARD A MORE EFFECTIVE ENDANGERED SPECIES ACT FOR PRIVATE LAND 2 (1996).
25. Chapter 10 contains a thorough discussion of safe harbor agreements, Candidate Conservation Agreements, Candidate Conservation Agreements with Assurances, and conservation banking. These topics will not be discussed in detail in this chapter.
26. 59 Fed. Reg. 65,782 (Dec. 21, 1994). The "No Surprises" Final Rule was issued 63 Fed. Reg. 8859, 8860 (Feb. 23, 1998) (codified at 50 C.F.R. § 17.32).
27. 61 Fed Reg. 63,854 (Nov. 22, 1996). *See* HCP HANDBOOK, *supra* note 22.
28. 65 Fed. Reg. 35,242 (June 1, 2000).
29. *See* Conservation Plans and Agreements Database, *supra* note 23.
30. *Id.*
31. *Id.*
32. *See* H.R. CONF. REP. NO. 97-835, *reprinted in* 1982 U.S.C.C.A.N. (Sept. 17, 1982) ("Although the conservation plan is keyed to the permit provisions of the Act which only apply to listed species, the Committee intends that conservation plans may address both listed and unlisted species.").
33. *See* Conservation Plans and Agreements Database, *supra* note 23.
34. *Id.*
35. *See, e.g.*, Barton H. Thompson Jr., *Managing the Working Landscape*, *in* 1 THE ENDANGERED SPECIES ACT AT THIRTY: RENEWING THE CONSERVATION PROMISE 107 (Dale Goble, J. Michael Scott, & Frank Davis eds., 2006).
36. *See* Conservation Plans and Agreements Database, *supra* note 23.
37. 63 Fed. Reg. 8859, 8863 (Feb. 23, 1998) (codified at 50 C.F.R. §§ 17.22(b)(8), 17.32(b)(8)).
38. HCP HANDBOOK, *supra* note 22, at 3-29.
39. 63 Fed. Reg. 8859 (Feb. 23, 1998).
40. Spirit of the Sage Council v. Norton, 294 F. Supp. 2d 67, 80 (D.D.C. 2003).
41. 64 Fed. Reg. 32,706, 32,709 (June 17, 1999).
42. *Id.*
43. 50 C.F.R. § 13.28(a)(5) (emphasis added).
44. 64 Fed. Reg. 32,706, 32,712, 32,714 (June 17, 1999) (emphasis added); 16 U.S.C. § 1539(a)(2)(B)(iv).
45. 5 U.S.C. § 553.
46. *Spirit of the Sage Council*, 294 F. Supp. 2d at 85, 90.
47. *Id.* at 91.
48. 69 Fed. Reg. 71,723, 71,724 (Dec. 10, 2004).
49. 69 Fed. Reg. 29,669 (May 25, 2004); 69 Fed. Reg. 29,681 (May 25, 2004).
50. 69 Fed. Reg. 71,723 (Dec. 10, 2004).
51. Spirit of the Sage Council v. Kempthorne, 511 F. Supp. 2d 31, 41–43 (D.D.C. 2007).
52. *Id.* at 43.
53. *Id.*
54. *Id.* at 44.

55. *Id.*
56. *See* HCP HANDBOOK, *supra* note 22. Although it is a guidance document, the *Handbook* was made available for public comment in the *Federal Register. See* 59 Fed. Reg. 65,782 (Dec. 21, 1994). The *Handbook* was eventually finalized on November 4, 1996. *See* 61 Fed. Reg. 63,854 (Dec. 2, 1996).
57. HCP HANDBOOK, *supra* note 22, at 3-24.
58. *Id.*
59. *Id.* at 3-25.
60. 65 Fed. Reg. 35,242 (June 1, 2000).
61. The Final Rule for the Addendum to the HCP Handbook (five-point policy) lists examples of the type of scientific uncertainty that may necessitate adaptive management provisions, including "lack of specific information about the ecology of the species or its habitat (*e.g.* food preferences, relative importance of predators, territory size), uncertainty in the effectiveness of habitat or species management techniques, or lack of knowledge on the degree of potential effects on the activity on the species covered in the incidental take permit." *Id.* at 35,252.
62. *Id.* at 35,250–56.
63. *Id.* at 35,252.
64. *Id.* at 35,253.
65. *See* J. B. Ruhl, *Adaptive Management for Natural Resources—Inevitable, Impossible, or Both?* 54 ROCKY MTN. MIN. L. INST. § 11.03(2)(a) (2008) (citing Tucker Pond Habitat Conservation Plan (Aug. 2006), *available at* http://www.fws.gov/ventura/endangered/hconservation/hcp/hcfiles/TuckerPond/TuckerPondHCP_HCP.pdf).
66. *Id.*
67. 65 Fed. Reg. 35,252 (June 1, 2000).
68. *See, e.g.*, Nancy Netherton, *State Agency Forest Plan to Provide Habitat Protection for Aquatic Species*, 37 ENVTL. REP. 1296 (2006) (describing Washington state's 50-year habitat conservation plan for streams and forests, which will protect approximately 70 aquatic species, and which embraces a flexible adaptive management approach).
69. 128 F. Supp. 2d 1274 (E.D. Cal. 2000).
70. *Id.* at 1278–82.
71. *Id.* at 1279.
72. *Id.* at 1281.
73. *Id.* at 1282.
74. *Id.* at 1290.
75. *Id.*
76. *Id.* at 1291, 1299. The same court again upheld the HCP in a subsequent challenge in 2005. Although the court mentioned how the adaptive management procedures in the final HCP allow the permit holders to "respond to monitoring, reviews, or new scientific data," the HCP was not challenged the second time on inadequacy of adaptive management grounds. Nat'l Wildlife Fed'n v. Norton, No. CIV-S-04-0579 DFL JF, 2005 WL 2175874, at *3, *19 (E.D. Cal. Sept. 7, 2005).
77. *See* Ruhl, *supra* note 65, at § 11.05(2).
78. 202 F. Supp. 2d 594, 641 n.54 (W.D. Tex. 2002).
79. For instance, a vegetation survey in the cave habitats would occur every five years and could produce data necessitating an adjustment to the management plan. *Id.* at 613 n.15.
80. 470 F. Supp. 2d 1118, 1144–45 (S.D. Cal. 2006).
81. *Id.*
82. *Id.* at 1146.
83. 506 F. Supp. 2d 322, 356–57 (E.D. Cal. 2007).
84. *Id.* at 352.
85. *Id.*
86. *Id.* at 353, 355.

87. *Id.* at 353.
88. *Id.* at 355 ("Although the *process* must be implemented by holding meetings and making recommendations, nothing requires that any *actions* ever be taken.").
89. No. 1:06-cv-00245-OWW-GS, 2008 WL 2223070, at *61 (E.D. Cal. May 20, 2008).
90. *Id.* at *64.
91. *Id.* The Eastern District of California later confirmed that the Services, not the courts, had discretion to choose and validate appropriate scientific methodologies for adaptive management strategies. *See* Lockyer v. U.S. Dep't of Agric., No. 2:05-cv-0211-MCE-GGH, 2008 WL 3863479, at *17, *27 (E.D. Cal. 2008) (citing Lands Council v. McNair, 2008 WL 264001, at *4). Other cases have tangentially approved of the flexibility of adaptive management provisions in HCPs. In *Hanson v. U.S. Forest Service*, the U.S. District Court for the Western District of Washington denied an injunction to halt logging in the Pacific Northwest forest region, partially on the grounds that the adaptive management provision in an HCP protecting northern spotted owls rendered the HCP sufficiently adaptable to changing environmental circumstances. 138 F. Supp. 2d 1295, 1304 (W.D. Wash. 2001). Similarly, in *In re Scotia Development*, a bankruptcy judge in the U.S. District Court for the Southern District of Texas found that changes made pursuant to adaptive management provisions within a timber company's HCP "have significantly improved HCP implementation, fixed oversights in the HCP, and reduced [timber harvest plan] costs." 375 B.R. 764, 769 (Bankr. S.D. Tex. 2007).
92. 42 U.S.C. §§ 4321 *et seq.* The Council on Environmental Quality (CEQ) regulations implementing NEPA require all federal agencies to analyze the impacts of their proposed actions. *See* 40 C.F.R. §§ 1500–1508.
93. 42 U.S.C. § 4332(2)(C).
94. *See* HCP HANDBOOK, *supra* note 22, at 5-5. An example of a combined HCP/NEPA analysis may be found in Appendix 8 of the *HCP Handbook. See also* CEQ regulation 40 C.F.R. § 1506.4, which specifically permits NEPA documents to be combined with other agency documents.
95. U.S. Fish & Wildlife Serv., Endangered Species Program, http://www.fws.gov/endangered/hcp/hcpplan.html (last visited May 30, 2009).
96. HCP HANDBOOK, *supra* note 22, at 1-6.
97. *Id.* at 5-1.
98. Categorical exclusions to NEPA are defined as "a category of actions which do not individually or cumulatively have a significant effect on the human environment and which have been found to have no such effect in procedures adopted by a Federal agency in implementation of these regulations (§ 1507.3) and for which, therefore, neither an environmental assessment nor and environmental impact statement is required." *See* 40 C.F.R. § 1508.4.
99. HCP HANDBOOK, *supra* note 22, at 5-2.
100. *Id.* at 1-8.
101. *Id.* at 1-9.
102. *Id.*
103. *Id.* at 1-14.
104. 40 C.F.R. § 1508.9.
105. *Id.* § 1508.27.
106. HCP HANDBOOK, *supra* note 22, at 1-6 & 5-4.
107. *Id.* at 5-3.
108. *Id.* at 1-14.
109. NEPA challenges are reviewed under the Administrative Procedure Act. *See* 5 U.S.C. § 553.
110. 146 F. Supp. 2d 1 (D.D.C. 2001).
111. *Id.* at 5. The district court's holdings on ESA challenges from *Gerber v. Babbitt* were appealed and overturned by the D.C. Circuit the following year. The NEPA claim, however, was not appealed. *See* Gerber v. Norton, 294 F.3d 173 (D.C. Cir. 2002).

112. Ctr. for Biological Diversity v. U.S. Fish & Wildlife Serv., 202 F. Supp. 2d 594, 663 (W.D. Tex. 2002).
113. Nat'l Wildlife Fed'n v. Babbitt, 128 F. Supp. 2d 1274 (E.D. Cal. 2000).
114. *Id.* at 1301–2.
115. *Id.*
116. Sierra Club v. Norton, 207 F. Supp. 2d 1310 (S.D. Ala. 2002).
117. Sierra Club v. Norton, No. 02-0258-CG-C, 2007 WL 891153 (S.D. Ala. 2007). On a subsequent challenge to the reissued ITPs, the permits and consequently the projects relying on the permits were again enjoined. Sierra Club v. Kempthorne, Civ. No. 07-216-WS-17, Order and Preliminary Injunction (Doc. No. 88) (S.D. Ala. May 31, 2007).
118. Atl. Green Sea Turtle v. County Council of Volusia County, Fla., No. 604CV1576OR L31KRS, 2005 WL 1227305 (M.D. Fla. 2005).
119. Envtl. Prot. Info. Ctr. v. U.S. Fish & Wildlife Serv., No. C 04-04647 CRB, 2005 WL 3021939, at *7 (N.D. Cal. 2005).
120. Glasser v. Nat'l Marine Fisheries Serv., No. C06-561 BHS, 2008 WL 2811156 (W.D. Wash. 2008).
121. Telephone interview with Dr. Mike Allen, Chair, Ctr. for Conservation Biology, Univ. of California, Riverside (May 28, 2009).
122. *Id.*
123. U.S. Fish & Wildlife Serv., Endangered Species Program, *supra* note 95.
124. Lloyd Dixon et al., Balancing Environment and Development: Costs, Revenues, and Benefits of the Western Riverside County Multiple Species Habitat Conservation Plan (2008).
125. *Id.* at 19–20.
126. *Id.* at xxi.
127. *Id.* at xxii.
128. *Id.* at 135.
129. *Id.*
130. *See* S.B. 375, ch. 728 (Cal. 2008), *available at* http://www.arb.ca.gov/cc/sb375/sb375.htm.
131. *See* 33 U.S.C. § 1344.
132. *See* Cal. Dep't of Fish & Game, Conservation and Mitigation Banking Policies, http://www.dfg.ca.gov/habcon/conplan/mitbank/cmb_genpolicies.html (last visited June 10, 2009).
133. *See* U.S. Fish & Wildlife Serv., Conservation Banking: Incentives for Stewardship, http://www.fws.gov/endangered/factsheets/conservation_banking.pdf (last visited June 10, 2009).
134. Food, Conservation, and Energy Act of 2008, § 2709, Pub. L. No. 110-234, 122 Stat. 923, *available at* http://www.usda.gov/documents/Bill_6124.pdf (last visited June 12, 2009). *See also* U.S. Dep't of Agric., News Release No. 0307.08, USDA Announces New Office of Ecosystem Services and Markets (Dec. 18, 2008).
135. *In re* Envtl. Trust, Inc., No. 05-02321-LA11 (Bankr. S.D. Cal. 2006).
136. *See, e.g.*, Barton H. Thompson, *Managing the Working Landscape*, and A. Dan Tarlock, *The Dynamic Urban Landscape*, *in* 1 The Endangered Species Act at Thirty: Renewing the Conservation Promise (Dale Goble, J. Michael Scott & Frank Davis eds., 2006).
137. Cal. Fish & Game Code §§ 2050 *et seq.* (2008). State implementing regulations for the California ESA are found at Cal. Code Regs. tit. 14, §§ 783–783.8 & 786–786.8.

12

Plants

Holly Wheeler

Introduction

Plants are essential to life on Earth: they fix energy from the sun through photosynthesis; form the beginning of the food chain upon which countless other species, including humans, depend; and categorically comprise the largest amount of biomass on the planet.[1] Yet plants are not usually the species that focus policy makers or the public on issues of biological diversity loss, the question of how to address the global extinction crisis, or debates on the economic costs of protecting species. Most attention focuses on charismatic fish and wildlife species such as gray wolves, Atlantic salmon, and, most recently, polar bears. But even with the majority of plants yet to be assessed, the experts agree that plants are in trouble. In 2008, the International Union for Conservation of Nature (IUCN) ranked 41,875 species of plants worldwide as threatened (critically endangered, endangered, or vulnerable).[2] According to the Center for Plant Conservation, in the United States an estimated one in 10 species of native plants is of conservation concern.[3]

As of December 2008, 749 species of plants had been listed as endangered or threatened under the Endangered Species Act (ESA)—40 percent of all listed species—from well-known species such as orchids and cacti to many lesser-known species such as the Roan Mountain bluet and the autumn buttercup.[4] Nearly all of the endangered and threatened plant listings are for species within the United States; only three of the 749 listings are foreign species.[5] In addition, nearly 29,000 species of plants are regulated under the Convention on International Trade in Endangered Species of Wild Fauna and Flora (CITES),[6] which is implemented in the United States through the ESA.

The Endangered Species Act of 1973 was the first statute in which Congress directly dealt with the problem of conserving endangered plants, although protection for plants in the new comprehensive law to address species extinction was not without controversy. A conference committee reconciled differences between the House and Senate bills on treatment of plants.[7]

In the end, Congress acknowledged the need to include plants in the comprehensive federal law that lays out the United States' role in addressing species loss, finding that plants, along with fish and wildlife, are of "esthetic, ecological, educational, historical, recreational, and scientific value to the Nation and its people."[8] Congress defined "plant" broadly to include any member of the plant kingdom—live or dead—and included any seeds, roots, or other plant parts within the definition.[9]

Congress has refined the role of the ESA in plant conservation over the years through a number of statutory amendments,[10] but the Act remains the primary federal statute to prevent plant extinctions and guide their path to recovery.

The views presented in this chapter represent the personal opinions of the author and do not necessarily represent the position or views of the U.S. Department of the Interior, the Office of the Solicitor, or the United States Government.

Current State of the Law

In a number of areas, Congress determined that measures necessary to realize the statute's purpose of providing a program for the conservation of endangered and threatened species were equally appropriate for plants and animals (i.e., fish and wildlife). In several areas, however, the law takes a different approach to plant conservation. Exploring these areas of similarity and contrast illustrates Congress's approach to plant conservation.

A Unified Approach to Plant and Wildlife Conservation

Any protection under the ESA begins with the process of adding a species to the lists of endangered or threatened species. The standards and procedures for adding plants to the list are identical to that for wildlife. The same standards and procedures also apply to reclassifying or removing a plant from the list; to the immediate listing of a plant where an emergency poses a significant risk to the well-being of the species; and to the listing of a plant due to similarity of appearance with an endangered or threatened species where the close resemblance between the species means that it is substantially difficult to differentiate between them, and this difficulty is a threat to the endangered or threatened species.[11]

Which agency has jurisdiction to determine listing status for any species—the Fish and Wildlife Service (FWS) or the National Marine Fisheries Service (NMFS)—is determined by Reorganization Plan Number 4 of 1970,[12] which, among other things, transferred the Bureau of Commercial Fisheries from the Department of the Interior to the newly established National Oceanic and Atmospheric Administration within the Department of Commerce.[13] A subsequent memorandum of understanding between the FWS and NMFS clarified jurisdiction between the agencies for wildlife but did not address jurisdiction for plants.[14] As of 2008, the FWS had listed 748 plant species while NMFS had listed one plant species.[15]

Once FWS or NMFS lists a plant as endangered or threatened, a recovery plan is developed and implemented unless the agency determines that such a plan would not promote the conservation of the species.[16] The agency designates critical habitat for plant species to the maximum extent prudent.[17] The agency may also establish experimental populations of plants as long as the new population is completely separate geographically from other populations of the same species.[18]

Many of the regulatory effects of listing under the ESA are also the same for plants and wildlife. Section 7(a)(1) directs all federal agencies to use their authorities to further the purposes of the ESA by carrying out programs for the conservation of listed species, with no differentiation between plants and wildlife.[19] Similarly, under section 7 federal agencies must ensure that any agency action is not likely to jeopardize the continued existence of any listed plant species or result in the destruction or adverse modification of its designated critical habitat, and must confer with FWS or NMFS on any agency action that is likely to jeopardize the continued existence of a plant species that is proposed for listing.[20] Federal agencies also must not make any irreversible or irretrievable commitment of resources that would have the effect of foreclosing the development of reasonable and prudent alternatives following initiation of consultation on a plant species.[21]

Section 9 of the ESA lays out the restrictions that apply to endangered species, a number of which apply equally to plants and wildlife, including import into and export from the United States; delivery, receipt, carrying, transport, or shipment in interstate or foreign commerce and in the course of a commercial activity; and sale or offer for sale in interstate or foreign commerce.[22] These activities may be authorized by FWS or NMFS, but only for certain specific purposes (scientific purposes or to enhance the propagation or survival of the species) or due to economic hardship.[23] For plant species designated as threatened, FWS or NMFS determines by regulation what restrictions and authorizations are necessary and advisable to provide for the conservation of the species.[24]

The ESA Diverges: Regulatory Differences Between Plants and Wildlife

Although in many areas of the ESA, Congress applied the same measures to plants and wildlife, in other areas Congress took a separate approach to plant and wildlife conservation.

The first distinction appears in the listing process itself. From the beginning of the Act, Congress gave FWS and NMFS the ability to delineate and manage taxa not only at the species and subspecies level but also at the population level. This allows the agencies to address extinction risk at a finer level and focus regulatory and recovery activities in the specific areas of a species' range where threats present an extinction risk. But listing at the population level can be applied only to vertebrate fish and wildlife,[25] leaving plants, along with invertebrate wildlife, to be managed at the broader systematic levels.[26]

Congress also recognized the Department of Agriculture's role in plant regulation. Although FWS or NMFS determines whether a plant species qualifies as endangered or threatened, works with other federal agencies to ensure their actions will not jeopardize the survival of the species, and enforces the plant prohibitions, Congress added the Department of Agriculture as another agency that has authority to enforce restrictions on import and export of terrestrial plants.[27]

But it is in section 9 of the ESA where Congress took a dramatically different approach to plant conservation—with consequences that reverberate throughout the statute. One of the centerpieces of the ESA is its prohibition against the "taking" of protected wildlife. But there is no prohibition against the taking of a protected plant. Rather, along with the restrictions described above relating to import, export, and the commercial movement of plants, Congress merely made it unlawful for any person subject to the jurisdiction of the United States to "remove or reduce to possession any such species from areas under Federal jurisdiction; maliciously damage or destroy any such species on any such area; or remove, cut, dig up, or damage or destroy any such species on any other area in knowing violation of any law or regulation of any state or in the course of any violation of a state criminal trespass law."[28] The extensive protections that attach to endangered or threatened wildlife through the take prohibition's restrictions against the intentional or unintentional (i.e., "incidental") harming, harassing, wounding, killing, or collecting of a listed individual—or attempting to engage in any such conduct—anywhere within the United States, in the territorial seas of the United States, or on the high seas, do not accrue to plants.

Thus for plants, restrictions are limited to import into and export from the United States; commercial movement in interstate or foreign commerce; violation of any applicable ESA regulation; certain acts on areas under federal jurisdiction;[29] and, similar to the legal framework of the Lacey Act,[30] certain acts in violation of a state's plant conservation laws or conducted in the course of a violation of state trespass law. The limitations of these restrictions in conserving endangered or threatened plants, especially in comparison to the broad prohibition against take for wildlife, are apparent. For the most part, only purposeful acts are restricted. For example, damaging or destroying a plant on federal lands is not unlawful if the damage or destruction is not malicious. Beyond areas under federal jurisdiction, there are no restrictions on killing, damaging, or removing plants or plant parts unless the state's law prohibits the act and the government can prove that the person "knowingly" violated the state law or committed criminal trespass. The prohibition also contains no habitat alteration component similar to that included in the definition of "harm" that applies to wildlife[31] in spite of the fact that habitat destruction and modification is a threat contributing to the risk of extinction for many endangered and threatened plants.

Because the taking of plants is not prohibited, there is no need for a person to seek authorization for any incidental take that may result during the course of conducting other activities.[32] The lack of any prohibition against take of plants also affects the consultation process for federal activities under section 7. As discussed earlier, federal agencies must ensure that any agency action is not likely to jeopardize the continued existence of any listed plant species or result in the destruction or adverse modification of its designated critical habitat. For wildlife, if FWS or NMFS determines that incidental take is reasonably certain to occur, the section 7 consultation process concludes with the issuance of an incidental take statement that specifies the amount of take anticipated, reasonable and prudent measures to minimize the take, and terms and conditions to implement those measures.[33] Because incidental take of plants is not unlawful, however, no incidental take coverage for the agency conducting the action is needed, nor is such coverage available for endangered plants.[34] FWS or NMFS may include cautions informing the agency of the prohibitions that do apply to plants, but also advise the agency that there is no prohibition against the taking of plants.

The lack of a taking prohibition for plants also affects provisions of the ESA addressing the relationship between the federal law and state laws. Thus, the substitute provision in section 6(g)(2), which provides that the prohibition against take for endangered and threatened species does not apply to the taking of any resident species within a state as long as certain requirements are met, applies only to listed wildlife.[35] Likewise, the provision that any state law regarding the taking of an endangered or threatened species may be more restrictive than any federal authorization or exemption, but not less restrictive than the federal taking prohibition, applies only to listed wildlife.[36] The lack of a plant taking prohibition also explains the limitation in section 4(d) applicable only to threatened wildlife whereby any federal restriction on take applies to resident wildlife only if a state with which FWS or NMFS has entered into a section 6 cooperative agreement has adopted the federal restriction.

Finally, there are other provisions that provide disparate treatment of endangered or threatened plants with no obvious connection to conservation need or assessment of threats. For example, a state must show that it has the authority to establish programs, including the acquisition of land or aquatic habitat, for the conservation of resident endangered and threatened wildlife in order to have an adequate and active program under section 6 of the ESA; no such authority is required to have an adequate and active program for plants.[37] Congress also provided an exemption from the standard import/export and regulatory restrictions for wildlife that were held in captivity at the time of the species' listing, provided that the holding and any subsequent holding or use is noncommercial.[38] No similar exemption was provided for plants in cultivation at the time of their listing.

The Role of CITES in Plant Protection

The Endangered Species Conservation Act of 1969,[39] precursor to the current ESA, called for the development of an international agreement for the conservation of endangered species. This direction, along with a 1963 IUCN Resolution, led to development of CITES in Washington, D.C., in 1973; CITES entered into force in 1975.[40] CITES is implemented in the United States through the ESA, which designates the FWS as the CITES Management and Scientific Authorities and makes it unlawful for any person subject to the jurisdiction of the United States to engage in trade in CITES specimens contrary to the provisions of the Convention.[41]

In most instances CITES regulates the import and export of plant and wildlife specimens in the same manner. There are, however, a few areas where the Parties to CITES, like Congress for the ESA, took a different approach to plant conservation. Like the ESA, these differences have generally resulted in lower standards of protection for plants than wildlife. For wildlife species, listing under Appendices I or II of CITES automatically includes any readily recognizable part or derivative of the species; it is only for listings under Appendix III that the listing Party specifies which parts and derivatives will be covered by the listing.[42] For plants, only Appendix I listings automatically include any readily recognizable part or derivative of the species; both Appendix II and Appendix III listings require the Parties to specify which parts and derivatives will be covered, thus allowing international trade in remaining parts or products to continue with no CITES controls.[43]

Emerging Issues and Future Directions

The recent direction of plant conservation efforts reflects the traditional tension between conservation and resource use: recognition of the importance of protecting plants from extinction and maintaining their key role in natural ecosystems while at the same time reluctance to regulate what are often commercially valuable commodities produced from species that have not traditionally had strong advocacy groups.

Much of the recent discussion on plant species conservation has involved regulation of commercial timber species and has taken place in the CITES arena. Recent proposals to list commercially valuable timber species under CITES have generated lively discussions during the biennial Conferences of the Parties. The Parties to CITES agreed to add bigleaf mahogany throughout its range of Central and South America to Appendix II in 2002.[44] Ramin, a timber species from Asia used for furniture production, was listed throughout its range under Appendix II in 2004.[45] A number of *Taxus* species, a tree from which cancer-treatment drugs are produced, were also listed under Appendix II in 2004.[46] At the most recent CITES Conference of the Parties in 2007, pernambuco or Brazil wood, a species valued for its high-quality wood for bows for musical instruments, was listed under Appendix II, although proposals to list three species of Central and South American rosewoods were rejected by the Parties.[47] Also in 2007, the CITES Strategic Plan Working Group presented its draft 2008–2013 Strategic Vision, which specifically called for CITES Parties to give greater attention to international trade in timber species.[48] The United States announced its commitment to global conservation of timber species in 2003 with the President's Initiative Against Illegal Logging, under which the United States assists developing countries in their efforts to combat illegal timber harvest.

Recent case law reflects this new attention on the conservation of timber species. In 2002, the U.S. government detained a number of shipments of bigleaf mahogany lumber and veneer from Brazil after information received from the Brazilian CITES Management Authority indicated that legal-acquisition findings had not been made prior to issuance of the export permits. Brazil had imposed a moratorium on harvest and export of bigleaf mahogany in 2001 and issued the CITES export permits only after a Brazilian court ordered the Brazilian Management Authority to do so. In spite of the Brazilian court orders, a series of communications between the Brazilian and United States Management Authorities established that the Brazilian Management Authority could not make legal acquisition findings for the detained shipments as required under CITES.[49] A number of U.S. timber importers sued the government, seeking to compel immediate clearance of the shipments and alleging that the U.S. government had no authority to detain the shipments when the importers had presented facially valid export permits issued by the Brazilian Management Authority.

The court held that the government's actions were "in all respects authorized by treaty, statute, and regulation."[50] Looking to the text of CITES, resolutions by the

CITES Parties, the seizure and forfeiture provisions of the ESA, and the Department of Agriculture's ESA enforcement regulations, the court agreed with the government's position that it has the authority not to accept CITES export permits from other countries at face value when there is reason to doubt their validity. The court of appeals affirmed the judgment, finding that the U.S. government had a reasonable basis for detaining the mahogany shipments until legal acquisition findings had been confirmed.[51]

Two years later, a United States environmental group and two Peruvian groups representing the interests of indigenous people sued the United States government to halt the importation of bigleaf mahogany timber from Peru. The plaintiffs alleged that the Peruvian government had issued, and the United States government was accepting, CITES export permits that were not supported by legitimate nondetriment and legal acquisition findings. The court denied the plaintiffs' motion for a preliminary injunction and granted the government's motion to dismiss, finding that it lacked subject matter jurisdiction.[52] Fewer than two months later, the Parties to CITES adopted an Action Plan for the Control of International Trade in Bigleaf Mahogany at their 14th Conference of the Parties, which called upon both range countries and importing countries to take specific conservation actions for the benefit of the species.[53]

Throughout this period, the CITES Parties have worked to ensure that timber species are not threatened due to their commercial value in trade. The Parties have encouraged range countries to "pay particular attention to internationally traded timber species within their territories for which the knowledge of the biological status and silvicultural requirements gives cause for concern" and have encouraged exporting countries to establish voluntary annual export quotas for Appendix II timber species.[54] But other provisions have lessened protections for timber species. The CITES resolution on implementation of the Convention for timber species also includes a provision that any timber from trees grown in monospecific plantations should be considered artificially propagated,[55] without the standard requirements to minimize or eliminate augmentation with plants taken from the wild.[56] The provision was later amended to also include nontimber products.[57] This same resolution also recommends that Parties consider "any possible deleterious conservation *and trade impacts* before they impose stricter domestic measures on trade in timber specimens of species included in Appendix II or III."[58]

Since 1994, the Parties to CITES have also taken a number of steps to strengthen the general plant conservation measures. The Parties defined "artificially propagated" and adopted other definitions to provide consistent interpretation of the term.[59] They clarified that plants grown from cuttings or divisions should be considered artificially propagated only if the specimens do not contain any material collected from the wild and that grafted plants be recognized as artificially propagated only if both the rootstock and the graft were taken from plants that qualify as artificially propagated.[60] The Parties have also encouraged stricter enforcement of the Convention for plants and recommended that each Party ensure that environmental modification within that country will not threaten the survival of any CITES plant species.[61] At the same time, the Parties have cut back protection for plants by providing that plants grown from wild-collected seeds or spores can be considered "artificially propagated" as long as certain conditions are met.[62] No similar exception has been made for wildlife specimens.[63] Of most concern is the Parties' vote to exempt from any CITES controls artificially propagated Appendix I orchids that are obtained in vitro in solid or liquid media and transported in sterile containers (the "flasked seedling" exemption),[64] contrary to the fundamental terms of the Convention for plants.[65]

Most, although not all, of these exemptions have focused on artificially propagated plants, which if appropriately regulated should not pose a threat to wild populations and may provide a conservation benefit by reducing pressure on wild populations. A similar provision applies to threatened plants under the ESA under the jurisdiction of the FWS: seeds of cultivated specimens are exempt from the standard prohibitions as long as a statement that the seeds are of "cultivated origin" accompanies the seeds or their container during the course of any activity otherwise subject to regulation.[66] No similar broad exemption has been provided for threatened wildlife species bred in captivity. Such exceptions for at-risk plants will achieve the goal of protecting the species in the wild while satisfying human demand only if they are adequately enforced and any removal from the wild to create or augment the parental stock is carefully regulated. It therefore must be asked whether lower protective standards and recent relaxations reflect a lack of commitment to plant conservation and a slide toward sacrificing protections that ensure species survival in favor of the economic gain from commercially valuable species.

Conclusion

Through the ESA, Congress recognized that both wildlife and plant species have already been lost due to economic growth and development and that other species are so depleted as to be threatened with extinction.[67] The statute provides a program to slow species' slide toward extinction and to coordinate efforts to manage threats and promote recovery. The ESA has accomplished its goals for many listed species. By late 2008, 20 species of plants and wildlife had recovered and been removed from the lists of endangered and threatened species, three of which were plants.[68] As of 2006 (the last date for which general statistics are available), 33 percent of listed wildlife and plants were reported as stable and 8 percent were reported as improving.[69] Only nine species have been removed from the lists due to extinction, none of which was a plant.[70] Another one percent of wildlife and plant species listed as endangered or threatened are believed to be extinct, although some of these species may have already been extinct at the time that they were added to the lists.[71] Without the protections of the ESA, it is unlikely that 41 percent of endangered and threatened species would be stable or improving, and more listed species would be at imminent risk of extinction or already gone.

Nonetheless, as of 2006, 34 percent of species protected under the Act were reported to be declining, and the status of 23 percent of listed species was reported as uncertain.[72] Thus, in spite of the Act's success in preventing extinctions, more could be done to improve the status of endangered and threatened plants, prevent future extinctions, and move more species toward recovery, particularly for species within the United States. Exceptions from conservation protections should be granted only when the best available data show that easing a restriction will not present a threat to the species and governments are able to adequately enforce laws that manage the threats that create the risk of extinction. Perhaps it is also time for stronger protections for plants under the ESA, in line with the prohibitions for wildlife.

A prohibition against the taking of endangered or threatened plants within the United States or the territorial seas of the United States or upon the high seas would dramatically increase protection for listed plants and would align conservation measures for plants with existing measures for wildlife. Any such restriction should address all take, as the majority of current impacts on listed plants is likely unintended and occurs during the course of conducting otherwise lawful activities. The prohibition should include a habitat component similar to the harm definition for wildlife.

Replacing the current limited restrictions on removal, damage, and destruction under section 9 with a full taking prohibition would reduce the disparities between protections for plants and wildlife. Current restrictions limited to federal lands or acts in violation of state laws would be replaced with a general restriction against any taking of a listed plant, regardless of where the act occurred and with no requirement to prove an underlying violation of law or malicious intent. A taking prohibition would also strengthen protections for plants by making other sections of the Act currently applicable only to wildlife applicable to plants. For example, the full strength of section 7 protections would apply, including the requirement for FWS or NMFS to provide reasonable and prudent measures to minimize any take that is likely to occur from a proposed federal action. Because taking of plants on private land would be prohibited, landowners would be encouraged to develop habitat conservation plans and participate in other programs that reduce threats and promote the recovery of listed species.

A taking prohibition applicable to plants would represent a new direction in plant conservation. There is a perception that because most plants are attached to the land, such a conservation measure would place an unfair burden on private landowners.[73] But many wildlife species have extremely restricted home ranges, as a result of which they are effectively limited to particular parcels of land. In addition, life history needs such as nesting or denning habitat, mating grounds, and specialized feeding areas limit many other wildlife species to particular habitat areas during at least certain portions of their lives. The FWS has developed a number of programs for landowners, including various types of agreements and grants, that help reduce the economic impact of a listing while accommodating the species' habitat needs.[74] These programs would likewise be appropriate for plant conservation.

A taking prohibition applicable to plants would also represent a new direction in conservation law. Natural vegetation, such as trees, shrubs, and grasses, produced by the powers of nature alone and rooted in the soil is *fructus naturales*.[75] At common law, unlike wildlife that is not owned by the person on whose land it occurs,[76] such vegetation is regarded as part of the land as long as it is unsevered from the soil, with ownership following ownership of the land.[77] Nonetheless, early versions of the ESA included plants in the general takings prohibition, indicating that such a prohibition may be appropriate.[78] Although some have raised concerns regarding constitutional takings claims,[79] there is precedent for the appropriateness of governmental regulation of activities with plants on private land. State and local laws and ordinances that restrict the removal of trees on private land have been upheld in a number of jurisdictions against constitutional takings, vagueness, and due process claims.[80]

If a national takings prohibition is not feasible, a logical first step would be to enact a takings prohibition for plant species on areas under direct federal or state jurisdiction. Such a prohibition would be consistent with federal agencies' existing responsibilities under section 7(a)(1) of the ESA and the co-management provisions with states under section 6 of the Act. Such a measure also would be consistent with traditional legal principles.[81] As an intermediate step in plant conservation, such a measure would increase protection for those species that occur primarily on areas under federal or state jurisdiction, without affecting private landowners.

In the end, it is up to the people of the United States to determine whether and how to protect the plants that have made life, as we know it, possible. The ESA has been a positive first step, with mixed results. With many plant species still at risk of extinction and with new environmental threats on the horizon such as global climate change and competition from nonnative invasive species, it is time to consider whether current measures are adequate for the coming decades.

Notes

1. *See* EDWARD O. WILSON, THE DIVERSITY OF LIFE 35–37 (W.W. Norton & Co. 1992).
2. International Union for Conservation of Nature, Red List of Threatened Species, Summary Statistics for Globally Threatened Species, http://www.iucnredlist.org/info/stats (last visited Dec. 23, 2008); 1997 IUCN Red List of Threatened Plants (Kerry S. Walter & Harriett J. Gillett eds., 1998).
3. *See* Ctr. for Plant Conservation, Frequently Asked Questions, http://www.centerforplantconservation.org (last visited Dec. 23, 2008).
4. *See* U.S. Fish & Wildlife Serv., Summary of Listed Species, http://ecos.fws.gov/tess_public/Boxscore.do (last visited Dec. 23, 2008); 50 C.F.R. § 17.12 (2007).
5. *Id.*
6. *See* Convention on International Trade in Endangered Species of Wild Fauna and Flora [hereinafter CITES], CITES Species, http://www.cites.org/eng/disc/species.shtml (last visited Dec. 23, 2008).
7. H.R. CONF. REP. NO. 93-740 (1973).
8. 16 U.S.C. § 1531(a)(3) (2000).
9. *Id.* § 1532(14).
10. *See* Vincent L. DeWitte, *Plants, in* ENDANGERED SPECIES ACT: LAW, POLICY, AND PERSPECTIVES 401–14 (Donald C. Baur & Wm. Robert Irvin eds., 2002).

11. *See* 16 U.S.C. § 1533(a), (b), (c), (e). As of December 2008, neither FWS nor NMFS had listed a plant due to its similarity of appearance with an endangered or threatened plant.
12. *See id.* § 1533(a)(2).
13. Reorg. Plan No. 4 of 1970, 35 Fed. Reg. 15,627–30, *reprinted in* 5 U.S.C. app. at 189–91 (2000).
14. Memorandum of Understanding Between the U.S. Fish & Wildlife Serv., U.S. Dep't of the Interior, and the Nat'l Marine Fisheries Serv., Nat'l Oceanic & Atmospheric Admin., U.S. Dep't of Commerce, Regarding Jurisdictional Responsibilities & Listing Procedures Under the Endangered Species Act (Aug. 28, 1974) (on file with author).
15. *See* 50 C.F.R. § 223.102(e) (2007) (noting listing of Johnson's seagrass by NMFS).
16. 16 U.S.C. § 1533(f).
17. *Id*. § 1533(a)(3), (b)(6)(C)(ii).
18. *Id*. § 1539(j).
19. *Id*. § 1536(a)(1).
20. *Id*. § 1536(a)(2), (a)(4).
21. *Id*. § 1536(d).
22. *Compare id.* § 1538(a)(1) *with* § 1538(a)(2).
23. *Id*. § 1539(a)(1)(A), (b). An exemption for economic hardship is available only within one year of the first notice in the *Federal Register* that the species is under consideration for listing as an endangered or threatened species. *Id*. § 1539(b)(1)(A).
24. *Id*. § 1533(d). Using this authority, FWS has developed general regulations that apply to all threatened plants, 50 C.F.R. §§ 17.71, 17.72 (2007), although it could also develop special rules specifically tailored to the conservation needs of a plant species as it has for some threatened wildlife species, *see id.* §§ 17.40–17.46.
25. *See* 16 U.S.C. § 1532(16) (definition of "species" includes "any distinct population segment of any species of vertebrate fish or wildlife which interbreeds when mature").
26. The ability, however, to list a species in one or more significant portions of its range applies to both plants and wildlife. *See id.* § 1532(6), (20) (definitions of "endangered species" and "threatened species").
27. *See id.* § 1532(15) (definition of "Secretary"); *see also* 7 C.F.R. pt. 355 (2008) (USDA regulations for import and export of terrestrial plants).
28. 16 U.S.C. § 1538(a)(2)(B).
29. In *Northern California River Watch v. Wilcox*, the court found that while the term "areas under federal jurisdiction" does not necessarily mean "owned by the federal government," it does not apply to private property that is merely subject to federal regulation. 547 F. Supp. 2d 1071, 1076 (N.D. Cal. 2008).
30. 16 U.S.C. §§ 3371–3378.
31. *See* 50 C.F.R. § 17.3 (2007) (definition of "harm").
32. *See* 16 U.S.C. § 1539(a)(1)(B) (referencing only prohibition against taking of fish and wildlife in providing for incidental take authorization); *see, e.g.*, 50 C.F.R. § 17.62 (2007) (authorizing otherwise prohibited acts for scientific purposes or enhancement of propagation or survival only).
33. *See* 16 U.S.C. § 1536(b)(4).
34. *Id*. § 1536(o).
35. *Id*. § 1535(g)(2).
36. *Id*. § 1535(f).
37. *Compare id.* § 1535(c)(1) *with* § 1535(c)(2).
38. *Id*. § 1538(b)(1).
39. Pub. L. 91-135, 83 Stat. 275 (1969).
40. Convention on International Trade in Endangered Species of Wild Fauna and Flora, Mar. 3, 1973, 27 U.S.T. 1087.
41. 16 U.S.C. §§ 1537a(a)–(c), 1538(c).
42. *See* CITES, art. I, para. (b)(ii) (definition of "species").
43. *See id.* art. I, para. (b)(iii).

44. Prop. 50, CITES Conference of the Parties 12 (2002), *available at* http://www.cites.org [hereinafter CoP]. The Parties had rejected earlier proposals at prior Conferences of the Parties following intense debate.
45. Prop. 50, CITES CoP 13 (2004).
46. Props. 47, 48, CITES CoP 13 (2004).
47. Props. 30, 31, 32, CITES CoP 14 (2007).
48. Doc. 11, CITES CoP 14, at 5 (2007). Following extensive work during the Conference of the Parties by a working group, a more spare final strategic vision was adopted, which dropped the specific reference to timber species.
49. When the Brazilian Management Authority was able to confirm that the timber in a particular shipment had been legally acquired, the Department of Agriculture cleared the shipment for import into the United States.
50. Castlewood Prod. v. Norton, 264 F. Supp. 2d 9 (D.D.C. 2003).
51. Castlewood Prod. v. Norton, 365 F.3d 1076 (D.C. Cir. 2004).
52. Native Fed'n of the Madre De Dios River & Tributaries v. Bozovich Timber Prod., Inc., 491 F. Supp. 2d 1174 (Ct. Int'l Trade 2007).
53. Dec. 14.145 & Annex 3, CITES CoP 14 (2007).
54. Res. Conf. 10.13 (Rev. CoP14), CITES CoP 10 (1997).
55. *Id.*
56. Res. Conf. 11.11 (Rev. CoP 14), CITES CoP 11 (2000).
57. Res. Conf. 10.13 (Rev. CoP 14).
58. *Id.* (emphasis added).
59. Res. Conf. 11.11 (Rev. CoP14).
60. *Id.*
61. *Id.*
62. *Id.*
63. The rearing in a controlled environment of wildlife specimens taken from the wild (i.e., "ranching") may be allowed under limited circumstances, but only with approval of the Parties. Res. Conf. 11.16 (Rev. CoP 14), CITES CoP 11 (2000).
64. Res. Conf. 11.11 (Rev. CoP 14).
65. CITES, art. I, para. (b)(iii).
66. 50 C.F.R. § 17.71(a) (2007).
67. 16 U.S.C. § 1531(a)(1), (2).
68. *See* U.S. Fish & Wildlife Serv., Report of Delisted Species, http://ecos.fws.gov/tess_public/DelistingReport.do (last visited Dec. 24, 2008).
69. U.S. Fish & Wildlife Serv., Recovering Threatened and Endangered Species: Fiscal Years 2005–2006, 27 (Apr. 2008), *available at* http://www.fws.gov/endangered/recovery (narrative summary for report to Congress).
70. *See* Report of Delisted Species, *supra* note 68.
71. Recovering Threatened and Endangered Species, *supra* note 69, at 27.
72. *Id.*
73. Many aquatic (freshwater or marine) plant species occur in areas under federal or state jurisdiction due to state ownership of the beds of navigable waterbodies and submerged lands. Many terrestrial plants in the United States, particularly those of the continental West, may also occur primarily on land in federal or state ownership.
74. *See* U.S. Fish & Wildlife Serv., Tools for State and Private Landowners, http://www.fws.gov/endangered/landowner (last visited Dec. 26, 2008).
75. BLACK'S LAW DICTIONARY 669 (6th ed. 1990); Kiehl v. Holliday, 251 P. 527, 528 (Mont. 1926).
76. Pierson v. Post, 3 Cai. R. 175, 177 (N.Y. Sup. Ct. 1805).
77. Triggs v. Kahn, 563 N.Y.S.2d 262, 264 (N.Y. App. Div. 1990); Childers v. Wm. H. Coleman Co., 118 S.W. 1018, 1021 (Tenn. 1909).
78. Endangered Species Conservation Act of 1972, H.R. 13081, 92d Cong. § 7(a) (1972) (committee staff print).

79. U.S. Const. amend. V.
80. *See* Greater Atlanta Homebuilders Ass'n v. DeKalb, 588 S.E.2d 694 (Ga. 2003); Webster v. Town of Candia, 778 A.2d 402 (N.H. 2001); Jensen v. City of Everett, No. 47077-9-1, 2001 Wash. App. LEXIS 2749 (Wash. Ct. App. Dec. 17, 2001).
81. *See* Kleppe v. New Mexico, 426 U.S. 529 (1976) (federal government has complete power over its own property analogous to police power, including power to regulate and protect wildlife).

13

Citizen Suits

Eric R. Glitzenstein

Introduction

Consistent with the statute's sweeping objectives, the Endangered Species Act (ESA) contains one of the most far-reaching citizen suit provisions that Congress has adopted in an environmental law. Section 11 of the Act provides, in pertinent part, that "any person" may "commence a civil suit" to "enjoin any person, including the United States and any other governmental instrumentality or agency (to the extent permitted by the eleventh amendment of the Constitution), who is alleged to be in violation of any provision of this chapter or regulation under the authority thereof."[1] It further authorizes citizen suits "against the Secretary [and by delegation the Fish and Wildlife Service (FWS) and National Marine Fisheries Service (NMFS)] where there is alleged a failure of the Secretary to perform any act or duty under section 1533 of this title which is not discretionary with the Secretary."[2] In turn, "section 1533 of this title [section 4 of the Act]" imposes obligations on the Secretary to list and designate critical habitat for endangered and threatened species, as well as to prepare and implement recovery plans for listed species.[3]

The statute expressly vests federal district courts with jurisdiction to order the Secretary to "perform any act or duty" arising under section 4, as well as to "enforce" any "provision or regulation" with which "any person" covered by the Act must comply.[4] The only exhaustion requirement is that 60 days' advance notice of a lawsuit must generally be provided to both the Secretary and any other "alleged violator."[5] Venue is in the "judicial district in which the violation occurs,"[6] and the reviewing court "may award costs of litigation (including reasonable attorney and expert witness fees) to any party, whenever the court determines such award is appropriate."[7]

Although these provisions seem relatively straightforward, a number of issues concerning the ability of citizens to pursue claims for violations of the ESA have arisen—and, for the most part, now been largely resolved—in the Supreme Court and lower federal courts. This chapter will not endeavor to address every such issue or every arguably pertinent precedent; rather, it will present an overview of the law as it applies to most of the ESA-related litigation that is brought to enforce the Act's most significant substantive provisions.

Current State of the Law

Standing

As in any lawsuit filed in federal court, plaintiffs in cases arising under the ESA citizen suit provision must satisfy the "irreducible constitutional minimum of standing," which consists of three elements: (1) there must be an "injury in fact" that is "concrete and particularized," (2) "there must be a causal connection between the injury and the conduct complained of," and (3) it must be "likely" as opposed to merely "speculative" that the injury will be redressed by a favorable decision.[8] However, because the citizen suit provision expressly authorizes "any person" to bring suit—an "authorization of remarkable breadth when compared with the language Congress ordinarily uses"—the Supreme Court has held that plaintiffs in such cases need not satisfy any "prudential" test for standing; that is, they need not meet any "zone-of-interests test to bring their claims under the ESA's citizen-suit provision."[9]

Also as in any federal litigation, the "manner and degree of evidence" required to establish standing varies with the particular "stage[] of the litigation."[10] Thus, at the pleading stage—that is, in response to a motion to dismiss—a plaintiff in an ESA case may ordinarily rely on "general factual allegations of injury resulting from the defendant's conduct," although, even at that preliminary stage, it is prudent to detail as much as possible in the complaint how the plaintiff is harmed by the particular ESA violation being alleged.[11] At the summary judgment phase, it is never sufficient for plaintiffs in ESA (or any other) cases to rely on the "'mere allegations'" of injury in their complaints; rather, even if a standing defense is not raised by the agency and/or private defendant in the case, it is the affirmative burden of the plaintiff to proffer, by affidavit or other appropriate evidence, "'specific facts'" supporting the plaintiff's standing as to each of the three elements required for Article III jurisdiction.[12]

In applying the "injury in fact" element in an ESA case, the Supreme Court has declared that "[o]f course, the desire to use or observe an animal species, even for purely esthetic purposes, is undeniably a cognizable interest for purpose of standing."[13] Accordingly, the crucial inquiry in cases involving potential impacts on an animal or plant species in the wild is whether the plaintiff seeking to advance conservation interests can allege (at the motion to dismiss stage) or proffer evidence (at the summary judgment stage) that the plaintiff has a *particularized* interest (whether it be aesthetic, scientific, or recreational) in the species at issue, and whether that interest is being threatened in some concrete "imminent" fashion.[14]

Hence, it is insufficient for a plaintiff to allege that she has *previously* visited a particular area to observe a species, because "'past exposure to illegal conduct does not in itself show a present case or controversy.'"[15] Nor is it adequate for an individual to assert (even in a sworn affidavit or declaration) that she intends to return to the area at some time in the future because "[s]uch 'some day' intentions—without any description of concrete plans, or indeed even any specifications of *when* the some day will be—do not support a finding of [an] 'actual or imminent' injury."[16] Accordingly, plaintiffs in the ordinary ESA case will be on the most solid footing when they can claim to actually live or work in very close proximity to the affected species or habitat[17] *and* they use the "area affected by the challenged activity" on an ongoing or recurrent basis.[18] In contrast, plaintiffs who are far removed from the area in question must be able to point to very tangible plans to visit the area within a specified time frame.

For members of the regulated community, injury in fact may be readily established through well-pled allegations (at the motion to dismiss stage) and sworn declarations (at the summary judgment stage) that an identifiable business or economic interest will likely be adversely affected through an agency's alleged misapplication of the ESA.[19] Indeed, the Supreme Court has declared (in an ESA case) that if the "plaintiff is himself an object" of "government action or inaction," then "there is ordinarily little question that the action or inaction has caused him injury" within the meaning of Article III.[20]

While these general principles govern "injury in fact" assessments in most ESA cases, there are certain cases where other kinds of asserted injuries may come into play. In *Lujan v. Defenders of Wildlife*, the Supreme Court observed that "[i]t is clear that the person who observes or works with a *particular animal* threatened by a federal decision is facing perceptible harm, since the very subject of his interest will no longer exist."[21] Thus, for example, a scientist who has radio-collared a particular animal may assert an injury based on imminent threats to that animal. Similarly, where persons have particularized interests in individual captive animals protected by the ESA, that may also afford a basis for challenging governmental or private actions threatening those particular animals.

In addition, in some contexts, plaintiffs in ESA cases may also assert that they have been injured by being deprived of information that they are statutorily entitled to receive under particular provisions of the ESA. For example, such a claim of "informational injury" was sustained in a case challenging a regulation issued by the FWS authorizing persons to take several listed antelope species without having to apply for individual permits under section 10 of the Act, which affords interested persons the right to obtain documents on which permit applications are based. The plaintiffs claimed that the regulation unlawfully deprived them of the information to which they would be entitled if the section 10 process were followed, and the court agreed that, as in a case arising under the Freedom of Information Act (FOIA) and other statutes requiring the dissemination of particular information to the public, section 10 "creates a right sufficient to support standing."[22]

With regard to the causation and redressability elements of Article III standing, the plaintiff in an ESA who can otherwise demonstrate injury in fact need not show that compliance with a procedure required by the ESA (such as section 7's consultation requirement) will necessarily lead to better protection for the species and/or habitat at issue.[23] It is sufficient for the plaintiff to demonstrate that violation of the statutory requirement "could impair a separate concrete interest" of the plaintiff's, that is, a "concrete" aesthetic, recreational, scientific, or similar interest in a species likely to be affected.[24]

Regardless of whether a case is challenging an agency decision of general effect, such as a regulation or management plan, or a site-specific determination, plaintiffs bear essentially the same burden of demonstrating that a violation of the ESA is likely to contribute to a concrete injury.[25] The Ninth Circuit has specifically held that the number of "steps" in the causal chain before harm to the plaintiff may occur is of little moment so long as it is reasonably foreseeable that the decision of general applicability will cause site-specific harms to the plaintiff's interests.[26] On the other hand, in a National Environmental Policy Act (NEPA) case frequently cited by defendants in ESA cases, the en banc D.C. Circuit held that the larger the number of steps in the causal chain, the more difficult it is to establish causation and redressability in cases challenging rules or other agency decisions of general applicability.[27] Of course, as in any case involving a challenge to a rule or other decision of general application, such challenges must overcome ripeness as well as standing hurdles.

Although claims may be brought directly against the FWS or NMFS for the Services' failure to properly implement section 7 of the Act, it is, at the least, prudent for the plaintiff to join the "action agency" to such suits. In *Lujan v. Defenders of Wildlife*, a four-Justice plurality held that, in a case challenging a Service regulation limiting the consultation requirement to agency actions within the United States and on the high seas, the plaintiff conservation groups lacked standing because they had not initially joined the federal agencies actually carrying out allegedly harmful projects in foreign countries and there was "no reason" that such agencies "should be obliged to honor an incidental legal determination the suit produced"—that is, even if a court had held that the regulation was unlawful because the consultation obligation did apply to agency actions affecting species in foreign countries, such a ruling "would not have been binding upon the agencies."[28]

On the other hand, in *Bennett v. Spear*, the Supreme Court held that when ranch operators and irrigation districts challenged a Biological Opinion issued by the FWS concerning an irrigation project operated by the Bureau of Reclamation, the plaintiffs had standing *without* joining the Bureau to the case because a Biological Opinion has a "powerful coercive effect on the action agency" and "alters the legal regime to which the action agency is subject."[29] Especially in view of the seeming tension between these rulings, plaintiffs in any section 7 case—even one directed at the Service's findings or omissions—would be well advised to join all of the action agencies that may ultimately be responsible for carrying out the action(s) of concern.[30]

Other Jurisdictional Issues

In addition to standing questions, ripeness and mootness issues often arise in ESA cases. Ripeness issues are frequently presented when a plaintiff brings a facial challenge to a Service regulation implementing the ESA or some other agency decision of general applicability.[31] In evaluating whether such a challenge is ripe, courts apply the familiar two-part test that requires the court to "evaluate (1) the fitness of the issues for judicial decision and (2) the hardship to the parties of withholding court consideration."[32]

At least in the D.C. Circuit, facial challenges to rules that present "purely legal" questions are deemed to be presumptively reviewable and, indeed, that court will frequently resolve them with little or no serious consideration of the hardship to the parties of withholding review.[33] In deciding such challenges on the merits, the court considers whether "faithful application" of the rule "would carry the agency beyond its statutory mandate," and the court does not assume that the agency will "exercise its discretion [under the rule] unlawfully."[34]

In contrast, mootness issues generally arise when plaintiffs in ESA cases challenge very specific actions or omissions—such as an agency's failure to consult with regard to a particular project or to comply with the ESA's deadlines in making listing decisions—and the agency defendant takes steps that arguably rectify the violation after the complaint is filed but before a court has resolved the claim.[35] Defendants in such cases bear a "heavy burden" of demonstrating that the case has been completely mooted, and the asserted violation rectified, by intervening actions.[36] Nonetheless, where such claims are based on agency failures to carry out discrete obligations imposed by the Act, courts often find that agencies have managed to moot claims through post-complaint efforts at compliance.[37]

As in all cases where defendants invoke a mootness defense, plaintiffs may attempt to argue that one of the recognized mootness "exceptions" applies: (1) the defendant has voluntarily ceased its allegedly unlawful conduct but could resume it once the case is dismissed[38] or (2) the agency's unlawful conduct is "capable of repetition yet evading review."[39] The latter exception applies where the "duration of the challenged action is too short to allow full litigation before it ceases" and "there is a reasonable expectation that the plaintiffs will be subjected to it again."[40]

In *Biodiversity Legal Foundation v. Badgley*, a case challenging the FWS's practice, in responding to listing petitions, of delaying "substantial information findings" even past the 12-month deadline for making final decisions on such petitions, the Ninth Circuit held that the Service's post-complaint resolution of the particular petitions at issue did not moot the case.[41] Rather, the court held that the "capable of repetition" exception applied because the "Service exhibits a pattern of making listing determinations shortly after suit is commenced," thus affording insufficient time for judicial review,[42] and because the plaintiffs' "litigation history with the Service, in conjunction with the pending petitions it has filed with the Service, reflects that [plaintiffs] have a reasonable expectation that they will again litigate the issue of the extent of the Service's discretion to delay a twelve-month finding."[43] The court held that under these circumstances, it could issue meaningful declaratory relief to the plaintiffs irrespective of whether there were any "live" petitions pending before the court.[44]

ESA versus APA Claims Following *Bennett v. Spear*

In *Bennett v. Spear*, the Supreme Court delineated the scope of the ESA citizen suit provision, while also establishing that certain claims that do *not* fall within that provision may nonetheless be pursued under the Administrative Procedure Act (APA). In *Bennett*, the plaintiffs challenged a Biological Opinion on various grounds, including that it was contrary to the requirement of section 7 of the ESA and that it "implicitly determine[d] critical habitat without complying with" the procedures mandated by section 4 for designating critical habitat.[45] The Court held that the latter claim did fall within the ESA citizen suit provision because section 11(g)(1)(A) of the ESA authorizes claims against the Secretary (and hence the Service) when there is "alleged a failure of the [Service] to perform any act or duty under [section 4] which is not discretionary" with the Service.[46] Of particular importance, the Court reasoned that a claim based on the proposition that the Service had ignored the *process* required by section 4—including that it use the best scientific data available and that it consider economic impacts in designating critical habitat—constituted a nondiscretionary duty claim even if the agency's ultimate decision "is reviewable only for abuse of discretion."[47]

Given the Court's reasoning in *Bennett*, most, if not all, challenges relating to the Services' implementation of their listing and critical habitat duties will be regarded by the courts as ESA, rather than APA, claims, even if the challenge may reasonably be characterized as one seeking review of a discretionary decision. For example, *Association of California Water Agencies v. Evans* involved a claim that NMFS, in using an "incremental effects" approach to evaluating the economic effects of critical habitat designation, had failed to perform a "*proper* economic impact analysis of the effects of designating a critical habitat," as mandated by section 4(b)(2) of the Act.[48] The government, in resisting a claim for attorneys' fees under the ESA citizen suit provision, argued that the Service's action was "discretionary" and hence judicial review could only be sought under the APA.[49] The court, however, held that, "as in *Bennett*[ ], Defendants had the 'categorical *requirement* to take into consideration the economic impact or any other relevant impact' in the designation of critical habitat," and thus the plaintiffs' claim that NMFS's approach failed adequately to do so was cognizable as a claim under the ESA citizen suit provision.[50] Under this reading of *Bennett*, *any* claim that the FWS or NMFS has violated a particular provision of section 4 in the course of making a listing or a critical habitat decision should be classified as an ESA, rather than APA, claim, regardless of whether the argument is that the agency ignored the provision entirely or simply misapplied it.

By the same token, however, even a claim that may appear to implicate section 4 but that does not assert a violation of any specific section of that provision may be pursued only under the APA (and, even then, plaintiffs may have difficulties obtaining judicial review). One example involves the Services' treatment of requests for emergency listing of species. Because there is "no separate process in the ESA or its implementing regulations for requesting an 'emergency listing' as opposed to a non-emergency listing," the D.C. Circuit has held that a plaintiff "had no statutory right to petition the Secretary for an emergency listing under [16 U.S.C.] § 1533(b)(7), and no right to a decision meeting any particular procedural or substantive standards."[51] On a request for rehearing, the court clarified that its ruling did "not resolve whether plaintiffs may seek to have the denial of an emergency listing request reviewed under the Administrative Procedure Act."[52]

With regard to claims that the Service has engaged in the "maladministration" of ESA provisions *other than* those in section 4 (and particularly a claim that the Service has issued a Biological Opinion that does not comport with section 7's requirements), *Bennett* holds that such claims do *not* come within the ambit of the ESA citizen suit provision because the Service's "conduct in implementing or enforcing the ESA is not a 'violation' of the ESA within the meaning of" section 11(g)(1)(A), which authorizes suit against any "'person . . . alleged to be in violation'" of the ESA or implementing regulations.[53] Rather, the Court accepted the government's position that this provision only allows plaintiffs to "enforce the substantive provisions of the ESA against *regulated parties*—both private entities and Government agencies—but is not an alternative avenue for judicial review of the [Services'] implementation of the statute."[54]

At the same time, however, the Court held that the Service's issuance of an unlawful or arbitrary Biological Opinion *may* be challenged under the APA, which "provides a right to judicial review of all 'final agency action[s] for which there is no other adequate remedy in a court.'"[55] The Court reasoned that "[n]othing in the ESA's citizen-suit provision expressly precludes review under the APA," nor is there is anything "in the statutory scheme suggesting a purpose to do so";[56] in addition, Biological Opinions constitute "final agency actions" within the meaning of the APA because the Opinions (and the accompanying incidental take statements) represent the "consummation" of the Service's analysis of a project's impacts on listed species and also "alter the legal regime to which the agency action is subject."[57]

The upshot of *Bennett*, therefore, is that certain violations of the ESA must be pled under the ESA citizen suit provision, and others must be pled under the APA. When the claim is that an agency is taking an action in violation of section 7—either by failing to consult at all or by *relying on* a faulty Biological Opinion (or concurrence in a "not likely to adversely affect" determination) issued by one of the Services—that claim is properly pled under the ESA citizen suit provision. Likewise, a claim that a party—whether a private entity or government agency—is taking a species in violation of section 9 must be pled as an ESA citizen suit. On the other hand, *except for* violations of section 4—that is, the Services' failures to comply with their section 4 duties to list species, designate critical habitats, or prepare or carry out recovery plans—claims against the Services concerning their implementation of the Act *must* be pled as APA claims. Most important, this means that challenges to all decision documents issued by the Services in implementing section 7—that is, Service concurrences in "not likely to adversely affect" determinations by action agencies, along with Biological Opinions themselves—as well as Incidental Take Permits and other permits issued by the Services under section 10 of the Act must be pled and pursued as APA claims.

Although *Bennett* appears to counsel that all claims that a Service has violated its section 4 obligations in the course of making a listing or critical habitat decision (whether a positive or negative decision) should be pled as ESA, rather than APA, claims, in one recent case a court held that a challenge to the FWS's refusal to list a species was properly pled as an APA claim and hence did not have to be preceded by the provision of 60 days' notice to the Secretary.[58] The court reasoned that the Service's listing decision was a "discretionary duty under the ESA," and that "[b]ecause this suit is brought under the APA, to review a discretionary decision of the FWS, *Bennett* dictates that the ESA notice requirement does not apply."[59] Plaintiffs should approach this ruling with caution, especially in view of the legal basis on which the court in that case actually ruled for the conservation group challenging a listing decision. The court held that the FWS had failed to comply with its statutory obligation to use the "'best science'" available in making its listing decision.[60] In *Bennett*, however, the Supreme Court held that a claim that the Service had failed to consider the best available science (in the course of making a decision on critical habitat designation) *did* implicate a nondiscretionary section 4 duty and hence fell within the ESA citizen suit provision.[61] Accordingly, plaintiffs contemplating *any* claims implicating section 4 duties would be well-advised to provide 60 days' advance notice and to plead their claims under the ESA citizen suit provision and, in the alternative, under the APA. This approach also ensures that the plaintiff may avail itself of the more generous attorneys' fees provision that is triggered for ESA claims.

Properly categorizing a particular claim is crucial because substantial legal and practical consequences attach to the classification. As noted, ESA claims *must* generally be preceded by 60 days' advance notice to the Secretary and any alleged violator,[62] whereas there is no exhaustion requirement before an APA claim may be filed.[63] On the other hand, plaintiffs bringing ESA claims need not satisfy any zone-of-interests standing test, whereas plaintiffs bringing APA claims must do so.[64]

Of even greater practical consequence, as *Bennett* makes clear, APA claims (except for those, discussed below, seeking review of "unreasonable" agency delay under 5 U.S.C. § 706(1)) may seek judicial review only of Service decisions constituting "final agency actions," whereas claims brought under the ESA citizen suit provision should not be confined by that limitation. Indeed, in explaining why it was declining to construe the term "violation" in the citizen suit provision to encompass "any errors on the part of the [Services] in administering the ESA," the Supreme Court in *Bennett* stated that this would "effect a wholesale abrogation of the APA's 'final agency action' requirement" and that "[a]ny procedural default, even one that had not yet resulted in a final disposition of the matter at issue, would form the basis for a lawsuit."[65] The necessary implication of this language would appear to be that for those claims that *do* fall within the citizen suit provision—such as claims that action agencies have violated section 7—a lawsuit may be pursued without meeting the APA's "final agency action" requirement.[66]

In one recent case, however, a district court held that even an action brought under the ESA's citizen suit provision must satisfy the "final agency action" requirement. In *Defenders of Wildlife v. Gutierrez*,[67] the plaintiffs challenged the Coast Guard's failure to engage in any section 7 consultation with respect to the establishment of "traffic separation schemes" that could adversely affect the northern right whale. Although this claim fell squarely within the ESA citizen suit provision, the court held that the plaintiffs were required to demonstrate that the Coast Guard had engaged in "final agency actions that are reviewable under the APA."[68] On appeal, the D.C. Circuit found it "unnecessary to resolve" the issue of "whether 'agency action' or '*final* agency action' is required in order to bring suit under the citizen-suit provision of the ESA" because the court found that the plaintiffs were "challenging final agency action by the Coast Guard" in any event.[69]

Another important ramification of claim classification is that plaintiffs who prevail in ESA claims may recover fees under the generous fee provision set forth in the ESA citizen suit provision, whereas plaintiffs who prevail on APA claims are restricted to seeking recovery under the Equal Access to Justice Act (EAJA).[70] Among other significant differences, EAJA limits fee awards to a "prevailing party,"[71] whereas the ESA citizen suit provision authorizes the court to award fees "whenever the court determines such award is appropriate."[72] This means that plaintiffs prevailing on ESA claims may recover fees when they have not obtained any actual judgment or court-ordered relief in their favor, but they can establish that their lawsuit served as a "catalyst" for a sought-after change in the defendant's conduct.[73] On the other hand, because the Supreme Court has construed the term "prevailing party" to foreclose a fee award for a party that has failed to secure either an "enforceable judgment on the merits" or a "court-ordered consent decree,"[74] plaintiffs prevailing on APA claims cannot recover fees based on the catalyst theory. In addition, EAJA limits the parties that are eligible for a fee award,[75] and also restricts the rates that may be assessed,[76] whereas the ESA citizen suit provision contains no such restrictions. EAJA further provides that the court must deny an award when the government can establish that its legal position, though erroneous, was "substantially justified or that special circumstances make an award unjust,"[77] whereas the pertinent ESA provision contains no such proviso.

When a claim is based on the FWS's or NMFS's failure to carry out an action that is required by section 4, but need not be carried out by a date certain—in other words, the duty is nondiscretionary but the specific time for compliance is not statutorily delineated—several courts have viewed such claims as arising under the APA's "unreasonable delay" provisions,[78] rather than under the ESA citizen suit provision.[79] For example, one case addressed the Services' duty to revise a critical habitat designation in light of an obligation that the agency had imposed on itself (in a Recovery Plan) to carry out the revision.[80] The court reasoned that only the FWS's failure to carry out a "clearly-mandated nondiscretionary duty must form the basis" for a suit under the ESA citizen suit provision;[81] hence, because the Service had "some discretion" under the ESA as to *when* to carry out a critical habitat revision the agency had deemed necessary, the plaintiffs' claims were cognizable only under the APA, which imposes on agencies "merely a 'general duty of timeliness'" in carrying out a "required action."[82] Other courts have pursued a similar analysis in the context of claims that agencies failed to carry out ESA-related obligations.[83]

In contrast, one court has held that a claim of agency delay in carrying out a duty arguably imposed by section 4 could not be brought under *either* the ESA citizen suit provision or the APA.[84] In that case, the plaintiffs had argued that the Recovery Plan for the grizzly bear required the FWS to initiate a NEPA process to evaluate methods for recovering a particularly imperiled population and that the Service had unlawfully and unreasonably delayed in carrying out that duty. Consistent with other cases, the court held that such a claim could not be brought under the ESA citizen suit provision.[85] But in conflict with those rulings, the court further held that the claim could not be pursued under the APA because section 4 does not impose any specific deadline by when duties imposed by recovery plans must be carried out.[86]

In reaching that conclusion, however, the court relied heavily on a D.C. Circuit ruling, *Sierra Club v. Thomas*,[87] which analyzed different kinds of unlawful agency delay claims in the Clean Air Act context, and held that a claim that an agency has failed to carry out a specific legal duty under a statute that lacks a "readily ascertainable deadline" for the action *should* be brought as an APA claim.[88] *Sierra Club*, in turn, is generally consistent with *Norton v. Southern Utah Wilderness Alliance*,[89] which held that unreasonable delay claims under the APA must be based on allegations that "an agency has failed to take a *discrete* agency action that it is *required to take*."[90] This test does *not* require a date-certain deadline for agency action, but does foreclose "broad programmatic attack[s]" on agencies' failures to carry out general statutory mandates,[91] and also requires that unreasonable delay claims be predicated on unequivocal obligations imposed by statute or that agencies have imposed on themselves through regulations or other formal documents.[92]

Standard of Review

Regardless of whether a claim comes within the ESA citizen suit provision or the APA, courts employ the same standard of review in assessing the legality of an agency's decision implementing the Act. Thus, because the citizen suit provision sets forth no separate standard of review, even where courts are called on to review actions that are clearly encompassed within the citizen suit provision, they apply the standard of review in section 706(2)(A) of the APA, which directs that agency actions be set aside when they are "arbitrary, capricious, an abuse of discretion, or otherwise not in accordance with law."[93] In addition, in evaluating whether the Services or action agencies have acted in "accordance with law," courts apply the familiar two-step *Chevron* framework,[94] which requires the court to assess (1) whether the court can infer, based on "traditional tools" of statutory interpretation (including legislative history), a clear congressional intention on the specific issue before the court and, if not, (2) whether the agency has adopted a "permissible" construction of the statutory provision at issue.[95]

Likewise, in reviewing all agency decisions—including those that are challengeable under the ESA's citizen suit provision—courts do not engage in de novo review but, rather, generally confine themselves to review of the administrative record that was before the agency at the time of its decision, in accordance with standard APA principles.[96] As in any case involving record review, however, courts in ESA cases occasionally find that particular documents fall within one of the recognized exceptions to the record review principle. Most important, some courts have permitted de novo affidavits or other extra-record materials in order to "allow the court to 'understand the issues more clearly'" in a complex case involving difficult scientific principles, as well as to assess whether "'the agency failed to consider factors which are relevant to its final decision.'"[97] Courts may also consider extra-record materials in deciding whether to craft equitable relief[98] and, in rare cases, may authorize a de novo factual investigation, including discovery, "where there is initially 'a strong showing of bad faith or improper behavior' by the agency."[99]

As in other administrative law cases, there are often disputes in ESA cases as to what actually *does* constitute the record for purposes of judicial review. While it is well established that the reviewing court must consider the "'full administrative record before the [decision maker] at the time" of the decision,[100] this does not mean that the record necessarily consists of *only* "those documents that the *agency* has compiled and submitted as 'the' administrative record."[101] Although the agency is afforded a "presumption that it properly designated the administrative record," the agency may not "unilaterally determine what constitutes" the record; rather, the presumption of regularity can be rebutted where one of the other parties to the litigation demonstrates that particular documents that were "before" the agency at the time of decision have been omitted because, for example, they were unfavorable to the agency's position.[102]

One important record-related issue that frequently arises in ESA litigation is the extent to which agencies (and particularly the Services) may invoke the deliberative process privilege as a basis for withholding from the reviewing court materials that would otherwise be deemed part of the record. Several courts have held that the privilege—which "is centrally concerned with protecting the process by which *policy* is formulated"[103]—cannot generally be invoked to withhold documents generated during the section 7 consultation process. These courts have reasoned that although "scientific expertise" is brought to bear on the process, it is insufficiently connected to any "policy-oriented judgment" to implicate the underlying purpose of the deliberative process privilege.[104]

In addition, in a FOIA case, a court rejected the government's argument that an action agency's Biological Assessment could be withheld as predecisional because it was part of "one long deliberative process" required by section 7 that did not end until after the action agency makes a "final decision after it receives the biological opinion from FWS."[105] The court held, instead, that the Biological Assessment was the "consummation of the [agency's] decision making process up to the time it submitted the assessment to FWS to initiate a formal consultation," and hence the Assessment "constitutes a final agency opinion and is, therefore, releasable to the public under the principles of FOIA."[106]

In contrast, in several cases concerning listing and critical habitat designation decisions, several courts have allowed the Services to invoke the deliberative process privilege more broadly. A district court, for example, allowed e-mails and other "internal" documents to be withheld from the record, reasoning that the documents "were generated as part of the deliberative process by which the listing decision was made and their disclosure to the public would expose that process in a way to discourage candid discussion within the agency and thereby undermine the agency's ability to perform its functions."[107]

Venue/Transfer Issues

With regard to claims that fall within the ESA citizen suit provision, the ESA provides that such claims may be brought "in the district in which the violation occurs."[108] APA claims based on ESA violations are governed by the general venue provision that applies to civil actions in federal courts.[109] Such cases—in which a "defendant is an officer or employee of the United States or any agency thereof acting in his official capacity" or an "agency of the United States"—may "be brought in any judicial district in which (1) a defendant in the action resides, (2) a substantial part of the events or omissions giving rise to the claim occurred, or a substantial part of [the] property that is the subject of the action is situated, or (3) the plaintiff resides."[110]

As a practical matter, this means that section 9 claims against nonfederal entities may certainly be brought where the unlawful "taking" is allegedly occurring, and perhaps where the decisions were made to proceed with actions that violate section 9, because those are the arguable locations where the "violation occurs" for purposes of such claims. For other claims covered by the ESA citizen suit provision—claims asserting violations of section 4 by the Services, or violations of sections 7 and 9 by action agencies—the violation arguably "occurs" (and hence venue is proper under the ESA venue provision) either in the area where the species is affected, or where the relevant agency decision makers are located. This means that such suits may be brought in the District of Columbia as well as any regional office with significant responsibility over the particular decision.[111]

Likewise, for APA-based claims—principally those brought against the Services for "maladministering" sections 7 and 10 of the ESA—suit may be brought in the District of Columbia (because that is where the "defendant" agency "resides"), in the area where the affected species exists (because that is where the "property that is the subject of the action is situated"), and arguably in the district where a regional office responsible for the particular action is located (because that is where a "defendant" "resides" if suit is brought against a regional official and/or where a "substantial part of the events or omissions giving rise to the claim occurred"). In addition, venue over APA-based claims is proper in any location in which at least one of the plaintiffs "resides."[112]

A federal claim that is filed in a district where venue is proper may nonetheless be transferred "to any other district or division where it might have been brought."[113] The standard for such a transfer is that it must be "[f]or the convenience of the parties and witnesses" and "in the interest of justice."[114] In ESA cases, the vast majority of transfer issues have arisen when cases were filed in Washington, D.C., and agency defendants (and/or private intervenors) moved to transfer to another location where the case could have been brought and was evidently regarded by the defendant as a more hospitable forum.[115] Although the Supreme Court has said that there is "ordinarily a strong presumption in favor of the plaintiff's choice of forum,"[116] the decision on transfer is committed to the broad discretion of the district court.[117] Accordingly, courts consider a wide variety of factors in ruling on transfer motions, including the location and convenience of the parties and witnesses, the court's ability to resolve the particular case based on an administrative record, and whether the case is deemed to involve a "localized controversy" rather than an issue of national concern.[118]

Given the inherently discretionary nature of transfer decisions, it is difficult to distill from the case law any clear criteria that will serve as reliable predictors of whether a particular case will be transferred. As a general matter, however, D.C. judges are somewhat less inclined to transfer cases pertaining to the Services' listing and critical habitat decisions[119] than cases involving challenges to permitting, licensing, or funding decisions involving particular projects located in other parts of the country.[120]

60-Day Notice Requirement

For cases that fall within the ESA's citizen suit provision, the provision's 60-day notice requirement is jurisdictional—the requirement *cannot* be waived by courts on equitable or any other grounds. Accordingly, unless adequate notice is afforded to *both* the relevant Secretary *and* to any other alleged violator of the Act, there is an "absolute bar to bringing suit under the ESA."[121] Thus, the principal issue that arises with regard to the notice provision is whether the notice letter sufficiently identifies the issue over which suit is brought.[122]

While there is no hard and fast rule on how detailed the notice must be, the basic principle endorsed by the courts is that the notice must "provide sufficient information of a violation so that the Secretary or [action agency] could identify and attempt to abate the violation."[123] Accordingly, the notice should, at the least, identify each listed species the plaintiff intends to sue over, each specific agency action that may form the basis of a claim, and each provision of the ESA the plaintiff claims has been violated.[124] When the plaintiff intends to seek relief for an ongoing pattern or practice of agency conduct that allegedly violates the ESA—such as a recurrent failure to engage in section 7 consultation with respect to a particular kind of agency action—the notice letter should also make that clear.[125]

Intervention

In ESA cases, as in other civil litigation, district courts apply a four-part test to determine whether a party may intervene as of right under Federal Rule of Civil Procedure 24(a): (1) the motion to intervene must be timely; (2) the applicant for intervention must have a protectable interest relating to the property or transaction that is the subject of the action; (3) the applicant must be so situated that the disposition of the action may, as a practical matter, impair or impede the applicant's ability to protect that interest; and (4) the applicant's interest must not be adequately represented by the existing parties in the lawsuit.[126] The circuits vary considerably, however, in how stringently they apply various features of that test. Accordingly, it is essential for any prospective applicant for intervention—whether it be a conservation group or a business interest—to become conversant with the particular manner in which each circuit approaches the intervention standards and to frame the intervention motion accordingly.

Most important, although the Supreme Court has held that the burden of showing inadequacy of representation by existing parties is "minimal," and that the applicant need only demonstrate that representation of its interests by existing parties "may be" inadequate,[127] in some circuits it is far more difficult to shoulder this "minimal" burden than in others. For example, in the Ninth, Tenth, and D.C. Circuits, it is relatively easy for would-be intervenors to establish that an agency defendant may not fully represent either a conservation group's interest in species preservation or a business's economic interest.[128] In contrast, it is much more difficult to establish that an agency's representation may be inadequate in the First Circuit.[129]

Relief

In its seminal ruling in *TVA v. Hill*, the Supreme Court held that, in enacting the ESA, Congress intended to deprive the courts of their ordinary equitable discretion in crafting relief for legal violations. Accordingly, in that case—in which it was conceded that the operation of the Tellico dam would likely cause the extinction of the snail darter—the Court held that injunctive relief against dam operation was required without the courts engaging in the equitable balancing that generally must precede the issuance of injunctive relief.[130] The Court reasoned that, in enacting the ESA, "Congress has spoken in the plainest of words, making it abundantly clear that the balance [of equities] has been struck in favor of affording endangered species the highest of priorities."[131]

In view of *Hill*, lower courts have generally held that appropriate injunctive relief *must* be fashioned for violations of any the substantive prohibitions in the ESA—for example, the prohibitions on jeopardizing species and impairing critical habitat embodied in section 7, or the unauthorized prohibition on taking species in section 9.[132] Similarly, the case law establishes that the "remedy for a substantial procedural violation of the ESA—a violation that is not technical or de minimis—must [also] be an injunction of the project pending compliance with the ESA."[133] Hence, when an action agency fails to follow the consultation process mandated by section 7, courts will ordinarily issue injunctions against the actions that should have undergone consultation, on the grounds that the "purpose of the consultation process [] is to prevent later substantive violations of the ESA."[134] Likewise, when the FWS or NMFS fails to abide by the time frames set forth in section 4 for making listing or critical habitat decisions, courts have determined that injunctive relief *must* be fashioned to bring the agency into compliance.[135]

This does not mean that a court lacks any discretion in crafting relief for an ESA violation; in deciding precisely what kind of injunctive (and/or declaratory) relief to fashion, a court may consider the nature of the ESA violation and how the purposes of the ESA would best be served under the particular circumstances. For example, notwithstanding a finding of a violation of the section 7 consultation process, the Ninth Circuit has "allowed nonjeopardizing agency actions to continue during the consultation process," while making clear that the agency—the "entity that has violated its statutory duty"—bears a heavy burden of proving that a particular action is "nonjeopardizing."[136] Similarly, while courts have held that the Services' plea of inadequate resources cannot be relied on to avoid injunctive relief for a violation of one of the section 4 deadlines for decisions on listing or critical habitat designation, a court *may* take resource capabilities into account in determining the nature of the required injunctive relief, that is, exactly how much time to allow the Service to bring itself into compliance.[137]

The courts' approach to the crafting of injunctive relief for ESA violations is largely the same in the context of requests for preliminary and permanent relief. Thus, when a court discerns a likely violation of the ESA that poses the potential for irreparable harm to a listed species, preliminary injunctive relief will ordinarily be forthcoming irrespective of the economic arguments or any other equitable factors counseling against such relief.[138] Indeed, in appropriate circumstances, courts will fashion preliminary injunctions that require affirmative changes in agency conduct—ones that alter, rather than maintain, the status quo—when that is necessary to prevent irreparable harm to listed species.[139] Once again, however, courts may consider economic and related interests in determining whether the specific injunctive relief sought by plaintiffs is broader than necessary to protect species while the court is resolving the merits and considering what kind of permanent relief may be appropriate.[140]

Emerging Issues and Future Directions

As the foregoing discussion reflects, while some legal issues bearing on the pursuit of citizen suits under the ESA (as well as under the APA for violations of the ESA) are still being fleshed out in the courts, for the most part the law is now well settled, particularly because of Supreme Court rulings that provide a fairly clear blueprint as to how these kinds of cases should (and should not) be brought. Nonetheless, there are several issues that have thus far received relatively little attention, but that may grow in importance in coming years.

As noted previously, there is some confusion in the current case law as to the extent to which APA principles and restrictions should be incorporated into the resolution of claims that are properly brought under the ESA's citizen suit provision. While the case law is consistent that reviewing courts should borrow the APA's standard of review in assessing, for example, listing and critical habitat decisions (because the ESA sets forth no other standard of review), the government is now going considerably further and arguing that significant *limitations* on review of agency action under the APA—and particularly the APA's requirement that agency action must be deemed "final" before it can be reviewed—should also be incorporated into the courts' consideration of claims brought under the ESA citizen suit provision.[141] Although *Bennett v. Spear* appears to conflict with that argument, it has been adopted by at least one district court and was then sidestepped by the D.C. Circuit on appeal.[142] Accordingly, there is likely to be further litigation on that issue in the future.

There have also been several recent district court cases holding that although claims may be brought under the ESA citizen suit provision against violators of the statute itself and the Services' implementing regulations, such claims *cannot* be predicated on violations of *permits* issued by the Services under the ESA. In one such case—which has since been vacated by the 11th Circuit on mootness grounds—the United States District Court for the Middle District of Florida held that the plaintiff could not bring a citizen suit based on an asserted violation of an "incidental take" permit issued under section 10(a)(1)(B) of the Act. The court reasoned that the ESA provides that various provisions of the ESA refer to enforcement of permit conditions by the "Secretary," but that "[i]n comparison, the ESA's citizen suit provision provides, in relevant part, for suits to enjoin violations only of the ESA and related regulations. The ESA, itself, simply does not provide a private enforcement mechanism covering the terms and conditions of incidental take permits."[143]

That ruling was relied on by another district court to hold that plaintiffs also could not base a claim on violations of permits authorizing otherwise prohibited activities that the Service has found will "enhance the propagation or survival of the affected species."[144] The court similarly reasoned that "[b]y specifically referencing permits" in various enforcement provisions of section 11 for which the Secretary has responsibility (relating to civil enforcement, criminal sanctions, administrative or judicial seizure and forfeiture), "but not referencing permits in subsection (g) (pertaining to citizen suits), Congress evidenced its intent to preclude private parties from permit enforcement."[145]

Although these rulings are ostensibly based on the plain terms of the ESA's citizen suit provision, on close inspection, they are in tension with the statutory language. Both rulings acknowledge that under the Act, citizen suits *may* be based on violations of the ESA implementing regulations. In both cases, moreover, the plaintiffs specifically argued that the regulations *themselves* were violated *because* there were violations of ESA permits at issue. Indeed, as acknowledged in *Atlantic Green Sea Turtle*, one such regulation flatly "requires '[a]ny person holding a permit under [the ESA] and any person acting under authority of such permit [to] comply with all conditions of the permit and with all applicable laws and regulations governing the permitted activity.'"[146]

Yet neither ruling clearly explains why a citizen suit cannot be based on asserted violations of the regulations, as authorized by the plain terms of the citizen suit provision—that is, why ESA regulations mandating compliance with general or specific permit conditions cannot be the basis for a citizen suit even if permit violations, standing by themselves, could not form the foundation for such a suit.[147] More important, neither ruling makes any effort to explain why Congress would have adopted what the Supreme Court has characterized as a citizen suit provision of "remarkable breadth when compared with the language Congress ordinarily uses" in such provisions[148] if it had also intended to foreclose all citizen suits in any way tied to permit violations.[149] Accordingly, other courts may decline to follow these rulings, especially as their full practical ramifications for effective enforcement of the ESA become evident.[150]

Conclusion

Citizen suits have been crucial to the enforcement of the ESA and they will continue to play a vital role in the Act's implementation regardless of who controls the political branches of government. Indeed, as the world's wildlife is increasingly jeopardized by climate change, habitat destruction, invasive species, and other grave threats, the federal courts will likely be asked to play even more of a role in construing and applying the Act's vital safeguards. While some may bemoan the central function played by the courts, the fact is that Congress saw fit to create a sweeping citizen suit provision in the ESA, and those seeking to stave off extinctions as well as those affected by the economic impacts of species preservation efforts will continue to call on the judiciary for redress, especially if the political branches are unwilling or unable to devise effective solutions to the far-reaching problems plaguing imperiled wildlife.

Notes

1. 16 U.S.C. § 1540(g)(1)(A).
2. *Id*. § 1540(g)(1)(C).
3. *Id*. § 1533.
4. *Id*. § 1540(g).
5. *Id*. § 1540(g)(2).
6. *Id*. § 1540(g)(3).
7. *Id*. § 1540(g)(4).
8. Lujan v. Defenders of Wildlife, 504 U.S. 555, 560–61 (1992) (internal quotations and citations omitted).
9. Bennett v. Spear, 520 U.S. 154, 162–66 (1997). As discussed below, however, certain cases asserting that the Secretary and/or Services have violated the Act may only be brought pursuant to the judicial review provisions of the Administrative Procedure Act (APA). As with all APA claims, plaintiffs in such cases must demonstrate that their claims fall within the "zone-of-interests" of the particular statutory provision at issue. *Id*. at 175–77.
10. *Defenders*, 504 U.S. at 561; *see also* Lujan v. Nat'l Wildlife Fed'n, 497 U.S. 871, 883–89 (1990).
11. *Defenders*, 504 U.S. at 562. It particularly behooves plaintiffs whose "asserted injury arises from the government's allegedly unlawful regulation (or lack of regulation) of *someone else*"—e.g., conservation organizations complaining that the Services have adopted inadequate or unlawful regulations implementing sections 7 or 10 of the ESA—to make detailed standing allegations in their complaint. *Id*. (emphasis added). This is because the Supreme Court has held that "when a plaintiff is not himself the object of the government action or inaction he challenges, standing is ordinarily 'substantially more difficult' to establish," particularly with regard to the causation and redressability elements of Article III standing. *Id*. (quoting Allen v. Wright, 468 U.S. 737, 758 (1984)).
12. *Defenders*, 504 U.S. at 561 (quoting Fed. R. Civ. P. 56(e)). In rare cases, an affidavit or other evidence on which a plaintiff relies for standing in an ESA case will be controverted by a defendant's proffer of contrary evidence, e.g., testimony in a deposition or some other evidence calling the plaintiff's allegations of injury into question. In that event, as in any situation in which there is a genuine issue of material fact, a trial will be necessary to resolve the factual conflict. *Id*.
13. *Id*. at 563.
14. *Id*. at 564.
15. *Id*. (internal quotation omitted). At the same time, the fact that a person *has* visited an area previously in an effort to observe a species—especially if done so periodically—may be used to buttress an argument that the individual is likely to *continue* doing so and hence suffer injury in the foreseeable future.
16. *Id*. (emphasis in original); *see also* Summers v. Earth Island Institute, 129 S. Ct. 1142, 1150–51 (2009) (A "vague desire to return is insufficient to satisfy the requirement of imminent injury.").

17. *Defenders*, 504 U.S. at 566 (recognizing that it is "plausible" to "think that a person who observes or works with animals of a particular species in the very area of the world where that species is threatened by a federal decision is facing such harm, since some animals that might have been the subject of his interest will no longer exist") (citing Japan Whaling Ass'n v. Am. Cetacean Soc'y, 478 U.S. 221, 231 n.4 (1986)).
18. *Id.* (citing Lujan v. Nat'l Wildlife Fed'n, 497 U.S. 871, 887–89 (1990)).
19. *Bennett*, 520 U.S. at 167 (ranch operators and irrigation districts had standing to challenge Biological Opinion where they alleged "that they currently receive irrigation" from a particular lake and that the Bureau of Reclamation would abide by a Biological Opinion that imposed restrictions on lake levels, which, in turn, would adversely affect the plaintiffs by "substantially reducing the quantity of available water").
20. *Defenders*, 504 U.S. at 561–62.
21. *Id.* at 566 (emphasis added); *see also* Am. Soc'y for the Prev. of Cruelty to Animals v. Ringling Bros. and Barnum & Bailey Circus, 317 F.3d 334, 335 (D.C. Cir. 2003) (a former circus employee had alleged sufficient injury in fact in a case contending that Asian elephants were being taken in violation of section 9 of the ESA where the employee asserted that he had formed a "strong, personal attachment" to the elephants and would visit them if the asserted mistreatment ceased) (citing Friends of the Earth, Inc. v. Laidlaw Envtl. Servs., 528 U.S. 167, 181–82, 184 (2000)); *see also id.* at 337–38 ("A person may derive great pleasure from visiting a certain river; the pleasure may be described as an emotional attachment stemming from the river's pristine beauty.... We can see no principled distinction between the injury that person suffers when discharges begin polluting the river and the injury Rider allegedly suffers from the mistreatment of the elephants to which he became emotionally attached during his tenure at Ringling Bros.—both are part of the aesthetic injury.").
22. Cary v. Hall, No. C 05-4363 VRW, slip op. at 20 (N.D. Ca. Sept. 30, 2006) (citing FEC v. Akins, 524 U.S. 11, 22 (1998) and Havens Realty Corp. v. Coleman, 455 U.S. 363, 373 (1982)); *see also* Gerber v. Norton, 294 F.3d 173, 179 (D.C. Cir. 2002)). On the other hand, it is *not* enough for a plaintiff simply to assert that the Services or other agencies have failed to comply with one of the procedural requirements imposed on agencies by the Act—such as the consultation process required by section 7. *Defenders*, 504 U.S. at 572–78. Rather, as in cases involving violations of the National Environmental Policy Act, plaintiffs in such cases must demonstrate that the failure to comply with the procedural requirement at least threatens to harm a "separate concrete interest of theirs." *Id.* at 572 ("This is not a case where plaintiffs are seeking to enforce a procedural requirement the disregard of which could impair a separate concrete interest of theirs (*e.g.*, the procedural requirement for a hearing prior to denial of their license application, or the procedural requirement for an environmental impact statement before a federal facility is constructed next door to them.").
23. *Defenders*, 504 U.S. at 572 n.7 (A plaintiff who claims that an agency's violation of a procedural duty harms the plaintiff's "concrete interests" can advance that claim "without meeting all the normal standards for redressability and immediacy. Thus, under our case law, one living adjacent to the site for proposed construction of a federally licensed dam has standing to challenge the licensing agency's failure to prepare an environmental impact statement, even though he cannot establish with any certainty that the statement will cause the license to be withheld or altered, and even though the dam will not be completed for many years.").
24. *Id.* at 572.
25. *See, e.g.*, Biodiversity Legal Found. v. Badgley, 309 F.3d 1166 (9th Cir. 2002) (conservation organizations had standing to seek declaratory judgment that FWS was unlawfully delaying making listing decisions where the organizations alleged that members derived concrete scientific, aesthetic, and other benefits from particular species whose existence was jeopardized by the delay); Citizens for Better Forestry v. U.S. Dep't of Agric., 341 F.3d 961, 975 (9th Cir. 2003) ("environmental plaintiffs have standing to challenge

not only site-specific plans, but also higher level, programmatic rules that impose or remove requirements on site-specific plans" so long as they can demonstrate that there is a "reasonabl[e] probability" that the challenged violation of the ESA will harm the plaintiffs' concrete interests) (internal quotation omitted).

26. *Citizens for Better Forestry*, 341 F.3d 961.
27. Fla. Audubon Soc'y v. Bentsen, 94 F.3d 658, 667 (D.C. Cir. 1996) (en banc); *id.* at 675 (Rodgers, J., dissenting) ("The majority's new rule places this circuit in conflict with the Ninth Circuit, which has frequently found standing in cases similar to this one."); *see also* Defenders of Wildlife v. Gutierrez, 532 F.3d 913, 923–25 (D.C. Cir. 2008) (finding standing and distinguishing *Fla. Audubon Soc'y* in a case challenging the Coast Guard's failure to comply with section 7 of the ESA before approving commercial shipping lanes in right whale habitat).
28. 504 U.S. at 570.
29. *Bennett*, 520 U.S. at 169–70.
30. The opinions suggest several possible distinctions between *Defenders* and *Bennett* (other than the identity of the plaintiffs). First, in *Bennett*, the Court was applying the motion to dismiss standard—which, once again, is "relatively modest at th[at] stage of the litigation," 520 U.S. at 171—whereas in *Defenders* the Court was applying the more stringent summary judgment standard. Second, *Bennett* involved a challenge to a specific Biological Opinion, which found that long-term operation of the project would jeopardize listed species, and hence set forth a "reasonable and prudent alternative" and an "incidental take statement," which the Court, based on the language and structure of section 7, found had a "virtually determinative effect" on the Bureau's ultimate decision. *Id.* at 170. In contrast, *Defenders* involved a challenge to a general regulation, which the plurality stated posed particular "difficulties insofar as proof of causation or redressability is concerned," especially because the plurality regarded it as "very much an open question" whether the Secretaries of Interior and Commerce had been authorized by Congress to issue binding regulations implementing section 7 of the Act. *Defenders*, 504 U.S. at 568. There is no analysis in the rulings (both authored by Justice Scalia) as to why Congress would want to afford the Services' Biological Opinions "virtually determinative" weight (hence allowing suit without joinder of the action agencies), but would *not* want the Services to have the authority to promulgate binding regulations implementing section 7 as a whole. Indeed, rather than squarely address the evident tension in the rulings, *Bennett* contains only the oblique statement that *Defenders* "does not exclude injury produced by determinative or coercive effect upon the action of someone else." 520 U.S. at 169.
31. *See, e.g.*, Spirit of the Sage Council v. Kempthorne, 511 F. Supp. 2d 31, 38–40 (D.D.C. 2007) (finding that facial challenges to two FWS rules implementing section 10 of the Act were ripe for review).
32. Nat'l Park Hospitality Ass'n v. Dep't of the Interior, 538 U.S. 803, 808 (2003). As discussed in the next section, certain claims that agencies have acted in contravention of the language or purpose of the ESA must be pled under the APA rather than the ESA citizen suit provision. Such claims must satisfy not only constitutional and prudential ripeness requirements, but must also meet the APA's "final agency action" requirement, 5 U.S.C. § 704, i.e., the agency action must be "final" rather than tentative or preliminary, and it must challenge a discrete agency action, rather than seeking more generic review and relief pertaining to an agency's programmatic implementation of the ESA. *See, e.g.*, Inst. for Wildlife Prot. v. Norton, 205 Fed. Appx. 483 (9th Cir. 2006) (affirming district court's dismissal of claims that did not come within ESA citizen suit provision and could not be reviewed under the APA "because they are programmatic challenges" rather than requests for review of any "final agency action.").
33. *See, e.g.*, Nat'l Ass'n of Home Builders v. U.S. Army Corps of Eng'rs, 440 U.S. 459, 464 (D.C. Cir. 2006) (reviewing facial challenge to regulation implementing the Clean Water Act because a "purely legal claim in the context of a facial challenge . . . is presumptively reviewable"); Nat'l Mining Ass'n v. Fowler, 324 F.3d 752, 756–57 (D.C. Cir. 2003).

34. Nat'l Mining Ass'n v. U.S. Army Corps of Eng'rs, 145 F.3d 1399, 1408 (D.C. Cir. 1998). Accordingly, even if such challenges overcome the ripeness hurdle, they may falter on the merits if a court concludes that the agency may exercise its discretion under the rule to avoid unlawful results. *See Spirit of the Sage Council*, 511 F. Supp. 2d at 41–45 (rejecting a facial challenge to the "No Surprises" rule under which Services provide incidental take permit holders with broad assurances that their permit conditions will not be modified; although the challenge was ripe, the rule was sustained on the merits because "[d]epending on the conditions imposed by the ITP [incidental take permit], it is certainly possible that issuing an ITP with No Surprises assurances may satisfy the no-jeopardy standard. Since this is a facial challenge, and the No Surprises Rule is not logically inconsistent with the no-jeopardy standard, it is appropriate for the Court to presume that the Services will faithfully execute their duties under Section 7 and reasonably determine whether an ITP complies with the no-jeopardy standard at the time of issuance").
35. If a violation is arguably rectified before the complaint is filed, the defense is properly analyzed on standing (i.e., injury in fact), rather than mootness, grounds. *See Laidlaw*, 528 U.S. at 189. This is a much more favorable legal posture for a defendant to be in because the plaintiff has the burden of demonstrating its standing, whereas the defendant has the burden of demonstrating that a case that presented a justiciable controversy at its inception has been rendered moot by intervening events. *Id.* at 189. Accordingly, an agency (or any other potential target of an ESA case) that wishes to avoid protracted litigation is well advised to take ameliorative steps, if possible, *before* litigation is initiated.
36. *Laidlaw*, 528 U.S. at 189.
37. *See, e.g.*, Voyageurs Nat'l Park Ass'n v. Norton, 381 F.3d 759, 765 (8th Cir. 2004) ("[A]fter the Park Service and the FWS completed their formal consultation . . . the procedural defect identified by the Association was cured and the Association's claim for relief—seeking the remedy of formal consultation—was rendered moot."); S. Utah Wilderness Alliance v. Smith, 110 F.3d 724, 727–28 (10th Cir. 1997) (same); Klamath Siskiyou Wildlands Ctr. v. Babbitt, 105 F. Supp. 2d 1132, 1134 (D. Or. 2000) (holding that suit to list six species was mooted by final listing); Ctr. for Biological Diversity v. Clark, 2000 WL 1842942 (N.D. Cal. 2000) (listing after suit was filed rendered case moot).
38. *Laidlaw*, 528 U.S. at 189 (the "defendant's voluntary cessation of a challenged practice does not deprive a federal court of its power to determine the legality of the practice"); *see also* United States v. W.T. Grant Co., 345 U.S. 629, 633 (1953) (same). Thus, in order for a defendant's shift in position to moot a claim—e.g., an agency's announcement that it will belatedly engage in section 7 consultation—it must make "absolutely clear that the allegedly lawful behavior could not be reasonably expected to recur." *Laidlaw*, 528 U.S. at 189.
39. *Biodiversity Legal Found.*, 309 F.3d at 1173 (citing S. Pac. Terminal Co. v. ICC, 219 U.S. 498, 515 (1911)).
40. Greenpeace Action v. Franklin, 14 F.3d 1324, 1329 (9th Cir. 1993).
41. *Biodiversity Legal Found.*, 309 F.3d at 1173–76.
42. *Id.* at 1174.
43. *Id.*
44. *Id.* at 1175–76 (citing Super Tire Eng'g Co. v. McCorkle, 416 U.S. 115, 122 (1974)).
45. 520 U.S. at 172.
46. 16 U.S.C. § 1540(g)(1)(C).
47. *Bennett*, 520 U.S. at 172.
48. 386 F.3d 879, 884 (9th Cir. 2004) (emphasis added).
49. *Id.*
50. *Id.* (quoting *Bennett*, 520 U.S. at 172) (emphasis in original).
51. Fund for Animals v. Hogan, 428 F.3d 1059, 1063–65 (D.C. Cir. 2005).
52. Fund for Animals v. Hogan, No. 03-5077, Order on Rehearing (D.C. Cir. Feb. 17, 2006). A district court, however, subsequently ruled that the Service's denial of a request for

emergency listing is not even reviewable under the APA because the "ESA does not set forth any specific criteria governing the exercise of the Secretary's discretion in choosing whether to invoke 'emergency' listing procedures as opposed to following the 'normal' listing process." Am. Bird Conservancy v. Kempthorne, Civ. No. 06-2641, slip op. at 20 (D.N.J. Oct. 11, 2007). In response to the plaintiffs' argument that the ESA contemplated rapid action in the event of an "emergency," the court found that "pursuant to the plain language of the statute, such an 'emergency' is merely a *prerequisite* to the exercise of the Secretary's emergency rulemaking authority, and it does not mandate such an exercise." *Id.* at 21 (emphasis in original); *cf.* Inst. for Wildlife Prot. v. Norton, 303 F. Supp. 2d 1175, 1180 (W.D. Wash. 2003) (a FWS letter declining to list a species on an emergency basis did not give rise to a claim under the ESA because "Congress intended the emergency listing mechanism to be an option which the agency could exercise if, in its discretion, it determined that the threats to a particular species" warranted such action; further finding that the letter could not be reviewed under the APA because it was not sufficiently definite on the issue of emergency listing to constitute a "final agency action").
53. *Bennett*, 520 U.S. at 173 (quoting 16 U.S.C. § 1540(g)(1)(A)).
54. *Id.* (emphasis added).
55. *Id.* at 175 (quoting 5 U.S.C. § 704).
56. *Id.*
57. *Id.* at 177–78.
58. *See* W. Watersheds Project v. U.S. Forest Serv., No. 4:06-cv-277-BLW, slip op. at 20–21 (D. Idaho Dec. 4, 2007).
59. *Id.*
60. *Id.* at 26 (citing 16 U.S.C. § 1533(b)(1)(a)).
61. 520 U.S. at 172 ("[T]he fact that the Secretary's ultimate decision is reviewable only for abuse of discretion does not alter the categorical *requirement* that, in arriving at his decision, he . . . use 'the best scientific data available.' It is rudimentary administrative law that discretion as to the substance of the ultimate decision does not confer discretion to ignore the required procedures of decisionmaking. . . . Since it is the omission of these required procedures that petitioners complain of, their § 1533 claim is reviewable under § 1540(g)(1)(C).") (emphasis in original; internal citations omitted).
62. The only exception is that an "action may be brought immediately after such notification in the case of an action" asserting that one of the Services has violated a mandatory duty under section 4 and that involves an "emergency posing a significant risk to the well-being of any species of fish or wildlife or plants." 16 U.S.C. § 1540(g)(2)(C). Although this "exception clearly demonstrates Congress's intent to stop imminent threats of injury to protected wildlife," Forest Conservation Council v. Rosboro Lumber Co., 50 F.3d 781, 786 (9th Cir. 1995), it applies only to claims brought to remedy violations of section 4 of the Act. *See, e.g.*, Protect Our Eagles' Trees v. City of Lawrence, 715 F. Supp. 996, 998 & n.3 (D. Kan. 1989)).
63. There may be strategic reasons for a plaintiff to provide advance notice to the Service even where it is not legally required. The Service may choose to modify its position, thus rendering litigation unnecessary. In addition, especially where injunctive relief is being sought, it may be helpful for a plaintiff to demonstrate to the court that it has taken all reasonable steps to resolve the conflict before seeking judicial intervention.
64. Satisfying the zone-of-interests (or prudential) standing test is not especially onerous because the plaintiff need only demonstrate that its interest is "arguably within the zone of interests to be protected or regulated by the statute" in question. Ass'n of Data Processing Serv. Orgs., Inc. v. Camp, 397 U.S. 150, 153 (1970). In *Bennett*, the Court explained that this analysis must be conducted "not by reference to the overall purpose of the Act in question (here, species preservation), but by reference to the particular provision of law" upon which the plaintiff relies. 520 U.S. at 175–76. In applying that test, the Court held that the "obvious purpose" of the requirement in section 7 that agencies

"use the best scientific and commercial data available" in assessing species impacts is to "ensure that the ESA not be implemented haphazardly, on the basis of speculation and surmise," and that this purpose is designed to further not only the "overall goal of species preservation," but also to "avoid needless economic dislocation produced by agency officials zealously but unintelligently pursuing their environmental objectives." *Id.* at 176–77. Given that very expansive reading of the "zone of interests" covered by section 7, there will be very few APA challenges to Service decisions implementing the ESA that raise serious prudential standing issues.
65. *Bennett*, 520 U.S. at 175.
66. *See, e.g.*, Wash. Toxics Coal. v. EPA, 413 F.3d 1024, 1034 (9th Cir. 2005) (claim that EPA had violated section 7 in approving pesticides was brought under the ESA because "suits to compel agencies to comply with the substantive provisions of the ESA arise under the ESA citizen suit provision, and not the APA"); *id.* (rejecting argument that the "district court erred by not applying the APA and its limited provision for judicial review of final agency action.... Because [the ESA] independently authorizes a private right of action, the APA does not govern the plaintiffs' claims. Plaintiffs' suits to compel agencies to comply with the substantive provisions of the ESA arise under the ESA citizen suit provision, and not the APA."); Forest Serv. Employees for Envtl. Ethics v. U.S. Forest Serv., 397 F. Supp. 1241, 1256–57 (D. Mont. 2005) ("There is no requirement for 'final agency action' with regard to the ESA claim because Plaintiff has brought suit under . . . the 'citizen suit' provision of the ESA."); Nat'l Wildlife Fed'n v. FEMA, 345 F. Supp. 2d 1151, 1160 (W.D. Wash. 2004) (the final agency action requirement "does not apply to suits brought under the ESA's broad citizen suit provision"); *cf.* Nat'l Wildlife Fed'n v. Brownlee, 402 F. Supp. 2d 1, 7 n.10 (D.D.C. 2005) ("[b]ecause I find that the present challenge meets the APA's standards for final agency action, I do not need to consider whether suits under the ESA's citizen suit provision . . . have a lower (if any) bar to surmount.").
67. 484 F. Supp. 2d 44 (D.D.C. 2007) , *rev'd in part on other grounds*, 532 F. Supp. 2d 913 (D.C. Cir. 2008).
68. 484 F. Supp. 2d at 56. In reaching that conclusion, the district court relied on confusing language in a D.C. Circuit ruling that applied, with little explication and no discussion of the ESA's citizen suit provision, the final agency action requirement to a claim that the FWS had failed to comply with notice and comment procedures in adopting "protocols" for identifying endangered species habitats. *See* Nat'l Ass'n of Home Builders v. Norton, 415 F.3d 8, 13 (D.C. Cir. 2005) ("There exists no statutory review provision in the ESA that authorizes judicial review of agency action beyond that provided for in the APA. . . . Thus, an agency action must be final in order to be judicially reviewable.").
69. *Defenders of Wildlife*, 532 F.3d at 925–26 (emphasis in original).
70. 24 U.S.C. § 2412.
71. *Id.* § 2412(d).
72. 16 U.S.C. § 1540(g)(4).
73. *See, e.g.*, Ass'n of Cal. Water Agencies v. Evans, 386 F.3d 879, 884–85 (9th Cir. 2004); Ctr. for Biological Diversity v. Norton, 262 F.3d 1077, 1081 (10th Cir. 2001).
74. Buckhannon Bd. & Care Home, Inc. v. W. Va. Dep't of Health & Human Res., 532 U.S. 598, 604 (2001).
75. *See, e.g.*, 28 U.S.C. § 2412(d)(2)(B) (providing that nonprofit (501(c)(3)) organizations with fewer than 500 employees are eligible for an award).
76. *Id.* § 2412(d).
77. *Id.*
78. *See* 5 U.S.C. §§ 555(e), 706(1).
79. On the other hand, even when a claim of unlawful delay in carrying out a mandatory duty clearly *does* fall within the citizen suit provision of the ESA, some courts have cited the language of the APA as mandating that *injunctive relief* be awarded for the violation. *See, e.g.*, Forest Guardians v. Babbitt, 174 F.3d 1178, 1187–88 (10th Cir. 1999) ("Having

determined that the Secretary violated his nondiscretionary duty to issue a critical habitat designation . . . we now look to the APA to determine the remedy to be prescribed upon judicial review. . . . The reviewing court '*shall . . . compel* agency action unlawfully withheld or unreasonably delayed.'") (emphasis in original; quoting 5 U.S.C. § 706(1)); *see also* Fla. Home Builders Ass'n v. Norton, 496 F. Supp. 2d 1330, 1335–36 (M.D. Fla. 2007) (citing section 706(1) in awarding relief for a section 4 violation, but relying on the government's protestations of limited resources in crafting a "reasonable" schedule for compliance; "[a]ccepting Defendants' schedule in no way excuses the Service's noncompliance with legislative mandates. In the future, Defendants should address budgetary concerns to Congress").

80. *See* Biodiversity Legal Found. v. Norton, 285 F. Supp. 2d 1 (D.D.C. 2003).
81. *Id.* at 8.
82. *Id.* at 8–9 (quoting Sierra Club v. Thomas, 828 F.2d 783, 791 (D.C. Cir. 1987)). Consequently, the court applied the factors adopted by the D.C. Circuit for evaluating whether an agency's delay in carrying out a legal duty has become unreasonable—generally known as the TRAC factors in light of a seminal D.C. Circuit ruling on unreasonable delay, *see* Telecommns. Research & Action Ctr. v. FCC, 750 F.2d 70, 76 (D.C. Cir. 1984).
83. *See* Ctr. for Biological Diversity v. Evans, 2005 WL 1514102, at *4 (N.D. Cal. 2005) (finding that NMFS had engaged in "unreasonable delay" under the APA where the agency had delayed "for at least nine years, if not 34 years" in revising a critical habitat designation for the right whale to encompass habitat in the Pacific Ocean); *cf. In re* Am. Rivers & Idaho Rivers United, 372 F.3d 413 (D.C. Cir. 2004) (applying the TRAC factors in granting a writ of mandamus compelling FERC to respond to a six-year old petition requesting that the agency formally consult with NMFS regarding the agency's ongoing regulatory authority over hydropower operations affecting listed fish species); *id.* at 418 ("In considering a charge of unreasonable delay, however, we must satisfy ourselves that the agency has a duty to act and that it has 'unreasonably delayed' in discharging that duty").
84. *See* Conservation Nw. v. Kempthorne, 2007 WL 1847143 (W.D. Wash. 2007).
85. *Id.* at *3.
86. *Id.* at *4 ("For the same reasons stated above regarding the discretionary nature of the time line of implementation of recovery plans under the ESA, the Court holds that this same conduct is discretionary when analyzed under the APA.").
87. 828 F.2d 783 (D.C. Cir. 1987).
88. *Id.* at 791.
89. 542 U.S. 55 (2004) (*SUWA*).
90. *Id.* at 64 (emphasis in original).
91. *Id.*
92. *See also* Wyoming v. U.S. Dep't of Interior, 360 F. Supp. 2d 1214, 1225, 1231 (D. Wyo. 2005) (dismissing a claim that the government "fail[ed] to manage and control the gray wolf population in Wyoming" in violation of the ESA because 5 U.S.C. § 706(1) does not authorize courts to inject themselves into "day-to-day agency management") (citing *SUWA*).
93. 5 U.S.C. § 706(2)(A); *see, e.g.*, Nw. Ecosystem Alliance v. U.S. Fish and Wildlife Serv., 475 F.3d 1136, 1140 (9th Cir. 2007); Biodiversity Legal Found. v. Babbitt, 146 F.3d 1249, 1252 (10th Cir. 1998) ("in examining whether the Service's [listing] actions violate the ESA, we rely on the standards of review provided in the APA").
94. *Nw. Ecosystem Alliance*, 475 F.3d at 1140 (applying *Chevron*'s "analytical framework" to FWS's "distinct population policy").
95. Chevron U.S.A., Inc. v. Natural Res. Def. Council, Inc., 467 U.S. 837 (1984).
96. *See, e.g.*, Sw. Ctr. for Biological Diversity v. Babbitt, 131 F. Supp. 2d 1, 5 (D.D.C. 2001) ("[I]f Congress permits judicial review of an agency's determination, expressly or implicitly, but has not set forth the standards by which that review is to be conducted, the courts limit review to the record before the agency. Building on that authority, the Court

of Appeals for this Circuit specifically held that the citizen suit provisions of the ESA merely provided a right of action to challenge agency action and did not permit *de novo* review. Instead, review of an agency decision made pursuant to the ESA is limited to the administrative record.") (citing Cabinet Mountains Wilderness v. Peterson, 685 F.2d 678, 684 (D.C. Cir. 1982)); *see also* Nw. Ecosystem Alliance, 475 F.3d at 1140; Newton County Wildlife Ass'n v. Rogers, 141 F.3d 803, 808 (8th Cir. 1998).

However, in several cases raising claims under the ESA citizen suit provision—and particularly claims that action agencies have failed to engage in any consultation as required by section 7—courts have suggested that they are *not* generally confined to review of an administrative record in evaluating whether the actions at issue have sufficient impacts to trigger consultation. *See* W. Watersheds Project v. Kraayenbrink, 2007 WL 1667618, at *19–20 (D. Idaho 2007) (finding that materials relied on to challenge agency's failure to consult were "all within the Administrative Record," but also stating that the "Court is not bound, however, to the Administrative Record" in its "review of an ESA citizen suit to compel consultation") (citing Wash. Toxics Coal. v. Envtl. Prot. Agency, 413 F.3d 1024, 1029–30 (9th Cir. 2005) (affirming district court ruling requiring consultation based on review "outside of an administrative record" of "evidence on the effects of the use of the challenged pesticides"); Defenders of Wildlife v. Martin, 2007 WL 641439, at *2 (E.D. Wash. 2007) ("Plaintiffs' current claims are brought under the citizen suit provision of the ESA, not the APA, and the Court may in its discretion consider materials outside the administrative record").

While these cases could be read as suggesting that traditional administrative record review precepts have nothing to do with claims brought under the ESA citizen suit provision, they may also be viewed as applying one of the well-recognized *exceptions* to the record review requirement, i.e., that courts may consider extra-record materials when the administrative record alone is simply inadequate to permit meaningful judicial review. *See* cases cited *infra* note 97. This understanding of the cases would place them more squarely within the generally accepted framework of administrative law principles.

97. Oceana, Inc. v. Evans, 384 F. Supp. 2d 203, 218 (D.D.C. 2005) (quoting Esch v. Yeutter, 876 F.2d 976, 991 (D.C. Cir. 1989)); *see also* Carlton v. Babbitt, 26 F. Supp. 2d 102, 108 (D.D.C. 1998) (allowing the plaintiff to supplement the record with a declaration by a scientist who disclaimed the FWS's "optimistic reading" of an article the scientist had written); Sw. Ctr. for Biological Diversity v. Norton, 2002 WL 1733618, at *7 (D.D.C. 2002) (considering a scientist's declaration that, in refusing to list a species, the FWS had misapplied listing criteria developed by the scientist).
98. *Wash. Toxics Coal.*, 413 F.3d at 1029.
99. Alabama-Tombigbee Rivers Coal. v. Kempthorne, 477 F.3d 1250, 1262 (11th Cir. 2007) (internal quotation omitted).
100. Trout Unlimited v. Lohn, 2006 WL 1207901, at *1 (W.D. Wash. 2006) (quoting Citizens to Pres. Overton Park, Inc. v. Volpe, 401 U.S. 402, 420 (1971)).
101. *Trout Unlimited*, 2006 WL 1207901, at *1 (emphasis in original; internal quotation omitted).
102. Fund for Animals v. Williams, 391 F. Supp. 2d 191, 197 (D.D.C. 2005) ("The agency may not skew the record in its favor by excluding pertinent but unfavorable information. . . . Nor may the agency exclude information on the grounds that it did not 'rely' on the excluded information in its final decision."); *id.* at 198 (finding that the plaintiffs had made a "showing" that the FWS had "exclude[d] information adverse to its position from the administrative record" because the "documents at issue (1) were known to the agency at the time it made its decision, (2) 'are directly related to the decision,' and (3) 'are adverse to the agency's decision.'") (internal quotation omitted); *see also* Common Sense Salmon Recovery v. Evans, 217 F. Supp. 2d 17, 20 (D.D.C. 2002) (the record must include all documents that the agency "directly or indirectly considered").
103. Petroleum Info. Corp. v. U.S. Dep't of the Interior, 976 F.2d 1429, 1435 (D.C. Cir. 1992) (emphasis in original). To qualify for withholding under the privilege—the contours of

which have been elucidated primarily in cases arising under exemption 5 of the Freedom of Information Act (FOIA), 5 U.S.C. § 552(b)(5)—information must be both "predecisional" and "deliberative." A document is predecisional if it was "prepared to assist an agency decisionmaker in arriving at his decision, rather than to support a decision already made." *Petroleum Info. Corp.*, 976 F.2d at 1435 (internal quotation omitted). A document is "deliberative" if its disclosure would "discourage candid discussion within an agency." Dudman Commc'ns v. Dep't of Air Force, 815 F.2d 1565, 1567–68 (D.C. Cir. 1987). Factual information ordinarily may not be withheld under the privilege, *see* EPA v. Mink, 410 U.S. 73, 87–91 (1973), although in some FOIA cases courts have held that the "disclosure of even purely factual material may so expose the deliberative process within an agency that the material is appropriately held privileged." *Petroleum Info. Corp.*, 976 F.2d at 1435 (internal quotation omitted); *see also* Montrose Chem. Corp. v. Train, 491 F.2d 63, 68 (D.C. Cir. 1974) (an EPA staffer's summary of voluminous scientific evidence presented at a hearing was exempt from FOIA disclosure because the act of culling out relevant evidence involved a "judgmental process" that could be compromised by disclosure).

Although FOIA precedents regarding the scope of the deliberative process privilege (or, for that matter, other governmental privileges, such as the attorney-client and work product privileges) are frequently invoked by courts in evaluating the Administrative Record that must be produced in challenges to agency decisions, there are potentially important distinctions. The deliberative process privilege is a "qualified" privilege so that, in a challenge to an agency's decision, a litigant may attempt to demonstrate that "his or her need for the materials" in a particular case "override[s] the Government's interest in nondisclosure." Ctr. for Biological Diversity v. Norton, 2002 WL 32136200, at *3 (D. Ariz. 2002). In particular, a plaintiff may argue that the agency is withholding so many documents as "deliberative" that the reviewing court's obligation to evaluate the "full administrative record" is being compromised. *Citizens to Pres. Overton Park*, 401 U.S. at 420.

104. Greenpeace v. Nat'l Marine Fisheries Serv., 198 F.R.D. 540, 544 (W.D. Wash. 2000) ("A determination of jeopardy and adverse modification under the ESA requires the agency to collect scientific facts and data, and to reach expert scientific conclusions based on these facts. However, the fact that scientific expertise is brought to bear does not transform interpretations of facts into communications protected by the deliberative process privilege.") (internal quotation omitted); *see also* Ctr. for Biological Diversity v. U.S. Marine Corps, 2005 WL 3262901, at *1 (D.D.C. 2005) (rejecting, in a FOIA case, an agency's invocation of the deliberative process privilege to withhold a Biological Assessment because the document "is almost an exclusively factual document. It contains a significant amount of scientific data, research, and statistical figures about Camp Pendleton and Defendant's activities on base. Such compilations of data include information about the ongoing military activities for which Defendant uses Camp Pendleton, detailed descriptions of the base's topography and the critical habitat areas, information about the endangered and threatened species of animals and plants that are at issue, and projected effects of ongoing military training and other base activities on the species in question. *None of this information is advisory or deliberative in any way, but a plain account of factual information.*") (emphasis added).

105. *Ctr. for Biological Diversity*, 2005 WL 3262901, at *2.

106. *Id.* at *3. The court held that various other consultation-related documents could not be withheld because, while predecisional, they contained factual information. *Id.* at *3–5. On the other hand, the court allowed several such documents to be withheld because they reflected individual agency employees' opinions of how to respond to the FWS's request for additional information. *Id.* at *4–5. In making these distinctions, the court conducted an in camera review of the documents at issue, *id.* at *1, as courts have also done in engaging in direct reviews of agency decisions implementing the ESA. *See, e.g.*, Trout Unlimited v. Lohn, 2006 WL 1207901, at *2 (W.D. Wash. 2006) (conducting an

in camera review of 21 withheld documents to determine whether they could properly be withheld under the deliberative process privilege in a case challenging a NMFS policy on the consideration of "hatchery-origin" fish in listing decisions).
107. Ctr. for Biological Diversity v. Norton, 336 F. Supp. 2d 1149, 1154 (D.N.M. 2004) (Magistrate), *aff'd*, Ctr. for Biological Diversity v. Norton, 336 F. Supp. 2d 1155, 1159–60 (D.N.M. 2004) (Chief Magistrate) (distinguishing *Greenpeace* because it did "not concern a listing decision by the agency" and "documents should be protected from disclosure so as to protect the integrity of government decision making and to avoid interference with candid and frank communications needed for future listing decisions of this nature."); *see also* Ctr. for Biological Diversity v. Norton, 2002 WL 32136200, at *2–3 (D. Ariz. 2002) (applying similar reasoning in sustaining government's invocation of deliberative process privilege with regard to documents pertaining to critical habitat designation). Because agency decisions implementing sections 4 and 7 of the ESA must both be based on the "best available" science concerning the particular species at issue, and do not generally involve broad policy considerations, it is difficult to justify treating such decisions differently from the vantage point of invocation of the deliberative process privilege.
108. 16 U.S.C. § 1533(g)(3)(A).
109. 28 U.S.C. § 1391.
110. *Id.* § 1391(e).
111. Several courts have held that because the ESA citizen suit provision uses the "permissive 'may,'" it supplements, rather than substitutes for, the general federal venue provisions. McCrary v. Gutierrez, 2006 WL 1748410, at *2 (E.D. Cal. 2006); *see also* Nw. Forest Council v. Babbitt, 1994 WL 908586, at *2 (D.D.C. 1994) ("the statute permits—but does not require—a lawsuit to 'be brought in the judicial district in which the violation occurs.' It merely expands the scope of permissible venues available for an ESA citizen suit."). The general federal venue provision in cases not based on diversity jurisdiction and not involving a federal defendant provides that a civil action may be brought in "(1) a judicial district where any defendant resides, if all defendants reside in the same State, (2) a judicial district in which a substantial part of the events or omissions giving rise to the claim occurred, or a substantial part of the property that is the subject of the action is situated, or (3) a judicial district in which any defendant may be found, if there is no district in which the action may otherwise be brought." 28 U.S.C. § 1391(b). The general venue provision that applies to claims against federal defendants is quoted in the text. *See* 28 U.S.C. § 1391(e).
112. *See generally* CHARLES A. WRIGHT, ARTHUR R. MILLER & EDWARD H. COOPER, FEDERAL PRACTICE AND PROCEDURE: JURISDICTION AND RELATED MATTERS § 3802.1, at 4, 6–7 n.9 (2d ed. 1986 (2005 Supp.)) ("there may be more than one district in which a claim may be thought to have arisen and in which venue should be proper").
113. 28 U.S.C. § 1404(a).
114. *Id.*
115. *See, e.g.*, Sierra Club v. Antwerp, Civ. No. 07-1756 (RCL), slip op. at 10 (D.D.C. Mem. Op. Dec. 4, 2007) (In denying a motion to transfer a case from D.C. where plaintiffs were accused of "forum shopping," the court stated that it was "well-aware that for each strategic rationale that motivated plaintiffs to file suit in this District, there is likely an equally compelling strategic basis—aside from the statutory standards of convenience and justice—for defendants and Intervenors' strong desire to ensure that this litigation takes place in the Middle District of Florida.").
116. Piper Aircraft Co. v. Reyno, 454 U.S. 235, 255 (1982).
117. *Id.*
118. Trout Unlimited v. U.S. Dep't of Agric., 944 F. Supp. 13, 19 (D.D.C. 1996); *id.* at 16 (section 1404(a) vests "discretion in the district court to adjudicate motions to transfer according to individualized, case-by-case consideration of convenience and fairness") (internal quotation omitted).

119. *See, e.g.*, Defenders of Wildlife v. Babbitt, No. 99-206, slip op. at 2 (D.D.C. Oct. 8, 1999) (declining to transfer challenge to listing decision despite "relevance to interests located [in Maine]" because court in D.C. had resolved "ample litigation of a similar nature under the ESA"); *but see* Nw. Forest Res. Council v. Babbitt, 1994 WL 908586, at *4 (D.D.C. 1994) (transferring to Western District of Washington challenge to final regulation listing species because "marbled murrelets do not inhabit land or water in—or anywhere near—the District of Columbia").
120. *See, e.g.*, Sierra Club v. Flowers, 276 F. Supp. 2d 62, 68 (D.D.C. 2003) (transferring to U.S. District Court for the Southern District of Florida case challenging Corps' issuance of mining permits that were alleged, among other impacts, to adversely affect the endangered wood stork; "Federal officials in Florida, not the District of Columbia, signed the final record of decision authorizing the permits" and the "decision to issue the permits is a controversy local to Florida and is one in which Florida and its residents have a great interest"); Hawksbill Sea Turtle v. FEMA, 939 F. Supp. 1, 3–5 (D.D.C. 1996) (transferring action where the "housing project, and the habitat of the sea turtle and tree boa are in the Virgin Islands, and the alleged violation of the [ESA] took place there"); *but see* Sierra Club v. Antwerp, Civ. No. 07-1756 (RCL) (D.D.C. Mem. Op. Dec. 4, 2007) (denying transfer in case contending that the Corps violated section 7 of the ESA in issuing a permit for a development project in Florida; the court relied on various factors including (1) at least one of the plaintiffs "has its headquarters in the District of Columbia" and "this plaintiff is entitled to a strong presumption in favor of the chosen forum"; (2) the "disposition of th[e] case will likely be based solely on the administrative record"; and (3) although there will "undoubtedly be a localized impact" on Florida residents, the plaintiffs had alleged violations that are "national in scope" and the ESA declares the "*national value* of endangered species") (emphasis in original)).
121. Sw. Ctr. for Biological Diversity v. U.S. Bureau of Reclamation, 143 F.3d 515, 520 (9th Cir. 1998) (citing Hallstrom v. Tillamook County, 493 U.S. 20, 26–28 (1989)). Although day-to-day implementation of the ESA has been delegated to FWS and NMFS, for purposes of the 60-day-notice requirement, notice must always be given directly to the Secretary of the Interior or Commerce. *See Sw. Ctr.*, 143 F.3d at 520 n.3 (notice letter to FWS was sufficiently detailed but nonetheless "failed to meet the notice requirements of the citizen suit provision of the ESA because it was not sent to the Secretary or to" the action agency).
122. *See, e.g., Sw. Ctr.*, 143 F.3d at 521; Marbled Murrelet v. Babbitt, 83 F.3d 1068, 1073 (9th Cir. 1996).
123. *Sw. Ctr.*, 143 F.3d at 522.
124. *Compare id.* at 521 (notice letter was deficient because it "said nothing about the Flycatcher or Southwest's intention to sue Reclamation based on the effects its operations were having on the Flycatcher's habitat at the Lake Mead delta"); Common Sense Salmon Recovery v. Evans, 329 F. Supp. 2d 96, 104 (D.D.C. 2004) (plaintiffs' notice letter "made no mention of the claim set forth in plaintiffs' third cause of action, which concerns the 'allow[ance of] fishing on listed salmon through adoption of regulations, incidental take permits and/or the ESA consultation process.' This letter therefore fails to satisfy the notice requirement as to this cause of action.") *with Marbled Murrelet*, 83 F.3d at 1073 (notice of section 7 violation was sufficient because "[a]lthough section 7 was referenced in only one part of the letter, the letter as a whole provided notice sufficient to afford the opportunity to rectify the asserted ESA violations"); Loggerhead Turtle v. County Council of Volusia County, 148 F.3d 1231, 1256 (11th Cir. 1998) (although notice letter mentioned leatherback sea turtles only once, the plaintiffs "provided sufficient notice that the leatherback sea turtle would be included in the allegations where, in its first paragraph, the letter expresses the need for 'immediate action ... to eliminate ... artificial beachfront lighting sources that take *protected sea turtles* during turtle nesting season' ... and in the next paragraph, the letter references the leatherback sea turtle as one of the three species of sea turtles that nest on Volusia County beaches") (emphasis in original).

125. *E.g.*, Water Keeper Alliance v. U.S. Dep't of Def., 217 F.3d 21, 30 (1st Cir. 2001) ("To say the Navy was not on notice that Water Keeper would object to the failure to prepare a biological assessment for its interim activities, when the Notice makes it clear that Water Keeper intended to challenge an ongoing delinquency in the preparation of a biological assessment, would be setting the bar for adequacy of notice too high"); Alabama v. U.S. Army Corps of Eng'rs, 441 F. Supp. 2d 1123, 1130 (N.D. Ala. 2006) ("The court finds that the express terms of the letter put the Corps on notice that Florida was challenging the ongoing operation of the reservoirs in the ACF Basin."). Because the function of the notice requirement is to allow an agency to take corrective action, the notice requirement should be deemed satisfied when notice is given that a proposed action will violate the ESA should it be adopted as a final decision. *See* Humane Soc'y of the United States v. Hodel, 840 F.2d 45, 61 n.28 (D.C. Cir. 1988).
126. *See* Nw. Forest Res. Council v. Glickman, 82 F.3d 825, 836 (9th Cir. 1996).
127. Trbovich v. United Mine Workers, 404 U.S. 528, 538 n.10 (1972).
128. *See* Coal. of Ariz./N.M. Counties for Stable Economic Growth v. Babbitt, 100 F.3d 837, 841, 845 (10th Cir. 1996) (activist could intervene in case challenging listing of Mexican spotted owl because of his past "involvement with the Owl in the wild and his persistent record of advocacy for its protection," and because the Department of the Interior "must represent the public interest, which may differ from Dr. Silver's interest in the protection of the Owl in the habitat where he has photographed and studied the Owl"; "DOI's ability to adequately represent Dr. Silver despite its obligation to represent the public interest is made all the more suspect by its reluctance in protecting the Owl, doing so only after Dr. Silver threatened, and eventually brought, a law suit to force compliance with the Act"); Fund for Animals, Inc. v. Norton, 322 F.3d 728, 736 (D.C. Cir. 2003) (the Natural Resources Department of the Ministry of Nature and Environment of Mongolia had a right to intervene in case challenging the FWS's rule allowing the importation of sport-hunted trophies of a threatened species; the Mongolian agency's "interests plainly are not adequately represented by the federal defendant.... For just these reasons, we have often concluded that governmental entities do not adequately represent the interests of aspiring intervenors.").

   It is noteworthy that, in NEPA cases, the Ninth Circuit has generally confined intervention to remedial issues on the theory that because only federal agencies can violate NEPA, a private party's only interest is in what relief a court crafts for a NEPA violation. *See* Forest Conservation Council v. U.S. Forest Serv., 66 F.3d 1489, 1499 (9th Cir. 1995). One district court has applied this reasoning to a claim that the Forest Service failed to fulfill its section 7 obligation to consult with the FWS before issuing grazing permits. *See* Sw. Ctr. for Biological Diversity v. U.S. Forest Serv., 82 F. Supp. 2d 1070 (D. Ariz. 2000); *but see* Friends of Animals v. Kempthorne, 452 F. Supp. 2d 64, 69 (D.D.C. 2006) (finding the Ninth Circuit's approach to be inconsistent with D.C. Circuit precedent).
129. Maine v. Dir., U.S. Fish and Wildlife Serv., 262 F.3d 13, 19 (1st Cir. 2001) (affirming denial of intervention motion by conservation group in case challenging listing of Atlantic salmon, although the group's prior litigation against the FWS had led to the listing; "[g]enerally, our decisions have proceeded on the assumption, subject to evidence to the contrary, that the government will adequately defend its actions, at least where its interests appear to be aligned with those of the proposed intervenor"; "[o]ur view is that the former adversary relationship between the government and proposed intervenors may raise questions about adequacy, but does not alone answer the questions. An earlier adverse relationship with the government does not automatically make for a present adverse relationship.").
130. TVA v. Hill, 437 U.S. 153, 193–95 (1978).
131. *Id.* at 194; *see also* Weinberger v. Romero-Barcelo, 456 U.S. 305, 313 (1982) (in passing the ESA, "Congress foreclosed the exercise of the usual discretion possessed by a court of equity").

132. *See, e.g.*, Sierra Club v. Marsh, 816 F.2d 1376, 1383 (9th Cir. 1987) (section 7 violation); Marbled Murrelet v. Babbitt, 83 F.3d 1068, 1073 (9th Cir. 1996) (section 9 violation).
133. Wash. Toxics Coal. v. EPA, 413 F.3d 1024, 1035 (9th Cir. 2005) (citing *Sierra Club*, 816 F.2d at 1389).
134. *Wash. Toxics Coal.*, 413 F.3d at 1035.
135. *See, e.g.*, *Biodiversity Legal Found.*, 309 F.3d at 1177 ("While neither this court nor the Supreme Court has yet ruled that an injunction must issue when the Service fails to comply with Section 4 of the ESA, as it has for violations of Section 7, Congress' purpose for passing the ESA applies to both provisions. . . . Congress has established procedures to further its policy of protecting endangered species. The substantive and procedural provisions of the ESA are the means determined by Congress to assure adequate protection. Only by requiring substantial compliance with the [A]ct's procedures can we effectuate the intent of the legislature.").
136. *Wash. Toxics Coal.*, 309 F.3d at 1035. It is important to note that *Washington Toxics Coalition* involved a ruling that section 7 safeguards applied to agency actions that had been ongoing for many years, i.e., EPA's registration of pesticides that, the plaintiffs maintained, were harming listed salmon and steelhead species in the waters of the Pacific Northwest. Accordingly, the court was called on to assess the kind of affirmative injunctive relief that would be appropriate where it was the "very maintenance of the 'status quo' that [was] alleged to be harming the endangered species." *Id.* In many (if not most) section 7 cases, the plaintiffs will be seeking relief that is designed to maintain the status quo by preventing the action agency from embarking on a *new* project that poses risks to listed species. In such cases, the scope of injunctive relief will generally be *broader* than in cases seeking to subject ongoing agency actions to the section 7 process, including because the section 7(d) prohibition on the "irreversible or irretrievable commitment of resources" during the consultation process will come into play, 16 U.S.C. § 1536(d); *see Wash. Toxics Coal.*, 413 F.3d at 1034–35 ("Section 7(d) was enacted to ensure that the status quo would be maintained during the consultation process, to prevent agencies from sinking resources into a project in order to ensure its completion regardless of its impacts on endangered species.").
137. *See* cases cited *supra* note 79.
138. *See, e.g.*, Nat'l Wildlife Fed'n v. NMFS, 422 F.3d 782, 793–94 (9th Cir. 2005) ("The traditional preliminary injunction analysis does not apply to injunctions issued pursuant to the ESA."). At the same time, "[t]his change in the preliminary injunction standard does not mean that courts are not required to look at the likelihood of future harm before deciding whether to grant an injunction." Seattle Audubon Soc'y v. Sutherland, 2007 WL 2220256, at *14 (W.D. Wash. 2007). Rather, plaintiffs must establish that the asserted violation creates at least a "reasonable likelihood" of harm to one or more members of a listed species, and hence that preliminary injunctive relief is necessary to prevent such harm. *Id.* at *15 ("The loss of a single listed species is an irreparable harm.") (citing Loggerhead Turtle v. Volusia County, 896 F. Supp. 2d 1170, 1180 (M.D. Fla. 1995)). Hence, to obtain either permanent or preliminary injunctive relief, a plaintiff need not establish that a particular action will result in extinction of the entire species. *Id.*; *see also* Greater Yellowstone Coal. v. Flowers, 321 F.3d 1250, 1257 (10th Cir. 2003) ("Plaintiffs contend that a proponent of a preliminary injunction under these circumstances, seeking to prevent harm to members of a threatened or endangered species, need not show harm to the species as a whole. We agree."); Am. Rivers v. U.S. Army Corps of Eng'rs, 271 F. Supp. 2d 230, 259 (D.D.C. 2003) ("While it is undisputed that high flow this summer will not lead to extinction of the [Piping plover] this year, the 2000 BiOp made clear that long term recovery of the species is dependent, in large part, on the long-planned implementation of low summer flow in 2003. Thus, the Court finds that implementation of the [agency action] will result in irreparable injury to the recovery and continued existence of these birds.") (footnote omitted); *id.* at 258–59 ("another

member of this District Court has concluded that even when there was 'not the remotest possibility that [the planned agency activity] during the period in which a preliminary injunction would be in place [would] eradicate the species,' the strong congressional mandate contained in the ESA to protect endangered and threatened species supported the finding that 'the loss even of the relatively few [individuals] that are likely to be taken through [an agency action] during the time it will take to reach a final decision in this case is a significant, and undoubtedly irreparable, harm.") (quoting Fund for Animals v. Turner, 1991 WL 206232, at *8 (D.D.C. 1991) (preliminarily enjoining a hunting season that would have killed an estimated three threatened grizzly bears)).

In *Winter v. Natural Resources Defense Council*, 129 S. Ct. 365 (2008), the Supreme Court addressed the traditional standard for the issuance of a preliminary injunction in the context of a NEPA claim that the Navy had failed to study adequately the effects of certain military training exercises on marine life. The Court stated that its "frequently reiterated standard requires plaintiffs seeking preliminary relief to demonstrate that irreparable injury is *likely* in the absence of an injunction," and not merely possible. *Id.* at 375 (emphasis in original). The Court's ruling, however, did not find that the plaintiffs had failed to make the requisite showing with respect to their recreational and other interests in marine mammals and other wildlife off the coast of California. Instead, while "not question[ing] the seriousness of [the plaintiff's] interests," *id.* at 377–78, the Court held that the national security need to "conduct training exercises with active sonar under realistic conditions" outweighed such interests, especially because the Navy had already adopted significant measures aimed at minimizing and mitigating wildlife impacts. *Id.* at 376–77. Although *Winter* is narrowly written and says nothing about the particular injunction analysis that should apply in ESA cases, it remains to be seen whether the ruling will have any bearing on how lower courts assess the propriety of preliminary relief in such cases or, indeed, whether the ruling will have ramifications beyond the national security context.

In one post-*Winter* ESA case—involving a claim that a Maine agency was violating section 9 by authorizing trapping in Canada lynx habitat—a district court reasoned that "[c]onsistent with *Winter*, the Court concludes that the correct test for irreparable injury is whether the Plaintiffs have demonstrated irreparable injury is likely if the injunction is not granted." Animal Welfare Institute v. Martin, 588 F. Supp. 2d 70, 102 (D. Me. 2008). The court held that the plaintiffs had satisfied that standard with regard to one type of trapping, which had resulted in the death of a lynx, although the plaintiffs "have not established that the death of one threatens the species as a whole." *Id.* at 106. On the other hand, the court declined to issue preliminary injunctive relief with respect to another form of trapping that had temporarily caught but not killed lynx, because the plaintiffs had "failed to establish that under the current state of Maine restrictions the lynx have suffered or will suffer irreparable harm." *Id.* at 105; *id.* at 105–6 ("the Court does not accept the view that 'any take and every take' of whatever definition meets the standard of irreparable harm").

139. *Nat'l Wildlife Fed'n*, 422 F.3d at 795 (affirming preliminary injunction requiring changes in the federal operation of the Columbia and Snake River dams because the district court had found that maintaining the status quo would "strongly contribute to the endangerment of the listed species and irreparable injury will result if changes are not made.").

140. *Id.* at 800 (remanding to the district court the "question of whether the [preliminary] injunction should be more narrowly tailored or modified").

141. *See* cases cited *supra* notes 67–69.

142. *Id.*

143. Atl. Green Sea Turtle v. County Council of Volusia County, Fla., 2005 WL 1227305, at *14 (M.D. Fla. 2005) (vacated as moot).

144. 16 U.S.C. § 1539(a)(1)(A).

145. Am. Soc'y for the Prevention of Cruelty to Animals v. Ringling Bros. and Barnum & Bailey Circus, 502 F. Supp. 2d 103, 112 (D.D.C. 2007).

146. *Atl. Green Sea Turtle*, 2005 WL 1227305, at *14 n.8 (quoting 50 C.F.R. § 13.48). In addition, the plaintiffs in *American Society for the Prevention of Cruelty to Animals* claimed that the defendant there was in violation of several specific regulations applicable to permits for individual animals held in captive situations. See 502 F. Supp. 2d at 111. Indeed, the "permit" at issue in that case itself takes the form of a regulation, i.e., a "captive-bred wildlife" regulation that provides that "any person may take . . . any endangered wildlife that is bred in captivity in the United States provided . . . that . . . [t]he purpose of such activity is to enhance the propagation or survival of the affected species." 50 C.F.R. § 17.21(g)(ii); *see also Am. Soc'y for the Prevention of Cruelty to Animals*, 502 F. Supp. 2d at 111 ("In addition to the [captive-bred wildlife regulation], entities that receive a permit must comply more generally with FWS regulations that apply to all permits issued under the ESA.").
147. The court in *Atlantic Green Sea Turtle* opined that allowing claims to be based on violations of the Service regulation mandating compliance with permit conditions "would require nothing less than the Court to police the County's permit compliance" and that, "[f]urthermore, it is the executive (not the judicial) branch that is generally charged with such duties." 2005 WL 1227305, at *14 n.8 (citing U.S. Const. Art. II § 3). But that charge could be leveled at *any* citizen suit based on *any* violation of the ESA or one of its implementing regulations. By creating an extremely broad citizen suit provision in the ESA, Congress evidently decided that citizen suit enforcement was needed to *supplement* Executive Branch oversight of the Act.
148. *Bennett*, 520 U.S. at 164–65.
149. Neither ruling cites any legislative history suggesting Congress's intent to restrict ESA citizen suits in this fashion.
150. For example, the Services have issued hundreds of incidental take permits that authorize the take of listed species on millions of acres of habitat. It is impossible for the chronically underfunded Services to effectively police compliance with all of these permits. Consequently, in the absence of citizen suit enforcement, it seems inevitable that violations of permits—including violations that may pose grave risks to species—will go largely unchecked. As courts increasingly recognize this reality, they may be more willing to entertain the seemingly strong legal arguments for construing the citizen suit provision to encompass permit violations, at least under certain circumstances.

14

The Endangered Species Act and the Constitutional Takings Issue

John D. Echeverria and Glenn P. Sugameli

Introduction

In the 35-year history of the Endangered Species Act (ESA), property owners have filed over a dozen lawsuits claiming that the Act resulted in a "taking" of private property under the Takings Clause of the Fifth Amendment to the U.S. Constitution.[1] In only one instance, however, has such a claim succeeded, in the controversial case of *Tulare Lake Basin Water Storage District v. United States*.[2] Applying an expansive "per se" takings theory, a U.S. Court of Federal Claims judge ruled that an ESA restriction on water deliveries from a California water project resulted in a taking. But six years later, in a similar case, *Casitas Municipal Water District v. United States*,[3] the same court (indeed, the same judge) repudiated the ruling in *Tulare Lake*. Thus, there is no surviving, final legal authority[4] supporting the argument that ESA restrictions result in constitutional takings.[5]

This chapter surveys the numerous, overlapping rationales courts have offered for rejecting takings claims based on government actions protecting threatened and endangered species. While the primary focus is on claims arising from restrictions imposed pursuant to the ESA, the chapter also discusses takings cases arising from other federal laws that serve at least in part to protect imperiled wildlife. Thus, it discusses a case based on denial of a Clean Water Act permit for a development that threatened bald eagles,[6] and a case based on a restriction on mining activity under the Surface Mining Control & Reclamation Act designed to avoid adverse impact on an endangered fish.[7] In addition, it discusses various takings cases based on application of state or local land use laws to protect threatened or endangered species.[8] With one arguable exception,[9] these decisions, like decisions based directly on ESA restrictions, have consistently rejected takings claims.

In theory, condemnation of private lands for species conservation purposes might raise interesting questions about the scope and proper application of the eminent domain power.[10] So far as we are aware, the United States has not exercised its condemnation power for ESA conservation purposes.

The chapter is organized as follows. First, it provides an overview of the relevant principles of regulatory takings doctrine, then describes the major provisions of the ESA that generate potential takings concerns. The primary reasons why takings challenges based on ESA restrictions have consistently failed are then summarized. The chapter then lays out in detail the various grounds on which courts have rejected takings claims based on restrictions on natural resource use designed to protect threatened and endangered species. We then discuss takings claims arising from private property damage caused by protected species, and the private property issues raised by government surveys for the presence of threatened and endangered species on private land. Finally, the chapter addresses takings claims arising from restrictions on the sale or transport of endangered animals or parts of endangered animals.

Overview of Relevant Takings Principles

In a regulatory taking case there are two basic questions: does the owner possess "property" and has the government "taken" the property? At the most simplistic level, plaintiff may not be the public or some third party, but must be an owner of the property. In addition, the owner must have a legal entitlement to use the property for the purpose he or she intends that is prohibited by the challenged law or regulation. The scope of private property interests is defined in part by "background principles" of nuisance or property law that limit what can be privately owned and what owners can lawfully do with their property.[11]

Assuming the owner can point to a protected property interest, the next question is whether the government action results in a "taking." As the Supreme Court explained in *Lingle v. Chevron U.S.A. Inc.*, the "common touchstone" of regulatory takings doctrine is government action that imposes such a severe burden on private property that it is "functionally equivalent to the classic taking in which government directly appropriates private property or ousts the owner from his domain."[12] Under this general principle, the Court has recognized two "relatively narrow"[13] categories of government action that will generally be regarded as per se takings. The first per se category, first recognized in *Loretto v. Teleprompter Manhattan CATV Corp.*,[14] involves the situation where the government "requires an owner to suffer a permanent physical invasion of her property."[15] A regulation imposing a physical occupation generally effects a taking regardless of whether all or only a part of the property is subject to the invasion. The second per se category, first recognized in *Lucas v. South Carolina Coastal Council*,[16] refers to regulation that renders an entire parcel of land valueless.

"Outside these two relatively narrow categories regulatory takings challenges are governed by the standards set forth in *Penn Central Transp. Co. v. New York City*."[17] In its landmark 1978 *Penn Central* decision,[18] the Supreme Court set out a three-part framework that remains the "polestar" of the Court's regulatory analysis today. The three factors include the "economic impact" of the government action, the extent to which the regulation has interfered with "investment-backed expectations," and the "character" of the government action.[19]

The economic impact factor addresses the degree of economic loss (if any) caused by the government action. Investment expectations, which the Supreme Court has said must be "reasonable,"[20] primarily turn on whether the regulatory program was in place at the time the claimant acquired the property, and whether the claimant knew or should have known that the property might be subjected to regulatory restrictions. The character factor has a somewhat more uncertain meaning, but largely turns on whether the regulation is designed to restrict harmful activity and whether the regulation singles out an owner to bear a particular burden or whether the burden is spread broadly across the community.[21]

In either a *Lucas* or a *Penn Central* regulatory taking case, the economic impact of the regulation must be assessed in relation to the property as a whole, not the portion of the property subject to the regulation. In general, in the case of land, "[t]he relevant parcel is defined to include the entire contiguous lot in the same ownership, with noncontiguous lots held by the same owner thrown in if part of an integrated development."[22] The resolution of the parcel question determines how difficult it will be to demonstrate the kind of severe economic impact necessary to support a taking claim: focusing on the affected portion, virtually any regulation will appear to have a burdensome effect; but under the property-as-whole approach it will be far more difficult to show a burdensome effect. In *Penn Central*, the Supreme Court seemingly resolved the issue in favor of the property-as-a-whole approach, but some dicta in two subsequent Supreme Court decisions appeared to cast doubt on this aspect of *Penn Central*.[23] However, in its 2002 decision in *Tahoe-Sierra Preservation Council v. Tahoe Regional Planning Agency*,[24] the Court definitively settled on the property-as-a-whole approach.

A special set of rules apply to regulatory "exactions," conditions attached to permits requiring owners to accept physical invasions of their property. Viewed independently, physical invasions ordinarily trigger the Supreme Court's per se takings rule. On the other hand, exactions are imposed as conditions to permits that government officials could generally deny without takings liability. In this special context, the Supreme Court has said that an individualized exaction will not be deemed a taking unless there is no "essential nexus" between the exaction and the government's regulatory objective,[25] or no "rough proportionality" between the burden imposed by the exaction and the projected impacts of development.[26] In *City of Monterey v. Del Monte Dunes at Monterey, Ltd.*[27] the Supreme Court refused to extend this test "beyond the special context of exactions—land-use decisions conditioning approval of development on the dedication of property to public use."[28]

The Supreme Court has drawn a distinction in its takings analysis between regulation of land and personal property. "In the case of personal property," the Court has stated, "by reason of the State's traditionally high degree of control over commercial dealings, [the owner] ought to be aware of the possibility that new regulation might even render his property economically worthless (at least if the property's only economically productive use is sale or manufacture for sale)."[29]

For many years, the Supreme Court maintained that a regulation constitutes a taking if it "fails to substantially advance a legitimate government interest,"[30] a verbal formula that appeared to call for relatively searching judicial review of government action under the Takings Clause. However, in *Lingle v. Chevron U.S.A.*,[31] the Supreme Court eliminated this test as a free-standing takings inquiry and ruled that this type of claim was "in the nature of a due process test," governed by the Court's traditional rational basis test. The *Lingle* decision makes clear that this ruling amounts to more than a matter of constitutional labels. Indeed, the *Lingle* decision is more important for reemphasizing the need for judicial deference to regulatory programs than for its rejection of the Takings Clause as the technical basis for judicial review.[32]

ESA Provisions Affecting Property Use

The regulatory apparatus of the ESA is triggered by the listing of a species as threatened or endangered.[33] Concurrent with the listing decision, the relevant agency (the U.S. Fish and Wildlife Service (FWS), or the National Marine Fisheries Service

(NMFS)) is required, when "prudent and determinable," to designate "critical habitat" for a listed species.[34] While the initial listing decision is to be made "solely on the basis of the best scientific and commercial data available," a critical habitat decision must be based both on scientific data and "economic impact and any other relevant impact."[35]

Listing decisions and critical habitat designations trigger substantive legal protections that may affect private property interests. Most significantly, section 9 of the ESA prohibits the "take" of an endangered species, which is defined to include any act endangering a species—including "to harass, harm, pursue, hunt, . . . capture or collect" a listed animal.[36] The Fish and Wildlife Service by regulation has defined "harm" to include "an act which actually kills or injures wildlife, . . . includ[ing] significant habitat modification or degradation where it actually kills or injures wildlife by significantly impairing essential behavioral patterns, including breeding, feeding, or sheltering."[37]

Section 10 of the ESA contains an important exception to section 9's takings prohibition. This provision authorizes the issuance on an Incidental Take Permit (ITP) for any taking otherwise prohibited by section 9 "if such taking is incidental to, and not for the purpose of, the carrying out of an otherwise lawful activity."[38] This provision allows permitted activities to proceed even if they harm individuals of a listed species. To obtain an ITP, an owner must prepare a habitat conservation plan (HCP) that includes proposed mitigation measures and discusses alternatives to the proposed action that were considered. "The purpose of the HCP is to ensure that the proposed action does not appreciably reduce the survival and recovery prospects of the species."[39]

The other provision of the ESA with the potential to generate takings concerns is section 7, which directs federal agencies in carrying out their responsibilities, such as deciding whether to issue a permit to a private party, to consult with the FWS or NMFS to ensure that their actions are "not likely to jeopardize the continued existence of any endangered species or threatened species, or result in the destruction or adverse modification of" designated critical habitat.[40] If the relevant service determines in a "biological opinion" that the proposed action will likely result in "jeopardy" or "adverse modification," it must prepare "reasonable and prudent alternatives" to the proposed action that would not violate the ESA. Once the agency ultimately adopts a reasonable and prudent alternative approved by the FWS or NMFS, then the service issues an incidental take permit and the activity can go forward.[41]

Finally, over the last decade, the FWS and NMFS have adopted various administrative measures designed to soften the burden of the ESA on the regulated community and private landowners in particular. Under safe harbor agreements, landowners who take steps to improve the quality of wildlife habitat on their land can subsequently return the land to its baseline condition without violating the ESA.[42] The so-called "No Surprises" policy provides property owners assurances that if they comply with the terms of an HCP, no additional restrictions or monetary obligations will be imposed during the term of the plan.[43] Finally, federal agencies have made increasingly aggressive use of "4(d) rules" for threatened species to establish relatively flexible wildlife protections.[44]

Overview of the ESA and Constitutional Takings Claims

In the sections that follow we discuss the grounds on which takings claims involving threatened and endangered species have been resolved. Before delving into these details, however, it may useful to focus on the big picture—the striking fact that so far the ESA has not produced any authoritative precedent upholding a taking claim. What accounts for this remarkable record? Several explanations come to mind.

First, regulatory takings doctrine, as recently clarified and simplified by the U.S. Supreme Court, provides an avenue for relief for landowners only in rare and extreme circumstances. Despite the efforts of property rights advocates to persuade the Supreme Court to adopt a broader view, the vast majority of regulatory takings claims fail under current law. Viewed in this larger context, the complete dearth of authoritative ESA takings precedents, though remarkable, basically reflects the current state of takings jurisprudence.

Second, the general failure of takings claims based on the ESA is consistent with a longstanding legal tradition upholding broad government authority to regulate private property to protect wildlife. As stated in a leading text on wildlife law, wildlife has long been "regarded as occupying a nearly unique status" in the law.[45] This special status is attributable to the deep-rooted idea that government (specifically state government) owns the wildlife within its borders in its sovereign capacity as representative of and for the benefit of the people. As a result of the doctrine of public ownership, wildlife is "not the subject of private ownership, except in so far as the people may elect to make it so; and they may, if they see fit, absolutely prohibit the taking of it, or the traffic and commerce in it, if it is deemed necessary for the protection or preservation of the public good."[46]

Historically, this doctrine has been invoked to support extensive fish and hunting regulations and substantial public immunity from liability for property damage caused by wildlife.[47] But, as a matter of logic, what the Washington Supreme Court has described as the public's "perfectly astounding" power to protect wildlife provides equally strong support for modern endangered species protections against constitutional takings challenges.[48]

Finally, despite frequent objections to the ESA by some development interests, the Act's regulatory mandates are actually quite flexible and carefully tailored to achieve conservation goals without unduly interfering with private property interests. As discussed, at various points the ESA requires consideration of economic effects on landowners, including in designating critical habitat and in defining reasonable and prudent alternatives. Before property owners can file a "ripe" taking claim, they must seek relief under the Act to determine what development will be allowed, ultimately reducing the volume of takings litigation under the ESA. Also, some endangered species restrictions are by their nature limited in area (e.g., applying only to acreage around a nesting tree); in scope (e.g., restricting some uses of property while allowing others); or in duration (e.g., addressing stresses caused by periodic droughts[49] or protecting a species during one particular part of its life cycle).[50]

For this combination of reasons, the ESA has proven essentially impregnable to regulatory takings claims. We now turn to a more detailed examination of the reasoning employed by different courts in rejecting takings claims based on the ESA and other laws that protect imperiled wildlife.[51]

Regulatory Restrictions on Natural Resource Use

The most common takings claims involving the ESA and other similar laws arise from regulatory restrictions on the use of land, water, and other natural resources. These types of takings claims have failed at a number of different points in the courts' legal analyses, as we discuss below.

Ripeness Issues

In order to get out of the starting gate with a taking claim, the claimant must present a "ripe" claim, and a number of ESA claims have been dismissed because they failed to overcome this hurdle. The ripeness requirement is rooted in the notion that "[a] court cannot determine whether a regulation has gone too far unless it knows how far the regulations go."[52] Accordingly, a taking claim is not ripe for adjudication until the government decision maker has made a "final" decision.[53] A corollary of the ripeness rule is that the mere imposition of a "requirement that a person obtain a permit before engaging in a certain use of his or her property does not itself 'take' the property in any sense: after all, the very existence of a permit system implies that permission may be granted."[54]

Thus, for example, the U.S. Court of Appeals for the Federal Circuit rejected on ripeness grounds a taking claim based on logging restrictions designed to protect the endangered spotted owl when the owner had never filed an application for an incidental take permit.[55] State courts have likewise rejected takings claims involving endangered species when the owners failed to pursue state administrative processes to their conclusion.[56]

In *Morris v. United States*,[57] the Federal Circuit rejected a test case mounted by the Pacific Legal Foundation that attempted to circumvent the ripeness barrier. The plaintiffs owned a half-acre lot on the Eel River in northern California with a half dozen old-growth redwoods that the owners wanted to harvest. Logging the trees represented a potential ESA "take" because it could adversely affect endangered fish in the river. The plaintiffs claimed their property had been taken without first seeking an incidental take permit, arguing that the claim was ripe on the theory that the $10,000 cost of preparing and processing a permit application exceeded the value of the timber. The government defended on the basis that the NMFS staff was willing to provide free assistance to the owners in preparing the application. On that understanding, the court ruled that the plaintiffs were required to seek an incidental take permit in order to ripen their taking claim.[58]

Threshold Property Issue

Assuming the claimant has overcome the procedural barriers to prosecuting a taking claim, the first substantive issue is whether the claimant has a protected property right to engage in the proposed activity. It can never be a taking to bar uses of property that are not part of the owner's title, or to "occupy" property in a way the owner does not have a right to prevent. In other words, do "background principles" of property or nuisance law bar the owner from claiming a vested property right and therefore preclude the taking claim at the threshold? The *Lucas* decision recognized that background limits can originate in either federal or state law.[59]

To date, only a handful of courts have carefully evaluated the background principles defense in the ESA context. Nonetheless, the available precedents indicate that relevant background principles of state law represent an important defense to takings claims based on protections for imperiled wildlife.

The doctrine of public ownership of wildlife, discussed above, readily fits into the background principles framework. In *Lucas*, the Court declared that a regulatory taking claim should fail if "the logically antecedent inquiry into the nature of the owner's estate shows that the proscribed use interests were not part of his title to begin with."[60] No regulation results in a taking, the Court continued, if the limitation "inhere[s] in the title itself, in the restrictions that background principles of the State's law of property and nuisance already place upon land ownership."[61] The public ownership doctrine is a rule of state property law that limits private rights impinging on wildlife and therefore qualifies as a background principle for the purpose of takings analysis. Both the courts and the commentators[62] have recognized that the venerable common-law doctrine of public ownership should generally bar takings claims based on restrictions to protect imperiled wildlife.

In *State v. Sour Mountain Realty*,[63] the Appellate Division of the New York Supreme Court invoked the public ownership doctrine to justify rejection of a taking claim arising from enforcement of the New York Endangered Species Act. The case involved a dispute between a property owner seeking to establish a mining operation and the New York Department of Environmental Conservation (DEC), which is responsible for enforcing the state act. A den of timber rattlesnakes, a threatened species in New York, was discovered on property a few hundred feet from the plaintiff's property line. The snakes undoubtedly utilized portions of the plaintiff's property as forage habitat. The landowner responded to the discovery of the den by constructing a "snake proof" fence to keep the snakes off its land. The DEC then sought an injunction requiring removal of the fence. The owner opposed the injunction, arguing that it would result in a regulatory taking.

The Appellate Division affirmed entry of an injunction against the landowner and rejected the taking claim. The court ruled that the plaintiff had failed to demonstrate the kind of severe intrusion on private property necessary to support a claim. In addition, however, the court stated that "the State, through the exercise of its police power, is safeguarding the welfare of an indigenous species that has been found to be threatened with extinction. The State's interest in protecting its wild animals is a venerable principle that can properly serve as a legitimate basis for the exercise of its police power" without payment of compensation. To support this conclusion, the court cited a New York statute codifying the doctrine of public ownership of wildlife.[64] The court also cited an early-twentieth-century New York decision rejecting an owner's objection to a requirement of a fishway at a private dam on the ground that the "petitioner cannot be deprived of a right [to obstruct wild fish] which it never possessed."[65]

Similarly, in *Sierra Club v. Department of Forestry & Fire Protection*,[66] the California Court of Appeals invoked the public ownership doctrine to support rejection of a taking claim based on an endangered species regulation. The case involved applications by the Pacific Lumber Company to harvest old growth timber on two parcels on which several endangered species, including the marbled murrelet and the spotted owl, had been detected. The timber company appealed a ruling invalidating its timber harvest plans for lack of necessary wildlife mitigation measures, contending that rejection of its plans was an unconstitutional taking. The Court of Appeals rejected the taking claim on ripeness grounds and, in the alternative, based on the doctrine of public ownership of wildlife. Surveying the extensive precedents on public ownership of wildlife, the court said that federal and state courts "have rejected the claim that a state or federal statute enacted in the interest of protecting wildlife is unconstitutional because it curtails the uses to which real property may be put." The court continued:

> A landowner whose valuable stands of old-growth forest are infested with protected species is subject to state regulation designed for the legitimate purpose of such protection. The . . . [precedents] clearly indicate that the federal and state governments may regulate and protect rare species on private lands without, ipso facto, triggering an unconstitutional taking of private property on which such species are present.

The court recognized that the then recently decided *Lucas* decision generally mandated compensation for regulations that eliminate all economic use. However, it observed that the Supreme Court had made its "total taking" inquiry subject to an exception for limitations consistent with "preexisting state common law of nuisance and property use," and that "wildlife regulation of some sort has been historically a part of the preexisting law of property."

Laws protecting endangered wildlife also can be defended against takings claims on the alternative ground that they parallel background principles of "nuisance" law. The *Restatement (Second) of Torts* defines a public nuisance to include, among other things, "an unreasonable interference with a right common to the general public."[67] Because the doctrine of public ownership of wildlife defines a common public right in wildlife, an activity that harms wildlife arguably represents not only an intrusion on public property rights but also a nuisance.

Reliance on the concept of public ownership in the context of endangered species regulation undoubtedly represents somewhat of a departure from the traditional applications of the doctrine. For the reasons discussed, however, application of the doctrine in the ESA context is entirely consistent with the logic underlying the doctrine. Moreover, the Supreme Court has recognized that the scope of background principles may evolve. As the Court stated in *Lucas*, "Changed circumstances or new knowledge may make what was previously permissible no longer so."[68] Even more to the point, Justice John Paul Stevens has observed, "New appreciation of the significance of endangered species . . . shapes our evolving understandings of property rights."[69]

The doctrine of public ownership of wildlife does not exhaust background principles that might be relevant in takings analyses. For example, the state courts have recognized that private interests in tidelands are subject to the public trust doctrine protecting the public's right to use tideland areas.[70] Wildlife protection is generally viewed as within the scope of the public trust doctrine.[71] Therefore, a restriction on development of tidelands that served in whole or in part to protect imperiled wildlife would fall within the scope of the public trust doctrine, providing an independent basis for rejecting a taking claim. Native American treaty rights might also represent background principles supporting ESA restrictions against a takings challenge.[72]

Finally, in *Palazzolo v. Rhode Island*, the Supreme Court explicitly recognized that at least some statutes can be background principles, but declined "to consider the precise circumstances when a legislative enactment can be deemed a background principle."[73] In *Tahoe-Sierra*, Chief Justice Rehnquist, in dissent, suggested that zoning restrictions might represent background principles, referencing the 1916 New York City zoning ordinance.[74] Query whether, under this view, given sufficient passage of time, certain federal or state statutes protecting wildlife or the ESA itself may be or might become background principles of property law.

Takings Analysis

Physical versus Regulatory Takings Analysis

A recurring issue in takings cases arising from endangered species regulation has been whether a regulatory restriction can be characterized as a physical occupation of private property. This is an important issue because, absent some applicable background principle, a permanent physical occupation is generally regarded as a per se taking no matter how modest the intrusion. By contrast, takings claims based on regulatory restrictions are evaluated using the property-as-a-whole approach, and generally based on the multifactor *Penn Central* analysis, with the result that few government actions rise to the level of compensable takings. In recent years, the issue has been hotly litigated in two contexts: trees and water.

In Oregon, the Boise Cascade Corporation and other timber companies mounted a concerted litigation campaign over the last decade seeking to establish that logging restrictions for the protection of endangered species should be regarded as a type of physical occupation. All of the cases involve the same basic pattern, with state forestry or federal wildlife officials drawing an imaginary circle around nest sites of spotted owls or bald eagles and prohibiting logging within the circles so long as the nests remain active. Some of the claims have been filed against the United States in federal court and other claims have been filed against the Oregon Board of Forestry in state court. The plaintiffs' theory has been that because the restrictions effectively required them to suffer the presence of wildlife that they would have driven from the area by logging, the restrictions constituted a physical taking of their property. Both the federal and state courts have roundly rejected the theory.

In *Boise Cascade Corp. v. United States*,[75] involving ESA restrictions designed to protect a nesting spotted owl, the Federal Circuit rejected the claim that a federal district court's injunction against logging constituted a per se physical-occupation taking of the property. In the Federal Circuit's words, "The government has no control over where the spotted owls nest, and it did not force the owls to occupy Boise's land. The government simply imposed a temporary restriction on Boise's exploitation of certain natural resources located on its land unless Boise obtained a permit."[76] The Federal Circuit followed the same reasoning in *Seiber v. United States*,[77] rejecting the argument that denial of an incidental take permit for logging activity that would harm an eagle nest site constituted a physical taking, stating, "The Supreme Court has long held that regulatory restrictions on the use of property do not constitute physical takings."[78]

The Oregon Supreme Court, in another case involving nesting eagles, also refused to accept the per se physical taking theory. Rejecting plaintiff's effort to analogize a restriction on tree harvesting to protect an endangered bird to a physical occupation, the court said that plaintiff's theory "fails to take into account the different character of regulatory action."[79]

As noted, the same issue also has been debated in the context of endangered species restrictions relating to water use. In the controversial *Tulare Lake* case,[80] U.S. Court of Federal Claims Judge John Wiese ruled that restrictions on water pumping in the Sacramento-San Joaquin Delta to protect endangered fish constituted a taking under the per se rule for physical occupations. Although the resulting shortfalls in water deliveries affected only a small portion of plaintiffs' entire water rights,[81] the court ruled that the restrictions constituted a compensable taking under this per se theory.[82]

The *Tulare Lake* decision has been the object of substantial judicial[83] and academic[84] criticism. The question whether the United States would appeal this adverse ruling became a matter of significant public controversy, especially after the National Oceanic and Atmospheric Administration (which includes the National Marine Fisheries Service), the California Attorney General's Office, and the California Water Resource Control Board advocated an appeal. Despite these recommendations, the U.S. Department of Justice decided not to appeal. Not surprisingly, the *Tulare Lake* decision prompted the filing of several similar takings claims based on ESA restrictions in water use.[85]

However, six years later, in *Casitas Municipal Water District v. United States*,[86] Judge Wiese issued a decision repudiating his ruling in the *Tulare Lake* case. In response to the listing of the steelhead trout as an endangered species, the National

Marine Fisheries Service prescribed new operating criteria for the Ventura River Project in southern California that limited the quantity of water the district could divert. Judge Wiese concluded that the Supreme Court's 2002 decision in *Tahoe-Sierra Preservation Council v. Tahoe Regional Planning Agency*[87] required that he abandon the analysis in *Tulare Lake*. In *Tahoe-Sierra* the Court rejected a claim that a development moratorium in the Lake Tahoe basin should be regarded as a per se taking, and in the process emphasized the narrowness of the physical occupation theory, stating that it was confined to "relatively rare, easily identified" cases. In *Casitas*, Judge Weise concluded that the Supreme Court's *Tahoe-Sierra* decision "compels us to respect the distinction between a government takeover of property (either by physical invasion or by directing the property's use to its own needs) and government restraints on an owner's use of that property."[88]

The decisions discussed above addressing the physical occupation takings theory in the context of endangered species restrictions affecting logging activity and water diversions have attracted a good deal of public attention. But these relatively recent decisions are only the latest examples in a long line of legal authority consistently rejecting the physical-occupation takings theory in cases involving similar (as well as other types) of restrictions on property use designed to protect endangered species and other wildlife.[89]

Applying Regulatory Takings Analysis

Setting aside the physical occupation theory, the next issue is how a taking claim based on ESA restrictions should be analyzed under the *Lucas* test or the *Penn Central* framework.

Because a *Lucas* claim must be evaluated using the property-as-a-whole approach, and ESA restrictions rarely if ever prohibit all economically productive use of an entire parcel, *Lucas* offers little promise to claimants challenging ESA restrictions. Accordingly, the courts that have addressed *Lucas* claims based on ESA restrictions have consistently dismissed them. The Oregon Supreme Court rejected a claim that restrictions on logging in the vicinity of a nesting bald eagle effected a taking under *Lucas*, stating that "in determining whether the regulation at issue ... deprived plaintiff of any economically viable use of its property, we focus on the plaintiff's ability to use the 40-acre parcel, not merely its ability to use the nine acres of timber" subject to the restrictions.[90] Similarly, the Federal Circuit rejected a *Lucas* claim based on logging restrictions where "the forty acres of regulated land were part of a larger two-hundred acre parcel of land."[91]

Absent a viable *Lucas* claim, a plaintiff challenging an ESA restriction must proceed under the *Penn Central* framework, which focuses on the economic impact of the regulation, the reasonableness of the owner's investment expectations, and the character of the regulation. Each of these factors has figured prominently in decisions rejecting ESA takings claims.

As with a *Lucas* regulatory taking claim, a *Penn Central* claim must be evaluated using the property-as-a-whole approach. Accordingly, some takings claims under

Penn Central have failed because the claimants did not make the kind of showing of adverse economic impact necessary to support their claims. In *Flotilla v. Florida Game & Fresh Water Fish Commission*,[92] the Florida Court of Appeals rejected a *Penn Central* claim where restrictions on development surrounding a bald eagle nest affected only 48 acres of the plaintiff's 173-acre holding. In *East Cape May Associates v. State of New Jersey*,[93] the New Jersey Court of Appeals reversed and remanded a takings award that was based on denial of a state wetlands permit because the trial court had not adequately considered whether a restricted parcel should be regarded as a part of a larger property.[94]

As noted, the narrow focus and limited duration of ESA restrictions tend to prevent the ESA from imposing the kinds of severe economic burdens that support a credible takings claim. For example, in *Seiber v. United States*,[95] the Federal Circuit affirmed rejection of a *Penn Central* claim when the FWS initially denied an incidental take permit because of the presence of an endangered bird, but 19 months later concluded that a permit was not necessary because the bird was no longer present on the property. The taking claim failed, the court said, because plaintiffs presented no evidence of "any economic impact imposed by the alleged temporary taking."[96] Similarly, in *Flotilla*,[97] the court rejected a taking claim because it was based on a temporary restriction that remained in place only until nesting eagles left the property.

The expectations factor also may militate against takings claims based on regulations imposed to protect endangered species. In *Palazzolo v. Rhode Island*,[98] the Supreme Court rejected the notion that an owner's knowledge of applicable regulations at the time he or she purchased the property should always bar a subsequent regulatory taking claim. However, in practice, a claimant's advance notice of a regulatory restriction is generally fatal to a taking claim.[99] Although we are not aware of any ESA takings case following this pattern, there is no reason to suppose that a property investor's advance notice of ESA constraints would not weigh against a takings challenge. If and when such a case is presented, an interesting set of questions may arise about whether the courts should regard the owner's expectations as having been primarily shaped by enactment of the ESA itself, the discovery of species on the property, and/or the formal designation of a particular species as threatened or endangered.

Another approach to the expectations issue is to ask whether the plaintiff was operating in a "highly regulated environment" and whether the plaintiff could have anticipated the regulation based on that environment and any foreseeable problems associated with the planned property use.[100] In *Good v. United States*,[101] the Federal Circuit affirmed rejection of a takings claim on this basis, stating: "In view of the regulatory climate that existed when Appellant acquired the subject property, Appellant could not have had a reasonable expectation that he would obtain approval to fill ten acres of wetlands in order to develop the land."[102] The developer purchased the land shortly before the ESA was enacted and started taking steps to obtain regulatory approval for development in 1980. The Army Corps of Engineers issued and reissued wetlands permits on several occasions. But, in the 1990s, after two endangered species were discovered on the property, the Corps denied a permit, prompting the takings claim. In rejecting the claim the court affirmed that it is not enough to sustain a claim that, when a property was acquired, a claimant "'had every reason to believe that necessary permits would be forthcoming.'"[103] Because Good "must have been aware that standards could change to his detriment . . . he lacked the reasonable, investment-backed expectations that are necessary to establish that a government action effects a regulatory taking."[104] The court also observed that during the lengthy application process, "rising environmental awareness translated into ever-tightening land use regulations," and that plaintiff "was not oblivious to this trend."[105]

The character factor tends to be the most elusive part of regulatory takings analysis and this has certainly been the case with takings claims involving ESA restrictions. A review of takings jurisprudence reveals a plethora of alternative, sometimes conflicting definitions of the character factor.[106] The limited space in this chapter requires a truncated examination of the issue, focusing specifically on how the character factor applies in the ESA context.

As initially introduced into takings law by the *Penn Central* decision itself, the character factor was defined as focusing on whether the government action could be characterized as a "physical occupation of private property."[107] As discussed, the courts have consistently rejected efforts to categorize property restrictions based on the presence of endangered species as physical invasions. Accordingly, this original definition of the character factor has apparently provided no support for takings claims involving imperiled wildlife.

Another approach to the character factor focuses on the importance of the goal the government is trying to achieve. Several cases involving ESA restrictions embrace this definition of the character factor, referring to the "strong public policy interest,"[108] or the "benefi[t] to the welfare and quality of life of the people"[109] served by species conservation.[110] Given that regulatory takings doctrine is a subset of condemnation law, the importance of the government's goal cannot properly be weighed directly against the burden imposed on a landowner to evaluate the merits of a takings claim. After all, it could never be contended that the government is entitled to take land for a road or a park without payment because the taking will serve some important transportation or open space need.

Nonetheless, the importance or value of a government policy, and of species conservation in particular, is critically important in takings analysis. The Supreme Court has long recognized that "[u]nder our system of government, one of the State's primary ways of preserving the public weal is restricting the uses individuals can make of their property. While each of us is burdened somewhat by such restrictions, we, in turn, benefit greatly from the restrictions that are placed on others."[111] While certain landowners are burdened by ESA restrictions, they are also benefited by the application of the ESA (and many other laws) to other landowners in the community. The more important the public purpose served by the law, the greater the reciprocal benefits. Because the ESA serves what is generally acknowledged to be a vital public goal, it produces very significant reciprocal benefits for landowners. In addition, the increasing presence of threatened and endangered species on private lands across the country[112] means that both the burdens and reciprocal benefits of ESA restrictions are becoming widely shared.[113]

The final alternative definition of character that appears relevant in the ESA context is the extent to which a restriction on activities to protect threatened or endangered species can be characterized as harm-preventing. In *Lucas*, Justice Scalia famously observed that the distinction between harm-preventing and benefit-conferring regulation "is difficult, if not impossible, to discern on an objective, value-free basis."[114] However, this statement runs counter to a long legal tradition of considering the harmfulness of a regulated activity in takings cases,[115] and probably should be read as applying only in a *Lucas*-type case, not a case under *Penn Central*.[116] In a variety of contexts the lower courts have addressed the degree to which regulations prevent harm in analyzing whether they result in takings.[117]

Regulations that prevent the death or extinction of fish and other wildlife can fairly be characterized as harm-preventing. Indeed, the ESA itself explicitly defines the primary regulatory provision of the Act as aimed at harm prevention. Section 9 of the Act makes it unlawful for any person to "take" endangered or threatened species, and defines "take" to mean, among other things, to "harm," which the Secretary of the Interior subsequently defined by regulation to include "significant habitat modification or degradation where it actually kills or injures wildlife." Consistent with this understanding, some lower courts addressing takings claims involving threatened or endangered species have explicitly relied upon the harm-preventing character of the restrictions in rejecting the claims.[118]

Restrictions on Defense of Property

Another type of regulatory taking claim involving threatened or endangered species arises when animals have directly caused damage to private property, such as by breaking down fences or attacking livestock. These cases are part of a much larger body of law relating to government liability for property damage caused by wildlife generally. Summarizing the larger body of law, the en banc U.S. Court of Appeals for the Tenth Circuit stated, "Of the courts that have considered whether damage to private property by protected wildlife constitutes a 'taking,' a clear majority have held that it does not and that the government thus does not owe compensation."[119] The handful of cases specifically involving threatened or endangered species have reached the same result.

The leading ESA decision is *Christy v. Hodel*,[120] decided by the U.S. Court of Appeals for the Ninth Circuit. Christy maintained a flock of sheep that was repeatedly attacked by endangered grizzly bears on land adjacent to Glacier National Park. After unsuccessful attempts to capture the bears or frighten them away, Christy shot and killed a bear. In response to the Department of the Interior's assessment of a civil penalty under the ESA, Christy asserted that the prohibition against killing endangered species in this circumstance was a taking. The court rejected the claim that the ESA effected either a physical or a regulatory taking, observing that "Numerous cases have considered, and rejected, the argument that destruction of private property by protected wildlife constitutes a governmental taking."[121]

Although the matter is debatable, the soundest legal basis for this ruling appears to the longstanding doctrine of public ownership of wildlife. In the venerable case of *Barrett v. State*,[122] the New York Court of Appeals rejected a landowner's claim for compensation for the value for timber destroyed by wild beavers based on the public ownership doctrine, stating:

> Whatever protection is accorded [to wildlife], harm may be done to the individual. Deer or moose may browse on his crops; mink or skunks kill his chickens; robins eat his cherries. In certain cases the Legislature may be mistaken in its belief that more good than harm is occasioned. But this is clearly a matter which is confided to its discretion.[123]

Similarly, the Colorado Supreme Court stated in a comparable case that the principle of governmental immunity from takings claims "is based largely on the circumstance that the property right to the wild game within [a state's] borders is vested in the people of the state in their sovereign capacity."[124]

Certain other decisions, including *Christy*, suggest that this rule is based on the different rationale that government officials have no ability to control the conduct of wild animals.[125] But, as noted, the concept of public rights in wild animals appears to represent the actual foundation for this rule. This conclusion is supported by decisions rejecting takings claims based on property damage even when government officials have physically transported and reintroduced the animals to an area where they were absent. *Barrett v. State*, the seminal public ownership precedent, involved beavers that state officials had trapped and transported to a new location where they destroyed the plaintiff's valuable trees. Likewise, in *Moerman v. California*,[126] the California County of Appeals ruled that the state did not take private property by reintroducing endangered tule elk that subsequently damaged the plaintiff's fences and ate his forage. If the rule that government is not liable for property damage caused by wild animals were based on a lack of government control over the animals, as opposed to sovereign public rights in wildlife, these cases probably would have come out the other way.

Official Access for Survey Purposes

As discussed, the Supreme Court has emphasized that government actions impinging on an owner's right to exclude others from private property generally trigger serious concerns under the Takings Clause. One ESA-related question raised by this aspect of takings doctrine is whether surveys of private land by government wildlife officials to determine whether endangered species are present constitute takings. Again, the answer is no.

In *Boise Cascade Corp v. United States*,[127] the U.S. Court of Appeals for the Federal Circuit ruled that a preliminary injunction granting the U.S. Fish and Wildlife Service permission to enter private property to conduct surveys for spotted owls over a five-month period did not a constitute a compensable taking. In rejecting the owner's takings theory, the court emphasized the transitory nature of the invasions:

> Transient, nonexclusive entries by the Service to conduct owl surveys do not permanently usurp Boise's exclusive right to possess, use, and dispose of its property. The government's incursion into Boise's property is more in the nature of a temporary trespass . . . rather than a permanent physical occupation or an easement of some kind.[128]

The court also observed that rejection of the claim was justified in this case by the purpose of these particular surveys, "which was to discover information necessary to the adjudication of a case that [the plaintiff] itself had initiated."[129]

Restrictions on Commercial Dealings

Finally, takings claims have arisen from restrictions on commercial sales or transportation of endangered animals or parts of endangered animals. These cases arise against the backdrop of the Supreme Court decision in *Andrus v. Allard*,[130] in which the Court found no taking based on a ban on the commercial sale of bird parts under the Eagle Protection Act and the Migratory Bird Treaty Act. The cases arising directly from enforcement of the ESA reach the same result.

In *United States v. Kepler*,[131] the U.S. Court of Appeals for the Sixth Circuit rejected a takings challenge to a criminal conviction for the illegal transportation of endangered species. The defendant had lawfully acquired two animals, a cougar and a leopard, but later, following the enactment of the ESA, transported the animals from Florida to Kentucky in violation of the ESA's ban on interstate transport. In *United States v. Hill*,[132] the federal district court refused to dismiss, based on a takings objection, a criminal indictment charging plaintiff with the sale of parts of endangered species (rhinoceroses, tigers, and leopards) in violation of the ESA provision barring such sales.

These decisions (and *Andrus*) appear to rest on two rationales. First, the courts invoked the property-as-a-whole rule to support the conclusion that the ESA restrictions did not destroy all or a substantial portion of plaintiffs' property interests. In *Kepler*, the court observed that the prohibition on interstate sales did not destroy the plaintiff's property because it did not apply to intrastate sales and was subject to an exception "for scientific purposes or to enhance the propagation or survival of the affected species."[133] Similarly, in *Hill*, the court said, "Hill has not been denied all economic value from his property. There are other uses for the animal parts in question."[134]

Second, the decisions are supported by the distinction between land and personal property. In *Lucas*, the Court, citing *Andrus v. Allard*, stated, "[I]n the case of personal property, by reason of the State's traditionally high degree of control over commercial dealings [the owner] ought to be aware of the possibility that new regulation might even render his property economically worthless (at least if the property's only economically productive use is sale or manufacture for sale)."[135] In *Hill*, the court explicitly invoked "the distinction between personal and real property" to justify rejection of the claim.[136] While the court in *Kepler* did not rely on this distinction, the result in that case can be explained on the same basis.

Conclusion

The central message of this chapter is that experience with takings claims based on the ESA and other legal restrictions designed to protect imperiled wildlife shows that these claims will be extremely difficult to sustain. The consistent rejection of this type of claim partly reflects the determination by the Supreme Court to reserve regulatory takings doctrine for rare cases. But it also reflects the flexibility inherent in the ESA and the strong legal tradition, long predating adoption of the ESA, upholding expansive public authority to protect the public's wildlife despite claimed impacts on private property interests.

Notes

1. "[N]or shall private property be taken for public use, without just compensation."
2. 49 Fed. Cl. 313 (2001).
3. 76 Fed. Cl. 100 (2007).
4. Technically, as a trial-level ruling, the decision in *Tulare Lake* never had binding precedential effect, even on the judge who issued the opinion. *See* Penzoil-Quaker State Co. & Subsidiaries v. United States, 62 Fed. Cl. 689, 696 (2004) (decisions by particular judges of the Court of Federal Claims not binding on other judges of the Court of Federal Claims); 18-134 MOORE'S FEDERAL PRACTICE—CIVIL § 134.02[1][d] (2006) ("A decision of a federal district court judge is not binding precedent in either a different judicial district, the same judicial district, or even upon the same judge in a different case.").
5. As this chapter was being prepared for publication, the U.S. Court of Appeals for the Federal Circuit, in a 2 to 1 ruling, reversed the grant of summary judgment to the government in *Casitas* and remanded for the federal claims court to determine whether requiring the plaintiff to divert water through a fish ladder would be a compensable taking. *See* 543 F.3d 1276 (Fed. Cir. 2008). The panel majority did not rule on whether Judge Wiese correctly repudiated his prior ruling in *Tulare Lake*, stating: "We do not opine on whether *Tulare* was rightly decided, but note that the *Tulare* decision has been criticized." *Id.* at 1295 n.16. On February 17, 2009, the Federal Circuit rejected an application for a rehearing en banc, with four members of the court dissenting. *See* 556 F.3d 1329 (Fed. Cir. 2009).
6. Forest Props., Inc. v. United States, 39 Fed. Cl. 56 (1997), *aff'd*, 177 F.3d 1360 (Fed. Cir. 1999).
7. Appolo Fuels, Inc. v. United States, 54 Fed. Cl. 717 (2002), *aff'd*, 381 F.3d 1338 (Fed. Cir. 2004).
8. *See, e.g.*, State v. Lake Lawrence Pub. Lands Prot. Ass'n, 601 P.2d 494 (Wash. 1979) (county denial of subdivision plat to protect bald eagles); E. Cape May Assocs. v. State of New Jersey, 693 A.2d 114 (N.J. Super. Ct. App. Div. 1997) (state denial of wetlands development permit to protect endangered bird nesting habitat).
9. The arguable exception is the Supreme Court decision in City of Monterey v. Del Monte Dunes at Monterey Ltd., 526 U.S. 687 (1999), upholding a takings award based on a city's rejection of a development application. The city's action was motivated by various factors, including a concern about potential impacts on an endangered butterfly. However, for several reasons the case provides little useful guidance on whether or under what circumstances restrictions to protect endangered wildlife might support a takings claim. The record was ambiguous on whether the butterfly was even present on the property

and therefore the endangered species issue did not loom large in the case. The jury was instructed that it could find a taking if it concluded that the regulatory action failed to substantially advance a legitimate state interest, a theory of takings liability subsequently repudiated by the U.S. Supreme Court in Lingle v. Chevron U.S.A. Inc., 544 U.S. 528 (2005). Finally, the case before the Supreme Court did not focus on the substantive issues of takings law discussed in this chapter, but instead addressed (1) whether the case was properly submitted to a jury, (2) whether the municipality's decision was subjected to overly intrusive judicial review, and (3) the scope of the Court's doctrine dealing with regulatory "exactions."

10. See Kelo v. City of New London, 545 U.S. 469 (2005).
11. Lucas v. S.C. Coastal Council, 505 U.S. 1003 (1992). See generally Michael Blumm & Lucus Ritchie, Lucas's Unlikely Legacy: The Rise of Background Principles as Categorical Takings Defenses, 29 HARV. ENVTL. L. REV. 321 (2005); Glenn P. Sugameli, Threshold Statutory and Common Law Background Principles of Property and Nuisance Law Define If There Is a Protected Property Interest, in TAKING SIDES ON TAKINGS ISSUES: PUBLIC AND PRIVATE PERSPECTIVES § 7 (Thomas E. Roberts ed., ABA 2002).
12. 544 U.S. 528, 539 (2005).
13. Id. at 538.
14. 458 U.S. 419 (1982).
15. Lingle, 544 U.S. at 538.
16. 505 U.S. 1003 (1992).
17. Lingle, 544 U.S. at 538.
18. 438 U.S. 104 (1978).
19. Id. at 124.
20. See Kaiser Aetna v. United States, 444 U.S. 164, 175 (1979).
21. See generally John D. Echeverria, Making Sense of Penn Central, 23 UCLA J. ENVTL. L. & POL'Y 171 (2005).
22. Robert Meltz, CRS Report to Congress, The Endangered Species Act and Claims of Property Rights "Takings" at CRS-9 (Dec. 18, 2006).
23. See Palazzolo v. Rhode Island, 533 U.S. 606, 631 (2001); Lucas v. S.C. Coastal Council, 505 U.S. at 1016 n.7.
24. 535 U.S. 302 (2002).
25. Nollan v. Cal. Coastal Comm'n, 483 U.S. 82 (1987).
26. Dolan v. City of Tigard, 512 U.S. 374 (1994).
27. 526 U.S. 687 (1999).
28. See John D. Echeverria, Revving the Engines in Neutral: City of Monterey v. Del Monte Dunes at Monterey, Ltd., 29 ENVTL. L. RPTR. 10,682 (1999).
29. Lucas, 505 U.S. at 1027.
30. Agins v. City of Tiburon, 447 U.S. 255, 260 (1980).
31. 544 U.S. 528 (2005).
32. J. Peter Byrne, Due Process Land Use Claims After Lingle, 34 ECOLOGY L.Q. 471, 475 (2007).
33. 16 U.S.C. § 1533.
34. 16 U.S.C. § 1533(a)(3).
35. 16 U.S.C. § 1533(b)(2).
36. 16 U.S.C. § 1532(19).
37. 50 C.F.R. § 17.3 (1994). See Babbitt v. Sweet Home Chapter of Cmtys. for a Great Or., 515 U.S. 687 (1995) (upholding the regulations as a reasonable interpretation of the statute).
38. 16 U.S.C. § 1539(a)(1)(B).
39. Robert Meltz, CRS Report to Congress, The Endangered Species Act and Claims of Property Rights "Takings" (Dec. 18, 2006).
40. 16 U.S.C. § 1536(a)(2).
41. 16 U.S.C. § 1536(b)(4). A rarely invoked provision authorizes the so-called Endangered Species Committee to exempt activities from section 7 despite the risk of species extinc-

tion based upon a finding that the action's benefits clearly outweigh the benefits of alternatives that would conserve the species or the habitat. 16 U.S.C. § 1536(e).
42. *See* 50 C.F.R. §§ 17.22(c), 17.32(c).
43. 50 C.F.R. §§ 17.22(b)(5), 17.32(b)(5) (FWS); 50 C.F.R. § 222.307(g) (NMFS).
44. *See* 16 U.S.C. § 1532(d).
45. MICHAEL J. BEAN & MELANIE J. ROWLAND, THE EVOLUTION OF NATIONAL WILDLIFE LAW 8 (3d ed. 1997).
46. Geer v. Connecticut, 161 U.S. 519, 529 (1896).
47. *See generally* Thomas A. Lund, *Early American Wildlife Law*, 51 N.Y.U. L. REV. 703 (1976).
48. Cook v. State, 74 P.2d 199, 201 (Wash. 1973). Some decisions, including decisions directly addressing takings claims involving threatened or endangered species, appear to reject the concept of public ownership of wildlife. *See* Christy v. Hodel, 857 F.2d 1324, 1335 (9th Cir. 1988) ("The federal government does not 'own' the wild animals it protects") (citing Douglas v. Seacoast Products, Inc., 431 U.S. 265, 284, (1977) ("[I]t is pure fantasy to talk of 'owning' wild fish, birds, or animals. Neither the States nor the Federal Government . . . has title to these creatures until they are reduced to possession by skillful capture.")). As one of us and a co-author have explained elsewhere, these statements are based on an overly broad reading of Supreme Court decisions invalidating state protectionist regulation of wildlife under the federal Constitution that do not (and could not) invalidate the common-law tradition of public ownership of wildlife. *See* John D. Echeverria & Julie Lurman, *"Perfectly Astounding" Public Rights: Wildlife Protection and the Takings Clause*, 16 TUL. ENVTL. L.J. 331 (2003).
49. *See, e.g.*, Klamath Irrigation Dist. v. United States, 67 Fed. Cl. 504 (2004) (takings claims based on shortfall in irrigation water supplies in extreme drought year).
50. State v. Lake Lawrence Pub. Lands Prot. Ass'n, 601 P.2d 494 (Wash. 1979) (temporary restriction to accommodate nesting bald eagle).
51. We are not aware of any cases focusing on the takings implications of legal protections for endangered plants and we therefore confine our attention to animals.
52. McDonald, Sommer & Frates v. Yolo County, 477 U.S. 340, 348 (1986).
53. *Id.*
54. United States v. Riverside Bayview Homes, 474 U.S. 121, 126–27 (1985).
55. Boise Cascade Corp. v. United States, 296 F.3d 1339 (Fed. Cir. 2002) (landowner failed to present ripe federal taking claim based on district court injunction barring logging because owner never sought an incidental take permit under the ESA).
56. *See, e.g.*, Sierra Club v. Dep't of Forestry & Fire Prot., 24 Cal. Rptr. 487 (Cal. App.) (dismissing challenge to logging restrictions designed to protect endangered species on the ground that the state department of forestry had not made a final administrative decision on proposed logging plan), *review denied*, 26 Cal. Rptr. 338 (1993) (ordering that court of appeals decision not be published). *Cf.* Boise Cascade Corp. v. Bd. of Forestry, 63 P.3d 598 (Or. Ct. App. 2003) (vacating grant of summary judgment to state board in takings challenge to logging restriction designed to protect spotted owl in order to give plaintiff opportunity to attempt to establish "futility" of filing an application for an ITP).
57. 392 F.3d 1371 (Fed. Cir. 2004).
58. Ripeness doctrine does not exhaust the list of potential procedural hurdles to successful takings claims based on regulations protecting threatened wildlife. For a sampling of decisions involving other procedural hurdles, see Gordon v. Norton, 322 F.3d 1213 (10th Cir. 2003) (affirming dismissal of taking claim based on Department of the Interior's reintroduction of the endangered gray wolf to the Yellowstone ecosystem on the ground that exclusive jurisdiction over takings claims over $10,000 against the United States lies in the U.S. Court of Federal Claims); Meredith v. Talbot, 828 F.2d 228 (4th Cir. 1987) (affirming dismissal of taking claim under both Pullman and Burford abstention doctrines where developers brought suit in federal court based on county's limitation of proposed subdivision to avoid adversely affecting endangered species habitat).

59. 505 U.S. at 1029 (citing as an example of a background limitation Scranton v. Wheeler, 179 U.S. 141 (1900), in which the claimant's property interest was limited by the federal navigational servitude).
60. 505 U.S. 1003, 1027 (1992).
61. *Id.* at 1029.
62. Michael Blumm & Lucus Ritchie, *Lucas's Unlikely Legacy: The Rise of Background Principles as Categorical Takings Defenses*, 29 HARV. ENVTL. L. REV. 321 (2005); John D. Echeverria & Julie Lurman, *"Perfectly Astounding" Public Rights: Wildlife Protection and the Takings Clause*, 16 TUL. ENVTL. L.J. 331 (2003); Oliver A. Houck, *Why Do We Protect Endangered Species, and What Does That Say About Whether Restrictions on Private Property to Protect Them Constitute "Takings"?*, 80 IOWA L. REV. 297, 308–31 (1995).
63. 714 N.Y.S.2d 78 (App. Div.), *leave to appeal denied*, 714 N.Y.S.2d 78 (App. Div. 2000). *See* Christopher A. Amato & Robert Rosenthal, *Endangered Species Protection in New York After* State v. Sour Mountain Realty, Inc., 10 N.Y.U. ENVTL. L.J. 117 (2001).
64. N.Y. ENVTL. CONSERV. LAW § 11-0105.
65. *In re* Del. River at Stilesville, 131 A.D. 303, 115 N.Y.S. 745 (3d Dep't 1909).
66. 24 Cal. Rptr. 487 (Cal. App.), *review denied*, 26 Cal. Rptr. 338 (1993) (ordering that court of appeals decision not be published).
67. *Lucas*, 505 U.S. at 1031.
68. *Id.*
69. *Id.* at 1069–70 (dissenting). In a different context, courts have relied in part on the new appreciation of the significance of endangered species to support a broad interpretation of the Commerce Clause. *See* Nat'l Ass'n of Home Builders v. Babbitt, 130 F.3d 1041, 1050, 1058 (D.C. Cir. 1997), *cert. denied*, 524 U.S. 937 (1998); Gibbs v. Babbitt, 214 F.3d 483 (4th Cir. 2000), *cert. denied*, 531 U.S. 1145 (2001).
70. McQueen v. S.C. Coastal Council, 580 S.E.2d 116 (S.C. 2003).
71. *See, e.g.*, Nat'l Audubon Soc'y v. Superior Court, 658 P.2d 709 (Cal. 1983) (applying the public trust doctrine to protect various species of birds). *See In re* Steuart Transp. Co., 495 F. Supp. 38, 40 (E.D. Va. 1980) ("[u]nder the public trust doctrine, the State . . . and the United States have the right and the duty to protect and preserve the public's interest in natural wildlife resources"). *See generally* Hope M. Babcock, *Should* Lucas v. South Carolina Coastal Council *Protect Where the Wild Things Are? Of Beavers, Bob-o-Links, and Other Things That Go Bump in the Night*, 85 IOWA L. REV. 849, 889–98 (2000).
72. *See* Glenn P. Sugameli, *Threshold Statutory and Common Law Background Principles of Property and Nuisance Law Define If There Is a Protected Property Interest*, in TAKING SIDES ON TAKINGS ISSUES: PUBLIC AND PRIVATE PERSPECTIVES § 7 (Thomas E. Roberts ed., ABA 2002).
73. 533 U.S. 606, 627 (2001).
74. 503 U.S. at 352 (Rehnquist, C.J., dissenting, joined by Scalia & Thomas, JJ.). *See* Glenn P. Sugameli, *The Supreme Court Confirms That Threshold Statutory and Common Law Background Principles of Property and Nuisance Law Define If There Is a Protected Property Interest*, in TAKING SIDES ON TAKINGS ISSUES: THE IMPACT OF TAHOE-SIERRA § 7, at 51–543 (Thomas E. Roberts ed., ABA 2003).
75. 296 F.3d 1339 (Fed. Cir. 2002).
76. *Id.* at 1354–55.
77. 364 F.3d 1356 (Fed. Cir. 2004).
78. *Id.* at 1366.
79. Coast Range Conifers, LLC v. State *ex rel.* Or. State Bd. of Forestry, 117 P.3d 990 (Or. 2005).
80. 49 Fed. Cl. 313 (2001).
81. Melinda Harm Benson, *The Tulare Case: Water Rights, the Endangered Species, and the Fifth Amendment*, 32 ENVTL. L. 551, 560 (2002) ("[t]he restrictions resulted in an

overall reduction in water availability of approximately 0.11% and 2.92%" for the two lead plaintiff irrigation districts).
82. 49 Fed. Cl. at 319.
83. *Klamath*, 67 Fed. Cl. at 538 ("[W]ith all due respect, Tulare appears to be wrong on some counts, incomplete in others, and distinguishable at all events."); Allegretti & Co. v. County of Imperial, 42 Cal. Rptr. 3d 122 (2006) ("we disagree with *Tulare Lake*'s conclusion that the government's imposition of pumping restrictions is no different than an actual physical diversion of water").
84. *See, e.g.*, Michael C. Blumm & Lucus Ritchie, *Lucas's Unlikely Legacy: The Rise of Background Principles as Categorical Takings Defenses*, 29 HARV. ENVTL. L. REV. 321, 329 (2005); Cari S. Parobek, *Of Farmers' Takes and Fishes' Takings: Fifth Amendment Compensation Claims When the Endangered Species Act and Western Water Right Collide*, 27 HARV. ENVTL. L. REV. 177, 212–23 (2003); Brittany K. T. Kauffman, *What Remains of the Endangered Species Act and Western Water Rights After* Tulare Lake Basin Water Storage District v. United States, 74 U. COLO. L. REV. 837 (2003); Melinda Harm Benson, *The Tulare Case: Water Rights, the Endangered Species, and the Fifth Amendment*, 32 ENVTL. L. 551 (2002).
85. *See, e.g.*, Stockton E. Water Dist. v. United States, 76 Fed. Cl. 497 (2007); Casitas Mun. Water Dist. v. United States, 76 Fed. Cl. 100 (2007).
86. 76 Fed. Cl. 100 (2007).
87. 535 U.S. 302 (2002).
88. 76 Fed. Cl. at 106. As noted *supra* note 5, on September 25, 2008, the U.S. Court of Appeals for the Federal Circuit, in a 2 to 1 ruling, reversed the federal claims court's grant of summary judgment to the government and remanded the case for further proceedings to determine whether a compensable taking occurred.
89. *See, e.g.*, Clajon Prod. Corp. v. Petera, 70 F.3d 1566, 1576 (10th Cir. 1995) ("[p]laintiffs resist framing their argument as a 'regulatory' takings claim" but "do not complain of a physical occupation"); Fallini v. United States, 56 F.3d 1378, 1383 (Fed. Cir. 1995) (protected wild "horses are not agents of the Department of the Interior"); Southview Assocs., Ltd. v. Bongartz, 980 F.2d 84, 106–07 (2d Cir. 1992) (no physical taking; developer retained deeryard and substantial power to control use or to sell it), *cert. denied*, U.S. 987 (1993); Christy v. Hodel, 857 F.2d 1324, 1335 (9th Cir. 1988) (management and protection of grizzly bears did not cause government occupation of land); *Mountain States Legal Found.*, 799 F.2d at 1428 (Wild Free-Roaming Horses and Burros Act is "nothing more than a land-use regulation"); Moerman v. California, 21 Cal. Rptr. 2d 329, 334 (Cal. App. 1993) (state relocated tule elk were not state "instrumentalities"); Flotilla v. Fla. Game & Fresh Water Fish Comm'n, 636 So. 2d 761 (Fla. App. 1994) (no physical occupation from establishment of bald eagle nest buffer zone; developer "lost neither the right to possess nor convey the affected areas, and further retained the right to use the property in any way that would not disturb the eagles' habitat."); State v. Lake Lawrence Pub. Lands Prot. Ass'n, 601 P.2d 494 (Wash. 1979) (en banc) (no physical or regulatory taking from denial of plat to protect eagle perching and feeding area), *appeal dismissed, cert. denied*, 449 U.S. 830 (1980).
90. *Coast Range Conifers*, 117 P.3d at 998.
91. *Seiber*, 364 F.3d at 1369. *See also* Forest Props., Inc. v. United States, 39 Fed. Cl. 56 (1997) (rejecting *Lucas* claim based on denial of permit to fill 9.4 acres of wetlands in order to protect several species of endangered animals and plants where wetland area was a portion of a larger 62-acre property), *aff'd*, 177 F.3d 1360 (Fed. Cir. 1999).
92. 636 So. 2d 761 (Fla. App. 1994).
93. 693 A.2d 114 (N.J. Super. Ct. App. Div. 1997).
94. *See also* Appolo Fuels, Inc. v. United States, 54 Fed. Cl. 717 (2002) (rejecting, based on the property-as-a-whole rule, taking claim based on restriction imposed pursuant to Surface Mining Control and Reclamation Act designed in part to protect endangered species), *aff'd*, 381 F.3d 1338 (Fed. Cir. 2004); State v. Lake Lawrence Pub. Lands Prot.

Ass'n, 601 P.2d 494, 500 (Wash. 1979) (rejecting taking claim under federal and Washington state takings clauses, stating, "Of crucial importance in this case is the fact that the Commissioners' decision to deny the plat leaves open the possibility of approving a less dense development of Woods Point.").
95. 189 F.3d 1355 (Fed. Cir. 1999).
96. *Id.* at 1361.
97. 636 So. 2d 761 (Fla. App. 1994).
98. 533 U.S. 606 (2001).
99. *See* John D. Echeverria, *Making Sense of* Penn Central, 23 J. ENVTL. L. & POL'Y 171, 183–84 (2005) (discussing post-Palazzolo case law addressing whether a purchaser's notice of regulatory constraints supports rejection of a subsequent taking claim).
100. Appolo Fuels, Inc v. United States, 381 F.3d 1338, 1349 (Fed. Cir. 2004).
101. Good v. United States, 189 F.3d 1355 (Fed. Cir. 1999), *cert. denied*, 529 U.S. 1053 (2000).
102. *Id.* at 1361–62.
103. *Id.* at 1363 (quoting Deltona Corp. v. United States, 657 F.2d 1184, 1193 (Ct. Cl. 1981), *cert. denied*, 455 U.S. 1017 (1982)).
104. *Id.* at 1363.
105. *Id.* at 1362. The court ruled in *Good* that even a total taking under *Lucas* does not "eliminat[e] the requirement that the landowner have reasonable, investment-backed expectations of developing his land." *Id.* at 1361. Subsequently, a different Federal Circuit panel claimed that this statement in *Good* was dictum and ruled that a lack of reasonable investment-backed expectations is a not a relevant factor in a *Lucas* case. Palm Beach Isles Assocs. v. United States, 208 F.3d 1374 (Fed. Cir.), *op. on reh'g*, 231 F. 3d 1354 (Fed. Cir. 2000). This characterization of the ruling in *Good* as dictum is at the very least highly debatable. *See* Glenn P. Sugameli, *The Supreme Court Confirms That Threshold Statutory and Common Law Background Principles of Property and Nuisance Law Define If There Is a Protected Property Interest*, in TAKING SIDES ON TAKINGS ISSUES: THE IMPACT OF TAHOE-SIERRA § 7, at 51, 53 (Thomas E. Roberts ed., ABA 2003) (discussing this intra-circuit conflict in greater detail). If the *Good* language is indeed a holding, then it remains the binding circuit rule on this question. *See* Newell Cos., Inc. v. Kenney Mfg. Co., 864 F.2d 757, 765 (Fed. Cir. 1988) ("This court has adopted the rule that prior decisions of a panel of the court are binding precedent on subsequent panels unless and until overturned in banc."), *cert. denied*, 493 U.S. 814 (1989).
106. John D. Echeverria, *Making Sense of* Penn Central, 23 J. ENVTL. L. & POL'Y 171 (2005).
107. 438 U.S. at 124.
108. State v. Lake Lawrence Pub. Lands Prot. Ass'n, 601 P.2d 494, 501 (Wash. 1979).
109. Fla. Game & Fresh Water Fish Comm'n v. Flotilla, Inc., 636 So. 2d 761 (1994).
110. In addition, the U.S. Supreme Court in TVA v. Hill, 437 U.S. 153 (1978), famously observed that the ESA elevated the government's interest in species conservation to the "highest of priorities."
111. *Id.* at 491.
112. According to a 1994 General Accounting Office report, 90 percent of protected species had some portion of their habitat on private land and 37 percent of them were entirely dependent on private land (GAO 1994). *See* U.S. Gen. Accounting Office, Endangered Species Act: Information On Species Protection On Nonfederal Land (1994).
113. The Supreme Court has also emphasized that the reciprocity of advantage concept includes the reciprocal advantages that citizens receive from the network of regulations that exist in modern society. In his famous dissent in *Pennsylvania Coal Co. v. Mahon*, 260 U.S. 393 (1922), Justice Louis Brandeis objected to the notion that regulations could only be defended based on the reciprocal benefits produced by the specific regulation at issue. Sometimes regulations can be defended, he said, based on "the advantages of living and doing business in a civilized society," *id*. at 142, an idea subsequently embraced

in majority Supreme Court decisions. *See, e.g.*, Kirby Forest Indus., Inc v. United States, 467 U.S. 1, 14 (1984); Andrus v. Allard, 444 U.S. 51, 67 (1979).
114. 505 U.S. at 1026.
115. *See, e.g.*, Mugler v. Kansas, 123 U.S. 623 (1887).
116. *See* John D. Echeverria, *Making Sense of* Penn Central, 23 UCLA J. ENVTL. L. & POL'Y 171, 195.
117. *See, e.g.*, First English Evangelical Lutheran Church v. County of Los Angles, 258 Cal. Rptr. 893, 904 (1989) (on remand from the Supreme Court, rejecting taking claim based on floodplain zoning ordinance that "involve[d] this highest of public interests—the prevention of death and injury").
118. *See, e.g.*, Appolo Fuels, Inc. v. United States, 381 F.3d 1338 (Fed. Cir. 2004) (affirming rejection of a taking claim based on designation of area as unsuitable for mining under the Surface Mining Control and Reclamation Act in order to protect an endangered fish species, and observing that the designation would prevent "harmful runoff" into local streams and represented "the type of governmental action that has typically been regarded as not requiring compensation for the burdens it imposes on private parties who are affected by the regulations"); State v. Sour Mountain Realty, Inc., 276 A.D.2d 8, 16 (N.Y. App. Div. 2000) (rejecting taking claim on the ground that "the State, through its exercise of its police power, is safeguarding the welfare of an indigenous species that has been found to be threatened with extinction").
119. Mountain States Legal Found. v. Hodel, 799 F.2d 1423, 1428 (10th Cir. 1986) (en banc), *cert. denied*, 480 U.S. 951 (1987). *Accord* Christy v. Hodel, 857 F.2d 1324, 1335 (9th Cir. 1988). Both the Ninth and Tenth Circuits disagreed with two state cases that ruled that crop damage caused by hunting bans on private land caused a taking. *See* State v. Herwig, 117 N.W.2d 335, 340 (Wis. 1962); Shellnut v. Ark. State Game & Fish Comm'n, 258 S.W.2d 570, 573–74 (Ark. 1953). Neither *Herwig* nor *Shellnut* discussed any of the contrary federal or state decisions preceding those cases that the Ninth and Tenth Circuits relied upon. *See also* Green Acres Land & Cattle Co. v. State, 766 S.W.2d 649, 652 (Mo. App. 1988) (rejecting *Herwig* and *Shellnut*).
120. 857 F.2d 1324, 1335 (9th Cir. 1988).
121. *Id.* at 1334.
122. 116 N.E. 99 (N.Y. 1917).
123. *Id.* at 100.
124. Maitland v. People, 23 P.2d 116, 117 (Colo. 1993).
125. 857 F.2d at 1335 ("the government [does not] control the conduct of such animals. . . . Plaintiffs assume that the conduct of the grizzly bear is attributable to the government but offer no explanation or authority to support their assumption").
126. 21 Cal. Rptr. 2d 329, 332–34 (Cal. App. 1993), *cert. denied*, 511 U.S. 1031 (1994).
127. 296 F.3d 1339 (Fed. Cir. 2002).
128. *Id.* at 1355.
129. *Id.* at 1357.
130. 444 U.S. 51 (1979).
131. 531 F.2d 796 (1976).
132. 896 F. Supp. 1057 (D. Colo. 1995).
133. 531 F.2d at 797.
134. 896 F. Supp. at 1063.
135. *Lucas*, 505 U.S. at 1027.
136. 896 F. Supp. at 1063.

15

The Convention on International Trade in Endangered Species of Wild Fauna and Flora

W. Michael Young and Holly Wheeler

Introduction

Prior to 1973, the cross-border shipment of animals and plants, or their parts or products, was regulated principally through a maze of national or subnational laws and regulations. There was no common set of conservation standards established under international law and adopted by a majority of countries for use in determining whether to permit trade in particular species. Nor was there international agreement on a standard permitting regime that would provide transparency for the regulated community while maintaining effective control over potentially deleterious trade. The results of the Plenipotentiary Conference that negotiated and adopted the Washington Convention, or the Convention on International Trade in Endangered Species of Wild Fauna and Flora (CITES),[1] in 1973 changed the landscape for the effective regulation and conservation of wildlife and plant species in international trade and filled a huge vacuum in international law.

Thirty-four years later, after years of experience involved in the issuance of thousands of CITES documents under somewhat cryptic implementing regulations, the U.S. Fish and Wildlife Service (FWS) replaced its archaic CITES regulations codified at 50 C.F.R. Part 23 with comprehensive regulations that implement fully the accumulated resolutions and decisions of 13 Meetings of the CITES Conference of the Parties. These new regulations were published on August 23, 2007.[2] They represent state-of-the-art legal and policy interpretations of CITES.

The new regulations provide a "user-friendly" guide to the regulated community in the United States on how to comply with CITES worldwide, whether from the perspective of an individual traveling with a CITES-listed pet, a tourist who purchases goods overseas composed in part of CITES-regulated animal or plant parts or products, a scientist engaged in the noncommercial international exchange of CITES-regulated animal or plant species or their parts, zoological institutions engaged in the acquisition of CITES-listed animals for public display or captive-breeding programs, or others who trade CITES-listed species internationally. They capture the evolution of CITES interpretation and practice over the last 34 years while providing regulatory guidance that can be used productively by tourists as well as attorneys who practice daily on sophisticated issues involved in compliance with CITES.

This chapter examines the structure, conservation standards, and processes of CITES from both a governmental and transactional perspective.

Current State of the Law

The Structure of CITES

One common misconception that flows principally from the inclusion of the term "endangered species" in its title is that the Convention applies solely to the trade

---

The views presented in this chapter represent the personal opinions of the authors and do not necessarily represent the position or views of the U.S. Department of the Interior, the Office of the Solicitor, or the United States Government.

in species that face threats to their continued existence in the wild. Instead, CITES applies to international trade[3] in wildlife and plant species[4] that may pose risks to the survival of that or other species unless effective trade controls are established. CITES addresses four different categories of species:

- Appendix I, "all species threatened with extinction which are or may be affected by trade";[5]
- Appendix II, "all species which although not necessarily now threatened with extinction *may* become so unless trade in specimens of such species is subject to strict regulation to avoid utilization incompatible with their survival";[6]
- Appendix II "look-alike" species ("other species which must be subject to regulation in order that trade in specimens of certain species . . . may be brought under effective control");[7] and
- Appendix III, all species designated by an individual CITES Party as subject to regulation within that Party's jurisdiction and as requiring the cooperation of the other Parties to control international trade.[8]

In short, CITES applies to species presently facing extinction threats (Appendix I species); species that are involved in international trade that may face extinction unless subjected to strict regulation (Article II(2)(a) Appendix II species); species that are similar in appearance to those that currently or may face extinction threats (Article II(2)(b) Appendix II species); and species involved in international trade that an individual CITES Party designates as requiring the regulatory assistance of the other Parties (Appendix III species).[9]

Another popular misconception, at least in the United States where CITES is implemented through sections 8A and 9(c) of the Endangered Species Act (ESA),[10] is that the listing of endangered and threatened species under section 4 of the ESA[11] is comparable to the process for adding species to Appendices I and II of CITES. In fact, the substantive standards and procedures are not the same. Whereas the listing of a species under the domestic ESA is conducted by regulation in accordance with the procedures and substantive standards of the ESA,[12] amendments to Appendices I and II are carried out through the parliamentary process of the Meeting of the Conference of the Parties[13] or by postal vote of the Parties.[14] Article XVI of CITES establishes the procedure for adding species to Appendix III.[15]

By acceding to CITES, a Party country agrees to regulate the import, export, re-export, and introduction from the sea of all species included in Appendices I, II, and III in accordance with the Convention requirements.[16] More importantly, the Party country agrees to implement the permitting controls, administrative requirements, and enforcement mandates of CITES for the species included in the Appendices.[17] This includes the all-important duty to take "appropriate measures" to enforce the Convention, which requires the penalization of any illegal trade or possession of illegally traded specimens,[18] and the confiscation, or return to the exporting country, of any illegally traded specimens.[19] Although a degree of prosecutorial discretion is allowed under CITES regarding the imposition of civil or criminal penalties on a person engaged in trade contrary to the provisions of the Convention, the mandate to confiscate illegally traded specimens is clear—such specimens are contraband and must be dealt with by the Party countries accordingly.[20]

In recent years, the CITES Parties have adopted guidance to assist in the identification and resolution of compliance problems at the governmental level. In Resolution 14.3, the Parties adopted a Guide to CITES compliance procedures and recommended that it be referred to by the Parties, the Standing Committee, and the Animals and Plants Committees when dealing with issues involving alleged lapses in compliance with CITES requirements by particular Party countries.[21] The purpose of this guide is to establish a uniform system of procedures that can be referred to by the various CITES committees when attempting to remedy infrastructural deficiencies (e.g., lack of budgetary resources to properly carry out reviews of permit applications or to adequately inspect shipments at a Party's ports of entry), permit violations, trade records or periodic reports problems, and other trade issues involving the effective implementation of the treaty that are identified by the Parties and communicated by the Secretariat. The provisions in the guide emphasize the need for transparency in identifying the specific compliance issue of concern to the Parties, as well as the need for due process in both notifying the responsible Party or Parties of the compliance issue and allowing an adequate opportunity for response. While specific penalties for noncompliance are not set out in the resolution or guide, the prospect for CITES-consistent suspensions of trade in one or more CITES-listed species is noted at paragraph 30 of the guide. Further examination of compliance issues is expected at the 15th Meeting of the Conference of the Parties (Doha, Qatar, March 2010).

Each Party to CITES must designate a Management Authority and a Scientific Authority to carry out the administrative requirements called for by the Convention.[22] The Management Authority is the governmental body that is authorized to issue CITES permits and certificates on behalf of a Party. It also has the responsibility to carry out communications with the other Management Authorities and the CITES Secretariat to effectuate arrangements for the return of illegally traded specimens to the country of export and to respond to inquiries regarding its own permits or certificates. The Scientific Authority, which need not necessarily be a governmental entity, provides technical and scientific advice or findings to the Management Authority as needed for the processing of permit applications.[23]

Although Parties that accede to the requirements of CITES must meet the minimum requirements of the treaty when engaging in trade in CITES-protected specimens, there is no preemptive effect on the Parties' authority[24] to adopt and enforce stricter domestic measures.[25] In the United States, there are a number of such "stricter domestic measures" that add procedural and substantive requirements that either preclude or further restrict the importation of CITES-listed specimens.[26] A number of states in the United States also impose restrictions on the importation of certain CITES-listed species, and nothing in the Convention preempts the enforcement of these state laws.[27]

The Conservation Standards of CITES

The substantive standards and procedural safeguards that must be met before allowing trade in CITES specimens is scaled according to the degree of conservation risk faced by a particular species. Each Party must adhere to these minimum requirements so that the documents issued by each Party can be accepted at each port of entry with a minimum of inspection and processing delay.

Species included in Appendix I receive the highest degree of substantive and procedural protection under CITES. As stated in Article II, paragraph 1 of the Convention, trade in Appendix I specimens "must be subject to particularly strict regulation in order not to endanger further their survival and must only be authorized in exceptional circumstances."

Article III of CITES sets out the standards and procedures for regulating trade in Appendix I specimens. As a general rule, no Appendix I specimen can be entered into international trade unless its use is not for primarily commercial purposes.[28] Further, trade in the specimen must not be "detrimental to the survival" of the species, and the acquisition of the specimen must not be in violation of the laws of the exporting country. Finally, Appendix I specimens are uniquely subjected to a dual-permitting regime. Generally, both the importing and exporting countries must issue permits to effectuate trade in an Appendix I specimen.[29]

Article IV of CITES sets out the standards and procedures for regulating trade in Appendix II specimens. Unlike Appendix I specimens, the issue of "not for primarily commercial purposes" for the use of the Appendix II specimen is irrelevant. Appendix II specimens can be freely traded for commercial purposes as long as the other requirements of Article IV are met.[30] As is the case with Appendix I specimens, the trade in Appendix II specimens must not be "detrimental to the survival" of the species,[31] and the acquisition of the specimen must not be in violation of the laws of the exporting country. The country of import does not have to issue a document to authorize the importation of an Appendix II specimen.[32]

Article V sets out the standards and procedures for regulating trade in Appendix III specimens. As a general matter, Appendix III specimens require an export permit from the country of export when that country has included the species in Appendix III.[33] An export permit can be granted if the specimen was not acquired in violation of the exporting country's laws for the conservation of that taxon. The export of Appendix III specimens from countries other than the country that added the species to Appendix III requires only the issuance of a certificate of origin.[34]

The Administrative Procedures of CITES

Under CITES, documents are issued by a Party's Management Authority to show that a particular CITES specimen can be traded consistent with the requirements of the Convention. These documents take the form of a "permit" or "certificate," and each must follow a standard form as prescribed by the Convention.[35]

Those persons who wish to trade internationally in CITES-listed species must apply to the appropriate Management Authority for any needed permit or certificate.[36] In the United States, the Management Authority is the FWS.[37] The remainder of the discussion in this chapter will focus on the procedures followed by the FWS in the review and final action taken on an application for a CITES document.[38]

Import permits under CITES are required only for the importation of Appendix I specimens.[39] FWS regulations require that applications for CITES import permits follow specific formats depending on the species at issue.[40] As noted earlier in this chapter, import permits may be granted[41] only if the Service's Scientific Authority issues a "nondetriment" finding,[42] the Service's Management Authority finds that the specimen "is not to be used for primarily commercial purposes,"[43] and, for living specimens, the Service's Scientific Authority finds that the recipient is "suitably equipped to house and care" for the specimen.[44] Import permits are valid for no more than 12 months from the date of issuance.[45]

Export permits may be issued for specimens included in Appendices I, II, or III. FWS regulations require that applications for CITES export permits follow specific formats depending on the species at issue.[46] For Appendix I specimens, export permits may be granted[47] only if the Service's Scientific Authority issues a "nondetriment" finding, the Management Authority finds that the specimen was legally acquired,[48] the Management Authority is satisfied that an import permit has been granted,[49] and, for living specimens, the Management Authority finds that the specimen "will be so prepared and shipped as to minimize the risk of injury, damage to health or cruel treatment."[50] For Appendix II specimens, export permits may issue only if the appropriate "nondetriment," "legal acquisition," and humane handling (for living specimens) findings are made.[51] For Appendix III specimens, export permits may issue only from a Party country that has included the species in Appendix III and that finds that the specimen was lawfully acquired and, for living specimens, meets humane handling requirements.[52] Export permits are valid for no more than six months from the date of issuance.[53]

Certificates are issued under CITES for a variety of reasons to authorize trade in species listed in Appendix I, II, or III. These documents must satisfy the basic documentary requirements of Article VI of the Convention and any substantive requirements specified in Articles III, IV, V, or VII.

After the initial export of a CITES specimen, every subsequent export to another country requires the prior issuance of a "re-export" certificate.[54] For Appendix I specimens, the certificate may be granted if the Service's Management Authority finds that the import of the specimen into the United States complied with all CITES requirements, that an import permit has been granted by the importing country for any living specimen, and that humane handling requirements have been met for any living specimen.[55] For Appendix II specimens, the certificate may be granted as long as the Management Authority finds that the import of the specimen into the United States complied with all CITES requirements and that, for living specimens, humane handling requirements have been met.[56] For Appendix III specimens, the Management Authority need only issue a certificate noting that the specimen was processed in the United States or that it is being re-exported.[57] Re-export certificates are valid for no more than six months from the date of issuance.[58]

Certificates for introduction from the sea are available for specimens of Appendix I and II species that are taken within the marine environment outside the jurisdiction of any country[59] and that are to be transported into a Party country.[60] For Appendix I specimens, a certificate may be granted if the Scientific Authority of the "State of introduction"[61] issues a "nondetriment" finding, the Management Authority of the "State of introduction" issues a finding that the specimen is not to be used for primarily commercial purposes, and, for living specimens, the Management Authority finds that the recipient is suitably equipped to house and care for the specimen.[62] For Appendix II specimens, a certificate may be granted based on "nondetriment" and "suitably equipped" findings.[63] However, special rules apply to those Appendix II specimens that are taken by ships registered by Party countries that are also parties to pre-Convention treaties that regulate the taking of such species. Under CITES Article XIV, paragraphs 4 and 5, Appendix II specimens taken consistent with the terms of such pre-Convention treaties need not secure introduction from the sea certificates. Instead, any export of such specimens "shall only require a certificate from a Management Authority of the State of introduction to the effect that the specimen was taken in accordance with the provisions of the other treaty."[64] Appendix III specimens are not subject to certificate requirements for introductions from the sea. However, any subsequent trade (export or re-export) of the specimen would be considered subject to CITES export permit or certificate of origin requirements.[65] Certificates for introduction from the sea are valid for no more than 12 months from their date of issuance.[66]

Certificates of origin are required by Article V, paragraph 3 of the Convention to allow the import of any Appendix III specimen if the exporting country did not include the species in Appendix III. Such certificates are issued by the Management Authority,[67] and they remain in effect for no more than 12 months from the date of issuance.[68]

Certificates are also available from the Management Authority to document compliance with the pre-Convention exemption of Article VII, paragraph 2;[69] to obtain a certificate of exemption for artificially propagated plants under Article VII, paragraph 5;[70] to obtain a "bred-in-captivity" certificate under Article VII, paragraph 5;[71] or to obtain a certificate of ownership that allows the transboundary shipment of personally owned pets for personal use.[72] These certificates remain in effect for no longer than three years from the date of issuance.[73]

Under certain circumstances scientific institutions that register with the Management Authority of their country may engage in the international trade of CITES specimens for purposes of the noncommercial loan, donation, or exchange of such specimens. Such trade, which is exempt from the requirements of CITES under Article VII, paragraph 6 of the treaty, does not require the issuance of a CITES document per se. Instead, upon registration, the Management Authority assigns to each eligible scientific institution a unique five-character code that must be provided on the customs declaration label. The institution code, plus the additional labeling requirements of 50 C.F.R. § 23.48, are included on the customs declaration label that is affixed to the shipping container or package. The contents of the label provide the necessary CITES authorization for specimens traded among registered scientific institutions.

As noted in 50 C.F.R. § 23.17, there is no exemption from CITES requirements for diplomatic, consular, military, or other persons exempt from customs duties or inspection who engage in international trade in CITES specimens. Such persons must obtain appropriate CITES documentation for their shipments or otherwise risk enforcement action, consistent with CITES Decision 9.15 and the preamble discussion.[74]

Specialized CITES Procedures

The CITES Parties have dealt with a number of recurring import/export problems involving the high-volume trade in commercially valuable specimens of wildlife and plants. Some of these problems flow from particular provisions of the Convention—such as the provision allowing for Appendix II treatment of specimens of Appendix I wildlife bred in captivity for commercial purposes or Appendix I plants artificially propagated for commercial purposes—that were remarkably vague in terms of procedure as well as standards for approval.[75] Others have arisen as a result of the unique features of the trade in tropical timber species, the scope and noncommercial aspects of the trade in personally taken hunting trophies, and the labeling and repackaging challenges presented by the sturgeon caviar trade. These issues are discussed below.

Bred in Captivity

Specimens of CITES-listed animal species that are bred in captivity are accorded special treatment under the Convention. The Parties placed great importance on reducing the need to remove animals from the wild where the use of captive-bred animals would fulfill trade demand for public display, scientific research, and other uses. Therefore, Article VII, paragraph 4 of the Convention provides that specimens of Appendix I animal species that are bred in captivity for commercial purposes are to be treated as Appendix II specimens for purposes of the trade restrictions of CITES.[76] This provides much-needed flexibility—both procedurally (no need to apply for an import permit) and substantively (the prohibition against primarily commercial trade is removed)—for those who wish to trade in Appendix I wildlife species, thereby creating a clear incentive to use captive-bred specimens rather than removing specimens from the wild. The procedures for registering a facility that engages in the captive breeding of Appendix I specimens for commercial purposes, as well as the conditions for maintaining that registration, are set out at 50 C.F.R. § 23.46.

Even greater flexibility is accorded to Appendix II animal specimens that are bred in captivity and Appendix I animal specimens that are bred in captivity for noncommercial purposes. Under Article VII, paragraph 5 of the Convention, once captive-breeding operations are registered with the CITES Secretariat, these captive-bred Appendix II specimens and Appendix I specimens (noncommercial captive-breeding operations only) can be traded internationally on the basis of a "captive-bred" certificate issued by the Management Authority of the exporting country. The procedures for the issuance of "captive-bred" certificates are set out at 50 C.F.R. § 23.41.

The FWS has developed regulatory criteria that set substantive limits on the types of captive-breeding operations that can qualify for the special treatment accorded by paragraphs (4) and (5) of Article VII. For example, to qualify for registration, such operations must maintain the complete separation of the breeding stock from specimens of the same species that exist in the wild. In other words, the captive-breeding operation must maintain a "controlled environment."[77] Further, if reproduction is sexual for the particular Appendix I species, the specimen must be "born to parents that either mated or transferred gametes in a controlled environment."[78] This means that the flexibility extended by paragraphs (4) and (5) of Article VII of the Convention extends only to those specimens that are the offspring of parents that mated in captivity (or were the product of artificial insemination conducted in captivity). *Neither the parental stock nor offspring derived from mating that occurred in the wild—regardless of whether the offspring were born in captivity—are eligible for trade under the relaxed procedures of paragraphs (4) and (5).*

Other conditions also attach to a "bred in captivity" finding, such as the determination that the establishment of the captive-breeding operation was not detrimental to the survival of the species in the wild;[79] that only occasional, limited introductions of specimens removed from the wild are done to prevent or alleviate deleterious inbreeding;[80] and that the operation has successfully produced offspring of the second or subsequent generations (or is managed in a manner demonstrated to be successful in producing second-generation offspring and has successfully produced first-generation offspring).[81] The last criterion is particularly important, especially for newly established captive-breeding operations that are attempting to qualify for a registration for a species that has yet to yield offspring in captivity at the second-generation level. It often requires a number of years of captive-breeding activities before second-generation progeny are successfully produced. Until that goal is accomplished, however, no registration may occur. Once the goal is accomplished, both first and subsequent generation progeny may be traded as "captive-bred." After the initial captive-breeding operation has demonstrated success in breeding specimens to the second generation, additional operations may qualify under this criterion by showing how they are implementing similar management regimes that are likewise capable of reliably producing second-generation stock.

Artificially Propagated

Specimens of CITES-listed plant species that are artificially propagated are also accorded special treatment under the Convention. As with animal species, the Parties placed great importance on reducing the need to collect plants from the wild where the use of artificially propagated plants would fulfill trade demand for horticultural, pharmaceutical, scientific research, and other uses. Therefore, Article VII, paragraph 4 of the Convention provides that specimens of Appendix I plant species that are artificially propagated for commercial purposes are to be treated as Appendix II specimens for purposes of the trade restrictions of CITES.[82] The procedures for obtaining permits for the trade in artificially propagated Appendix I plant specimens for commercial purposes are set out at 50 C.F.R. § 23.47.

Even greater flexibility is accorded to Appendix II plant specimens that are artificially propagated and Appendix I plant specimens that are artificially propagated for noncommercial purposes. Under Article VII, paragraph 5 of the Convention, all Appendix II plant specimens and Appendix I plant specimens (noncommercial artificial propagation only) can be traded internationally on the basis of an "artificial propagation" certificate issued by the Management Authority of the exporting country. The procedures for the issuance of "artificial propagation" certificates are set out at 50 C.F.R. § 23.40.

The FWS has issued regulatory criteria that govern the determination of whether certain plant specimens qualify as "artificially propagated."[83] Particular attention should be given to plants derived from a cutting or division, grafts, and specimens grown from wild-collected seeds or spores.[84]

For the special case presented by flasked seedlings of Appendix I orchids, the FWS has determined by regulation that such specimens are exempt from CITES requirements if they qualify as artificially propagated specimens under 50 C.F.R. § 23.64.[85] Wild-collected Appendix I orchid seedlings do not qualify for this regulatory exception.

Timber Trade

As a result of the actions of the CITES Parties to add a number of commercially valuable tropical timber species (such as big-leaf mahogany) to Appendices II and III, the Parties were prompted to address the commercial realities of the international trade in such species through the perspective of CITES compliance. In Resolution 10.13,[86] the CITES Parties addressed the need for uniform definitions of particular timber products in trade[87] and the consistent application of the "artificially propagated" concept to tropical timber species.[88] The FWS regulations further recognize the realities of the international trade in mahogany and other commercially valuable timber species, which often involve post-export changes in the ultimate destination of particular shipments and the need for flexibility in providing extensions on the validity of the export or re-export documents. For example, the FWS regulations allow the Management Authority of the importing country to change the name and address of the importer noted on the face of the CITES export permit or re-export certificate if there is no change in the quantity of timber products noted on the face of the CITES document, if the import occurs before the expiration of the CITES document (and no extension has been granted), and once other formalities are addressed.[89] A further change to usual CITES procedures involves the authority granted by the regulations to the Management Authority of the importing country to extend the validity date of a CITES export permit or re-export certificate for a period not to exceed six months from the original expiration date.[90]

Trade in Hunting Trophies

The CITES Parties have traditionally treated the international trade in hunting trophies of Appendix I and II specimens to be for the personal, noncommercial purposes of hunters who desire to return to their country of origin with their lawfully taken trophies. Therefore, regardless of the safari fees, taxes, and other revenues flowing from the hunting activity in the exporting country, Appendix I trophy animals have been approved for importation because the purposes of the importation into the hunter's country of origin have not been considered to be primarily commercial in nature. The United States has followed this interpretation for the importation of Appendix I, lawfully taken trophy specimens.[91]

However, problems do arise with respect to the trade in sport-taken trophies when dealing with the quantity of trade, the scope of the term "trophy," and the interplay with the Endangered Species Act for trophies that involve species listed under both the ESA and CITES. The FWS regulations deal with the quantity question by prescribing limits on the number of trophies that a single hunter may import within one calendar year for leopards, markhor, and black rhinoceros.[92] To avoid an overly broad construction of the term "sport-hunted trophy," the FWS has defined the term narrowly to exclude any coverage for articles or products manufactured from the animal other than the "bones, claws, hair, head, hide, hooves, horns, meat, skull, teeth, tusks, or any taxidermied part, including, but not limited to, a rug or taxidermied head, shoulder, or full mount."[93] Lastly, the importation of sport-taken trophies of animals listed as endangered species under the ESA and included on Appendix I of CITES receive the highest degree of protection[94] under U.S. law, and these specimens must be evaluated for import authorization under the rigorous procedural and substantive requirements of both laws. However, Congress has provided a special "exception" from the requirements of the ESA for the importation of any Appendix II fish or wildlife species that is not listed as endangered under the ESA (nonlisted or threatened species are eligible for the exception) as long as CITES requirements are satisfied; any applicable licensure, declaration, and designated port requirements are met; and the importation is not made in the course of a commercial activity.[95]

Disagreements sometimes occur between the Scientific Authority of the importing country and the Scientific Authority of the exporting country on whether the proposed export of an Appendix I hunting trophy will not be detrimental to the survival of the species. While encouraging the Parties to defer to the exporting country's findings "unless there are scientific or management data to indicate otherwise,"[96] the Parties have adopted a resolution that upholds the independence of each Scientific Authority to conduct its own scientific examination on whether the proposed export will be detrimental to the survival of the Appendix I species.[97]

Trade in Caviar

The international trade in caviar derived from sturgeon species, including American paddlefish, has received increased attention from the CITES Parties in recent years.[98] The increasing demand for sturgeon caviar from the Caspian Sea region, as well as the complexity of complying with harvest and export quotas for shared stocks of various sturgeon species, has prompted the Parties to develop a variety of monitoring, documentary, and enforcement measures to promote the sustainable harvest and trade in sturgeon caviar. These measures are set out in the FWS regulations at 50 C.F.R. § 23.71.

The FWS regulations set out the specific labeling and documentation requirements that attach to shipments of sturgeon caviar.[99] Exports of commercial shipments of sturgeon caviar that contain specimens from shared populations must satisfy export quota verification requirements.[100] To enhance adherence to export quotas, the FWS regulations limit the re-export of sturgeon caviar to a period that must not exceed 18 months from the date noted on the original export permit.[101] Further, the FWS regulations disallow the use of pre-Convention certificates for trade in sturgeon caviar.[102]

The international transport of sturgeon caviar as personal effects of an individual continues to be covered by the exemption in Article VII, paragraph 3 and therefore does not generally require the issuance of a CITES document. However, the Parties recently decreased the amount of sturgeon caviar that will qualify for the personal-effects exemption to no more than 125 grams.[103]

Emerging Issues and Future Directions

Coordination Between CITES and Other Multilateral Environmental Agreements

With 174 Party nations as of January 2009, CITES has successfully provided consistent conservation standards that facilitate international trade in wild animals and plants while meeting species' conservation needs and ensuring their survival. Building on this success, the Parties have increasingly moved toward working with other intergovernmental bodies and coordinating with the bodies of other multilateral environmental agreements (MEAs) to promote a globally integrated approach to species conservation.

The Convention itself calls for such cooperation. The United Nations and its specialized agencies and international bodies, either governmental or nongovernmental, that are technically qualified in the protection, conservation, or management of wild fauna or flora may participate in the biennial meetings of the Conferences of the Parties.[104] The Convention also calls for the Secretariat to consult with appropriate intergovernmental bodies on any proposed listing of a marine species in Appendix I or II.[105]

Through Decisions and Resolutions, the Parties have recognized the value of such intergovernmental cooperation. At the 11th Meeting of the Conference of the Parties in 2000, the Parties adopted a strategic vision to guide CITES priorities through 2005.[106] The fifth goal called for increased cooperation and development of strategic alliances with international stakeholders.[107] In 1999, the Governing Council of the United Nations Environment Programme (UNEP) had "noted the importance of promoting interlinkages among multilateral environmental conventions and international processes in an effort to achieve a better focus on international policy-making."[108] Consistent with this message, the Parties adopted four specific objectives. One called for greater coordination with scientific and technical organizations and more efficient distribution of responsibilities with partners such as the International Union for Conservation of Nature (IUCN), the UNEP-World Conservation Monitoring Centre, and TRAFFIC.[109] Two of the objectives called for close coordination with relevant MEAs, conventions, and associations.[110] The fourth objective specifically acknowledged CITES's link with the World Trade Organization (WTO) by calling for the Parties to work to ensure the continuing recognition and acceptance of CITES measures by the WTO and the mutual support of decision-making processes between the two bodies.[111]

In 2007 at the 14th Meeting of the Conference of the Parties, the Parties adopted a new strategic vision for 2008–2013. In the new strategic vision, the Parties continued to move in the direction of coordinating CITES activities with other MEAs. In particular, the planning document took into account CITES's potential contribution to relevant United Nations' Millennium Development Goals and the World Summit on Sustainable Development's (WSSD) target of significantly reducing the rate of biodiversity loss by 2010.[112] To that end, the third of the plan's three goals is to "contribute to significantly reducing the rate of biodiversity loss by ensuring that CITES and other multilateral instruments and processes are coherent and mutually supportive."[113] Five specific objectives will measure the Parties' success in achieving this goal.[114]

To address issues with particular groups of animals and plants, the Parties have adopted a number of specific resolutions that call for coordination with particular intergovernmental bodies or other multilateral agreements. For example, two resolutions urge the Parties to work with bodies such as the International Tropical Timber Organization, the Asian-Pacific Timber Trade Organization, the Food and Agriculture Organization of the United Nations (FAO) Forestry Department, and IUCN on timber listing and enforcement issues.[115] A Memorandum of Understanding also was agreed to between the Secretariats of CITES and the Convention on the Conservation of Migratory Species of Wild Animals (CMS),[116] while a resolution calls for CITES initiatives on certain species to "as far as possible, benefit from the regional collaboration already being undertaken or envisaged in the framework of CMS."[117] In Resolution 12.4, the Parties to CITES moved beyond information sharing when they recommended adoption of toothfish catch documents set by the Commission for the Conservation of Antarctic Marine Living Resources (CCAMLR) and urged all Parties to cooperate in CCAMLR's efforts to control illicit, unregulated, and unreported fishing by implementing verification procedures for any import, export, or transit.[118]

One of the most consistently contentious issues among CITES Parties has been that of whaling, whale conservation, and the relationship between CITES and the International Convention for the Regulation of Whaling. All of the cetaceans (whales, dolphins, and porpoises) are protected under CITES, with 21 genera, species, or populations listed under Appendix I and the remainder listed under Appendix II.[119] Many of the species most valuable to the whaling industry are listed under Appendix I, thus restricting their trade for commercial purposes and preventing trade in commercially valuable products such as whale meat and oil.

A few CITES Parties, primarily Japan, Norway, and Iceland, have taken reservations to the whale listings,[120] thereby allowing them to continue trade in whale products with non-Parties and other Parties that have taken reservations. These countries have submitted numerous proposals to transfer whale species from Appendix I to Appendix II, which would allow for commercial trade;[121] have attempted to distance CITES from the management measures of the International Whaling Commission (IWC);[122] and have attempted to use CITES to force changes in whale management by the IWC.[123]

Such proposals have been largely unsuccessful. The majority of Parties, including the United States, have consistently opposed such initiatives. These Parties have introduced documents at the meetings of the Conference of the Parties to address illegal trade in whale meat[124] and to strengthen the relationship between CITES and the management measures of the IWC.[125] At the 14th Meeting of the Conference of the Parties, a number of countries declared that the CITES Parties should not revisit the status of Appendix I cetaceans while the IWC moratorium against commercial whaling is in place, and reiterated the primary competence of the IWC with regard to management and conservation of cetaceans.[126] The current Resolution 11.4 addresses illegal trade in whale meat, encourages all Parties to cooperate in monitoring illegal trade in whale parts such as meat, and recommends that no Party issue an import or export document for primarily commercial purposes for any species protected from commercial whaling. Future Conferences of the Parties will no doubt continue to debate whale conservation issues and the relationship between implementation of CITES and the IWC. With most of the world's countries being Parties to CITES and only a few Parties having entered reservations for whale listings, so far the Convention has been an effective tool in aiding the recovery of whale populations around the world.

The multilateral agreement that has recently received the most attention, however—and the one likely to generate the most discussion in coming years—is the Convention on Biological Diversity (CBD). This convention, which entered into force in 1993, addresses the conservation of biological diversity, sustainable use of biological diversity components, and equitable benefit sharing of the use of genetic resources.[127]

Nearly every Party to CITES other than the United States is also a Party to CBD.[128] Since 1997, the majority of Parties to CITES have pressed to incorporate CBD principles into CITES processes. The Parties first addressed the relationship between CITES and CBD in Resolution 10.4, which recognized a Memorandum of Understanding between the two Secretariats; suggested that Parties to both conventions, as appropriate, coordinate and reduce duplication of activities between their national authorities for each agreement; and recommended that the CITES Secretariat "investigate opportunities whereby CITES can become a partner in the implementation of appropriate provisions of [CBD]."[129]

Since this beginning, the relationship between CITES and CBD has been on the agenda for discussion and adoption of further measures at nearly every meeting of the Conference of the Parties.[130] At the 13th Meeting of the Conference of the Parties, the submission of two proposals triggered spirited discussions. First, following a 2004 experts workshop in Vilm, Germany, the member countries of the European Community and Kenya submitted a draft decision that would have directed the CITES Secretariat to work with the CBD Secretariat to improve synergies between the two conventions, with particular emphasis on the WSSD target of significantly reducing the rate of biodiversity loss by 2010.[131] The United States proposed that the recommendations from the Vilm workshop first be referred to the CITES Standing Committee to determine which were applicable to CITES.[132] Following further discussion in committee,[133] the Parties adopted a decision directing the Secretariat to work with the Animals and Plants Committees to review the findings and recommendations of the Vilm report and identify relevant aspects.[134] The Standing Committee was then directed to consider the Vilm report, along with the Secretariat's conclusions and comments by the Parties, and identify priority actions to improve synergies between CITES and CBD.[135]

At this same meeting, Namibia submitted a document in which it presented a series of principles and guidelines on sustainable use of biological diversity (the Addis Ababa Principles and Guidelines) that the Conference of the Parties to CBD had adopted earlier that year.[136] Namibia reasoned that the concept of sustainable use is "the cornerstone of both CITES [through the required nondetriment findings] and CBD" and linked biodiversity conservation with trade in wildlife and sustainable development, arguing that "[d]eveloping countries in particular have encountered significant barriers to trade within the CITES framework."[137] For the purpose of "expedit[ing] synergy between and harmonization of CITES and CBD," Namibia proposed a new resolution that would urge Parties to make use of the Addis Ababa Principles and Guidelines when making CITES nondetriment findings.[138] It also presented two draft decisions that would have directed the Secretariat to incorporate work on the Principles and Guidelines into its work plan and incorporate the Principles and Guidelines into the Secretariat's capacity-building program, and would have directed the Animals and Plants Committees to develop case studies on how the Principles and Guidelines could be used in specific cases of exports of CITES Appendix II species.[139] Following vigorous discussion on a number of issues in both the draft resolution and draft decisions, Namibia agreed to consider the various drafting suggestions and return to the Committee with revised proposals.[140]

Namibia returned to the Committee three days later with a revised draft resolution, to which two Parties, one of which was the United States, raised concerns.[141] Following discussion of these concerns, Namibia moved that the debate be closed and the motion put to a vote, at which the draft resolution was agreed. The adopted resolution noted that 164 of the 166 Parties to CITES at the time were also Parties to CBD, urged the CITES Parties to make use of the Addis Ababa Principles and Guidelines when making nondetriment findings, and urged that Parties ensure that their Management and Scientific Authorities participate in the work of CBD.[142] The resolution then urged CITES Parties that were also Parties to CBD "to take effective measures at [the] policy and institutional level to ensure synergy between their implementation of CITES and CBD at the national level,"[143] thus presumably calling for coordination between CITES's goal of protecting wild plants and animals from overexploitation from trade and CBD's goals of conserving biological diversity and ensuring sustainable use of wildlife and plant resources. It is unclear to what extent the resolution also would include consideration of CBD's goal of equitable benefit sharing of the use of genetic resources.

Namibia also returned to the Committee with revised draft decisions, following discussion of which Namibia presented a further revised draft.[144] The final adopted decisions laid out a process for the Animals and Plants Committees to identify the Addis Ababa Principles and Guidelines of most relevance to CITES, taking into account case studies provided by the Parties on how they could be used in the export of Appendix II species, and directed the Secretariat to incorporate consideration of the Addis Ababa Principles and Guidelines into its work plan and, following the work of the Animals and Plants Committees, incorporate the relevant principles and guidelines into its capacity-building program.[145] Decision 13.6 also called for the Animals and Plants Committees to report to the Parties at the next meeting of the Conference of the Parties.[146]

In 2007 at the 14th Meeting of the Conference of the Parties, the Animals and Plants Committees fulfilled their mandate. The Committees' efforts represented the most substantial work to date in assessing how certain principles under CBD are relevant in the context of CITES—in this case the making of the nondetriment findings that are critical in protecting CITES-listed species from overexploitation in trade. The Committees issued eight recommendations, with mixed conclusions on the linkages between CITES and CBD. They began by recognizing the differences between the two Conventions: CBD provides general guidance on a broad range of biodiversity issues whereas CITES is regulatory, species-specific, and focused on trade. They found that a number of the Addis Ababa Principles and Guidelines are, on a case-by-case basis, relevant to the work of CITES; may be used as a voluntary additional tool in making nondetriment findings; and would be valuable to the development of taxa-specific guidelines.[147] But case studies showed that the Addis Ababa Principles and Guidelines are not always applicable or relevant to the CITES decision-making process, and the Committees acknowledged questions regarding the complications of using socioeconomic aspects of the Principles and Guidelines in making nondetriment findings.[148] The Secretariat, which has been an advocate for increasing integration of and cooperation between CITES and CBD, concurred with the recommendations but declared its belief that all of the Addis Ababa Principles and Guidelines are pertinent to the implementation of CITES "in a wider sense."[149] Based on the Committees' document, the Parties amended Resolution 13.2 to include the Committees' recommendations.[150]

Thus, for more than a decade, the Parties to CITES have focused on coordinating their responsibilities under the Convention with their responsibilities under other MEAs. In the case of coordination between CITES and CBD, the United States has repeatedly raised concerns when it has perceived that other Parties are going too far in advocating for integration of standards that are incompatible with the fundamental purpose of CITES. But the United States has supported appropriate coordination between CITES and other MEAs. As explained by the CITES Secretariat in 2000, "as one of the more practically oriented and mature conventions, [CITES] is certainly in a position to play a leading role in promoting [concrete synergy between biodiversity-related MEAs]."[151] The Parties have also taken significant steps to coordinate with other intergovernmental bodies and multilateral agreements, thus working toward an integrated, consistent approach to global species conservation. This trend will certainly continue as countries recognize that a coordinated approach is needed to tackle the world's tough species conservation problems.

The Effects of Conservation Restrictions on People's Livelihoods

Consideration of how regulating wildlife trade affects people's lives, especially the livelihoods of the poor and people in developing countries, has always been an undercurrent during CITES discussions on restrictions needed to ensure a species' survival. For example, at the 13th Meeting of the Conference of the Parties, Namibia proposed to allow trade in certain products made in that country from African elephant ivory. The committee rejected Namibia's proposal, but Namibia proposed to reopen debate on the issue during the plenary session at the end of the meeting.[152] During the debate, the delegate from Namibia emphasized the strict control mechanisms in place and that 90 percent of the ivory to be used came from elephants that had died from natural causes.[153] But he also spoke passionately about the economic needs of the people of his country and the need to support local communities that have supported elephant conservation programs.

These considerations have most recently taken form during debates on synergy between CITES and CBD—specifically the relationship between CBD's goal of sustainable use and CITES's goal of species conservation. The goals of the two conventions can be compatible. Through the nondetriment findings, CITES strives to ensure that trade in listed species is sustainable. While trade is regulated under CITES through documentation requirements, it is not the intent that these requirements unduly restrict trade, particularly for Appendix II and III species, which may be traded for commercial purposes.[154] The preamble to CITES specifically recognizes the importance of wild fauna and flora for its economic value. As long as the Scientific and Management Authorities have made the required findings, trade in CITES species is wholly appropriate. In fact, it has been suggested that CITES documents could serve as "green" certifications, promoting trade in sustainable products by assuring consumers that their purchase is environmentally sound. But there can be differences, particularly where sustainable use under CBD targets use of natural resources to address human economic needs. For example, the CBD Addis Ababa Principles and Guidelines for the Sustainable Use of Biodiversity include the principle that the needs of indigenous and local communities should be reflected in the equitable distribution of the benefits of resource use.[155] In pursuing the goal of sustainable use, the focus of some CITES Parties has shifted at times from an emphasis on species conservation to an emphasis on people's economic needs, particularly people in developing countries. Two examples illustrate this tension within CITES between species conservation and the effects of species conservation on people's livelihoods.

In 2000, the Parties to CITES adopted their first strategic vision to provide policy direction for the coming years. The plan included seven goals, all of which focused on species conservation, capacity building, or administration of the treaty.[156] With the period for the first strategic plan ending, at the 13th Meeting of the Conference of the Parties, the Parties adopted a decision to form a working group to draft a new strategic vision.[157] At the 2006 Standing Committee meeting, the Strategic Plan Working Group presented its draft strategic plan. The Working Group discussed the two main themes that it adopted in approaching its task. The first theme, not surprisingly, was about making CITES work effectively.[158] But the second theme discussed the role of CITES not only in providing for the sustainable use of wildlife but also in providing benefits for people.[159] Thus, along with the goals of ensuring compliance and enforcement of the Convention, securing the financial basis for the Convention, and reducing the rate of global biodiversity loss, the Working Group had included the goal of adopting "balanced wildlife trade policies compatible with human well-being, livelihoods and cultural integrity."[160]

A number of Parties expressed concern about the trend in CITES, as reflected in the draft document, away from the core functions of the treaty and into areas such as the United Nations' Millennium Development Goals.[161] The Standing Committee requested that the Working Group prepare a revised plan that took the comments into account, and the Working Group submitted the revised Strategic Vision for consideration by all of the Parties at the 14th Meeting of the Conference of the Parties.[162] The goal on adopting wildlife trade policies compatible with people's livelihoods was gone (although the Secretariat commented that it did not share the concern of some commenters that the present draft still looked too far beyond the core purpose of CITES).[163] References to the Millennium Development Goals remained, although now more clearly tied to reducing rates of biodiversity loss and ensuring sustainable international trade in wildlife and plants.[164] Following further revision at the Meeting of the Conference of the Parties, the new Strategic Vision for 2008–2013 was adopted.[165]

The second example involves the amendment of Resolution 8.3 on "Recognition of the Benefits of Trade in Wildlife" in 2004 to recognize that "implementation of CITES-listing decisions should take into account potential impacts on the livelihoods of the poor." This change emerged quietly from a report that the chair of the Plants Committee presented on the second day of the Meeting of the Conference of the Parties. In her report, the chair noted that the proposed inclusion of the medicinal plants known as Devil's Claw in Appendix II had shown that implementation of CITES decisions may impact the livelihoods of poor people.[166] The Plants Committee therefore recommended a new decision on options for including information on the impact of listings on poor peoples' livelihoods.[167] Instead, Australia proposed adding the new language to the resolution.[168]

At the 14th Meeting of the Conference of the Parties, Argentina, China, Germany (on behalf of the European Community), and Nicaragua submitted a document titled "CITES and Livelihoods," building on the new paragraph in Resolution 8.3.[169] They reported on a CITES and Livelihoods Workshop held in September 2006 and provided three reasons that "the impacts of CITES regulation on the livelihoods of poor should not be ignored."[170] Interestingly, only one of the three reasons related to the goal of furthering species conservation—that addressing livelihoods in the course of implementing CITES can promote support for CITES and conservation at the local, national, and international levels.[171] The other two reasons were ethical and political: (1) that the impacts of CITES regulation on the livelihoods of the poor should not be ignored, and (2) that the goal of reducing poverty has been endorsed globally at the political level and the Parties should ensure that CITES regulation is compatible with this overarching goal.[172] The document then presented 14 recommendations from the workshop. The recommendations included that guidance should be developed on how to implement CITES in a way that mitigates negative impacts and supports positive impacts on livelihoods; that consideration of livelihood issues should be included in the Wildlife Trade Policy Review framework; that ways of incorporating livelihood issues into relevant CITES processes should be explored; and that CITES implementation should be linked to other national initiatives on poverty alleviation and livelihoods.[173] The Parties emphasized that their focus was on how CITES listing decisions are to be implemented, rather than on whether to list species on the Appendices due to livelihood concerns. The document included two proposed decisions to continue the work on livelihoods and implement the recommendations.[174]

Vigorous discussion followed, stretching out over several days of Committee II sessions. The United Kingdom noted the concern by several Parties and organizations that the proposals would prioritize consideration of livelihoods over species conservation, although the introducing Parties again stressed that this was not the intention and that the draft decisions should not lead to any changes in the criteria for whether a species should or should not be protected under CITES.[175] On the second day of debate, a number of Parties and organizations argued that CITES's strength lay in scientifically based decision-making and again stressed that livelihood considerations should not affect listing decisions, but noted that livelihood considerations could be addressed as part of the implementation process.[176] The United States noted that some Parties appeared to be disregarding scientific advice regarding listings if local livelihood interests were at stake.[177] India acknowledged the importance of livelihoods for local communities but argued that other MEAs were better placed to address the issue and CITES should focus on the core mandate of species conservation.[178] Following the discussion, the chair of Committee II requested that South Africa convene a working group to revise the document and then report back to the Parties in committee.[179]

Eight days later, the Parties returned with two revised draft decisions. Following additional discussion on precise language changes, the decisions were adopted by consensus.[180] The primary decision calls for the Standing Committee to continue work on livelihood issues by supervising a process to develop voluntary tools for the Parties to assess both positive and negative impacts of implementing CITES listing decisions on the livelihoods of the poor.[181] The Standing Committee is also to supervise development of voluntary guidelines for the Parties to address these impacts, particularly in developing countries.[182] To address some of the concerns raised during discussions, the final decision specifically clarified that "the process shall not include consideration of . . . the requirement to make nondetriment findings" or the criteria for determining whether to list a species in the Appendices.[183] Discussions on the appropriate role of livelihood considerations in CITES decision-making will surely continue into the future when the processes initiated by this decision are reported back to the next meeting of the Conference of the Parties in 2010.

Thus, the Parties continue to grapple with the need to protect species threatened by trade while considering the impact on people's livelihoods—livelihoods that are affected positively and negatively by both the trade itself and restrictions on the trade. A multinational treaty whose purpose is to ensure that trade in wildlife and plants does not threaten their survival will always have an impact on people's livelihoods due to the need to limit or regulate the use of those resources. That impact is particularly poignant when economic costs fall on those people with the fewest resources to absorb the effects. Nevertheless, by trying to use CITES to address broader social problems such as poverty and inequitable economic benefit distribution, the Parties risk weakening this strong conservation mechanism whose success contributes to making it an attractive vehicle to address other problems. The strengths of CITES are its clear purpose of species conservation, specific procedures, focus on science-based decision making, and mutually supportive implementation. Initiatives to address broader societal issues such as poverty should proceed carefully, with a strict eye to adhering to CITES's core mandate of species conservation.

Conclusion

As CITES moves into its fourth decade of implementation, a further acceleration in the breadth and scope of international trade in animal and plant parts and derivatives regulated by the Convention can be anticipated. This will undoubtedly increase the complexity of the compliance issues presented to the Parties. Controversial issues pertaining to the trade in whale meat, in caviar, in elephant ivory and tiger products, and in tropical timber species and the familiar tension between collaborative, multilateral conservation measures versus unilateral "stricter domestic measures" will continue to take the spotlight before future meetings of the conference of the CITES Parties.

The trends in favor of multilateral plant and wildlife conservation measures is expected to continue, as well as the continuing effort to build synergies between CITES and other international conservation and trade treaties. The CITES Parties will continue to preside over the never-ending tension between taking appropriate measures to stem excessive trade that threatens the survival of certain plant and animal species versus allowing limited trade, stipulated in terms of quotas or parts or derivative annotations, as an incentive to maintain trade at sustainable levels.

Meanwhile, hundreds of shipments including CITES specimens will pass through U.S. ports daily, many of which involve commercial transactions. The new CITES regulations adopted by the FWS provide a helpful primer to all U.S. citizens, whether tourist, animal or plant dealer, zoo or aquarium curator, or scientist, on how to conduct their trade in a lawful, efficient, and effective manner. The regulations also help to inform U.S. citizens on how the CITES process operates on an international level and how multilateral positions are shaped and implemented through meetings of the Conference of the Parties. These regulatory developments should provide a productive platform for the future evolution of CITES implementation, both in the United States and internationally.

However, the continued international success of CITES to further the conservation of wildlife and plant species in trade will depend not only on the constructive implementation of legal requirements, but on addressing enforcement needs and livelihood impacts in developing countries as well. The special conservation and enforcement problems presented by the cross-border trade in bushmeat (Resolution 13.11) and the international trade in traditional medicines containing parts or derivatives of CITES species (Resolution Conf. 10.19 (Rev. CoP 14)) will continue to require extra attention from the CITES Parties—beyond the standard measures carried out at official ports of entry—if these avenues for the international movement of rare species and their parts and products are to be brought under control.

Meanwhile, the CITES Parties will continue to meet every two to three years to address *and resolve* vital interpretive and scientific questions regarding the trade in important wildlife and plant species. And the history of CITES has shown that when the Parties meet as the "Conference of the Parties" they succeed—in a period that never exceeds two weeks—in reaching a consensus or near-consensus decision on many important conservation and regulatory questions that require global attention for the international trade in wildlife and plants. This successful record of decisive and collaborative international action, especially when coupled with the broad-scale level of day-to-day communication among the Parties' Management Authorities and the CITES Secretariat, offers reason for optimism that the long-term conservation success of CITES will match its success in international implementation.

Notes

1. 27 U.S.T. 1087 (1973).
2. 72 Fed. Reg. 48,402 (Aug. 23, 2007).
3. CITES defines trade as including "export, re-export, import and introduction from the sea." CITES art. I, para. (c). "Re-export" is defined as the export of any specimen that was previously imported. *Id.* para. (d). "Introduction from the sea" is defined as the transportation of a CITES specimen that was "taken in the marine environment not under the jurisdiction of any State" into a country. *Id.* para. (e). As shown by these definitions, "trade" in CITES specimens need not involve any commercial aspects whatsoever. The key factor is the movement of CITES specimens from one country to another (or the taking of such specimens on the high seas and eventual movement of such specimens into the resource or territorial jurisdiction of a country). CITES exempts the in-transit shipment of animals and plants through the territory of a Party as long as the specimens remain within customs control. Art. VII, para. 1. However, the exporting and importing countries remain obligated to see that all CITES requirements are satisfied for such shipments.
4. Under CITES, the term "species" is defined as "any species, subspecies, or geographically separate population thereof." Art. I, para. (a). Generally, a plant or wildlife hybrid of a CITES-listed species must be covered by CITES documentation if entered into trade. For plant hybrids, the appropriate permit or certificate will depend upon the Appendix listing (I, II, or III) of the CITES species in the specimen's lineage. If more than one CITES species is included in the specimen's lineage, the more restrictive Appendix listing (Appendix I being the most restrictive) will control. (Special rules exist for artificially propagated Appendix I hybrid plants.) 50 C.F.R. § 23.42. For animal hybrids, general CITES permitting requirements attach to a hybrid specimen that "contains a CITES species in its recent lineage," 50 C.F.R. § 23.43(e), which includes the last four generations of the specimen's "direct line of descent." *Id.* § 23.43(a). Wildlife hybrids are generally

exempt from permitting requirements if there are no purebred CITES species within the last four generations of the specimen's lineage. However, a hybrid between two CITES wildlife species is subject to permitting requirements. *See* 50 C.F.R. § 23.43(f)(1).

5. Art. II, para. 1.
6. Art. II, para. 2(a) (emphasis added).
7. Art. II, para. 2(b).
8. Art. II, para. 3.
9. The official list of species included in CITES Appendices I, II, and III is found at the Secretariat's Web site: http://www.cites.org/eng/app/appendices.shtml.
10. 16 U.S.C. §§ 1537A, 1538(c) (2006).
11. *Id.* § 1533.
12. *Id.* The ultimate substantive standards for determining a species to be an "endangered species" or a "threatened species" are set out in the definitions of those terms in section 3 of the ESA. *Id.* § 1532(6), (20).
13. CITES arts. XI, XV.
14. The CITES Parties have adopted a resolution that sets out the criteria for proposing and adopting amendments to Appendices I and II. *See* Res. Conf. 9.24 (Rev. CoP 14). The FWS has summarized the amendment standards and procedures in 50 C.F.R. § 23.89.
15. CITES art. XVI. The CITES Parties have adopted a resolution that further explains the procedure that a Party should follow to add or remove a species from Appendix III. *See* Res. Conf. 9.25 (Rev. CoP 14). The FWS has summarized the procedures for amending Appendix III in 50 C.F.R. § 23.90.
16. CITES art. II, para. 4. Upon accession to CITES, a Party country may choose to enter specific reservations against the implementation of the Convention for particular species included in Appendices I, II, or III, or it may choose to assert a reservation regarding any parts or derivatives of an Appendix III species. *See* CITES art. XXIII. After accession, a Party country may choose to assert a reservation against any subsequent addition of a species to Appendix I, II, or III. *See* CITES arts. XV, para. 3; XVI, para. 2; XXIII.
17. No general reservations are allowed by CITES. *Id.* art. XXIII, para. 1.
18. CITES defines the term "specimen" to include any animal or plant of a species included in Appendix I, II, or III, whether living or dead. *Id.* art. I, para. (b)(i). For animal species included in Appendices I and II, the term "specimen" also includes "any readily recognizable part or derivative thereof." *Id.* para. (b)(ii). For animal species included in Appendix III, the term "specimen" includes any readily recognizable part or derivative of the species that is specified in Appendix III. *Id.* For plant species included in Appendix I, the term "specimen" includes any readily recognizable part or derivative thereof. *Id.* para. (b)(iii). For plant species included in Appendices II or III, the term "specimen" includes only those readily recognizable parts or derivatives that are specified in the appropriate Appendix. *Id.* Obviously, CITES does not regulate any parts, products, or derivatives of a species that are not "readily recognizable." The FWS defines the phrase "readily recognizable" to mean "any specimen that appears from a visual, physical, scientific, or forensic examination or test; an accompanying document, packaging, mark, or label; or any other circumstances to be a part, product, or derivative of any CITES wildlife or plant, unless such part, product, or derivative is specifically exempt from the provisions of CITES of this part." 50 C.F.R. § 23.5.
19. CITES art. VIII, para. 1. *See* Res. Conf. 9.9; Res. Conf. 11.3 (Rev. CoP 13). Pursuant to Resolution 9.10 (Rev. CoP 14) the CITES Parties have agreed that illegally traded Appendix I specimens, once confiscated and forfeited or returned to the country of origin or re-export, may be transferred only for *"bona fide* scientific/educational or enforcement/identification purposes, and that Parties save in storage or destroy those excess specimens whose transfer for these purposes is not practicable." *Id.* para. (e).
20. Illegally traded specimens are treated as contraband by the United States and are subject to seizure and forfeiture without a showing of knowledge by the importer. *See* 16 U.S.C. §§ 1538(c)(1), 1540(e) (2006). Furthermore, it is unlawful in the United States for a person to possess or engage in domestic trade in any specimen traded in violation of CITES,

see 16 U.S.C. § 1538(c)(1) (2006), and the FWS interprets this prohibition to extend to the offspring of illegally imported specimens as well. *See* 72 Fed. Reg. 48,405–06 (Aug. 23, 2007) (preamble to the CITES regulations). The civil penalty and criminal enforcement provisions of the ESA, 16 U.S.C. § 1540(a)(1), (b)(1) (2006), also apply to knowing violations of the terms and conditions contained in or attached to CITES documents issued by the FWS and to knowing violations of regulatory requirements that pertain to use restrictions after importation occurs. *See* 50 C.F.R. §§ 23.55, 23.56.

21. Draft resolutions are submitted for discussion at Meetings of the Conference of the Parties to CITES. They are adopted by consensus or, if dissent is noted, by a two-thirds majority of the Parties present and voting. Once adopted, a resolution represents an interpretation or recommendation of the Conference of the Parties that can inform the implementation of the Convention but is not binding on a particular Party. *See* CITES art. XI, para. 3(e).
22. *Id.* art. IX, para. 1.
23. *See* 50 C.F.R. § 23.6 (explanation of the roles played by the U.S. Management and Scientific Authorities).
24. At either the national or subnational (state or local) levels.
25. CITES art. XIV, para. 1.
26. *See, e.g.,* 16 U.S.C. §§ 668 *et seq.* (Bald and Golden Eagle Protection Act), §§ 703–712 (Migratory Bird Treaty Act), §§ 1361 *et seq.* (Marine Mammal Protection Act), §§ 1531–1544 (Endangered Species Act), §§ 4201 *et seq.* (African Elephant Conservation Act), §§ 4901 *et seq.* (Wild Bird Conservation Act), §§ 5301 *et seq.* (Rhinoceros and Tiger Conservation Act) (2006). In addition to enacting stricter domestic measures for certain CITES-listed species involved in international trade, the Congress also gave extraterritorial effect to the prohibition against CITES-inconsistent trade. Section 9(c)(1) of the ESA, 16 U.S.C. § 1538(c)(1) (2006), establishes a federal offense for *any* international trade in CITES specimens by citizens of the United States, whether or not the actual import, export, or re-export occurs at U.S. ports of entry. Therefore, the CITES regulations prohibit not only the import, export, or re-export of CITES specimens but also engaging "in international trade," wherever that may occur. 50 C.F.R. § 23.13(a); 72 Fed. Reg. 48,409 (Aug. 23, 2007).
27. However, state and local restrictions on the importation of endangered and threatened species is preempted if such importation or interstate commerce is authorized by permit or regulation issued under the ESA. *See* H. J. Justin & Sons, Inc. v. Deukmejian, 702 F.2d 758 (9th Cir.), *cert. denied*, 104 S. Ct. 91 (1983); Man Hing Ivory & Imps., Inc. v. Deukmejian, 702 F.2d 760 (9th Cir. 1983); 16 U.S.C. § 1535(f) (2006).
28. If a specimen was acquired before the effective date of CITES (or the effective date of the particular species listing under Appendix I or II), it is exempt from the requirements of Article III as long as the Management Authority of the country of export issues a certificate to that effect. CITES art. VII, para. 2. If an Appendix I specimen is to be imported as a personal or household effect (i.e., contained in accompanying personal baggage of the importer), it is exempt from Article III as long as that specimen was not "acquired by the owner outside his State of usual residence." *Id.* para. 3. Special permitting and certificate requirements attach to specimens bred in captivity or artificially propagated, *id.* paras. 4, 5, or loaned, donated, or exchanged between scientists or scientific institutions, *id.* para. 6.
29. *Id.* art. III, paras. 2, 3.
30. The exemptions mentioned *supra* note 28 apply to Appendix II specimens, except that the "personal or household effect" exemption is generally available unless the exporting country requires the issuance of a permit under its domestic law. *See id.* art. VII, para. 3(b).
31. For "look-alike" species listed under CITES art. II, para. 2(b), the "nondetriment" finding focuses on the survival of the species in Appendix I or listed under paragraph 2(a) of Article II.
32. *Id.* art. IV, paras. 2, 4.
33. *Id.* art. V, para. 2.

34. *Id.* para. 3.
35. *Id.* art. VI, para. 3. *See* Res. Conf. 12.13 (Rev. CoP 13). FWS regulations indicate specific information that must be included in CITES documents. 50 C.F.R. § 23.23.
36. 50 C.F.R. § 23.32. If the original CITES document is lost, damaged, stolen, or accidentally destroyed, the permittee may apply to the FWS for a replacement document. The application procedure and issuance criteria for securing a replacement document are set out at 50 C.F.R. § 23.52. Under limited circumstances (especially rare for Appendix I specimens), retrospective CITES documents—permits or certificates issued *for the first time after the export or re-export has occurred*—are available under the narrow criteria set out in 50 C.F.R. § 23.53, but may only issue before the importing country has cleared the shipment. Once the CITES specimen clears the port of entry, any violation of CITES requirements cannot be cured through the issuance of a retrospective document.
37. 16 U.S.C. § 1537a(a) (2006). The FWS is also designated as the Scientific Authority for purposes of CITES. *Id.*
38. Unlike the ESA, where public notice and comment requirements attach to the review process for any application for a permit under section 10 of the Act, 16 U.S.C. § 1539(c) (2006), CITES permit applications do not require public notice and an opportunity to comment.
39. In certain instances species included in Appendix II may be subject to a substantive "annotation" (see definition at 50 C.F.R. § 23.5) that identifies populations, export quotas, or particular parts or derivatives. The terms of such annotations identify particular populations or specimens that should be treated as included within Appendix I for purposes of the substantive and documentary requirements of CITES.
40. 50 C.F.R. § 23.35(b).
41. CITES art. III, para. 3.
42. The regulations at 50 C.F.R. § 23.61 explain how the Service evaluates the facts regarding a proposed importation of a specimen to determine whether the "no-detriment" test is satisfied. For Appendix I specimens, the Service gives particular focus to whether the proposed trade would or would not cause an increased risk of extinction for the species or population from which the specimen was derived, whether the shipment would or would not interfere with the recovery of the species, and whether additional trade in the species would be stimulated by the issuance of a permit. 50 C.F.R. § 23.61(e).
43. The regulations at 50 C.F.R. § 23.62 explain how the Service evaluates the facts regarding a proposed importation of a specimen to determine whether the "not for primarily commercial purposes" test is satisfied. The criteria identified in this regulatory section, which are derived principally from Resolution 5.10, examine all aspects of the intended use of the specimen in the United States. The basic rule followed by the FWS is that if "the noncommercial aspects do not clearly predominate, we will consider the import or introduction from the sea to be for primarily commercial purposes." 50 C.F.R. § 23.62(a)(4). As noted in the regulations, the focus is not on whether a broker arranged the transaction or whether money changed hands in the conveyance of the specimen from exporter to importer—the key is the intended use of the specimen. *Id.* § 23.62(a)(5).
44. *Id.* § 23.65.
45. *Id.* § 23.54(b)(2).
46. *Id.* § 23.36(b).
47. CITES art. III, para. 2.
48. Factors considered by the FWS in making a finding of legal acquisition are identified in 50 C.F.R. § 23.60.
49. FWS regulations generally require that an import permit be issued or that the importing country's Management Authority confirm in writing that an import permit will be issued to satisfy this criterion. *See id.* § 23.35(e)(1). However, if an emergency situation exists where the life or health of the specimen is at risk "and no means of written communication is possible," oral confirmation will be accepted from the foreign Management Authority that the import permit will be issued. *Id.* § 23.35(e)(2).
50. CITES art. III, para. 2(c).

51. *Id*. art. IV, para. 2.
52. *Id*. art. V, para. 2.
53. *Id*. art. VI, para. 2; 50 C.F.R. § 23.54(b)(1).
54. *See* 50 C.F.R. § 23.37 for FWS requirements regarding re-export certificates.
55. CITES art. III, para. 4. The Service's examination of the specimen's permitting history will be relevant to the determination whether CITES requirements have been met. Questions regarding the lawful acquisition of the specimen under relevant foreign laws can be raised.
56. *Id*. art. IV, para. 5.
57. *Id*. art. V, para. 4.
58. 50 C.F.R. § 23.54(b)(1).
59. The landing in U.S. ports of Appendix I or II fish or other aquatic species taken in the waters of the U.S. exclusive economic zone constitutes domestic trade only and would not implicate CITES requirements. The recent interpretation of the phrase "the marine environment not under the jurisdiction of any State"—reached by the CITES Parties at CoP 14—supports this view. Resolution 14.6 defines the phrase to mean "those marine areas beyond the areas subject to the sovereignty or sovereign rights of a State consistent with international law, as reflected in the United Nations Convention on the Law of the Sea."
60. FWS regulations regarding introduction from the sea are found at 50 C.F.R. § 23.39.
61. It is ambiguous whether the "State of introduction" mentioned in CITES art. III, para. 5(a), refers to the country where the specimen is first landed, the country of registry for the vessel that has or will take the specimen, or the country whose exclusive economic zone or territorial waters are first traversed by the vessel that captured the specimen.
62. CITES art. III, para. 5.
63. *Id*. art. IV, para. 6.
64. *Id*. art. XIV, para. 5. *See* 50 C.F.R. § 23.39(d), (e).
65. *See* 50 C.F.R. § 23.39(f).
66. *Id*. § 23.54(b)(2).
67. *See* FWS regulations at *id*. § 23.38.
68. *Id*. § 23.54(b)(2).
69. *See id*. § 23.45.
70. *See id*. § 23.40.
71. *See id*. § 23.41.
72. *See id*. This certificate is issued consistent with the provisions in CITES Article VII, paragraph 3, that exempt noncommercial trade in certain CITES specimens that are transported as personal or household effects.
73. *See* 50 C.F.R. § 23.54(b)(3), (4).
74. 72 Fed. Reg. 48,411 (Aug. 23, 2007).
75. CITES art. VII, para. 4.
76. This means that all permitting requirements set out in Article IV of the Convention apply to Appendix I animal specimens that are bred in captivity for commercial purposes. However, for purposes of the other exemptions allowed by CITES, the specimen would continue to be treated as an Appendix I specimen. *See* 50 C.F.R. § 23.46(a).
77. 50 C.F.R. § 23.63(b)(1).
78. *Id*. § 23.63(c)(1).
79. *Id*. § 23.63(c)(3)(ii).
80. *Id*. § 23.63(c)(3)(iii), (d).
81. *Id*. § 23.63(c)(3)(iv).
82. This means that artificially propagated plants originating from a commercial nursery would be traded under the more flexible permitting requirements set out in Article IV of the Convention. However, such specimens would continue to be treated as included in Appendix I for purposes of the other exemptions to CITES. *See* 50 C.F.R. § 23.47(a).

83. 50 C.F.R. § 23.64.
84. *Id.*
85. *See id.* § 23.92(b)(3); Res. Conf. 11.11 (Rev. CoP 14), at 3.
86. Revised at both the 13th and 14th Meetings of the Conference of the Parties.
87. The resolution sets out recommended definitions of the terms "logs," "sawn wood," "veneer sheets," and "plywood" for use in accurately identifying products noted in annotations to timber species included in the CITES Appendices. These definitions have been adopted by the FWS. *See* 50 C.F.R. § 23.73(b). The resolution recommended the uniform use of parts and derivatives definitions based on the tariff classifications of the Harmonized System of the World Customs Organization. Res. Conf. 10.13 (Rev. CoP 14) at para. (d).
88. The resolution recommends that "timber and nontimber products derived from trees grown in monospecific plantations be considered as being artificially propagated in accordance with the definition contained in Resolution Conf. 11.11 (Rev. CoP 14)." Res. Conf. 10.13 (Rev. CoP 14) at para. (g). The FWS has adopted this recommended interpretation with the proviso that "the seeds or other propagules from which the trees are grown were legally acquired and obtained in a nondetrimental manner." 50 C.F.R. § 23.64(f).
89. *See* 50 C.F.R. § 23.73(c)(1).
90. *Id.* § 23.73(c)(2).
91. *See id.* § 23.62(c)(1).
92. *Id.* § 23.74(d)(1).
93. *Id.* § 23.74(b).
94. Endangered, Appendix I marine mammal species would receive the ultimate level of protection under U.S. law, but none of those species are involved in the international trade in hunting trophies.
95. 16 U.S.C. § 1538(c)(2) (2006). This "exception" is actually a statutory presumption that the importation is not in violation of the ESA or any of its implementing regulations. One court has found that the statutory presumption of section 9(c)(2) of the ESA can be overcome by the adoption of regulations by the Secretary of the Interior under section 4(d) of the ESA, 16 U.S.C. § 1533(d) (2006), that establish more restrictive provisions for the conservation of a threatened species. *See* Safari Club Int'l v. Babbitt, No. MO-93-CA-001 (W.D. Tex., Aug. 12, 1993). Further, the "exception" does not extend to the acquisition of specimens in foreign commerce in the course of a commercial activity. *See* 50 C.F.R. § 17.8(b)(1); 72 Fed. Reg. 48,404 (Aug. 23, 2007).
96. Res. Conf. 2.11 (Rev. CoP 9), at para. (b).
97. *Id.* para. (c).
98. *See* Res. Conf. 12.7 (Rev. CoP 14).
99. 50 C.F.R. § 23.71(b), (c). Additionally, for caviar shipments that consist of roe from more than one species, the CITES document must identify the exact quantity of roe from each species. *Id.* § 23.71(g).
100. *Id.* § 23.71(d).
101. *Id.* § 23.71(e).
102. *Id.* § 23.71(f).
103. The FWS has amended its regulations at 50 C.F.R. § 23.15(c)(3) to reduce the personal-effects limit for sturgeon caviar from 250 grams to 125 grams. 73 Fed. Reg. 40,983 (July 17, 2008).
104. CITES, art. XI, paras. 6, 7(1).
105. *Id.* art. XV, para. 2(b).
106. Dec. 11.1. The strategic vision was later extended into 2007.
107. CoP 11 Doc. 11.12.2 (draft strategic vision for adoption by the Parties).
108. *Id.* goal 5.
109. *Id.* goal 5, objective 5.3. At the time of the Strategic Vision, IUCN was known as the World Conservation Union.

110. *Id.* goal 5, objectives 5.1, 5.2. As of early 2009, the CITES Secretariat had entered into 14 cooperative agreements with groups such as ICPO-INTERPOL, the World Customs Organization, and the U.S. Fish and Wildlife Service National Fish and Wildlife Forensic Laboratory. *See* CITES Secretariat, http://www.cites.org/eng/disc/sec/index.shtml (last visited Jan. 17, 2009) (list of current memoranda of understanding).
111. CoP 11 Doc. 11.12.2, goal 5, objective 5.4.
112. Res. Conf. 14.2, Annex.
113. *Id.* Goal 3.
114. *Id.* At the meeting of the Conference of the Parties during which the new strategic vision was adopted, the Parties also approved three new decisions specific to cooperation with other multilateral processes: to collaborate on the global strategy for plant conservation under the Convention on Biological Diversity (CBD), to further discuss cooperation with the Food and Agriculture Organization of the United Nations on forestry issues, and to harmonize nomenclature and taxonomy with other multilateral environmental agreements. *See* Dec. 14.15–14.18.
115. Res. Conf. 14.4.
116. The United States is not a Party to this agreement.
117. Res. Conf. 13.3.
118. Res. Conf. 12.4.
119. CITES Secretariat, Appendices I, II, and III (valid from July 1, 2008), http://www.cites.org/eng/app/appendices.shtml.
120. CITES Secretariat, Reservations Entered by Parties (in effect from Sept. 13, 2007), http://www.cites.org/eng/app/reserve_index.shtml.
121. *See, e.g.*, CoP 10 Prop. 10.19–10.23 (submitted by Japan and Norway), CoP 11 Prop. 11.15–11.18 (submitted by Japan and Norway); CoP 12 Prop. 4 (submitted by Japan). These countries argue that CITES Parties have rejected proposals to transfer species from Appendix I to Appendix II because of the IWC moratorium on commercial whaling rather than for scientific reasons. CoP 14 Com. I Rep. 3 (Rev. 2), at 2–3.
122. *See, e.g.*, CoP 10 Doc. 10.34 (Rev.) (submitted by Japan).
123. *See, e.g.*, CoP 14 Doc. 51 (submitted by Japan).
124. CoP 9 Doc. 9.57 (submitted by the United States); CoP 10 Docs. 10.40, 10.40.1 (submitted by the United States);
125. CoP 12 Doc. 16.4 (submitted by Mexico).
126. CoP 14 Com. I Rep. 3 (Rev. 2), at 3. The IWC, in turn, has expressed its appreciation of the CITES Parties' recognition of the IWC's expertise in evaluating the status of whale stocks and reaffirmed the role of CITES in supporting IWC management decisions. *Id.*
127. Convention on Biological Diversity, *opened for signature* June 5, 1992, art. 1, 1760 U.N.T.S. 79.
128. For the list of Parties to CBD, see http://www.cbd.int/information/parties.shtml (official Web site of the CBD Secretariat) (last visited Jan. 17, 2009).
129. Res. Conf. 10.4 (Rev. CoP 14). These steps resulted from a study on how to improve the effectiveness of CITES, with recommendations and a draft Memorandum of Cooperation between the Secretariats of CITES and CBD presented to the Parties at the 10th Meeting of the Conference of the Parties. *See* CoP 10 Docs. 10.20, 10.21, 10.22 (submitted by the Secretariat).
130. *See, e.g.*, CoP 11 Doc. 11.12.3 (document on cooperation and synergy with CBD and other biodiversity-related conventions).
131. CoP 13 Doc. 12.1.1, Doc. 12.1.1 Annex 1 (Rev. 1).
132. CoP 13 Com. II Rep. 4, at 2.
133. CoP 13 Com. II Rep. 9 (Rev. 1), at 1–2.
134. Decs. 13.4, 13.5.
135. Dec. 13.2. *See also* Dec. 13.3.
136. CoP 13 Doc. 12.1.2.
137. *Id.* at 1, 2.

138. *Id.* Annex 2 (Rev. 1).
139. *Id.* Annex 3.
140. CoP 13 Com. II Rep. 4, at 2–3.
141. CoP 13 Com. II Rep. 9 (Rev. 1), at 2–3.
142. Res. Conf. 13.2.
143. *Id.*
144. *See* CoP 13 Com. II, at 4, 24 (revised draft decisions).
145. Decs. 13.6, 13.7.
146. *Id.*
147. CoP 14 Doc. 13, Annex.
148. *Id.*
149. CoP 14 Doc. 13, at 2.
150. CoP 14 Com. II, at 17. *See also* Res. Conf. 13.2 (Rev. CoP 14) (revised Resolution).
151. CoP 11 Doc. 11.12.3, at 7.
152. *See* CoP 13 Plen. 5 (Rev. 1), at 2 (Oct. 14, 2004) (summary report from fifth session of plenary).
153. *See id.*
154. For example, the Parties are to ensure that specimens pass through any formalities required for trade with a minimum of delay. *See* CITES, art. VIII, para. 3.
155. *See* Res. Conf. 13.2 (Rev. CoP 14), Annex 1 (Principle 12).
156. *See* Dec. 11.1. The goals were to enhance the ability of Parties to implement the Convention, strengthen the scientific basis for decision-making, contribute to the reduction of illegal trade, promote understanding of the Convention, increase cooperation with international stakeholders such as other MEAs and the WTO, strive for full global membership, and provide a secure financial and administrative basis for the Convention.
157. *See* Dec. 13.1.
158. *See* SC54 Doc. 6.1, at 2.
159. *Id.*
160. *See id.*, Annex 2.
161. *See* SC54 Summary Record, at 3.
162. *See* CoP 14 Doc. 11.
163. *See id.* at 3.
164. *Id.*
165. *See* Res. Conf. 14.2, Annex.
166. *See* CoP 13 Doc. 9.2.1, at 6.
167. *Id.*
168. *See* CoP 13 Com. I Rep. 10 (Rev. 1), at 1–2.
169. *See* CoP 14 Doc. 14.
170. *Id.*
171. *See id.* at 2.
172. *Id.*
173. *Id.*
174. *Id.*
175. *See* CoP 14 Com. II Rep. 2 (Rev. 1), at 3.
176. *See* CoP 14 Com. II Rep. 3 (Rev. 1), at 1.
177. *See id.*
178. *See id.*
179. *See id.* at 2.
180. *See* CoP 14 Com. II Rep. 15 (Rev. 1), at 1.
181. *See* Dec. 14.3.
182. *See id.*
183. *Id.*

16

State Endangered Species Acts

Susan George and William J. Snape III

Introduction

The role of state governments in protecting not just endangered species but all species can be summed up with one fact: state governments traditionally have been the chief stewards of wildlife within their borders. The states therefore serve a vital role in protecting and conserving their own plants, animals, and habitats. Yet while states historically were given the role of protecting the wildlife within their borders and still retain significant rights and powers, the federal government in many instances has assumed primary responsibility over these national resources under its constitutional authorities.[1] Under the Commerce Clause, inter alia, Congress enacted a wide range of environmental laws, including the Endangered Species Act of 1973 (ESA).[2]

Through the ESA, the federal government now exercises its vitally important power to regulate listed species and their associated habitat to achieve conservation and recovery. But the role of the states in endangered species protection was recognized from the outset, as the ESA authorized the Secretary of the Interior to enter into cooperative agreements with states that established "adequate and active" programs of protection. This chapter will explore those programs, enacted statutorily and dubbed "state endangered species acts," as well as their history, current status, and role.

The role of the states, and how to enhance the conservation of threatened and endangered species through greater state involvement, has been and likely will continue to be a topic of national discussion. Although many states have lacked the capacity, both legal and programmatic, to protect nongame species, many states are significantly increasing their focus on nongame management. By increasing their capacity, the states not only can increase their ability to manage threatened and endangered species as an extra safety net but, more important, can fulfill their trust responsibility for all wildlife species in a way that supplements and complements irreplaceable federal protections.

Current State of the Law

The laws in place today vary as widely as the landscapes from which they come. These laws range from simply prohibiting either the "taking" of or trafficking in an endangered species to more comprehensive schemes for their listing, management, and protection. Nevada, in 1969, was the first state to declare that its people had a legal obligation to conserve and protect native species threatened with extinction.[3] Kentucky was the most recent state to enact a law protecting imperiled species, passing its Rare Plant Recognition Act in 1994.[4]

The authors wish to thank Matthew Padilla, J.D. candidate, American University Washington College of Law, and Aaron Weisbuch, J.D. candidate, American University Washington College of Law, for their assistance.

Most of the existing state endangered species acts merely provide a mechanism for listing and prohibit the taking of or trafficking in listed species. No mechanisms for recovery, consultation, or critical habitat designation exist in 32 state acts. Such a framework exists in states such as Florida, where the only provisions relating to endangered species provide for listing and make it "unlawful for a person to intentionally kill or wound any fish or wildlife of a species designated by the Fish and Wildlife Conservation Commission as endangered, threatened or of special concern."[5] Kentucky prohibits only the import, transport, possession for resale, or sale (trafficking) of an endangered species listed by the state.[6] Georgia, although it has an Endangered Wildlife Act, is primarily governed by rules and regulations, and has no specific statutory provisions related to endangered species other than penalty provisions.[7] Five states have no act at all; they simply rely on the federal act or nongame programs.[8]

The California Endangered Species Act is the most comprehensive of the state acts. Modeled after the federal act, it provides a mechanism for listing and prohibits the taking of or trafficking in listed species.[9] In addition, it covers both plants and animals and requires recovery plans and agency consultation on the impact of proposed state agency projects on endangered species.[10] Acts in several other states, including Kansas and Hawaii, also provide substantial measures.[11] In general, however, most acts lack all but the most basic elements of a legislative scheme to protect a state's imperiled species.

History

Before enactment of the ESA, 16 states had adopted legislation classifying certain wildlife species as endangered and tried to protect them through import and sale restrictions. The focus of these acts was on taking and commerce prohibitions rather than habitat protection. Then, with the enactment of the 1973 legislation, Congress adopted a federal scheme to improve state efforts. In 1973, Section 6(f) of the federal act was created in part to bolster more state participation by defining what state acts must look like. An acceptable state program had to do the following:

1. Include the authority for a state agency to implement the program;
2. Establish acceptable conservation programs for all resident listed species;
3. Include the authority to determine the status and survival requirements for resident fish and wildlife;
4. Authorize the establishment of programs to conserve listed species; and
5. Provide for public involvement in decisions on the listing species.

Federal funding was provided as an incentive.

Twenty-one states responded to the call. Seeking to encourage even greater state participation, Congress amended the ESA in 1977 to create an alternative. The 1977 amendment authorized the Secretary to enter into more limited cooperative agreements with those states that met the final three criteria and whose programs addressed those species in the greatest need of attention. The loosened requirements appear to have had the desired effect, as eight states adopted laws following the amendment. Today, 46 states have some form of endangered species legislation on the books.

Listing

Listing is the first step in the protection of imperiled species. Under this procedure, plants and animals are classified according to the degree of risk to the species. Based on this classification, a species is then given varying degrees of protection.

The courts have confirmed that states can list animals that are not on the federal endangered list. In *Nettleton Co. v. Diamond*,[12] a New York court found that because scientific uncertainty sometimes exists as to whether an animal should be classified at the federal level as threatened or endangered, states can step in and list species that the federal government decides not to list. Further, the court in *Nettleton* stated that this state authority applied not only to species indigenous to the state but to nonindigenous species as well.[13]

Every state with its own act requires or authorizes promulgation of a list of endangered species within the state. Listing is required in each of these states except New Jersey, where by law the Commission of the Department of Environmental Protection may list species that are endangered.[14] Three other state statutes require that species be listed but provide significant exceptions to the rule. In Oregon, the Fish and Wildlife Commission can decide not to list if the species is secure outside the state and is not of "cultural, scientific or commercial significance to the state."[15] And in Kentucky, the listing of plants "shall not serve to impede the development or use of private or public lands."[16]

Most acts, however, are written to exclude cost/benefit considerations from the decision about whether or not to list a species for protection.[17] In general, the rationale is that socioeconomic impacts can be considered when protective regulations are actually implemented and that an honest accounting of the state's biota is owed to the public. In California, for example, which has a comprehensive process for listing, "sufficient scientific information" is necessary for a listing decision.[18] An amendment to New Mexico's Wildlife Conservation Act states that listings cannot be based on public information concerning social and economic impact, but input from affected landowners and resource managers must be taken and kept in a public repository.[19]

An additional criterion used in listing a species is geographic location. Unlike the federal act, which lists a species found to be imperiled within its entire geographic range, most state acts focus on the species' status within that state's geographic borders. Typical language can be seen in Maine's act: protected species are those "in danger of being rendered extinct within the State of Maine."[20] This protection is extended to subspecies in almost three-quarters of the state acts. Connecticut goes further, extending protection to distinct populations of imperiled species.[21]

In addition to listing state endangered species, 37 states also adopt the federal list. New Mexico is one exception. In that state, the Game and Fish Commission must adopt the federal list by regulation, and to date, only select species from the federal list have become part of the state list.[22] The Mexican spotted owl is federally listed in New Mexico but does not appear on the state list, although the Mexican gray wolf appears on both lists.[23]

Listing procedures vary in complexity. Typically, the state wildlife commission, agency, or division is empowered to make listing decisions. North Carolina, however, until recently permitted a species to be listed only after several independent bodies concurred—a Scientific Council, a Nongame Wildlife Advisory Committee, and the Wildlife Resources Commission.[24] Montana allows a wildlife administrator to make recommendations about listing, but final decisions are reserved for the legislature.[25]

While all states with acts recognize both threatened and endangered status for listed species, 12 states also authorize the listing of "candidate species" or "species of special concern." For example, Minnesota designates a "species of special concern" if it is uncommon in the state or has "unique or highly specific habitat requirements."[26] As with the federal act, however, these species are not given any protection except in California, where the state's prohibitions on taking apply to candidate species.[27]

One legal issue that has arisen recently is whether an environmental analysis must be performed prior to listing decisions at the state level. Several states have statutes requiring an environmental analysis for agency actions similar to the process under the National Environmental Policy Act (NEPA).[28] At least one state court has held that before delisting a state species, an environmental impact report under the state's "little NEPA" must be prepared.[29] In that case, the California Supreme Court held that before delisting the Mojave ground squirrel under the California Endangered Species Act, the state Fish and Game Commission must prepare a report under the California Environmental Quality Act, the state's "little NEPA." The court reasoned that an impact analysis was necessary when a state action lessened protections for a species, as would delisting. It is too early to say whether other states will follow this trend, as the federal courts currently are split on the issue of whether the federal NEPA applies to the designation of critical habitat under the ESA.[30]

Critical Habitat

The designation of critical habitat, or other explicit habitat protection, is one of the protections sometimes given to listed species at both the state and federal level. This requirement is based on an understanding that habitat is crucial to species' survival and recovery, and that the habitat most important to a species should be identified at the time the species is listed under the federal ESA. Critical habitat designation does not affect private landowners unless they are applying for a federal permit or funding, but it requires that government agencies review the impact of their actions to ensure that this habitat is not adversely affected.

Only six states have a provision requiring critical habitat designation, and it is rarely used. For example, Connecticut directs the Commissioner of Environmental

Protection to adopt regulations to identify "essential" habitat for threatened and endangered species.[31] Critical or essential habitat has never been designated in that state, however. In Maine, critical habitat designations are not required, although the Commissioner of Inland Fisheries and Wildlife has the authority to make such designations.[32] And in New Hampshire, critical habitat is designated for purposes of consultation, similar to the federal act.[33]

Many of the remaining states authorize the purchase of land to protect threatened and endangered species. The authority of a state wildlife agency to acquire land or aquatic habitat "for the conservation of resident endangered or threatened species" is one of the requirements that a state program must satisfy to be deemed "adequate and active" under Section 6 of the federal ESA, which authorizes federal funding for state cooperative programs. Nonetheless, only 32 states explicitly authorize the acquisition of habitat for imperiled species.[34]

Prohibitions

Restrictions on certain commercial activities and on the taking of listed species are common in state statutes. Most, though not all, prohibit the take of listed species, generally defined as the killing, injuring, or harming of listed species. Forty-one state acts prohibit, in some form, the import, export, transportation, sale, or take of listed species.

The most variety exists in how or whether the term "take" is defined. While the federal act includes habitat modification as a take in its implementing regulations,[35] only Massachusetts has followed the federal lead. In that state, "take" is defined as including the disruption of an animal's "nesting, breeding, feeding, or migratory activity."[36] A separate section explicitly prohibits the alteration of significant habitat.[37] Alaska, on the other hand, follows the majority of states in narrowly defining the term to include only harvesting, actually injuring, or capturing listed species.[38]

Some states have statutory or regulatory language that might be construed to prohibit habitat modification, but they have chosen not to do so. The language of Nebraska's statute, for example, is similar to the federal act and might support a similar interpretation, but the state has taken no position on the question. In California, until recently, the term "take" was administratively interpreted by the state Department of Fish and Game (DFG) to parallel the federal definition, which includes habitat modification. Both the legislative counsel for DFG and the state's attorney general have changed courses, however, opting for a narrow definition that does not include habitat modification.[39] Recent legislative changes in the state continue to exclude references to impact on habitat.[40]

The take prohibition, not surprisingly, has landed in the state courts for interpretation. The issue, as in the federal courts, is whether a take constitutes only a direct killing or whether it can include indirect threats such as habitat modification. The recent U.S. Supreme Court ruling in *Babbitt v. Sweet Home Chapter of Communities* for a Great Oregon[41] may set the stage for a more consistent line of rulings on the species takings issue at the state level. In *Sweet Home*, the Court found that federal regulations that defined "take" of an endangered species to include harm to its habitat were reasonable and valid.

Rulings on the issue, however, are not consistent in state courts across the country. In *Department of Fish and Game v. Anderson-Cottonwood Irrigation District*,[42] the California Department of Fish and Game sought to prevent an irrigation district from operating its pump diversion, which was killing chinook salmon. On appeal, the court found that the terms "take" and "possess" applied to incidental killings of endangered species and that the killings violated the state's endangered species act.

Different results were obtained in Hawaii. In *Stop H-3 Association v. Lewis*,[43] the U.S. District Court found that destruction of habitat was not covered by the state's statutory definition of "take." Thus, construction of a highway through the habitat of an endangered species of bird, even when it destroyed its habitat, was not considered to be illegal.

Permits

Many states' acts recognize exceptions to the take and commerce prohibitions, just as sections 7 and 10 of the federal act do. Thirty-nine states authorize permits for taking listed species under limited circumstances. Typically, permits are authorized for scientific, educational, or zoological purposes, or to enhance the propagation or survival of listed species. A number of states include provisions to capture or destroy species to reduce property damage or to protect human health. Others permit the capture, removal, or devastation of a listed species without a permit if an immediate threat to human life exists. Louisiana, Maine, and Michigan authorize permits for "regulated takings" where population pressures cannot otherwise be relieved.[44]

Six states also permit incidental takings of listed species pursuant to a habitat conservation plan. California, Hawaii, Illinois, Massachusetts, Maine, and Wisconsin allow incidental takes if individuals proposing to alter significant habitat submit detailed plans that include mitigation.[45] California, Illinois, and Maine amended their acts specifically to add a procedure for incidental take permits.[46] The new provision in California retroactively validates take permits previously authorized by the state without statutory authority. Hawaii's provision goes beyond the federal Section 10 habitat conservation plan provision by codifying a "No Surprises" policy into its provision as well.[47]

Conservation Agreements

Recognition is growing that programs are needed to foster voluntary private landowner conservation. Two states have begun to experiment with conservation agreements designed to encourage private landowners to conserve species and habitat.

Kansas amended its act in early 1997, authorizing three new types of agreements—prelisting, safe harbor, and no-take agreements.[48] The prelisting agreement allows management activities "without penalties of law enforcement action or permitting requirements if the species is listed at a late-date."[49] The intent of the safe harbor agreement is to "protect the contracting entity from any restrictions on land use that might otherwise occur if a listed species immigrates into the habitat."[50] No-take agreements provide "assurance that the management activities specified in the agreement would not lead to penalties of law enforcement action or permitting requirements if future changes in land use are needed."[51] Hawaii followed soon after, adding a provision for safe harbor agreements.[52] Unlike Kansas, this provision contains several restrictions, such as the requirement that the agreement increase the likelihood of recovery. In general, however, explicit language authorizing voluntary conservation agreements does not appear in most state acts.

Penalties and Enforcement

State endangered species acts are no exception to the rule that a law must be enforced to be effective, yet most states suffer from a lack of proper enforcement. Although most of the state acts provide for penalties, little consistency exists in this area. In Minnesota, for example, violation of the state's provisions constitutes a misdemeanor,[53] with fines up to $1,000 and/or 90 days' imprisonment. In Massachusetts, violation can result in penalties from $5,000 up to $10,000 and imprisonment of 180 days. Furthermore, if the violation involved significant habitat, the offender may also be required to restore the habitat.[54] Some states, such as Oklahoma, authorize the seizure and forfeiture of property used as an aid in violation of any provision of the state's endangered species act.[55] Prohibitions and permit provisions typically are enforced by the state through its wildlife wardens and the state attorney general's office.

Citizen enforcement also can aid government efforts, especially when the government is unable or unwilling to pursue enforcement.[56] Yet none of the state endangered species acts has a citizen suit provision that allows lawsuits to force compliance with the law.

Because no state endangered species act has a mechanism for citizen enforcement, the public has been forced to rely on other means. Several states have statutes that grant standing to citizens to protect the environment.[57] Yet few of these laws define "environment" to include wildlife or plants, and fewer courts have interpreted the word as broadly. A citizen from Illinois was once trapped in this very dilemma.

In 1989, the city of Marion, Illinois, submitted an application under the Clean Water Act[58] to build a dam. Dr. Joseph Glisson, a 24-year resident, had evidence that the project would extirpate two state-listed species, the Indiana crayfish and the least brook lamprey. He sued, alleging a violation of the Illinois Endangered Species Act,[59] but his complaint was dismissed for lack of standing. He appealed, arguing that the Illinois Constitution, which gives standing to citizens to promote a "healthy environment," should include wildlife.[60] The appellate court reversed, finding that he had standing.[61] The Illinois Supreme Court, however, agreed with the trial court, ruling that wildlife is not part of the "environment" and that Dr. Glisson therefore had no standing to sue.[62]

Without the ability to enforce endangered species laws, these acts have no teeth. In the Southwest, for example, nearly every federal listing of an endangered species in the last decade was the result of a citizen suit or petition against the U.S. Fish and Wildlife Service. Citizen suit provisions are often the only means of ensuring compliance with environmental laws.

Recovery Plans

The purpose of a recovery plan is to detail what is needed to restore the listed species and its habitat so that the provisions of the endangered species act are no longer necessary. Yet states rarely require recovery plans, and the few that do have not promulgated final recovery plans. Of the five states that require a plan, only two—California and New Mexico—set deadlines for its implementation.[63] Maine requires a recovery plan only when a species will be transplanted, introduced, or reintroduced.[64] North Carolina requires recovery plans, although they can't restrict the use or development of private property.[65] Kansas law establishes a volunteer local advisory committee to assist in drafting recovery plans.[66]

Most of the states requiring recovery plans rely on a model in which recovery efforts are directed at a single species. Two states are moving toward an ecological model emphasizing a multispecies approach to protection. In New Mexico, recovery plans must include multiple threatened and endangered species if the species use similar habitats or share a common threat or both.[67] Kentucky also is beginning to use a multispecies approach to management.

Consultation

Consultation provisions are designed to ensure that government agency actions do not jeopardize a listed species or adversely modify critical habitat. Eight states have laws that require agency consultation on proposed state projects to ensure that any action funded, authorized, or carried out by a state agency is not likely to jeopardize an endangered or threatened species or adversely impact its habitat. These requirements are similar to requirements under the federal act, except that they extend only to state and local agency actions.[68] Unlike the federal act, however, none of the state statutes requires the preparation of a biological assessment by the action agency.

If no feasible alternative to a project exists, exemptions can be approved in California, Connecticut, and Minnesota. California also can require mitigation if a state project will "result in the destruction or adverse modification of habitat essential to the continued existence of the species."[69] Several states, such as Hawaii, do not require consultation but state that the governor shall "encourage" other agencies to ensure that their actions do not jeopardize listed species.[70]

Plant Protection

The different treatment given to plants and animals reflects a legal rather than a scientific reality. While wild animals are held in trust by a state for the benefit of its citizens, plants "attach" to the real property on which they are found. The result is that plants and animals generally receive different statutory treatment, even at the federal level, where both plants and animals are covered by the ESA.

Differences abound as to whether the various state provisions cover plants and animals, just animals, or plants and animals separately. Only 15 state acts include plants within the definition of "species." Seventeen states have separate acts for plants, and the remaining 13 protect only animals. Alaska, for example, protects only vertebrate species and subspecies,[71] while Connecticut statutes protect both plant and animal species.[72] In Kansas, where innovative new measures have been incorporated, no protection for plants is included.

In states such as Kentucky, separate provisions exist to protect animals and plants.[73] Even in such cases, however, most states provide less protection for plant species than for animals. The Kentucky Rare Plant Recognition Act requires that threatened and endangered plant species be listed and that location and population information be kept.[74] The species, however, are declared to be the property of the landowner, and no interference with construction projects is allowed.[75] Maine's act requires the listing of imperiled plants, but no other protections exist.[76] The New Hampshire Native Plant Protection Act of 1987 prohibits the taking of listed plant species, but from public property only; an exception exists for private property owners.[77] In California, on the other hand, the "take" prohibitions apply on public as well as private land. South Dakota's prohibitions also apply equally to plants and animals.[78]

Funding

A critical element in any program is adequate funding. Without it, even the best-written laws will stay unimplemented. Funding mechanisms and funding levels for the various statutory programs vary widely, with sources generally falling into three categories: federal, state, and private.

Typically, the majority of funding for a state program comes from the federal government. Under Section 6 of the federal ESA, the federal government can enter into cooperative agreements "with any state which establishes and maintains an adequate and active program for the conservation of endangered species and threatened species."[79] To date, each state has a signed cooperative agreement with the U.S. Fish and Wildlife Service (FWS) for vertebrates; fewer have cooperative agreements for plants.[80] Along with the cooperative agreements comes the incentive of funding.

Under the cooperative agreements, Congress can appropriate to the states up to 5 percent of the combined amounts collected by the Federal Aid in Wildlife Restoration Act and the Federal Aid in Fish Restoration Act.[81] The appropriation is distributed to the seven FWS regions based on the number of listed Section 6 species within that region. States then submit proposed projects to the regional FWS office for approval. The federal government will fund up to 75 percent of project costs for a single state, or up to 90 percent if the project involves a joint agreement by two or more states for the conservation of a species.[82] These federal acts generated over $740 million in 2009,[83] with over $57 million available to the states for threatened and endangered species protection efforts.[84]

In addition to federal monies, state general funds also provide a percentage of funding.[85] Kentucky's Nature Preserves Commission receives a significant amount of its plant protection budget from state general fund revenues. In Nebraska, over half of the nongame and endangered species funding, totaling $495,000,[86] comes from a legislative appropriation from the general fund.[87]

Most states also have private funding mechanisms. Louisiana, for example, authorizes the issuance of endangered species stamps.[88] Nebraska and Texas laws both create a Nongame and Endangered Species Conservation Fund.[89] Missouri voters established a conservation sales tax in 1976, portions of which go to support endangered species conservation;[90] Arkansas has passed similar legislation.[91] Tax check-offs also are common, although revenues from these programs have been declining; in South Carolina, revenues from check-offs for endangered wildlife have dropped to nearly half of 1989 figures, most likely due to competition with other check-off programs. Wildlife license plate sales show promise as a significant source of income, available for purchase in 42 states.[92] In Massachusetts, sales of wildlife plates have generated more than $16 million since the program began in 1994.[93] Bald eagle and other wildlife conservation plates brought in over $1.5 million for conservation in 2003 in Ohio.[94] Other programs include Minnesota's successful Critical Habitat Matching Program, which provides a dollar-for-dollar match to buy wildlife management areas, restore wetlands, and protect spawning sites.[95] Over $26 million in land and cash donations have been matched by the state since 1986.[96]

States Without Acts or Provisions

States without statutory provisions related specifically to endangered species protection rely predominantly on the federal ESA and other nongame programs, such as habitat acquisition, and scattered regulatory measures. Wyoming, Utah, and West Virginia, for example, simply abide by the federal ESA and rely on their nongame wildlife programs to protect threatened and endangered species. Alabama and Arkansas have their own lists of endangered, protected, or "special concern" species based on regulatory authority, but except for nongame programs, they have no other program of protection.

While Arizona does not have a state endangered species act for animals, it does have a protective framework. In addition to having a statute protecting imperiled plants,[97] the state Game and Fish Department prepared procedures for the reestablishment of threatened native wildlife. This was the result of a Game and Fish Commission policy approved in June 1987 requiring the department to "pursue an active program of re-establishing, where appropriate to do so, all species on the Commission's list of Threatened Native Wildlife in Arizona."[98] The program does not include recovery plans or critical habitat designation but is designed to work in conjunction with the federal ESA. Thus, Arizona has an established program, though not legislative in nature.

Emerging Issues and Future Directions

State endangered species acts have a vital role to play in endangered species protection. First, they give a state the ability to protect non-federally listed species. In the Northeast, for example, upland sandpiper numbers are declining, though not widely enough to warrant federal protection. In an effort to stem the decline, several states have put the bird on their state lists and have begun local recovery efforts. Nearly everyone agrees that if the states stopped working on the species, it would need federal protection. So, state listing can be the first line of defense on behalf of recovery.

Second, for species already on the federal list, a state act can provide another line of defense. Most acts include a prohibition against taking; others give the state the authority to do research and acquire land for protection. In New Mexico, the federally endangered Rio Grande silvery minnow was uplisted on the state list from threatened to endangered, giving the state the ability to prepare a recovery plan, prohibit taking of the species, and authorize research. The state Department of Game and Fish has stated that it won't prepare a separate recovery plan but instead will pool its resources with the FWS and coordinate its activities to aid the federal efforts, including providing biological research and a species database.

Finally, states can play an innovative role in preventing ecosystem fragmentation. In cooperation with their neighbors and the federal government, states could develop regional ecosystem plans to identify key habitats, protect ecologically important areas, and allow human development in the least sensitive areas. A regional ecosystem plan would maintain each state's wildlife program's flexibility while guaranteeing that whole ecosystems are rationally protected. State wildlife action plans are also important in this regard.[99]

Conclusion

In today's world of changing climates, increasing human populations, and decreasing federal budgets, the need to find creative solutions for wildlife protection is evident. The states, with their historical jurisdiction over wildlife and local resources, are one obvious focus. The states' need for increased legal authority, responsibility, and programmatic resources, however, means that these serious gaps must be addressed in order for the states to become truly effective partners in the management of threatened and endangered species.

Although most states have enacted their own state endangered species laws, these laws remain far from comprehensive, and many fall short of what is mandated for a state program under the federal ESA. State-level statutory changes are needed to shore up species coverage, enforcement provisions, and recovery requirements. Also needed, of course, is infrastructure in the form of funding and staffing to support those improved programs. With such changes, the next phase of wildlife protection in this country could see a greatly enhanced state role, not just in managing endangered species, but in conserving wildlife and habitat as an integral part of each state's natural infrastructure, as part of the national conservation fabric and as part of the worldwide effort to address the impacts of global climate change. Biological diversity needs help at all levels of government if we are to pass along a healthy natural estate to future generations, keeping intact the world we inherited.

Notes

1. The current doctrine recognizes a state's primary responsibility over wildlife but subjects it to strict constitutional limits. *See* Hughes v. Oklahoma, 441 U.S. 322 (1979) (explicitly overturning the state ownership doctrine but recognizing a state's right to the wildlife within its borders).
2. 16 U.S.C. §§ 1531–1543 (1973). The federal government's role of protecting migratory waterfowl, birds of prey, marine mammals, and species listed as threatened or endangered under the Endangered Species Act of 1973 has arisen because of the decline of these species nationwide and a concomitant failure on the part of the states to protect these species locally. *See* DEFENDERS OF WILDLIFE & CTR. FOR WILDLIFE LAW, SAVING BIODIVERSITY: A STATUS REPORT ON STATE LAWS, POLICIES, AND PROGRAMS (July 1996). *See also* DEFENDERS OF WILDLIFE, ESA SECTION 6: THE ROLE OF THE STATES (Sept. 2005).
3. NEV. REV. STAT. ANN. §§ 503.584–.589, 527.260–.300.
4. KY. REV. STAT. ANN. §§ 146.600–619.
5. FLA. STAT. ANN. § 379.411.
6. KY. REV. STAT. ANN. § 150.183.
7. GA. CODE ANN. §§ 27-3-130, -133.
8. These states are Alabama, Arkansas, Utah, West Virginia, and Wyoming.
9. CAL. FISH & GAME CODE §§ 2050–2100.
10. *Id.* Amendments in the 1997 legislative session may negate some of the protective measures, however.
11. *See* KAN. STAT. ANN. §§ 32-957 to -963, HAW. REV. STAT. ANN. §§ 195D-1 to -10.
12. Nettleton Co. v. Diamond, 315 N.Y.S.2d 625 (1970).
13. *Id.* at 631.
14. N.J. STAT. ANN. § 23:2A-4.
15. OR. REV. STAT. § 496.176(9)(a).
16. KY. REV. STAT. ANN. § 146.615.
17. *See* Amy Ando, *Delay on the Path to the Endangered Species List: Do Costs and Benefits Matter?*, in RESOURCES FOR THE FUTURE (1997).
18. CAL. FISH & GAME CODE § 2062.
19. N.M. STAT. ANN. § 17-2-40.
20. ME. REV. STAT. ANN. tit. 12, § 12801.
21. CONN. GEN. STAT. ANN. § 26-304(6).
22. N.M. STAT. ANN. § 12-2-41.
23. N.M. Dep't of Game & Fish, Biota Information System of N.M., http://www.bison-m.org.

24. N.C. Gen. Stat. § 113-334.
25. Mont. Code Ann. § 87-5-107.
26. Minn. Stat. Ann. § 84.0895.
27. Cal. Fish & Game Code § 2085.
28. National Environmental Policy Act of 1969, 42 U.S.C. §§ 7601 *et seq.* This law requires an analysis of the impacts of federal agency actions on the environment. States with similar requirements include California, Connecticut, Georgia, Hawaii, Indiana, Maryland, Massachusetts, Minnesota, Montana, New York, North Carolina, Virginia, Washington, and Wisconsin.
29. Mountain Lion Found. v. Fish & Game Comm'n, 51 Cal. Rptr. 2d 408 (Cal. Ct. App. 1996), *aff'd*, 939 P.2d 1280 (1997).
30. *See* Douglas County v. Babbitt, 48 F.3d 1495 (9th Cir. 1995); Catron County Bd. of Comm'rs v. U.S. Fish & Wildlife Serv., 75 F.3d 1429 (10th Cir. 1996) (Secretary of the Interior must comply with NEPA when designating critical habitat).
31. Conn. Gen. Stat. Ann. § 26-306.
32. Me. Rev. Stat. Ann. tit. 12, § 12804.
33. N.H. Rev. Stat. Ann. § 212-A:9.
34. The fact that all 50 states have active cooperative agreements in place indicates that the various state agencies have at least general authority to acquire habitat, even if that authority does not explicitly mention endangered species.
35. 62 Fed. Reg. 32,183.
36. Mass. Gen. Laws Ann. ch. 131A, § 1.
37. *Id.* § 2.
38. Alaska Stat. §§ 16.20.195, .200.
39. Tara Mueller, The Wilson Administration's Interpretation of CESA and CEQA, paper presented at Saving Biodiversity in the United States: A Conference for Wildlife Advocates, Catholic University, Washington, D.C. (Feb. 8, 1997).
40. Cal. Fish & Game Code § 2062.
41. 515 U.S. 687 (1995).
42. 11 Cal. Rptr. 2d 222 (1992).
43. 538 F. Supp. 149 (D. Haw.), *aff'd in part, rev'd in part*, 740 F.2d 1442 (9th Cir. 1984).
44. La. Civ. Code Ann. art. 56, § 1904G; Me. Rev. Stat. Ann. tit. 12, § 12804; Mich. Comp. Laws Ann. § 324.36505.
45. Cal. Fish & Game Code § 2080.1; Haw. Rev. Stat. Ann. § 195D-4(G); Mass. Gen. Law Ann. ch. 131A, § 5; Wis. Stat. Ann. § 29.604(6).
46. Cal. Fish & Game Code § 2081, 520 Ill. Comp. Stat. 10/1; Me. Rev. Stat. Ann. tit. 12, § 12808.
47. Haw. Rev. Stat. § 195D.
48. Kan. Stat. Ann. § 32-962(b)(1).
49. *Id.*
50. *Id.* § 32-962(b)(1)(i).
51. *Id.*
52. Haw. Rev. Stat. Ann. § 195D-22. Note that no new safe harbor agreements, HCPs, or incidental take licenses shall be approved or issued under the statute after July 1, 2012.
53. Minn. Stat. Ann. § 84.0895(9).
54. Mass. Gen. Laws Ann. ch. 131A, § 6.
55. Okla. Stat. Ann. tit. 29, §§ 5-402, -412.
56. For a thorough analysis and discussion of citizen suit laws, see Defenders of Wildlife & Ctr. for Wildlife Law, The Public in Action: Using State Citizen Suit Statutes to Protect Biodiversity (1996).
57. *Id.*
58. 33 U.S.C. §§ 1365 *et seq.*
59. 520 Ill. Comp. Stat. 10/1.

60. Defenders of Wildlife and the Illinois chapter of the Sierra Club filed an amicus brief in both the appellate and state supreme court actions. *See* Glisson v. City of Marion, 97-CH-7 (Ill. App. Ct.).
61. Glisson v. City of Marion, 697 N.E.2d 433 (Ill. App. Ct. 1998).
62. Glisson v. City of Marion, 720 N.E.2d 1034 (Ill. 1999).
63. Cal. Fish & Game Code §§ 2105–2116; N.M. Stat. Ann. §17-2-40.1.
64. Me. Rev. Stat. Ann. tit. 12, § 12804.
65. N.C. Gen. Stat. § 113-333(6).
66. Kan. Stat. Ann. § 32-960.
67. N.M. Stat. Ann. § 17-2-40.1.
68. State consultation requirements cannot be applied because of the Supremacy Clause of the U.S. Constitution, art. VI, cl. 2.
69. Cal. Fish & Game Code §§ 2052.1, 2054.
70. Haw. Rev. Stat. Ann. § 195D-5(B).
71. Alaska Stat. § 16.20.180.
72. Conn. Gen. Stat. Ann. § 26-303.
73. Ky. Rev. Stat. Ann. §§ 150.183, 146.600–.619.
74. *Id.* §§ 146.600–.619.
75. *Id.*
76. Me. Rev. Stat. Ann. tit. 5, § 13078.
77. N.H. Rev. Stat. Ann. § 217-A:3.
78. Cal. Fish & Game Code § 2080; S.D. Codified Laws § 34A-8-9. The federal act prohibits takings on federal lands, while takings on private lands are banned only if state law forbids the practice. Very few states have such laws.
79. 16 U.S.C. § 1535(c).
80. Only 20 states have full cooperative agreements for plants; 15 have limited agreements.
81. 16 U.S.C. § 1535 (i).
82. 16 U.S.C. § 1535 (d)(2)(D)(i)–(ii).
83. U.S. Fish and Wildlife Serv., Final Apportionment of Wildlife Restoration Funds 3 (2009), http://wsfrprograms.fws.gov/Subpages/GrantPrograms/WR/WRFinalApportionment2009.pdf.
84. Press Release, Secretary Salazar Announces $57.8 Million in Grants to Support Land Acquisition and Conservation Planning for Endangered Species, U.S. Fish and Wildlife Serv. (Apr. 20, 2009).
85. A report by the International Association of Fish and Wildlife Agencies found that in 1995, states spent over $11 million of nonfederal money on federally listed species. Int'l Ass'n of Fish & Wildlife Agencies, Endangered Species Survey Final Report for 1996.
86. Rick Schneider, Program Manager, Nebraska Natural Heritage Program (June 26, 2009).
87. Neb. Stat. § 37-811.
88. La. Civ. Code Ann. art. 56:1906.
89. Neb. Rev. Stat. § 37-431; Tex. Parks & Wild. Code Ann. §§ 68.001, 11.051–056.
90. A constitutionally mandated sales tax of one-eighth of 1 percent provides the funding. Mo. Const. art. 4, § 43(a).
91. Arkansas voters passed a constitutional amendment in 1996 that provides for a one-eighth-cent sales tax for conservation. Ark. Code Ann. § 19-6-484.
92. Conn. Dep't of Envtl. Prot., Wildlife License Plates (2009), http://www.ct.gov/Dep/cwp/view.asp?a=2723&q=325714&depNav_GID=1655.
93. Mass. Office of Energy and Envtl. Affairs, Environmental License Plates (2009), http://www.mass.gov/?pageID=eoeeasubtopic&L=5&L0=Home&L1=Grants+%26+Technical+Assistance&L2=Grant+%26+Loan+Programs&L3=Massachusetts+Environmental+Trust+(MET)&L4=Environmental+License+Plates&sid=Eoeea.
94. Ohio Dep't of Nat. Res., Wildlife License Plates (2009), http://www.dnr.state.oh.us/Home/license_platesplaceholder/WildlifeLicensePlates/tabid/9467/Default.aspx.

95. Trust for Pub. Lands, *GreenSense 4* (Spring 1997).
96. Minn. Dep't of Nat. Res., Reinvest in Minnesota: Critical Habitat Match Program (2009), http://www.dnr.state.mn.us/grants/land/rim.html.
97. Ariz. Rev. Stat. Ann. § 3-903.
98. The Arizona Game and Fish Department now designates these species as "species of special concern." *See, e.g.*, Preserving Humpback Chud from Extinction, http://www.azgfd.gov/w_c/research_loach_minnow.shtml.
99. *See* Ass'n of Fish & Wildlife Agencies, State Wildlife Action Plans, http://www.wildlifeactionplans.org/.

17

Nanotechnology and the Endangered Species Act

J. Michael Klise, Steven P. Quarles, and Wm. Robert Irvin

Introduction

Why Nanotechnology?

The recent emergence of nanotechnology has implications for many federal environmental and natural resource laws, including the Endangered Species Act (ESA).[1] Nanotechnology is the science and technology of using and controlling matter at the nanoscale. It involves material that has at least one dimension of 100 nanometers or less. A nanometer—one billionth of a meter—is small indeed. It is roughly 1/100,000 the width of a human hair.[2] By the end of this decade, nearly every Fortune 500 company will be involved in nanotechnology.

Nanotechnology's diverse areas of potential use include medical (for example, for drug delivery), cosmetic (sunscreens), electronic (carbon nanotubes), consumer (stain-resistant clothing; eyeglass coatings), and environmental cleanup (zero-valent iron for groundwater remediation). But with these and other beneficial uses come concerns about the effects of exposure to nanomaterials on human health and the environment.

Our understanding of nanotechnology is still in its infancy. Thus, it remains to be seen how fully and effectively nanomaterials can be regulated under existing federal environmental laws such as the Toxic Substances Control Act (TSCA),[3] the Federal Insecticide, Fungicide, and Rodenticide Act (FIFRA),[4] the Clean Air Act,[5] the Comprehensive Environmental Recovery, Compensation, and Liability Act,[6] and the Resource Conservation and Recovery Act.[7] With a potential range of coverage this broad under the principal federal environmental statutes, it is not surprising that nanotechnology would have implications for federal wildlife law as well.

Overview of the Endangered Species Act

The ESA furnishes protections for species listed as "threatened species" or "endangered species" (listed species) and habitat designated as "critical habitat" by the Secretary of the Interior (through the U.S. Fish and Wildlife Service) or the Secretary of Commerce (through the National Marine Fisheries Service). Species listings and critical habitat designations occur through a rulemaking process, either on a Service's own initiative or in response to a citizen petition. The ESA's language is broad enough to apply to virtually any conduct or substance that affects listed species and critical habitat, including the development, use, and disposal of nanoscale materials.

The ESA's two main protective mechanisms are the interagency cooperation provisions for federal agency actions in section 7(a)(2) and the take prohibition in section 9. Section 7(a)(2) imposes the obligation on federal agencies, through consultation with the U.S. Fish and Wildlife Service and National Marine Fisheries Service (Services) to ensure that agency actions are not likely to "jeopardize" listed species or "result in the destruction or adverse modification" of critical habitat. Section 9 applies to the conduct of any private or public "person" and prohibits the take of listed wildlife species. Remedies for take include injunctions, civil penalties, and criminal sanctions.

Both of these protective statutory provisions can apply to the effects of nanoscale materials. As this chapter explains, however, section 7(a)(2) may apply more effectively and fairly than section 9 for now, until more becomes known about the environmental impact of nanotechnology. The Supreme Court's gloss on section 9 in the leading ESA take case, *Babbitt v. Sweet Home Chapter of Communities for a Great Oregon*,[8] complicates, and creates uncertainties about, applying the take prohibition to nanoscale materials and other technologies on the frontiers of science. Under *Sweet Home*, establishing take from nanoscale materials may be difficult because section 9 requires proof that a given material is a "proximate cause" of harm—that is, that the material's effects were reasonably foreseeable, and not a scientific unknown. *Sweet Home* also requires proof of actual injury to or death of an identifiable member of a listed wildlife species—a challenging evidentiary standard even where adverse effects of activities or substances on listed wildlife species are clearly known and understood. Further, section 9's breadth and the potentially harsh penalties for violations may give rise to use of prosecutorial discretion by the U.S. Department of Justice to refrain from prosecuting end-users who in good faith are unaware of a nanoscale material's potential effects on wildlife. Nevertheless, fear of potential criminal and civil liability for take may also discourage companies from pursuing research and development of nanoscale technology, including its use for environmentally beneficial purposes.

By contrast, the protections afforded by ESA section 7(a)(2) do not raise the same concerns or complications. Instead of imposing a tort-like prohibition, section 7(a)(2) establishes a *process* for involving private stakeholders and the federal agencies that oversee nanoscale materials as part of their responsibilities under organic statutes such as the TSCA and FIFRA. As is appropriate for emerging technologies, section 7(a)(2) can trigger protections early in product development and marketing (when federal permits are needed) and high in the chain of commerce (at the pre-consumer level), without the section 9 demands of demonstrating proximate cause. Further, since section 7(a)(2) contains built-in measures for minimizing take, as well as means to excuse liability should take occur in the course of otherwise legitimate activity, it can protect listed species and their habitat and still provide an incentive for exploring emerging areas such as nanotechnology without fear of legal sanctions should inadvertent take occur.

Current State of the Law

The Endangered Species Act and Nanotechnology

Protection of imperiled wildlife and plants under the ESA has evoked superlatives from many quarters. A National Academy of Sciences study referred to the ESA as "the broadest and most powerful wildlife-protection law in U.S. history."[9] Professor Coggins, in his public land law treatise, stated that the "[f]ederal endangered species law is the closest thing to an absolute legislative command in public natural resources law."[10] The Supreme Court in its first opinion on the ESA over a quarter century ago rendered effusive descriptions of the law's might: The "plain intent of Congress in enacting this statute was to halt and reverse the trend toward species extinction, whatever the cost"; the ESA "admits of no exception" and "reveals a conscious decision to give endangered species priority over the 'primary missions' of Federal agencies."[11] The statute reflects the judgment of Congress about how best to protect imperiled species and their habitat from the threats of endangerment and extinction arising from a variety of human actions.

Implementation of the ESA most often occurs and is most visible in the context of major land-disturbing activities, such as residential or commercial development, highway construction, energy and mining projects, and timber harvesting. But it also applies to new technologies, including, most recently, Navy sonar and wind energy turbines. Nanotechnology, in turn, will receive ESA attention, even when it may be the source of potential benefits to biodiversity by providing the means to remediate environmental contamination or to develop smaller, smarter medical or surveillance devices to protect threatened or endangered species. While nanotechnology may pose new questions to be examined under the ESA, the Act's broad language is sufficient to address this technology in the same manner it addresses others.

The ESA protects species at risk and the "ecosystems upon which [they] depend."[12] Nanotechnology has implications for both. ESA section 4 provides the criteria and rulemaking procedures for the Services to list species as "endangered" or "threatened" species and designate those species' "critical habitat," thereby extending the ESA's protections to those species and habitats.[13]

The ESA identifies the criteria to be considered in determining whether to list a species:[14] "the present or threatened destruction, modification, or curtailment of [the species'] habitat"; "overutilization for commercial, recreational, scientific, or educational purposes"; "disease or predation"; "the inadequacy of existing regulatory mechanisms"; and "other natural or manmade factors affecting [the species'] continued existence."[15] Listing determinations must be made "solely on the basis of the best scientific and commercial data available."[16] The factors that lead to listing can include the effects of nanoscale materials, and may do so increasingly as the use and environmental presence of those materials expand and more is understood about their biological and ecological effects.

The criteria for designating "critical habitat" are contained in the ESA's definition of the term: areas within the geographical area occupied by the species at the time of listing that contain "physical or biological features essential to the conservation of the species" and "may require special management considerations or protection," and areas not occupied at the time of listing if the Secretary determines the entire "areas . . . are essential for the conservation of the species."[17] Once critical habitat is designated, impacts to it—including any impacts from nanoscale materials—are scrutinized under ESA section 7.

The ESA contains two principal protective mechanisms for listed species that can apply to impacts from nanoscale materials: the take prohibition of ESA section 9, which protects individual members of a species; and the procedures for consultation between federal agencies and the Services on federal agency actions under ESA section 7(a)(2), which is aimed at avoiding "jeopardy" to entire species. The effects of nanoscale materials could be subject to either or both of these mechanisms. Each mechanism presents its own set of issues generally, as well as in the context of nanotechnology.

Protecting Against Effects of Nanotechnology Using the ESA Section 9 Take Prohibition

ESA section 9(a)(1)(B)[18] prohibits the take of any endangered wildlife.[19] Take is defined broadly to encompass "harass, harm, pursue, hunt, shoot, wound, kill, trap, capture or collect" listed wildlife or any "attempt to engage in . . . such conduct."[20] By regulation, the Services define "harm" in the definition of take to include the concept that habitat disturbance, as might conceivably occur through the use or disposal of nanoscale materials, can be a cause of wildlife take—"significant habitat modification or degradation where it actually kills or injures wildlife by significantly impairing essential behavioral patterns, including breeding, feeding or sheltering."[21]

Several features make the take prohibition the ESA's preeminent wildlife protection mechanism:

- Section 9(a)(1)(B)'s take prohibition arguably prohibits any action that adversely affects a *single member* of a species. In contrast, as explained below, ESA section 7(a)(2) bars actions that are likely to threaten the survival of an entire species, not its individual members, or that likely adversely modify habitat that is designated by rulemaking as critical habitat pursuant to ESA section 4(b).
- The take prohibition has the broadest application to human actors. Private citizens—companies and individuals—are affected by section 7(a)(2) only if they require a federal permit or other federal authorization and the issuance of that permit or authorization is deemed to be a federal "agency action." Otherwise, section 7(a)(2) is applicable only to, and establishes obligations only for, federal agencies. In contrast, section 9(a)(1) applies equally to any "person"—federal employees, state and local government officials, and private-sector companies and individual citizens.
- The take prohibition contains no *scienter* element—it applies to all conduct, whether inadvertent, negligent, or intentional.
- Penalties for take can be severe. Violations are subject to civil and criminal sanctions: civil penalties of not more than $25,000 if the take is done "knowingly" and $500 otherwise;[22] a maximum criminal penalty of $50,000 and/or one year in jail against anyone who "knowingly" commits a take.[23]
- ESA sections 11(e)(6) and (g)(1)[24] authorize the Department of Justice through enforcement actions, and private citizens through citizen suits, to seek injunctions to halt or bar any activity that causes a take or other violation of the ESA.

In some instances, the development and use of nanoscale materials could result in a take of a listed wildlife species. For example, use of a nanopesticide could be toxic to members of listed species, resulting in their death or injury.[25] Similarly, release of nanoscale materials into the environment resulting in the destruction of plants, insects, or other organisms that serve as food sources for listed species could constitute habitat destruction that results in actual death or injury to members of those species and, therefore, could be a prohibited take.

Protecting Against Effects of Nanotechnology Using Federal Agency Consultation with the Services Under ESA Section 7(a)(2)

ESA section 7(a)(2)[26] requires federal agencies to carry out their actions in ways that are not likely to jeopardize the continued existence of listed species or destroy or adversely modify critical habitat. This provision may protect against nanoscale materials more handily than the take prohibition, especially until more is known about the properties and behavior of those materials. It better addresses scientific uncertainty, is more fair, and (unlike section 9) also covers plants.

ESA section 7(a)(2) applies to all federal agencies and to private parties who seek federal permits or funding or whose activities have some other nexus to federal agency actions. The provision establishes a two-part standard by requiring each federal agency to ensure, through consultation with the pertinent Service, that any agency action "authorized, funded, or carried out" by the agency "is not likely to jeopardize the continued existence of any" listed species "or result in the destruction or adverse modification of [any designated critical] habitat of such species."[27]

As with the initial listing of a species under the ESA, section 7(a)(2) looks to the current state of knowledge: "In fulfilling the requirements of this paragraph each agency shall use the best scientific and commercial data available."[28] On its face, this standard does not contemplate the need for an exhaustive body of data proving that a new program or technology does not pose any risks of harm. It is a procedural requirement to consider the best science currently available, not a substantive duty to conduct new studies.[29] The Supreme Court has interpreted the "best scientific and commercial data available" standard as intended not only to "advance the ESA's overall goal of species preservation" but also to prevent the "haphazard" implementation of the ESA that could lead to "needless economic dislocation."[30] The standard balances competing interests of species preservation and the original intent of the triggering agency action.

The "best available data" requirement is not technology specific. While nanotechnology may pose new considerations of possible effects on listed species or habitat, it nevertheless fits into section 7(a)(2)'s existing procedural paradigm and should be subject to the same requirements as other new technologies. Fundamentally, the ESA's consultation requirements function as a tool to ensure that federal agencies (and the public) are aware of their actions' effects on listed species and their critical habitats, and that the agencies consider and adopt alternatives or protective measures when appropriate. The consultation process will serve the same functions when the agency actions involve nanotechnology applications.

The Services have adopted joint regulations that establish a triage system for procedural compliance with ESA section 7(a)(2). The regulations require no consultation if the action agency determines that its action will have "no effect" on listed species or critical habitat; "informal consultation" if the action agency determines, and the relevant Service concurs, that the action is "not likely to adversely affect" a listed species/critical habitat; and the "formal consultation" described in section 7(a)(2) and (b) if the "not likely to adversely affect" finding cannot be made.[31] If formal consultation occurs, the Service prepares a biological opinion (BiOp) on the agency action's impacts.[32]

Under ESA sections 7(b)(4) and (o)(2), the Service submits to the action agency (and the applicant for a federal permit, license, grant, etc., if that is the agency action) in a BiOp an incidental take statement that provides immunity from prosecution for the action agency (and applicant) for any incidental take otherwise barred by section 9 if the agency (and applicant) adopts the "reasonable and prudent measures" (RPMs) the Service includes in the statement to "minimize" (but not mitigate for) the "impact" of the expected incidental take. The agency (and applicant) must also adhere to the "terms and conditions" the Service specifies for implementing the RPMs.[33] The RPMs are the increment above the section 7(a)(2) minimum of avoiding "jeopard[y]" or "adverse modification" that the Service believes will minimize take and still allow the desired action to proceed. If the Service determines that the federal agency action would likely result in jeopardy or adverse modification, it must offer to the agency (and applicant) in the BiOp any possible "reasonable and prudent alternatives" (RPAs) to the action (which, here, might include mitigation steps).[34] While the RPMs and RPAs are not mandatory, an agency that disregards the BiOp "does so at its own peril."[35]

ESA section 7(a)(2) applies broadly to all federal agencies and to private parties who seek federal permits or funding or whose activities have some other nexus to federal agency actions, and covers listed plants as well as wildlife. Federal environmental statutes already reach many nanoscale materials. Thus, any number of federal actions regarding nanotechnology could trigger the section 7(a)(2) analysis. Pesticide registration, drug approval, or federal approval of environmental remediation or issuance of a research grant involving nanotechnology could each create a need for this review.

While complete information regarding all aspects of the environmental impact of nanotechnology is not currently available, section 7(a)(2) does not require that level of certainty. The consultation process encompasses societal decision-making at or beyond the bounds of scientific certainty. The ultimate fate of Pacific salmon, the northern spotted owl, and numerous other species cannot be known with certainty. To protect listed species and designated critical habitat, the relevant action agencies and the Services regularly employ cutting-edge scientific models, technologies, and strategies to protect these animals and lands—the "best available data"—without complete knowledge of their effectiveness. The same analysis can, and should, be applied in section 7(a)(2) consultations involving nanotechnology.

Emerging and Future Directions

Use of the Take Prohibition to Address Nanoscale Materials

Using the ESA's take prohibition to protect against the effects of nanoscale materials raises issues of effectiveness, fairness, and economic incentives. The first of these is primarily a legal concern, whereas the other two involve questions of policy.

Effectiveness

Considering how much muscle Congress gave the take provision as described above, ESA section 9 would seem to be a highly effective means of policing against any adverse effects of nanoscale materials on ESA-listed wildlife. Yet its effectiveness in this context is tempered by the reality that scientific understanding of many nanoscale materials is in its infancy. In *Babbitt v. Sweet Home Chapter of Communities for a Great Oregon*,[36] the Supreme Court upheld a challenge to the Services' regulation defining the "harm" form of take likely most applicable to nanotechnology, but identified three compulsory elements to establish "harm" and thus "take": (1) there must be death or actual injury (2) to an identifiable member of a listed wildlife species (3) that is *proximately caused* by the conduct in question.[37]

Given the current limitations on scientific understanding, the need to demonstrate proximate cause may make it difficult to establish ESA take from nanoscale materials, even assuming there has been death of, or injury to, an identifiable member of a protected species. In *Sweet Home*, the Court stressed the foreseeability component of proximate cause. The majority opinion explained that ESA take violations incorporate "ordinary requirements of proximate causation and foreseeability"; and Justice O'Connor specifically conditioned her concurrence on the understanding that the "ordinary principles of proximate causation, which introduce notions of foreseeability," apply.[38]

The novelty of many aspects of nanotechnology may compound the difficulty of demonstrating the foreseeability of its effects on wildlife. Even when adverse effects of a certain nanoscale material on listed species may be foreseeable, the nascent state of knowledge of the effects may render the task of proving that use of the material caused actual injury to, or death of, a member of a listed wildlife species virtually impossible. Thus, while the ESA's stringent take prohibition no doubt would apply to the effects of nanoscale materials, as a practical matter the prohibition may lack the punch it has in other contexts in which, for example, a conventional material's behavior is more fully understood and predictable.

Fairness

The take prohibition's broad scope, the potential harshness of penalties for violations, and the current state of scientific and public knowledge about the behavior of nanoscale materials also raise concerns about the fairness of using ESA take prohibitions to police the effects of nanoscale materials on wildlife. For example, given the nature of some of the prohibited conduct ("hunt," "shoot," "wound," "kill"), it may not be equitable to impose take liability on a consumer, if damage to wildlife results from nanoscale materials disposed of by a consumer who has no knowledge of the potential for damage, no role in placing the materials in the stream of commerce, and no economic stake in marketing or distributing the materials. Further, the ESA's principal take-avoidance mechanism for the private sector—to prepare a habitat conservation plan and obtain an incidental take permit, as discussed in the next section—has proven enormously costly and time-consuming.

Economic Incentives

The threat of section 9 take liability, without some sort of safe harbor for harm that occurs incidental to some otherwise lawful activity, may also prove a disincentive for companies to invest in the emerging nanotechnology field. In 1982, Congress added provisions that enabled the Services to allow landowners to take listed species when that take is "incidental" to otherwise lawful land uses. This "incidental take" permission comes in the form of either an incidental take permit (ITP) when no other federal permit or authorization for the particular land use is sought[39] or an incidental take statement where such other federal permit or authorization is involved.[40] To obtain the ITP, the landowner must prepare, and secure the pertinent Service's approval of, a conservation plan (often called a habitat conservation plan, or HCP) for the affected listed species covering the contemplated land use.[41] To approve the HCP and issue an ITP, the Service must find that the "taking" identified in the ITP application "will be incidental"; that "the applicant will, to the maximum extent practicable, minimize and mitigate the impacts" of the taking; that "the applicant will ensure that adequate funding" will be provided for the HCP; and that "the taking will not appreciably reduce the likelihood of the survival and recovery of the species in the wild."[42] The Service may add any "measures" that it "may require as being necessary or appropriate for purposes of the" HCP.[43] Meeting the substantive requirements for an HCP may prove difficult if not impossible given what little is known about the biological effects of many nanoscale materials.

Use of ESA Section 7(a)(2) to Address Effects of Nanoscale Materials

ESA section 7(a)(2) provides comparable protections to those available under section 9, without the attendant drawbacks discussed above.

Effectiveness

Section 7(a)(2) protects against "jeopardy" to species as a whole, not against take of individual species members as such. But that seeming reduction in protection for individual species members is offset by other protections that are available under section 7(a)(2) and unavailable in a section 9 take prosecution.

The threshold for protection under section 7(a)(2) is lower and more flexible than the showing required for take under section 9, and therefore may be better suited for situations involving nanotechnology, where scientific understanding is in an emergent stage. There is no need to demonstrate death or injury to an identifiable member of a species under section 7(a)(2), or to establish proximate cause, which could prove difficult if a nanoscale material's effects are unknown and therefore not foreseeable. Rather, section 7(a)(2) is triggered any time an agency determines that an action it has authorized, funded, or carried out "may affect" a listed species or critical habitat; and formal consultation between the action agency and the Service must occur for any action that is "likely to adversely affect" the species or habitat.

These lower and more flexible thresholds will provide protections not available in a pure section 9 enforcement action (which by its terms does not apply until take has occurred), as formal consultation produces a BiOp that, if followed by the action agency, will protect wildlife against jeopardy and take. A BiOp will contain recommended RPMs to protect the species against all but incidental take;[44] and a BiOp that finds a likelihood of species jeopardy will identify the RPAs to the proposed agency action that, if taken, would avoid jeopardy at the species level.[45]

Fairness

In situations involving emerging technologies, the section 7(a)(2) consultation process enhances fairness by focusing appropriately on the upstream levels of the chain of commerce—the manufacturers and marketers who are responsible for introducing, and have the greatest economic stake in the environmental consequences of, these new products, and whose need for federal permits or licenses, or other authorizations or federal funding, brings them within the purview of section 7(a)(2).[46] The process would place the burden of complying with the RPMs or implementing RPAs jointly on the authorizing or funding agencies and on the appropriate economic interests that apply for the authorizations or funding. These parties are in the best position to determine (agencies) and implement (applicants) the RPMs to protect listed species and designated critical habitat and, by doing so, "earn" the protection of the incidental take statement. Meanwhile, at the other end of the chain of commerce, end-users (i.e., consumers), who may be unaware of, and likely are unable to address effectively, the species and habitat consequences, would benefit from that incidental take statement acquired through the consultation process.

Economic Incentives

As already noted, the potential for take liability under ESA section 9, and the costs and potential unavailability of an HCP and accompanying ITP, can provide disincentives for companies to do business in emerging areas of nanotechnology, where environmental effects are so unknown and could well be beneficial. Consultation under section 7(a)(2) avoids that deterrent, because it provides a means, based on *currently available* scientific and commercial data, to proceed with business in an emerging technology while still enjoying the protection from liability for incidental take of protected wildlife and habitat.

The ESA's Conservation Goal and Nanotechnology

The ESA's ultimate goal is the *conservation* of endangered and threatened species and the ecosystems on which they depend.[47] ESA section 3(2) defines "conservation" to mean actions that permit eventual recovery of the listed species to the point that it no longer requires ESA protection.[48]

Protective measures such as the section 7(a)(2) consultation process and the section 9 take prohibition can help achieve conservation. Other ESA provisions address the conservation goal more directly, but do so without the same force of law. For example, in recognition that "conservation" is the ultimate objective of the ESA and to enlist those who are most knowledgeable, section 4(f) directs the Services to prepare "recovery plans" for most listed species and suggests the appointment of "recovery teams" to draft those documents.[49] But a recovery plan, while it could address the effects of nanotechnology, is not a legally binding document.[50] Similarly, section 7(a)(1) requires that federal "agencies shall, in consultation with" the Services, "utilize their authorities in furtherance of the purposes of this Act by carrying out programs for the conservation of" listed species.[51] Although section 7(a)(1) consultations have been found to be legally enforceable,[52] the level of generality of the provision (which addresses entire programs and not individual agency actions) and the degree of discretion it confers on agencies[53] limit its use as a tool for regulating a specific subject such as nanotechnology.

Conclusion

Nanotechnology intersects the ESA at many points, including the initial listing of species, protecting wildlife against harm at the individual and species level, and safeguarding wildlife habitat. Both the take prohibition in ESA section 9 and federal agency consultation with the Services under section 7(a)(2) protect wildlife and habitat from adverse effects of nanotechnology. But given the difficulties of proving take, the nascent state of scientific understanding of the behavior and environmental impacts of nanoscale materials, and questions of fairness and commercial incentives, section 7(a)(2) may be the more appropriate of these two approaches for addressing nanotechnology under the ESA until science and society achieve a fuller understanding of the biological effects of the use and presence of nanoscale materials in the environment.

Notes

1. 16 U.S.C. §§ 1531 *et seq.*
2. ENVTL. LAW INST., NANOTECHNOLOGY DESKBOOK 3 (Lynn Bergeson & Tracy Hester primary auths., 2008) [hereinafter ELI DESKBOOK].
3. 15 U.S.C. §§ 2601–2692. For a discussion of the current and potential applicability of the principal federal environmental statutes to nanotechnology, see ELI DESKBOOK 12–54.
4. 7 U.S.C. §§ 136–136y.
5. 42 U.S.C. §§ 7401 *et seq.*
6. 42 U.S.C. §§ 9601 *et seq.*
7. 42 U.S.C. §§ 6901 *et seq.*
8. 515 U.S. 687 (1995).
9. COMM. ON SCIENTIFIC ISSUES AND THE ENDANGERED SPECIES ACT, SCIENCE AND THE ENDANGERED SPECIES ACT 19 (Nat'l Acad. Press 1995).

10. II Coggins & Glicksman, Public Natural Resources Law § 156.01[1].
11. TVA v. Hill, 437 U.S. 153, 184–85 (1978).
12. 16 U.S.C. § 1531(b).
13. 16 U.S.C. § 1533. An endangered species is "any species which is in danger of extinction throughout all or a significant portion of its range." *Id.* § 1532(6). A threatened species is one "which is likely to become an endangered species within the foreseeable future throughout all or a significant portion of its range." *Id.* § 1532(20).
14. Under the ESA, "species" includes "any subspecies of fish or wildlife or plants, and any distinct population segment [DPS] of any species of vertebrate fish or wildlife which interbreeds when mature." 16 U.S.C. § 1532(16). A species, subspecies, or DPS can be listed in only a portion of its range. *Id.* § 1532(6).
15. 16 U.S.C. § 1533(a)(1). The endangered and threatened species are "listed" in 50 C.F.R. § 17.11 (animals) and § 17.12 (plants).
16. 16 U.S.C. § 1533(B)(1)(A).
17. 16 U.S.C. § 1532(5). The critical habitats are mapped and described in 50 C.F.R. § 17.95 (animals) and § 17.96 (plants).
18. 16 U.S.C. § 1538.
19. The Section 9 take prohibition applies only to *endangered* wildlife species, not to *threatened* wildlife species. Another ESA provision, section 4(d), grants to the Services discretion to extend by regulations the take prohibition and/or any other section 9 prohibitions to threatened wildlife species. 16 U.S.C. § 1533(d). The Services have adopted different approaches under this authority: The Fish and Wildlife Service fastened the take prohibition generically to almost all threatened wildlife species in a single rule (50 C.F.R. § 17.31(a)); whereas the National Marine Fisheries Service makes decisions on whether to apply the prohibition by specific rules addressed to individual threatened wildlife species or groups of such species. Take of listed *plant* species is not proscribed; other section 9 prohibitions not likely to be relevant to the use of nanotechnology do apply to listed plant species. *See* 16 U.S.C. § 1538(a)(2).
20. 16 U.S.C. § 1532(19).
21. 50 C.F.R. §§ 17.3, 222.102.
22. 16 U.S.C. § 1540(a)(1).
23. 16 U.S.C. § 1540(b)(1). The maximum fines have been increased by general legislation to $100,000 for individuals and $200,000 for corporate violators, per violation. 18 U.S.C. §§ 3559, 3571.
24. 16 U.S.C. §§ 1540(e)(6), (g)(1).
25. *See, e.g.*, Defenders of Wildlife v. Adm'r, EPA, 882 F.2d 1294 (8th Cir. 1989) (finding ESA "take" when endangered species died after ingesting strychnine from agricultural pesticides that had been applied to crops).
26. 16 U.S.C. § 1536(a)(2).
27. 16 U.S.C. § 1536(a)(2).
28. 16 U.S.C. § 1536(a)(2).
29. *See* Sw. Ctr. for Biological Diversity v. Norton, 215 F.3d 58, 60–61 (D.C. Cir. 2000).
30. Bennett v. Spear, 520 U.S. 154, 169 (1997).
31. 50 C.F.R. §§ 402.13, 402.14.
32. 16 U.S.C. § 1536(b), (c).
33. 16 U.S.C. § 1536(b)(4), (o). The Services also have discretion to extend the coverage of the incidental take statement beyond the action agency and applicant to anyone involved in a related action whose impacts were fairly considered in a BiOp (here, for example, a consumer or user of a product containing nanoscale material). Ramsey v. Kantor, 96 F.3d 434, 440, 440–42 (9th Cir. 1996).
34. 16 U.S.C. § 1536(b), (c), (o).
35. *Bennett*, 520 U.S. at 169–70.
36. 515 U.S. 687 (1995).
37. 515 U.S. at 696–97 n.9, 700 n.13, 708–08.

38. 515 U.S. at 696 n.9, 700 n.13, 709.
39. 16 U.S.C. § 1539(a)(1)(B).
40. 16 U.S.C. § 1536(b)(4), (o).
41. 16 U.S.C. § 1539(a)(2).
42. 16 U.S.C. § 1539(a)(2)(B).
43. 16 U.S.C. § 1539(b)(2).
44. 16 U.S.C. § 1536(b)(4)(C)(ii).
45. 16 U.S.C. § 1536(b)(3)(A).
46. *See* 16 U.S.C. § 1536(a)(3), (b)(1)(B) (describing permit or license applicant's role in consultation process).
47. 16 U.S.C. § 1531(b).
48. 16 U.S.C. § 1532(2).
49. 16 U.S.C. § 1533(f).
50. Fund for Animals v. Rice, 85 F.3d 535, 547 (11th Cir. 1996).
51. 16 U.S.C. § 1536(a)(1).
52. Sierra Club v. Glickman, 156 F.3d 606 (5th Cir. 1998).
53. *See, e.g.*, Defenders of Wildlife v. Babbitt, 130 F. Supp. 2d 121, 135 (D.D.C. 2001) ("[t]he case law is well settled that federal agencies are accorded discretion in determining how to fulfill their 16 U.S.C. § 1536(a)(1) obligations") (citing Coal. for Sustainable Res. v. U.S. Forest Serv., 48 F. Supp. 2d 1303, 1315–16 (D. Wyo. 1999) (and cases cited therein)).

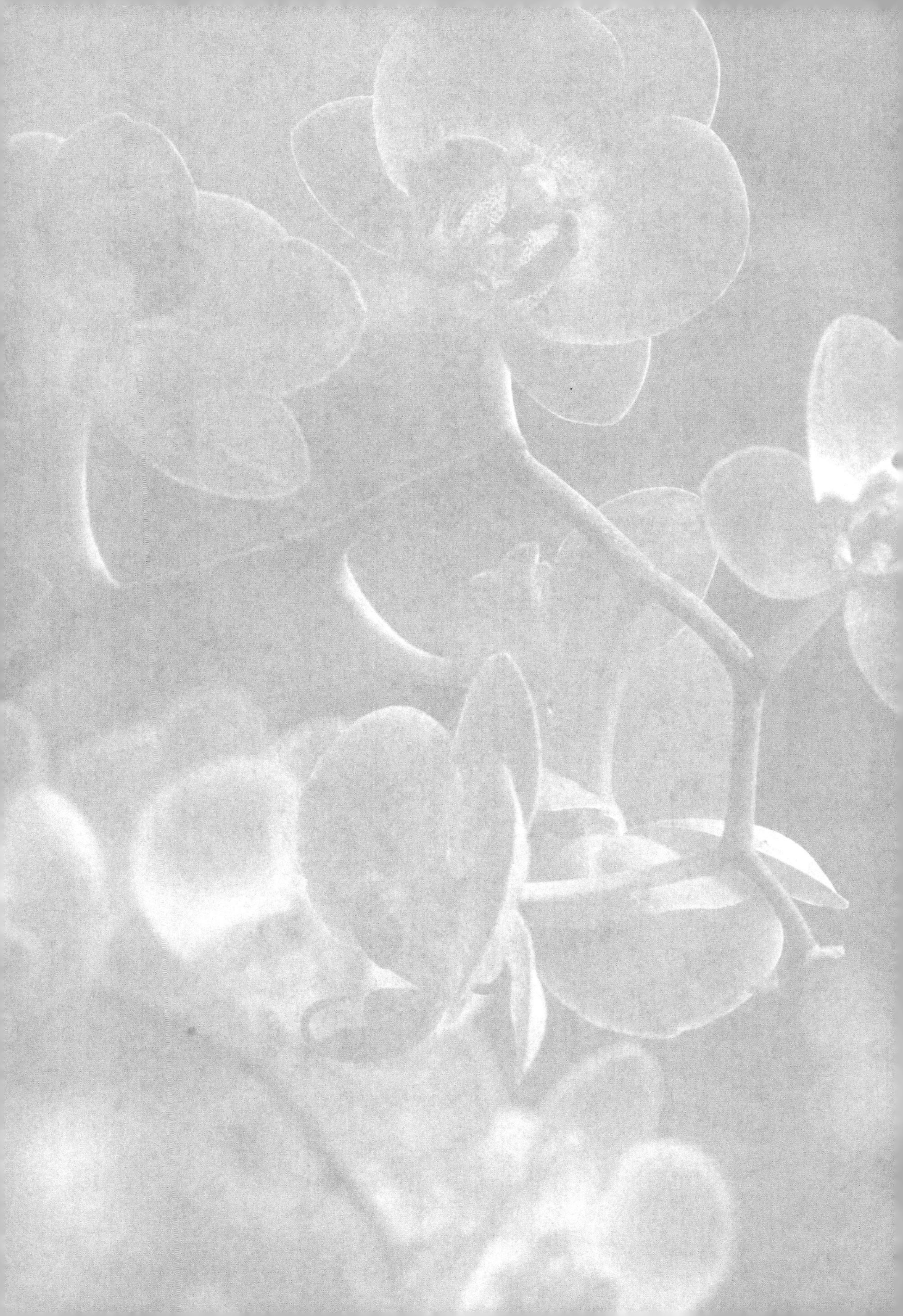

18

Conserving Endangered Species in an Era of Global Warming

An Environmental Community Perspective

John Kostyack and Dan Rohlf

Introduction

As the Endangered Species Act reaches its 36th anniversary, the nation has much to celebrate. Time and again, the Act has demonstrated its crucial role as the nation's safety net for imperiled fish, wildlife, and plant species. Thanks to the ESA, we have been able to stave off hundreds of extinctions.[1] Each of these species represents incalculable biological wealth. Our commitment and actions to maintain these species in the wild in the face of severe extinction threats, and to ensure that they are available to future generations, represent a moral act for which we as a nation should be proud.

But not too proud. The 1,400 or so species to which we have afforded ESA protection represent a small fraction of those at risk of extinction.[2] Most of the thousands of imperiled species in the United States awaiting ESA protections lack any alternate safety net of protection and remain highly vulnerable to extinction. More important, despite the ESA's stated purpose of conserving the ecosystems on which listed species depend, U.S. ecosystems are greatly imperiled due to the combined impacts of global warming and more direct forms of habitat destruction and degradation such as road-building and the spread of invasive species. Thus, many of the species that we have rescued in the past 35 years of ESA implementation, as well as many others, easily could be lost to extinction in the next 35 years if we fail to take aggressive action.

How can we prevent such a tragic loss of the nation's biological wealth? After reviewing the current state of the ESA and the nation's ecosystems, this chapter makes recommendations about how the ESA can be updated and improved and how it can be integrated within a broader conservation framework focused on greenhouse gas emissions reductions and climate change adaptation. If these steps are taken, we can maximize our chances of conserving species and ecosystems for future generations.

A Record of Success Despite Significant Obstacles

Considering the many political and economic forces that have hindered endangered species protection and recovery in the past few decades, the Endangered Species Act has an impressive conservation record. Of the listed species for which there are reliable data, a significantly greater number are stabilized or recovering than are declining.[3] More important, as the amount of time a species enjoys ESA protection increases, so does its chances of moving from a declining to a stable condition and from a stable to improving condition.[4] Of the 1,400-plus domestic species ever protected by the Act, only a handful have gone extinct after listing, and each of these was probably already a hopeless cause at the time of listing.[5] In contrast, a significant number of declining species without ESA protection have gone extinct.[6] There can be little dispute that the ESA has so far succeeded in achieving its goal of preventing extinction of species in the United States and improving the prospects for species survival and recovery.[7]

Critics of the ESA have argued that the law is a failure because, except in a few cases, it has not achieved its stated goal of recovering species to the point where they no longer need the Act's protections.[8] This argument is misleading because it blames the ESA for factors well beyond the law's control. Through no fault of the Act, the populations of most species are severely depleted, and their habitats are greatly reduced and degraded, by the time they receive ESA protection. The ESA's mandates apply primarily to measures that limit harm to species; in contrast, measures to improve the condition of species—such as species reintroductions, land acquisitions and habitat restorations, and management measures such as prescribed fire and invasive species removal—are largely voluntary and dependent on congressional appropriations. Inadequate funding, not any inherent flaw with the ESA, is the proximate cause of the slow pace of recovery.[9]

The underlying drivers of species and ecosystem decline—human population growth, an expanding human development footprint, unsustainable technologies and consumption habits, and excessive carbon emissions—are also well beyond the scope of the ESA. Given the scope of these challenges, the ESA can hardly be faulted for failing to achieve species recovery during the few decades of its existence.

The assaults against the Endangered Species Act for its supposed failure to help endangered species recover have not come from objective observers. They are part of a 16-year campaign by regulated interests to undermine public support for the law so that they can carry out their business with fewer regulatory restraints.[10] In many respects, this campaign has failed. With a few narrow exceptions, Congress and the courts have repeatedly rejected efforts to weaken the law by industry groups and their allies in the conservative think tanks. The public continues to favor maintaining a strong ESA.[11]

The campaign to undermine the Act made significant inroads, however, during the 16 years of the Clinton and George W. Bush administrations, which failed to ask for the funding needed to fully implement the law. Congress reciprocated by appropriating woefully inadequate amounts—with amounts ranging from $100 million to $500 million annually for the U.S. Fish and Wildlife Service (FWS) and National Marine Fisheries Service (NMFS), the two agencies with primary responsibility for ESA implementation.[12] These failures to appropriate the funds needed to maintain the nation's biological wealth took place without serious political opposition because the ESA's allies in the Congress and the Clinton administration were on the defensive, fighting a battle largely on the terms of ESA antagonists.

The campaign to undermine the Act reached its zenith during the George W. Bush administration. Former Representative Richard Pombo led a widely publicized effort to weaken the law in Congress; although this effort ultimately failed, conservationists saw a majority of the House of Representatives vote in 2005 to drastically weaken the law. Meanwhile, anti-ESA zealots at the political levels of the Bush administration were working on behalf of favored industry groups to undercut the wildlife professionals charged with carrying out the ESA on a day-to-day basis. In three different instances, longstanding ESA regulations were overturned to greatly reduce the independent scientific input of FWS and NMFS into the approval of federal actions affecting listed species and their habitat.[13] Other attacks on the integrity of the ESA involved interference in specific listings, critical habitat designations, and project reviews and consultations.[14] As reported by the Department of the Interior's inspector general, administration officials repeatedly thwarted protection measures despite clear legal and scientific mandates to implement them.[15] One official, Deputy Assistant Secretary Julie MacDonald, resigned in disgrace after she was found, among other things, to have instructed wildlife professionals to remove scientific studies from the public record because they pointed toward the need for greater ESA protection.

It is remarkable that despite this hostility from the political officials in charge of implementing agencies, the ESA has nonetheless continued protecting habitat, fostering active management and recovery efforts, and otherwise bringing public attention, effort, and funding to stewardship of the natural world. The Act continues to function in large measure due to its clear mandates for protective measures and its directive that officials use the best available science in applying those measures. Of equal importance, the Act's citizen enforcement mechanism has enabled conservation groups to ensure compliance with the law's strong mandates.

The Act also has continued to function because its core concepts have become ingrained in the thinking of so many public and private actors. Most people who operate in or near the habitat of a listed species embrace the Act's concept of "looking before you leap," even if they may grumble about the resulting costs and delays. The Act's consultation and habitat conservation planning features also provide a crucial forum for disparate stakeholders to ensure that their concerns are heard and that species protection measures are designed with other societal goals taken into account. As a result, many economic activities in or near endangered species habitats continue to be adjusted to minimize harmful impacts on listed species, resulting in significant benefits to the ecosystems on which both people and wildlife depend. Similarly, many activities in or near the habitats of species not yet listed are being conserved as agencies, landowners, and others seek to avoid the need for ESA listings.

The campaign to undermine the ESA nonetheless has exacted a significant toll on species and ecosystem conservation in the United States. Enormous resources, both financial and intellectual, have been expended in the past 16 years on needless courtroom battles and in less-than-constructive debates in Congress and in the media. These resources would have been better spent on finding creative ways to use the ESA's existing tools (such as recovery plans) to strengthen scientific understanding of complex natural resource issues and on developing new collaborative processes for resolving those issues. These resources also could have been spent on defining the ESA's role within the larger societal effort to save the planet. By defining the ESA's niche in the broader conservation framework, policy makers and interest groups could end, once and for all, the pretense that the ESA alone can recover imperiled species and ecosystems.

Entering an Era of Rapid Climate Change and Ecosystem Disruptions

Even without taking climate change into account, many scientists have warned that ecosystems in the United States and around the globe are in a degraded condition and increasingly threatened by human economic activity.[16] Although many public agencies and private industries have made important strides toward sustainability in recent years, many still are operating in ways incompatible with species conservation. For example, the real estate and transportation sectors continue to rely primarily on low-density, automobile-dependent development models, resulting in large-scale habitat loss and fragmentation. The agricultural sector continues to rely primarily on heavy inputs of chemical fertilizers and pesticides, resulting in polluted runoff and serious degradation of aquatic habitats. Whereas in past centuries ecosystems could recover from localized disturbances of terrestrial and aquatic systems, the size of human populations and the scale of economic activity and resource consumption today make ecosystem restoration much more difficult.

Today, scientists recognize climate change as the leading threat to the future of biological diversity on the planet. The 2007 reports of the Intergovernmental Panel on Climate Change (IPCC) conclude that human activity is "very likely" causing the world to warm. These reports also note that the average surface temperature of the earth increased 0.76°C (1.4°F) in the 20th century and predict that this temperature will likely increase by another 1.8 to 4.0°C (3.2 to 7.2°F) in the 21st century, depending on pollution levels.[17] The IPCC also finds that 20 to 30 percent of species worldwide are likely to be at increased risk of extinction if increases in average global temperatures exceed 2–3°C (3.6–5.4°F) above pre-industrial levels.[18]

Since the release of the IPCC reports in early 2007, the Arctic has experienced a dramatic loss of summer sea ice, a loss that exceeds the worst-case IPCC projections. This and other changes recently observed in natural systems suggest that unless aggressive greenhouse gas (GHG) emissions cuts are made, climate disruptions and species extinctions will be even worse than projected in 2007.

No ecosystem on earth is immune to the effects of global warming. Many ecosystems have already undergone rapid transformations as a result of a combination of one or more climate-change-related events, such as sea level rise, intensified hurricanes and other storms, intensified droughts, spreading pests and invasive species, warming streams, evaporating lakes and wetlands, disappearing glaciers and mountain snowpack, melting permafrost, and shrinking polar ice. These disruptions are expected to worsen as warming trends accelerate in the coming decades.[19]

In addition to these ecosystem-level disturbances, two serious problems are also surfacing at the species level: changes in phenology (timing of seasonal life-cycle events) and changes in distribution (most notably, the shift of U.S. plant and animal species northward and to higher elevations). An example of the former phenomenon is the shift in the time of springtime peak insect abundance, which affects the reproductive success of songbirds that depend on high insect levels during the critical nestling phase. The 90 percent decline of the northwestern Minnesota moose population in the past 20 years, which biologists have attributed to excessive heat, provides an example of the latter.[20] Another example is the decline of the American pika, a small rabbit-like mammal that inhabits talus fields in the mountains of the western United States. One study of Great Basin pikas found that their range had shifted upslope by 900 feet and that 36 percent of populations had been extirpated.[21]

As different species respond to changes in climate in idiosyncratic ways, ecological communities will begin the process of disassembling. There is no precedent in the historical record for such a rapid disassembly, and considerable uncertainty surrounds how species in any particular place may reassemble, and the functional characteristics of such reassembled communities. Without any analog to guide them, scientists and natural resource managers will face great difficulty anticipating and preparing for key changes on the landscape and ensuring the continuing viability of species and habitat types in the wild.

The Need for Climate Change Safeguards

Aggressive action to reduce GHG emissions is necessary, but not sufficient, to protect species and ecosystems from the dramatic changes caused by global warming. Because GHGs remain in the atmosphere for decades, levels of atmospheric carbon dioxide (CO_2) will inevitably increase in the coming decades regardless of the emissions policies that are put in place. Moreover, there is a lag time between emissions and effects on the earth's systems. Some of the effects of today's GHG emissions (e.g., increased surface air and stream temperatures) will be felt for decades; other effects (e.g., disappearing polar ice caps, sea level rise) will continue for centuries. Thus, regardless of where we live, the climate that we knew from our childhood will not be returning—certainly not in our lifetimes and potentially never again.

In at least three ways, the practice of wildlife conservation will need to be transformed to address these massive changes on the landscape. First, natural resource managers and policy makers will no longer be able to rely upon unstated assumptions that the climate of the future will mirror that of the past; they must now develop sophisticated tools to account for a rapidly changing climate. Second, they will need to augment conservation to strengthen the resilience of ecosystems and thereby help species and habitats to withstand the new climactic stressors. Third, they will need to increase the flexibility of institutions and programs, so that natural resource managers are equipped to deal with the many unavoidable and unpredictable changes that climate change will bring.

We refer to this kind of adaptation to climate change as putting in place "climate change safeguards" for species and ecosystems.

To date, the federal government has not adopted climate change safeguards for any listed species or any land management unit within its jurisdiction. This is likely due to the political controversies surrounding climate change; in such a highly politicized climate, the safest approach is to avoid action on adaptation and to claim that there is still too much uncertainty surrounding climate change and its effects.[22] However, while there will always be uncertainty about the *degree* to which the effects of climate change will be felt, there is virtually no scientific debate over whether those effects will arrive. In recognition of this, experts have begun developing approaches for carrying out climate change vulnerability assessments for species and ecosystems designed to inform both the incorporation of climate change into conservation resource management efforts and the development of climate change adaptation plans.[23]

A review of the various methods of assessing vulnerability of species and habitats to climate change, and developing adaptation strategies, is outside the scope of this chapter. However, such vulnerability assessments and adaptation strategies must be integrated into recovery plans, biological opinions, habitat conservation plans, and other ESA tools to safeguard listed species and their habitats from the most harmful effects of climate change. Considering that numerous other institutions will likely be undertaking similar efforts to address climate change, the challenge for ESA practitioners will be to determine how best to learn from those efforts and to integrate their climate change adaptation planning into those efforts. This question of ESA's role in the larger framework of adaptation—both preparing for and responding to climate change—is addressed later in this chapter.

Making the ESA More Effective

Updating the ESA to address climate change is just one of many needs that must be addressed to ensure that the Act remains effective in conserving species and ecosystems for future generations. While the ESA broke new ground decades ago as a bold and visionary approach to conservation, there is no doubt that the statute, as currently implemented, is inadequate to address the comprehensive and complex forces accelerating the pace of species declines and extinctions.

Already a variety of perspectives have arisen among experts and stakeholders as to how to proceed. Some highlight a need for triage, focusing limited conservation resources on the species deemed to have the best chances for rehabilitation. Others emphasize a need to overhaul the statute itself, convincing Congress to add to the ESA an even greater sense of urgency and still sharper legal teeth. Finally, many call for significant increases in funding for all aspects of ESA implementation.

The most effective way to protect imperiled species likely involves a nuanced approach rather than simply more sophisticated trade-offs between listed species, more stringent regulatory mandates, or more dollars. Congress could enhance the ESA's effectiveness with modest adjustments to the law itself, but agencies implementing the statute should put its existing tools to use with much greater effectiveness. And while increased investment in biodiversity conservation will nearly always generate environmental and economic returns, financial resources must be used more strategically, efficiently, and with a stronger commitment to science-driven conservation blueprints. Lastly, perhaps the most important step toward furthering the

ESA's conservation goal will be to integrate the ESA into an overarching conservation framework, implemented by all levels of government and the private sector, that drastically reduces GHG emissions while ensuring that species, habitats, and functioning ecosystems thrive in a warming climate.

Modest Legislative Updates

Despite two decades of efforts to change the ESA, both by conservation interests seeking to strengthen the Act as well as by industry groups looking to loosen it, Congress has remained unwilling or unable to alter the statute since 1988. Looking forward into the next 20 years, Congress would find that a few minor statutory adjustments would make the statute more efficient and effective while not generating significant controversies among ESA fans or foes.

Lawmakers could build on some of the thoughtful discussions fostered by the Senate's last serious evaluation of the ESA's structure to enact modest reforms likely to increase the Act's efficiency and effectiveness. Currently, Section 4 requires designation of critical habitat, that is, habitat judged to be essential to recovery of a particular species, concurrent with a species' initial listing as threatened or endangered.[24] On the other hand, recovery planning, a process designed to define what "recovery" means for a particular species and outline the steps to get there, often takes place many years after listing because the law places no deadlines on the process. ESA critics and proponents alike have pointed out the incongruity of identifying habitat needed for a species' recovery well before defining what recovery for that species looks like, an argument that has even spilled over into legal challenges to critical habitat designation.[25] While moving the critical habitat designation process into recovery planning would improve the scientific basis of the former by allowing more time for evaluation of important habitat in light of a species-specific definition of recovery, the lack of any deadline for the latter could doom both to interminable delays, particularly in the case of more widespread or controversial listings. Working proposals for a Senate ESA bill in 2006 called for moving critical habitat designation into the recovery planning process and placing a three-year deadline on completion of a recovery plan that included identification of critical habitat.[26] Improving the process for critical habitat designations would increase reliability of the results and thus hopefully decrease litigation over designations themselves. Moreover, a specified deadline for completion of recovery plans could decrease uncertainty over the implications of specific listings by defining within a relatively short timeframe the ultimate conservation benchmarks for each listed species, as well as the steps needed to achieve these goals.

A broad, consensus-based work group on possible ESA modifications (in which the authors of this chapter participated) released a report in 2006 encouraging Congress to build into the Act and related legislation a suite of financial and other incentives to encourage landowners to improve species conservation efforts on nonfederal land.[27] Suggestions for nonmonetary means to bolster such actions included codification of the so-called safe harbor program, whereby landowners may manage their land in a manner that provides increased habitat for listed species but still retain the right to take management actions that return the land to its original "baseline" condition; establishment of administrative timeline targets to encourage swift decisions by the Services on issuance of incidental take permits based on habitat conservation plans; and improved cooperation and partnerships between the states and the federal government.[28] The group also identified many possible strategies for Congress to use financial incentives to spur conservation of habitat for listed species on non-federal land, such as widening financial incentives for endangered species conservation under the Farm Bill's Conservation Reserve Program, reducing capital gains and estate taxes when properties or conservation easements are sold to buyers planning to protect habitat on the land, and allowing income tax credits for landowners' expenditures that are part of specified species conservation programs.[29]

A variation on this last recommendation was accepted by the 110th Congress in the most recent Farm Bill. With the support of a diverse group of conservation nongovernmental organizations (including the National Wildlife Federation) and landowner interests, Congress provided a tax deduction for farmers who agree to carry out measures that implement recovery plans for listed species.[30] This was an important breakthrough on ESA policy, which (as noted above) had not been updated by Congress since 1988 due to a lack of consensus among key interest groups. A more ambitious proposal to give tax credits for recovery actions by a wider array of landowners was not accepted by the 110th Congress, but could become the focus of ESA legislative activity in future Congresses.

Using Existing Tools to Enhance the ESA's Effectiveness

Aside from the modest legislative "tune-up" outlined above, there are many additional ways to improve protections for listed species without modifying the ESA itself. Under George W. Bush, the FWS and the NMFS enacted a series of regulatory and policy changes in an effort to substantially modify the workings of the statute itself, most of them diminishing rather than improving protections for imperiled species. Administrative tools could similarly be used to alter the Act's day-to-day functions toward more productive ends.

The statute's listing process ground to a near-standstill during Bush's tenure, but policy shifts by FWS and NMFS could substantially strengthen identification of species in need of protection. To address the increasingly acute listing backlog, FWS should reinvigorate a 1994 policy emphasizing an ecosystem-based listing approach under which a single listing decision could result in protection of a suite of species dependent on a particular ecosystem or habitat type in peril.[31] The Services should also reevaluate recent interpretations of two statutory terms crucial to the listing process—"distinct population segment" and "significant portion of the range" of species. For example, FWS has often used a narrow construction of what constitutes a "distinct population segment" to avoid listing populations in need of protection, such as the reproductively isolated population of bald eagles that have adapted to survive in the harsh Sonora Desert of Arizona.[32] It also has interpreted the requirement that a species be at risk in a "significant portion of the range" as allowing consideration only of the area where a species currently exists rather than its historic range, again making it easier to avoid listings, as well as easier for the Service to remove ESA protections from portions of presently listed species.[33] This "museum piece" approach to conservation is at odds with Aldo Leopold's wise advice to save species in many places, as well as with Congress's intent to give high priority to conservation of listed species and their ecosystems.[34] Recent scientific findings that restoration of keystone predators can improve species diversity and enhance ecosystem function reveal the shortsightedness of efforts to restrictively read ESA protections for populations and wide-ranging species.[35]

In recent years, the Services have also worked to stymie rather than effectively implement the Act's protections for species' critical habitat. Section 4 directs FWS and NMFS to designate critical habitat when listing species as threatened or endangered, and gives them discretion to exempt otherwise eligible areas from designation if the agencies determine that the economic or other costs of this designation outweigh its benefits. Whereas the Clinton administration used this exemption authority relatively sparingly, its successor took the opposite approach. A study by a coalition of conservation groups found that FWS during the Bush administration used this exemption authority in over 90 percent of its critical habitat designations, and on average protected less than one-quarter of the land area it determined was essential to recovery of listed species.[36] During that same time period, FWS also never listed critical habitat without a court order, conducted time-consuming and expensive economic analyses of every designation, and often ignored the identified economic *benefits* of critical habitat designation in deciding whether to exclude areas from protection.[37] NMFS also made dubious critical habitat determinations. For example, as a result of settling a lawsuit with interests opposed to critical habitat protections for salmon and steelhead in the Columbia River Basin, the agency in 2005 withdrew its critical habitat designations for most listed runs and issued new designations with extensive exclusions.[38] All of these trends could and should be immediately reversed by a simple commitment to implementing the ESA as Congress intended. Critical habitat designation plays a key role in furthering the ESA's primary goal—recovery of listed species—and prompt adherence to the Act's designation requirement, a balanced examination of critical habitat's costs and benefits, and strategic rather than blanket use of the statute's authority to exclude otherwise eligible areas from designation as critical habitat would significantly advance species recovery efforts.

As noted above, the Bush administration attempted to permanently weaken protections for listed species with a series of changes to regulations implementing the interagency consultation requirements set forth in section 7 of the Act. A common theme of these amendments was giving federal agencies whose actions may affect listed species or designated critical habitat authority to avoid entering into consultation with FWS or NMFS. The consultation process essentially requires that one or sometimes both of the Services "sign off" on a proposed project before it proceeds; this de facto sharing of decision-making authority often results in modifications to agency actions that reduce or offset impacts on listed species and designated critical habitat. A district court struck down new section 7 regulations aimed at easing consultation requirements for pesticide registrations, while new rules loosening consultation on federal logging projects under the U.S. Forest Service's National Fire Plan at least temporarily survived a court challenge.[39] Finally, in the Bush administration's waning days, the Services made the first modifications in over two decades to general regulations implementing section 7(a)(2)'s consultation process, enacting broad exemptions for impacts on listed species and critical habitat related to "global processes" such as climate change, as well as impacts that project proponents unilaterally decide are not harmful to listed species or "not capable of being measured or detected in a manner that permits meaningful evaluation." Using authority provided by the 111th Congress, the Obama administration quickly revoked these changes to the consultation regulations early in 2009.[40]

The Obama administration could further strengthen the ESA's consultation provisions by expanding the scope of section 7(a)(2) review. The Services have historically read this section as merely preventing near-catastrophic impacts to listed species and designated critical habitat, an interpretation that has often allowed incremental impacts that threaten to "nickel and dime" many species to the brink of extinction. However, recent judicial interpretations of section 7's jeopardy standard and its ban against "adverse modification" of critical habitat have emphasized that these benchmarks also play a role in fostering recovery of listed species.[41] FWS and NMFS could finally use section 7(a)(2) consultation as a tool for advancing species recovery by routinely including as part of their jeopardy assessments a meaningful consideration of how proposed federal actions affect species' chances for recovery, as well as by finally recognizing that the ESA's protections for critical habitat do not allow piecemeal reductions in land identified as essential for recovery. The Services could advance both of these steps by recognizing a link between section 7(a)(2) consultations and recovery plans for affected species. The latter represent a significant federal investment in both scientific analysis and planning aimed at species recovery. Requiring an evaluation of the impact of a proposed action on recovery plan goals and objectives would be a logical means of introducing enhanced consideration of recovery in the section 7 process.

FWS and NMFS should also make species recovery an important consideration in implementing sections 9 and 10 of the Act. The Services for many years have placed a very low priority on enforcing section 9's ban on "taking" (actually killing or injuring) listed species, particularly takings that result from destruction or alterations of listed species' habitat on nonfederal land. FWS should carry out a program of targeted enforcement of take prohibitions on nonfederal land in a manner designed to end the most egregious and widespread actions that harm listed species. For example, after conservation groups (and later FWS) threatened to sue farmers over water withdrawals that virtually dried up Washington's Walla Walla River in the summer—

killing many of the river's threatened salmon—three irrigation districts entered into a series of temporary agreements to leave more water instream, as well as committed to formulating a habitat conservation plan (HCP) pursuant to section 10 that would set forth a long-term strategy to provide more water for fish.[42]

The Services have often touted HCPs as a means of garnering conservation benefits for listed species on nonfederal land, and the number of approved HCPs has skyrocketed over the past 15 years. While many HCPs provide some benefits for listed species, those benefits are often quite modest compared to the impacts on listed species and their habitat authorized by the incidental take permits issued in conjunction with HCP approvals. This imbalance between conservation benefits and development allowances in HCPs stems in great part from the Service's overly narrow interpretation of the jeopardy and adverse modification prohibitions as well as its legal conclusion that HCPs need not provide a benefit to listed species or even address the species' recovery needs.[43] As noted above, the jeopardy and adverse modification prohibitions require that the recovery needs of species be addressed. Moreover, Congress's use of the term "conservation plan" in Section 10 indicated an intention that these plans address the challenge of species recovery. Section 10's legislative history also provides a clear indication that lawmakers saw conservation plans and incidental take permits as tools to foster win-win scenarios benefiting both landowners and species recovery efforts. Drawing from this background, as well as from the conclusions of a federal court decision linking HCP approval with conservation benefits for listed species, FWS and NMFS should insist that nonfederal parties seeking permission to incidentally take listed species in the course of their activities build into their HCPs a means of providing a meaningful boost to species recovery efforts rather than merely avoiding pushing species appreciably closer to extinction.[44]

In sum, the ESA has suffered a litany of both overt and veiled Executive Branch attacks under the Bush administration. If the Obama administration interprets the Act faithfully and consistently with Congress's intent, the Act could become a far more effective tool for conserving species and ecosystems.

New Energy and New Initiatives

While improving implementation of the ESA's key provisions is a crucial ingredient for enhancing the statute's effectiveness, more is needed to adequately address the accelerating loss of biodiversity. Congress and the Obama administration must dedicate substantial funds to the ESA and other conservation programs; investments in species conservation will provide present and future generations with economic, environmental, and social dividends. At the same time, however, it is unlikely that even substantial increases in species conservation appropriations—assuming that such increases are even possible given current economic realities—will be sufficient to stem the myriad threats that species now face. Therefore, FWS and NMFS must find ways to get more conservation benefits from their limited resources. Enhancing and developing new conservation partnerships, bringing new kinds of skills and expertise to bear on conservation problems, and developing new and creative initiatives will help federal agencies meet this challenge.

The Services must continue and even expand their efforts to rely on cooperative partnerships to provide species conservation benefits. States and local governments, for example, are key players in managing and protecting species and their habitats. FWS and NMFS already work closely with these entities in many ways, as well as provide federal dollars under section 6 of the ESA for state species and habitat conservation programs. However, federal agencies must find ways to make these relationships even more productive. For example, federal funds under section 6 are currently allocated in a more or less ad hoc basis. The resulting projects provide benefits for listed species, but more strategic uses of these funds could enhance their effectiveness. The Services should consider linking funding under section 6 to states' commitments to updating and implementing strategic blueprints for conserving vulnerable species.[45] In updating these plans, the states should work collaboratively with the Services to take a hard look at climate change and the myriad other large-scale forces contributing to extinctions or otherwise posing a barrier to ecological restoration. Section 6 funds would be awarded based on projects' relative contributions toward conserving listed species and advancing these overall plans.

The Services should also develop nonmonetary incentives for state and local governments to increase their protection of species and habitats, such as reemphasizing and expanding an NMFS program in the 1990s that used section 4(d) regulations to cede more control over threatened species to state and local governments in exchange for a promise by those governments to regulate threats to these species and their habitat.[46] The recent NMFS biological opinion governing the impact of the National Flood Insurance Program (NFIP) on threatened salmon and orcas in the Pacific Northwest potentially serves as a model here. NMFS found that the subsidized flood insurance was jeopardizing listed species and adversely modifying critical habitat, and it concluded that such jeopardy and adverse modification could be avoided only if local governments substantially curtailed NFIP-subsidized development in the floodplain habitat.[47] Thus, the "carrot" of the flood insurance subsidy was made conditional upon the "stick" of local government regulation of development in floodplains.

The Services also need to rely on new skills and expertise to efficiently deliver conservation benefits. For example, FWS and NMFS often "reinvent the wheel" when they consider species for listing or develop recovery plans. By better understanding how to integrate science and policy elements in these processes, as well as by developing more standardized approaches to these decisions, the agencies could make decisions and put together recovery strategies more rapidly and efficiently and thus with less cost, allowing them to accomplish more with their limited budgets. Hiring personnel with expertise in cutting-edge fields such as climate change and ecological modeling, environmental economics, and ecosystem management could also allow the Services to develop innovative conservation techniques that may be able to accomplish more conservation with the same or even fewer resources used in more strategic ways.

Finally, the Services need to look for nontraditional partners to collaborate with on species conservation. For instance, multi-stakeholder organizations such as the Willamette Partnership are using innovative techniques to bring together financial and environmental benefits; increased federal involvement with such organizations could take advantage of their new strategies while ensuring that these techniques provide promised conservation.[48] Similarly, the Services can better connect ESA implementation with Farm Bill programs by working with farm agencies to ensure that their conservation incentives are more targeted toward endangered species recovery. They also could reach out to other federal agencies and finally make a serious effort to develop and implement conservation programs for listed species as required by section 7(a)(1). This sort of planning could place both the Services and other federal agencies in a proactive position rather than their customary reactive modes; species conservation efforts would undoubtedly be the better for it.

Integrating the ESA into the Larger Climate Change and Conservation Framework

Conservation leaders are now recognizing that because climate change is thoroughly disrupting ecosystems, the old ways of doing business will no longer suffice. From the top levels of the Obama administration down to the business meetings of the city council, much of conservation policy and planning is boiling down to two priority agenda items: *combating* climate change, and *safeguarding* natural resources threatened by an array of stressors, with climate change at or near the top of the list. Failure to act quickly to address these threats could mean that many of our most precious species and habitat types are lost to extinction or reduced to mere remnants.

Designing a conservation policy or plan that takes climate change into account is difficult and complex. Very few global circulation models have been downscaled to sufficiently local levels to allow policy makers and natural resource managers to understand future physical conditions such as temperature and precipitation. Even the relatively simple task of modeling the impact of sea level rise on coastal wetland habitats has not yet been completed for most of the United States. Climate change adaptation is still very much a new field, with no widely accepted approaches and plenty of experimentation.

Given the complexity, no single agency will be making definitive judgments anytime soon about the best ways to conserve species and ecosystems in a warming world. One thing is clear, however: animal and plant species are already on the move and will be moving at an increasing clip as climate change accelerates. Thus, it makes little sense to plan at small geographic scales. Agencies implementing the ESA must participate in a reinvigorated conversation about how best to carry out regional or ecosystem-level planning and management. This means collaborating with other federal, state, local, and tribal agencies working to conserve natural systems in the same region as the targeted listed species. These agencies must begin sharing and synthesizing data sets and developing uniform protocols for climate change modeling, vulnerability assessments, monitoring, and adaptive management. Ultimately, they must collaborate in protecting and restoring habitats.

Natural resource agencies alone will not be able to achieve these results. Congress must enact rules and guidelines and provide substantial dedicated funding to facilitate such strategic collaboration and conservation action. Fortunately, lawmakers have already taken steps in this direction. Several climate change bills introduced in the 110th Congress explicitly recognized the need to protect natural resources from the effects of global warming and provided policy direction and substantial funding to accomplish this objective. The American Clean Energy and Security Act of 2009, approved by the House of Representatives in June 2009, would provide $1.7 billion annually for two decades using the proceeds from the auction of global warming emission allowances.[49] These funds would be used to develop and implement natural resources adaptation strategies at the federal and state levels, new federal scientific research and monitoring capabilities, and a host of new species and ecosystem conservation actions on the part of federal, state, and tribal agencies. It is crucial that Congress build on this strong foundation and move quickly to enact climate change legislation with aggressive GHG emission reduction mandates and substantial dedicated funding for natural resources adaptation.

Conservationists must use a wide array of tools to achieve immediate emissions reductions and to persuade the federal government to confront climate change through comprehensive legislation. Among these should be state and regional laws and agreements and an expanded use of anti-pollution laws such as the Clean Air Act. Although the ESA arguably could be used as part of this emissions reduction effort—GHG emissions sources are covered by the ESA to the same extent as any other contributors to species decline and extinction[50]—such a use of the ESA has a number of inherent flaws. First, because all GHG emissions from federal actions affect at least some listed species, it is difficult to see what legal doctrine could be invoked to limit the application of ESA section 7 to just a small subset of those actions. Carrying out a full-blown section 7 review of the millions of federal actions that take place each year, or even a subset of them, would divert substantial resources from the Services' core responsibilities under ESA and would require a vast expansion of their budgets that Congress would not likely support.[51] Moreover, the benefits of such an exercise are questionable. Although the Services may be able to conclude scientifically that additional global warming pollution will further jeopardize an already imperiled species, it is very unlikely that they would ever be able to provide permit applicants with a level of GHG emissions reductions (except to zero) that would eliminate the harm caused by GHGs. Without such scientific data, the Services will never have the scientific or political fortitude to force the emissions reductions that have eluded conservation advocates in other legal and political forums.

For these reasons, the Act simply cannot serve as a driver of GHG emissions reductions. To protect imperiled species and for a host of other reasons, Congress must act quickly to enact comprehensive federal climate change legislation that rapidly reduces

GHG emissions and provide programs and dedicated funding to safeguard natural resources from the impacts of climate change. At the same time, agencies implementing the ESA should focus on the Act's strengths: protecting habitats and ecosystems from direct forms of habitat destruction and fragmentation, while developing safeguards against the new climate-related stressors such as sea level rise, intensified storms and droughts, warming streams, and disappearing mountain snowpack.

The concept of ecosystem-oriented climate change safeguards that we advocate here is just one of several legitimate adaptation concepts currently competing for the attention of policy makers and natural resource managers. Other adaptation approaches focus primarily on helping human communities deal with the impacts of climate change on public infrastructure, private property (including homes, industries, and agriculture), and public health. Wherever possible, policy makers and agency managers must design adaptation strategies to benefit both human and biological communities. They also must ensure that ecosystem-oriented adaptation receives its fair share of attention and financial resources.

Policy makers and natural resource agencies alone will not be sufficient to ensure species and ecosystems gain attention and resources. Conservation advocates must explain to these decision makers and to the broader public how conserving species and ecosystems makes economic sense: coastal wetlands provide not only nursery habitat for important fisheries, but also provide buffers against sea level rise and storm surges; natural floodplains provide not only movement corridors for wildlife, but also help protect people and property from intensified rainfall events and droughts; native species pollinate our food crops; ecosystems provide us with clean water, assimilate our wastes, and provide still other vital but often unseen services. Community leaders, educators, and parents must help people reconnect with nature and remind them about how conservation is the backbone not just of our economy, but also our quality of life. Finally, we all must remember the ethical imperative of stewarding the other species with which we share our planet.

Conclusion

The future presents enormous challenges for species conservation. Climate change, human population growth, unsustainable technologies, and excessive per-capita consumption of natural resources put species in serious jeopardy. The ESA is essential for helping to meet these challenges, but the agencies responsible for implementing the statute must use their tools more effectively, engage in more large-scale landscape planning, and enter more creative partnerships. Perhaps most of all, these agencies must participate, and ensure that species conservation is fully addressed, in the broader decision-making processes surrounding adaptation to climate change and the shift to a more sustainable society.

Many people beyond the natural resource agencies have an important role to play. Conservationists of all stripes must help the ESA evolve into an effective legal tool for protecting imperiled species and their habitat not just from direct threats such as habitat destruction and fragmentation, but also from the enormous indirect threat known as climate change. The most important variable in determining the success of species protection efforts is both simple and enormously challenging: our continued resolve to ensure the secure future of all life on Earth.

Notes

1. M. W. Schwartz, *Choosing an Appropriate Scale of Reserves for Conservation*, 30 ANN. REV. ECOLOGY & SYSTEMATICS 83 (1999). Because the ESA pays only a small amount of attention to species occurring solely in foreign countries, this chapter focuses primarily on domestic species.
2. D. S. Wilcove & L. L. Master, *How Many Endangered Species Are There in the United States?* 3 FRONTIERS IN ECOLOGY & ENV'T 414 (2005). Natureserve, a nonprofit research organization, has classified more than 8,000 U.S. species as being at elevated risk of extinction.
3. *See* U.S. Fish & Wildlife Serv., Recovery Reports to Congress, http://www.fws.gov/endangered/recovery/index.html.
4. Timothy D. Male & Michael S. Bean, *Measuring Progress in US Endangered Species Conservation*, 8 ECOLOGY LETTERS 968 (2005); J. J. Rachlinski, *Noah by the Numbers: An Empirical Evaluation of the Endangered Species Act*, 82 CORNELL L. REV. 356 (1997).
5. M. Taylor et al., *The Effectiveness of the Endangered Species Act: A Quantitative Analysis*, 55 BIOSCIENCE 360 (2005).
6. *Id.*
7. For a useful review of the literature on ESA effectiveness, see M. W. Schwartz, *The Performance of the Endangered Species Act*, 39 ANN. REV. ECOLOGY & SYSTEMATICS 279 (2008).
8. *See, e.g.*, CHARLES C. MANN & MARK L. PLUMMER, NOAH'S CHOICE (1995); Competitive Enterprise Inst., Endangered Species Act Still a Failure, http://cei.org/gencon/003,02720.cfm.
9. Male & Bean, *supra* note 4.
10. *See, e.g.*, SourceWatch, http://www.sourcewatch.org (detailing campaign to weaken the ESA carried out by National Endangered Species Act Reform Coalition).
11. Memorandum from B. Meadow & M. Mehringer (Decision Research Apr. 16, 2004) (describing national poll finding that 86 percent of registered voters support the ESA) (on file with the authors).
12. The Congressional Research Service's regular reports on ESA appropriations levels can be found at the Biodiversity section of http://ncseonline.org/NLE/CRS/. The most recent is E. H. Buck et al., The Endangered Species Act (ESA) in the 111th Congress: Conflicting Values and Difficult Choices (Congressional Research Service, Apr. 10, 2009), http://ncseonline.org/NLE/CRSreports/09Mar/R40185.pdf (table 2).
13. *See* 68 Fed. Reg. 68,254 (Dec. 8, 2003) (loosening section 7 consultation requirements for logging under the National Fire Plan); 69 Fed. Reg. 47,732 (Aug. 5, 2004) (loosening consultation requirements for pesticide registrations, later overturned by a federal district court in Washington); 73 Fed. Reg. 76,272 (Dec. 16, 2008) (loosening consultation requirements for all federal actions and placing climate change considerations largely outside the scope of consultations).
14. For an extensive discussion of political pressures altering decision-making under the statute, see OFFICE OF INSPECTOR GENERAL, U.S. DEP'T OF THE INTERIOR, INVESTIGATIVE REPORT: THE ENDANGERED SPECIES ACT AND THE CONFLICT BETWEEN SCIENCE AND POLICY (2008), *available at* http://wyden.senate.gov/newsroom/interior_ig_report.pdf.
15. *Id.; see also* OFFICE OF INSPECTOR GENERAL, U.S. DEP'T OF THE INTERIOR, INVESTIGATIVE REPORT: ALLEGATIONS AGAINST JULIE MACDONALD, DEPUTY ASSISTANT

SECRETARY, FISH, WILDLIFE, AND PARKS (2007), *available at* http://wyden.senate.gov/DOI_IG_Report.pdf.
16. MILLENNIUM ECOSYSTEM ASSESSMENT, ECOSYSTEMS AND WELL-BEING: CURRENT STATE AND TRENDS (2005); HEINZ CTR., STATE OF THE NATION'S ECOSYSTEMS (2008).
17. IPCC, CLIMATE CHANGE 2007: THE PHYSICAL SCIENCE BASIS: CONTRIBUTION OF WORKING GROUP I TO THE FOURTH ASSESSMENT REPORT OF THE INTERGOVERNMENTAL PANEL ON CLIMATE CHANGE (Susan D. Solomon et al. eds., Cambridge Univ. Press 2007).
18. IPCC, CLIMATE CHANGE 2007: IMPACTS, ADAPTATION, AND VULNERABILITY: CONTRIBUTION OF WORKING GROUP II TO THE FOURTH ASSESSMENT REPORT OF THE INTERGOVERNMENTAL PANEL ON CLIMATE CHANGE (Martin L. Parry et al. eds., Cambridge Univ. Press 2007).
19. *See generally* John Kostyack & Daniel Rohlf, *Conserving Endangered Species in an Era of Global Warming*, 38 ENVTL. L. REP. 10,203 (2008).
20. D. L. Murray et al., *Pathogens, Nutritional Deficiency, and Climate Influences on a Declining Moose Population*, 166 WILDLIFE MONOGRAPHS 1–30 (2006).
21. Erik A. Beever et al., *Patterns of Apparent Extirpation Among Isolated Populations of Pikas in the Great Basin*, 84 J. MAMMOLOGY 37–54 (2003).
22. Fortunately, in the waning months of the Bush administration, the political controversies had died down sufficiently to enable the Interior Department to release a series of discussion papers outlining adaptation options. *See, e.g.*, Dep't of Interior, Task Force on Climate Change, Report of the Subcommittee on Science, http://www.usgs.gov/global_change/docs/science.pdf.
23. *See, e.g.*, HEINZ CTR., STRATEGIES FOR MANAGING THE EFFECTS OF CLIMATE CHANGE ON WILDLIFE AND ECOSYSTEMS, http://www.heinzctr.org.
24. 16 U.S.C. § 1533(a)(3)(A)(i).
25. In *Arizona Cattle Growers' Ass'n v. Kempthorne*, 534 F. Supp. 2d 1013, 1025 (D. Ariz. 2008), the court rejected plaintiffs' argument that FWS must first determine exactly when a species could be considered "recovered" in order to designate critical habitat; while finding this argument "tempting in its logical simplicity," the court found that Congress drew a distinction between the ESA's critical habitat designation and recovery planning processes.
26. *See* FINAL REPORT, KEYSTONE WORKING GROUP ON ENDANGERED SPECIES HABITAT ISSUES (2006), *available at* http://keystone.org/files/file/about/publications/ESA-Report-FINAL-4-25-06.pdf.
27. *Id.*
28. *Id.* at 23–24.
29. *Id.* at 19–28.
30. *See* Pub. L. No. 110-234, § 15303 (2008) (popularly known as the 2008 Farm Bill).
31. *See* Notice of Interagency Cooperative Policy for the Ecosystem Approach to the Endangered Species Act, 59 Fed. Reg. 34,274 (1994). While the Services in recent years have largely ignored ecosystem approaches to listing and recovery, there are a few bright spots. For example, FWS has worked to develop and fund the Hawaiian Plant Conservation Strategy, an ecosystem approach to saving the islands many endemic plants. *See* Marie M. Bruegmann, *A Plan for Hawaiian Plants and Their Ecosystems*, 28(4) ENDANGERED SPECIES BULL. 28 (2003), *available at* http://www.fws.gov/endangered/bulletin/2003/07-12/28-29.pdf.
32. *See* Ctr. for Biological Diversity v. Kempthorne, 2008 WL 659822 (D. Ariz. 2008) (overturning FWS's determination that bald eagles in Arizona are not eligible for listing as a distinct population segment).
33. The Interior Solicitor's Opinion setting forth this determination is available at http://www.doi.gov/solicitor/opinions/M37013.pdf.
34. *See* Aldo Leopold, *Wilderness for Wildlife*, *in* A SAND COUNTY ALMANAC WITH ESSAYS ON CONSERVATION FROM ROUND RIVER 277 (Oxford Univ. Press 1966).

35. For an excellent synthesis of recent scientific findings detailing the crucial ecological roles of top-level predators, including accounts of "trophic cascades" of ecological harms when these predators disappear, see W. STOLZENBURG, WHERE THE WILD THINGS WERE (2008).
36. *See* CTR. FOR BIOLOGICAL DIVERSITY ET AL., BUSH ADMINISTRATION ATTACKS ENDANGERED SPECIES ACT (2008), http://www.biologicaldiversity.org/publications/papers/esa_attack.pdf.
37. *See* CTR. FOR BIOLOGICAL DIVERSITY, POLITICIZING EXTINCTION: THE BUSH ADMINISTRATION'S DANGEROUS APPROACH TO ENDANGERED WILDLIFE (2007), *available at* http://www.biologicaldiversity.org/publications/papers/PoliticizingExtinction.pdf.
38. *See* 70 Fed. Reg. 52,630 (Sept. 2, 2005).
39. Wash. Toxics Coal. v. U.S. Fish & Wildlife Serv., 457 F. Supp. 2d 1158 (W.D. Wash. 2006) (striking down pesticide counterpart regulations); Defenders of Wildlife v. Kempthorne, 2006 WL 2844232 (D.D.C., 2006) (upholding counterpart regulations for projects that support the U.S. Forest Service's National Fire Plan).
40. 73 Fed. Reg. 76,272, 76,287 (2008) (codified at 50 C.F.R. § 402.03(b)(3)). In March 2009, Congress granted the Secretary of the Interior and Secretary of Commerce extraordinary authority to withdraw the Bush administration's section 7 regulations and reinstate the previously existing regulations without first complying with normal procedural requirements for rulemaking. *See* 2009 Omnibus Appropriations Act, Pub. L. No. 111-8, § 429, —Stat.—(2009). The Secretaries exercised their authority to withdraw the section 7 regulations and reinstated the prior existing regulations. 74 Fed. Reg. 20,421 (May 4, 2009).
41. In Nat'l Wildlife Fed'n v. Nat'l Marine Fisheries Serv., 524 F.3d 917, 932–33 (9th Cir. 2008), the Ninth Circuit Court of Appeals noted that the regulatory definition of the term "jeopardize the continued existence of" listed species includes a consideration of a proposed action's impact on species recovery, and overturned a biological opinion that considered only a proposal's impacts on the survival of the affected species. The Ninth Circuit also has held that the "purpose of establishing 'critical habitat' is for the government to carve out territory that is not only necessary for the species' survival but also essential for the species' recovery." Gifford Pinchot Task Force v. U.S. Fish & Wildlife Serv., 378 F.3d 1059 (9th Cir. 2004).
42. For more information on the Walla Walla Basin HCP and water management issues, see Matthew Preusch, Walla Walla Basin Sidesteps a Water War, HIGH COUNTRY NEWS, Aug. 19, 2002, *available at* http://www.hcn.org/issues/232/11356.
43. The Services' *HCP Handbook* specifies that the ESA "does not explicitly require an HCP to recover listed species, or contribute to their recovery objectives outlined in a recovery plan." U.S. DEP'T OF INTERIOR, FISH & WILDLIFE SERV., & U.S. DEP'T OF COMMERCE, NAT'L OCEANIC & ATMOSPHERIC ADMIN., NAT'L MARINE FISHERIES SERV., HABITAT CONSERVATION PLANNING AND INCIDENTAL TAKE PERMIT PROCESSING HANDBOOK 3-20 (Nov. 4, 1996), *available at* http://www.fws.gov/endangered/hcp/hcpbook.html.
44. *See* Sw. Ctr. for Biological Diversity v. Bartel, 470 F. Supp. 2d 1118, 1136 (S.D. Cal. 2006) (holding that FWS must consider the recovery plan for affected species in deciding whether a proposed HCP is adequate under section 10).
45. In some states, the Wildlife Action Plans already provide such a strategic blueprint for conservation of listed and other at-risk species. In other states, the Wildlife Action Plans are focused primarily on preventing the need to list additional species and a strategic approach to ESA-listed species is still needed. See Ass'n of Fish & Wildlife Agencies, Teaming with Wildlife, http://www.teaming.com/.
46. *See* Robert L. Fischman and Jaelith Hall-Rivera, *A Lesson For Conservation From Pollution Control Law: Cooperative Federalism For Recovery Under The Endangered Species Act*, 27 COLUM. J. ENVTL. L. 45 (2002).
47. *See* NATIONAL MARINE FISHERIES SERVICE, FINAL BIOLOGICAL OPINION, IMPLEMENTATION OF THE NATIONAL FLOOD INSURANCE PROGRAM IN THE STATE OF WASHINGTON,

September 22, 2008, *available at* https://pcts.nmfs.noaa.gov/pls/pcts-pub/sxn7.pcts_upload.download?p_file=F3181/200600472_fema_nfip_09-22-2008.pdf.
48. The Willamette Partnership attempts to use markets for ecosystem services to provide financial incentives for polluters, governments, and landowners to carry out actions with conservation benefits. For more information, see http://www.willamettepartnership.org/.
49. H.R. 2454 (2009).
50. In its 2008 revisions to the ESA's section 7 regulations, the Bush administration excused federal agencies from consulting regarding the impacts of "global processes" (meaning climate change) whenever such processes could not be measured at the local scale, their impacts were insignificant, or their risks to species and habitats were remote. 50 C.F.R. § 402.03(b)(2). These regulatory changes, which as noted earlier were reversed by the Obama administration, arbitrarily assumed that some GHG emissions would have negligible impact on listed species while others would have significant impact. In fact, if a listed species is threatened by climate change, any source of GHG emissions poses a threat to some degree.
51. *See* Kostyack & Rohlf, *supra* note 19, for our recommendation on how the Services could develop a streamlined approach to reviewing new GHG emissions sources.

19

Refocusing the Endangered Species Act

A Regulated Community Perspective

W. H. "Buzz" Fawcett

The Challenge of the Act

> And what do you do about aridity if you are a nation accustomed to plenty and impatient of restrictions and led westward by pillars of fire and cloud? You may deny it for a while. Then you must either try to engineer it out of existence or adapt to it.
> —Wallace Stegner, *Where the Bluebird Sings to the Lemonade Springs*

The regulated community generally enjoys a post-enlightenment attitude toward endangered and threatened species. We understand how important it is that we reestablish the human relationship to these species in distress. We have been employed for most of our adult lives with the security, conservation, and perfection of habitat for endangered and threatened species. We have been associated with the creation or protection of more habitat for threatened or endangered species in America than most of the stereotype(r)s could conjure up in their imaginations.

The United States has changed mightily since the Endangered Species Act was born. Landowners now regularly employ a biologist's sophistication (and plenty of biologists) in problem solving and base their actions on an understanding of natural processes not attainable in 1973. An understanding of the complex and interrelated nature of habitat is common not just to environmentalists but also, in the course of doing business, to owners and developers themselves. Who would doubt that state and private managers and biologists know more about the asset they manage than the federal government?

What do we want out of the Act? If you sit in front of a blank computer monitor and ask yourself this question you quickly realize that the Act is (place best euphemism available here) in need of focus and leadership. However, there are things that can be done to put the Act in its proper perspective and begin to address the challenges that have so hindered its operation.

So, representing myself as a member of the regulated community for the purposes of this chapter, I believe that at a minimum a landowner should expect to be able to know the requirements of the Act; have the rules applied uniformly, fairly, and without undue delay; and have the manner and the costs of doing business accurately described. That is not happening now.

The Act Is a Reflection of Its Time and Congressional Neglect

One cannot blame the drafters of the ESA for their lack of prescience. Consider the times. Social revolution and a growing awareness of the interconnectedness of the planet led to the passage of the Clean Air Act of 1970, the 1970 National Environmental Protection Act, the 1972 amendments to the Clean Water Act, and the Safe Drinking Water Act (1974); and the establishment of both the Environmental Protection Agency and the Council on Environmental Quality. In the ESA, Congress sought to make a fundamental change in the way the species with whom we live are respected, but members of Congress never could have predicted the fundamental changes that have occurred in the life sciences they fostered.

Passed in 1973, the Act is long on ideals and short on specificity. In particular, it has a paucity of provisions that lead to effective and efficient conservation on the ground. The Act has not enjoyed political consensus and therefore has not received the necessary support, through congressional amendment, that its sister statutes have received over the years. It has a singular beauty in that it prevents federal government agencies from doing anything to contribute to the jeopardy of a listed species,[1] but it does very little else well. What it does accomplish is certainly not achieved transparently. This is one of the reasons that the Act is considered a difficult one to master. Because of its curious style, very little of the information necessary to a complete understanding of the subject matter is in the Act itself. The Code of Federal Regulations, guidance documents issued to instruct staff, past and current litigation, and current practice collectively make up the messy fabric of one of this nation's primary conservation laws: the effort to save endangered species from extinction.

Time and time again, we are drawn back to the words of that Congress almost 35 years ago. As usual, when dealing with the Act, one must go to the beginning. How did the drafters intend to protect species and what authority did they give to the Secretaries of the Interior and Commerce?

The Act Is Primarily a Jurisdictional Statute

If the drafters wanted species protected, why did they not stop with section 9, the prohibition on taking listed species? They could have simply made it a crime to "harm" a species, as defined by the Service in its regulations to include habitat modification that actually kills or injures listed species. Any act, whether on federal or private land, that harmed species would draw stern condemnation and an appropriate penalty. But they did not stop with section 9. Why? Because they knew that prosecutions under Section 9 would never succeed as a strategy for the future. Section 9 requires a dead animal and a chain of proof. Section 9 responds to an act after it is completed. Secretary of the Interior Kempthorne used to refer to the option for the scoundrel as "shoot, shovel and shut up." The harm is already done. No matter how egregious the injury, a successful prosecution of the crime of take of a species does not often succeed without actual proof of injury to the species. This is also why so few Section 9 cases are actually filed.

How then could the drafters extend the effect of the Act without the proofs necessary under section 9? How could the federal government become proactive on species without running afoul of the rights of states? The federal government has no zoning function absent congressional action and therefore effective planning for species can only be enforced on federal property.

Congressional authority over the funding of the Executive Branch meant that the drafters could use their power to control the acts of federal agencies. Through this avenue, no proof "beyond a reasonable doubt" would be needed to effect the change sought, and no injury would be needed to initiate action. Only the opinion of the federal agency exercising its duties would be needed so long as that opinion was not arbitrary or capricious.[2]

Within the federal family, actions that "may affect" species were reviewed and, if the effect was adverse, mitigation required from the acting agency typically would be required under the consultation process of section 7(a)(2). If the acting agency was responding to a request for a license or permit, then that mitigation is borne in proportion to the interference by the licensee or permittee.

That is the power of section 7; it controls future events. Unlike section 9, which needs an act and a chain of proof, Section 7 asks how the Service's (Fish and Wildlife Service or National Marine Fisheries Service) "special management" can be best interposed between the agency action and completion of the project. This authority is hypothetically absolute over federal lands, barring the political clout of the Department of Defense and its ability to force an exception.[3]

Within the federal family, this means that the Service will be heard on the question of long-term federal lands plans, licenses, and permits, which are themselves acts of the government that "may affect" endangered species.[4] The agencies will act at federal speed and with certain deliberation, which usually means that none of the timelines of section 7 are ever really met.

The value of section 7 for the Service is that with the Service's finding that any action agency project, license, or permit has an adverse effect, as a modification of critical habitat[5] impacting jeopardy (or recovery), the Service can require mitigation for the harm to be done to the habitat. This mitigation required can, depending on the circumstances, range in extent from 1:1 replacement value to even moderately higher ratios with a ceiling carefully influenced by the strictures of Fifth Amendment eminent domain law. The value of section 7 is that the Service can, unlike under section 9, affirmatively address a project, license, or permit before harm occurs.

The input the Service is afforded by the Act during action agency plan formulation is one of the few opportunities that the Service will have to address the long-term benefits to supporting habitat without the full support of the various federal agencies. Accordingly, the only connection the Service has to the privately owned critical habitat is often through the section 7 process, and the Service is therefore left to the vagaries of license and permit application. This does not give the Service any platform for sound planning for species or the land that they inhabit.

Essentially, the Act is about the separate relationships between the Secretary and the federal family, the states, the courts, and nonfederal parties.[6] Considering its focus and its history, the ESA is a statute drafted to save species from going extinct by requiring the Secretary to list species and protect their habitat from the acts of other agencies or from the exercise of their jurisdiction over the habitat without the prior agreement of the Secretary.

The ESA is not an act that creates effective tools for recovering species, conserving habitat, or bringing about wise future planning. The ESA does not maximize the benefit to species or reduce the cost of taking species off the list. In practice, the ESA is not designed to recognize real-world situations relating to species whose ranges cross international boundaries or to deal with scientific realities unknown at the time of its drafting, like genetic coding or global warming.

It might be said that considering the importance placed on endangered species in this country, the subject deserves an act that is specific, informed, and transparent. Perhaps we should have an act that recovers and conserves habitats and is amenable to planning for the future. Unfortunately this is not the case. Congress has utterly failed to housekeep the Act and make the Act more relevant to the critical needs of endangered and threatened species.[7] The same ideological divide that stopped reform in 1997 (when a concerted effort to achieve ESA reauthorization failed) continues to prevent meaningful reform today. Congress has been satisfied with a stale debate, devoid of a decade's new thinking. The lack of serious-minded reauthorization attempts in Congress means that no effort will be made to improve agency performance in administering the Act. With no progress visible in Washington, D.C., in addressing the existing problems between the Act and its application, some continue to try to make the Act something it never was intended to be—a sweeping legal mechanism to not only prevent extinction and harm but also to achieve recovery through a vast federal planning mechanism.[8]

Transparency and the Administration of the Act

In the 103rd Congress, Secretary Babbitt announced his ten-point plan for the ESA.[9] A cornerstone of his policy was utilizing the planning available to the U.S. Fish and Wildlife Service (FWS) in section 10 habitat conservation plans (HCPs). Babbitt and the administration persuaded large private property owners to negotiate ecosystem-wide, multispecies HCPs locking in mitigation requirements and locking down environmental baselines all in the name of take avoidance. HCPs were hailed by members of Congress on both sides of the Senate Environment and Public Works Committee as the new solution for civilized ESA planning. Landowners began to negotiate agreements with the Service, convinced that this was a better way to proceed rather than trying to defend against an action under section 9 take. By planning habitat for multiple species, including unlisted species, both landowners and the environment benefited. The investment in time and money that landowners made in reliance on the 10-point plan has been substantial.

The best part of the policy for landowners was that they could ensure their compliance with the Act and quantify their future expenditures. No more would be asked of them because a "deal was a deal" with the Department of the Interior. Secretary Babbitt promised this with the endorsement of President Clinton.

Unfortunately, Secretary Babbitt took a few hits on his way out of town and the environmental community soon forgot their commitments and obligations to No Surprises and HCPs generally. Adaptive management, as often incorporated in HCPs, is an appropriate scientific tool to test and verify hypotheses and deal with uncertainty, but that solution posed a threat to those who wished to use the Act to stop land use. Finally, by steadily increasing the requirements for HCPs, the Services have made HCPs in general less attractive to large landowners.[10]

The failure of Congress over the last decade to codify this uniformly praised policy invited multiple interpretations of its application in the Executive Branch, spurred wasteful litigation, and raised questions over the efficacy of conservation programs. The cost of HCPs discouraged most land use managers from using it as a tool. In light of the failure of the Congress to use Land and Water Conservation Funds for conservation, using farm-program-styled conservation purchase programs cannot substitute for proper planning if we are to recover species off the list.

Critical Habitat: The Agony of Expectations Unfulfilled

In the United States, there are currently a grand total of 1,314 endangered and threatened species.[11] Critical habitat has been designated for 489 species, about half of them plants.[12] The Bush administration did its best to relieve the backlog; there are currently three species proposed for listing, thus suggesting that the best way to avoid the strictures of the Act is to not use it in the first place. But there are 248 recognized candidate species waiting in the wings for an administration with a less highly developed sense of avoiding undue species privilege. And when the Obama administration does begin to list new species, the problems inherent in the act will return with a vengeance.

Under pressure to designate critical habitat for species within one year of listing,[13] the Service is in most cases operating in the dark. A dispassionate analysis of the science with an eye to the proofs necessary to succeed inevitably yields sufficient evidence questioning the conclusions of biological staff. Sometimes the science to support the hypothesis on primary constituent elements of habitat, the criteria that must be satisfied for designation, just does not exist. Furthermore, when science does exist, it is off-point or not determinative. During the pygmy owl redesignation, for example, the Service was saddled with trying to hide the fact that the science it was relying on was old State of Arizona data that would not bear scrutiny.

The best solution to the inability to meet the one-year timeline is to either delay designation of critical habitat to the recovery plan stage or (and this is less harsh than it sounds) do away with the concept of critical habitat completely. The arguments that surround delay of designation depend on whether you want to use the proposed designation of critical habitat as a rallying cry or a fund raiser (by raising concern among those who would be regulated), or just hope to delay designation of proposed habitat to a point where you just might get something akin to competent compliance.

The Department of the Interior is, as of the writing of this chapter, deliberating streamlining the consultation process under new regulations that allow action agency biologists to make the initial determination that a particular project has "no effect" on a listed species. This determination is now made solely by FWS biologists and contributes to the indisputably slow review as duties are piled up on FWS staff without additional appropriations.

> [The] new regulations streamline the process by which agencies work with each other and institutionalize ESA review within responsible action agencies. This will better insure species are protected, and eliminate unnecessary bureaucracy attributed to administration of the ESA.[14]

This idea originally surfaced during then Senator Kempthorne's bipartisan S.1180, which was cosponsored by Senators Reid, Baucus, and Chafee. The basis for the idea was that this low bar of the ESA could easily be scaled by action agency biologists whose determination would be subject to review under the civil enforcement provisions of the Act. In turn, action agency review would alleviate some of the workflow on the FWS. The quid pro quo for this action agency review was the elimination of critical habitat as a concept under the Act: something all agency heads have sought for over a decade.[15]

The idea of doing away with critical habitat still has lots of supporters. It can be politically risky since it seems counterintuitive that critical habitat does not do anything to the administration of the Act that listing did not do in the first place. Despite this, there seemed to be general agreement in the work product coming out of various drafting sessions in Washington, D.C., about eliminating critical habitat as a concept in the Act.

Having said all of this, I still believe that, for the time being, the safest political course would be to maintain critical habitat as a concept yet holding the line on any concession to the principle that there is a recovery duty. To make the Act transparent and discourage useless litigation, Congress should amend section 4 of the Act to delay designation of critical habitat by the Secretary until the recovery plan is adopted and encourage habitat planning through a new recovery statute and a new authorization for recovery.

The Polar Bear Paradox

On May 14, 2008, complying with a court-imposed deadline, the Department of the Interior announced a final rule listing the polar bear (*Ursus maritimus*) as a threatened species under the Act. FWS concluded that the polar bear's sea ice habitat "is declining throughout the species' range, that this decline is expected to continue for the foreseeable future, [and] that this loss threatens the species throughout all of its range."[16] To most onlookers this was a necessary and proper application of the Act to protect a species in decline as a result of global warming. But just as light can act both as a particle and a wave, so too does the designation serve as both a show of compassion and an illustration of one of the acute failures of the Act. The Act's propensity for misuse is a direct result of its lack of clarity.

The purposes clause of the Act authorizes, in pertinent part: "a means whereby the ecosystems upon which endangered species and threatened species depend may be conserved [and] to provide a program for the conservation of such endangered species and threatened species."[17] Polar bear habitat will not be conserved by using either section 7 or section 9, the two principal forcing mechanisms under the Act.[18] Designation of critical habitat for the polar bear based only on the evidence spread across the *Federal Register* on global warming is a useless act fated to neither conserve the habitat of the polar bear nor curb global warming. The very structure of the Act as a jurisdictional document prevents it from being used as an agent of change for such a purpose.

Almost by definition global warming can be addressed only by a systemic change in the carbon zeitgeist of America. No one has so far proved that utilization of the civil or criminal penalties under the Act can realistically affect the future of the bear, humanity, or any other species at risk from global warming.

What is the utility of using the Act to protect endangered and threatened species if both people and the wildlife species are threatened by the same source? The Act was intended to prevent individuals and specific agency actions from frustrating the purpose of a listing or designation. The Act was never intended to empower the Department of the Interior to impose mitigations and restrictions for acts with no nexus to the subject habitat save living in the same world. What principle of judicial relativism causes one to ignore the fact that the courts cannot order a cooler planet like they can order the FWS to churn out critical habitat designations without sufficient science? Were we threatened by an asteroid collision it is doubtful we would look to the Act for policy inspiration to ensure species safety.

The Act does not possess the mechanisms necessary to enforce the designation. The FWS was not authorized by Congress to regulate and impose mitigations on the consumption of carbon benefits that could be theoretically restricted by the Act. Under section 7, federal agencies would surely have to evaluate their (and their licensees' and permittees') thermal impacts within the Arctic Circle, but relative to what—to the immediate impact of their action, or to a globally warmed planet? Could FWS agents in the lower 48 states evaluate the impact of a single diesel electric generator's operation on jeopardy to the polar bear as a species? By what mechanism in the Act does the Secretary commit or require what ungodly sum be directed to saving the polar bear?[19] What possible costs could be borne in mitigation?

Now that listing has occurred, presumably the next step is critical habitat designation. Rather than designate critical habitat for the polar bear, the Secretary should take into account the costs of FWS enforcement under sections 7 and 9. Section 4(b)(2) states that "[t]he Secretary shall designate critical habitat . . . after taking into consideration the economic impact, *and any other relevant impact,* of specifying any particular area as critical habitat."[20]

The cost of enforcement and the costs of mitigation are so wildly unknown that designating Arctic Circle habitat for the polar bear, solely for the sake of its own designation, is unnecessary. Furthermore, rather than simply rejecting the designation for cost, the Secretary would have had a firm foundation to find that introduction of the facts of global warming necessitate an examination of the costs of survival and recovery occasioned by those facts, which would then trigger the protection of section 4(b)(2).

The Act almost demands such a construction. Section 4(b)(2) goes on to say that "the Secretary may exclude any area from critical habitat if he determines that the benefits of such exclusion outweigh the benefits of specifying such area as a part of the critical habitat."[21] Surely acknowledging global warming as a fact does not mean that every legislative vehicle chosen for its resolution is appropriate. As Secretary of the Interior Dirk Kempthorne stated:

It should be without debate that the ESA as written compelled the listing of the polar bear. We cannot however confuse the literal application of the Act with its practical utility as a means of saving the species. The Act must confront itself. Designation of critical habitat for the polar bear, or any species threatened with global warming, will not be the forcing principle behind its survival or conservation. Only systemic and innovative change in our utilization of specific power resources for specific purposes can turn the tide of global warming once set in motion.[22]

This is not to say that we ignore the threat of global warming or that we do not wish more had been done by Congress to address the issue. Nor do I wish polar bears ill. I love polar bears. But since polar bears are not actually in decline (yet), could we not fool ourselves into believing that the Act can be the instrument of change to save them? Such actions divert attention from the problem and the remedy and provide a false sense that the Act can contribute to the solution of the problem. If we really want to save endangered species, should we try not killing them for sport or subsistence?[23]

That is the polar bear paradox. The ESA has not stopped humans from consuming the same salmonids our government has spent billions trying to save. The Service could more easily roll back the tides than bear up to the costs and pressures necessary to bring back the species by stopping people from eating them.[24] Similarly, the Act is powerless to affect global warming, the greatest threat to "ecosystems upon which endangered and threatened species depend"[25] without a new foundation to plan for recovery of endangered threatened species. The continued abrogation of congressional responsibility to endangered and threatened species invites the abuse of the Act and defers action on global warming at a time when action is critical.

The *Pinchot* Conundrum[26]

Gifford Pinchot Task Force v. U.S. Fish and Wildlife Service drew recovery battle lines in the sand between opposing poles in the critical habitat debate and ended the discussion about deleting critical habitat as a concept in the Act. In this decision, the Ninth Circuit ruled that the regulatory definition of adverse modification of critical habitat and jeopardy to the species (as both acts are prohibited by section 7(a)(2)) could not have the same meaning. Instead, the court observed, adverse modification of critical habitat includes a concept of recovery rather than mere avoidance of extinction or maintaining the species status quo. Until *Pinchot*, there was no functional difference between adverse modification of critical habitat and jeopardy to the species.

Perhaps *Pinchot* could be understood more easily if we were to change the frame of reference the *Pinchot* court developed and bring the Act back to its roots. The Secretary protects habitat under the Act through a variety of means.[27] Under Section 7(a)(2), Congress granted the Secretary a very powerful tool to protect habitat from infringement against federal agencies.[28] This is the dual prohibition on (1) jeopardy to species and (2) adverse modification to critical habitat under section 7(a)(2).

These two prohibitions lead to the obvious question: what constitutes "jeopardy" and what "adverse modification"? As discussed above, prior to the Fifth Circuit decision in *Sierra Club v. U.S. Fish and Wildlife Service*[29] and the Ninth Circuit decision in *Pinchot*, FWS defined both terms in the same way. As it defined adverse modification:

> [A] direct or indirect alteration that appreciably diminishes the value of critical habitat for both the survival and recovery of a listed species. Such alterations include, but are not limited to alterations adversely modifying any of those physical or biological features that were the basis for determining habitat to be critical.[30]

And as it defined jeopardy: "[i]n contrast, (to the adverse modification standard) the jeopardy standard addresses the effect of the action itself on the survival and recovery of the species."[31] Is it the difference between the use of "or" and "and" in the agency regulations that has so vexed the courts? As a result, two circuits have invalidated the definition as it is used for "adverse modification." Neither addressed the definition of "jeopardy." The courts have not provided guidance on this question. Thus, how should these two terms be defined?

The rule as written, and struck down in *Sierra Club* and *Pinchot*, defines adverse modification in terms of the intrinsic values (both subjective and objective) of critical habitat that are detrimentally altered.[32] It is a practical impossibility to write language in any rule or statute that can encompass all conceivable adverse modifications to the diverse habitats of the United States. An adverse modification of habitat that would be adverse for the Banbury Springs limpet may not necessarily be adverse for the pygmy owl. The challenge is, therefore, to develop a regulation that speaks to recovery, as required by the Fifth and Ninth Circuits, while at the same time being flexible enough to apply to a wide range of species habitat areas.

To redefine the term, it is instructive to parse the definition of adverse modification as it stands today. A "direct or indirect alteration" is surely a subjective standard. As applied, it is anything any party would like to claim it is. The requirement that the adverse modification "appreciably diminishes the value of critical habitat for both the survival and recovery of a listed species" is, as the courts have ruled, simply an awkward attempt to redefine a provision in the statute without actually adding anything to the administration of the term.

From the application of the definition, what the drafters of the regulation were apparently trying to reach for was a way to memorialize an alteration adversely modifying any of those physical or biological features that were the basis for the Secretary's statutory determination that the habitat is critical. And it is here that we find what is really needed by a definition. The statute cries out for a regulatory definition of those acts controlling how the Secretary orders the relationship with federal agencies that may infringe on the very broad statutory power granted by Congress through section 7(a)(2).

The definition in the regulation,[33] as it stands today, does not define the authority of the Secretary under the statute to prevent federal agencies from rendering judgments moot. The rule does imply some premium on physical and biological features altered. We must give it credit for recognizing that the issue at question is the "basis" for determining the habitat as a whole to be critical.[34] But there is a better definition for the rule that can, if implemented, augur a new and more flexible administration of the Act and that has a platform for a new conservation ethic in this country.[35]

Federal actors are not allowed to act in a way that will, by deed or misdeed, inevitably lead to the complete extirpation of the species.[36] This is the jeopardy standard. It is the congressional protection of Secretarial decisions from federal agency action regarding the continued existence of species and the habitat it relies on as determined by the Secretary.

Federal actors also are not allowed to act in a way that will, by deed or misdeed, lead to the destruction or adverse modification of critical habitat.[37] As the conjunctive "or" suggests in the sentence, destruction of critical habitat and adverse modification of critical habitat are similar but differing states, in relative descending order.

Destruction of any critical habitat forever renders ineffective or useless, nullifies, neutralizes, or invalidates the *purpose of the designation of critical habitat* by the Secretary. Destruction of habitat, in law and fact, effects a redesignation of critical habitat without process required in the Act and which only the Secretary by specific act can pronounce in order to redesignate critical habitat.[38] Destruction of habitat by the offices of a federal actor would therefore interfere by federal action with a designation that only the Secretary by authority can modify by acting to approve a permit.

The existing definition of adverse modification is a problem for the Secretary because the original definition was flawed. The original definition attempted to define a state of action toward habitat; an individual act physically modifying habitat to its detriment. However, destruction and adverse modification can be much more easily and logically defined by their affect on the jurisdiction and authority of the Secretary. Based upon these concepts, a revised definition of adverse modification of critical habitat would read:

> *Destruction or adverse modification* means the net effect of a direct or indirect alteration that appreciably diminishes the value of the physical or biological features of the designated area such that they no longer meet the needs considered by the Secretary to be essential to the conservation of the species at the time of designation.

Under this definition, the standard set by the Fifth and Ninth Circuits would be satisfied; clear guidance would be provided to affected parties; incentive would be provided to look for ways to promote critical habitat creation or enhancement; and the Secretary's judgment and authority would be protected and strengthened.

Toward a Conservation Economy

The Act does one thing well and that is placing species that have fallen victim to one or more of the five factors for ESA listing under federal special management.[39] However, the Act does not include a functional recovery section. The extent of recovery in the Act is covered by the direction that "[t]he Secretary shall develop and implement [recovery] plans."[40] Unless the current Secretary is able to gain the consensus of the Service on development of a structure and formality behind recovery plans, Congress must act to develop a recovery planning regimen. Long-term habitat planning should occur at the landscape level and should be integrated with elements of a conservation economy.

The drafters of the Act were primarily concerned with federal action that might, without consensus or review, extirpate or jeopardize a species. They addressed this need through the authority of the Secretary to demand mitigation through the power of section 7(a)(2). This is in keeping with the essentially jurisdictional nature of the Act, and section 7(a)(2) is the heart of interfederal relationships on the subject. It is one of the single most powerful tools a government has ever laid at the feet of biologists. Without a doubt, section 7(a)(2) has produced more directed conservation than any other portion of the Act precisely because biologists are able to impose mitigation requirements, methods, and procedures without real negotiation.

Consultations that may result in a jeopardy opinion effortlessly halt or significantly alter federal and nonfederal nexus projects alike. The threat of a jeopardy opinion can change an agency's underlying mission. Mitigation costs and their multiplying effect to avoid a jeopardy opinion are of great concern to action agencies and nonfederal applicants for federal approval alike. The application and scope of section 7 is without limits, expansive, and sometimes without relationship to the underlying project.

However, an unintended consequence of this power is that it has masked the fact that Section 7-inspired conservation is anathema to planned conservation or attempts to apply a logical framework to recovery. Section 7(a)(2) is triggered through an agency action, most often to approve a federal permit or license administered by an agency. The haphazard nature of the conservation this process produces relies on the vagaries of the application process. This generates within its biological reviewers a yearning need to "get while the getting is good." This precise attitude is one that generates a great deal of dissatisfaction with FWS and causes representative constituencies to complain about the Act. All of this is because a logical framework for recovery planning does not exist.

Instead of exacting as much as can be snatched from each proposed action under section 7(a)(2), the Act should be applied through one of the many existing models of habitat and property valuation that will consider the impact of the federal action in relationship to the whole of the habitat unit designated by the Secretary. What is the landowner's cost in acquiring, replacing, or improving a specific portion of habitat? At what point does any modification of habitat so diminish the value of critical habitat as a whole as to frustrate the intent of the Secretary in designating the habitat in the first place?

By establishing the cost of replacing and repairing habitat we can, just as the law of supply and demand compels, foster fluctuations in value that can amount to the beginning of a conservation economy. The cost of replacing habitat could then be bought, sold, or traded as any other item in commerce.

It is necessary to begin a debate on recovery. We must begin a lexicon of hope and a legislative structure that results in a transparent process with a permanent appropriation for recovery. A new recovery section in the Act would provide an organized planning process with timetables and public input for recovery plans, tax incentives to promote conservation consistent with recovery planning, and the ability of action agencies to accept mitigation across FWS regional boundaries to give greater strength to planning priorities. Most important, a new recovery section would mean a new source of permanent funding that could not be appropriated for other means. The loss of funds for land and water conservation for budget balancing and other purposes is a national disgrace. If endangered and threatened species are important enough to us, and they are, and we want to see them recover, and we do, why not recognize that real federal funding for real species recovery is critical?

The Act is a time capsule, and each time it is opened we have to deal with the fact that its fabric is crumbling over time. The sooner we realize the limitations of the current statutory text and open ourselves up to the possibilities of the future, the better. In many ways, we have become prisoners of the words at the expense of the job at hand.

I have advocated some specific changes that should be made to make the Act more transparent, thereby decreasing the incentive for litigation. This amounts to legislative housekeeping; but our current house is in disorder. With recognition of the considerable benefits of doing away with critical habitat as a concept, I have recommended only a delay in designation until Congress has a plan for recovery. I have recommended a new recovery statute with its own separate appropriation.

Nearly twenty years ago, the Keystone Center in Colorado came up with the recommendation that landowner incentives should be promoted as a way to involve property owners into the administration of the Act. These recommendations became Secretary Babbitt's 10-point plan. This was, for its time, a revolution in ESA philosophy. By promoting HCPs and planning, Keystone and Secretary Babbitt signaled their willingness to accommodate the capitalistic motives of the owners of property. The attempt was ultimately frustrated, but the lesson was clear. By utilizing the forces of the economy, we have a much better chance of making real change for the environment than our current and failed model for conservation planning.

Rather than depend on slipshod conservation driven by the vagaries of section 7(a)(2) biological opinions, the implementation of the Act should be focused on the need to plan habitat conservation; assign a cost for its acquisition, repair, or creation; and fund that cost on an open market driven by mitigation costs for landowners in poor quality habitat areas. Rather than require on-site mitigation on development in poor quality habitat areas, we should acquire, repair, or create habitat.

Fixing the cost of habitat remediation and conservation would create a market for conservation credits. The purchase, sale, and trade of credits related to endangered and threatened species is not a new idea. Many parties have written about this idea adapted from wetlands banking. Much more work on the structure of market mitigation needs to be done.

An owner of property with marginal habitat that could be efficiently conserved or improved to recover species and fit within a overall strategy for recovery (wrapped with the appropriate restrictions) ought to be able to certify the cost of improving the quality of the habitat and offer those improvements for sale to those landowners of property who cannot, without extraordinary or disproportionate cost, improve their poor quality, low value habitat.

Rather than perpetuating a test of wills at the biological level, we must change the nature of the discussion into how can we utilize the structure of our market economy, a conservation economy, to change the environment for the better while adding planning, informed designation, and other positive changes to the process.

By being able to quantify the cost of mitigation, development could continue knowing that the quantifiable debt to the environment will be paid per acre and that the cost of that debt will be borne in portion by each purchaser. Infill projects could be encouraged with incentives to avoid mitigation costs. The scourge of patchwork conservation would end its inefficient reign over the Act.

Notes

1. Albeit without the use of the God Squad (the Endangered Species Committee Section7(e)–(o)), a concept the drafters felt so compelling that they devoted pages to procedures for exemptions allowing the take of species and hardly anything for the recovery of them.
2. Federal action agencies also are not allowed to act in a way that will, by deed or misdeed, jeopardize the continued existence of a species or lead to the destruction or adverse modification of critical habitat. As the conjunctive "or" suggests in the sentence, destruction of critical habitat and adverse modification of critical habitat are similar but differing states, in relative descending order. 16 U.S.C.§ 1536(a)(2).
3. *Id.* § 1533(a)(3)(B). The Secretary's wings are clipped when it comes to designating habitat. In (B)(iii), "[n]othing in this paragraph affects the obligation of the Department of Defense to comply with section 1538 of this title, including the prohibition preventing extinction and taking of endangered species and threatened species."
4. The oft-stated primary purpose of the designation of critical habitat is to ensure that all federal agencies consult with the Service so that "any action authorized, funded, or carried out" by an agency "is not likely to jeopardize the continued existence of any endangered species or threatened species or result in the destruction or adverse modification of [critical] habitat of such species," unless the agency has been granted an exemption. 16 U.S.C. § 1536(a)(2); *see also* 16 U.S.C. § 1536(a)(3) (requiring federal agencies to consult with the Service on any prospective agency action at the request of a prospective permit or license applicant).
5. *Id.* § 1533(4)(b)(2). The Secretary shall designate critical habitat, and make revisions thereto, under subsection (a)(3) of this section on the basis of the best scientific data available and after taking into consideration the economic impact, the impact on national security, and any other relevant impact, of specifying any particular area as critical habitat. The Secretary may exclude any area from critical habitat if he determines that the benefits of such exclusion outweigh the benefits of specifying such area as part of the critical habitat, unless he determines, based on the best scientific and commercial data available, that the failure to designate such area as critical habitat will result in the extinction of the species concerned. *Id.* § 1536(a)(2); *see also id.* § 1536(a)(3) (requiring federal agencies to consult with the Service on any prospective agency action at the request of a prospective permit or license applicant).

6. Sections 8 and 9 establish the Secretary's relationship with the International community and criminal violators of the Act.
7. The last attempt at a major reauthorization of the Act was made a decade ago. A pragmatic ESA reauthorization bill in 1997 was torpedoed by the House Western Republican Caucus after the bill received clearance to proceed from the White House, the Senate, and House leadership in a bipartisan fashion. That the self-same author of that legislation (Dirk Kempthorne as sponsor along with cosponsors Senators Chafee, Baucus, and Reid) now sits as the Secretary of the Department of Interior is just irony.
8. The ESA was not an attempt by Congress to add an affirmative duty to recover species to the jurisdiction of federal agencies. The ESA merely considers recovery and does so without even a proper definition. Recovered off the list is a point on a continuum between extinction, jeopardy, survival, conservation, and recovery. It is not possible to twist a duty to recover out of the Act.
9. Administration's New Assurance Policy Tells Landowners: "No Surprises" in Endangered Species Planning ("Interior News Release") (Aug. 11, 1994).
10. Numerous examples of the long delays in HCP approval and associated high costs for plan operation and review have degraded the value of this administration tool for prompting conservation.
11. http://ecos.fws.gov/tess_public/TESSBoxscore. These figures change consistently enough that a daily summary is posted.
12. *Id.*
13. 16 U.S.C. § 1533(b)(6).
14. Interview with Secretary of Interior Dirk Kempthorne (Nov. 17, 2008).
15. Then Senate Majority leader Trent Lott's representatives had insisted on no change to the critical habitat process. Intensive negotiation resulted in S. 1180's forward-thinking provisions.
16. 73 Fed. Reg. 28,212 (May 15, 2008).
17. 16 U.S.C. § 1531(b).
18. Section 6 state agreements are not considered here.
19. The costs are astronomical. For a well-cited discussion on the costs in the United Kingdom of addressing planet-wide warming, see STERN REVIEW ON THE ECONOMICS OF CLIMATE CHANGE pt. III (HM Treasury, Office of Climate Change, 2006), *available at* http://www.hm-treasury.gov.uk/stern_review_report.htm.
20. 16 U.S.C. § 1533(b)(2) (emphasis added).
21. *Id.*
22. Interview with Secretary of Interior Dirk Kempthorne (Nov. 17, 2008).
23. Affirmative actions, such as ensuring adequate food supplies, maintaining genetic variability, and limiting competition, should be considered.
24. Insofar as the species is concerned there is probably little difference between waiting for global warming and the human palate.
25. 16 U.S.C. § 1531(b).
26. Gifford Pinchot Task Force v. U.S. Fish and Wildlife Serv., 378 F.3d 1059 (9th Cir. 2004). To paraphrase the court, a critical habitat designation must serve alternately as survival habitat, recuperation habitat, and recovery habitat for all threatened and endangered species. Therefore, according to the court, designation of critical habitat, which occurs at the beginning of the listing process, must also take into account the habitat necessary for recovery of the species. By requiring the Secretary to consider survival and recovery within the initial designation of critical habitat, the court is requiring the Secretary to do what is not required by statute. How does the Secretary consider recovery in the final designation of critical habitat? The Secretary has not yet gone through the recovery planning process in section (4)(f). The Secretary has not had an opportunity to determine if a recovery plan is not necessary section under (4)(f), and the public has not yet had an opportunity to comment on recovery measures applied to the habitat section

4)(f)(4). The Secretary's authority to consider recovery does not even trigger until the procedures of section 4(b) have been completed.
27. 16 U.S.C. §§ 1533, 1535, 1536, 1538.
28. *Id.* § 1536.
29. Sierra Club v. U.S. Fish and Wildlife Serv., 245 F.3d 434 (5th Cir. 2001). In this case, the Sierra Club asserted that the definition of adverse modification that was applied by the Service "set(s) the bar too high, because the adverse modification threshold is not triggered by a proposed action until there is an appreciable diminishment of the value of critical habitat for both survival *and* recovery." The court agreed.
30. 50 C.F.R. § 402.02.
31. *Id.*
32. *Id.*
33. *Id.*
34. ". . . modifying any of those physical or biological features that were the basis for determining the habitat to be critical." *Id.*
35. It should be clear to even the most detached observers that the real crisis facing threatened and endangered species is a lack of funding from Congress. This is because seldom, if ever, does a constituent slap a congressperson on the back and offer congratulations for the exactions required to get a permit through the FWS. It is unlikely that funds necessary to proactively address the problem will be forthcoming considering the current funding shortfalls and the unfortunate general lack of funding regard for the FWS.
36. "appreciably diminishes the value of critical habitat for . . . survival . . . of a listed species." 50 C.F.R. § 402.02.
37. 16 U.S.C. § 1536(a)(2).
38. *Id.* § 1533(a)(3)(A)(ii).
39. *Id.* § 1533(b)(2).
40. *Id.* § 1533(f)(1).

Table of Cases

Adair, United States v., 143n47
Agins v. City of Tiburon, 310n30
Alabama v. U.S. Army Corps of Eng'rs, 151, 186n65, 186n71, 187n78, 190n132, 288n125
Alabama-Tombigbee Rivers Coal. v. Dep't of Interior, 38n114
Alabama-Tombigbee Rivers Coal. v. Kempthorne, 65n69, 156n21, 284n99
Allegretti & Co. v. County of Imperial, 313n83
Allen v. Wright, 277n11
Alsea Valley Alliance v. Evans, 24, 37n82
Am. Bald Eagle v. Bhatti, 151, 158n54, 185n42, 186n69, 187n75
Am. Bird Conservancy v. Kempthorne, 281n51
Am. Rivers & Idaho Rivers United, *In re*, 283n83
Am. Rivers v. U.S. Army Corps of Eng'rs, 289–290n138
Am. Soc'y for the Prev. of Cruelty to Animals v. Ringling Bros. and Barnum & Bailey Circus, 317 F.3d 334 (D.C. Cir. 2003), 278n21
Am. Soc'y for the Prev. of Cruelty to Animals v. Ringling Bros. and Barnum & Bailey Circus, 502 F. Supp. 2d 103 (D.D.C. 2007), 290n145, 291n146
Am. Wildlands v. Kempthorne, 37n72
Amoco Prod. Co. v. Vill. of Gambell, 186n73, 187n80
Andrus v. Allard, 308, 315n113
Animal Protection Institute v. Holsten, 153
Animal Welfare Institute v. Martin, 290n138
Appolo Fuels, Inc. v. United States, 309n7, 313n94, 314n100, 315n118
Arizona v. California, 130, 141n31, 142nn44–46
Arizona v. San Carlos Apache Tribe, 142n45
Ariz. Cattle Growers Ass'n v. Fish & Wildlife Serv., 123n66, 124n100, 170, 186n59, 189n120
Ariz. Cattle Growers Ass'n v. Kempthorne, 391n25

Ass'n of Cal. Water Agencies v. Evans, 266, 282n73
Ass'n of Data Processing Serv. Orgs., Inc. v. Camp, 281n64
Atl. Green Sea Turtle v. County Council of Volusia County, Fla., 233, 245n118, 276, 290n143, 291nn146–147
Babbitt v. Sweet Home Chapter of Cmtys. for a Great Or., 7n29, 62n5, 64n45, 148, 150–151, 156nn13–19, 162, 165, 168–169, 173–177, 183n17, 184n29, 310n37, 349–350, 362, 367
Barrett v. State, 307
Bennett v. Spear, 26, 149, 264, 265–268, 277n9, 278n19, 279nn29–30, 280n47, 280n50, 281–282nn64–65, 281nn53–57, 291n148, 371n30, 371n35
Bensman v. U.S. Forest Serv., 103n191, 151
Bernstein/Glazer, LLC v. Babbitt, 38n137
Billie, United States v., 130–133, 143n51, 143n53, 143n63, 143n68, 143nn65–66, 157n41
Biodiversity Legal Found. v. Babbitt, 63 F. Supp. 2d 31 (D.D.C. 1999), 38n109
Biodiversity Legal Found. v. Babbitt, 146 F.3d 1249 (10th Cir. 1998), 65n78, 283n93
Biodiversity Legal Found. v. Babbitt, No. 96-00227-SS, 1996 U.S. Dist. LEXIS 15322 (D.D.C. Oct. 10, 1996), 37n87
Biodiversity Legal Found. v. Badgley, 309 F.3d 1166 (9th Cir. 2002), 68n137, 265, 278n25, 280n39, 280nn41–44, 289n135
Biodiversity Legal Found. v. Badgley, 1999 WL 1042567 (D. Or. 1999), 38n109, 55, 68n137
Biodiversity Legal Found. v. Norton, 65n71, 65n73, 103n194, 283nn80–82
Boise Cascade Corp. v. Dep't of Forestry, 156n25, 311n56
Boise Cascade Corp. v. United States, 148, 302, 307–308, 311n55
Bouchard, United States v., 141n33
Brendale v. Confederated Tribes and Bands of the Yakima Indian Nation, 140n16

Bresette, United States v., 143n69
Buckhannon Bd. & Care Home, Inc. v. W. Va. Dep't of Health & Human Res., 282n74
Building Industry Association of Superior California v. Babbitt, 51, 66nn92–94
Butte Environmental Coalition v. White, 51
Cabinet Mountains Wilderness v. Peterson, 284n96
Cabinet Res. Group v. U.S. Forest Serv., 103n188
California v. Kempthorne, 125n146
California v. Watt, 186n65
Cal. Farm Bureau Fed'n v. Dep't of Interior, 38n138
Cal. Plant Soc'y v. Norton, 35n8
Cal. Sportfishing Prot. Alliance v. Fed. Energy Regulatory Comm'n, 125n146
Cape Hatteras Access Pres. Alliance v. U.S. Dep't of Interior, 45, 61, 63nn36–37, 64n55
Carlton v. Babbitt, 36n69, 89, 103n179, 284n97
Carlton v. Interior Dep't, 36n68
Carroll Towing Co., United States v., 92n15
Cary v. Hall, 278n22
Casitas Mun. Water Dist. v. United States, 76 Fed. Cl. 100 (2007), 293, 302–303, 313n85
Casitas Mun. Water Dist. v. United States, 2008 WL 4349234 (Fed. Cir. 2008), 156–157nn28–29
Castlewood Prod. v. Norton, 264 F. Supp. 2d 9 (D.D.C. 2003), 258n50
Castlewood Prod. v. Norton, 365 F.3d 1076 (D.C. Cir. 2004), 258n51
Catron County Bd. of Comm'rs v. U.S. Fish & Wildlife Serv., 61, 357n30
CBD v. Point Marina Development, 152
Cetacean Cmty. v. Bush, 157n46
Cherokee Nation v. Georgia, 128, 139n4, 140nn18–19
Chevron U.S.A., Inc. v. Natural Res. Def. Council, 185n33, 283n95
Childers v. Wm. H. Coleman Co., 258n77
Christy v. Hodel, 37n96, 148, 306–307, 311n48, 313n89, 315n119
Citizens for Better Forestry v. U.S. Dep't of Agric., 278–279nn25–26
Citizens to Pres. Overton Park v. Volpe, 158n56, 284n100, 285n103

City of Las Vegas v. Lujan, 37nn74–77
City of Monterey v. Del Monte Dunes at Monterey Ltd., 295, 309–310n9
Clajon Prod. Corp. v. Petera, 313n89
Coal. for Sustainable Res. v. U.S. Forest Serv., 372n53
Coal. of Ariz./N.M. Counties for Stable Economic Growth v. Babbitt, 288n128
Coast Range Conifers, LLC v. State *ex rel.* Or. State Bd. of Forestry, 312n79, 313n90
Coastside Habitat Coal. v. Prime Props., Inc., 189n120
Cobell v. Norton, 140n21, 140n23
Cold Mountain v. Garber, 185n43
Colo. River Water Conservation Dist. v. United States, 142n45
Colorado Wildlife Federation v. Turner, 53
Colorado Wildlife Federation v. U.S. Fish and Wildlife Service, 52
Colville Confederated Tribes v. Walton, 143n47
Common Sense Salmon Recovery v. Evans, 217 F. Supp. 2d 17 (D.D.C. 2002), 284n102
Common Sense Salmon Recovery v. Evans, 329 F. Supp. 2d 96 (D.D.C. 2004), 287n124
Confederated Salish & Kottenai Tribes v. Namen, 143n47
Confederated Tribes of the Umatilla Reservation v. Alexander, 140n22, 143n70
Conner v. Burford, 116
Conservation Council for Haw. v. Babbitt, 51, 68n137
Conservation Northwest v. Kempthorne, 85, 283nn84–86
Cook v. State, 311n48
Covelo Indian Cmty. v. FERC, 140n21
CropLife Am. v. Wash. Toxics Coal., 158n76, 282n66, 284n96, 284n98, 289n136, 289nn133–134
Ctr. for Biological Diversity v. Babbitt, 283–284n96
Ctr. for Biological Diversity v. Badgley, 38n108
Ctr. for Biological Diversity v. Bureau of Land Mgmt., 58–59, 103n181, 103n191
Ctr. for Biological Diversity v. Clark, 280n37
Ctr. for Biological Diversity v. Evans, 52–53, 283n83

Ctr. for Biological Diversity v. Hamilton, 54–55

Ctr. for Biological Diversity v. Kempthorne, 2008 WL 659822 (D. Ariz. 2008), 391n32

Ctr. for Biological Diversity v. Kempthorne, No. CV-08-5546 (N.D. Cal. 2008), 125n145

Ctr. for Biological Diversity v. Lohn, 37n100

Ctr. for Biological Diversity v. Marina Point Dev. Co., 185n44

Ctr. for Biological Diversity v. Morganweck, 37n102

Ctr. for Biological Diversity v. Norton, 240 F. Supp. 2d 1090 (D. Ariz. 2003), 45, 63nn39–40

Ctr. for Biological Diversity v. Norton, 262 F.3d 1077 (10th Cir. 2001), 282n73

Ctr. for Biological Diversity v. Norton, 304 F. Supp. 2d 1174 (D. Ariz. 2003), 55

Ctr. for Biological Diversity v. Norton, 336 F. Supp. 2d 1149 (D.N.M. 2004) (Magistrate), 286n107

Ctr. for Biological Diversity v. Norton, 2002 WL 32136200 (D. Ariz. 2002), 285n103, 286n107

Ctr. for Biological Diversity v. Norton, 2003 WL 22225620 (S.D. Cal. 2003), 68n140

Ctr. for Biological Diversity v. U.S. Fish & Wildlife Serv., 202 F. Supp. 2d 594 (W.D. Tex. 2002), 103n188, 229, 232, 243nn78–79, 245nn112–114

Ctr. for Biological Diversity v. U.S. Fish & Wildlife Serv., 450 F.3d 930 (9th Cir. 2006), 65n72

Ctr. for Biological Diversity v. U.S. Fish & Wildlife Serv., 2005 WL 2000928 (N.D. Cal. Aug. 19, 2005), 38n112

Ctr. for Biological Diversity v. U.S. Marine Corps, 285–286nn104–106

Ctr. for Marine Conservation v. Brown, 183n10

Defenders of Wildlife v. Adm'r, EPA, 371n25

Defenders of Wildlife v. Babbitt, 130 F. Supp. 2d 121 (D.D.C. 2001), 83, 93n32, 372n53

Defenders of Wildlife v. Babbitt, 958 F. Supp. 670 (D.D.C. 1997), 36n70

Defenders of Wildlife v. Babbitt, 1999 U.S. Dist. LEXIS 10366 (S.D. Cal. June 14, 1999), 37n99

Defenders of Wildlife v. Babbitt, No. 99-206 (D.D.C. Oct. 8, 1999), 287n119

Defenders of Wildlife v. Bernal, 169–170, 176, 186n55, 186n70, 187n75, 189n120, 189nn116–118

Defenders of Wildlife v. EPA, 152, 158nn74–76

Defenders of Wildlife v. Gutierrez, 268, 279n27, 282n69, 282nn67–68

Defenders of Wildlife v. Hall, 89–90, 98n142, 103n195

Defenders of Wildlife v. Kempthorne, 392n39

Defenders of Wildlife v. Lujan, 98n134

Defenders of Wildlife v. Martin, 121n12, 284n96

Defenders of Wildlife v. Norton, 258 F.3d 1136 (9th Cir. 2001), 39n152

Defenders of Wildlife v. Norton, 340 F. Supp. 2d 9 (D.D.C. 2002), 37n89

Defenders of Wildlife v. Norton, Civ. A. No. 04-1230 (D.D.C. Aug. 27, 2007), 39n148

Del. River at Stilesville, *In re*, 312n65

Delbay Pharms. v. Dep't of Commerce, 204n57

Deltona Corp. v. United States, 314n103

Dep't of Fish & Game v. Puyallup Tribe, 141n33, 143n67, 143nn47–48

Dep't of Fish and Game v. Anderson-Cottonwood Irrigation District, 350

Dep't of Transp. v. Pub. Citizen, 190n129

Dion, United States v., 130–133, 141n27, 143n49, 143nn54–62

Dolan v. City of Tigard, 310n26

Douglas v. Seacoast Products, Inc., 311n48

Douglas County v. Babbitt, 60–61, 357n30

Douglas County v. Lujan, 60

Dow v. Bernal, 157n38, 158n54, 158n61

Dudman Commc'ns v. Dep't of Air Force, 285n103

E. Cape May Assocs. v. State of New Jersey, 304, 309n8

Endangered Species Comm'n v. Babbitt, 38n113

Enos v. Marsh, 36n46

Envtl. Def. Ctr. v. Babbitt, 68nn135–136

Envtl. Integrity Proj. v. EPA, 185n42

Envtl. Prot. Info. Ctr. v. NMFS, 37n100

Envtl. Prot. Info. Ctr. v. Simpson Timber Co., 124n115, 124n118, 158n61

Envtl. Prot. Info. Ctr. v. Tuttle, 191n150
Envtl. Prot. Info. Ctr. v. U.S. Fish & Wildlife Serv., 245n119
Envtl. Trust, Inc., *In re,* 245n135
EPA v. Mink, 285n103
Esch v. Yeutter, 284n97
Fallini v. United States, 313n89
FEC v. Akins, 278n22
Fed'n of Fly Fishers v. Daley, 218n18
First English Evangelical Lutheran Church v. County of Los Angles, 315n117
Fla. Audubon Soc'y v. Bentsen, 279n27
Fla. Game & Fresh Water Fish Comm'n v. Flotilla, Inc., 314n109
Fla. Home Builders Ass'n v. Kempthorne, 38n139
Fla. Home Builders Ass'n v. Norton, 283n79
Flotilla v. Fla. Game & Fresh Water Fish Comm'n, 304, 313n89
Forest Conservation Council v. Roseboro Lumber Co., 157n34, 158n54, 189n113, 281n62
Forest Conservation Council v. U.S. Forest Serv., 288n128
Forest Guardians v. Babbitt, 53, 55, 65n78, 67n109, 67nn114–116, 282–283n79
Forest Props., Inc. v. United States, 309n6, 313n91
Forest Serv. Employees for Envtl. Ethics v. U.S. Forest Serv., 124n122, 282n66
Friends of Animals v. Kempthorne, 288n128
Friends of Endangered Species v. Jantzen, 241nn11–13
Friends of the Earth, Inc. v. Laidlaw Envtl. Servs., 157n43, 278n21, 280n35, 280n38
Friends of the Wild Swan, Inc. v. U.S. Fish and Wildlife Serv., 36n71, 37n87, 218n18
Fund for Animals, Inc. v. Norton, 288n128
Fund for Animals v. Babbitt, 82–83, 93n31, 97–98n115
Fund for Animals v. Fla. Game and Fresh Water Fish Comm'n, 185n43
Fund for Animals v. Hogan, 35n26, 280n51
Fund for Animals v. Rice, 98n126, 103nn185–188, 372n50
Fund for Animals v. Turner, 290n138
Fund for Animals v. Williams, 284n102
GDF Realty Ltd. v. Norton, 156n21
Geer v. Connecticut, 14n7, 311n46
Gerber v. Babbitt, 232, 244nn110–111

Gerber v. Norton, 244n111, 278n22
Gibbs v. Babbitt, 156n21, 312n69
Gifford Pinchot Task Force v. U.S. Fish & Wildlife Serv., 48, 59, 62n14, 90n2, 100n150, 102n175, 123n90, 392n41, 402–404, 408n26
Glasser v. Nat'l Marine Fisheries Serv., 233, 245n120
Glenn-Colusa Irrigation Dist., United States v., 157n39, 190n133
Glisson v. City of Marion, 697 N.E.2d 433 (Ill. App. Ct. 1998), 358nn60–61
Glisson v. City of Marion, 720 N.E.2d 1034 (Ill. 1999), 358n62
Glover River Org. v. U.S. Dep't of Interior, 36n62
Good v. United States, 304–305, 314nn101–105
Gordon v. Norton, 311n58
Grand Canyon Trust v. Norton, 98n125
Greater Atlanta Homebuilders Ass'n v. DeKalb, 259n80
Greater Yellowstone Coal. v. Flowers, 289n138
Green Acres Land & Cattle Co. v. State, 315n119
Greenpeace v. Nat'l Marine Fisheries Serv., 106 F. Supp. 2d 1066 (W.D. Wash. 2000), 152
Greenpeace v. Nat'l Marine Fisheries Serv., 198 F.R.D. 540 (W.D. Wash. 2000), 285n104
Greenpeace Action v. Franklin, 280n40
Gwaltney of Smithfield, Ltd. v. Chesapeake Bay Found., 189n111
Hallstrom v. Tillamook County, 157n49, 287n121
Hamilton v. Babbitt, 202n11
Hamilton v. City of Austin, 187n79
Hanson v. U.S. Forest Service, 244n91
Hart v. Lucas, 185n42
Havens Realty Corp. v. Coleman, 278n22
Hawksbill Sea Turtle v. FEMA, 11 F. Supp. 2d 529 (D.V.I. 1998), 186n66, 188n98
Hawksbill Sea Turtle v. FEMA, 126 F.3d 461 (3d Cir. 1997), 157n50
Hawksbill Sea Turtle v. FEMA, 939 F. Supp. 1 (D.D.C. 1996), 287n120
Heartwood v. U.S. Forest Serv., 103n191
Herwig, State v., 315n119

Hill, United States v., 308–309
H.J. Justin & Sons, Inc. v. Deukmejian, 333n27
Home Builders Ass'n of N. Cal. v. Norton, 58
Home Builders Ass'n of N. Cal. v. U.S. Fish & Wildlife Serv., 268 F. Supp. 2d 1197 (E.D. Cal. 2003), 45, 56, 63n38, 63n41, 64n54
Home Builders Ass'n of N. Cal. v. U.S. Fish & Wildlife Serv. 2006 WL 3190518 (E.D. Cal. Nov. 2, 2006), 46, 56, 63n33
House v. U.S. Forest Serv., 90–91n3, 152, 158n70
Hughes v. Oklahoma, 356n1
Humane Soc'y of the United States v. Kempthorne, 193
Humane Soc'y of the United States v. Hodel, 288n125
Idaho Farm Bureau Fed'n v. Babbitt, 37n103
In re ———. See name of party
Inst. for Wildlife Prot. v. Norton, 205 Fed. Appx. 483 (9th Cir. 2006), 279n32
Inst. for Wildlife Prot. v. Norton, 303 F. Supp. 2d 1175 (W.D. Wash. 2003), 281n51
Int'l Ctr. for Tech. Assessment v. Thompson, 121n21
Japan Whaling Ass'n v. Am. Cetacean Soc'y, 278n17
Jensen v. City of Everett, 259n80
Johnson v. McIntosh, 128, 139n4
Jumping Frog Research Inst. v. Babbitt, 67n96
Kaiser Aetna v. United States, 310n20
Kake v. Egan, 142n35
Kelo v. City of New London, 310n10
Kepler, United States v., 308–309
Kimball v. Callahan, 142n38, 142n42
Kirby Forest Indus., Inc v. United States, 315n113
Kittitas Reclamation Dist. v. Sunnyside Valley Irrigation Dist., 143n47, 143n70
Klamath Irrigation Dist. v. United States, 148, 311n49, 313n83
Klamath Siskiyou Wildlands Ctr. v. Babbitt, 280n37
Klamath Tribes v. United States, 140n22, 141n25, 143n70
Kleppe v. New Mexico, 259n81
Lac Courte Oreilles Band of Lake Superior Chippewa Indians v. Voigt, 141n33
Lac Courte Oreilles Band of Lake Superior Chippewa v. Wisconsin, 141n25, 141n33
Lake Lawrence Pub. Lands Prot. Ass'n, State v., 309n8, 311n50, 313n89, 313–314n94, 314n108
Lands Council v. McNair, 244n91
Lingle v. Chevron U.S.A. Inc., 294, 295, 310n9, 310n15, 310n17
Lockyer v. U.S. Dep't of Agric., 244n91
Loggerhead Turtle v. County Council of Volusia County, Fla., 92 F. Supp. 2d 1296 (M.D. Fla. 2000), 103n180, 180, 191n151
Loggerhead Turtle v. County Council of Volusia County, Fla., 148 F.3d 1231 (11th Cir. 1998), 153, 157n40, 158n54, 159n94, 190n142, 287n124
Loggerhead Turtle v. Volusia County, 289n138
Lone Wolf v. Hitchcock, 139n6
Loretto v. Teleprompter Manhattan CATV Corp., 294
Louisiana *ex rel.* Guste v. Verity, 183n10, 204n56
Lucas v. S.C. Coastal Council, 294, 299, 300–301, 303, 306, 310n11, 310n23, 310n29, 312nn67–69, 314n105, 315n135
Lujan v. Defenders of Wildlife, 36n63, 157n42, 263–264, 277–278nn10–18, 277n8, 278nn20–24, 279n30
Lujan v. Nat'l Wildlife Fed'n, 157n45, 277n10, 278n18
Maine v. Dir., U.S. Fish and Wildlife Serv., 288n129
Maitland v. People, 315n124
Man Hing Ivory & Imps., Inc. v. Deukmejian, 338n27
Marbled Murrelet v. Babbitt, 121n20, 151, 157n51, 159n94, 188n89, 287n124, 289n132
Marbled Murrelet v. Lujan, 37n104
McCrary v. Gutierrez, 286n111
McDonald, Sommer & Frates v. Yolo County, 311n52
McKittrick, United States v., 155n2, 197–198, 203n23
McLanahan v. Ariz. State Tax Comm'n, 139n5
McQueen v. S.C. Coastal Council, 312n70

Table of Cases | 415

Menominee Tribe v. United States, 141nn26–27, 141–142n34, 142nn40–42
Meredith v. Talbot, 311n58
Merrion v. Jicarilla Apache Tribe, 139n5
Miccosukee Tribe of Indians of Fla. v. United States, 144n75
Miccosukee v. United States, 124n129
Middle Rio Grande Conservancy Dist. v. Norton, 61–62, 103n191
Minnesota v. Mille Lacs Band of Chippewa, 141n33
Mitchell, United States v., 140n23
Moden v. U.S. Fish & Wildlife Serv., 37n102
Moerman v. California, 307, 313n89
Montana, United States v., 142n35
Montana v. United States, 140n16
Montrose Chem. Corp. v. Train, 285n103
Morrill v. Lujan, 98n125, 151, 186n65, 190n134
Morris v. United States, 149, 157nn30–31, 298–299
Mountain Lion Found. v. Fish & Game Comm'n, 357n29
Mountain States Legal Found. v. Hodel, 315n119
Muckelshoot v. Hall, 143n70
Mugler v. Kansas, 315n115
N. Spotted Owl v. Hodel, 22–23, 36nn64–67
N. Spotted Owl v. Lujan, 53
Nance v. EPA, 140n21
Native Fed'n of the Madre De Dios River & Tributaries v. Bozovich Timber Prod., Inc., 258n52
Nat'l Ass'n of Home Builders v. Babbitt, 103n178, 156n21, 312n69
Nat'l Ass'n of Home Builders v. Defenders of Wildlife, 118–119, 121, 121nn16–17, 124n116, 190n145
Nat'l Ass'n of Home Builders v. Evans, 57, 69nn156–157
Nat'l Ass'n of Home Builders v. Kempthorne, 37n81
Nat'l Ass'n of Home Builders v. Norton, 309 F.3d 26 (D.C. Cir. 2002), 66–67n94
Nat'l Ass'n of Home Builders v. Norton, 340 F.3d 835 (9th Cir. 2003), 37n80
Nat'l Ass'n of Home Builders v. Norton, 415 F.3d 8 (D.C. Cir. 2005), 282n68
Nat'l Ass'n of Home Builders v. U.S. Army Corps of Eng'rs, 279n33

Nat'l Audubon Soc'y v. Hester, 84–85, 98nn127–129
Nat'l Audubon Soc'y v. Superior Court, 312n71
Nat'l Mining Ass'n v. Fowler, 279n33
Nat'l Mining Ass'n v. U.S. Army Corps of Eng'rs, 280n34
Nat'l Park Hospitality Ass'n v. Dep't of the Interior, 279n32
Nat'l Wildlife Fed'n v. Babbitt, 228, 245n113
Nat'l Wildlife Fed'n v. Brownlee, 282n66
Nat'l Wildlife Fed'n v. Burlington N. R.R., 154, 186n72, 186n74, 187n75, 187n77
Nat'l Wildlife Fed'n v. FEMA, 282n66
Nat'l Wildlife Fed'n v. Nat'l Marine Fisheries Serv., 254 F. Supp. 1196 (D. Or. 2003), 218n18
Nat'l Wildlife Fed'n v. Nat'l Marine Fisheries Serv., 422 F.3d 782 (9th Cir. 2005), 289n138, 290nn139–140
Nat'l Wildlife Fed'n v. Nat'l Marine Fisheries Serv., 481 F.3d 1224 (9th Cir. 2007), 59, 118–119, 123n72, 123n86, 123n90, 124nn131–132
Nat'l Wildlife Fed'n v. Nat'l Marine Fisheries Serv., 524 F.3d 917 (9th Cir. 2008), 102n175, 392n41
Nat'l Wildlife Fed'n v. Nat'l Park Serv., 84–85, 98nn130–131, 122n34
Nat'l Wildlife Fed'n v. Norton, 332 F. Supp 2d 179 (D.D.C. 2004), 123n82
Nat'l Wildlife Fed'n v. Norton, 386 F. Supp. 2d 553 (D. Vt. 2005), 92n24, 93n32
Nat'l Wildlife Fed'n v. Norton, No. CIV-S-04-0579 DFL JF, 2005 WL 2175874 (E.D. Cal. Sept. 7, 2005), 243n76
Natural Resources Defense Council v. Kempthorne, 59–60, 230, 243–244nn83–88
Natural Resources Defense Council v. U.S. Department of the Interior, 51, 66nn90–91
Nettleton Co. v. Diamond, 347, 356n12
Nevada v. United States, 141n26, 141n28
New Mexico, United States v., 142n44, 143n46
New Mexico v. Mescalero Apache Tribe, 139n6
New Mexico Cattle Growers Ass'n v. U.S. Fish and Wildlife Service, 57

Newell Cos., Inc. v. Kenney Mfg. Co., 314n105
Newton County Wildlife Ass'n v. Rogers, 284n96
N.M. Citizens for Clean Air & Water v. Espanola Mercantile Co., 157n52
Nollan v. Cal. Coastal Comm'n, 310n25
Northern California River Watch v. Wilcox, 257n29
Norton v. Southern Utah Wilderness Alliance, 270
Nuesca, United States v., 200
Nw. Ecosystem Alliance v. U.S. Fish & Wildlife Serv., 37n79, 283nn93–94, 284n96
Nw. Envtl. Advocates v. U.S. E.P.A., 121n11
Nw. Forest Res. Council v. Babbitt, 286n111, 287n119
Nw. Forest Res. Council v. Glickman, 288n126
Nw. Sea Farms v. Army Corps of Eng'rs, 141n25
Oceana, Inc. v. Evans, 284n97
Office of Pers. Mgmt. v. Richmond, 190n138
Ohio Mfrs. Ass'n v. City of Akron, 185n42
Or. Natural Res. Council v. Brown, 37n99
Or. Natural Res. Council v. Daley, 37n86
Or. Natural Res. Council v. Turner, 82, 97nn110–114
Oregon Natural Desert Ass'n v. Lohn, 59
Pac. Coast Federation of Fisherman's Ass'ns v. Gutierrez, 230, 244nn89–91
Pac. Legal Found. v. Andrus, 38nn110–111, 60
Pac. Rivers Council v. Brown, 2002 WL 32356431 (D. Or. 2002), 190n143
Pac. Rivers Council v. Brown, 2003 WL 21087974 (D. Or. 2003), 187n77, 190n143
Pac. Rivers Council v. Brown, 2004 WL 2091471 (D. Or. 2004), 180–181, 191n152
Pac. Rivers Council v. Thomas, 121n19, 122n28
Palazzolo v. Rhode Island, 301, 304, 310n23
Palila v. Haw. Dep't of Land & Natural Res., 471 F. Supp. 985 (D. Haw. 1979), 64n45, 88, 147, 163, 183n19, 189n123, 241n9

Palila v. Haw. Dep't of Land & Natural Res., 649 F. Supp. 1070 (D. Haw. 1986), 147, 155–156nn11–12, 164, 183n25, 183n26, 185n37, 188–189n110, 189n114, 242n21
Palm Beach Isles Assocs. v. United States, 314n105
Parravano v. Babbitt, 141n25, 141n31
Penn Central Transp. Co. v. New York City, 294, 301, 303–306
Pennsylvania Coal Co. v. Mahon, 314–315n113
Penzoil-Quaker State Co. & Subsidiaries v. United States, 309n4
Petroleum Info. Corp. v. U.S. Dep't of the Interior, 284–285n103
Pierson v. Post, 258n76
Piper Aircraft Co. v. Reyno, 286nn116–117
Protect Our Eagles' Trees v. City of Lawrence, 281n62
Protect Our Water v. Flowers, 186n65, 187n75, 189n120
Puyallup Tribe v. Dep't of Game, 391 U.S. 392 (1968), 141n33, 142n36
Puyallup Tribe v. Dep't of Game, 443 U.S. 165 (1977), 141n33
Pyramid Lake Paiute Tribe of Indians v. U.S. Dep't of the Navy, 90n3, 121n6, 121n10, 190n131
Pyramid Lake Paiute Tribe v. Morton, 140n21, 140n22, 141n24
Ramsey v. Kantor, 371n33
Rancho Viejo LLC v. Norton, 156n21
Rio Grande Silvery Minnow v. Keys, 103n191
Riverside Bayview Homes, United States v., 311n54
Riverside Irrigation Dist. v. Andrews, 123n75
S. Appalachian Biodiversity Project v. U.S. Fish & Wildlife Serv., 67n133
S. Dakota v. Yankton Sioux Tribe, 141n27
S. Pac. Terminal Co. v. ICC, 280n39
S. Utah Wilderness Alliance v. Smith, 280n37
Safari Club Int'l v. Babbitt, 341n95
Salmon Spawning & Recovery Alliance v. Basham, 124n116, 191n149
San Carlos Apache Tribe v. United States, 151, 186n65

San Luis & Delta Mendota Water Auth. v. Dep't of Interior, 38n138
San Luis & Delta-Mendota Water Auth. v. Badgley, 37n88
Santa Clara Pueblo v. Martinez, 140n14
Save Our Springs v. Babbitt, 37n85, 218n18
Save the Yaak Committee v. Block, 150
Schloeffler v. Kempthorne, 54–55
Scotia Development, *In re*, 244n91
Scranton v. Wheeler, 312n59
Seattle Audubon Soc'y v. Sutherland, 2007 WL 1300964 (W.D. Wash. 2007), 159n83, 190n143, 191n153
Seattle Audubon Soc'y v. Sutherland, 2007 WL 1577756 (W.D. Wash. 2007), 181, 190n143, 191n154
Seattle Audubon Soc'y v. Sutherland, 2007 WL 2220256 (W.D. Wash. 2007), 289n138
Seiber v. United States, 156n25, 302, 304, 313n91
Seminole Nation v. United States, 140n20
Shellnut v. Ark. State Game & Fish Comm'n, 315n119
Sierra Club v. Antwerp, 286n115, 287n120
Sierra Club v. Babbitt, 121n9, 124n115
Sierra Club v. Clark, 37n96, 193
Sierra Club v. Dep't of Forestry & Fire Prot., 300, 311n56
Sierra Club v. EPA, 157n44
Sierra Club v. Flowers, 287n120
Sierra Club v. Glickman, 121n11, 121n14, 158n55, 372n52
Sierra Club v. Kempthorne, 245n117
Sierra Club v. Lujan, 81–82, 84–85, 97nn105–109, 98nn135–136
Sierra Club v. Marsh, 122n35, 289nn132–133
Sierra Club v. Norton, 233, 245nn116–117
Sierra Club v. Peterson, 158n57
Sierra Club v. Thomas, 269–270, 283n82
Sierra Club v. U.S. Fish and Wildlife Serv., 47–48, 51, 59, 62n14, 403, 408n29
Sierra Club v. Yeutter, 157n35, 157n49, 177, 189nn121–122
Silver v. Thomas, 68n135
Sohappy v. Smith, 142n35
Sour Mountain Realty, State v., 299–300, 315n118
Southview Assocs., Ltd. v. Bongartz, 313n89

Species of Wildlife, United States v., 204n57
Spirit of the Sage Council v. Kempthorne, 242–243nn51–55, 279n31, 280n34
Spirit of the Sage Council v. Norton, 242n40, 242nn46–47
State v. ———. *See name of opposing party*
Steuart Transp. Co., *In re*, 312n71
Stockton E. Water Dist. v. United States, 313n85
Stop H-3 Ass'n v. Lewis, 350
Strahan v. Coxe, 103n177, 152–153, 157n36, 158–159nn77–83, 159n94, 180, 190n141
Strahan v. Linnon, 97n115, 98n125, 191n147
Strahan v. Pritchard, 180, 187n75, 191n146
Summers v. Earth Island Institute, 277n16
Super Tire Eng'g Co. v. McCorkle, 280n44
Sw. Ctr. for Biological Diversity v. Babbitt, 215 F.3d 58 (D.C. Cir. 2000), 37n73
Sw. Ctr. for Biological Diversity v. Babbitt, 939 F. Supp. 49 (D.D.C. 1996), 37n87
Sw. Ctr. for Biological Diversity v. Babbitt, 1999 WL 33438081 (D. Ariz. Sept. 3, 1999), 98nn120–122
Sw. Ctr. for Biological Diversity v. Bartel, 89, 98n125, 229–230, 392n44
Sw. Ctr. for Biological Diversity v. Norton, 215 F.3d 58 (D.C. Cir. 2000), 371n29
Sw. Ctr. for Biological Diversity v. Norton, 2002 WL 1733618 (D.D.C. 2002), 37n98, 284n97
Sw. Ctr. for Biological Diversity v. U.S. Bureau of Reclamation, 157n51, 287nn121–124
Sw. Ctr. for Biological Diversity v. U.S. Forest Serv., 288n128
Swan View Coal., Inc. v. Turner, 158n70, 186n65, 188n99
Sweet Home Chapter of Cmtys. for a Great Or. v. Babbitt, 37n92, 161–166, 183n8, 184–185nn31–35, 185nn37–39, 187n83, 188–189nn105–110, 188nn92–94, 188nn101–103, 189–190nn126–128, 189n112, 189n114, 191n159
Sweet Home Chapter of Cmtys. for a Great Or. v. Lujan, 165, 168–169, 173–177, 184n29
Sweet Home Chapter of Cmtys. for a Great Or. v. Turner, 165, 184n28

Tahoe-Sierra Pres. Council, Inc. v. Tahoe Reg'l Planning Council, 156n24, 295, 301, 303
Telecommns. Research & Action Ctr. v. FCC, 283n82
Tennessee Valley Authority v. Hill, 35n9, 41, 43, 107, 117, 132, 153–154, 184n33, 204n56, 221, 274, 288nn130–131, 314n110, 371n11
Tinno, State v., 142n38
Town of Plymouth, United States v., 153, 157n37
Trbovich v. United Mine Workers, 288n127
Tribal Vill. of Akutan v. Hodel, 124n99
Triggs v. Kahn, 258n77
Trout Unlimited v. Lohn, 2006 WL 1207901 (W.D. Wash. 2006), 284nn100–101, 285–286n106
Trout Unlimited v. Lohn, 2007 WL 1795036 (W.D. Wash. June 13, 2007), 24–25
Trout Unlimited v. U.S. Dep't of Agric., 236n118
Tulare Lake Basin v. United States, 148
Tulare Lake Basin Water Storage District v. United States, 293, 302–303, 309nn4–5
United States v. ———. *See name of opposing party*
Voyageurs Nat'l Park Ass'n v. Norton, 280n37
W. Coast Forest Res. Ltd. Partnership, United States v., 1997 WL 33100698 (D. Or. 1997), 158n66, 186n67, 289n115
W. Coast Forest Res. Ltd. Partnership, United States v., 2000 WL 298707 (D. Or. 2000), 151, 174, 186n68, 188nn95–96
W. Watersheds Project v. Foss, 37n101
W. Watersheds Project v. Hall, 37n79
W. Watersheds Project v. Kraayenbrink, 284n96
W. Watersheds Project v. Matejko, 121n22, 124n116
W. Watersheds Project v. U.S. Forest Serv., 281nn58–60
Wash. Envtl. Council v. Nat'l Marine Fisheries Serv., 191n159

Wash. Toxics Coal. v. EPA, 158n76, 282n66, 284n96, 284n98, 289n136, 289nn133–134
Wash. Toxics Coal. v. U.S. Fish & Wildlife Serv., 392n39
Wash. Trout v. McCain Foods, Inc., 157n52
Washington, United States v., 135 F.3d 618 (9th Cir. 1998), 141n33, 142n37, 142n39
Washington, United States v., 384 F. Supp. 312 (W.D. Wash. 1974), 136, 141n33, 142n38, 145n93
Washington, United States v., 502 F.2d 676 (9th Cir. 1975), 140n17
Washington, United States v., 506 F. Supp. 187 (W.D. Wash. Sept. 26, 1980), 136–138, 140n22, 145n95
Washington, United States v., 626 F. Supp. 1405 (W.D. Wash. 1985), 142n41
Washington, United States v., No. CV 9213RSM, 2007 WL 2437166 (W.D. Wash. 2007), 145nn102–107
Washington v. Confederated Tribes of the Colville Reservation, 140n14
Washington v. Wash. State Commercial Passenger Fishing Vessel Ass'n, 142n34, 145n92
Water Keeper Alliance v. U.S. Dep't of Def., 187n79, 288n125
Webster v. Town of Candia, 259n80
Weinberger v. Romero-Barcelo, 187n76, 288n131
Wheeler, United States v., 140n7
White Mountain Apache Tribe v. United States, 140n23
Whitefoot v. United States, 142n42
Winans, United States v., 129–130, 141n30, 142n37
Winter v. Natural Resources Defense Council, 186n71, 290n138
Winters v. United States, 129–130, 142n43, 143n46
Worcester v. Georgia, 128, 139n4, 140n19
W.T. Grant Co., United States v., 280n38
Wyoming v. U.S. Dep't of Interior, 283n92
Wyo. Farm Bureau Fed'n v. Babbitt, 91n5, 198, 203nn23–25

Table of Cases | 419

Index

A

actual injury, 168–178
adaptive management, 227–231, 398
Administrative Procedure Act
    arbitrary and capricious standard of, 150, 270–271, 275
    citizens suits using, 265–272, 275
    critical habitats and, 49
    incidental take permit revocation and, 226–227
    listing and, 28
Alabama beach mouse, 233
Alabama sturgeon, 28
Alabama v. Corps of Engineers, 151
Alameda whipsnake, 56
Alaskan Native Americans, 132, 200
Aleutian cackling goose, 75–76, 77, 79
Alsea Valley Alliance v. Evans, 24–25
American alligator, 76
American Bald Eagle v. Bhatti, 151
American Clean Energy and Security Act of 2009, 388
American pika, 379
Andrus v. Allard, 308
Animal Protection Institute v. Holsten, 153
antique articles, 201
Appalachian Mountain Club, 78
Arizona Cattle v. Fish and Wildlife Service, 170
Arizona v. California, 130
artificially propagated plants, 324–325
Association of California Water Agencies v. Evans, 266
Atlantic Green Sea Turtle v. County Council of Volusia County, 233, 276

B

Babbitt, Bruce, 133, 138–139, 224–225, 398, 406
Babbitt v. Sweet Home Chapter of Communities for a Great Oregon, 148, 150–151, 162, 168–169, 173–177, 349–350, 362, 367. *See also Sweet Home Chapter of Communities for a Great Oregon v. Babbitt*
Baird's sparrow, 27
Bald and Golden Eagle Protection Act, 131–132
bald eagles, 76, 131–133, 151–152, 169, 302, 303–304, 382
Barrett v. State, 307
Barton Springs salamander, 25
beach mouse, 151, 233
bear
    black, 54–55
    grizzly, 23, 82–83, 84–85, 88–89, 154, 269, 306
    polar, 34, 119–120, 181–182, 400–402
Beebe, William, 10
Bennett v. Spear, 26, 149, 264, 265–268, 275
Bensman v. U.S. Forest Service, 151
Bernhardt, David, 119
bigleaf mahogany, 252–253, 325
Billie, United States v., 130–133
Biodiversity Legal Foundation v. Badgley, 55, 265
biological assessments, 106–108
Biological Opinions, 110, 111–116, 223, 265–270, 366
bison, 198–199
black bear, 54–55
blue shiners, 54
Boise Cascade Corp. v. United States, 148, 302, 307–308
bred-in-captivity species, 323–324
brown pelican, 76
Building Industry Association of Superior California v. Babbitt, 51
bull trout, 23, 59
Bureau of Biological Survey, 10–11
Bureau of Indian Affairs, 134
Bureau of Land Management, 78
Bureau of Sport Fisheries and Wildlife, 11–12
Bush administration, 148, 210, 376, 382, 383, 385, 393n50, 399
Butte Environmental Coalition v. White, 51
butterflies, 194, 222

Index | 421

C

California condor, 84, 85
Canada lynx, 23, 153
Candidate Conservation Agreements, 211–213
Cape Hatteras Access Preservation Alliance v. U.S. Department of the Interior, 45, 61
Carlton v. Babbitt, 89
Carolina parakeet, 11
Casitas Municipal Water District v. United States, 293, 302–303
Catron County Board of Commissioners v. U.S. Fish and Wildlife Service, 61
caviar, 326–327
CBD (Convention on Biological Diversity), 329–332
CBD v. Point Marina Development, 152
Center for Biological Diversity v. Bureau of Land Management, 58–59
Center for Biological Diversity v. Evans, 52–53
Center for Biological Diversity v. Hamilton, 54–55
Center for Biological Diversity v. Norton, 45, 53, 55
Center for Biological Diversity v. U.S. Fish and Wildlife Service, 229, 232
Center for Plant Conservation, 247
certificates. *See* permits/certificates
cerulean warbler, 73
Cherokee Nation v. Georgia, 128
Chinook salmon, 230, 350
Christy v. Hodel, 148, 306–307
CITES (Convention on International Trade in Endangered Species of Wild Fauna and Flora)
  administrative procedures of, 320–323
  artificial propagation procedures, 324–325
  bred-in-captivity procedures, 323–324
  caviar trade procedures, 326–327
  conservation standards of, 319–320
  Convention on Biological Diversity and, 329–332
  coordination with other environmental agreements, 327–331
  economic impact of, 331–335
  history of, 12–13, 317
  hunting trophy procedures, 325–326
  plant regulation under, 247, 251–254, 324–325
  recovery plans and, 75–76
  structure of, 317–319
  timber trade procedures, 252–253, 325
citizen suits
  advance notification of, 267–268, 273, 281nn62–63, 287–288nn124–125
  emerging issues with, 275–276, 291nn146–150
  ESA *versus* APA claims, 265–270, 280–281n52, 281–282nn61–68, 282–283n79, 283nn82–83
  intervention standards for, 273–274, 288nn128–129
  legal fees for, 268–269
  mootness issues in, 264–265, 280nn35–38
  on permit violations, 275–276
  relief as result of, 274–275, 289n136, 289–290nn138–140
  ripeness issues in, 264, 279–280nn32–34
  standards of review for, 270–271, 275, 283–284n96, 284–286nn102–107
  standing in, 261–264, 268, 277–279nn9–30, 281–282n64, 351–352
  state endangered species laws on, 351–352
  on take prohibition, 149–150, 162, 168, 275–276
  unreasonable delays prompting, 269–270, 282n79, 283nn82–83
  venue/transfer issues with, 271–273, 286n111, 286n115, 287nn119–120
City of Monterey v. Del Monte Dunes at Monterey Ltd., 295
civil litigation. *See* citizen suits
Clean Air Act (1970), 361, 388
Clean Water Act (1972), 46, 75, 88, 106, 213, 237, 293, 351
climate change
  conservation framework including, 387–389
  critical habitats impacted by, 33–34, 400–402
  duty to consult impacted by, 119–120
  ecosystem disruptions due to, 378–379
  ESA updates to address, 380–387
  habitat conservation plans impacted by, 237
  legislation on, 388

listings impacted by, 33–35
safeguards against, 379–380
vicarious liability and, 181–182
Clinton administration, 4–5, 144n74, 224, 376, 383, 398
Colorado Wildlife Federation v. Turner, 53
Colorado Wildlife Federation v. U.S. Fish and Wildlife Service, 52
Columbian white-tailed deer, 76–79
commercial trade. *See* trade of endangered species
Commission for the Conservation of Antarctic Marine Living Resources, 328
Committee on Rare and Endangered Wildlife Species, 11–12
Comprehensive Environmental Recovery, Compensation, and Liability Act, 361
condor, 84, 85
Cone, Ben, 208
Conner v. Burford, 116
conservation
    beginning of conservation movement, 10
    CITES standards on, 319–320
    conservation banking, 213–214, 238, 406–407
    critical habitat designation and, 55–56
    defined, 41
    duty to conserve, 105
    economic impact of, 331–335, 404–407
    ESA support by conservationists, 6
    framework, 387–389
    habitat conservation plans (*see* habitat conservation plans (HCPs))
    incentives for (*see* incentives, landowner; incentives, state/local government)
    by landowners, 6, 178, 194–195, 208–217, 238, 296–297, 350–351, 381–382, 406–407
    listing impacted by conservation efforts, 25, 31, 212
    nanotechnology and, 369–370
Conservation Council of Hawaii v. Babbitt, 51
Conservation Northwest v. Kempthorne, 85
Conservation Reserve Programs, 382
constitutional claims
    character factor in, 305–306
    on defense of property, 306–307
    Eleventh Amendment as basis of, 129
    Fifth Amendment as basis of, 6, 130, 148–149, 181, 293
    knowledge of landowner impacting, 304–305
    on official access for surveys, 307–308
    regulatory restrictions on natural resource use in, 298–306
    ripeness issues in, 298–299, 311nn55–58
    take prohibition challenges in, 148–149, 152–153, 181, 293–309
    takings analysis in, 301–306
    Tenth Amendment as basis of, 152–153
    threshold property issues in, 299–301
    on trade restrictions, 308–309
consultation
    biological assessments and, 106–108
    Biological Opinions issued on, 110, 111–116, 223, 366
    climate change impact on, 119–120
    court decisions on, 116–119
    critical habitat, 383–384
    discretionary *versus* nondiscretionary agency action, 118–119
    duty to consult, 4, 45, 47–48, 58–60, 105–121, 223, 365–366
    early, 110–111
    effect of actions for, 112–113
    emergency, 117
    Endangered Species Committee exemptions in, 117–118
    environmental baselines for, 112
    formal, 111–116, 366
    incidental take statements for, 115–116, 178, 223, 366
    incremental, 116
    informal, 108–110, 366
    jeopardy determination for, 113–114
    listing, 29, 383–384
    nanotechnology and, 363–364, 365–366, 368–370
    with Native Americans, 4–5, 118
    politics impacting procedures for, 383–384
    preparing for formal, 106–111
    reasonable and prudent alternatives as result of, 114–115
    recovery, 384
    regulation modification for, 120
    reinitiation of, 116–117
    state endangered species laws on, 352–353

Index | 423

Convention on Biological Diversity (CBD), 329–332
Convention on International Trade in Endangered Species of Wild Fauna and Flora. *See* CITES
Convention on Nature Protection and Wildlife Preservation in the Western Hemisphere, 11
Convention on the Conservation of Migratory Species of Wild Animals, 328
coral, 34, 119
Council on Environmental Quality, 60, 232, 395
courts. *See also* Supreme Court
   critical habitat decisions in, 41–43, 44–45, 47–48, 51–62, 402–404
   on duty to conserve, 105
   on duty to consult, 116–119
   on habitat conservation plans, 226–227, 229–230, 232–233
   on incidental take permit revocation, 226–227
   on jeopardy prohibitions, 5, 17, 121, 402–404
   listing-related decisions in, 22–31, 347
   on Native American rights, 127–133, 136–139
   procedural listing challenges in, 27–28
   recovery plan decisions in, 81–85, 88–90
   substantive listing challenges in, 22–26
   take prohibition decisions in, 147–154, 161–166, 168–171, 173–182, 226–227, 293–309, 349–350, 367
critical habitats
   Administrative Procedure Act impacting, 49
   adverse modification of, 4, 45, 47–48, 58–60, 105, 113–115, 147, 150–152, 163–179, 402–404
   biological assessments of, 106–108
   climate change impacting, 33–34, 400–402
   conservation goals and, 55–56
   constituent elements of, 46–47, 114
   consultation on, 383–384
   court decisions on, 41–43, 44–45, 47–48, 51–62, 402–404
   defined, 3, 42–48
   on Department of Defense land, 50, 54
   designation of, 3, 48–58, 348–349, 383, 399–400, 407nn3–5
   economic impact of designation of, 56–58
   effect of actions on, 112–113
   elimination of, 399–400
   environmental baselines for, 112, 209–210
   funding impact on, 41–42, 50, 55
   generally, 41–42
   imprudence exception to, 50–51
   listing concurrently with, 49
   nanoscale material impact on, 363
   National Environmental Policy Act compliance, 60–62
   number of, 3, 41, 399
   occupied *versus* unoccupied habitat as, 44, 46
   petitions for, 49–50
   physical/biological features of, 46–47, 403–404
   recovery requirements on, 43, 77–78, 381, 406
   revisions to, 48–49
   state endangered species laws on, 348–349
   take prohibitions including, 147, 150–152, 163–166, 167–168
   on tribal lands, 135
   undeterminable, 52–53

D

Daley, William, 138
deer, 76–79
Defenders of Wildlife v. Babbitt, 83
Defenders of Wildlife v. Bernal, 169–170, 176
Defenders of Wildlife v. EPA, 152
Defenders of Wildlife v. Gutierrez, 268
Defenders of Wildlife v. Hall, 89–90
defense of property, 306–307
Delhi Sands flower-loving fly, 88
delisting, 22, 32, 74–79, 85–87
Delmarva fox squirrel, 232
delta smelt, 32, 60, 230
Department of Agriculture, 10, 211, 249
Department of Commerce. *See also* National Marine Fisheries Service (NMFS)
   implementation responsibilities of, 1–2, 17–19
   Secretarial Order No. 3206, 127, 133–136

Department of Defense, 50, 54
Department of Fish and Game v. Anderson-Cottonwood Irrigation District, 350
Department of the Interior. *See also* Fish and Wildlife Service
    Bureau of Sport Fisheries and Wildlife, 11–12
    history of conservation legislation implemented by, 11–13
    implementation responsibilities of, 1–2, 17–19
    Secretarial Order No. 3206, 127, 133–136
desert tortoise, 24, 88
Dingell, John, 13
Dion, United States v., 130–133
distinct population segments, 24–25, 77, 85–86, 382
Douglas County v. Babbitt, 60–61
Douglas County v. Lujan, 60
duty to conserve, 105
duty to consult. *See* consultation

E

eagles, 76, 131–133, 151, 152, 169, 302, 303–304, 383
East Cape May Associates v. State of New Jersey, 304
economic impacts
    of conservation, 331–335, 404–407
    of critical habitat designations, 56–58
    of international trade (CITES) restrictions, 331–335
    of listing, 199–200, 347
    of takes, 294–295, 303–304, 368
ecosystems
    climate change disrupting, 378–379
    habitat conservation plans addressing, 234–237, 239–241
    recovery impact on, 86–87
elephants, 332
Eleventh Amendment, 129
Elkhorn coral, 119
emergency consultation, 117
emergency listing, 21
eminent domain power, 293
endangered species. *See also* plants, endangered/threatened; *specific species by name*
    actual injury to, 168–178
    biological assessments of, 106–108
    bred in captivity, 323–324
    defense of property from, 306–307
    definition of, 18
    distinct population segments of, 24–25, 77, 85–86, 382
    effect of actions on, 112–113
    environmental baselines for, 112, 209–210
    experimental populations of, 196–199, 201–202
    listing of (*see* listing)
    multiple, and habitat conservation plans, 234–237
    number of, 3, 12, 13, 22, 375, 399
    trade/sale of (*see* trade of endangered species)
Endangered Species Act (ESA) (1973)
    administration of, 398–399
    amendments to, 42, 43–46, 222–224, 238–240
    Babbitt administrative reforms to, 224–225, 240, 398, 406
    challenges facing, 395–407
    conservation framework including, 387–389
    duty to consult under (*see* consultation)
    effectiveness of, 380–387
    funding, 376, 385–386, 388, 409n35
    generally, 1
    goals of, 2–3, 207–208
    history of, 9–14, 221–225, 395–399
    as jurisdictional statute, 396–398
    limitations of, 395–407
    listing under (*see* listing)
    nanotechnology and, 361–370
    plant provisions in (*see* plants, endangered/threatened)
    purposes/perceptions of, 221–222
    responsibility for implementation of, 1–2, 17–19
    successes, 375–377
    transparency of, 398–399, 406
Endangered Species Committee, 4, 117–118
Endangered Species Conservation Act (1969), 12
Endangered Species Preservation Act (1966), 12
environmental assessments/impact statements, 60–62, 231–233, 348

environmental baselines, 112, 209–210
Environmental Protection Agency, 395
Equal Access to Justice Act, 268–269
ESA. *See* Endangered Species Act (ESA) (1973)
experimental populations, 196–199, 201–202

F

fairy shrimp, 51
Farm Bill (2008), 216, 238, 382, 387
Federal Advisory Committee Act, 28
federal agencies. *See also* Fish and Wildlife Service; National Marine Fisheries Service (NMFS)
  biological assessments by, 106–108
  discretionary *versus* nondiscretionary action by, 118–119
  duty to conserve, 105
  duty to consult, 4, 45, 47–48, 58–60, 105–121, 223, 365–366, 383–384
  early consultation by, 110–111
  effect of actions by, 112–113
  emergency consultation by, 117
  Endangered Species Committee exemptions for, 4, 117–118
  formal consultation by, 111–116, 366
  incidental take statements by, 115–116, 178, 223, 336
  incremental consultation by, 116
  informal consultation by, 108–110, 366
  jeopardy prohibition for, 4–5, 17, 45, 47–48, 58–60, 105–121, 385, 402–404
  listing notifications to, 20
  National Environmental Policy Act analysis in, 231–233
  Native American consultation with, 4–5, 118
  plant protection by, 248–249
  preparation for formal consultations by, 106–111
  reasonable and prudent alternatives for, 114–115
  reinitiation of consultation by, 116–117
Federal Aid in Fish Restoration Act, 354
Federal Aid in Wildlife Restoration Act, 354
Federal Insecticide, Fungicide and Rodenticide Act, 76, 361

Federal Register
  consultation regulation notification in, 120
  critical habitat designation notification in, 49
  delisting notification in, 86
  emergency rulemaking notification in, 21
  listing notification in, 20, 21
  take exemption notification in, 199–200
Fifth Amendment, 6, 130, 148–149, 181, 293
Fish and Wildlife Service
  collaboration efforts of, 386–387, 388–389
  funding of, 376, 385–386, 388, 409n35
  implementation responsibilities of, 1–2, 17–19
  No Surprises rule of, 224, 225–227, 296–297, 398
  nontraditional partnerships with, 387
  Partners for Fish and Wildlife Program, 210–211
  policy changes at, 382–385
  Secretarial Order No. 3206 addressing, 134–136
  state cooperative agreements with, 353–354, 386
Florida panther, 88, 132–133
Flotilla v. Florida Game & Fresh Water Fish Commission, 304
Food, Conservation, and Energy Act (2008), 216, 238
Forest Guardians v. Babbitt, 53, 55
formal consultation, 111–116, 366
Fort Hood Army Base, 214
fox squirrel, 232
Frank, Billy, 138–139
Fund for Animals v. Babbitt, 82–83
funding/finances
  critical habitat impacted by, 41–42, 50, 55
  of ESA programs, 376, 385–386, 388, 409n35
  of habitat conservation plans, 223, 231, 235–236, 239
  of landowner conservation incentives, 210–211, 216
  listing impacted by, 31
  recovery planning impacted by, 81, 376, 406
  of state endangered species programs, 346, 353–354, 386

G

Gerber v. Babbitt, 232
giant garter snake, 229, 233
Gifford Pinchot Task Force v. U.S. Fish and Wildlife Service, 48, 59, 402–404
Gila trout, 83
Glasser v. National Marine Fisheries Service, 233
Glisson, Joseph, 351–352
global warming. *See* climate change
gnatcatcher, 28, 51
God Squad (Endangered Species Committee), 4, 117–118
golden-cheeked warbler, 214
goldline garter, 54
Good v. United States, 304–305
goose, 11, 75–76, 77, 79
gray whale, 76
gray wolf, 85–87, 89, 193, 197, 198, 348
greenhouse gas emissions, 33–34, 119–120, 181–182, 237, 378, 388–389
Greenpeace v. National Marine Fisheries Service, 152
grizzly bear, 23, 82–83, 84–85, 88–89, 154, 269, 306
Gulf sturgeon, 51

H

habitat conservation plans (HCPs)
    adaptive management provisions in, 227–231, 398
    cost-benefit assessment of, 235–237, 399
    court decisions impacting, 226–227, 229–230, 232–233
    ESA history with, 221–225, 398–399
    funding for, 223, 231, 235–236, 239
    HCP Handbook guidelines on, 224, 227–228
    incidental take permits in association with, 178, 222–227, 231–233, 296–297, 368
    landowners creating, 6, 178, 195, 221–240, 296–297, 368, 385, 398–399
    lessons learned from, 238–240
    mitigation role in, 237–238
    National Environmental Policy Act impact on, 195, 223, 231–233
    No Surprises assurances in, 224, 225–227, 296–297, 350, 398
    number/duration of, 224–225
    San Bruno Mountain Area, 222–223
    Western Riverside Country Multiple-Species, 234–237, 240–241
habitats, critical. *See* critical habitats
Hall, Dale, 120
harass, defined, 166–167
harm rules
    actual injury under, 168–178
    affirmative action *versus* inaction, 177–178
    definitions under, 162–166, 167–168
    living individuals and, 175–176
    permanent injunction under, 168–171
    preliminary injunction under, 171–172
    proximate causation under, 177–178
    vicarious liability under, 179–182
hawks, 229, 233
HCPs. *See* habitat conservation plans (HCPs)
Healthy Forest Reserve Program, 211
heath hen, 11
Hill, United States v., 308–309
Home Builders Association of Northern California v. Norton, 58
Home Builders Association of Northern California v. U.S. Fish and Wildlife Service, 45, 47, 56
Hoover's woolly-star, 76
House v. U.S. Forest Service, 152
Humane Society of the United States v. Kempthorne, 193
hunting/fishing, 129–133, 136–138, 200, 325–326

I

Idaho springsnail, 24, 27
incentives, landowner
    Candidate Conservation Agreements, 211–213
    conservation banking, 213–214, 238, 406–407
    emerging and future directions in, 214–217
    funding, 210–211, 216
    increasing effectiveness of, 381–382
    prelisting agreements, 351
    safe harbor agreements, 194, 208–211, 296, 351
    state-level, 350–351
    tax incentives, 216, 382
incentives, state/local government, 386

incidental takes
    Biological Opinions on, 115–116, 223, 366
    conservation banking and, 213
    enhancement and, 193–196
    habitat conservation plans and, 178, 222–227, 231–233, 296–297, 368
    harm rule on, 169–170
    history of, 5–6
    incidental take statements, 115–116, 178, 223, 366
    permit revocation rule, 225–227
    of plants, 250
    safe harbor agreements and, 209–210
    state-authorized, 350
incremental consultation, 116
Indians. *See* Native Americans
informal consultation, 108–110, 366
interagency consultation. *See* consultation
Intergovernmental Panel on Climate Change, 378
international agreements
    CITES as (*see* CITES)
    Convention on Biological Diversity, 329–332
    Convention on Nature Protection and Wildlife Preservation in the Western Hemisphere, 11
    Convention on the Conservation of Migratory Species of Wild Animals, 328
    International Convention for the Regulation of Whaling, 328
    Multilateral Environmental Agreements, 327–331
International Convention for the Regulation of Whaling, 328–329
international trade of endangered species
    artificially propagated, 324–325
    bred in captivity, 323–324
    caviar from, 326–327
    coordination of multiple agreements on, 327–331
    economic impact of regulation of, 331–335
    hunting trophies and, 325–326
    permits/certificates for, 320–323, 325
    plants, 247, 252–253, 324–325
    regulation of (*see* CITES)
    timber trade, 252–253, 325

International Union for the Conservation of Nature, 11, 247, 327
International Whaling Commission (IWC), 328–329
interstate commerce regulations, 11, 201, 308–309

J
Jefferson, Thomas, 9
jeopardy
    determination of, 113–114, 403
    prohibition, 4–5, 17, 45, 47–48, 58–60, 105–121, 385, 402–404
Johnson v. McIntosh, 128
jurisdiction
    citizen suit standing requirements for, 149–150
    ESA as jurisdictional statute, 396–398
    Native American tribal, 127–128, 134–135
    state *versus* federal, 1–2, 13, 215–216, 250–251

K
kangaroo rats, 234
Kempthorne, Dirk, 119, 396, 401–402, 408n7
Kepler, United States v., 308–309
Klamath Irrigation District v. United States, 148

L
Lacey, John, 10
Lacey Act (1900), 10–11
land use activities
    actual injury from, 168–178
    affirmative action *versus* inaction, 177–178
    ESA provisions affecting, 295–297
    habitat modification through, 163–166, 167–168
    harm rule and, 163–166, 167–179
    incentives for conservation in, 194, 208–217, 238, 296–297, 350–351, 381–382, 406–407
    landowner options for, 169–170, 178–179
    living individuals and, 175–176
    permanent injunction against, 168–171
    physical occupation restricting, 301–303

preliminary injunction against, 171–172
as proximate cause of injury, 177–178
regulatory restrictions on natural resource use, 298–306
threshold property issues with, 299–301
vicarious liability for, 152–153, 179–182
Landowner Incentive Program, 210, 216
landowners
   Candidate Conservation Agreements with, 211–213
   conservation banking by, 213–214, 238, 406–407
   conservation measures by, 6, 178, 194–195, 208–217, 238, 296–297, 350–351, 381–382, 406–407
   critical habitat on private land of, 51
   habitat conservation plans by, 6, 178, 195, 221–240, 296–297, 368, 385, 398–399
   incentives for conservation for, 194–195, 208–217, 238, 296–297, 350–351, 381–382, 406–407
   knowledge of, 304–305
   no-take agreements with, 351
   physical intrusion on private land of, 301–303
   prelisting agreements with, 351
   safe harbor agreements with, 194, 208–211, 296, 351
   take prohibitions options for, 169–170, 178–179
   take prohibitions *versus* property rights of, 6, 148–149, 181, 256, 293–295, 299–301, 306–307
   take-avoidance duty of, 177–178
   tax incentives for, 216, 382
legislation. See also state endangered species laws
   Administrative Procedure Act, 28, 49, 150, 226–227, 265–270, 275
   American Clean Energy and Security Act of 2009, 388
   Bald and Golden Eagle Protection Act, 131–132
   Clean Air Act (1970), 361, 388
   Clean Water Act (1972), 46, 75, 88, 106, 213, 237, 293, 351
   climate change, 388
   Comprehensive Environmental Recovery, Compensation, and Liability Act, 361
   Endangered Species Act (1973) (*see* Endangered Species Act (ESA) (1973))
   Endangered Species Conservation Act (1969), 12
   Endangered Species Preservation Act (1966), 12
   Equal Access to Justice Act, 268–269
   Federal Advisory Committee Act, 28
   Federal Aid in Fish Restoration Act, 354
   Federal Aid in Wildlife Restoration Act, 354
   Federal Insecticide, Fungicide and Rodenticide Act, 76, 361
   Food, Conservation, and Energy Act (2008), 216, 238
   Lacey Act (1900), 10–11
   Marine Mammal Protection Act (1972), 200–201
   Migratory Bird Treaty Act, 75
   National Defense Authorization Act (2003), 54
   National Environmental Policy Act (1970), 28, 60–62, 195, 223, 231–233, 348
   Nonindigenous Aquatic Nuisance Prevention and Control Act, 75
   nuisance laws, 300
   Partners for Fish and Wildlife Act (2006), 211
   Reclamation Act (1902), 119
   Resource Conservation and Recovery Act, 361
   Safe Water Drinking Act (1974), 395
   Surface Mining Control & Reclamation Act, 293
   Toxic Substances Control Act, 361
Lingle v. Chevron U.S.A. Inc., 294, 295
listing
   Administrative Procedure Act and, 28
   administrative reform of, 28–31
   best available science used in, 26, 28
   climate change impacting, 33–35
   conservation efforts impacting, 25, 31, 212
   consultation, 29, 383–384
   court actions on, 22–31, 347
   criteria for, 3, 18–19, 363
   critical habitat designation with, 49
   current status of, 18
   definitions and standards for, 18–19

listing *(continued)*
    delisting, 22, 32, 74–79, 85–87
    distinct population segments, 24–25, 382
    economic impact of, 199–200, 347
    emergency rulemaking, 21
    Federal Advisory Committee Act and, 28
    five-year status reviews of, 22, 31–32
    generally, 17–18
    implementation procedures for, 19–22
    insufficient biological support for, 23–24
    listing action rulemaking, 20–21
    nanoscale material impact on, 363
    National Environmental Policy Act and, 28
    number of listed species, 3
    petition review, 19–20
    plants, 249
    political interference with, 32–33
    post-decisional listing program duties, 21–22
    prioritization of, 30–31
    procedural challenges to, 27–28
    risk assessment for, 74–75
    state endangered species laws on, 347–348
    substantive challenges to, 22–26
    as threatened *versus* endangered, 25–26
local governments, 153, 179–181, 386
Locke, Gary, 120
Loggerhead Turtle v. County Council of Volusia, 153, 180
Loretto v. Teleprompter Manhattan CATV Corp., 294
Lucas v. South Carolina Coastal Council, 294, 299, 300–301, 303, 306
Lujan v. Defenders of Wildlife, 263–264
lynx, 23, 153

M

MacDonald, Julie, 32–33, 39n146, 39n148, 377
Marbled Murrelet v. Babbitt, 151
marbled murrelets, 151, 300
Marine Mammal Protection Act (1972), 200–201
Marshall, John, 127–128
Marshall, Thurgood, 131
McKittrick, United States v., 197–198

MEAs (Multilateral Environmental Agreements), 327–331. *See also* CITES
Melville, Herman, *Moby-Dick*, 9–10
Mexican spotted owl, 45, 348
Middle Rio Grande Conservancy District v. Norton, 61–62
Migratory Bird Treaty Act, 75
milk-vetch, 58–59
mission blue butterflies, 194, 222
mitigation, 237–238, 401, 405
Moby-Dick (Melville), 9–10
Moerman v. California, 307
moose, 379
mootness issues, 264–265, 280nn35–38
Morrill v. Lujan, 151
Morris v. United States, 149, 298–299
Multilateral Environmental Agreements (MEAs), 327–331. *See also* CITES

N

nanotechnology, 361–370
National Association of Home Builders v. Defenders of Wildlife, 118–119, 121
National Association of Home Builders v. Evans, 57
National Audubon Society, 10
National Audubon Society v. Hester, 84–85
National Defense Authorization Act (2003), 54
National Environmental Policy Act (1970)
    critical habitat designation and, 60–62
    habitat conservation plans and, 195, 223, 231–233
    listing and, 28
    state compliance with, 348
National Marine Fisheries Service (NMFS)
    collaboration efforts of, 386–387, 388–389
    funding of, 376, 385–386, 388
    implementation responsibilities of, 1–2, 17–19
    No Surprises rule of, 224, 225–227, 296–297, 398
    nontraditional partnerships with, 387
    policy changes at, 382–385
    Secretarial Order No. 3206 addressing, 134–136
    state cooperative agreements with, 353–354, 386
National Wildlife Federation, 13

National Wildlife Federation v. Babbitt, 229
National Wildlife Federation v. Burlington Northern Railroad, Inc., 154
National Wildlife Federation v. National Marine Fisheries Service, 59, 118–119
National Wildlife Federation v. National Park Service, 84–85
Native Americans
  Alaskan, 132, 200
  case law ambiguity regarding, 130–133
  court decisions on ESA and, 127–133, 136–139
  duty to consult with, 4–5, 118
  emerging issues with, 136–139
  federal trust responsibility to, 128–129, 134–135
  habitat management plans by, 135
  hunting/fishing rights of, 129–133, 136–138, 200
  reserved rights of, 129–130
  Secretarial Order No. 3206 impacting, 127, 133–136
  take exemptions for, 200
  treaties with, 127–132, 136–139, 144–145n92, 301
  tribes as sovereign governments, 127–128, 134–135
  water rights of, 130
Natural Resources Defense Council v. Kempthorne, 59–60, 230
Natural Resources Defense Council v. U.S. Department of the Interior, 51
Nature Conservancy, 78
nene (Hawaiian goose), 11
NEPA. *See* National Environmental Policy Act (1970)
Nettleton Co. v. Diamond, 347
New Mexico Cattle Growers Association v. U.S. Fish and Wildlife Service, 57
New York Zoological Society, 10
Nixon administration, 13
No Surprises rule, 224, 225–227, 296–297, 350, 398
Nonindigenous Aquatic Nuisance Prevention and Control Act, 75
northern spotted owl
  critical habitat for, 47, 53, 60
  listing of, 22–23
  take prohibitions for, 148, 151, 164–166, 170–171, 173–174, 300, 302

Northern Spotted Owl v. Hodel, 22–23
Northern Spotted Owl v. Lujan, 53
Norton v. Southern Utah Wilderness Alliance, 270
no-take agreements, 351
Nuesca, United States v., 200
nuisance laws, 300

O

Obama administration, 86, 120, 191n161, 385, 387, 399
O'Connor, Sandra Day, 148, 156n17, 156n19, 165, 166, 174–175, 177, 367
Oregon coast coho salmon, 25
Oregon Natural Desert Association v. Lohn, 59
Oregon Natural Resource Council v. Turner, 82
otter, 198
owl. *See* northern spotted owl; pygmy owl; spotted owl

P

Pacific Coast Federation of Fisherman's Associations v. Gutierrez, 230
Pacific Legal Foundation v. Andrus, 60
Pacific Rivers Council v. Brown, 180–181
Pacific salmon, 24–25, 136–138, 386
Palazzolo v. Rhode Island, 301, 304
Palila v. Hawaii Department of Land & Natural Resources, 88, 147, 163, 164
panther, 88, 132–133
parakeet, 11
Partners for Fish and Wildlife Act (2006), 211
Partners for Fish and Wildlife Program, 210–211
passenger pigeon, 10
peer reviews, 28
Peirson's milk-vetch, 58–59
pelican, 76
penalties, 351–352, 365
Penn Central Transp. Co. v. New York City, 294–295, 301, 303–306
Perdido Key beach mouse, 151
peregrine falcon, 76, 77, 79
permits/certificates
  artificially propagated, 325
  bred-in-captivity, 323
  CITES export/import, 320–323, 325
  state-issued, 350

Index | 431

petitions, 19–20, 49–50
physical takings analysis, 301–303
pigeon, 10
pika, 379
piping plover, 153
plants, endangered/threatened
    artificially propagated, 324–325
    CITES' role in protecting, 247, 251–254, 324–325
    emerging issues with, 252–254
    history of legislation protecting, 12–13, 247
    listing, 249
    number of, 247, 254–255
    recovery of, 254–255
    regulatory differences with wildlife, 249–251
    regulatory similarities with wildlife, 248–249
    state endangered species laws on, 250–251, 353
    take prohibitions for, 162, 249–251, 255–256
    timber restrictions protecting, 252, 325
polar bears, 34, 119–120, 181–182, 400–402
Policy for Evaluation of Conservation Efforts When Making Listing Decisions (PECE Policy), 212
politics. *See also specific presidential administrations*
    climate change controversies in, 379–380
    consultation procedures impacted by, 383–384
    critical habitat designations impacted by, 383
    ESA obstacles due to, 375–377
    listing decisions impacted by, 32–33
Pombo, Richard, 376
prelisting agreements, 351
private property owners. *See* landowners
Private Stewardship Grants Program, 210, 216
property rights
    in defense of property, 306–307
    take prohibitions *versus*, 6, 148–149, 181, 256, 293–295, 299–301, 306–307
    threshold property issues with, 299–301
public hearings
    on critical habitat designation, 49
    on habitat conservation plans, 195, 226–227, 228
    on incidental take permits, 195, 226–227
    on listing action rulemaking, 21
    on take exemptions, 200
pygmy owl, 24, 176, 399

R

Rand Corporation study, 235–237
razorback sucker, 53
Reclamation Act (1902), 119
recovery plans
    best available science used in, 87–90
    case law on, 81–85, 88–90
    consultation on, 384
    contents of, 82–83
    critical habitat as facet of, 43, 77–78, 381, 406
    delisting and, 74–79, 85–87
    distinct population segments in, 77, 85–86
    funding impact on, 81, 376, 406
    goals of, 4, 79–81
    habitat management in, 77–79
    implementation of, 83–85, 405
    number of, 4, 80
    obligation to develop, 81–82
    plant, 254–255
    recovery, defined, 71–79
    regulatory mechanisms impacting, 75–80
    revision of ESA provisions for, 405–407
    risk assessment and, 72–79
    state endangered species laws on, 352
    viability thresholds in, 85–87
red-cockaded woodpecker, 177, 208–209
Rehnquist, William, 301
Resource Conservation and Recovery Act, 361
right whales, 52–53, 88, 152, 268
Rio Grande silvery minnow, 53, 61–62, 355
ripeness issues, 264, 279–280nn32–34, 298–299, 311nn55–58
risk assessments, 72–79
Robbins' cinquefoil, 76, 78–79
Roosevelt, Theodore, 10

S

Sacramento splittail, 23
safe harbor agreements, 194, 208–211, 296, 351
Safe Water Drinking Act (1974), 395

salamander, 25, 228
Salazar, Ken, 119–120
salmon, 24–25, 136–138, 230, 350, 386
San Bruno Mountain Area Habitat Conservation Plan, 222–223
San Carlos Apache Tribe v. United States, 151
Sanders, Marren, 135
Santa Cruz long-toed salamander, 228
Save the Yaak Committee v. Block, 150
Scalia, Antonin, 148, 165, 174–175, 177, 306
Schloeffler v. Kempthorne, 54–55
scrimshaw, 200–201
sea lions, 152
sea otter, 198
sea turtle, 88, 153, 180, 233
Seattle Audubon Society v. Sutherland, 181
Secretarial Order No. 3206, 127, 133–136
Seiber v. United States, 302, 304
shrimp, 51
Sierra Club v. Clark, 193
Sierra Club v. Department of Forestry & Fire Protection, 300
Sierra Club v. Lujan, 81–82, 84–85
Sierra Club v. Norton, 233
Sierra Club v. Thomas, 269–270
Sierra Club v. U.S. Fish and Wildlife Service, 47–48, 51, 59, 403
Sierra Club v. Yeutter, 177
silvery minnow, 53, 61–62, 355
snail darter, 221
snake, 56, 229, 233, 299–300
Sour Mountain Realty, State v., 299–300
Southwest Center for Biological Diversity v. Bartel, 89, 229–230
southwestern willow flycatcher, 57
Spirit of the Sage Council, 226–227
spotted owl
    critical habitat for, 45, 47, 53, 60
    listing of, 22–23, 348
    Mexican, 45, 348
    northern, 22–23, 47, 53, 60, 148, 151, 164–166, 170–171, 173–174, 300, 302
    take prohibitions for, 148, 151, 164–166, 170–171, 173–174, 300, 302
springsnail, 24, 27
staghorn coral, 34, 119
state endangered species laws
    conservation agreements under, 350–351
    on consultation, 352–353
    cooperative agreements on, 353–354, 386
    on critical habitats, 348–349
    current state of, 345–346
    emerging issues in, 355
    history of, 345, 346–347
    incentives to improve, 386
    jurisdiction of state *versus* federal, 1–2, 13, 215–216, 250–251
    on listing, 347–348
    penalties and enforcement of, 351–352
    permits under, 350
    on plants, 250–251, 353
    program funding, 346, 353–354, 386
    on recovery plans, 352
    states without, 354–355
    on take prohibitions, 349–350
State v. ———. See name of opposing party
states
    endangered species acts of (*see* state endangered species laws)
    HCP implementation by, 239–240
    interstate commerce between, 11, 201, 308–309
    listing consultation with, 29
    listing notification to, 20, 21
    vicarious liability for take of, 153, 179–181
steelhead trout, 59, 302–303
Steller sea lions, 152
Stephens' kangaroo rats, 234
Stevens, John Paul, 148, 156n15, 165, 301
Stop H-3 Association v. Lewis, 350
Strahan v. Coxe, 152–153, 180
sturgeon, 28, 51, 326–327
Supreme Court
    on best available science, 365
    on citizen suits, 262, 265, 268–269, 273
    on constitutional claims, 294–295, 301, 305–306
    on critical habitats, 41, 43
    on ESA power, 363
    on jeopardy prohibitions, 5, 17, 121
    on Native American rights, 127–128, 130–133
    on take prohibitions, 147, 149, 165–166, 168–169, 173–177, 294–295, 367
Surface Mining Control & Reclamation Act, 293
surveys, 307–308

Swainson's hawks, 229, 233
Sweet Home Chapter of Communities for a Great Oregon v. Babbitt, 161–166, 168–169, 173–177. *See also Babbitt v. Sweet Home Chapter of Communities for a Great Oregon*
Sweet Home Chapter of Communities for a Great Oregon v. Lujan, 165
Sweet Home Chapter of Communities for a Great Oregon v. Turner, 165

T

Tahoe-Sierra Preservation Council v. Tahoe Regional Planning Agency, 295, 301, 303
take prohibitions
  actual injury, defined, 172–175
  Alaskan natives exemptions to, 132
  antique article exemptions to, 201
  citizen suits on, 149–150, 162, 168, 275–276
  constitutional challenges to, 148–149, 152–153, 181, 293–309
  court decisions on, 147–154, 161–166, 168–171, 173–182, 226–227, 293–309, 349–350, 367
  definitions under, 147, 161–167, 172–175, 193, 349
  economic impact of, 294–295, 303–304, 368
  exceptions/exemptions to, 5–6, 132, 193–202
  experimental populations and, 196–199, 201–202
  generally, 147
  habitat conservation plans addressing, 222–223
  habitat modifications and, 147, 150–152, 163–166, 167–168
  harass, defined, 166–167
  hardship exemptions to, 199–200
  injunctions on, 153–154, 168–172
  land use activities and, 163–168
  nanotechnology and, 363–365, 367–370
  noncommercial transshipment exemptions to, 201
  penalties for violating, 365
  for plants, 162, 249–251, 255–256
  pre-ESA endangered species parts exemptions to, 200–201
  property rights *versus*, 6, 148–149, 181, 256, 293–295, 299–301, 306–307
  regulatory causes of take, 147–148, 179–181, 298–306
  requirements for, 5
  ripeness issues and, 298–299, 311nn55–58
  state endangered species laws on, 349–350
  statutory and regulatory framework of, 147–148
  take, defined, 147, 193, 349
  take-avoidance duty, 177–178
  takings analysis, 301–306
  for threatened species, 25, 161–162, 178, 181
  threshold property issues and, 299–301
  vicarious liability for, 152–153, 179–182
tax incentives, 216, 382
Tennessee Valley Authority v. Hill, 41, 43, 107, 118, 132, 153–154, 221, 274
Tenth Amendment, 152–153
threatened species
  definition of, 18
  experimental populations of, 196–199
  listing as endangered *versus*, 25–26
  plants as (*see* plants, endangered/threatened)
  take prohibitions for, 25, 161–162, 178, 181
threshold property issues, 299–301
tidelands, 301
timber industry, 164–166, 252–253, 298–299, 300, 301–302, 303–304, 325, 328
timber rattlesnake, 299–300
Town of Plymouth, United States v., 153
Toxic Substances Control Act, 361
trade of endangered species
  artificially propagated, 324–325
  bred in captivity, 323–324
  caviar from, 326–327
  CITES regulation of (*see* CITES)
  constitutional claims on, 308–309
  coordination of multiple agreements on, 327–331
  economic impact of regulation of, 331–335
  hunting trophies and, 325–326
  international (*see* international trade of endangered species)
  interstate commerce regulations on, 11, 201, 308–309

permits/certificates for, 320–323, 325
plants, 247, 252–253, 324–325
pre-ESA exemptions to, 200–201
state endangered species laws on, 349
timber trade, 252–253, 325
TRAFFIC, 327
transparency, 398–399, 406
treaties. *See* international agreements; Native Americans, treaties with
tribes/tribal land. *See* Native Americans
trout, 23, 59, 83, 302–303
Trout Unlimited v. Lohn, 24–25
Tulare Lake Basin v. United States, 148
Tulare Lake Basin Water Storage District v. United States, 293, 302–303
turtle/tortoise, 24, 88, 153, 180, 233

U

United Nations Environment Programme (UNEP), 327
United Nations Millennium Development Goals, 328
United States v. ———. *See name of opposing party*
upland sandpipers, 355
U.S. Departments. *See Department entries*
U.S. Fish and Wildlife Service. *See* Fish and Wildlife Service
U.S. Forest Service, 78, 117, 151–152

V

viability thresholds, 85–87
vicarious liability, 152–153, 179–182

W

Washington, United States v., 136–138
Washington Convention. *See* CITES
water rights, 130, 302–303
West Coast Forest Resources, United States v., 151, 174
Western Riverside Country Multiple-Species HCP, 234–237, 240–241
wetlands, 237–238, 304–305
whale
    citizen suits involving, 268
    commercial fishing and, 88, 152, 180
    conservation history and, 11, 12
    critical habitat of, 52–53
    gray, 76
    Moby-Dick on, 9–10
    parts of, 200–201
    right, 52–53, 88, 152, 268
    whaling industry, 9–10, 328–329
white-tailed deer, 76–79
whooping crane, 11
Wiese, John, 302–303
Wildlife Conservation Society, 10
Willamette Partnership, 387
Winans, United States v., 129–130
Winters, United States v., 129–130
wolf, 85–87, 89, 193, 197, 198, 348
Worcester v. Georgia, 128
World Summit on Sustainable Development, 328
World Trade Organization (WTO), 327–328
Wyoming Farm Bureau v. Babbitt, 198

Y

yellow-billed cuckoo, 27–28

Z

zoos, 194